INTERNATIONAL ORGANIZATIONAL BEHAVIOR

Text, Readings, Cases, and Skills

ANNE MARIE FRANCESCO   BARRY ALLEN GOLD

Lubin School of Business, Pace University

PRENTICE HALL
Upper Saddle River, New Jersey 07458

To

Henry, Jennie, Hua, Anthony, and Giancarlo

Bonnie, Lauren, and Ian

Acquisitions Editor: Stephanie Johnson
Editorial Assistant: Dawn Marie Reisner
Associate Editor: Lisamarie Brassini
Editor-in-Chief: Natalie Anderson
Marketing Manager: Tammy Wederbrand
Associate Managing Editor: David Salierno
Production Coordinator: Carol Samet
Managing Editor: Dee Josephson
Manufacturing Buyer: Diane Peirano
Manufacturing Supervisor: Arnold Vila
Manufacturing Manager: Vincent Scelta
Senior Designer: Ann France
Design Manager: Patricia Smythe
Interior/Cover Design: Donna Wickes
Project Management/Composition: University Graphics, Inc.
Cover Art: Hua Lee

Copyright © 1998 by Prentice-Hall, Inc.

Upper Saddle River, New Jersey 07458

Library of Congress Cataloging-in-Publication Data

Francesco, Anne Marie.
    International organizational behavior: text, readings, cases, and skills /Anne Marie Francesco, Barry A. Gold.
      p.   cm.
    Includes bibliographical references and index.
    ISBN 0-13-192485-0
    1. Organizational behavior. 2. International business
enterprises. I. Gold, Barry A.   II. Francesco, Anne Marie.   III. Title.
HD58.7.G646 1997
658′.049—dc21
                                                97-17400
                                              CIP

Prentice-Hall International (UK) Limited, London
Prentice-Hall of Australia Pty. Limited, Sydney
Prentice-Hall Canada, Inc., Toronto
Prentice-Hall Hispanoamericana, S.A., Mexico
Prentice-Hall of India Private Limited, New Delhi
Prentice-Hall of Japan, Inc., Tokyo

Editora Prentice-Hall do Brasil, Ltda., Rio de Janeiro

Printed in the United States of America

10 9 8 7

BRIEF CONTENTS

CONTENTS

PREFACE

Twenty years ago the year 2000 loomed like a colossus on the horizon. Futurologists speculated on what types of societies would evolve and wondered whether humanity would be better or worse off. Some envisioned a future of unlimited freedom and wealth; space travel would be common, poverty and disease would be eradicated, and happiness would abound. Others viewed the future pessimistically: overpopulation, environmental deterioration, war, famine, and alienation would pervade all civilizations.

We awaited dramatic changes.

The year 2000 is almost here and neither of these scenarios developed. We still don't know what the future holds. Of course, communism disintegrated—a few predicted it and even fewer expected it—and there have been other momentous social, economic, and political events. However, depending on one's ideology, these events can be interpreted as either the foundations of utopia or a headlong rush into irreversible disaster.

The change that has affected most of the world's population the greatest is the increase in globalization of social, cultural, and economic activity. From the vantage point of 1998 it appears that globalization will continue and probably accelerate.

Organizations are global. Business is global. Communication is global. Finance is global. Work is global.

This book is global.

International Organizational Behavior: Text, Readings, Cases, and Skills *provides a guide to changes in organizations and ways that we understand organizations. Organizations are important to understand because they affect most of our lives. Organizations connect us, control us, enrich us, and often frustrate us. We are born in organizations, work in organizations, purchase the products made in them, receive health care from them, are educated and play in them, and we die in them.*

Are we entering the global "Iron Cage" of organizations that Max Weber viewed as part of the disenchantment of the world? Or are we about to encounter a new era of freedom through understanding and the humane management of organizations?

For either scenario, we need to understand the emerging globalization of organizations to understand and shape our present and future. International Organizational Behavior: Text, Readings, Cases, and Skills *increases our knowledge of the impact of globalization on human behavior.*

Aims of the Text

The primary aim of this text is to provide students and instructors with an introduction to the field of international organizational behavior and management. Understanding the functioning of Western—European and American—

organizations has been an ongoing effort for most of the twentieth century. Now, on the verge of the twenty-first century, it is important to understand how organizations function in a wide variety of cultures.

A related aim is to present the material as global rather than from a North American or Western European perspective. This is difficult to accomplish for several reasons. First, the authors are U.S. citizens and were trained in American universities. This is countered, in Francesco's case, with extensive international business experience, and in Gold's case, with a long-term interest in comparative organizational and sociological studies. Second, much of the management and organizational literature—research, theory, and speculation—is either North American or Western European. In fact, American scholars dominate the field. Third, many countries view the West as a model for economic development, including management principles, and often embrace it uncritically. In many instances, articles and cases written by native writers about their cultures borrow extensively from American research and theory, making the cultural variations difficult to detect. Fourth, related to the last point, over the past twenty years, the distinction between United States/Western European and non-Western—particularly Asian—management and organization has been blurred by the selective borrowing of management theories and practices. Fifth, major parts of the globe (e.g., Russia, China, and South Africa) are changing rapidly, making it difficult to generate reliable knowledge—what we know quickly becomes old news. Finally, the concept of organization in the United States—a major influence on other cultures—is undergoing what appears to be fundamental changes as this book is being written. For example, U.S. firms are downsizing, consolidating through mergers, globalizing, and introducing technological innovations.

Throughout the text the terms *international* and *global* management and organizational behavior are used interchangeably. There is, however, an important difference between them. International refers to companies that do business in one country other than their own. Global refers to companies that do business in many countries, often with the objective of reducing the emphasis on a home country as the organization's headquarters. More important, global refers to the process of globalization as discussed in chapter 1, as a process that changes consciousness from a focus on domestic events toward awareness of global events. The major issue of this book is the effects and implications of globalization on management and organizational behavior. Globalization anticipates the future.

Another intention is to present a cultural perspective on organizational behavior and management. The emphasis on culture differs from other approaches. It views culture not only as important for understanding other societies and managing organizations, but as a major cause of much behavior in organizations. We discuss the other causal variables—technology, strategy, size, and goals—as they relate to culture. Finally, an increasingly important variable, the organization's environment, is the national, and increasingly international, culture within which an organization operates. To a great extent, exploring the environment's effect on organizations is the subject of this text.

The text is selective in the theories it presents. There is no attempt to cover every organizational behavior or management theory. We select those theories that elucidate the cultural perspective. The reader interested in a comprehensive treatment of organizational behavior and management theories can consult a standard textbook.

Finally, an aim of this text is to provide material to improve students' interpersonal behavior concerning the cultural variations found in international organizations. The skill exercises are provided for this purpose. They highlight aspects of cultural variation, attempt to increase student sensitivity to culture, and provide an opportunity to experiment with new behaviors.

Uses of the Text

The primary use of *International Organizational Behavior: Text, Readings, Cases, and Skills* is as a self-contained text for classes that focus on global aspects of management and organizational behavior. In addition to text, the book includes readings, cases, and skills. This comprehensive approach provides instructors with an opportunity to choose from a variety of materials and shape the class as they desire. For example, some instructors may not make extensive use of the readings but prefer to focus on the text, cases, and skills.

Another use of the book is as a supplement to standard organizational behavior texts based on research and theories developed in the United States. Of course, many of the theories and examples in *International Organizational Behavior: Text, Readings, Cases, and Skills* are from the United States.

This text can be used in the following courses: Organizational Behavior, Global Organizational Behavior, International Organizational Behavior, Global Management, International Management, and Comparative Management. It assumes that students have taken an introductory course in management or organizational behavior.

Because of the richness of material contained in the text, it can be used for both advanced undergraduate and MBA students. The instructor can tailor the text, readings, cases, and skills to the students' needs.

Organization of the Text

International Organizational Behavior: Text, Readings, Cases, and Skills is more comprehensive than existing international organizational behavior texts. It is divided into six sections:

    I. Understanding International Organizational Behavior

    II. Managing International Organizational Behavior

    III. Emerging Issues in International Organizational Behavior

    IV. Readings in International Organizational Behavior

    V. Cases in International Organizational Behavior

    VI. Skills Exercises in International Organizational Behavior

Fourteen chapters cover the essential topics for understanding modern organizations from a global comparative perspective. Each chapter has these pedagogical features:

- **Learning Objectives.** A preview and guide to each chapter.
- **Culture at Work.** A vignette illustrating practical implications of concepts in the text.
- **Key Concepts.** Definitions, concepts, and theories indicated in bold type.
- **Examples from various cultures.** Examples from a variety of cultures demonstrate how culture affects behavior in organizations.
- **Tables and Figures.** Tables and figures illustrate complex concepts and processes.
- **Convergence and Divergence.** A section that discusses forces creating similarities or differences in cultures worldwide.
- **Implications for Managers.** A section outlining practical issues that managers in a global economy face now and in the future.
- **Summary.** A summary of each chapter's major points.
- **Discussion Questions.** Questions for use in classroom discussion or assignment.

In addition to the text, there are 14 readings, 12 cases, and 15 skill exercises. The learning strategy for including this array of material is that the chapters provide the basic concepts for each topic; the readings explore an important topic in depth; the cases provide extended real-life examples plus an opportunity to improve students' analytical skills; and the skill exercises provide an opportunity for students to develop more sensitivity to intercultural variations as well as more effective managerial behaviors.

▌▌▌ TEXT

Fourteen chapters cover the essential topics for understanding modern organizations from a comparative global perspective. Chapter 3 (Ethics and Social Responsibility), Chapter 10 (International Human Resource Management), and Chapter 13 (Managing Diversity) are not usually found in organizational behavior texts. These topics are included because culture influences them, and they are critical for understanding relationships in organizations.

▌▌▌ READINGS

In selecting readings for this text, as we suspected, more material is available about the United States, Western Europe, and Asia than other parts of the world. Interest is increasing in former communist nations, but scant attention is paid to Africa, Latin America, and to developing nations in general.

▌▌▌ CASES

The situation of cases is similar to that of readings. There are comparatively few cases for developing nations, whereas many exist about the issues in advanced nations. The result is a bias toward the United States, Western Europe, and Asia. However, included in this text are cases from Latin America and the Middle East.

▌▌▌ SKILLS EXERCISES

The skills exercises are intended to demonstrate issues and problems in cross-cultural understanding and interaction. When used in a college classroom, they often raise as many issues as they resolve. In most instances, they are designed to be used in one class period and require little, if any, preclass preparation. Also, an attempt has been made to select exercises that involve as many students as possible.

Integrating Text, Readings, Cases, and Skills Exercises

Instead of locating the readings, cases, and skills exercises at the end of each chapter or section, they are grouped after the text. This permits creative and flexible use because many address multiple topics. To aid the instructor, the following chart correlates the 14 chapters with the readings, cases, and skills exercises.

Part/Chapter	Readings	Cases	Skills Exercises
I. Understanding International Organizational Behavior			
1. The Management of International Organizational Behavior	1	1	1
2. Culture and Organizational Behavior	All	All	All
II. Managing International Organizational Behavior			
3. Ethics and Social Responsibility	2	2,10	8
4. Communication	All	All	All
5. Negotiation and Conflict Resolution	3	1,3,4,10	2,3,4,10
6. Motivation	4,7	3,12	11,14
7. Groups and Teams	5	5	12
8. Organizational Culture	6,10	9,12	13
9. Leadership	6,7	4,6,10	4,14
10. International Human Resource Management	8,9,12,13,14	3,7,12	11,15
11. Organizational Structure	6,10	8,9	13
12. Organizational Change	10,11	9,10	13
III. Emerging Issues in International Organizational Behavior			
13. Managing Diversity	12,13,14	5,11,12	4
14. The Globalization of Organizational Behavior: Future Trends	10,12,13,14	6,9,12	15

Language Conventions

People who speak the same language often use different words for the same thing. In some cases, different usages are confusing or offensive to others. The text refers to the United States of America as the United States, to Americans as those people from the United States, and to North Americans as those from the United States and Canada. Latin America refers to Central and South America, including Mexico and the Caribbean. Concerning gender, the text adopts the policy of referring to both genders simultaneously.

Teaching Support

Support materials available for this text include an Instructor's Manual with answers to end-of-chapter questions, and teaching notes for the readings, cases, and skills exercises; a Test Item File with multiple choice, true/false, and essay questions for each chapter; and PH Custom Test for Windows, a computerized version of the Test Item File, which allows easy test preparation.

Acknowledgments

This book involved many people beyond the authors. We thank the following people for their contributions, encouragement, and patience.

Amit Devgan, Karen Keasler, and Regina Poleschuk, graduate students at Pace University, provided cultural insights and excellent assistance with library research.

Drs. Peter Eichhorn, University of Mannheim, and K. C. Yu, Dalian Technology University, wrote original papers on important topics.

Many people from Prentice Hall made this book possible. Natalie Anderson provided encouragement for the book from beginning to end. Bill Oldsey demonstrated strong interest in the project when it was in the proposal stage. Chrissy Statuto supplied expert administrative assistance and David Salierno capably guided the book through production.

The following reviewers each read several draft chapters and provided detailed, thoughtful, and useful comments: Cindy Pavett, University of San Diego; Joseph Cheng, University of Illinois; Edwin Miller, University of Michigan; Maryann Watson, University of Tampa; Wendy Kleptar, College of St. Benedict; Carol Carnevale, Empire State College; Erich Kerchler, Universitat Wien Austrial; Paul Fadil, Valdosta State University; Doug Ross, Towson State University; Mikael Sondergaard, Odense University; Fred Ware, Valdosta State University; and Steve Cady, Bowling Green State University. Of course, any deficiencies in the text are ours alone.

The authors, who are listed alphabetically, thank each other for constructive disagreements, perseverance, a sense of achievement, and several interesting lunches in Manhattan.

Anne Marie Francesco and Barry Allen Gold

Part I

UNDERSTANDING INTERNATIONAL
ORGANIZATIONAL BEHAVIOR

The Management of International Organizational Behavior

Today or Mañana?

"The U.S. team members are driven by the exact dates on the schedule," explained Marianne Torrcelli, leader of an AT&T team working in Mexico and the United Kingdom. "The team members are disappointed and feel a sense of urgency when the schedule is not met. We believe that 'Time is Money' and missed dates equate to potential jeopardy in project completion, which results in lost revenue. To prevent this, the American AT&T team responds quickly to jeopardy situations, focuses on critical issues, engages additional resources, and works extensive overtime. The job takes priority over family."

"But in Mexico," Marianne observed, "as long as work items are being addressed—even if they are not on schedule—the United States team members feel comfortable that they will be completed at some point. The 'schedule' is not in jeopardy. We understand that in Mexico there isn't the sense of urgency that American AT&T team members feel when critical task delivery times are missed. The 'mañana syndrome' is real. The Mexican team members have outstanding commitment and dedication to the project, but they place their family before work. The work can be done 'mañana.'"

"It's different in the UK. There employees understand the concept of 'schedule' the way Americans do. They also understand the need to complete tasks on time and that when a jeopardy situation

After reading this chapter, you should be able to:

1. Define international organizational behavior.
2. Understand why it is important to study international organizational behavior.
3. Compare industrialization and culture as explanations for international organizational behavior.
4. Know the role of theory in the study of international organizational behavior.
5. Explain the benefits of the comparative perspective for studying international organizational behavior.

> occurs, the team needs to respond quickly. But the British team members maintain a balance between work and their personal lives. For example, they never work extensive overtime to resolve a critical issue. The U.S. expatriates, however, would work extensive overtime, putting work ahead of their personal lives."
>
> *Source*: Marianne Torrcelli

Organizations are becoming global. Multinational corporations formulate global strategies to expand into new markets, reduce their dependence on expensive labor, restructure into network organizations, and capitalize on novel international financial arrangements. In the last decades of the twentieth century, many organizations transcend geographic, economic, political, and cultural boundaries. Globalization of commerce will increase in the next decades.

Society is becoming global. Much of the world is experiencing **globalization**, "A social process in which the constraints of geography on social and cultural arrangements recede and in which people become increasingly aware that they are receding" (Waters 1995, p. 3). During the 1990s, a profound shift in consciousness, the globalization process, has affected the daily lives of people around the world in diverse ways, such as the following:

- The Internet and World Wide Web connected people around the globe.
- College graduates in the United States competed for entry level positions with candidates worldwide.
- CNN broadcast the assault on the Russian White House as the aborted revolution unfolded.
- Workers in Paris and Kansas City were unemployed because labor was cheaper in Mexico, Sri Lanka, and Morocco.
- Newspapers throughout the world reported on China's takeover of Hong Kong in July 1997.

As a result of globalization, which is accelerating, it is important to know how to manage culturally diverse, cross-cultural, and geographically dispersed organizations. Because the management of modern corporations consists of more than accounting and finance, business strategy, or site location, managers should understand the behavior of people in organizations. Knowing how culture—particularly that of other countries—affects organizational behavior is essential. Some of the questions the global manager needs answers to follow:

> As a result of globalization, which is accelerating, it is important to know how to manage culturally diverse, cross-cultural, and geographically dispersed organizations.

- Do all cultures have the same understanding of ethics?
- Are people in different cultures motivated in different ways?
- Are leadership styles the same in all cultures?
- How do different cultures manage diversity?
- Do all cultures negotiate business deals the same way?

What is International Organizational Behavior?

International organizational behavior is the study of behavior in organizations around the world. In studying international organizational behavior, the influence of national culture on organizations is important because "despite all of the discussion of globalization of the world economy and the so-called multinationalization of corporations, different societies continue to have distinctive organizational arrangements" (Fligstein and Freeland 1995, p. 33).

Even if globalization and multinational corporate structures eventually cause national cultures to become more alike, it is improbable that indistinguishable values will emerge across cultures to produce the same management techniques and organizational behavior. National values, attitudes, traditions, customs, and ideologies produce distinctive organization structures, cultures, and dynamics. To be successful, a manager in the global economy must understand the effect of diverse cultures on organizational behavior.

▌▌▌ DIFFERENCES FROM ORGANIZATIONAL BEHAVIOR IN THE UNITED STATES

There are three reasons why organizational behavior theories developed in the United States are different from international organizational behavior theories.

First, the study of organizational behavior in the United States is not sensitive to variations in national cultures (Hofstede 1993). Until recently, American researchers assumed that organizations existed within the culture of the United States or one that was similar—for example, Western Europe. Not all societies, however, are based on capitalist economic principles or an ideology that emphasizes individualism, achievement, and equality. In fact, even capitalist societies other than the United States organize and manage differently as a result of culture. In addition, many U.S. theories receive either minimal or mixed support from data collected in the United States. It is unlikely, then, that these theories apply in other countries. One way to avoid the dominance of U.S. organizational theory is to develop theories in other cultures rather than merely test U.S. theories with international samples.

Second, the units of analysis in studies conducted in the United States are usually individual roles and the functioning of groups. Although sociologists have studied organizations as entities, there are few studies that view organizations holistically as the product of a specific culture.

Finally, much U.S. organizational behavior research emulates natural science methods that emphasize narrow research questions, hypothesis testing, and quantifiable data. In contrast, culture is hard to quantify, and it is difficult to measure the multiple, often subtle ways that it influences behavior. Another way of studying culture is using qualitative and ethnographic techniques. These methods produce rich, descriptive data presented in case studies that help researchers to understand life from inside organizations. Often, despite limitations of representativeness and researcher bias, these methods capture the meaning of culture more adequately than quantitative studies (Adler and Boyacigiller 1996).

Because of these limitations, the approach to international management and organizational behavior presented here extends the American model by using culture as the context and explanation.

Why Study International Organizational Behavior?

▌▌▌ COMPETITIVE ADVANTAGE

One result of globalization is that organizations confront an external environment that is more complex, dynamic, and competitive. To succeed in the new economy, it is essential to have knowledge of other cultures and behavior in their organizations.

> **O**ne result of globalization is that organizations confront an external environment that is more complex, dynamic, and competitive.

A practical aspect of studying global organizational behavior is understanding the nature of competition in the global marketplace. To remain competitive, companies must learn about the technologies, management practices, strategies, and product development of firms around the globe as well as domestic rivals. This is particularly important with the increased emphasis on international product quality and global finance and the ability to purchase products from companies located anywhere.

A related reason to know about the activities of businesses throughout the world is to evaluate prospects for collaboration with other companies. Increasingly, strategic alliances are common between competitors. For example, Mitsubishi, a Japanese company, collaborates with Chrysler, an American firm, to create new automotive products.

Another reason for learning about global organizational behavior is to borrow ideas from other cultures to improve performance in your organization. Since the late 1970s, Great Britain and the United States have borrowed Japanese management techniques, including total quality control and just-in-time manufacturing (Oliver and Wilkinson 1992). On a larger scale, former East European Communist countries are eager to apply capitalist economic principles to improve their businesses and factories.

Finally, as a result of immigration in some countries and the use of temporary guest workers in others, multiculturalism in the workforce is increasing. The management of people with diverse cultural backgrounds improves when managers apply organizational theories based on cultural explanations.

▌▌▌ ORGANIZATIONAL ANALYSIS

The second reason to study international organizational behavior is that formal organizations are a major social structure in modern societies. The influence of organizations on daily life is pervasive, and their leaders have significant power. A systematic analysis of organizations is essential for interpreting the social control and economic production structures of advanced and developing societies.

Of course, many of the issues addressed in the academic study of organizations have implications for improvement of management theory and practice. Much of the research reported in this book had its origin in academic studies, but it also relates directly to the improvement of global management practices.

▌▌▌ THE ANALYSIS OF CULTURE

The third reason for studying international organizational behavior is intellectual curiosity about cultures other than one's own. Critical examination of management techniques across societies helps us understand how people interact and justify their relationships under conditions of power and resource inequalities.

In addition, knowledge of other cultures generates insights into one's own culture and behavior. Without systematic comparisons, it is difficult to appreciate how culture influences one's own behavior. This is because most of us believe that our culture is preferable, possibly superior, to other cultures. We only question our cultural assumptions when practices from other cultures appear to be strange, unethical, or more effective.

Explaining International Organizational Behavior

The history of management and organizational behavior reflects continuous refinement of models of human behavior. Explanations have evolved from single cause theories to models of behavior based on interaction among multiple variables. For example, early researchers focused on finding universals: What is the most effective way to lead, motivate employees, or structure an organization? Recent research findings and theories usually emphasize that there is no single or "best" approach that applies to all situations. But there are still competing theories and debates over complex issues—for example, whether industrialization or culture exerts more influence on organizational structures and processes.

INDUSTRIALIZATION

The industrialization argument is that the logic of industrialization—movement from animal and human to steam, electric and petroleum energy sources for manufacturing—is a powerful economic force unaffected by culture (Harbison and Myer 1959). This view concludes that industrialization creates organizational structures and cultures that are fundamentally the same regardless of national culture.

Research has also identified influences on organizational behavior and structure as diverse as strategy (Chandler 1962), technology (Perrow 1967), size (Blau and Schoenherr 1971), and ecology, the social environment's influence on the evolution of organizational types (Hannan and Freeman 1989). Some of these studies support the industrialization thesis. For example, specific technologies are associated with particular organizational structures, and large size, an indicator of organization growth, is a measure of industrial success.

CULTURAL EXPLANATIONS

Recently, culture has become accepted as an explanation of organizational behavior. One reason is the increase in competitiveness of nations beginning in the 1980s. For example, the superior quality of Japanese automobiles prompted researchers and managers to ask: Is there something about Japanese culture that contributes to high quality standards in the workplace?

A second reason is that business executives encounter different cultures in their contacts with people from other nations. It has become more important to understand how members of other cultures behave. How should we communicate with them? Can we trust them? What leadership style do they think is effective? Answers to these questions require understanding the various external and internal cultural influences on organizations and how they interact.

> Culture has become accepted as an explanation of organizational behavior.

Multiple Cultures   Nations and organizations have multiple cultures. National cultures have roots in ethnic identity, religion, social class, or some combination of these. Subcultures form within nations that are based on these variables. These subcultures shape attitudes and values that affect behavior in organizations such as motivation, obedience to authority, and interpersonal relations. In organizations, subcultures develop from job specialization, departmentalization, friendship, and other factors.

External Culture   Until recently, organizational theorists viewed the boundary between organizations and external culture as rigid. New models conceptualize **external culture**, which includes multiple national and local cultures, as influencing internal organizational culture.

For example, social class, an external basis for distinctive cultures, seldom appears in organizational behavior studies conducted in the United States. However, the assumption of most research is that a managerial class controls organizations—but does not own them—and a class of lower level participants—the workers—is managed. A model of organizations sensitive to external culture would make these assumptions explicit and use them to explain behavior.

Internal Organizational Culture   Each organization creates a particular culture that influences its members' behavior in complex ways. **Internal organizational culture** is composed of artifacts, values, and basic assumptions that create meaning for organizational insiders and present it to those outside the organization. Interest in organizational culture arises from the increase in global competition and recognition that the management of culture creates competitive advantages.

▌▌▌ LIMITATIONS OF CULTURAL EXPLANATIONS

There are limits to the use of culture to explain organizational behavior. First, there are numerous definitions of culture; it is not entirely clear what composes culture. Related to this, many conceptualizations of culture originated in anthropological studies of "primitive" cultures and may not apply to industrial and postindustrial societies or complex organizations.

Second, culture is a multifaceted concept that is difficult to measure. An additional measurement issue is that researchers often use forced choice questionnaires that impose predetermined categories instead of developing grounded theories with data from specific cultures and organizations.

Third, culture can explain organizational behavior too comprehensively. **Cultural determinism**, the position that all behavior is the product of culture, ignores economic, political, technological, and biological factors as plausible explanations. A counter argument to this criticism is that technology and the economy are products of culture. However, industrialization and related variables are complex processes that are distinct from culture and contribute to organizational behavior. In this text, culture is a key variable but not the exclusive cause of organizational behavior.

Theory and International Organizational Behavior

Despite Kurt Lewin's aphorism, "There is nothing as practical as a good theory," people are often put off by the prospect of learning theories. Their response is, "It's just a theory. It has *nothing* to do with what happens in the *real world.*" Another frequent criticism of theory is that, "It all depends. Every situation is unique. It's *impossible* to make meaningful generalizations."

REAL WORLD THEORY

Theories *can explain* what happens in the real world. Social science is an attempt—often incomplete and frequently revised—to develop theories that accurately explain social life. Theories organize data into meaningful patterns and provide explanations of observed behavior.

> Theories *can explain* what happens in the real world.

Normative and Descriptive Theory   Two types of theory are normative and descriptive. In management and organizational behavior, **normative theories** formulate the way organizations *ought* to function. An example of a normative theory is the view that a properly designed and managed organization does not experience internal conflict. The assumption is that conflict has negative influences on organizational effectiveness. But few organizations are conflict free. In fact, organizations without conflict may be harmonious, nonproductive places where few people care enough about the organization's goals to engage in conflict.

   Descriptive theories attempt to portray organizations realistically. From this perspective, if conflict exits in organizations and whether it hinders or advances the goals of an organization are matters for empirical investigation. If a pattern of conflict emerges in different types of organizations, it requires an explanation. Of course, findings from descriptive studies contribute to policies and practices intended to improve organizations.

   The difference between descriptive and normative theories has important implications for managers. For example, if a normative theory views conflict as a product of ineffective management, the objective is to eliminate conflict. However, if empirical research indicates that all organizations experience conflict, the issue is finding ways to manage it effectively.

Values   A related issue is the role of values in research. **Value judgments** are culturally biased assessments of behavior. It is pointless to pretend that people escape culture. Indeed, it is natural to use one's own culture as the basis for comparison. However, researchers attempt to recognize values and perceptual biases that their culture and experience impose and reduce their influence. Two common forms of value judgment, ethnocentrism and culture shock, demonstrate these issues.

Ethnocentrism   **Ethnocentrism** is the belief that "one's own group is the center of everything, and all others are scaled and rated with reference to it" (Sumner 1906, p. 28). The Culture at Work vignette that opens this chapter illustrates the tendency to use one's own culture as the comparative and evaluative framework for behavior in other cultures. For Marianne Torrcelli, an American employee of AT&T, work is more a central life concern than it is for her British and Mexican coworkers. Marianne views the Mexicans as capable workers and accepts that they eventually perform their tasks but, nevertheless, appears to wish they were punctual like Americans. At the same time, Marianne recognizes that the Mexicans and British have different priorities in their relationship to work and family life than the American workers. Marianne believes her priorities are preferable while the other cultures' values are acceptable but inferior.

Culture Shock   Behavior in cultures other than our own often appears to be exotic, harmful, irrational, or meaningless. **Culture shock**, an adverse or confused reaction to behavior in other cultures, challenges understandings between ourselves and others. What is "normal" behavior becomes problematic.

From a Western perspective, examples of culture shock encountered in organizations are child and prison labor. A less dramatic example is pay differentials between executives and workers. Americans are surprised that Japanese executives receive only slightly more compensation than Japanese workers. Similarly, Japanese executives find it unusual that American executives often earn more than ten times the salary of workers. Another example is Americans in foreign countries who discover that most of the world does not have American style lavatories.

The Comparative Perspective

One way to reduce or eliminate ethnocentrism, culture shock, and other forms of culture bias is the comparative method. The **comparative method**, a technique for the systematic study of behavior in multiple cultures, reduces reliance on a single set of values. It is also a highly effective way to construct descriptive organizational behavior theories.

Although all empirical social research is comparative—either through the use of statistical methods or implicit comparisons with pure cases—international organizational behavior attempts to explicitly and systematically compare the effects of national culture on organizations (Ragin 1987). The comparative perspective can discover differences or similarities in behavior across cultures (Inkeles and Sasaki 1996, Punnett and Shenkar 1996).

▌▌▌ TWO EXAMPLES OF THE COMPARATIVE PERSPECTIVE

Two recent studies illustrate the comparative method in international management and organizational behavior. The first study identifies changes in international finance that created similar types of organizations in three cultures. These changes resulted in specific organizational cultures in knowledge-intensive organizations. This study's theoretical framework expands the scope of research on organizations by identifying large-scale global trends shaping post-modern society and organizations.

The second study discovered differences in management philosophies and practices in four industrial societies. These findings were unexpected because the theoretical viewpoint of many researchers is that management in industrial nations is similar because of industrialization.

Both studies present extensive data and complex theoretical arguments. The following are brief descriptions of some of their major themes.

Global Processes   Saskia Sassen's *The Global City* (1991) illustrates the discovery of similarities—convergence—across cultures produced by global economic activity. Sassen's thesis is that beginning in the 1980s New York, London, and Tokyo have "undergone massive and *parallel* changes in their economic base, spatial organization, and social structure" (1991, p. 4). Instead of control and power becoming decentralized with the dispersion of business around the globe, New York, London, and Tokyo have become global cities because they are the control centers of the new global economy. This development affects organizations throughout the world because, according to Sassen, "though large firms have increased their subcontracting to smaller firms, and many national firms in the newly industrializing countries have grown rapidly, this form of growth is ultimately part of a chain. Even industrial homeworkers in remote rural areas are now part of that chain" (1991, pp. 4–5).

Within the global cities are sections in which postindustrial production sites—knowledge industries—are concentrated. Knowledge industries specialize in financial and marketing services needed by complex organizations for running spatially dispersed networks of factories, offices, and service outlets.

One consequence of this is a division of the workforce into specialized high-salary work and low-wage support services. New organizational cultures arose that focus on financial knowledge and services. The same processes also reduced large segments of urban populations to marginal employment.

The similarity across cultures of these processes is observable only through the comparative method. Study of a single culture would not detect the simultaneous changes affecting the global economy and consequently the social structure of cities and organizations.

Management Pluralism   *Models of Management* (1994) by Mauro Guillén is a comparative historical study of the United States, Great Britain, Germany, and Spain during the twentieth century. It demonstrates that these industrial societies adopted different paradigms of management philosophies and practices at different times: scientific management, the human relations school, and structural analysis.

Scientific management, based on the ideas of Frederick Taylor and others, was prevalent in the United States and Germany during the early part of the century but was rejected as an ideology and practice in Great Britain and Spain.

The human relations movement, a reaction against scientific management, found favor in the United States, Great Britain, and Spain where it was consistent with social and political values. Germany, where social values did not support its practices, did not adopt it.

The last paradigm, structural analysis, is a critique of the search for "the one best way" to organize that was the driving force behind scientific management and the human relations school. It was formulated and adopted with the creation of complex multinational organizations and was in widespread use beginning in the 1960s in Great Britain, the United States, and Germany. It was rejected as an ideology and practice in Spain.

Guillén concludes that cultural factors influence the selection of management models, not only their scientific credibility or economic and technological factors. "Managers," Guillén writes, "in different countries adopted the three paradigms in selective ways during the twentieth century, depending on the problems they were facing and such institutional factors as their mentalities and training, the activities of professional groups, the role of the state, and the attitude of the workers" (1994, pp. 1–2).

In addition to the political and social factors that influenced managerial ideology and practice, Guillén found that religion—an important cultural element—also was significant in the adoption of a management model. Guillén writes:

> Guillén concludes that cultural factors influence the selection of management models, not only their scientific credibility or economic and technological factors.

Catholicism has generally emphasized the community, self-actualization, paternalism, and organicism, while Protestantism has emphasized individualism, instrumentalism, independence, and contractualism. In Germany, Protestant management intellectuals generally supported the scientific management paradigm, while Catholic ones took sides with the human relations school. In Spain, the dominant Catholic background played a key role in the reception, adoption, and adaptation to local conditions of American ideas about human relations at work. In Britain, Christian humanist ideals similar to those proposed by the Roman Catholic Church prompted management intellectuals to accept human relations. In the United States, religion did not play a role either in the formulation or in the widespread adoption of the human relations paradigm (1994, p. 297).[1]

Guillén's research demonstrates two important issues. First, institutional arrangements, not only the type of economy, technology, or a particular definition of industrial efficiency, create ideologies that become guidelines for the way people manage organizations. One implication of Guillén's research is that national and organizational cultures influence the adoption of management paradigms and shape managers' and workers' behavior. Management philosophies and practices embody culture and constrain aspects of work behaviors in nations and organizations.

Second, comparative analysis is a more productive way of understanding management and organizational behavior than single-culture studies. Without the systematic comparisons at the level of nation states, it is difficult to determine which variables affect the adoption of management models and the factors that cause them to change periodically. In addition, without comparisons, the misleading conclusion would be that all countries adopted the same managerial models at similar stages in economic development.

Convergence or Divergence?

If cultures are converging—that is, becoming more alike—there is less reason to study specific management practices and organizing principles. This echoes the logic of early management theorists in the United States who searched for the single most effective way to manage all types of business organizations. If organizations throughout the world are similar, the same management techniques apply.

However, if cultures diverge by remaining distinctive or becoming more dissimilar, culture is an important factor in management. This viewpoint suggests that it is urgent to become familiar with diverse cultures and develop culturally sensitive ways to manage organizations.

▌▌▌ FORCES FOR CONVERGENCE

Sassen concludes that globalization, which affects the economy and culture of cities, is a force for convergence. Part of the change in urban areas is transformation of work; major cities become centers of power and control in the global economy. The primary negative consequence of this is concentrations of power and wealth that produce urban centers with two social classes, affluent knowledge workers and economically marginal support workers. The process of globalization of cities was produced by economic activities but affected the culture of cities and organizations.

---

[1]Excerpt from *Models of Management* by M. Guillén. Reprinted by permission of The University of Chicago Press.

▌▌▌ FORCES FOR DIVERGENCE

Guillén's study concludes that distinctive cultural elements influence the management of organizations. Unless globalization produces a uniform religion or other value system, there will continue to be differences in management philosophies and practices. These findings and interpretation support the divergence view.

Implications for Managers

For international managers to perform successfully in the global economy, accurate information on how culture affects organizational behavior in different cultures is essential. Reliance on theories developed in one culture is not sufficient.

Managers also must distinguish between normative and descriptive theories. Normative theories can reinforce practices that "are fine in theory, but not in practice." The implication is that managers must evaluate theories by assessing whether data support them.

Although Guillén's and Sassen's studies are descriptive, normative theories can be derived from them. Guillén's findings imply that managers who work across cultures must acquire an extensive knowledge of management practices that are different from their own. For example, not only do international managers from the United Kingdom have to adapt to the style of management in Spain, they also have to understand the management practices of former Communist countries as well as other countries.

Sassen's study suggests that managers must become more familiar with abstractions and the management of knowledge workers who are, to a large extent, immune from specific cultures because their focus is the global flow of capital.

▬ Summary

International organizational behavior describes and explains behavior in organizations located in diverse national cultures. It differs from traditional organizational behavior as developed in the United States because it adds the dimension of culture as an explanation.

Three reasons for studying international organizational behavior are to gain competitive advantage, to improve understanding of behavior in organizations and modern society, and to appreciate other cultures.

Organizational and national cultures influence organizational behavior. Multiple cultures, including those based on ethnic identity, religion, and social class, affect behavior in organizations. However, there are limits to the use of culture as an explanation for organizational behavior. Technology, the organization's competitive environment, strategy, and size also account for organizational structure and behavior.

An objective of the study of international organizational behavior is to develop theories of behavior. Normative theory focuses on ways that organizations should operate and how people ought to behave. Descriptive theory attempts to describe and analyze behavior objectively without making judgments or prescriptions.

Ethnocentrism and culture shock can influence one's view of another culture, often negatively. Self-awareness in analyzing another culture reduces bias created by these processes. The comparative study of organizational behavior is a systematic method for reducing the entry of cultural values into the study of international organizational behavior. The comparative method often results in challenges to the implicit superiority of the investigator's own culture and social arrangements. Also, comparisons often result in unexpected findings. For example, Gullién's research concluded that industrial countries use different management philosophies and practices, not necessarily based on scientific reasons, but because of cultural factors such as religion.

Finally, although much global organizational behavior research is comparative, additional research using systematic comparisons, especially studies of developing nations, will provide data for more comprehensive theories. In addition, these studies will contribute to understanding whether cultures and organizations in them are becoming more alike or different. This has implications for the management of international organizational behavior.

■ Discussion Questions

1. Define and discuss international organizational behavior.
2. Why is international organizational behavior a subject that should be taught in business schools?
3. What role does research on organizations in the United States have on the study of organizations in other cultures?
4. Why is theory important for the study of international organizational behavior?
5. What is the comparative method?
6. What is an example of a business issue that could benefit from the approach of international management and organizational behavior?
7. From your understanding of international management and organizational behavior, what personal goals do you expect to achieve by taking this class?

References

ADLER, N. and BOYACIGILLER, N. (1996), "Global Management and the 21st Century," in Punnett, B. and Shenkar, O. eds. *Handbook for International Management Research*. Cambridge, MA: Blackwell Publishers.

BLAU, P. and SCHOENHERR, R. (1971), *The Structure of Organizations*. New York: Basic Books.

CHANDLER, A. (1962), *Strategy and Structure*. Cambridge, MA: MIT Press.

FLIGSTEIN, N. and FREELAND, R. (1995), "Theoretical and Comparative Perspectives on Corporate Organization," *Annual Review of Sociology*. Palo Alto, CA: Annual Reviews, 21–43.

GUILLÉN, M. (1994), *Models of Management: Work, Authority, and Organization in a Comparative Perspective*. Chicago: University of Chicago Press.

HANNAN, M. and FREEMAN, J. (1989), *Organizational Ecology*. Cambridge, MA: Harvard University Press.

HARBISON, R. and MYERS, C. (1959), *Management in the Industrial World: An International Study*. New York: McGraw-Hill.

HOFSTEDE, G. (1993), "Cultural Constraints in Management Theories," *Academy of Management Executive*, 7(1), 81–94.

INKELES, A. and SASAKI, M. (eds.). (1996), *Comparing Nations and Cultures: Readings in a Cross-Disciplinary Perspective*. Upper Saddle River, NJ: Prentice Hall.

OLIVER, N. and WILKINSON, B. (1992), *The Japanization of British Industry: New Developments in the 1990s*. Cambridge, MA: Blackwell Publishers.

PERROW, C. (1967), "A Framework for the Comparative Analysis of Organizations," *American Sociological Review*, 32, 194–208.

PUNNETT, B. and SHENKAR, O. (1996), *Handbook for International Management Research*. Cambridge, MA: Blackwell Publishers.

RAGIN, C. (1987), *The Comparative Method: Moving Beyond Qualitative and Quantitative Strategies*. Berkeley, CA: University of California Press.

SASSEN, S. (1991), *The Global City: New York, London, Tokyo*. Princeton, NJ: Princeton University Press.

SUMNER, W. (1906), *Folkways*. Boston: Ginn.

WATERS, M. (1995), *Globalization*. New York: Routledge.

Culture and Organizational Behavior

I Need New Clothes?

The secretary and administrative assistant came into the office and closed the door. "We need to talk to you, Paula. We want to help you get used to living in Hong Kong. We think you need some new clothes. Women managers in Hong Kong don't dress like that. You need to be more feminine, more fashionable. It's better if you wear a dress. We can take you shopping if you like."

Paula Sorrento, the new American expatriate manager at Home Bank's branch in Hong Kong, was totally taken aback. She had been wearing her normal work clothes—tailored slacks and a jacket with a button down shirt, her usual dress-for-success formula from back home. Why were these women telling her this? Were the Chinese so hung up on clothes? And, *how dare* her assistants be so forward! They hardly knew her.

Source: A.M. Francesco

After reading this chapter, you should be able to:

1. Understand what culture is and levels of culture.
2. Explain how culture develops.
3. Describe the major frameworks for explaining the cultures of different societies.
4. Discuss the relation of culture to the study of organizational behavior.
5. Debate the issue of cultural convergence versus divergence.

People from different countries often do things in different ways. One way to explain variations in behavior is the idea of culture. Models of culture provide ways of understanding behavior encountered in business situations that at first may appear odd, mysterious, or inscrutable. As business becomes more international and global, sophisticated models for understanding cultures become a necessity. National culture affects, to some extent, much management and organizational behavior.

The Culture at Work vignette illustrates that interpretations of something as basic as dress are different in different countries. In Hong Kong, people make judgments based on appearance. Paula's tailored look, appropriate for her U.S. workplace, did not create the impression of a high powered female manager in Hong Kong. The secretary and administrative assistant, as part of their roles in the Chinese business world, tried to protect the image of their boss. They did not hesitate to tell her she was wearing inappropriate clothes.

What is Culture?

Culture can explain differences in business dress and its meaning. To gain a deeper understanding of how culture influences organizational behavior, it is important to understand what culture is. In general terms, **culture** is a way of life of a group of people. Researchers from diverse fields, including anthropology, sociology, and management, have studied culture for a long time, but only recently have organizational scholars used culture to understand why people from different countries behave differently in organizations.

A narrow meaning of *culture* refers to the arts. A "cultured society" appreciates fine art, dance, drama, and intellectual discourse and develops institutions that support them such as museums, theaters, and schools. Although culture as used here does not exclude the arts, its meaning is much broader.

▮▮▮ DEFINING CULTURE

A single definition of culture is not adequate because the concept is complex. Indeed, defining culture has become a study in itself. In 1952, researchers identified more than 160 definitions of culture (Kroeber and Kluckhohn 1952). Tylor (1871, p. 1) proposed one of the earliest definitions as "that complex whole which includes knowledge, belief, art, morals, law, custom, and any other capabilities and habits acquired by man as a member of society." Ferraro's more recent and simpler definition is "everything that people have, think, and do as members of society" (1994, p. 17).

▮▮▮ LEVELS OF CULTURE

The analogy of an onion or an iceberg helps conceptualize the different levels of culture (see Figure 2-1). Certain aspects of culture are more apparent, just as the outside layers of an onion or the tip of an iceberg are visible. These aspects are the **manifest culture** (Sathe 1985), containing easily observable elements such as behaviors, language, music, food, and technology. The manifest culture represents the first contact with a new culture, for example, people's speech, dress, interactions with each other, and possessions. Although the manifest level is easily accessible, it provides only a partial understanding of a particular culture. Seeing alone does not make the meaning of the culture clear.

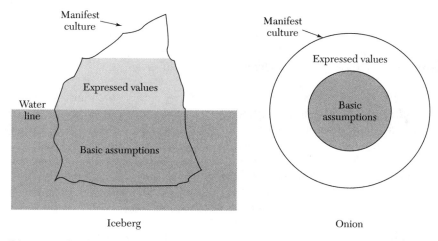

Figure 2-1   **Sathe's Levels of Culture**

A deeper meaning of culture comes from peeling away the outer layers of the onion or looking below the tip of the iceberg. The **expressed values level** represents how people in the culture explain the manifest level. In other words, it is the culture's own explanation of itself. For example, in the Chinese culture, leaving chopsticks sticking out from a bowl of rice is inappropriate because it looks similar to an offering made to one's ancestors. The expressed values level provides additional insight into a culture beyond the manifest level, but some aspects remain unclear.

The core of the onion or the base of the iceberg represent the level of **basic assumptions**. These are the foundations of the culture: shared ideas and beliefs about the world and society as a whole that guide people's thoughts and actions. For example, in Hindu Indian society, people believe true happiness only comes through spiritual enlightenment, not the possession of material wealth (Gannon 1994). Knowing the basic assumptions of a culture provides insight into the principles on which the other levels rest.

How is Culture Learned?

All of us learn a specific culture as we grow up. This complex, nonexplicit, prolonged process is **primary socialization** (Berger and Luckmann 1967, pp. 129–37). We learn appropriate age, gender, ethnic, and social class behavior from families, friends, schools, religious institutions, even advertising and television programs. In some instances, instead of "normal" behavior, people acquire deviant or pathological behavior from role models who do not conform to the central values of the society. In either case, culture is learned from the environment; it is not something we are born knowing.

Countries have specific cultures. People from one country usually behave differently from people who live in other countries. Groups within a country can also have distinctive cultures or **subcultures**. They develop because a group's ethnic background, language, or religion is different from the majority population. For example, in England there is a subculture of ethnic Asian Indians.

Immigrant children growing up in a culture different from their parents' are subject to the influences of both the new and old cultures. For example, the children of Chinese immigrants in the United States often represent a blend of their parents' native culture and American culture. As a result, these people may be very independent and individualistic like Americans yet show strong respect for elders, a Chinese value. In some cases, the values of the two cultures can conflict.

> Culture is so much a part of us that trying to identify our own culture is often difficult. Because culture is "natural" to its members, they experience it as the only way of doing things.

The socialization process is usually not explicit. Parents try to teach their children "what is right," but they rarely consider that this is culturally determined. Culture is so much a part of us that trying to identify our own culture is often difficult. Because culture is "natural" to its members, they experience it as the only way of doing things.

Another type of socialization is **secondary socialization** (Berger and Luckmann 1967). Secondary socialization occurs after primary socialization and usually equips people with the knowledge, skills, and behavior to achieve adult roles successfully, particularly occupational roles. In management and organizational behavior, secondary socialization includes training, organizational socialization, and the influence of organizational culture. This continuous process affects work behavior in important ways, including organizational motivation, planned change, career development, and to some extent, the acceptance of culturally diverse members of an organization.

Frameworks for Examining Cultures

Because understanding a culture's basic assumptions is important for understanding the culture itself, researchers have developed frameworks to classify the cultures of the world. These frameworks are averages or norms of the value systems that compose a culture rather than exact descriptions. In other words, they represent approximate expected behavior in a culture. Obviously, not everyone in a particular culture behaves in the same way. In fact, there is often greater variation within single cultures than across cultures.

KLUCKHOHN AND STRODTBECK'S VARIATIONS IN VALUES ORIENTATIONS

American anthropologists Kluckhohn and Strodtbeck (1961) developed a framework of six dimensions to describe the values orientation of a culture as presented in Table 2-1. The **values orientations** represent how different societies cope with

Table 2-1   Kluckhohn and Strodtbeck's Variations in Values Orientations

Values Orientation	*Variations*		
Relation to Nature	Subjugation	Harmony	Mastery
Time Orientation	Past	Present	Future
Basic Human Nature	Evil	Neutral/Mixed	Good
Activity Orientation	Being	Containing/Controlling	Doing
Relationships among People	Individualistic	Group	Hierarchical
Space Orientation	Private	Mixed	Public

Source: Table adapted from "Kluckhohn and Strodtbeck's Variations in Values Orientations" by H.W. Lane, J.J. DiStefano and M.L. Maznevski from *International Management Behavior*, 3e, 1997. Reprinted by permission of Blackwell Publishers.

various issues or problems. In the Kluckhohn and Strodtbeck framework, a culture may favor one or more of the **variations** or approaches associated with a particular values orientation. In the following discussion, each of Kluckhohn and Strodtbeck's dimensions is identified along with how it influences organizational behavior.

Relation to Nature   Kluckhohn and Strodtbeck consider a culture to cope with its **relation to nature** through subjugation to it, harmony with it, or mastery of it. For example, the Inuit Eskimo culture of Canada, Russia, and the United States has a **subjugation orientation**. The Inuit see whatever happens to them as inevitable. They accept nature as it is rather than try to change it.

A culture that is in **harmony** with nature, such as the Chinese, attempts to orient behavior to coexist with nature. *Feng shui*, "wind water," is a good example of this. The Chinese believe artificial aspects of the environment must be in harmony with nature; the orientation and layout of buildings such as homes and offices affect the lives of those who live and work in them. In selecting or building new office space, a *feng shui* expert or geomancer's advice often helps assess the *feng shui* of the location. When the *feng shui* is good, business should prosper. Table 2-2 presents examples of some of the basic principles of *feng shui*.

Mastery cultures—North America and Western Europe are examples—attempt to change aspects of the environment through technology when necessary or desirable. Land reclamation, air-conditioned buildings, chemical fertilizer, and immunization against disease reflect this orientation. For example, after the discovery of oil at Prudhoe Bay in Alaska, engineers did not consider the severe climactic conditions an insurmountable barrier to extracting it.

Some cultures—Canadian society is one example—demonstrate an almost equal preference for harmony and mastery in relation to nature (Maznevski and DiStefano 1997). Canadians accept the harsh winter weather of their geographic location but at the same time attempt to limit its deleterious effects through a wide array of modern techniques.

Time Orientation   The **time orientation** dimension is a society's focus on the past, present, or future. A **past orientation** emphasizes tradition and using time-honored approaches. For example, Italians respect and value craftsmanship based on years of traditional practice, and an Italian organization treasures time-tested ways of making a product.

A **present-oriented** culture generally focuses on the short-term. For example, in the United States businesses evaluate employee performance yearly,

Table 2-2   Examples of Basic *Feng Shui* Principles

- An ideal building site is on elevated ground with a hill or mountain behind to act as a protective shield and a slow moving river or serene lake in the front.
- A poor location for a building is at a dead-end or blind alley or facing a Y-or T-junction.
- Entry doors into a home should not be too dark or too narrow.
- Windows should be able to receive fresh air and shield the residents from direct glare and heat.
- Good design results from balance.

Source: Table adapted from *Feng Shui for the Home* by E. Lip. Reprinted by permission of Times Editions Pte. Ltd., Singapore.

managers look at financial results quarterly, and people are highly conscious of time.

A **future-oriented** society emphasizes the long term. For example, some large Japanese corporations hire employees for life and consider profitability of a venture only after several years of operation. Similarly, the Japanese often do things to benefit future generations.

Basic Human Nature   **Basic human nature** assesses a culture's belief in people as good, evil, or neutral/mixed. A society seeing **good** in people is basically a trusting one. For example, in Japan executives often trust each other enough to make only verbal agreements for major business deals.

In a culture that believes that people are basically **evil**, there is a lack of trust. In making a business deal, a New Yorker, who often exhibits skepticism, is careful to guard against being cheated. He might have an attorney examine the terms of a contract and insist that every detail be in writing.

A society with a **mixed or neutral orientation** believes people are basically good, however, in some situations they do behave in an evil manner; therefore, it is important to be cautious to protect yourself. Many parts of Canada display this ambivalence; there, a legal contract accompanies verbal business arrangements.

Activity Orientation   A culture's **activity orientation** is either doing, being, or containing/controlling. In a **doing** culture, emphasis is on action, achievement, and working. For example, in the United States, people are hard working and want recognition for their accomplishments. Motivation is through increases in salary, promotions, and other forms of recognition.

A **being** country emphasizes enjoying life and working for the moment; people work to live rather than live to work. For example, in Mexico, businesspeople socialize and enjoy each other's company before discussing their business.

> A **being** country emphasizes enjoying life and working for the moment.

Finally, a **containing/controlling** culture emphasizes rationality and logic. People restrain their desires to try to achieve a mind/body balance. As an example, the French approach to decision making emphasizes pragmatism, logic, and rationality.

Relationships Among People   **Relationships among people** can be individualistic, group, or hierarchical. People in **individualistic** societies define themselves through personal characteristics and achievements. For example, in the United States employees receive rewards for their own accomplishments; individuals have their own work goals, and managers often encourage competition.

In a **group**-oriented society, a positive relationship to the collective is important. People relate to and take responsibility for members of the family or community. Emphasis is on harmony, unity, and loyalty. For example, the Japanese usually base organizational decisions on consensus, working from the lower levels and moving upward.

Hierarchical societies also value group relationships, but emphasize the relative ranking of groups within an organization or society as a whole, making them more class conscious than group societies. For example, in India, as a result of the caste system, birth largely determines position in society, and people from certain groups are more likely to have higher- or lower-prestige jobs.

Space Orientation   The **space orientation** dimension indicates how people relate to the ownership of space. Is it public, private, or mixed? In a **public** society, space belongs to all. For example, Japanese companies arrange office space in an open plan. The desks of both employees and their supervisor are in the same large room with no partitions. In a society that values **privacy** such as the United States, employees consider it important to have their own space. Because privacy is highly valued, higher-status members of an organization often have larger, more private space. Finally, in a **mixed** society, views on space fall somewhere in the middle; a combination of public and private spaces. For example in Hong Kong, lower level employees may share a common work area while managers have private offices.

▌▌▌ HOFSTEDE'S DIMENSIONS OF CULTURAL VALUES

A more recent study of culture focuses specifically on **work-related values**. In a large-scale research program of 40 countries, Geert Hofstede (1980), a Dutch researcher, collected data from IBM employees on work-related values and attitudes. Because the employees were from the same organization, the differences Hofstede found can be more reliably attributed to national culture differences rather than any differences in company cultures or practices.

In analyzing the data from more than 116,000 employees, Hofstede extracted four dimensions of values to explain the differences among cultures: individualism/collectivism, power distance, uncertainty avoidance, and masculinity/femininity. Using the average scores for each country, Hofstede developed national profiles that explain differences in work behaviors. Table 2-3 and Figure 2-2 present these profiles.

Individualism/Collectivism   In **individualistic** countries, people have concern for themselves and their families, rather than others. The individual is important, and each person's rights are valued. Organization systems attempt to honor individual preference and choice, and an employee's evaluation and reward are based on

Table 2-3 Hofstede's Dimensions of Cultural Values—Country Abbreviations

ARG	Argentina	FRA	France	JAP	Japan	SIN	Singapore
AUL	Australia	GBR	Great Britain	MEX	Mexico	SPA	Spain
AUT	Austria	GER	Germany (West)	NET	Netherlands	SWE	Sweden
BEL	Belgium	GRE	Greece	NOR	Norway	SWI	Switzerland
BRA	Brazil	HOK	Hong Kong	NZL	New Zealand	TAI	Taiwan
CAN	Canada	IND	India	PAK	Pakistan	THA	Thailand
CHL	Chile	IRA	Iran	PER	Peru	TUR	Turkey
COL	Colombia	IRE	Ireland	PHI	Philippines	USA	United States
DEN	Denmark	ISR	Israel	POR	Portugal	VEN	Venezuela
FIN	Finland	ITA	Italy	SAF	South Africa	YUG	Yugoslavia

Source: Geert Hofstede, "Motivation, Leadership, and Organization: Do American Theories Apply Abroad?" *Organizational Dynamics* (Summer 1980), p. 50.

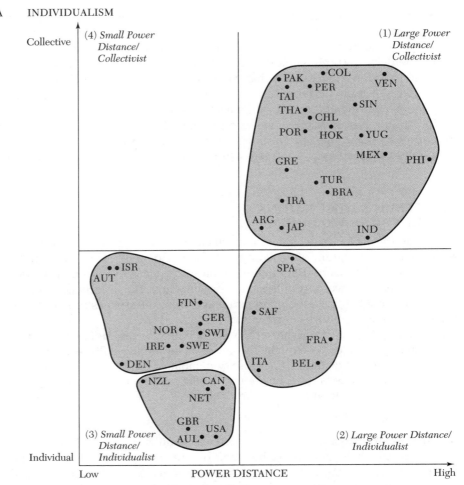

Figure 2-2 **Hofstede's Dimensions of Cultural Values Illustrated**

Source: Figure "Position of Forty Countries on Power Distance and Individualism" from "Organizational Dynamics," Summer 1980, by Geert Hofstede. Copyright © 1980 by Geert Hofstede. Reprinted by permission of the author.

individually agreed-upon objectives. In the individualistically oriented United Kingdom, for example, individual initiative is important, and even when they belong to a team, employees are recognized for individual achievements.

Collectivist cultures value the overall good of the group. The expectation is that people subordinate their individual interests and needs for the benefit of the group. Because being part of the group is so important, it is often very clear how people in the group should behave. In collectivist countries such as Mexico, people look after each other in exchange for loyalty, emphasize belonging, and make group decisions.

Power Distance **Power distance** is the extent to which less powerful members of organizations accept that power is unequally distributed. It ranges from small to large. A **small power distance** society is less comfortable with power differences such as social class distinction or organizational ranking. Rank differences are ignored in certain situations, for instance, when a subordinate makes a complaint to her boss's boss. It is positive for someone in a high-level position to treat those in lower-level

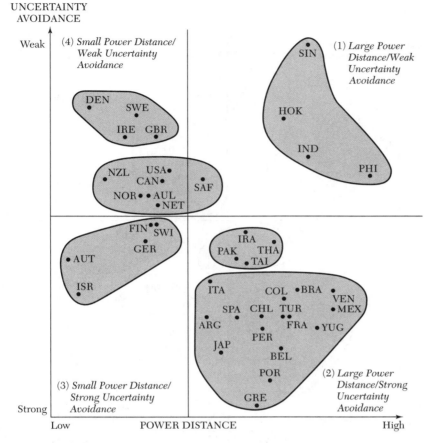

B UNCERTAINTY AVOIDANCE

Figure 2-2 *(Continued)*

positions as equals. In Denmark, a small power distance country, there is more participation in decision making and disregard of hierarchical level to some extent.

In a **large power distance** culture, differences among people with different ranks are accepted, and an individual's societal or organizational position influences how he acts and how others treat him. A person in a high-level position treats those at lower levels with dignity, but the differences in rank are always clear. Delegating decision making implies incompetence because the rank of a manager's position requires him to make decisions himself. In a large power distance country such as Venezuela managers tend to use an autocratic or paternalistic style, most decisions are made at the top, and organizations have many layers of management.

Uncertainty Avoidance   **Uncertainty avoidance**, which ranges from strong to weak, indicates the preferred amount of structure. **Strong uncertainty avoidance** countries prefer more structure, resulting in explicit rules of behavior, either written or unwritten. These nations have strict laws with heavy penalties for offenders, a high need for security, and great respect for experts. Concern about doing things correctly is great, and people are not likely to start a new venture without very thorough research. For example, in a strong uncertainty avoidance country such as Greece, managers are risk-averse and likely to work for the same company for a long time.

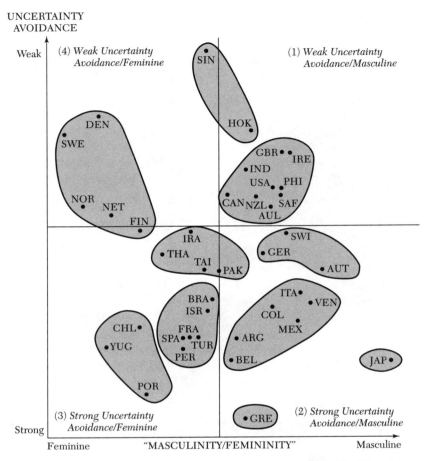

Figure 2-2 **Hofstede's Dimensions of Cultural Values Illustrated** *(Continued)*

In contrast, **weak uncertainty avoidance** cultures favor unstructured situations. The culture is more flexible and people more easy going; a wider range of behaviors is acceptable. In Hong Kong, where uncertainty avoidance is weak, individuals have strong feelings of personal competency, and entrepreneurial behavior is common.

Masculinity/Femininity In a **masculine** society, the "tough" values—including success, money, assertiveness, and competition—are dominant. There are often significant differences between men's and women's roles. The label "masculine" is used because these tough values are almost universally associated with men's roles. Countries such as Germany and Austria ranked highly masculine because their cultures value earnings, recognition, advancement, and challenge. This type of society encourages independent decision making.

Feminine cultures place importance on "tender" values such as personal relationships, care for others, the quality of life, and service. Gender roles are less distinct and often equal. This dimension is termed "feminine" because these traits are usually part of the female role. People in feminine Finland value cooperation, a friendly atmosphere, employment security, and group decision making.

▌▌■ THE CHINESE VALUE SURVEY

Because Hofstede's study presents a Western view of values, some researchers thought that his European values influenced his findings and theory. Consequently, Michael Harris Bond, a Canadian who lives and works in Hong Kong, and a group of Chinese colleagues developed a questionnaire reflecting Chinese cultural values. To prevent Western values from influencing the study, Chinese social scientists developed the Chinese Value Survey (CVS) in Chinese (Chinese Culture Connection 1987), then translated it into other languages and administered it to students in 23 different countries on five continents. Twenty of the countries were also in Hofstede's study.

Four dimensions of culture emerged from the study, three similar to Hofstede's dimensions of power distance, individualism/collectivism, and masculinity/femininity. The fourth dimension, however, represents Chinese values related to Confucianism. Originally called Confucian work dynamism, it was eventually labeled long-term/short-term orientation by Hofstede.

Cultures high on **Confucian work dynamism**, or **long-term oriented**, have greater concern with the future and value thrift and persistence. Such societies consider how their current actions could influence future generations. In a long-term oriented country such as Japan, companies take a longer-term view of investments. It is not necessary to show profits year by year, but rather, progress toward a longer-term goal is most important.

In countries low in Confucian work dynamism, or **short-term oriented**, values are toward the past and present. There is respect for tradition and fulfilling social obligations is a concern, but the here and now is most important. In the short-term oriented United States, for example, companies focus on quarterly and yearly profit results, and managers evaluate employee performance on a year-to-year basis.

Table 2-4 presents the scores of ten countries for long-term and short-term orientation with their four Hofstede dimension scores.

T a b l e   2 - 4   Cultural Dimension Scores for Ten Countries

	PD	*ID*	*MA*	*UA*	*LT*
USA	40L	91H	62H	46L	29L
Germany	35L	67H	66H	65M	31M
Japan	54M	46M	95H	92H	80H
France	68H	71H	43M	86H	30*L
Netherlands	38L	80H	14L	53M	44M
Hong Kong	68H	25L	57H	29L	96H
Indonesia	78H	14L	46M	48L	25*L
West Africa	77H	20L	46M	54M	16L
Russia	95*H	50*M	40*L	90*H	10*L
China	80*H	20*L	50*M	60*M	118H

PD=Power Distance; ID=Individualism; MA=Masculinity; UA=Uncertainty Avoidance; LT=Long-Term Orientation. H=top third, M=medium third, L=bottom third (among 53 countries and regions for the first four dimensions; among 23 countries for the fifth)

*estimated

Source: Hofstede, G. (1993), "Cultural Constraints in Management Theories," *Academy of Management Executive,* 7, p. 91.

❚❚❚ TROMPENAARS' SEVEN DIMENSIONS OF CULTURE

Fons Trompenaars, a Dutch economist and consultant, also developed a framework to examine cultural differences. Using Kluckhohn and Strodtbeck's theory (1961) described previously, Hampton-Turner's dilemma theory (1983), and Parsons' pattern variables (1951), Trompenaars analyzed the questionnaire responses of approximately 15,000 employees representing 47 national cultures.

Trompenaars describes national cultural differences using seven dimensions. Five dimensions are about how people relate to others, including universalism versus particularism, individualism versus collectivism, neutral versus affective, specific versus diffuse, and achievement versus ascription. The sixth dimension is time orientation: past, present, or future and sequential or synchronous. The final dimension is relationship to nature: internal- or external-oriented. Just as with the Kluckhohn and Strodtbeck work, Trompenaars' dimensions represent how societies develop approaches to handling problems and difficult situations.

In measuring a country's score on each dimension, Trompenaars used more than one question. Depending on the question used, the country responses vary somewhat. Therefore, it is difficult to make an absolute categorization of countries on Trompenaars' dimensions.

Universalism Versus Particularism   In a **universal** culture, people believe the definition of goodness or truth applies to every situation. Judgments are made without regard to circumstance. A **particularist** society is more contingency oriented, believing circumstances and relationships are more important in deciding what is right or good. Business contracts illustrate the differences between these two types. In a universalist culture such as the United States, lawyers are an essential part of most negotiations because they write the contract defining a business relationship. Reliance is on the contract, and the parties refer to it when disputes arise. In a particularist country such as China, a legal contract carries very little weight. The situation and the particular individuals involved define the relationship. The contract is a starting point, and the parties' behavior toward each other evolves as circumstances develop.

Individualism Versus Collectivism   This dimension is similar to Hofstede's. In an **individualist** society, the focus is on self. The society structures laws and rules to preserve the rights of the individual and to allow individual development and achievement. In individualist Netherlands, employees receive recognition for their personal contributions and achievements at work.

A **collectivist** society emphasizes group membership. Belonging and contributing to a group is an essential part of the culture. However, within different countries, the definition of "group" varies. For example, although China and Japan are both collective societies, in China the reference group is the clan, an extended network of family and friends. In Japan the reference group is society as a whole.

Neutral Versus Affective Relationships   Expression of emotions is the focus of the **neutral versus affective relationships** dimension. In **affective** cultures, expressing emotions is natural and appropriate. Not to express these may be considered dishonest. In contrast, **neutral** cultures try to control emotion so as not to interfere with judgment. Expressing emotion at a culturally inappropriate time may be considered irrational. In a business situation, someone from an affective culture such as Mexico naturally expresses emotions such as anger or happiness. Singaporeans, representing a neutral culture, view such displays of emotion as unprofessional or out of control.

Specific Versus Diffuse Relationships   The **specific versus diffuse relationships** dimension focuses on how a culture treats privacy and access to privacy. In **specific** countries, people usually have large public spaces and relatively smaller private spaces. There is a separation between the public and private spaces, and the private space tends to remain more private, with access to it limited. In **diffuse** cultures, the relationship of the public and private spaces is the reverse. The public space is relatively smaller and more carefully guarded than the private space.

In practice, people in a specific culture, such as the United States, tend to compartmentalize their public and private lives. Whereas it is easy to access someone in a work situation (public space) to conduct business, an American executive does not automatically allow a business associate to share his private life. In a diffuse culture, such as Spain, gaining access to an individual to transact business is more complicated. Building a relationship precedes negotiating the deal. "Breaking into" the public space of a Spanish executive is initially more difficult, but once there, access to the private or personal life often accompanies it.

Achievement Versus Ascription   The **achievement versus ascription** dimension describes how people in a culture gain power and status. An **achievement** society emphasizes attainment of position and influence. Competence determines who occupies a particular position. People in more powerful positions hold them because of their skills, knowledge, and talents. Members of **ascriptive** cultures believe people are born into influence. Those in power naturally have the right to be there because of their personal characteristics.

In achievement-oriented Australia, a person wins respect on the basis of how well she performs in a position. Age, gender, and family background are not relevant in making hiring or promotion decisions. An ascription-oriented society such as Indonesia generally places people in positions on the basis of who they are, and background, age, and gender are all important. Senior members of an organization are respected because of who they are and their length of service.

Relationship to Time   Trompenaars looks at two aspects of a culture's **relationship to time**. The first is a country's focus on the past, present, or future and how these relate to each other. In a **past-oriented** society, tradition and history are important. In Ethiopia, for example, there is respect for great historical events and well-known people. A **present-oriented** country focuses on what is going on now, including activities and relationships. For example, the Indonesians consider the present more important than the past or future. For them actions are viewed in relation to current impact and style. The **future-oriented** culture uses the past and present to gain future advantage. In the United States, for example, there is great concern with planning, prospects, and future achievements.

The second aspect of the time dimension is **sequential versus synchronic**. People in **sequential** cultures do one thing at a time, make appointments and arrive on time, and generally stick to schedules. Organizations in sequential cultures such as England use detailed plans and evaluate performance every six months or annually based on meeting objectives by a certain date. In **synchronic** countries, people do several activities simultaneously, the time for appointments is approximate, and interpersonal relationships are more important than schedules. The synchronous

Mexicans often evaluate performance based on the whole person, looking at someone's history with the company, present accomplishments, and future potential. Rather than basing evaluations on objectives, they focus on the employee's own aspirations and how these relate to the organization.

Relationship to Nature   Trompenaars' final dimension is **relationship to nature. Internal-oriented** cultures believe nature is controllable. The individual, group or organization is in control of a situation. In Australian businesses, for example, there may be open discussion of conflicts and disagreements because this is a way of controlling them. **External-oriented** societies are more flexible. They try to harmonize with the environment and have more focus on the "other." In Egypt, organizational conflict is managed quietly over a longer period of time because this is less upsetting.

▌▌▌ HALL'S HIGH- AND LOW-CONTEXT CULTURAL FRAMEWORK

Edward T. Hall (1976), an American anthropologist, uses the concept of context to explain differences in communication styles among cultures. "**Context** is the information that surrounds an event; it is inextricably bound up with the meaning of that event" (Hall and Hall 1995, p. 64). Cultures can be categorized on a scale from high- to low-context. "A **high-context (HC)** communication or message is one in which most of the information is either in the physical context or internalized in the person, while very little is in the coded, explicit, transmitted part of the message. A **low-context (LC)** communication is just the opposite; i.e., the mass of the information is vested in the explicit code" (Hall 1976, p. 79). Table 2-5 gives examples of high- and low-context countries.

In a high-context culture, such as Saudi Arabia, family, friends, coworkers, and clients have close personal relationships and large information networks. Because of this, people in high-context cultures know a lot about others within their networks; they do not require extensive background information. People in low-context cultures such as Switzerland separate their lives into different aspects such as work and personal lives. Therefore, when interacting with others, they need to receive more detailed information.

In a high-context culture, people do not rely on language alone for communication. Tone of voice, timing, facial expression, and behaving in ways considered

Table 2-5   **High- and Low-Context Countries**

High-Context	Low-Context
China	Australia
Egypt	Canada
France	Denmark
Italy	England
Japan	Finland
Lebanon	Germany
Saudi Arabia	Norway
Spain	Switzerland
Syria	United States

acceptable in the society are major means of expression. A low-context culture depends on the use of words to convey meaning. Expressing complete, accurate meaning through appropriate word choice is important. The key difference between the two types of cultures is the amount of information supplied in communicating.

DO THE CULTURAL FRAMEWORKS REALLY EXPLAIN CULTURAL DIFFERENCES?

Each cultural framework attempts to explain cultural differences. Some are built on and elaborate the work of others, resulting in some overlap. None of the frameworks is absolutely correct or better than the others, yet each contributes to our understanding of why people from different cultures behave differently.

As noted previously, a framework represents an average of people's behavior within a particular culture. Of course, there are always exceptions to the average, and sometimes particular behaviors common across a whole culture seem to be contrary to a theory's categorization. For example, at a conference, a Taiwanese scholar disagreed with the classification of Taiwan as collective, asking, "Have you ever been in a traffic jam in Taipei? The individualistic behavior of the drivers certainly disproves Hofstede's classification!" Many countries classified as similar may not view themselves as so. The Americans and the British are classified similarly on many dimensions yet often find their two cultures quite different—even the English spoken in one country may be incomprehensible to someone from the other!

> "Have you ever been in a traffic jam in Taipei? The individualistic behavior of the drivers certainly disproves Hofstede's classification!"

The use of different frameworks can provide useful insights. Where more than one framework uses a dimension in the same way and classifies a country similarly, it provides greater reliability. For example, Hofstede, Trompenaars, and Kluckhohn and Strodtbeck all have a dimension focusing on relationships among people. The United States is classified as highly individualistic in all three frameworks, giving more confidence in this classification.

However, France varies from individualistic in the Hofstede model to collective on Trompenaars' dimension to hierarchical in the Kluckhohn and Strodtbeck framework. What explains these differences? Is it because the definitions of the dimension vary? Is it due to differences in the samples of French respondents for the three models? These are some plausible explanations for the differences. Therefore, for foreigners approaching the French, what behavior to expect based on these cultural frameworks is far less clear.

CULTURAL METAPHORS

A different approach to understanding culture is the use of metaphors. Martin Gannon and his associates (1994) identify an important phenomenon or activity of a culture as a metaphor to describe it. Gannon discusses the history and culture of 17 countries and how the metaphor leads to greater understanding of cultures. In explaining each metaphor, typical behaviors in the culture are related to the metaphor. Table 2-6 outlines some of these.

For example, the metaphor for the United States is American football. Americans belong to several groups or teams as part of their work and social life. Membership in these groups is usually temporary, and even though contributing to the team

Table 2-6 **Another Perspective: Metaphors of Culture**

Country	*Metaphor*
England	the traditional British house
Germany	the symphony
Italy	the opera
Japan	the garden
Nigeria	the marketplace
Russia	the ballet
Turkey	the coffeehouse
United States	football

Source: Table from *Understanding Global Cultures: Metaphorical Journeys through 17 Countries* by M.J. Gannon and Associates. Copyright (©) 1994 by Sage Publications, Inc. Reprinted by permission of Sage Publications, Inc.

is an important value, rewards go to individuals. Gannon compares this behavior to the huddle in American football. Members of the team come together and decide what to do as a group. Then, individuals receive rewards for individual performance.

The various frameworks and metaphors are useful for understanding one's own and others' cultures, but knowing the scores of a country on these frameworks, or being able to identify an insightful metaphor, will not make one an expert in that country's culture. Only through in-depth study of the history, traditions, and institutions of a culture, coupled with interaction with its people, can one begin to understand their behaviors, values, and overall approach to life.

How Culture Relates to Organizational Behavior

The cultural frameworks can help one understand how culture relates to organizational behavior. As mentioned in Chapter 1, research in the field of organizational behavior originated primarily in the United States. Therefore it reflects American culture and values, such as the worth and uniqueness of the individual, the correctness of capitalism as an economic system, and the use of natural science models to study human behavior. However, as the study of organizational behavior becomes widespread in other cultures and the concepts of comparative management and internationalization develop in the United States, more researchers are examining whether U.S. models of organizational behavior apply to other cultures.

One source of critical appraisal of U.S. theories is the many documented failures of U.S. multinationals attempting to apply American management theories abroad. Because of this, both academics and businesspeople want to understand why the failures occurred and what approaches might be more successful. They recognize that U.S. models are not universal. In trying to understand how other countries differ from the United States, researchers have considered several variables, such as government, economy, language, technology, and geography.

It can be argued, however, that culture is the most useful variable in discussing differences in how people behave. The examples of cultural differences in this chapter strongly suggest that the application of American management and organizational behavior approaches is destined for failure when applied to cultures differing significantly from the United States. Consequently, throughout this book the frameworks for describing cultures are used to help us understand organizational behavior around the world.

Convergence or Divergence?

FORCES FOR CONVERGENCE

As communication technologies advance and countries become more closely linked through trade, more information about other cultures becomes available. Products are sold worldwide and in some cases marketed in the same way everywhere. Because of this, some might say that cultures are becoming more alike and that the study of culture is therefore irrelevant. At some levels there may be a certain truth to the idea of cultural convergence. For example, in virtually any country you can find someone eating a McDonald's hamburger while sitting in a Honda filled with Shell gasoline; and Christmas, a Christian holiday, is celebrated around the world.

FORCES FOR DIVERGENCE

However, a closer look at what seem to be cultural universals reveals many differences. Having a McDonald's hamburger in Moscow or Beijing is somewhat trendy and the cost is well above average; in Washington, D.C., eating at McDonald's is a mere convenience as well as one of the cheapest meals available. Christmas for the Italians is a family holiday with religious meaning. In Hong Kong it is an occasion for fun among friends, time off work, commercial decorations, and no family obligations. Looking below the surface, cultures attach different meanings to what appear to be the same acts.

On another level, the effect of cultural differences can be clearly seen. Ethnic conflicts continue to flare around the world. These conflicts are often the result of attempts to maintain distinct cultural identities. In many cases the interventions of the United Nations or other countries not involved in the conflict did little to settle the violence. Although there is a World Trade Organization, trade disputes continue. In many cases, arguments over trade reflect the cultural differences of the countries involved.

Culture, although not the only variable of importance, contributes significantly to explaining key differences in societal behavior. With an appreciation of the role of culture in organizations comes a better understanding of management and organizational behavior around the world.

Implications for Managers

Understanding culture can make you a better manager even if you never leave home. In our increasingly interdependent world, managers in every country must be global in their thinking. Even in a large market, such as the United States, that has so many of its own producers, the large majority of products faces foreign competition at home. Whatever your product or your market, global competition is a reality.

Another reason for studying culture is that in any country today an organization's stakeholders could be from another culture. Customers,

> Understanding culture can make you a better manager even if you never leave home.

competitors, suppliers, shareholders, or employees may be from another country. Worldwide, there are also increasing numbers of immigrant and guest workers who bring their own cultures to their new homes. Learning how to integrate them into the existing workforce is essential. Consequently, it is important to understand your stakeholders in order to serve them better and to make your organization more successful.

Even acts that appear similar on the surface may in fact have different meanings for different cultures. Realizing the importance of these cultural differences helps a manager to understand his international partners and ultimately to be a better manager.

■ Summary

Definitions of culture abound, but a simple one is the way of life of a group of people. The levels of culture range from manifest to expressed values to basic assumptions. Understanding the deeper, less apparent, levels produces a more profound understanding of a culture. Culture develops through primary and secondary socialization processes whereby culture is transmitted to individuals.

Cultural frameworks classify national cultures. The frameworks of Kluckhohn and Strodtbeck, Hofstede, the CVS, Trompenaars, and Hall give an initial understanding of the cultures they describe and are useful for understanding differences in cultures.

In discussing the relation of culture to the study of organizational behavior, we note that organizational behavior theories developed in the United States may not apply elsewhere because of cultural differences. A debate on the issue of cultural convergence and divergence shows simultaneous trends in both directions.

The world is becoming increasingly more interdependent and better connected through improved communications technology, allowing managers access to more people and organizations. The implication for managers is that understanding culture is becoming a critical management skill.

■ Discussion Questions

1. What is culture? How is it useful in studying international organizational behavior?
2. Choose a familiar culture. Give examples of each of Sathe's three levels of culture.
3. Think about your own culture. How did the socialization process take place in your own life? Try to recall some of the behaviors and values you were taught early in life. How do these affect you now?
4. Using Hofstede's dimensions of cultural values, contrast two different cultures. What potential problems would people from these two cultures have in doing business with each other?
5. How did the results of the CVS complement the work of Hofstede?
6. Compare the five cultural frameworks from the chapter. What are their similarities and differences? Do you like any better than the others? Why?
7. From your own experience, how do you think understanding culture can help you become a better manager?
8. Do you think that cultures are becoming more similar or more dissimilar? Why?

References

ADLER, N.J. (1991), *International Dimensions of Organizational Behavior*, 2d Ed. Boston: PWS-Kent.

BENEDICT, R. (1934), *Patterns of Culture*. Boston: Houghton Mifflin Company.

BERGER, P. and LUCKMANN, T. (1967), *The Social Construction of Reality*. New York: Doubleday.

Chinese Culture Connection (1987), "Chinese Values and the Search for Culture-Free Dimensions of Culture," *Journal of Cross-Cultural Psychology*, 15, 417–33.

BOND, M.H. and HOFSTEDE, G. (1989), "The Cash Value of Confucian Values," *Human Systems Management*, 8, 195–200.

FERRARO, G.P. (1994), *The Cultural Dimension of International Business*, 2d Ed. Upper Saddle River, NJ: Prentice Hall.

GANNON, M.J. and Associates (1994), *Understanding Global Cultures: Metaphorical Journeys Through 17 Countries*. Thousand Oaks, CA: Sage Publications.

HALL, E.T. (1976), *Beyond Culture*. Garden City, NY: Anchor Press/Doubleday.

HALL, E.T. and HALL, M.R. (1997), "Key Concepts: Underlying Structures of Culture," in Lane, H.W., DiStefano, J.J., and Maznevski, M.L. *International Management Behavior*, 3rd Ed. Cambridge, MA: Blackwell, Publishers.

HOECKLIN, L. (1994), *Managing Cultural Differences: Strategies for Competitive Advantage*. Wokingham, England: Addison-Wesley.

HOFSTEDE, G. (1993), "Cultural Constraints in Management Theories," *Academy of Management Executive*, 7, 81–94.

———. (1980), *Culture's Consequences: International Differences in Work-Related Values*. Thousand Oaks, CA: Sage Publications.

———. and BOND, M.H. (1988), "The Confucian Connection: From Cultural Roots to Economic Growth," *Organizational Dynamics*, 16, 4–21.

KLUCKHOHN, F. and STRODTBECK, F.L. (1961), *Variations in Value Orientations*. Evanston, IL: Peterson.

KROEBER, A.L. and KLUCKHOHN, F. (1991), *Culture: A Critical Review of Concepts and Definitions*, *Peabody Museum Papers*, vol. 47, no. 1, cited in Adler, N.J. (1991), *International Dimensions of Organizational Behavior*, 2d Ed. Boston: PWS-Kent.

LANE, H.W., DiSTEFANO, J.J., and MAZNEVSKI, M.L. (1991), *International Management Behavior*, 3rd Ed. Cambridge, MA: Blackwell Publishers.

LIP, E. (1996), *Feng Shui for the Home*. Torrance, CA: Heian International.

MAZNEVSKI, M.L. and DiSTEFANO, J.J. (1997), "Culture and Its Impact on Management," presented at the 4th International Organizational Behavior Teaching Conference, Hong Kong, January.

PARSONS, T. (1951), *The Social System*. New York: The Free Press.

ROBBINS, S.P. (1993), *Organizational Behavior: Concepts, Controversies, and Applications*, 6th Ed. Upper Saddle River, NJ: Prentice Hall.

SATHE, V. (1985), *Culture and Related Corporate Realities*. Homewood, IL: Richard D. Irwin.

SOROKIN, P. (1939–41), *Social and Cultural Dynamics*, 4 vols. New York: American Book Company.

TROMPENAARS, F. (1993), *Riding the Waves of Culture: Understanding Diversity in Global Business*. London: The Economist Books.

TYLOR, E. (1871), *Origins of Culture*. New York: Harper & Row.

WESTWOOD, R.I. (1992), *Organizational Behaviour: Southeast Asian Perspectives*. Hong Kong: Longman.

Part II

MANAGING INTERNATIONAL ORGANIZATIONAL BEHAVIOR

Ethics and Social Responsibility

My Brother's Keeper

"I lived in Brooklyn, New York for three years and met only a handful of people from my town in Nigeria. One of my Nigerian friends, who is from the eastern protectorate of Umuahia, worked in a public welfare shelter in Brooklyn. One day she called to tell me that she had a new inmate whom she suspected came from my town in Nigeria.

"I asked: 'What is her name?' She told me. I knew right away that her suspicion was 99% correct. Although I didn't recognize her surname, I was certain that she didn't belong in the shelter. I resolved to do all I could to get her out.

"I made some phone calls to the people from Nigeria who lived in Brooklyn. I asked them if they recognized her surname. Eventually, I was able to track down her father, who also lived in Brooklyn. When I mentioned my name he recognized my village, my family, and my father. I told him what I had heard.

"He was unaware that his daughter had run away from home and was living in a public shelter. He was divorced and his daughter was supposed to be living with his ex-wife. He quickly made arrangements to get his daughter out of the shelter. He then took her back to Nigeria, where she now lives with his mother and is doing very well in school."

Source: Cecilia C. Onwuasoanya

After reading this chapter, you should be able to:

1. Define ethics and understand the importance of ethical behavior for organizations.

2. Discuss four perspectives on ethics and arguments for ethical relativism and universalism.

3. Understand the efficiency and social responsibility perspectives of corporate social responsibility.

4. Know how ethics affect individual behavior in organizations.

5. Consider ways of scientifically studying organizational ethics.

6. Know methods for resolving cross-cultural ethical conflicts.

7. Analyze your ethics and how they affect your understanding of management and organizational behavior.

Ethics and social responsibility are major concerns in the global economy. One reason for the heightened awareness of moral issues is the notoriety of recent unethical business behavior. The Wall Street scandals of the 1980s in the United States, product piracy in China, multinational corporate bribery, the prominence of the Russian Mafia in the 1990s, and the destruction of the Brazilian rain forest have increased concerns about the conduct of business throughout the world.

A second reason ethics and social responsibility are important is that as the global economy develops, diverse cultures come into contact. Dissimilar societal values, cultural assumptions, and social norms create conflicts that raise ethical and moral issues.

What are Ethics?

Ethics are moral standards, not governed by law, that focus on the human consequences of actions. Ethics often require behavior that meets higher standards than that established by law, including selfless behavior rather than calculated action intended to produce a tangible benefit.

> Ethics are moral standards, not governed by law, that focus on the human consequences of actions.

Ethics are a product of a society's culture, which includes its traditions, customs, values, and norms. Within a society, ethical behavior is usually taken for granted. Members implicitly understand how relationships, duties, and obligations among people and groups ought to be conducted and distinguish between their self-interests and the interests of others. When there is conflict between groups, it is usually because subcultures within a society have different ethical standards. Under these conditions, the resolution of competing group interests becomes problematic. Similarly, when two or more countries interact, they often find their ethics and understanding of social responsibility differ.

The Culture at Work vignette demonstrates a fundamental quality of ethics. No law required the rescue of a fellow Nigerian from a homeless shelter in Brooklyn, New York. The bonds of nationality and culture, however, created an unquestioned moral obligation to intercede on behalf of a stranger. It felt as though it was the correct, and perhaps only, way to behave.

Most ethical issues are not so clear. An example is the ethical, moral, and legal behavior of industrializing nations toward intellectual property developed and copyrighted by companies in economically advanced countries. The following incident in China illustrates the complexity of the issues:

Pu Xanghua, a plump man given to nervous giggling, leaned back in the witness box as he was asked whether the factory he manages had illegally copied compact disks, several of which were displayed before him in the courtroom.

"It's been a long time," Mr. Pu said, trying to suppress a laugh. "Maybe we made some like this, but I don't remember."

The chief judge, Yang Jun, raised an eyebrow. Lawyers said later that under an agreement that had been worked out before the court session, Mr. Pu was supposed to admit wrong-doing in exchange for avoiding further prosecution. Now Mr. Pu was apparently thumbing his nose at the agreement.

For the foreign plaintiff, an association of music companies from the United States and elsewhere, represented by Mr. Steven Chang, a U.S. citizen, Mr. Pu's testimony in Shanghai Intermediate Court one recent morning was a sign that on top of all the many other frustrations in navigating China's evolving legal system the court was now unable to enforce its own decisions.

Only recently has it even become possible for a foreign company in China to take a local defendant to court and win. More than half the battle is simply getting into a courtroom, where proceedings are generally scripted to validate a decision that has already been made.

But if Chinese courts are inching toward greater fairness in disputes involving foreign companies, they are also becoming less able to control Chinese defendants. Fast-paced economic growth and receding regulation are making Chinese companies less accountable and harder to prosecute.

In the Shanghai case, the factory evaded any attempt at tough prosecution because Mr. Pu and other managers agreed to admit guilt, to produce previously withheld evidence and to promise not to copy any more CDs illegally. But the agreement turned out to be worthless.

After observing Mr. Pu's courtroom performance, Steven Chang, whose organization initiated the complaint, observed:

"It's probably true that they didn't know much about the law when this case started. When I first visited their factory, they gave me a freshly copied CD as a gift. Can you believe it?" (Faison 1995, p. D1).[1]

This example demonstrates the complex interaction among culture, law, and ethics. Different cultures and political regimes have different interpretations of legality and ethics. Countries also control and punish unethical and illegal behavior in a variety of ways. To untangle these complexities, it is useful to explore various ways of thinking about ethics.

Four Perspectives on Ethics

Four perspectives for understanding ethics are the descriptive, conceptual, normative, and practical. The interests of the individual person or group exploring ethical questions influence the appropriateness of each perspective.

The **descriptive approach** is the study of ethics using the methods and theories of social science. Researchers study the ethics of a particular society or corporation and explain their effect on behavior without making judgments regarding their correctness. For example, social scientists can ask executives in various industries to fill out a questionnaire about their business practices. When compared across industries or nations, the data provide insight into behaviors executives consider ethical.

The **conceptual approach** focuses on the meaning of key ideas in ethics such as obligation, justice, virtue, and responsibility. The emphasis in this approach is to refine definitions of important ethical concepts through philosophical analysis. This approach is useful for students of ethics, including academics and members of the legal system.

The **normative approach** involves constructing arguments in defense of basic moral positions and prescribing correct ethical behavior. These arguments may rely on social science studies and conceptual clarification, but they focus primarily on the rationale for a particular position, often on the basis of logic as much as empirical evidence.

Finally, the **practical approach**, a variant of the normative perspective, involves developing a set of normative guidelines for resolving conflicts of interest to improve societal well-being (French and Granrose 1995). This approach is the most widely used by members of organizations.

---

[1]Excerpt from "Fighting Piracy and Frustration in China" by Seth Faison from *The New York Times*, May 17, 1995. Copyright © 1995 by *The New York Times*. Reprinted by permission.

Ethical Relativism and Universalism

Who determines what is right or wrong? Ethical relativism and universalism are different views on whether a person or group should set ethical standards and to whom the standards apply.

Individual ethical relativism is the view that there is no absolute principle of right and wrong, good or bad, in any social situation. The individual persons in a particular situation determine what is right and wrong. In its extreme form, ethics are a personal judgment independent of societal norms and values.

Cultural ethical relativism is the doctrine that what is right or wrong, good or bad, depends on one's culture. If the values of a society support certain acts as ethical and morally correct, then they are acceptable behavior for that society. The counter argument, **ethical universalism**, maintains that there are universal and objective ethical rules located deep within a culture that also apply across societies.

Moral philosophers usually reject ethical relativism because "despite differing practices and beliefs, people often do not disagree about ultimate moral standards" (Beauchamp and Bowie 1993, p. 9). For example, anthropological research demonstrates that behaviors in a wide variety of societies that appear to be unethical or immoral from a particular cultural perspective—usually Western culture—reflect similar ultimate values upon closer inspection.

For corporations, however, moral relativism has considerable appeal. First, it is an attractive position when the business ethics of other cultures are difficult to understand and interpret. It avoids these problems because it permits a business to use its own ethical standards. A second, more compelling reason for accepting relativism is reluctance to give competitive advantage to cultures that conduct business using different, often less stringent, moral and ethical standards. What, then, should be an organization's approach to ethics?

The Social Responsibility of Corporations

> Two fundamental perspectives of corporate ethical and social responsibility are the efficiency perspective and social responsibility theory.

Two fundamental perspectives of corporate ethical and social responsibility are the efficiency perspective and social responsibility theory. Neither can be demonstrated to be preferable by scientific analysis. The positions are grounded in different assumptions about the relationships among human action, economic principles, and desirable social outcomes.

■■■ THE EFFICIENCY PERSPECTIVE

The **efficiency perspective** of corporate social responsibility argues that the obligation of business is to maximize profits for shareholders. Milton Friedman, a Nobel Prize winning economist, strongly endorses this position. According to Friedman (1970, p. 32):

> In a free-enterprise, private-property system, a corporate executive is an employee of the owners of the business. He has direct responsibility to his employers. That responsibility is to conduct the business in accordance with their desires, which generally will be to make as much money as

possible while conforming to the basic rules of the society, both those embodied in law and those embodied in ethical custom.[2]

In this view, a corporation does not serve the interests of its owners by donating funds to charities. However, shareholders are free to support charitable causes or do whatever they want with their profits. Similarly, a corporation should not act to fulfill the needs of a particular segment of society, for example, by recycling packaging material to satisfy environmentalists, unless it creates profit for shareholders. In fact, from the efficiency perspective, managers should not recycle waste products unless it results in profit.

Social responsibility is the function of government, not business. Businesspeople are not elected, and they erroneously impose a tax on their customers, employees, and principals if they allocate profits for social programs. The government, however, can collect taxes and spend them on social programs.

From a cross-cultural perspective, a limitation of the efficiency perspective is that not all societies are based on the free enterprise system. Political systems that intervene in the economy often alter the free exchange that occurs in competitive markets. Of course, even nominally free markets are not without practices such as monetary intervention by central banks, monopolies, cartels, and tariffs. However, because this perspective applies primarily to advanced capitalist economies, it may be less useful for understanding management and organizational behavior in non-capitalist and emerging capitalist countries.

The Social Responsibility Perspective   Corporate social responsibility theory differs from the efficiency perspective

> by replacing the notion that managers have a duty to stockholders with the concept that managers bear a fiduciary relationship to stakeholders. Stakeholders are those groups who have a stake in or claim on the firm. [These] include suppliers, customers, employees, stockholders, and the local community, as well as management in its role as agent for these groups (Evan and Freeman 1993, p. 76).

Along with recognizing multiple stakeholders, this theory regards stakeholder groups not as uninvolved actors, as efficiency theory does, but as active participants "in the future direction of the firm in which they have a stake" (Evan and Freeman 1993, p. 76). Another reason for including a variety of stakeholders in addition to shareholders is the argument that society—the stakeholders—grants corporations the right to exist.

Although stakeholder theory appears straightforward, there are practical problems with implementing it. First, it is difficult to identify an organization's stakeholders. For example, are unborn future generations stakeholders? If the answer is yes, who should represent them? Second, conflict often exists among stakeholders. Sources of stakeholder conflict are differential claims to participation in the corporation's activities and contention over the distribution of its outputs, particularly profits. Finally, it is uncertain that managers can adequately identify socially responsible actions.

By articulating two different understandings of the relationships among groups in society, the efficiency and stakeholder perspectives provide different orientations toward the ethical and social conduct of business. Multinational corporations,

---

[2]Excerpt from "A Friedman Doctrine: The Social Responsibility of Business" by Milton Friedman from *The New York Times Magazine*, September 13, 1970. Copyright © 1970 by *The New York Times*. Reprinted by permission.

operating in diverse socio-cultural environments, either formulate ethical and social policies within these frameworks or develop modifications based on particular circumstances. As globalization increases, it is likely that corporations will move toward the stakeholder perspective because their behaviors will be scrutinized more by diverse outside groups.

The social responsibility perspective an organization adopts toward its environment affects, to some extent, the actions of individuals within the organization by specifying their obligations.

Ethics and Individual Behavior

Individual employees act within an organizational context, including its value system, business philosophy, ethical codes, and business practices. These may not be congruent with employees' personal moral beliefs and ethics. Nonetheless, the organization influences its members' behavior in critical ways, including relations with superiors, subordinates, customers, and competitors. To understand variation in individual persons' ethics, it is important to know the differences between universal and situational ethical theories.

A THEORY OF MORAL DEVELOPMENT

Lawrence Kohlberg, an American psychologist, takes a universal perspective in his theory of moral development. He posits six stages that form an invariant and universal sequence in individual development (Kohlberg 1976); people go through the same stages in the same sequence. It is possible, however, that a person could become "stuck" at one stage and fail to progress to the next. The six stages of Kohlberg's theory follow:

- **Stage 1.** The "obedience and punishment" stage. The only criterion of right for a person at this stage of moral development is obedience to those in authority who have the power to punish.
- **Stage 2.** The "individualism and reciprocity" stage. What is right at this stage is the greatest good for the individual person making the decision. Often, to obtain the greatest good a person enters into agreements with others and forms reciprocal relationships. However, these always have the motive of self-interest.
- **Stage 3.** The "interpersonal conformity" stage. What is right is determined by what is expected of a person by people close to him or her and people in general.
- **Stage 4.** The "social system" or "law-and-order" stage. Morality is playing one's role in the social system, doing one's duty, and obeying rules.
- **Stage 5.** The "social contract" stage. Here, there is individual thinking on morality and less reliance on the society's recognized rules or duties. The principle of "the greatest good for the greatest number" is the criterion for right and wrong used by rational people.
- **Stage 6.** The stage of "universal ethical principles" is the highest stage. Moral decisions are made on the basis of principles that are selected freely by a person and that the individual is willing for everyone to live by.

Most American adults are fixated at Stage 4; they obey rules and fit into the social system, seeking to maintain it. From the perspective of management and organizational behavior, most organizations, not only bureaucracies, rely on and reinforce this level of moral reasoning.

Some American adults reach Stage 5. These people accept the idea that there are moral values or rights independent and prior to the actual laws of society. They see the rules and ethics of organizations as arbitrary constructions favoring one social group over another, rather than tenets based on universal ethical principles.

Only a few Americans reach Stage 6. They believe in a higher set of ethical principles that go beyond what a society expects. They subscribe to "higher ethical laws beyond simple utilitarianism. People are to be treated as ends in themselves, not just as means to one's ends or even to the ends of a whole group or society" (French and Granrose 1995, p. 7). In other words, few people rise to a state of ethical awareness that involves viewing people as inherently valuable.

One criticism of Kohlberg's theory is that it is incomplete. A more profound type of social and political freedom than Stages 5 or 6 would become the seventh stage (Habermas 1979).

Another criticism involves the extent to which the stages are invariant and universal. Although individuals experience moral evolution, elements of earlier stages persist into later stages. In this view, moral development is not a sequential process.

There are also several important criticisms of Kohlberg's theory from the perspective of culture. First, the stage model applies to masculine moral development but not to feminine moral development, which centers on the concept of "caring" (Gilligan 1982).

Second, regarding universalism, Kohlberg's theory may not apply to all cultures because of the wide variety of social, economic, and political conditions that shape values and behaviors. It is possible, however, that within a particular culture there may be universal stages of moral development.

Finally, for management and organizational behavior, a limitation is that organizational culture and corporate ethical policies influence group norms, individual attitudes, and organizational members' actions. This is particularly true when organizations encounter different ethical behavior outside their home countries. Under these conditions, organizations often challenge and redefine ethical behavior to accommodate the other culture.

These criticisms support arguments for ethical relativism. Gender, national culture, and organizational culture can contribute to notable differences in moral orientation and ethical development. Another approach is to view these variables as situational modifiers of Kohlberg's stage theory rather than as fundamentally challenging it or providing alternative theories.

▍▍▉ FACE AND ETHICAL BEHAVIOR

A situational approach to ethical behavior is the concept of **"face."** Usually identified as exclusively part of Asian culture, face is a social process that is found in many cultures, including Western societies. It is an ethical concept because face displays a person's understanding of culturally defined moral codes as they apply to and maintain a particular social situation. Behavior that sustains the definition of the situation supports a person's face. Erving Goffman (1967, p. 5), an American sociologist, defines face as follows:

> The positive social value a person effectively claims for himself by the line others assume he has taken during a particular contact. Face is an image of self delineated in terms of approved social attributes—albeit an image that others may share, as when a person makes a good showing for his profession or religion by making a good showing for himself.

However, face has a central importance in Asian cultures that is not present in Western cultures (Redding and Ng 1983). The meaning of face in Asian cultures refers "to behavior that meets criteria of harmony, tolerance, and solidarity" (Mead 1994, p. 291). In addition, it differs from institutionalized rules found in organizations—for example, codes of ethics—because it is part of the general culture and internalized by individual persons. Finally, the Asian understanding of face reflects concern with social virtue instead of Western concerns with truth. This translates into a collectivist, high–power distance cultural behavior in which "saving one's face and that of other group members—in particular the superior—is of central importance in highly integrated and authoritarian cultures" (Mead 1994, p. 291).

An example of face involves an Australian negotiating with a Taiwanese. At the end of the negotiation, rather than saying no to the Australian, the Taiwanese tells him that his company decided not to purchase any products. Actually, the Taiwanese decided to deal with another company. To maintain harmony between himself and the Australian he fabricates an excuse. For him, the ethical action is to maintain face. The Australian, however, will become incensed if he discovers the real reason. From his perspective, telling the truth, even if it is uncomfortable, is ethical behavior.

Organizational Ethics

Ethical conflicts develop as a result of variations in ethical codes, moral standards, social values, and laws in different cultures.

Ethical conflicts develop as a result of variations in ethical codes, moral standards, social values, and laws in different cultures. Complicating these issues is that not all organizations within a society adhere to the same ethics, morality, or respect for law. Of course, ethical relativism challenges the idea that these are ethical issues.

One way to examine ethical and social responsibility issues is to distinguish between those that are primarily internal to organizations and those that affect interactions between organizations. Frequently, when internal organizational issues raise ethical concerns, they eventually affect relations between organizations.

▌▌▌ INTERNAL ETHICAL ISSUES

Internal ethical issues primarily affect the conduct of organization members. These can include explicit policies and practices of organizations, laws in a particular place, or cultural values that prescribe certain behaviors, such as the following:

- **Discrimination.** Many societies give preference to members of certain groups. Race, ethnicity, age, gender, geographic region, and religion are variables used to discriminate. In some cultures, not being a native of the society is a basis for employment discrimination. Discrimination can be overt or covert and can be used in hiring and promotion. It can also discourage group members from seeking certain types of employment or expecting career advancement.

- **Safety.** In many countries—both developing and developed—worker safety standards fail to provide adequate protection and create conditions that threaten workers' health. Unsafe working conditions, along with child and prison labor, are often part of a strategy to gain competitive advantage. They can also be a manifestation of indifference to human suffering.

- **Compensation.** Workers' wages vary considerably around the world. In many countries, a worker's annual salary may be what a person with a similar job in another country earns in a week. From the Western perspective, many developing nations pay incredibly low wages. However, because Western companies transplant their manufacturing facilities to low-wage countries, they reinforce this practice. It should also be noted that even in economically advanced societies, for example, the United States, "sweat shop" conditions still exist in urban areas with immigrant populations.

- **Child labor.** Widespread child labor is found in many less-developed countries. It raises questions similar to those of prison labor with the additional concern of corporate responsibility for establishing appropriate social welfare and educational institutions in a society.

Within a society, these practices may not only be ethical but legal. Only when cultures with different value systems object do they become ethical issues. An example of change caused by ethical value conflict is the formation of a coalition of major Western European and U.S. sporting goods manufacturers and child advocacy groups to combat the sale of soccer balls stitched by children in Pakistan.

Because of impoverishment, Pakistani parents in the Sialkot region of Punjab province force their children into soccer ball stitching as early as 6 years of age. According to one estimate, "Close to 10,000 Pakistani children under the age of 14 work up to 10 hours a day stitching the leather balls, often for the equivalent of $1.20 a day" (Greenhouse 1997, p. A12). In Western Europe and the United States, where the soccer balls are marketed, this practice is illegal and unethical.

To avoid the experience of other efforts aimed at eliminating child labor that resulted in the unemployed children entering other occupations, including making bricks and prostitution, the coalition plans to educate the children and place parents and older siblings in jobs or provide small loans to start their own businesses.

CROSS-CULTURAL ETHICAL ISSUES

With economic globalization, ethical issues increasingly affect the interaction of organizations across cultures, including the following:

- **Theft of intellectual property.** Not all countries honor copyrights and patents, and many encourage piracy. This is a significant issue with the increased use of computer software, compact music discs, and other forms of proprietary information that are difficult to protect.

- **Bribery and corruption.** Two common forms of bribes are whitemail and lubrication bribes. **Whitemail** is a payment made to a person in power for favorable treatment that is illegal, or not warranted on an efficiency, economic benefit scale. **Lubrication bribes** are payments to facilitate, speed up, or expedite otherwise routine government approvals for things such as licenses or inspections.

- **Intentionally selling dangerous products.** Companies sometimes export products that either are considered dangerous in their own country or are not entirely appropriate for the needs of the recipient culture. An example of the former is the sale of cigarettes in developing nations by firms, often from nations that have public policies to discourage smoking, such as the United States. An example of the latter is the exportation of infant formula to countries where there is a high likelihood of improper and harmful use.

■ **Environmental pollution.** Not all countries demonstrate concern for the natural environment, particularly because it is expensive to manufacture without polluting. Environmental degradation—such as toxic emissions from factories, radiation from nuclear power plants, and the destruction of vast forests—contributes to worldwide environmental problems.

■ **Intentional misrepresentation in negotiations.** Bluffing, fraud, intimidation, and various other forms of deception may be acceptable negotiation tactics in some cultures yet considered unethical, or even illegal, in others.

▌▐ THE INTERACTION OF INTERNAL AND CROSS-CULTURAL ETHICS

On occasion, internal ethical issues evolve into ethical and social responsibility concerns between organizations or countries. This occurs either because of a shift in corporate and public attitudes toward certain practices or exposure of hidden practices that were always objectionable. Examples include negative reactions to clothes imported from countries that use child or prison labor and the export of cigarettes to developing nations.

Some cases are extremely complex because they involve the use of products in ways other than intended. An example is the experience of H.B. Fuller in Central America. Fuller, a manufacturer of industrial glues, coatings, and paints located in St. Paul, Minnesota, prides itself on being a socially responsible company. Among its products is Resistol, a glue used for making shoes. For many years Resistol has been sniffed by children in Central America because it provides a temporary euphoria that relieves hunger and hopelessness. But Resistol's fumes are addictive and can cause brain damage and, in some cases, death.

Fuller has tried to stop Resistol's use as a drug by reducing the toxicity of the glue and putting restrictions on its sale in Honduras and Guatemala. It has not, however, followed other companies by adding mustard oil to the glue, which, when sniffed, induces vomiting, not euphoria. The addition of mustard oil has greatly reduced sales for these companies.

Lawsuits have been filed against Fuller challenging its self-image and public perception as an ethical, socially responsible company (Henriques 1995). The ethical issue for Fuller is whether it should do more to prevent the abuse of its product, including withdrawing it from the market.

Can Fuller use scientific techniques to resolve its ethical dilemma?

Studying Ethics

Researchers use social science methods to study ethics in organizations.

Researchers use social science methods to study ethics in organizations. Participant observers, social scientists who assume organizational roles to study organizations, document how managers confront ethical dilemmas and adjust their behavior to them (Jackall 1988). Another approach is examining consequences of potentially compromised decision making. An example is a reconstruction of the ethical climate at the National Aeronautical and Space Administration (NASA) in the United States that led to the Challenger space shuttle disaster. Organizational culture and the bureaucratic process created the normalization of deviance; when a manufacturer produced a part that did not meet specifications, because of time pressures and social conformity, the integrity of the approval process became undermined (Vaughan 1996). Finally, researchers can use interviews or questionnaires to study managers' and other organization members' policies and practices concerning ethics.

ETHICS IN THE UNITED KINGDOM AND UNITED STATES

Studies comparing the United Kingdom and the United States suggest that managers in both countries face similar management issues because they are almost the same on several cultural variables. For example, in Hofstede's framework they are similar in power distance, uncertainty avoidance, individualism, and masculinity. The United Kingdom and United States also share a common Anglo-Saxon heritage, system of law, economic system, and language.

Despite these similarities, a study of 813 U.K. and U.S. companies found important differences in their approaches to ethical issues (Robertson and Schlegelmilch 1993). First, U.K. companies are more likely to communicate ethics policies through senior executives, whereas U.S. companies rely more on their human resources and legal departments. Second, U.S. firms consider most ethical issues more important than do their U.K. counterparts, particularly employee actions that may harm the firm. Third, U.K. managers consider external corporate stakeholders more important than do U.S. managers. Finally, with the exception of the right to privacy, U.K. firms are more protective of employee rights and more likely to specify policies forbidding employee conduct counter to the firm's interests.

In summary, although the basic value orientations of the two countries are similar, corporations vary in the emphasis of different aspects of ethics and how they are managed. If countries as similar as the United States and United Kingdom emphasize and manage ethics differently, more significant variation probably exists in countries that have extensive cultural differences. This leads to consideration of ways to resolve ethical conflicts.

Resolving Cross-Cultural Ethical Conflicts

Differences in values are the core of cross-cultural ethical conflicts because ethical value systems vary across cultures. When cultures come into contact, even when they are similar, there is the potential for conflict over what is right and wrong.

One method for regulating ethical conflict is to transform ethics into **laws.** Rather than voluntary compliance with an action, there is mandatory compliance accompanied by formal punitive sanctions. An example from the United States is the Foreign Corrupt Practices Act (FCPA) of 1977, which was amended in 1988. The primary concern of the FCPA is the use of bribes by American firms to influence foreign executives to purchase their products. Instead of relying on voluntary compliance, the FCPA makes it illegal for U.S. firms to offer bribes or otherwise corrupt the actions of foreign executives, politicians, or candidates for office. The penalties include fines and prison terms.

American firms have found ingenious ways to comply with the FCPA yet achieve their objectives. An example is the strategy of the Chubb Corporation, an insurance company located in New Jersey. To enter the Chinese marketplace—a potentially huge insurance market—Chubb set up a $1 million program to teach insurance at a Shanghai university, naming as board members officials who can eventually grant Chubb its license to do business in China (Milbank and Brauchli 1995).

Another method for resolving ethical conflict is corporate **codes of ethics**. Although these are not laws, they codify behavior that is unacceptable under certain conditions. Organizations expect employees to adhere to them or suffer penalties ranging from reprimands to dismissal. In other words, ethical codes—involving issues as diverse as sexual harassment, the use of company property, and giving or receiving gifts—reduce ambiguity by specifying appropriate behavior. In some cases, for example, sexual harassment in the United States, the violation of an ethical code can result in legal action.

Laws and ethical codes do not cover all situations. To resolve problems raised by ethical relativism and absolutism, managers facing ethical conflicts should consider the nature of the specific ethical situation. The response, according to Kohls and Buller (1994, p. 32), "depends on the centrality of values at stake, the degree of social consensus regarding the ethical issue, the decision-maker's ability to influence the outcome, and the level of urgency surrounding the situation."

Managers can take one of seven approaches for resolving ethical conflicts (Kohls and Buller 1994, p. 32)[3]

1. **Avoiding.** One party simply chooses to ignore or not deal with the conflict.
2. **Forcing.** One party forces its will upon the other. Forcing is often used when one party is stronger than the other.
3. **Education–persuasion.** One party attempts to convert others to its position through providing information, reasoning, or appeals to emotion.
4. **Infiltration.** One party introduces its cultural values to another society hoping that an appealing idea will spread.
5. **Negotiation–compromise.** Both parties give up something to negotiate a settlement.
6. **Accommodation.** One party adapts to the ethics of the other.
7. **Collaboration–problem solving.** Both parties work together to achieve a mutually satisfying solution, a win-win outcome meeting the needs of both.

How does a manager select among these actions? First, he or she considers the **centrality of values**. Values form a continuum arranged from core values of universal concern and central to the ethical conduct of business to those on the periphery.

Following the continuum idea, ethical decisions preserve core values and focus less attention to those on the periphery (Kohls and Buller 1994). Core values include freedom from torture, the right to nondiscriminatory treatment, the right to

---

[3]"Seven approaches for resolving ethical conflicts" and figure illustrating "Core and Periphery" from "Resolving Cross-cultural Ethical Conflict: Exploring Alternative Strategies" by John Kohls and Paul Buller from *Journal of Business Ethics*, 12:33, 1994. Copyright © 1994 by Kluwer Academic Publishers. Reprinted with kind permission from Kluwer Academic Publishers.

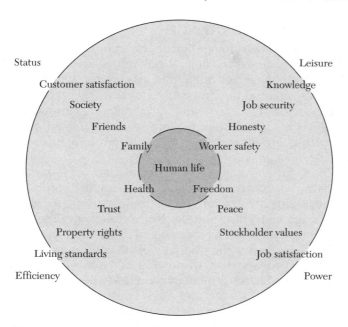

F i g u r e 3 - 1   Values: Core and Periphery

Source: John Kohls and Paul Buller from *Journal of Business Ethics*, 12:33, 1994. Copyright © 1994 by Kluwer Academic Publishers. Reprinted with kind permission from Kluwer Academic Publishers.

freedom of speech and association, and the right to political participation (Donaldson 1989). Figure 3-1 presents a continuum of values from core to periphery based on Western preferences.

Second, values are classified according to **home culture consensus**. Values widely shared by the home culture should be maintained in an ethical decision (Kohls and Buller 1994).

The third factor is the **influence** a manager has over the situation. There is a continuum from no ability to change the situation to complete control over the situation. When managers have no influence over the situation, they must accommodate to the other culture. If important values are involved, managers should take themselves out of the situation or not get involved (Kohls and Buller 1994).

The final factor is **urgency**. How quickly or slowly something must be done influences the choice of conflict resolution strategy. Urgency limits the options to avoidance, forcing, or accommodation because infiltration, education, negotiation, and collaboration require extended time.

Convergence or Divergence?

With increasing globalization will pressures emerge for standardization of ethics to facilitate interaction among organizations in different cultures? Will there be a set of mechanisms that permit diverse ethical codes to adjust to one another? Or, will ethics be a crazy quilt dependent on cultural preferences and individual corporate interests?

FORCES FOR CONVERGENCE

As organizations modernize through bureaucratization, a bureaucratic ethic could replace local ethics based on religion, social values, and customs. For example, Jackall (1988) analyzed the ethics of an American corporation and argues that a bureaucratic ethic has replaced the Protestant ethic. In other words, deeply held religious beliefs that provided business with its values were cast aside for an ethics of efficiency. As developing countries modernize and multinational companies expand, the ethics of knowledge workers will probably influence ethical codes (see Sassen 1991), hastening this process.

Another force for convergence is the emergence of international regulatory agencies that enforce ethical standards on multinational corporations (Frederick 1991). These codes, along with international trade agreements such as the General Agreement on Tariffs and Trade and the North American Free Trade Agreement, may eventually contribute to the replacement of local moral and ethical norms.

Another factor increasing the similarity of ethical standards and social responsibility is the diffusion of capitalism worldwide. In the late 1990s the effects of capitalism are mixed. On one hand, growth of organized crime and deterioration of traditional social controls in Russia and the People's Republic of China suggest unfettered, opportunistic, and amoral behavior under the guise of capitalism. On the other hand, economic reforms in these countries have led to greater availability of consumer products and new business opportunities. This may produce the ethical and cultural contradictions of American capitalism in the new capitalist countries (Bell 1976).

FORCES FOR DIVERGENCE

Religion is the most complex, deep rooted, and persistent force for ethical divergence. Although there are significant areas of agreement on ethical practices among the world religions, perhaps the areas of disagreement are more important (see Terpstra and David 1991).

The treatment of women and their role in organizations provides an example of ethical conflict based in religion. In Muslim societies—as well as other cultures with fundamentalist interpretations of religious texts—women are the social inferiors of men. A typical conflict arises when a Western company assigns a female to work in a culture that does not recognize principles of gender equality and objects to dealing with a woman.

Another issue raised by religion is the definition of insiders and outsiders, those who believe in a religious doctrine as opposed to those who do not. This often results in ethical particularism, the view that insiders adhere to a superior set of ethics and moral behavior compared with outsiders (Nelson 1969).

National and ethnic cultures are reasserting themselves in a variety of ways. For example, armed conflicts are continually waged to preserve a way of life based on religious and cultural identity. Because of nationalism and ethnic and cultural patterns, cultures are resistant to significant change and, in the late twentieth century, may be in the process of reestablishing themselves as major sources of international conflict (Huntington 1996).

Finally, countries have different economic systems and are at various stages of economic development. These may contribute to maintaining or creating different ethical standards. For example, developing countries frequently protest that it is unjust to hold them to the same environmental standards as developed countries because the expense impedes their economic development.

Implications for Managers

Managers do not share the same ethical code and understanding of social responsibility. They also cannot assume that their own corporation's ethical conduct is superior. As a result, cross-cultural managers must develop a framework for evaluating ethical codes and determining their own ethics.

Cross-cultural managers must understand other societies' religion, values, culture, law, and ethics. What may be a shocking breach of ethics to a Western business person—child labor, a wage of pennies a day, or blatant gender discrimination—may be acceptable behavior in another culture. Knowing the behaviors and ethics of other cultures can help determine which course of action is appropriate. The suggestions in this chapter for resolving cross-cultural ethical conflict can also be useful.

■ Summary

Ethics are intimately connected to culture. They are the translation of abstract cultural values into rules governing everyday interactions. Ethical issues are important when there is conflict over what is proper conduct.

Ethics can be viewed from four perspectives: the descriptive, conceptual, normative, and practical. Ethics can also be understood from the viewpoint of relativism or objectivism. Cultural relativism is the position that ethics vary with a specific culture. Objectivism or absolutism is the position that there are identifiable common ethics across cultures. Most philosophers argue for absolutism as do influential theories such as Kohlberg's moral development theory.

At the level of the organization three prominent theories are the efficiency perspective, the stakeholder perspective, and the group social responsibility perspective. The efficiency perspective argues that managers' only ethical responsibility is to satisfy corporate stockholders. The social responsibility perspective suggests considering various stakeholders of a firm in decision making. Finally, the concept of face—found primarily in Asian cultures—is an ethic of individual responsibility to and for the group that incorporates situational elements.

Cross-cultural studies indicate that ethics and the way they are managed are not the same in different cultures. Transforming ethics into laws or developing international corporate ethical codes are two ways to regulate organizational ethics across cultures. Managers can handle cross-cultural ethical conflicts through avoidance, forcing, education–persuasion, infiltration, negotiation–compromise, accommodation, and collaboration–problem solving.

Finally, there are various forces creating worldwide convergence of organizational ethics such as bureaucratization, professionalization, and the resurgence of capitalism. Forces for maintaining different ethical standards include religion, culture, economic systems, and varying stages of societal development. Managers can prepare for cross-cultural ethical issues by understanding the societies in which they do business.

■ Discussion Questions

1. What are ethics?
2. How do ethics differ from law?
3. What role do culture and societal values play in creating ethics?

4. Are ethics in business situations relative or absolute?
5. How does the efficiency view differ from the stakeholder view of corporate social responsibility?
6. Does the concept of face apply to behavior in your university?
7. Why do ethics create conflict?
8. Under what conditions would education be a useful approach to resolving a cross-cultural ethical conflict?
9. In your opinion, as the global economy develops, will ethics and social responsibility become more similar or distinctive across cultures?
10. What are your views on the role of ethics in multinational organizations?

References

BEAUCHAMP, T. and BOWIE, N. (1993), *Ethical Theory and Business*, 4th Ed. Upper Saddle River, NJ: Prentice Hall.

BELL, D. (1976), *The Cultural Contradictions of Capitalism*. New York: Basic Books.

DONALDSON, T. (1989), *The Ethics of International Business*. New York: Oxford.

EVAN, W. and FREEMAN, R. (1993), "A Stakeholder Theory of the Modern Corporation: Kantian Capitalism," in Beauchamp, T. and Bowie, N. eds., *Ethical Theory and Business*, 4th Ed. Upper Saddle River, NJ: Prentice Hall.

FAISON, S. (1995), "Fighting Piracy and Frustration in China," *The New York Times* (May 17), D1.

FREDERICK, W. (1991), "The Moral Authority of Transnational Corporate Codes," *Journal of Business Ethics*, 10, 22–37.

FRENCH, W. and GRANROSE, J. (1995), *Practical Business Ethics*. Upper Saddle River, NJ: Prentice Hall.

FRIEDMAN, M. (1970), "The Social Responsibility of Business Is to Increase Its Profits," *New York Times Magazine* (September 13), 32–33, 122, 126.

GILLIGAN, C. (1982), *In A Different Voice: Psychological Theory and Women's Development*. Cambridge, MA: Harvard University Press.

GOFFMAN, E. (1967), *Interaction Ritual: Essays in Face-to-Face Behavior*. Garden City, NY: Anchor Books.

GREENHOUSE, S. (1997), "Sporting Goods Concerns Agree to Combat Sale of Soccer Balls Made by Children," *The New York Times* (February 14), A12.

HABERMAS, J. (1979), *Communication and the Evolution of Society*. Boston: Beacon Press.

HENRIQUES, D. (1995), "Black Mark for a 'Good Citizen,'" *The New York Times* (November 26), 1, 11.

HUNTINGTON, S. (1996), *The Clash of Civilizations and the Remaking of World Order*. New York: Simon & Schuster.

JACKALL, R. (1988), *Moral Mazes: The World of Corporate Managers*. New York: Oxford University Press.

KOHLBERG, L. (1976), "Moral Stages and Moralization, the Cognitive-Developmental Approach," in Lickona, T. ed., *Moral Development and Behavior*. New York: Holt, Rinehart and Winston.

KOHLS, J. and BULLER, P. (1994), "Resolving Cross-Cultural Ethical Conflict: Exploring Alternative Strategies," *Journal of Business Ethics*, 13, 31–38.

MEAD, R. (1994), *International Management: Cross Cultural Dimensions*. Cambridge, MA: Blackwell.

MILBANK, D. and BRAUCHLI, M. (1995), "How U.S. Concerns Compete in Countries Where Bribes Flourish," *The Wall Street Journal* (September 9), 1, 16.

NELSON, B. (1969), *The Idea of Usury: From Tribal Brotherhood to Universal Otherhood*. Chicago: University of Chicago.

REDDING, S. and NG, M. (1983), "The Role of 'Face' in the Organizational Perceptions of Chinese Managers," *International Studies of Management and Organization*, 13 (3), 92–123.

ROBERTSON, D. and SCHLEGELMILCH, B. (1993), "Corporate Institutionalization of Ethics in the United States and Great Britain," *Journal of Business Ethics*, 12, 301–12.

SASSEN, S. (1991), *The Global City*. Princeton, NJ: Princeton University Press.

TERPSTRA, V. and DAVID, K. (1991), *The Cultural Environment of International Business*. Cincinnati: South-Western.

VAUGHAN, D. (1996), *The Challenger Launch Decision: Risky Technology, Culture, and Deviance at NASA*. Chicago: University of Chicago Press.

Communication

A Day at the Market

It was one of my first days in Hong Kong. I had gone to the market to buy some household items for my apartment. I picked out a few items and asked the seller, "How much?" I wasn't totally sure, given his strong accent, but it sounded like six dollars. "Very reasonable," I thought. "Okay," I said, "I'll take it. How much did you say it was?" The seller's hand went up with his thumb and little finger outstretched, and the three middle fingers folded over his palm. It looked like a sign for "two" to me. "If he only wants two dollars," I thought, "that's an even better deal for me." So I paid the seller two dollars and was ready to leave, but he held up his hand in the same gesture as before. This time there was no mistake; it was clearly the English word "six" coming out of his mouth. I paid the six dollars and walked off wondering what had happened.

Later, I asked a Chinese colleague, who laughed and said, "Yes, if we want to indicate the number five, we hold up a whole hand, but for six we use one hand with the thumb and little finger sticking out. It's very convenient, and everyone knows what it means." Except me . . .

Source: A.M. Francesco

After reading this chapter, you should be able to:

1. Explain the basic communication process and define cross-cultural communication.
2. Understand how language affects communication and how different cultures use the four styles of verbal communication.
3. Discuss various types of nonverbal communication.
4. Identify major barriers to communicating cross-culturally.
5. Enhance your cross-cultural communication skills.

Communication is central to culture and the management of organizational behavior. Language is intricately linked to culture, and communication expresses and changes cultural values. Organizations are communication systems. Without effective communication, organizations experience difficulty and even failure.

But it is challenging to achieve effective communication within cultures and organizations. It becomes more complex across cultures and organizations. As the Culture at Work vignette illustrates, even comparatively simple communication across cultures is open to misunderstanding.

What is Communication?

▮▮▮ THE COMMUNICATION PROCESS

Communication is the process of transmitting thoughts or ideas from one person to another. The person who initiates the process is the **sender**, and the other person is the **receiver**. Figure 4-1 summarizes the communication process.

The communication process begins with the sender, who has a **thought** or idea to relay to another person. The sender expresses this thought in a form he believes the receiver will understand, whether verbal or nonverbal. When the message is **encoded**, that is, expressed in an understandable format, it is then **transmitted** or sent via a medium such as voice, fax, memo, or e-mail. Once the receiver **receives** the message, he then **decodes** or interprets the meaning of the symbols used by the sender to **understand** or comprehend the meaning of the message. To the extent that the receiver's understanding and the sender's thought are the same, communication is effective. Although not an essential part of communication, the receiver can give the sender feedback, letting the sender know if his message was received and understood. The **feedback** process uses the same six steps, with the receiver and sender switching roles.

Distortion and interruption often enter the communication process. Factors responsible for distortion or interruption are called **noise**. Examples of noise include actual noise such as traffic or other people talking and technological problems, for instance, a fax machine breaking down. More important sources of noise are cultural and social differences between the sender and receiver that make it difficult for them to understand each other.

Cross-Cultural Communication Differences

Cross-cultural communication occurs when people from more than one culture communicate with each other. This is more difficult than communication among people of the same culture. Noise develops due to differences in language, values,

Figure 4-1   The Communication Process

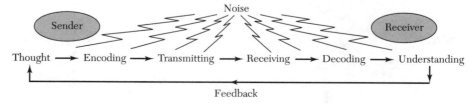

and attitudes, among other factors. The major differences in how people from different cultures communicate with each other are language usage, verbal style, and nonverbal communication.

▮▮▮ LANGUAGE USAGE

Two people may speak the same language but speak it quite differently. For example, people from the United States and England both speak English, but the meaning of certain words is quite different, sometimes even opposite, in the two countries. Americans call the storage compartment of a car the "trunk"; the English call it the "boot." To get to the 50th floor, Americans take an "elevator," but the English use a "lift." When the English "table" an item in a meeting, they act on it immediately. When Americans table something, they expect to deal with it later!

A more challenging situation is when native speakers of two different languages need to communicate. One or both may be able to speak a language that the other can understand, or they may require an interpreter. Complicating matters, words and concepts in one language may not have equivalents in another language. For example, as discussed in Chapter 6, the concept of *achievement* is almost impossible to translate into a language other than English (Hofstede 1980b). The Chinese have many different terms for the single English word *dumpling*. In the Inuit Eskimo language, there are more than 50 words for various types of snow (Deresky 1994). The precise meaning of *achievement* in the United States and the fine distinctions the Chinese give to dumplings and the Inuits to snow reflect their importance in those cultures.

Because of language and cultural differences, corporations must consider brand or product names when selling in international markets. Inadequate translations can result in a negative image for the product and company. An early translation of *Coca-Cola* into Chinese meant "bite the wax tadpole." Coca-Cola has since found and trademarked a new Chinese name that means "refreshing and delicious" (Warner 1996). The original brand name of a product can also create an unintended image in another language. The Chinese "White Elephant" brand name conveys a positive meaning in Chinese but has a negative connotation in the United States. Table 4-1 lists additional international marketing blunders based on language differences.

> An early translation of Coca-Cola into Chinese meant "bite the wax tadpole."

In some cases, differences in languages and cultures can make the interpreter's job almost impossible. Consider the case of a U.S. television news reporter trying to interview a local villager during the Vietnam War:

Table 4-1   International Marketing Blunders

- The Chevrolet Nova car had trouble selling in Puerto Rico because it sounded like *no va*, meaning "it doesn't go."
- A Finnish brewery found sales of Koff and Siff beers in the United States were slow because the names sounded unappealing in English.
- The soft drink Fresca was marketed in Mexico without a change of brand name. The company later discovered that *fresca* is slang for *lesbian* in Mexico.

Adapted from Ricks, D.A. (1983), *Big Business Blunders: Mistakes in Multinational Marketing*. Homewood, IL: Dow Jones-Irwin.

A Foreign Service linguist, while watching the evening news, discovered that a Vietnamese interpreter had simply given up when trying to bridge the gap between a CBS reporter and a Vietnamese villager. The TV audience watched the reporter ask a question, heard it go back and forth between the interpreter and the villager, and then heard the answer back in English. What the interpreter had done was simply ask the villager to count to ten, which he did. Then the interpreter reported what the villager *might* have said had he been able to understand the abstract ideas in the original question (Fisher 1980, p. 60).

▌▌▐ VERBAL COMMUNICATION STYLES

Verbal communication styles are another way that cultures vary in their communication patterns. Gudykunst and Ting-Toomey (1988) identify four different verbal communication styles: direct versus indirect, elaborate versus succinct, personal versus contextual, and instrumental versus affective. "Verbal interaction styles reflect and embody the affective, moral, and aesthetic patterns of a culture" (Gudykunst and Ting-Toomey 1988, p. 100). The words used and the way they are put together tell much about a particular culture. Gudykunst and Ting-Toomey associate the four verbal styles with cultural characteristics by referring to Hofstede's (1980a) dimensions of cultural values and Hall's (1976, 1983) high- and low-context culture descriptions.

The verbal styles are part of a culture. Often countries that speak the same language have similar cultures but not always. Therefore, it is possible that speakers of the same language from different cultures employ different verbal styles. For example, East Indian English speakers use the contextual style, in contrast to the personal style of American or British English (Gudykunst and Ting-Toomey 1988). This presents a communication barrier that neither party may expect. Table 4-2 presents the major characteristics of the four verbal styles.

Direct Versus Indirect Style   The **direct versus indirect style** differs in the degree of explicitness of the verbal message. In the **direct style**, the speaker tries to convey her true feelings through the choice of words. In the **indirect style**, the speaker selects words to hide his real feelings. For example, North Americans using

T a b l e   4 - 2   **Major Characteristics of the Four Verbal Styles**

Verbal Style	Variation	Major Characteristic	Cultures Where Found
Direct versus Indirect	Direct	Message is more explicit.	Individualistic, low-context
	Indirect	Message is more implicit.	Collective, high-context
Elaborate versus Succinct	Elaborate	Quantity of talk is relatively high.	Moderate uncertainty avoidance, high-context
	Exacting	Quantity of talk is moderate.	Low uncertainty avoidance, low-context
	Succinct	Quantity of talk is relatively low.	High uncertainty avoidance, high-context
Personal versus Contextual	Personal	Focus is on speaker, "personhood."	Low power distance, individualistic, low-context
	Contextual	Focus is on role of speaker, role relationships.	High power distance, collective, high-context
Instrumental versus Affective	Instrumental	Language is goal oriented, sender focused.	Individualistic, low-context
	Affective	Language is process oriented, receiver focused.	Collective, high-context

the direct style say, "No" or "I can't do that," if they are unable to make a particular deal. In contrast, a Korean speaker might say, "It might be possible," or "It's interesting in principle," rather than say "no" directly.

The direct style is common in individualistic, low-context cultures, and the indirect style in collective, high-context cultures. The direct style allows the individualist to express her own ideas clearly. The collectivist's orientation is to maintain group harmony and concern for the feelings of others.

Elaborate Versus Succinct   The second style is **elaborate versus succinct**, focusing on the quantity of talk with which people feel comfortable. There are three recognizable styles: the elaborate, the exacting, and the succinct. In the **elaborate style**, the quantity of talk is relatively high, description includes great detail, and there is often repetition. The use of metaphors, similes, and proverbs is frequent, many adjectives modify the same noun, and verbal elaboration and exaggeration are typical. People from Arabic countries use the elaborate style.

The emphasis in the **exacting style** is on precision and using the right amount of words to convey the desired meaning. The exacting style is typical in England, Germany, and Sweden. In these cultures, it is important to use words in a clear manner, in just the right quantity, with just the meaning intended. Using too many words is considered exaggeration, and using too few words, ambiguous.

Finally, for the **succinct style**, people are comfortable with a relatively low quantity of talk. Understatements, pauses, and silence convey meaning. Individuals in China, Japan, Korea, and Thailand use the succinct style. Particularly in unfamiliar situations, they tend to use silence and understatement rather than use talk and risk a loss of face.

The elaborate style is found in moderate uncertainty avoidance, high-context cultures; the exacting style in low uncertainty avoidance, low-context cultures; and the succinct style in high uncertainty avoidance, high-context cultures.

Personal Versus Contextual Style   **Personal versus contextual style** is the third verbal communication style. In the **personal style**, the focus is on the speaker, and "meanings are expressed for the purpose of emphasizing 'personhood'" (Gudykunst and Ting-Toomey 1988, p. 109). In the **contextual style**, focus is on the "role" of the speaker, and "meanings are expressed for the purpose of emphasizing role relationships" (Gudykunst and Ting-Toomey 1988, p. 109).

North American English speakers use the personal style, addressing each other informally and directly on an equal basis. First names are common, and there is no special manner of addressing people of different status levels or different gender. In contrast, the Japanese speak in the contextual style; words reflect the role and hierarchical relationship of those in the conversation. Males and females use different vocabulary, and the speaker chooses words to indicate his status relative to the receiver's.

The personal verbal style is spoken by members of low power distance, individualistic, low-context cultures such as Australia, Denmark, and Canada. The contextual style is associated with high power distance, collective, high-context cultures including Japan, India, Ghana, and Nigeria.

Instrumental Versus Affective Style   The last verbal style is the **instrumental versus affective**. In the **instrumental style**, the sender uses goal-oriented, sender-focused language. The **affective style** speaker is process oriented and receiver focused. People from Australia, for example, use the instrumental style. In

Table 4-3 Verbal Styles Used in 10 Countries

Country	Direct Versus Indirect	Elaborate Versus Succinct	Personal Versus Contextual	Instrumental Versus Affective
Australia	Direct	Exacting	Personal	Instrumental
Canada	Direct	Exacting	Personal	Instrumental
Denmark	Direct	Exacting	Personal	Instrumental
Egypt	Indirect	Elaborate	Contextual	Affective
England	Direct	Exacting	Personal	Instrumental
Japan	Indirect	Succinct	Contextual	Affective
Korea	Indirect	Succinct	Contextual	Affective
Saudi Arabia	Indirect	Elaborate	Contextual	Affective
Sweden	Direct	Exacting	Personal	Instrumental
United States	Direct	Exacting	Personal	Instrumental

speaking, the goal may be to persuade the listener, and the message is developed with this in mind. In contrast, Puerto Ricans use the affective style, so that neither the speaker nor the receiver is put in an uncomfortable position. The speaker listens to and closely observes the receiver to interpret how a message is being taken. Often, meaning is expressed nonverbally or intuitively. What is not said could be just as important as what is said.

The instrumental style is found in individualistic, low-context cultures such as the United States, Denmark, and Switzerland. Collective, high-context cultures— such as those in the Middle East, Latin America, and Asia—use the affective verbal style.

Because of differences in verbal styles, it can be difficult to express one language's precise meaning in another language. Beyond that, someone speaking a second language, unless she is extremely fluent or very familiar with the culture of the second language, may attempt to speak the second language using the verbal style of her native language. This too makes communication more difficult. Table 4-3 lists the four verbal styles used in 10 countries.

▌▌▌ NONVERBAL COMMUNICATION

Nonverbal communication includes the part of the message other than the words, such as facial expressions, gestures, and tone of voice (see Table 4-4). The verbal styles described previously may also include nonverbal aspects—for example, the affective style. When people are not speaking their native language or are relying on

Table 4-4 Forms of Nonverbal Communication

Kinesics	Communication through body movements, including facial expression, gestures, and posture
Oculesics	Communication through eye contact and gaze
Haptics	Communication through the use of bodily contact
Proxemics	Communication through the use of space
Chronemics	Communication through use of time within a culture
Chromatics	Communication through the use of colors

an interpreter, it is likely that nonverbal aspects of communication take on greater meaning. Indeed, people often assume they can understand gestures even if they can't understand words. However, nonverbal meanings in different cultures vary tremendously. To be an effective communicator, it is important to know both the language and the nonverbal aspects.

Emotions   Emotional expression is one area where there seems to be universal agreement. Studies in cultures as diverse as Brazil, Sweden Greece, Japan, the United States, and New Guinea show a high degree of agreement in recognizing the basic emotions of joy, sadness, and surprise (Gudykunst and Ting-Toomey 1988). However, why and when people in different cultures show these emotions differ. For example, in a culture low on Hofstede's power distance dimension such as Finland, people are uncomfortable with differences in rank and can become angry when they are present. In a high power distance country such as Venezuela, rank differences are an acceptable part of the culture and do not cause anger in most people (Gudykunst and Ting-Toomey 1988). Because of these different causes of emotions in different cultures, cross-cultural communication can leave a person feeling he is "missing something" or that the other person is reacting inappropriately.

> Studies in cultures as diverse as Brazil, Sweden, Greece, Japan, the United States, and New Guinea show a high degree of agreement in recognizing the basic emotions of joy, sadness, and surprise.

Kinesic Behavior   **Kinesic behavior** or **kinesics** is communication through body movements, including facial expression, gestures, and posture. For example, the smile usually indicates happiness or pleasure, but for Asians, it can also be a sign of embarrassment or discomfort (Samovar and Porter 1991). In the United States, maintaining eye contact is the sign of a good communicator; and in the Middle East, it is an integral part of successful communication; but for the Chinese and Japanese, it can indicate distrust. Communication through eye contact and gaze is **oculesics**.

The meaning of gestures also varies significantly among countries. In Italy, Greece, and certain Latin American countries, the level of gesturing is so high that people appear to be speaking with their hands. In North America, the level of gesturing is moderate. Other than waving hello or good-bye, gestures with the elbow higher than the shoulder are rare. For Chinese and Japanese speakers, using gestures is less common; keeping hands and arms close to the body is the norm (Chaney and Martin 1995).

Greeting gestures also differ. In a business situation, North Americans shake hands, Japanese bow, and Middle Easterners of the same sex kiss on the cheek (Abbasi and Hollman 1993). In a cross-cultural situation, a Japanese usually shakes hands because the non-Japanese is not expected to be acquainted with the complex etiquette of bowing. Communicating through the use of bodily contact is referred to as **haptics**.

The meaning of hand gestures varies in different countries too, as the Culture at Work vignette illustrates. The "V" for victory sign is common in the United States and England; it involves extending two fingers with the palm and fingers facing outward. However, in England reversing the gesture so that the palm and fingers face inward changes the meaning entirely so that it has an offensive connotation. Putting the thumb and forefinger together to form an "O" means "okay" in the United States, but "zero" or "worthless" in southern France. It stands for money in Japan and is an obscene gesture in Brazil (Chaney and Martin 1995; Hodgetts and Luthans 1994). The side-to-side wave for hello, common in many cultures, may be interpreted by Indians as "no" or "go away" (Besher 1991).

Posture while standing or seated can also convey different meanings. The casual, sometimes slouching, standing or seating posture of people from the United States might be interpreted as rude or conveying a lack of interest by others. In the Middle East, crossing your legs or showing the sole of your shoe to others conveys the message that they are worthy of being stepped on and is highly insulting (Abbasi and Hollman 1993).

Proxemics **Proxemics** is the use of space, either personal or office, to communicate. Hall (1966) believes people control intimacy by using personal space to regulate sensory exposure. For example, in the United States, people use one of four zones (Hall 1966). The **intimate zone**, a distance of less than 18 inches (46 cm) is used by very close friends. The distance from 18 inches to about four feet (46 cm to 1.22 m), the **personal zone**, is for a close working situation or to give instructions. In most business situations, Americans use the **social zone**, a distance of four to 12 feet (1.22 to 3.66 m). The **public zone**, distances over 12 feet (over 3.66 m), is used infrequently for formal occasions such as a speech.

The distances people feel comfortable with vary significantly by culture. South Americans, Southern and Eastern Europeans, and Middle Easterners prefer closer distances in communicating. Asians, North Europeans, and North Americans do not want to stand as close to others (Sussman and Rosenfeld 1982). These behaviors relate to a culture's overall tendency to be high contact or low contact. People in a **high-contact culture** like to stand close and touch each other. High-contact cultures usually are in warmer climates, have a greater interpersonal orientation, and are seen as interpersonally "warm." Those from **low-contact cultures** prefer to stand farther apart and touch infrequently. These cultures are often in cooler climate zones, and people there are task oriented and interpersonally "cool" (Gudykunst and Ting-Toomey 1988).

Use of office space is another aspect of proxemics. Where an office is and the type and arrangement of the furniture communicate a nonverbal message. For example, in the United States a senior executive usually occupies a large private corner office on an upper floor. The high floor, large size, and greater number of windows indicate the executive's prestige and status. In contrast, a high-level French manager sits in the middle of an office area. The central location allows him to monitor the activities of all the subordinates (Chaney and Martin 1995).

Chronemics **Chronemics** reflect the use of time in a culture. Two dominant patterns are characteristic. In a culture with a **monochronic time schedule (M-time)**, things are done in a linear fashion, one activity at a time. Time schedules are important, and an appointment is treated seriously. Time is seen as something that can be controlled or wasted by people. M-time is found in individualistic cultures such as those in Northern Europe, Germany, and the United States. With a **polychronic time schedule (P-time)**, people tend to do several things at the same time. Schedules are less important than personal involvement and the completion of transactions. In a P-time culture, schedules are subordinate to personal relationships. The P-time pattern is common in collective countries such as in Latin America and the Middle East (Gudykunst and Ting-Toomey 1988; Hall 1983).

The importance put on time also varies with culture. Those with monochronic time schedules generally emphasize time much more. For example, in Germany, an M-time country, punctuality is extremely important, and being even a few minutes late for a business appointment is an insult. In Ecuador with a P-time culture, business executives come to a meeting 15 or 20 minutes late and still consider it "on time" (Morrison, Conaway, and Borden 1994).

Chromatics   **Chromatics** is communication through colors. Colors of clothing, products and packaging, or gifts send intended or unintended messages when communicating cross-culturally. For example, in Hong Kong red signifies happiness or good luck. The traditional bridal dress is red, and at Chinese New Year lucky money is distributed in *hong bao*, red envelopes. Red packaging is common, particularly around the Chinese New Year. Men in Hong Kong, however, often avoid green because the Cantonese expression "He's wearing a green hat," means "His wife is cheating on him." In Chile, a gift of yellow roses conveys the message "I don't like you" while in the Czech Republic giving red roses indicates a romantic interest (Morrison, Conaway, and Borden 1994).

▌▐█ HOW CROSS-CULTURAL COMMUNICATION DIFFERENCES AFFECT THE COMMUNICATION PROCESS

Language usage, verbal styles, and nonverbal communication affect the communication process at two points. The first point is when the sender encodes a thought. The choice of language, the verbal styles used, and the nonverbals expressed carry a meaning that the sender expects the receiver to understand. To the extent that the sender encodes her thought in a manner that the receiver can comprehend, the accuracy of the communication is enhanced.

The second point where cross-cultural differences affect the communication process is when the receiver decodes and tries to understand the message. If the receiver is familiar with the sender, he can decode the language, verbal styles, and nonverbals and gain a better understanding of the message.

Barriers To Cross-Cultural Communication

With the many verbal and nonverbal differences in communication, people from different cultures often misunderstand each other. Edward T. Hall once said, "All human beings are captives of their culture" (Hall and Hall 1994, p. 3). People tend to interpret the words and actions of those from other cultures just as they would those of individuals from their home culture. This is a major barrier to cross-cultural understanding. Even after studying an unfamiliar culture in advance, when in it, an individual still confronts the totality of a different communication approach

> "All human beings are captives of their culture."

that can include a different language, a different verbal style, and numerous different nonverbals. Along with these different approaches, variation in culture, perception, and experience also make communication difficult (Bell 1992).

▌▐█ CULTURE, PERCEPTION, AND EXPERIENCE

Culture becomes a barrier when people from two different cultures have different ways of reacting to the same situation. Throughout this book and particularly in Chapter 2, the emphasis is on how cultural differences affect people's behavior. For example, if a Canadian manager asks his subordinates in Canada for ideas about a particular task, the subordinates would probably understand this as a positive message. They would think the manager has an interest in their ideas and wants to encourage participation. If this manager asks the same question while on assignment in India, however, the understanding of the message would be different. The subordinates would probably receive a negative message, believing the manager incompetent, as Indian subordinates expect their managers to know what they want subordinates to do.

Perception is an individual's personal view of the world. Whether it is correct or not, it is a person's definition of reality. In intercultural communication, a potential perceptual barrier is stereotyping. **Stereotyping** is a shortcut: Someone sees another person, categorizes her as a member of a particular group, and then assigns her the characteristics of that group. Stereotyped characteristics may be based on data—for example, the cultural frameworks presented in this book—or learned from other sources. For example, a child hears his parents say that people from Country X are rigid and set in their ways and later holds this stereotype of Country X'ers.

Stereotyping acts as a barrier to communication when it sets up expectations that may be untrue. However, if a person is able to use a stereotype as an initial expectation of how someone from another culture might behave, it could be helpful. When the person actually meets someone from the other culture, then he needs to gain an understanding of this individual to make communication more effective. One study (Ratiu 1983) found that managers judged as "most internationally effective" could change their stereotypes as they learned more about the real people they were working with. Those considered "least internationally effective" failed to change their stereotypes even when the people they encountered acted differently.

Experience barriers arise due to differences in life events between two individuals. When two people are from different cultures, it is likely that their life experiences have varied in many ways. The type of home, how they worship, their educational systems, what they eat, and how they spend their free time could all be different. Lacking a common body of experience is likely to make communication more difficult. For example, in the course of comparing the quality of students in Canada and the United States, one of the authors discovered that U.S. and Canadian universities attach different numerical scales to the letter grades given in courses. Without this knowledge, the information would have been understood very differently.

The experience of the expatriate manager in the following example illustrates how the three barriers of culture, perception, and experience all made understanding difficult.

> When my husband, Asbjorn, was on his first African assignment, he realized that understanding the words in Burkina Faso was not enough. To be effective in that country, expatriates need a good command of French and a respectable smattering of Moré, the principal African dialect. One day he was sitting on a large mat on the ground, meeting with a group of Mossi villagers. An older man spoke a short phrase in Moré and everyone nodded in agreement. Seeing Asbjorn's puzzled look, someone translated the phrase into French, thinking that might help. It turned out to be a parable, the gist of which was something like, 'the bird flew over.' Since the Mossi often employ parables and use them to capture the essence of what is occurring, Asbjorn's understanding of individual words was not enough; he needed an understanding of the cultural context as well (Osland 1995, pp. 70–71).[1]

---

[1]Excerpt from *The Adventure of Working Abroad: Hero Tales from the Global Frontier*, pp. 70–71 by Joyce Sautters Osland. Copyright © 1995 by Jossey-Bass Inc., Publishers. Reprinted by permission of Jossey-Bass Inc., Publishers.

▮▮▮ CULTURE, PERCEPTION, AND EXPERIENCE AND THE COMMUNICATION PROCESS

Differences in culture, perception, and experience influence the communication process by creating noise. The differences make it difficult for the sender and receiver to relate to each other. These differences can also influence the encoding and decoding of the message. Without a common frame of reference, the sender and receiver have greater difficulty understanding one another. Even when people from the same culture are communicating, perception and experience can create barriers. With a cross-cultural situation, these barriers are usually greater.

Although the barriers to communication are presented as distinct, in the process of communication they simultaneously interact. Awareness of and sensitivity to these barriers is the first step in improving intercultural communication effectiveness.

Enhancing Cross-Cultural Communication

Because many barriers to cross-cultural communication derive from differences in cultures, the first step for enhancing cross-cultural communication is an understanding of the other person's culture. The cultural frameworks of Hofstede, Trompenaars, and Kluckhohn and Strodtbeck found in Chapter 2 are a useful start. Some communication style differences relate directly to these cultural profiles. However, knowing that South Africans are individualist and Panamanians are collective is not enough. It is important to study details of the specific culture and learn about communication patterns such as verbal style and nonverbals. The more you know about the individual with whom you want to communicate, the more likely it is that your message will be understood.

Because cross-cultural communication often takes place with at least one of the parties speaking a non-native language or through an interpreter, using simple language and speaking slowly will be helpful. Also, try to avoid colloquial expressions, slang, and technical terms that may be unfamiliar to the other party. A short sentence with a clear meaning is easier to understand than a longer sentence. As you become familiar with the other person, try to match his level of speech. If the other person is speaking too quickly or beyond your level of understanding, let him know. If your foreign language ability is not adequate, request an interpreter.

Repeating major points or summarizing is also helpful. Ask for feedback from time to time to make sure that each party understands the other. Merely asking a yes or no question for confirmation is not sufficient; in some cultures such as Korea and Japan, a yes only indicates the other party was listening and not necessarily that she understands or agrees. Asking a question such as, "What is your view of this situation?" or "How do you feel about our proposal?" tests understanding and gives the important reaction of the other party.

Finally, underlying these suggestions, it is important in cross-cultural communication to express respect for other people and their cultures, to strive for equality by allowing each party an equal opportunity to be heard, and to be flexible enough to handle the inevitable differences.

Convergence or Divergence?

▌▌▌ FORCES FOR CONVERGENCE

With the increasing sophistication of communication technology, it is more common and much easier for people from different places to communicate. Fax and electronic mail (e-mail) all but replace letters and memos sent by post or messenger. Large corporations often have internal e-mail systems that allow their employees to communicate with each other worldwide. Globally, the Internet is bringing this form of communication to more people. The increasing ease of communication is a force for convergence.

Another force for convergence is the widespread use of English, particularly for business communication. More people speak English than any other language (*International Encyclopedia of Linguistics* 1992).

As new words develop in technology and business, often in English, they become part of many languages, sometimes using the same sound as the English and sometimes using an equivalent meaning. For example, the Japanese have a distinct set of characters for foreign words used to make a Japanese "word" that sounds the same as the foreign word. The Chinese word for *computer* translates literally as "electric brain." The extent to which words and concepts are similar in different languages represents a force for convergence.

▌▌▌ FORCES FOR DIVERGENCE

The number of different languages spoken around the globe, however, represents a force for divergence. Approximately 4,000–5,000 different languages are spoken in 140 different countries. Mandarin Chinese has the largest number of native speakers, followed by English (*International Encyclopedia of Linguistics* 1992). Even if people learn English, their levels of proficiency may vary if they are not native speakers.

For example, in a recent experiment, students from universities in different countries formed "**virtual teams**" on the Internet to complete a case study in business strategy. One of the teams' major problems was that native speakers of English had difficulty communicating with non-native speakers. Because English was the language required for the final paper, the native English speakers felt it unfair for them to have to rewrite the contributions from the others (Simmers 1996). The objective of having people from different countries work together is to bring together more ideas and to develop synergies from the interaction of perspectives. If language acts as a barrier, working in a multinational group becomes frustrating and counterproductive.

The various barriers to cross-cultural communication discussed in this chapter also represent forces for divergence. Communication approaches vary significantly with culture, even when using the same language. Verbal style and nonverbal communication are also strongly associated with culture.

Are communication approaches converging or diverging? There is evidence of both. As more people use a common language, there is pressure toward convergence. However, to the extent that culture retains or gains influence, there is movement toward divergence. Perhaps over time, as people's exposure to and interactions with each other increase, there will be a greater understanding of other cultures and more effective cross-cultural communication.

Implications for Managers

Communication is a large part of every manager's job. By one estimate a typical manager spends as much as 80 percent of his day in communication activities (Greenberg 1996). As the worldwide trend toward increased global business continues and domestic labor forces in many countries become more diverse, the ability to communicate cross-culturally is critical.

Communication serves as the foundation for a relationship between individuals. If a manager is effective in expressing herself, the other aspects of managing international organizational behavior become easier. For example, effective leadership relies on communication skill, motivation depends on making subordinates understand job requirements and how their actions affect consequences, and organizational culture develops as a result of effective communication. Thus, by gaining a better understanding of cross-cultural communication and working to enhance cross-cultural communication skills, there may be an impact on many areas of behavior.

> A typical manager spends as much as 80 percent of his day in communication activities.

In analyzing where in the communication process barriers arise, most are due to problems with the sender encoding a thought, the receiver decoding a message to achieve understanding, or with noise affecting the overall communication process. This implies that managers need greater knowledge about their communication partners to help minimize these problems. A sensitivity to the possibility of different approaches to language, verbal styles, and nonverbals can lead to more accurate encoding and decoding. Being aware of differences in culture, perception, and experience can help to reduce noise and also enhance the encoding and decoding process.

In considering trends toward convergence or divergence in communication approaches, language is still a major force for divergence. Because of this, knowledge of other languages is an important skill for an international manager. English and Mandarin Chinese are good choices of second languages, as these are the most commonly spoken worldwide. English is widely used in business, and with the continuing economic developments in China, it is likely that the use of Chinese for business communication will increase.

Summary

A variety of factors influences communication across cultures. The basic communication process of encoding and decoding is at the core of communication. Noise affects all aspects of communication and is a recurrent issue in effective communication. Also important are differences in language usage, verbal style, and nonverbal communication in different cultures. These differences represent major barriers to effective cross-cultural communication. Other barriers include culture, perception, and experience. To enhance intercultural communication, it is important to understand other cultures and become sensitive to differences.

Another issue for managers to consider is whether approaches to communication are converging or diverging worldwide. Improved communication technology and widespread use of English, particularly in business situations, represent forces for convergence. Yet, the large number of languages spoken worldwide and the strong effects of culture on communication, even when using the same language, are strong forces for divergence.

Finally, because communication represents such an important part of a manager's job, an understanding of cross-cultural communication can lead to more effective management of international organizational behavior. By studying other languages and cultures and learning more about their communication partners, managers can become more effective cross-cultural communicators.

■ Discussion Questions

1. Consider the basic communication model. At each point, discuss possible problems two individuals from different cultures could have in communicating with each other.
2. Think of your own experiences in communicating with people from another culture. What difficulties did you experience? What did you do to try to make yourself understood? How could you have handled the situation more effectively?
3. Using your own language, give examples of each variation of the four verbal styles.
4. In this chapter are examples of nonverbals from different cultures. Think about your own culture. Give examples of each type of nonverbal communication.
5. Give an example of a stereotype. How could it act as barrier to effective communication? How could it be helpful?
6. "The Internet and e-mail are making it easier to communicate with people across cultures." Do you agree or disagree? Why?

References

ABBASI, S.M. and HOLLMAN, K.W. (1993), "Business Success in the Middle East," *Management Decision*, 31 (1), 55–59.

ADLER, N.J. (1991), *International Dimensions of Organizational Behavior*, 2d Ed. Boston: PWS-Kent.

BELL, A.H. (1992), *Business Communication: Toward 2000*. Cincinnati, OH: South-Western.

BESHER, A. (1991), *The Pacific Rim Almanac*. New York: Harper Collins.

CHANEY, L.H. and MARTIN, J.S. (1995), *Intercultural Business Communication*. Upper Saddle River, NJ: Prentice Hall.

DERESKY, H. (1994), *International Management: Managing Across Borders and Cultures*. New York: Harper Collins.

ELASHMAWI, F. (1991), "Multicultural Business Meetings and Presentations: Tips and Taboos," *Tokyo Business Today*, 59 (11), 66–68.

FATEHI, K. and DESILVA, D. (1996), "International Communication and Negotiation," in *International Management: A Cross-Cultural and Functional Perspective*. Upper Saddle River, NJ: Prentice Hall.

FISHER, G. (1980), *International Negotiation: A Cross-Cultural Perspective*. Chicago: Intercultural Press.

GOLDMAN, A. (1994), "A Briefing on Cultural and Communicative Sources of Western-Japanese Interorganizational Conflict," *Journal of Managerial Psychology*, 9 (1), 7–12.

GREENBERG, J. (1996), *Managing Behavior in Organizations*. Upper Saddle River, NJ: Prentice Hall.

GUDYKUNST, W.B. and TING-TOOMEY, S. (1988), *Culture and Interpersonal Communication*. Newbury Park, CA: Sage Publications.

HALL, E.T. (1966), *The Hidden Dimension*. New York: Doubleday.

———. (1976), *Beyond Culture*. New York: Doubleday.

———. (1983), *The Dance of Life*. New York: Doubleday.

———. and HALL, E. (1994), "How Cultures Collide," in Weaver, G.R. (ed.) *Culture, Communication, and Conflict: Readings in Intercultural Relations*, Needham Heights, MA: Ginn Press.

HODGETTS, R.M. and LUTHANS, F. (1994), *International Management*, 2d Ed. New York: McGraw-Hill.

HOFSTEDE, G. (1980a), *Culture's Consequences: International Differences in Work-Related Values*. Beverly Hills, CA: Sage Publications.

————. (1980b), "Motivation, Leadership, and Organization: Do American Theories Apply Abroad?" *Organizational Dynamics*, 9, 42–62.

International Encyclopedia of Linguistics (1992), Vols. 1, 2. New York: Oxford University Press.

MORRISON, T., CONAWAY, W.A., and BORDEN G.A. (1994), *Kiss, Bow, or Shake Hands: How to Do Business in Sixty Countries*. Holbrook, MA: Bob Adams.

OSLAND, J.S. (1995), *The Adventure of Working Abroad: Hero Tales from the Global Frontier*. San Francisco: Jossey-Bass.

RATIU, I. (1983), "Thinking Internationally: A Comparison of How International Executives Learn," *International Studies of Management and Organization*, 13, 139–50.

RICKS, D.A. (1983), *Big Business Blunders: Mistakes in Multinational Marketing*. Homewood, IL: Dow Jones-Irwin.

SAMOVAR, L.A. and PORTER, R.E. (1991), *Communication Between Cultures*. Belmont, CA: Wadsworth.

SHENKAR, O. and RONEN, S. (1987), "The Cultural Context of Negotiations: The Implications of Chinese Interpersonal Norms," *Journal of Applied Behavioral Science*, 23 (2), 263–75.

SIMMERS, C. (1996), "The Internet in the Classroom: Case Analysis Across the Network: Across the Globe," paper presented at the Tenth Annual Mid Atlantic Regional Organizational Behavior Teaching Conference, Philadelphia, March 9.

SUSSMAN, N.M. and ROSENFELD, H.M. (1982), "Influence of Culture, Language, and Sex on Conversational Distance," *Journal of Personality and Social Psychology*, 42, 66–74.

WARNER, F. (1996), "Western Goods in Asia Lose Something in Translation," *The Asian Wall Street Journal Weekly*, (February 12), 6.

Negotiation and Conflict Resolution

Ellie the Elephant Versus Geoffrey the Giraffe

Redgwood's Holdings Ltd., the owner of Reggie's Toy Store, legally registered the Toys "R" Us trademark during South Africa's apartheid regime. In post-apartheid South Africa, when trade embargoes vanished and the opportunity existed to participate more extensively in international trade, Redgwood's had to confront the possibility of a challenge to its trademark. The four Redgwood Toys "R" Us stores were similar to the original Toys "R" Us chain in the United States, except Redgwood used Ellie the Elephant as its mascot instead of Geoffrey the Giraffe.

As expected, the U.S.-based Toys "R" Us objected to Redgwood's use of its trademark. Rather than fighting in court, where Redgwood's might have won, Redgwood's decided to negotiate with Toys "R" Us.

The result was a win-win solution. Redgwood's agreed to sell back the trademark to the U.S. company and simultaneously buy the rights to its use in South Africa. The South African government approved the deal in March 1996, making Redgwood's the seventh foreign franchise of Toys "R" Us .

Source: Excerpt from "Restoring Their Good Names: U.S. Companies in Trademark Battles in South Africa" by Donald G. McNeil, Jr. from *The New York Times*, May 1, 1996. Copyright © 1996 by The New York Times. Reprinted by permission.

After reading this chapter, you should be able to:

1. Define negotiation and understand the basic negotiation process.
2. Explain how culture influences the negotiation process.
3. Consider the impact of situational factors and negotiating tactics on negotiation outcomes.
4. Analyze the differences between intracultural and cross-cultural negotiations.
5. Discuss the role of culture in the conflict resolution process.
6. Appreciate how approaches to conflict influence negotiation.
7. Identify ways to become a better cross-cultural negotiator.

In the global economy, companies increasingly do business outside their home countries. Because the majority of transactions involves two or more organizations deciding the terms of an agreement, cross-cultural negotiating is an important skill that occupies as much as 50% of an international manager's time (Perlmutter 1983, 1984).

> **C**ross-cultural negotiating is an important skill that occupies as much as 50% of an international manager's time.

Imagine the potential conflicts executives from the two companies in the Culture at Work vignette faced. Each company had a large stake in the outcome of the negotiation and wanted to make sure it received a fair deal. Yet it is likely that at the start of the negotiation neither side had much information about the other. In addition, the United States and South Africa have different cultures, laws, and economic systems, making it very challenging for the two sides to communicate and reach agreement. In this case, despite the difficulties created by cultural differences, both sides won.

What Is Negotiation?

Negotiation is the process of bargaining between two or more parties to reach a solution that is mutually acceptable. Negotiating, either in a personal or work role, is something everyone does every day. The subject of the negotiation could be quite simple—two friends deciding whether to go to a movie or a soccer match—or it could be much more complex—companies from two different countries planning a joint venture.

Negotiation is a communication process; consequently, topics presented in Chapter 4 also apply. Traditionally, negotiating involves a face-to-face meeting, but it also happens through telephone, fax, e-mail, and letter.

The Negotiation Process

THE GOAL

The overall goal of negotiation is to arrive at a solution acceptable to all. In some cultures, the optimum outcome is a **win-win** or **integrative solution**. With a win-win solution, all parties are able to achieve their objectives. In some cultures, negotiators feel they must **compromise** to reach agreement. In fact, the compromise requires that all parties give up something, a **lose-lose** solution, which may be acceptable to all parties. In still other cultures, the goal of the negotiation is **win-lose;** one party receives all it wants by forcing or demanding the other to concede defeat.

The negotiation process consists of five steps: (1) preparation, (2) relationship building, (3) information exchange, (4) persuasion, and (5) agreement (Adler 1991; Deresky 1994).

PREPARATION STAGE

In the **preparation stage**, negotiators plan how to approach the actual negotiation and try to learn as much as possible about their negotiating partners. This stage typically takes place at the home office before the face-to-face meeting. The negotiators must understand their own positions and anticipate the positions of the other party through considering each party's objectives, needs, and interests (Ury 1993).

RELATIONSHIP-BUILDING STAGE

The second stage, relationship building, starts when the parties begin their discussion, typically, at one of their offices or at a mutually acceptable neutral location. The objective of the **relationship-building stage** is for the parties to get to know one another. This could involve a brief exchange of names and business cards or many days of conversation, dinners, and other forms of entertainment.

How much each party needs to know about the other depends on culture. Americans, for example, do not spend extensive time in the relationship-building stage. Once the parties establish that they represent their respective companies, they move to the next stage of negotiation. For much of the rest of the world, this rapid progression is inappropriate, even offensive. For example, Mexican negotiators usually prefer to spend time dining together and discussing matters other than those to be negotiated. When foreigners travel to Mexico for a negotiation, their Mexican hosts often arrange visits to important cultural sights and allow the foreigners to learn more about Mexico and themselves. For the Mexican negotiators, getting acquainted with their negotiating partners is a critical stage in the process.

INFORMATION EXCHANGE

Information exchange, the third stage, involves each party stating an initial position, usually in a presentation, followed by questions, answers, and discussion. The meaning of this stage varies depending on the negotiator's cultural background. An American typically thinks this the beginning of the "real" negotiation. The American expects each party to present relevant information followed by a logical discussion based on the presentation. The Mexican negotiator, in contrast, may be suspicious and indirect, presenting little substantive material (Deresky 1994). In negotiating with Mexicans, exploring issues informally and reaching some understanding with key individuals before the formal information exchange may be more beneficial (Fisher 1980).

PERSUASION

The fourth stage of the negotiation process is **persuasion**; the parties try to convince their counterparts to accept their proposals. This might involve the parties consciously trying to work toward a mutually acceptable solution or one party using persuasive arguments to influence the other. (Cultural variations in persuasion tactics are presented subsequently in the chapter.)

AGREEMENT

The final stage of negotiation is **agreement**, in which the parties come to a mutually acceptable solution. In the process, each may decide to make concessions to the other. Cultural variations exist at this stage as well. For example, American negotiators prefer to negotiate in a linear fashion, deciding one issue at a time and concluding with a binding legal contract. Russians, in contrast, prefer to develop the final agreement at the end based on all the items (Pettibone 1990), and they attach less meaning to the contract (Deresky 1994). Russians also view concessions as a sign of weakness and consequently make very few (Adler 1991).

How Culture Influences the Negotiation Process

Cultural variation exists at every stage of the negotiation process. Even the concept of the negotiation process itself varies from culture to culture. The following examples indicate the wide range of approaches.

Japanese culture highly values harmony. The Japanese typically make organizational decisions using the group consensus processes known as *nemawashi* and *ringi seido* discussed in Chapter 7. For the Japanese, the negotiation session functions as more of a ceremony to formalize a consensus decision previously reached. The Japanese prefer that the agreement not be too restrictive, as it represents a beginning position. Emphasizing the tentativeness of negotiations, the Japanese culture even provides a mechanism for breaking a contract. The idea of *naniwabushi* allows a party to explain why he can not follow a contract and provides an honorable out if circumstances change (Chen 1995).

In contrast, Americans view the negotiation session as a place for the parties involved to solve problems. Americans take a factual approach, based on logic (Glenn, Witmeyer, and Stevenson 1984). They expect to give and take on various issues and compromise along the way. A legal contract confirms the agreement. For Americans, the contract is an endpoint and deviations from it a cause for dispute.

The French also approach negotiation in a problem-solving mode. However, the French see negotiation more as an art and the negotiation table as a place "for searching out the solutions for which they have so carefully prepared. To them, the negotiation setting becomes more of a debating forum, with flexibility and accommodation simply for the sake of agreement less of an expectation" (Fisher 1980, p. 19).

These three examples illustrate the wide cultural variation in the concept of negotiation. Because of these variations, negotiating tactics also differ greatly.

Situational Factors and Negotiating Tactics

The circumstances of the negotiation and the tactics used by the negotiating parties such as geographical location, room arrangements, selection of negotiators, and time limits influence the success of the negotiation. Tactics include verbal aspects, which are the words spoken, and nonverbal, tactics, which include everything other than the words, such as tone of voice, facial expressions, gestures, and body posture. (Chapter 4 presents a general discussion of cross-cultural differences in verbal and nonverbal communication.)

▐▐▐▌ SITUATIONAL FACTORS

Geographical Location   One of the first decisions negotiators make together is where they will meet. When people are working on opposite sides of the globe, the selection of a **geographical location** has implications for all. Generally, the choice is the home location of one of the parties or a neutral location. It is usually advantageous to conduct the negotiations in one's own home office. The home party does not incur extra expenses for travel and hotel, has greater access to information and advice, and lives in the comfort of home. When one or both of the parties are away from the home office, there is usually pressure to come to agreement more quickly as costs increase daily. Home office managers often expect the negotiators to finalize an agreement in order to consider such a trip worthwhile.

The choice of a neutral location is usually one equidistant from both parties. For example, North American and Asian negotiators may meet in Hawaii, and South American and European teams may meet in New York. People from some countries have difficulty traveling abroad due to visa restrictions or financial constraints; others have a strong preference for conducting negotiations at home. For example, the Mainland Chinese like to hold major negotiating sessions at home (Chen 1995). This gives them the advantage of time because every day a foreigner is there is costly and stressful. A successful negotiator from Hong Kong claimed the secret of his success was to get to China, settle in, and appear that he was in no hurry to leave.

Room Arrangements   Another situational factor is **room arrangements**, the physical setup of the place for the negotiations. The shape of the table and where the negotiators sit can create greater competition or cooperation. For example, a rectangular or square table with the negotiating parties sitting on opposite sides leads to greater competition. Everyone sitting together at a round table may create a more cooperative climate.

Selection of Negotiators   The **selection of negotiators** involves the number of people and which ones will represent a team. The number chosen often reflects the organization's national culture. For example, U.S. companies often send a small team or only a single individual to represent them. The American concern for efficiency views sending a large group as "a waste." The Japanese, in contrast, prefer a large group. The size of their team can create an advantage by overwhelming the other side. The large team also allows them to have representatives from different areas within the company (Chen 1995).

Who is sent also reflects culture. U.S. companies select negotiators on the basis of position and competence. If the negotiation is a matter related to someone's position, that is the person most likely to represent the company. Personal factors such as age, gender, or race are not important if an individual is a good performer. In a Mexican organization, in contrast, personal qualities and social connections influence the selection of a negotiator (Fisher 1980).

Time Limits   **Time limits** are the real or presumed deadlines under which negotiating parties operate. The expected time for a negotiation varies with culture. If a negotiating team is away from home, their counterparts can find out how long they expect to stay by making hotel reservations or reconfirming air tickets on their behalf. Using this information to delay an agreement until close to the departure deadline makes the visitors more anxious to grant concessions.

A culture's view of time affects their expectations of the length of a negotiation. The U.S., Swiss, and German cultures view time as a commodity and want to conduct negotiations as efficiently as possible. For other cultures, such as those in the Middle East and Asia, the time perspective is longer term, and the extended negotiation time helps build a long-term relationship.

VERBAL TACTICS

Verbal tactics include spoken negotiating behaviors such as initial offer made, promises, threats, and recommendations. Certain behaviors greatly influence the outcome of the negotiation. Negotiators increase their profits by (1) asking more questions, (2) making fewer commitments before the final agreement stage, and (3) increasing the amount of the initial request—that is, seller asking for more and buyer offering less (Adler 1991).

Initial Offer   The **initial offer**, a beginning statement of intent made by each party, is one tactic influenced by culture. Chinese and Russian negotiators typically begin the negotiation with extreme initial offers (Adler 1991; Chen 1995). Negotiators from the United States and Sweden are more likely to make an initial offer closer to their actual bottom line (Adler 1991; Graham 1985). The Japanese typically do not like to make extreme offers, which they refer to as *banana no tataki uri*, the "banana sale approach"; but they sometimes do so when negotiating with foreigners (Chen 1995).

> The Japanese typically do not like to make extreme offers, which they refer to as banana no tataki uri, the "banana sale approach"; but they sometimes do so when negotiating with foreigners.

Other Verbal Negotiating Behaviors   Other verbal negotiating behaviors include promises, threats, recommendations, warnings, rewards, punishments, normative appeals, commitments, self-disclosure, questions, and command (see Table 5-1).

Table 5-2 illustrates variation in verbal behaviors in Japan, the United States, and Brazil. The verbal tactics of Americans and Japanese are similar compared with those used by Brazilians. For example, Brazilians make extensive use of much higher initial offers, fewer promises, fewer commitments, and more "no's" compared with American and Japanese negotiators.

NONVERBAL TACTICS

Nonverbal tactics include negotiating behaviors other than the words used—for example, tone of voice, facial expressions, gestures, and body position. As discussed in Chapter 4, there is great variation in the nonverbal behaviors used by people from different cultures in daily conversation. These variations, as well as more specific behaviors relating to negotiating, make the cross-cultural negotiation situation a challenge. Nonverbal behaviors often send a "louder" message than verbal behaviors, and people tend to interpret behaviors of people from other cultures as meaning the same thing that they mean in their own culture.

Silence   Table 5-3 presents an example of the nonverbal negotiating behaviors of negotiators from Japan, the United States, and Brazil. As with the verbal negotiating behavior, American and Japanese behaviors are more similar to each other than to the Brazilians'. The Japanese use of **silence**, a period of nonresponsiveness, during negotiations is well documented (Chen 1995; Fisher 1980). The Japanese often pause to reflect on what has been said, what should be said, or if a problem arises. Japanese consider this a normal part of conversation, yet an American or Brazilian may find it awkward or uncomfortable. Americans typically say something to break the silence after only a few seconds. In some cases, they may interpret silence as rejection and offer further concessions to get the negotiation moving again.

Table 5-1   Commonly Used Verbal Negotiating Tactics

Tactic	Description	Example
Promise	I will do something you want me to do if you do something I want you to do. (conditional, positive)	I will lower the price by $5 if you increase the order by 100 units.
Threat	I will do something you do not want me to do if you do something I don't want you to do. (conditional, negative)	I'll walk out of the negotiation if you leak this story to the press.
Recommendation	If you do something I want you to do, a third party will do something you want. (third party positive)	If you lower the price, all of the teenagers will be able to buy your product.
Warning	If you do something I don't want you to do, a third party will do something you don't want. (third party negative)	If you don't settle, the press will spill this whole sordid story on the front page of every newspaper in the country
Reward	I will give you something positive (something you want), now, on the spot. (unconditional, positive)	Let's make it easier on you tomorrow and meet closer to your office. I have really appreciated your willingness to meet at my building.
Punishment	I will give you something negative (something you don't want) now, on the spot. (unconditional, negative)	I refuse to listen to your screaming. I am leaving.
Normative Appeal	I appeal to a societal norm.	Everybody else buys our product for $5 per unit.
Commitment	I will do something you want. (unconditional, positive)	I will deliver 100 units by June 15th.
Self-Disclosure	I will tell you something about myself.	We have had to lay off 100 employees this month. We really need to sign a major contract by the end of the year.
Question	I ask you something about yourself.	Can you tell me more about your Brazilian operation?
Command	I order you to do something.	Lower your price. (or) We are going to talk about delivery now.

Source: Adler, N.J. (1991), *International Dimensions of Organizational Behavior*, 2d Ed. Boston: PWS-Kent, pp. 206–7, based on Graham, J.L. (1985), "The Influence of Culture on Business Negotiations," Table 3, *Journal of International Business Studies*, 16, 81–96.

Conversational Overlaps   The opposite behavior of silence is **conversational overlaps**, when more than one person speaks at the same time. Interrupting or having two people speak at the same time is common behavior for the Brazilians but considered rude or inappropriate by Americans and Japanese, who usually stop if someone else starts to speak.

Facial Gazing   **Facial gazing** is looking at the counterpart's face. Eye contact is one of the most intense forms of facial gazing. Referring back to Table 5-3, the Brazilians use the most facial gazing, followed by the Americans, then the Japanese. This reflects the level of intimacy between two persons. The norm for a business situation such as a negotiation varies widely. The polite Japanese directs his gaze somewhere around the neck or chest, rather than to the eyes (Goldman 1992). Americans like to maintain eye contact but with less intensity than the Brazilians are comfortable with.

Table 5-2   **A Comparison of Verbal Negotiating Behaviors Used by Negotiators from Japan, the United States, and Brazil**

Behavior (Tactic)	Japan	United States	Brazil
(Average number of times tactic was used in a half-hour bargaining session)			
Promise	7	8	3
Threat	4	4	2
Recommendation	7	4	5
Warning	2	1	1
Reward	1	2	2
Punishment	1	3	3
Normative Appeal	4	2	1
Commitment	15	13	8
Self-Disclosure	34	36	39
Question	20	20	22
Command	8	6	14
"No's" (per 30 minutes)	5.7	9.0	83.4
Profit level of first offers (80 maximum)	61.5	57.3	75.2
Initial concessions	6.5	7.1	9.4

Source: Adler, N.J. (1991), *International Dimensions of Organizational Behavior*, 2d Ed. Boston: PWS-Kent, p. 207, based on Graham, J.L. (1985), "The Influence of Culture on Business Negotiations," Tables 1 and 3, *Journal of International Business Studies*, 16, 81–96.

Touching   **Touching** behaviors are also strongly related to culture. The Japanese and American negotiators in the Table 5-3 example only touch via a handshake. For the Brazilians, touching is a way to make the relationship closer; they may interpret the lack of touching as rejection. Mexicans also use physical contact to signal confidence. Mexican men often use the *abrazo*, or hug, to indicate a relationship is deepening (Fisher 1980).

Table 5-3   **A Comparison of Nonverbal Negotiating Behaviors Used by Negotiators from Japan, the United States, and Brazil**

Behavior (tactic)	Japanese	Americans	Brazilians
Silent periods (Number of periods greater than 10 seconds, per 30 minutes)	5.5	3.5	0
Conversational overlaps (Number per 10 minutes)	12.6	10.3	28.6
Facial gazing (Minutes of gazing per 10 minutes)	1.3	3.3	5.2
Touching (Not including handshaking, per 30 minutes)	0	0	4.7

Source: Adler, N.J. (1991), *International Dimensions of Organizational Behavior*, 2d Ed. Boston: PWS-Kent, p. 210, based on Graham, J.L. (1985), "The Influence of Culture on Business Negotiations," *Journal of International Business Studies*, 16, 81–96.

Differences Between Intracultural and Cross-Cultural Negotiations

The variations to negotiation discussed so far primarily apply to **intracultural negotiations**, in which members of one culture negotiate with each other. What happens in **cross-cultural negotiations**, when members of different cultures negotiate with each other?

The dynamics of cross-cultural negotiation are different from intracultural negotiations. A study comparing Japanese, American, Francophone Canadian, and Anglophone Canadian negotiators found that all groups were different in the cross-cultural compared with the intracultural situation (Adler and Graham 1989). The nature of these differences, however, is quite varied. Francophone Canadians took a more cooperative approach to negotiating with Anglophone Canadians than with other Francophones, and Anglophone Canadians took longer and had lower joint profits when negotiating with Francophone Canadians. Japanese found American negotiators more attractive than other Japanese, even though they ended up with lower profits. Americans did not act differently in the cross-cultural negotiations, but they experienced more satisfaction negotiating with the Japanese than with other Americans.

Another study comparing executives from the People's Republic of China and Canada found no differences in strategy in a cross-cultural situation (Tse, Francis, and Walls 1994). Managers from both countries used the same conflict resolution strategy and were motivated by the same underlying factors whether they were in an intracultural or cross-cultural situation. However, executives from both countries preferred negotiating with Canadians rather than Chinese.

These two studies do not provide clear conclusions about cross-cultural negotiations. Perhaps the study methods influenced their results. Maybe negotiators from certain countries have a more appealing or flexible approach. Further research is needed to provide greater insight into cross-cultural negotiating behavior.

How Culture Influences Conflict Resolution

Negotiation is a communication process. From the discussion of situational factors and verbal and nonverbal tactics in negotiating, it is clear that the approach to negotiation varies widely with culture. Negotiation is also a means to resolve conflict, as the parties begin with different positions from which they move to an agreement.

The way a society perceives conflict reflects other aspects of that culture. Intercultural communications expert Stella Ting-Toomey has developed a theory of culture and conflict that explains cultural differences using Hall's low-and high-context framework (Gudykunst and Ting-Toomey 1988; Hall 1976, Ting-Toomey 1985). (Hall's framework is discussed in Chapters 2 and 4.)

People in low-context cultures see conflict as **instrumental oriented**. These cultures view the world in analytic, linear logic terms, and separate issues from people. In a high-context culture, conflict is **expressive oriented**. People in these cultures do not separate person from issue. The consequence is that in low-context cultures, public disagreements are acceptable; people can have a conflict and still maintain a friendly relationship afterwards. In the high-context culture, open disagreement and public confrontation are highly insulting and cause both parties involved to "lose face" (Gudykunst and Ting-Toomey 1988; Ting-Toomey 1985).

> In the high-context culture, open disagreement and public confrontation are highly insulting and cause both parties involved to "lose face."

Why conflict develops in the two types of cultures also differs. Because the low-context culture is more individualistic, there is less specification of appropriate ways to behave. Conflict often arises because one party violates the other's expectations. In the high-context culture, which has more specific rules of behavior, conflict usually occurs when a person violates cultural expectations.

Attitudes toward conflict is the third aspect of the conflict situation. In the low-context culture, people are oriented toward action. This results in a direct, confrontational response to conflict, with all parties wanting a quick resolution. In the high-context setting, the attitude toward conflict is evasive and nonconfrontational, leading to an indirect, inactive approach. This often results in avoiding or ignoring the conflict.

The final aspect of the conflict situation is how the conflict evolves or the style used to handle the conflict. In low-context cultures, people favor a factual-inductive or axiomatic-deductive style of argument. The **factual-inductive style** uses relevant facts and moves toward a conclusion using an inductive approach. The **axiomatic-deductive style** reasons from the general to the specific, going from basic ideas to their implications. Both of these depend on linear approaches to logic in making an argument. The **affective-intuitive style** is more common in high-context cultures. This approach uses circumlocution or flowery speech to make an emotional appeal and ambiguity and understatement to diffuse conflict. People in low-context cultures take a more intellectual view of conflict; those from high-context cultures see it from an emotional point of view. Table 5-4 summarizes the main ideas of Ting-Toomey's theory.

Two studies comparing a high- and low-context culture illustrate Ting-Toomey's model. Male business students in Hong Kong (high-context) and the

Table 5-4   Conflict Characteristics of Low- and High-Context Cultures

Key Questions	Low-Context Conflict	High-Context Conflict
Why	analytic, linear logic; instrumental oriented; dichotomy between conflict and conflict parties	synthetic, spiral logic; expressive oriented; integration of conflict and conflict parties
When	individualistic oriented; low collective normative expectations; violations of individual expectations create conflict potentials	group oriented; high collective normative expectations; violations of collective expectations create conflict potentials
What	revealment; direct, confrontational attitude; action and solution oriented	concealment; indirect, nonconfrontational attitude; "face" and relationship oriented
How	explicit communication codes; line-logic style: rational-factual rhetoric; open, direct strategies	implicit communication codes; point-logic style: intuitive-affective rhetoric; ambiguous, indirect strategies

Source: Table from *Communication, Culture, and Organizational Processes* by W. Gudykunst, L. Stewart, and S. Ting-Toomey. Copyright (©) 1985 by Sage Publications, Inc. Reprinted by permission of Sage Publications, Inc.

United States (low-context) varied on how they handled conflict (Chiu and Kosinski 1994). The Hong Kong Chinese preferred avoidance and accommodation as ways of handling conflict, whereas the Caucasian Americans chose direct methods of handling conflict more frequently.

Another example of these differences is responses to verbal insults. In a study comparing Chinese and North Americans (Bond et al. 1985), the Chinese advised an executive to speak to a person who insulted someone and the target of the insult separately to avoid conflict. The North Americans suggested the executive hold a meeting with the two parties to resolve the conflict.

How Approach to Conflict Influences Negotiation

The way different cultures view conflict affects their approaches to negotiation. Differences exist between high -and low-context cultures in thinking patterns, individualistic versus collective orientation, differing expectations, direct versus indirect attitude, and implicit versus explicit communication codes. These affect the behavior of persons from high- and low-context cultures within the negotiation situation.

Negotiators from a high-context culture often behave in ways that appear harmonious on the surface. They express differences in opinion less directly and communicate real feelings through implicit language and nonverbal means. In high-context cultures, the identity of the negotiator is important, and the "persona" of the negotiator is integrated into how the negotiation is handled. In contrast, negotiators from low-context cultures are open and direct. They take an action orientation and see negotiation as a problem-solving process. There is a clear difference between who the negotiator is as a person and how well she performs in the negotiating situation.

These examples illustrate the major differences *between* negotiators from high- and low-context cultures. However, there are also differences *among* high- or low-context cultures. An earlier example in the chapter illustrates differences among negotiators from Japan, the United States, and Brazil. Japanese and Americans are more alike in their use of verbal and nonverbal negotiating behaviors than Brazilians. However, Brazil and Japan are both high-context cultures, and the United States is a low-context culture. Clearly, these differences reflect another aspect of cultural difference not represented by high- and low-context.

How to Become A Better Cross-Cultural Negotiator

Substantial differences exist among cultures in the goals and behaviors associated with the negotiation process. How can a good cross-cultural negotiator handle these? First, it is important to understand one's negotiating partner. At the cultural level, a basic understanding of values, attitudes, and typical behaviors is helpful. There are many popular and academic publications on negotiating with individuals from China, Mexico, France, Japan, the United States, and Russia (see Chen 1995; Fisher 1980; Goldman 1992; Shenkar and Ronen 1987). These offer specific examples of how people from a particular country behave in a negotiation situation.

When you are aware of culture and how it influences negotiating style, consider the specifics of your situation. Who is your negotiating counterpart—the organization and its representatives—and what experience do they have with your organization and your culture? Also think about your own and the other party's needs, interests, and possible goals.

Finally, after you understand the background of your negotiating partner, you must consider how to handle the actual negotiation. Often, people do not behave the same way in a cross-cultural negotiation as in an intracultural negotiation. You might believe that doing what the natives do is the most effective approach; however, a foreigner trying to behave as a native may not be treated as a native.

In a study of how Americans responded to Japanese and Korean business people who attempted to adapt varying degrees of American behavior in a negotiation, a moderate adaptation of native behavior produced better outcomes than no adaptation or substantial adaptation (Francis 1991). Although these results are tentative, they suggest that neither totally following the approach of another culture nor totally ignoring the cultural differences is very effective.

> **N**either totally following the approach of another culture nor totally ignoring the cultural differences is very effective.

Cross-cultural negotiation researcher Stephen Weiss (1994) offers another viewpoint on this issue. He presents eight different culturally responsive strategies for cross-cultural negotiations. Negotiator familiarity with the counterpart's culture and the likelihood of explicitly coordinating the approaches determine the choice of strategy. When neither party is familiar with the other, Weiss suggests hiring an agent or advisor. One party can follow the style of the other when only that party is very familiar with the other's culture. When both are familiar with the other's culture, the parties can develop a synergistic approach. In summary, there is an appropriate strategy whether the negotiators know very little about or are entirely familiar with the other party's culture and language.

Can someone totally adapt a negotiation strategy different from his own cultural style? Professional negotiators from Spain and Denmark received identical negotiation training from a U.S. consulting firm specializing in communication and management (Grindsted 1994). The program goal was to train individuals to employ an appropriate negotiation style and to negotiate in a cooperative fashion. The training was administered in the home country and language of each group. The programs were otherwise identical. Despite the same training, each group negotiated in culturally dissimilar ways. The Spanish group was more people oriented compared with the Danish group, who were more task oriented. Even though these two groups had the same training, they continued to behave in ways reflecting their own cultures.

Convergence or Divergence?

▌▌▌ FORCES FOR CONVERGENCE

As our knowledge and understanding of other cultures increase, some convergence in the approach to negotiation may occur. For example, two parties adopting the approach suggested by Weiss (1994) and being explicit about how to handle their relative familiarity with the other's culture may provide a means for converging. Also, if moderate adaptation proves to be more effective than complete or no adaptation, as in the study discussed previously (Francis 1991), cross-cultural negotiators may use more convergent approaches.

▌▐█ FORCES FOR DIVERGENCE

However, people from various cultures seem to retain a specific pattern of negotiation, even when trained in a different approach, as in Grindsted's (1994) study. Ingrained cultural patterns of behavior are difficult to change, and, even if people could totally match their behavior to that of another culture, the result may not be effective.

An additional source of divergence is the perception that a particular culture's negotiation style is effective. If people from one culture believe they are effective negotiators, it is unlikely that they will change.

Implications for Managers

Cross-cultural negotiations are an important part of the international manager's job. Understanding the dynamics of the negotiation process and the influence of culture can improve negotiating outcomes substantially. Although the evidence is not clear as to the differences between intracultural and cross-cultural negotiations, a moderate adaptation to the approach of the negotiating partner may be most effective. The different strategies suggested by Weiss (1994) are also helpful when considering which approach to take.

■ Summary

The basic negotiation process includes five steps: (1) preparation, (2) relationship building, (3) information exchange, (4) persuasion, and (5) agreement. Culture influences every step of this process, as well as situational factors and negotiating tactics, both verbal and nonverbal. Location, room arrangements, choice of negotiators, and time limits can affect the final outcome for both parties. In comparing intracultural and cross-cultural negotiations, there is some evidence that people may behave differently depending on their negotiating partner. However, the nature of these differences is not clear.

High- and low-context cultures handle conflict differently. Differences in conflict resolution style affect the approach to negotiation, but other cultural factors create differences between negotiators who are both from either a high- or low-context culture.

Increasing knowledge of one's negotiating partner is a way to become a better cross-cultural negotiator. Learn as much as possible about the cultural background of both the people and the organization they represent. Also consider their approach to negotiation and specific concerns such as goals, needs, and interests. A moderate amount of adaptation to the other party's way of negotiating can lead to greater effectiveness. The two parties can also make their differences explicit and choose an appropriate means to negotiate on the basis of each party's familiarity with the other's culture.

Negotiation approaches differ considerably because of culture. However, through greater understanding of these differences and by following suggestions for improving cross-cultural negotiations, there may be greater convergence in the future. Because international managers spend such a large amount of time negotiating, it is important to understand the negotiation process and how culture influences it.

■ Discussion Questions

1. Describe the steps in the negotiation process. For each step, give an example of how someone from your own culture might differ in comparison with someone from another culture.

2. Situational factors and negotiating factors can have a strong impact on the ultimate outcome of a negotiation. How can you handle these to maximize your potential result?

3. Are you from a high-context or low-context culture? According to Ting-Toomey, how will this influence your approach to conflict? Do you agree or disagree? What are some characteristics of your culture that support your answer?

4. Identify another culture with which you have some familiarity. What differences would you expect to find between your approach and the other culture's approach to negotiation? Which differences are the most challenging? How would you attempt to handle these differences?

5. In negotiating with someone from another culture, which of the recommendations suggested do you think would be useful for you? Why? Can you think of other good advice to give those preparing for cross-cultural negotiations? (Hint: consider Chapter 4.)

References

ADLER, N.J. (1991), *International Dimensions of Organizational Behavior*, 2d Ed. Boston: PWS-Kent.

———. and GRAHAM, J.L. (1989), "Cross-Cultural Interaction: The International Comparison Fallacy?" *Journal of International Business Studies*, 20, 515–37.

BOND, M.H., WAN, K., LEUNG, K., and GIACALONE, R. (1985), "How Are Responses to Verbal Insults Related to Cultural Collectivism and Power Distance?" *Journal of Cross-Cultural Psychology*, 16, 111–27.

CHANEY, L.H. and Martin, J.S. (1995), *Intercultural Business Communication.* Upper Saddle River, NJ: Prentice Hall.

CHEN, M. (1995), *Asian Management Systems: Chinese, Japanese, and Korean Styles of Business.* New York: Routledge.

CHIU, R.K. and KOSINSKI, F.A. (1994), "Is Chinese Conflict-Handling Behavior Influenced by Chinese Values?" *Social Behavior and Personality*, 22, 81–90.

DERESKY, H. (1994), *International Management: Managing Across Borders.* New York: HarperCollins.

FISHER, G. (1980), *International Negotiations: A Cross-Cultural Perspective.* Chicago: Intercultural Press.

FISHER, R. and Ury, W. (1981), *Getting to Yes: Negotiating Agreement Without Giving In.* Boston: Houghton Mifflin.

FRANCIS, J.N.P. (1991), "When in Rome? The Effects of Cultural Adaptation on Intercultural Business Negotiations," *Journal of International Business Studies*, 22, 403–28.

GLENN, E.S., WITMEYER, D., and STEVENSON, K.A. (1977), "Cultural Styles of Persuasion," *International Journal of Intercultural Relations*, 1, 52–66.

GOLDMAN, A. (1992), "Intercultural Training of Japanese for U.S.–Japanese Interorganizational Communication," *International Journal of Intercultural Relations*, 16, 195–215.

GRAHAM, J.L. (1983), "Brazilian, Japanese, and American Business Negotiations," *Journal of International Business Studies*, 47–61.

———. (1985), "The Influence of Culture on the Process of Business Negotiations," *Journal of International Business Studies*, 16, 81–96.

———. and HERBERGER, R.A., Jr. (1983), "Negotiators Abroad—Don't Shoot from the Hip," *Harvard Business Review* (July–August), 160–68.

GRINDSTED, A. (1994), "The Impact of Cultural Styles on Negotiation: A Case Study of Spaniards and Danes," *IEEE Transactions on Professional Communication*, 37, 34–38.

GUDYKUNST, W.B. and TING-TOOMEY, S. (1988), *Culture and Interpersonal Communication.* Newbury Park, CA: Sage Publications.

HALL, E.T. (1976), *Beyond Culture*. New York: Doubleday.

MCNEIL, D.G., Jr. (1996), "Restoring Their Good Names: U.S. Companies in Trademark Battles in South Africa," *The New York Times* (May 1), D1, D19.

PERLMUTTER, H. (1983, 1984) cited in Adler, N.J. (1991), *International Dimensions of Organizational Behavior*, 2d Ed. Boston: PWS-Kent, 182, 220.

PETTIBONE, P.J. (1990), "Negotiating a Joint Venture in the Soviet Union: How to Protect Your Interests," *Journal of Business Strategy* (November/December) 5–12.

———. (1991), "Negotiating a Business Venture in the Soviet Union," *The Journal of Business Strategy* (January/February) 18–23.

PYE, L. (1982), *Chinese Commercial Negotiating Style*. Cambridge, MA: Oelheschlager, Gunn and Hain.

RAJAN, M.N. and GRAHAM, J.L. (1991), "Nobody's Grandfather Was a Merchant: Understanding the Soviet Commercial Negotiation Process and Style," *California Management Review* (Spring) 40–57.

SHENKAR, O. and RONEN, S. (1987), "The Cultural Context of Negotiations: The Implications of Chinese Interpersonal Norms," *The Journal of Applied Behavioral Science*, 23, 263–75.

SMITH, P.B. and BOND M.H. (1994), *Social Psychology Across Cultures: Analysis and Perspective*. Boston: Allyn and Bacon.

TING-TOOMEY, S., (1985), "Toward a Theory of Conflict and Culture," in Gudykunst, W., Stewart, L., and Ting-Toomey, S (eds.) *Communication, Culture, and Organizational Processes*. Beverly Hills, CA: Sage Publications.

TSE, D.K., FRANCIS, J., and WALLS, J. (1994), "Cultural Differences in Conducting Intra- and Inter-Cultural Negotiations: A Sino-Canadian Comparison," *Journal of International Business Studies*, 25, 537–55.

URY, W. (1993), *Getting Past No: Negotiating Your Way from Confrontation to Cooperation*, Rev. Ed. New York: Bantam.

WEISS, S.E. (1994a), "Negotiating with 'Romans'—Part 1," *Sloan Management Review* (Winter) 51–61.

WEISS, S.E. (1994b), "Negotiating with 'Romans'—Part 2," *Sloan Management Review* (Spring) 85–99.

Motivation

Avon Anybody?

Eroildes C. Castro is on her way to work. Maneuvering her way around puddles in the unpaved streets or down the Amazon River in northern Brazil, the Avon saleswoman faces the hazards of poisonous water snakes, flesh-eating piranhas, and customers who do not pay. Although her monthly salary is often barely above US$110, Brazil's minimum wage, Ms. Castro is clearly motivated by Avon's system of incentive prizes. An iron, a suitcase, and a plastic coffee cup set mean so much to her that Ms. Castro works despite the hardships.

In Russia, when Avon calls, Svetlana Morosova is at the door. Ms. Morosova, who holds advanced degrees in mathematics and economics and has two small children, sold her first Avon products to other mothers at a children's playground in 1994. By 1996, she was an Avon manager, driving a company car and making US$2,000 a month, more than 15 times the national average salary. In addition to the material benefits, Ms. Morosova gains self-assurance and independence from her Avon position.

Sources: Brooke, J. (1995), "Who Braves Piranha Waters? Your Avon Lady!" *The New York Times* (July 7), A4; Stanley, A. (1996), "New Face of Russian Capitalism: Avon and Mary Kay Create Opportunities for Women," *The New York Times* (August 14) D1, D16.

After reading this chapter, you should be able to:

1. Define and understand the nature of motivation.
2. Explain major content and process theories of motivation and how culture influences their application.
3. Discuss how culture influences rewards.
4. Explain how the meaning of *work* in different countries influences motivation.
5. Consider ways of developing cross-cultural motivation systems.

What motivates people to work in different countries is not always the same. Organizations are beginning to realize that a reward an employee considers valuable in one culture could be meaningless or even insulting in another. As organizations globalize, the task of developing motivation systems to fit the values and preferences of workers in a variety of cultures is becoming more demanding.

Why do people work? Is it for money, sales prizes, and company cars? Is it the job itself that people find satisfying? Does culture influence the answers to these questions? For example, is a Brazilian more appreciative of sales prizes than a Russian?

What Is Motivation?

One definition of **motivation** is the amount of effort that an individual puts into doing something. Motivation is also "a basic psychological process which explains why employees behave the way they do in the workplace" (Kanungo and Mendonca 1995, p. 16). Another view of motivation is "the willingness to exert high levels of effort toward organizational goals, conditioned by the effort's ability to satisfy some individual need" (Robbins 1996, p. 212).

Motivation is a key organizational concept. Organizations seek motivated employees, and view managers who have the ability to motivate others as successful. The vast majority of motivation theories, as with most organizational behavior research, originates within an American cultural context. Although some of the theories have been tested outside of the United States, it is not clear whether these models are appropriate for understanding the motivation of non-Americans (Hofstede 1980).

American Motivation Theories and Their Applicability Outside the United States

Two types of motivation theories are content and process. **Content theories** focus on the "what," identifying factors that cause people to put effort into work. **Process theories** concern the "how," the steps an individual takes in putting forth effort.

▌▐ CONTENT THEORIES

Three major content theories are Maslow's Hierarchy of Needs, Herzberg's Motivation-Hygiene Theory, and McClelland's Learned Needs Theory. This section gives a description of the basic ideas of each theory and a discussion of how the theory might apply in different cultures.

Maslow's Hierarchy of Needs   **Maslow's Hierarchy of Needs** (Maslow 1954) is a theory of general motivation developed in the United States in the 1950s. Abraham Maslow, an American psychologist, theorized that an individual would try to satisfy one category of needs at a time and that the hierarchical order of needs is the same for everyone.

Specifically, Maslow proposed five levels of needs:

- **Physiological needs** are the basic requirements for survival, including air, food, water, and sex drives;

- **Safety and security needs** are shelter and protection from outside threat;
- **Affiliation needs** include affection, friendship and belonging;
- **Esteem needs** focus on the need for respect, positive regard, status, and recognition from others;
- **Self-actualization needs** relate to developing one's full potential.

From the perspective of organizational behavior, employers could fulfill an employee's physiological needs by providing free or subsidized food. Safety and security needs could come in the form of job security and free or subsidized housing. Employers can meet employee social needs through a team structure or various company-sponsored social events. Employees' self-esteem needs can be fulfilled when they receive praise or recognition for performance. Finally, organizations can help employees self-actualize by assigning them meaningful, fulfilling work.

Money can satisfy any level of needs to some extent. It can purchase material goods to satisfy lower-level needs, provide a feeling of self worth, or create opportunities for self development to satisfy the higher levels.

According to Maslow, when a level of needs is satisfied, it no longer motivates behavior, and an individual moves to the next higher level, which then motivates behavior. This progression continues, and when an individual reaches the highest level of self-actualization, behavior is motivated indefinitely because in Maslow's view, no one could ever be totally self-actualized.

Although Maslow's theory has appeal in its simplicity and ease of application, "research has not been able to establish the validity of the need hierarchy itself" (Steers, Porter, and Bigley 1996, p. 15). Even in the United States, other needs motivate people—for example, spiritual needs. People can also operate on more than one needs level at the same time and move to a lower level of needs if their life circumstances change (Alderfer 1969). For example, professionals motivated by self-actualization can become motivated by physiological or security needs if they suddenly find themselves "downsized" and unable to find work.

In an international context, the circumstances and values of a particular culture can influence the ordering and importance of needs. The values of individualism and collectivism can make the hierarchy more or less relevant. For example, if a culture is collectively oriented, the individualistic higher-order needs of self-esteem and self-actualization could be irrelevant. Trompenaars (1993, pp. 65–66) writes:

> Western theories of motivation have individuals growing out of early, and hence primitive, social needs into an individually resplendent self-actualization at the summit of the hierarchy. Needless to say, this does not achieve resonance the world over, however good a theory it may be for America and Northwest Europe. The Japanese notion of the highest good is harmonious relationships within and with the pattern of nature; the primary orientation is to other people and the natural world.

In cultures that are high on uncertainty avoidance, safety and security needs might be most important. For example, in Japan, throughout their lives, people are highly motivated to compete for entrance into elite schools so that upon graduating, they can get jobs in large corporations that provide lifetime employment.

A masculine or feminine orientation, according to Hofstede's framework, can also influence the importance of different needs. In a feminine culture such as Sweden or Finland, people value the tradi-

In a feminine culture such as Sweden or Finland, people value the traditionally feminine ideals such as quality of life and working relationships, so social needs could dominate the motivation of workers over productivity.

tionally feminine ideals such as quality of life and working relationships, so social needs could dominate the motivation of workers over productivity (Adler 1997).

Economic and political circumstances can also influence the importance of needs. For example, a study of Libyan managers after the 1973 Libyan People's Revolution found that social needs were more fulfilled than security needs (Buera and Glueck 1979). Because the Revolution made Libyan managers more subject to dismissal, their security needs were less satisfied compared with non-Libyan managers working in the country. Maslow's theory would incorrectly predict that these managers could not focus on social needs until their security needs were met.

In conclusion, Maslow's hierarchy of needs theory is potentially useful for managers. It is clear, however, that the five needs in the order proposed by Maslow do not motivate everyone. Also, circumstances can cause an individual to return to a more basic needs level, and more than one needs level can be important at the same time. Despite these limitations, considering what needs are meaningful and in what order they might influence people in a particular culture can provide insight into how managers can motivate employees.

Herzberg's Motivation-Hygiene Theory Herzberg's Motivation-Hygiene Theory (Herzberg 1968; Herzberg, Mausner, and Snyderman 1959) was developed in the 1950s and 1960s and built on Maslow's theory. The premise of Herzberg's theory, often called **Two-Factor Theory**, is that satisfaction and dissatisfaction are two dimensions rather than opposite ends of a single dimension. Working from this assumption, Herzberg questioned American engineers and accountants to determine which job factors caused them to feel satisfaction or experience dissatisfaction.

Herzberg believed that the resulting two factors, hygiene and motivation, have differential effects on motivation. The **hygiene factors**, also called extrinsic or context factors, are factors outside the job itself that influence the worker. They include company policy and administration, supervision, relationship with a supervisor, work conditions, salary, relationships with peers, and security. These factors are associated with dissatisfaction. If they are absent, a worker feels dissatisfied, but their presence only brings a person to a neutral state.

The **motivation factors**, also called intrinsic or content factors, are aspects of the job itself, including achievement, recognition, interesting work, responsibility, advancement, and growth. The presence of these factors satisfies and motivates workers.

To apply his theory, Herzberg recommends **job enrichment**. In Herzberg's view, to motivate workers, a job must include many motivation factors. This is similar to Maslow's theory, with the hygiene factors corresponding to the lower-level needs and the motivation factors similar to the higher-level needs on the hierarchy.

In the United States, some workers, mainly professional and semiprofessional, did respond well to job enrichment, supporting Herzberg's model of motivation. However, blue-collar and farm workers often did not like having an enriched job and could experience reduced levels of satisfaction and motivation as a result. Even in the culture in which it originated, the limitations of Herzberg's model are significant.

Research on Herzberg's model in New Zealand, which has similar scores to the United States on Hofstede's four cultural dimensions, did not support the model (Hines 1973). The factors of supervision and interpersonal relationships had a significant relationship with satisfaction and motivation for both middle managers and salaried employees.

Despite inconclusive results, Herzberg's theory is widely used by managers in Europe, Latin America, and the Pacific Rim (Gibson, Ivancevich, and Donnelly 1994). Most likely this is because of its simplicity and the attractiveness of the basic concept. Different factors can produce satisfaction and motivation, but culture, and perhaps specific situations, influence which factors (Adler 1997).

McClelland's Learned Needs Theory   A third content theory is **Learned Needs Theory** (McClelland 1966, 1985). American psychologist David McClelland proposed that three major needs influence people's behavior. These needs are not instinctive desires, as in Maslow's theory, but learned. The learned needs, which help explain individual differences in motivation, are need for achievement, need for power, and need for affiliation.

Need for achievement is a concern for establishing and maintaining high levels of performance quality. Individuals with a high need for achievement want personal responsibility for their success or failure, like calculated—that is, moderate—risks, and like to receive immediate, concrete feedback on their performance. As a result, tasks that are too easy or too difficult do not appeal to them because they have less responsibility for the outcome.

Need for power is a concern for reputation, responsibility, influence, impact, and control over others. People high on this need prefer leadership positions, and others usually rate them as effective leaders. In addition, individuals with a high need for power are usually good performers and have above-average attendance at work (Steers and Braunstein 1976).

Need for affiliation is a concern for establishing and maintaining social relationships. People who have a high need for affiliation like close, friendly relationships with others and prefer cooperative rather than competitive situations.

How do these needs relate to organizational behavior? Research indicates that individuals with a high need for achievement strive for personal success. They are often dynamic entrepreneurs but do not necessarily make good managers, because the achievement of others is not their concern. Jobs with responsibility, moderate challenge, and the opportunity to receive feedback motivate people with a high need for achievement. In contrast, successful managerial performance is related to high power need and low affiliation need (McClelland and Burnham 1976).

Much of McClelland's work focuses on the need for achievement. McClelland theorizes that improving the level of need achievement among less economically successful groups would encourage the groups' economic development (McClelland 1966). McClelland and his colleagues developed a training course to increase need for achievement and instructed several groups with it, including executives in the United States and Mexico, underachieving high school boys, and businessmen in India. With the exception of one group in Mexico, those who received the training were more successful two years later than those who took another management course or no course. However, to continue the gains, the participants had to work in an environment that supported achievement-oriented behavior.

Subsequent research indicates that the business executives in India could not sustain the gains. Perhaps this was because of lack of social support for personal achievement in the culture (Misra and Kanungo 1994). This could also have been the reason that the course was not successful in Mexico. Both cultures have a group orientation, and the need for achievement is clearly an individualistic need.

Studies of actual and aspiring Russian entrepreneurs in the 1990s found a strong need for achievement (McCarthy, Puffer, and Shekshnia 1993; Tullar 1992). However,

> Achievement, ambition, and initiative have been denigrated in Russia. People with a high need for achievement have been condemned for being individualistic, antisocial, and enemies of the people. Personal ambition has aroused feelings of envy, vindictiveness, and derision. And initiative has typically been received with indifference, at best, and punishment, at worst. Negative attitudes towards these characteristics are so deeply ingrained in the Russian psyche that many Russians who want to realize their ambitions feel pressure from two sources—public scorn and their own guilt from violating the values they were raised with. . . . If Russians seem reluctant to take initiative or be ambitious, they might respond positively to proposals that emphasize benefits to the collective or that reward individuals in ways that do not arouse feelings of envy. One should respect requests for not publicizing personal achievements, material possessions or privileges (Puffer 1993, p. 479).[1]

In a study of Confucianism and needs in the People's Republic of China, MBA students in China scored lower than their North American counterparts in achievement, affiliation, change, cognitive structure, and impulsivity, and higher on autonomy and harm avoidance (Punnett 1995). It is possible that these needs affect the motivation of Chinese employees. For example, it might be more effective to put less emphasis on individual performance and short-term goals, to tie rewards to position and proper behavior, and to make rewards long term rather than immediate.

Another concern with Learned Needs Theory is that the concept of achievement is difficult, if not impossible, to translate into languages other than English (Hofstede 1980). Hofstede found that countries that scored high on achievement need in McClelland's research were those that had weak uncertainty avoidance and high masculinity on his cultural dimensions. This combination is found only in countries in the Anglo-American group and some of their former colonies. This includes Great Britain, the United States, Canada, New Zealand, Ireland, Hong Kong, Australia, India, South Africa, and the Philippines. Almost all of these countries use English as a primary language. Whether the concept of achievement and need for achievement applies outside these countries is open to question.

Conclusions about the Content Theories   All of the content theories identify factors or needs related to motivation. By focusing on content, each theory restricts its explanation of motivation to a particular set of factors and explains how to motivate people using these factors. Because values across and within cultures are not universal, it is difficult to find a set of motivating needs or factors that applies to everyone. Because of this, research results on the content models indicate a lack of conclusive support.

Does this mean that content theories are useless for understanding motivation? No. Their important contribution is to identify concepts useful for gaining a better understanding of motivation. The theories are valuable as a starting point for examining cultural and even individual differences in motivation. For example, managers can consider what, if any, hierarchies of needs exist for their employees, what factors motivate or dissatisfy them, or what major needs influence organizational behavior.

---

[1]"A Riddle Wrapped in an Enigma: Demystifying Russian Managerial Motivation" by Sheila M. Puffer from *European Management Journal*, 11 (4), 473–80. Copyright © 1993 by Elsevier Science, Ltd. Reprinted by permission of Elsevier Science, Ltd., Langford Lane, Kidlington OX5 1GB, UK.

PROCESS THEORIES

Reinforcement or Learning Theory, Goal Setting Theory, Expectancy Theory, and Equity Theory are examples of process theories. Like content theories, process theories were developed in the United States. However, because they focus on *process* rather than content, these theories are more applicable in other countries. Process theories attempt to discover universal mechanisms to explain motivation. To apply these theories, managers can incorporate specific cultural and other factors into the model to adapt it to the individuals whom they wish to motivate.

Reinforcement Theory   The premise of **Reinforcement or Learning Theory** is that the environment determines people's behavior (Skinner 1971). As people grow from children into adults, what they learn is a result of the outcomes of their behavior. If individuals receive a reward or **reinforcement** for what they do, it is likely that they will repeat it. If no one acknowledges the behavior, a person could stop it. When people receive a negative outcome or **punishment** for their behavior, they usually stop doing it at the moment; but punishment does not guarantee that undesirable behavior will end.

    Organizational behavior modification or **OBMod** is the application of Reinforcement Theory to motivating workers in organizations. A typical OBMod program involves a four step process (Komaki, Coombs, and Schepman 1996):

1. Ensure that workers know the behaviors they are expected to carry out as part of the job.
2. Train observers and have them record the workers' correct and incorrect behaviors.
3. Reinforce workers who practice correct behaviors and provide corrective feedback.
4. Evaluate the effects of the program on behavior.

    Many studies in the United States have tested this approach, with the majority of them showing positive results. Behaviors improved include performance, attendance and punctuality, safety and health-related behaviors, and service to customers (Komaki, Coombs, and Schepman 1996).

    One test of the applicability of OBMod outside the United States is a study of Russian textile workers (Welsh, Luthans, and Sommer 1993). Using a similar approach to an earlier study in which OBMod improved performance in retail sales workers in the United States, the researchers trained Russian supervisors to give positive reinforcers—attention, praise, and positive feedback—to their workers when they observed them performing specific behaviors identified as leading to high-quality work outputs. The program was successful in producing a positive change in the workers' behavior. However, when the reinforcers were withdrawn, the positive behavior changes continued. The theory predicts that the positive behaviors should have eventually stopped.

    Why the positive behaviors did not stop is unclear from the study. One explanation suggested by the authors is that coworkers provided social reinforcers that maintained the behaviors even after the supervisors formally stopped administering positive reinforcers. Because of the collective nature of Russian culture, approval from peers could be as rewarding, or even more rewarding, than from the supervisor. In other words, the positive behaviors might have continued because of positive reinforcers coming from a different source.

The ideas of Reinforcement Theory are simple, and the theory appears to be a convincing explanation for behavior. To apply it, managers must understand what is rewarding to the people they wish to motivate. At the organization level, managers can take into account reward preferences of the workforce. For example, if a Japanese company is establishing a subsidiary in the United States, the reward systems in the subsidiary must be more individualistic than in the home office to motivate American workers. In the vignette at the beginning of the chapter about the two Avon employees, both material incentives and feelings of accomplishment function as reinforcers of performance.

Reinforcement Theory might not be a successful explanation of behavior in cultures where people do not perceive a connection between their own behavior and its consequences. For example, in the Middle East many Muslims believe that whatever happens is God's will. Therefore, an OBMod program might have no effect because people would consider rewards as what God had willed rather than a consequence of their own desirable behavior.

In societies such as Argentina and Uruguay, status is based on personal characteristics—ascription, rather than achievement. People believe high status deserves rewards: It might be inappropriate to reward the performance of a lower-level worker directly; everyone associated with a successful performance should receive a reward in relation to his or her relative status. For example, in a sales situation, "the superior is by definition responsible for increased performance, so that relative status is unaffected by higher group sales. If rewards are to be increased, this must be done proportionately to ascribed status, not given to the person closest to the sale" (Trompenaars 1993, pp. 110–11).

When managers do give rewards to encourage performance, the rewards should be something an employee values. What an individual perceives as rewarding is subject to cultural influence. For example, praise and appreciation motivate members of family-dominated cultures such as Greece, Italy, Japan, Singapore, and South Korea more than money (Trompenaars 1993). Certain material rewards can also carry unexpected connotations. For example, in India, the reward of a cowhide leather wallet or key case with a corporate logo would be extremely offensive, because the cow is a sacred animal in the predominant Hindu religion.

> **P**raise and appreciation motivate members of family-dominated cultures such as Greece, Italy, Japan, Singapore, and South Korea more than money.

Goal Setting Theory   **Goal Setting Theory** involves the effect that goal setting has on performance. Research on Goal Setting Theory, begun in the late 1960s, has been conducted primarily in the United States and is largely supportive (Locke and Latham 1990; Pinder 1984). The theory is based on the idea that people are motivated by intentions to work toward a goal (Locke 1968). Researchers have found that performance increases when specific, rather than vague, goals are set. Setting a difficult but achievable goal generally leads to higher performance than setting an easy goal. In addition, feedback, especially that which comes from workers reviewing their own outputs, usually results in higher performance than no feedback does.

For Goal Setting Theory to work, an individual must be committed to the goal that is set. It does not matter whether a person participates in setting a goal or it is assigned by someone else, as long as there is commitment to it. However, people are usually more committed to goals they are involved in setting. A second condition for Goal Setting Theory is self-efficacy, that someone believes that he or she has the ability to do a particular task.

Studies of Goal Setting Theory comparing the United States with England and

Israel indicate that culture can affect the goal setting process. For example, American workers in one study responded equally well to a goal-setting program introduced by either a shop steward or a supervisor. However, the program initiated by the shop steward was more effective for a group of British workers (Earley 1986). Two studies with Israelis suggest that the effects of group participation in goal setting are stronger in a collective-participative culture (Erez 1986) and that participation in goal setting produces a stronger result in countries lower on power distance (Erez and Earley 1987).

Although the precise nature of the influence of culture on goal setting is unclear (Locke and Latham 1990), taking into account how values influence goal commitment can enhance the effects of the goal setting process. For example, in the studies just mentioned, the Israelis were higher on collectivism and lower on power distance than were the Americans. Therefore, in the collective-participative culture of Israel, participating in goal setting produces a more favorable result because people are more committed to a goal they participate in setting. Relative to the Israelis, Americans have higher power distance, and it seems that they are more willing to commit to a goal set by a supervisor. Therefore, in a high–power distance culture, employees might be more willing to commit to a goal set by their supervisor, and direct participation might not be necessary or even desirable.

Because self-efficacy is also an important aspect of the goal setting process, cultural values that influence individual beliefs about personal ability to perform a task should also have an influence. For example, in China, a collective country, it is often important to use *guanxi*, a relationship, to accomplish certain tasks. As a result, if a person lacks *guanxi*, for a particular task, self-efficacy could be low regardless of personal talents or ability.

Expectancy Theory   The **Expectancy Theory** of motivation (Nadler and Lawler 1991; Porter and Lawler 1968; Steers, Porter, and Bigley 1996; Vroom 1964) rests on important assumptions about people's behavior. First, behavior is a result of both personal and environmental factors. Second, people's decisions about whether to belong to an organization and how much effort to put into performing influence their behavior in organizations. Third, because of different needs, people seek different rewards from the organization. Finally, people decide how to behave on the basis of beliefs about what leads to the most desirable outcomes.

Using these assumptions, researchers developed Expectancy Theory to describe how an individual decides how much effort to put into a task. Figure 6-1 presents one model of Expectancy Theory.

The process an individual follows in deciding how much effort to put into a particular behavior is dependent on several things. First, a person considers whether trying or making an effort could lead to successful performance. This is identified as the **E→P expectancy**, effort leading to performance expectancy, in the model. If a person believes that trying can lead to success, he or she is more likely to put effort into a particular behavior.

Second, a person thinks about the likelihood that successful performance would lead to an outcome or reward. In the model, this is called the **P→O expectancy**, performance leading to outcome expectancy. Associated with each outcome is a **valence**, which is the value of the reward to the individual receiving it. If a person feels that performance will be rewarded with a valued outcome, this will increase the amount of effort. If the person sees no connection between performance and outcome or the outcome is not desirable, he or she is less likely to exert effort.

Finally, a person considers **instrumentality**, the likelihood that a first-level

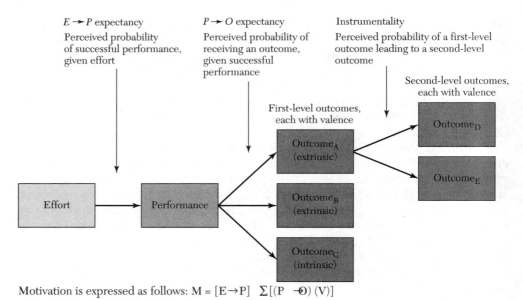

$E \rightarrow P$ expectancy
Perceived probability
of successful performance,
given effort

$P \rightarrow O$ expectancy
Perceived probability of
receiving an outcome,
given successful
performance

Instrumentality
Perceived probability of a first-level
outcome leading to a second-level
outcome

Second-level outcomes,
each with valence

First-level outcomes,
each with valence

Effort → Performance

$Outcome_A$ (extrinsic)
$Outcome_B$ (extrinsic)
$Outcome_C$ (intrinsic)

$Outcome_D$
$Outcome_E$

Motivation is expressed as follows: $M = [E \rightarrow P] \ \sum [(P \rightarrow O) (V)]$

Figure 6-1   The Expectancy Model of Motivation

Source: Nadler, D.A and Lawler, E.E., (1977), "Motivation: A Diagnostic Approach," in Hackman, J.R., Lawler, E.E., and Porter, L.W., (eds.) *Perspectives on Behavior in Organizations.* New York: McGraw-Hill. p. 34.

outcome would lead to a second-level outcome. This means that an immediate reward could lead to further rewards; for example, if a supervisor praises an employee for a job well done, will the supervisor later give the employee a salary increase? If an immediate outcome can lead to something positive in the future, that also increases effort. The amount of effort a person expends then depends on how he or she evaluates each of the factors in the Expectancy model in relation to other possible choices of behavior.

Tests of the Expectancy model in the United States support some aspects of it, but there are also criticisms. One problem is that the model is difficult to test. Researchers disagree on the measurement of variables in the model, and some question whether individuals consciously make choices the way the theory predicts. Although it seems complicated, Expectancy Theory does help understanding motivation and can provide a basis for evaluating organizational reward policies and practices (Steers, Porter, and Bigley 1996).

Expectancy Theory can explain the motivational processes of some people outside the United States. As with Reinforcement Theory, in applying Expectancy Theory, a manager must understand what is rewarding to his or her employees. Expectancy Theory also assumes people make conscious choices and have some control over their work environment. As mentioned previously, some societies' values are not congruent with these assumptions. For example, in high–power distance countries, people view their behavior in organizations as totally dependent on the orders of their superiors, and in a culture that has a subjugation orientation to nature, people do not try to control their environment.

As Adler (1997, p. 164) concludes, "Expectancy Theories work best in explaining cultures that emphasize internal attribution." When people in a culture believe they can control the work environment and their own behavior, such as in the United States, England, and Canada, Expectancy Theory can explain motivation. In cultures where people believe the work environment and their own behavior are not completely under their control, such as in Brazil, Saudi Arabia, or China, an Expectancy model might not be totally applicable (Adler 1997).

Equity Theory   Equity Theory also developed in the United States (Adams 1963). The basic premise of the theory is that people try to balance their inputs and outcomes in relation to others. **Inputs** are what someone brings to a situation. An employee's inputs include education, previous work experience, personality, and personal characteristics. **Outcomes** are what one takes from a situation—for example, pay, benefits, working conditions, coworker relationships, and training opportunities. Each person has his or her own perception of the value of these inputs and outcomes.

Motivation results through the process of comparing one's own perceived outcomes to inputs ratio with the perceived ratio of a comparison other. When the individual's ratio is about equal to the comparison other's, equity is achieved and there is no motivation. However, if the two ratios are unequal, the person experiences a tension or discomfort that motivates him or her to try to bring the two ratios into perceived equity. In mathematical terms, equity exists when

$$\frac{\text{Outcomes}_{\text{self}}}{\text{Inputs}_{\text{self}}} = \frac{\text{Outcomes}_{\text{other}}}{\text{Inputs}_{\text{other}}}$$

Inequity exists if the self ratio (on the left side of the equation) is either less than or greater than the other ratio (on the right side of the equation).

Equity theory predicts a variety of possible means to reduce inequity, including an individual distorting perceptions of the elements or changing the inputs or outcomes of the self or other. For example, if an individual perceives inequity due to his or her own outcomes being less than a comparison other's, the person might ask the supervisor for a raise.

Distributive justice, the issue of how rewards can be distributed in a fair manner, is an aspect of Equity Theory. One way is according to the equity norm defined in Equity Theory. This means that an outcome to input ratio should be relatively equal for every employee. A second approach is an equality norm in which each employee receives the same outcomes regardless of inputs. Finally, a need norm suggests each employee be given outcomes according to his or her need.

Some research suggests that collective cultures prefer an equality norm, in contrast to individualistic cultures, which favor an equity norm (Chen 1995). An equality norm allows collective societies to maintain interpersonal harmony, and the equity norm provides an opportunity for individualists to achieve. However, Chen (1995) suggests that moves toward greater collectivism in the United States and greater individualism in China could influence reward allocation preferences. In a comparison of employees at all levels from companies in the United States and China, Chinese employees used an equity norm for distributing both material and socioemotional rewards. American employees preferred to distribute material rewards on an equity basis but gave socioemotional rewards on an equality basis. Material rewards included pay and bonus, and socioemotional rewards were managerial friendliness, display of the employee's photo at the workplace, and social events.

> Moves toward greater collectivism in the United States and greater individualism in China could influence reward allocation preferences.

Process Theories: Conclusions   To summarize, process theories that focus on the "how" could be more effective than content theories are in explaining motivational constructs that can apply both inside and outside the United States. However, just as with the process theories, in applying any of these models outside of the United States, managers must consider the cultural differences between the United States and the other country. For example, cultural factors influence whether the basic assumptions in the models are met. Cultural variations can also be taken into consideration to enhance the effectiveness of a particular model. Although the evidence is not conclusive, the ability of the process theories to consider a deeper level of analysis and to allow for individual differences makes them more likely to fit people from a wider range of cultures.

Because rewards can have a great impact on motivation, in the next section we consider how culture influences the choice of rewards.

How Culture Influences Rewards

All motivation theories consider the effects of a reward or need fulfillment on behavior. Different cultural preferences influence the value of different rewards and affect motivational practices in organizations.

HOW CULTURAL FACTORS INFLUENCE THE VALUE OF REWARDS

Western motivation models are culturally individualistic; applying them to a collectivist culture might be inappropriate. For example, a Japanese saying is, "The nail that sticks out gets hammered down." This means that no individual should stand out from the group. Giving an individual reward to a Japanese employee could embarrass the recipient and thus be demotivating. In high-context collective cultures, there are often expected norms of behavior for particular situations. Offering rewards for individual behavior that runs counter to group norms is unlikely to have a positive influence on motivation.

Hofstede's masculinity versus femininity dimension also suggests what could be rewarding for different societies. If a culture is masculine, people prefer to receive money, titles, or other materialistic or status-oriented rewards. In a feminine society, meaningful rewards are time off, improved benefits, or symbolic rewards.

In some countries, the perception of material items is as gifts rather than as rewards for performance. In China for example, organizations often distribute food to all employees as holiday gifts. People in higher positions get more or better quality items, but employees make no connection between their performance and the gifts.

Even within countries, a variety of factors influence the reward preferences of employees. For example, in the Bahamas, hotel workers ranked higher wages, good working conditions, appreciation and praise for work done, and interesting work as the top four of ten motivational factors (Charles and Marshall 1992). However, age, gender, education, organizational level, and tenure also influenced individual preferences. For instance, males and supervisors ranked higher wages as being more important than did females and nonsupervisors.

Employees in Taiwan also responded to benefits differentially on the basis of their personal characteristics (Hong et al. 1995). Benefits that employees thought had the most impact on their performance were year-end bonuses, dividends, pensions, holidays and leave, and working disease and damage compensation. However, there were many differences among groups based on gender, marital status, age, education, and position level. Single employees emphasized further education, career development, and flexible work time, whereas married employees thought day care, dividends, child education subsidies, and pensions more important. Men emphasized entertainment, further education, loan, dividends, and laundry benefits, compared with women who liked maternity leave, commuting subsidies, and flexible work time.

ORGANIZATIONAL REWARD PRACTICES

Organizations often equate rewards with employee motivation. The following examples are a sample of current motivation practices.

A 1995 Asia-wide survey, including 500 top companies listed in the stock exchanges in ASEAN countries (The Association for Southeast Asian Nations includes Singapore, Thailand, Malaysia, Indonesia, the Philippines, Brunei, and Vietnam), China, Taiwan, and India, found cash, travel, and promotions to be the most popular motivational tools (Desker-Shaw 1996). Of the 65% of companies in the survey that have a motivational program, Thai companies use them most and Indonesian companies least. Travel is a new incentive in Asia, and major corporations are the only ones to use it to improve morale, productivity, and sales.

An example is DHL International's cash and travel incentive program for sales staff in Hong Kong, which began in 1995. After training to increase employee knowledge and expertise, the company gave each salesperson a model air cargo container. When salespeople exceeded their monthly sales targets, they received small blocks to fill the container as a reward. The salespeople could choose whether to redeem the blocks immediately for cash or accumulate them for a travel prize. Because the models were on employees' desks, colleagues could see one another's progress; those with full containers consistently beat monthly sales targets. Anyone needing help closing a difficult sale would approach someone with a full container for advice. DHL sales exceeded targets as a result of the program.

In the United States, cutting-edge companies are developing novel rewards to retain workers and encourage their productivity (Dolan 1996). At Illinois Trade, a bartering company employing 50 people, workers can get company, paid alternative medical care such as herbal therapy and a once-a-month free massage on company time. Employees can volunteer for community projects, also on company time. Because training employees is extremely expensive, Illinois Trade hopes not to lose even one.

Andersen Consulting in Chicago offers a concierge service that waits at employees' homes for deliveries and repairs. Another motivational device is a company-sponsored public school on the work sites at American Bankers Insurance Group, Barnett Banks, and Hewlett-Packard in the United States. Companies offer new types of rewards because they believe they help attract and retain the best talent.

The Meaning of Work Across Cultures

A major concern with the motivation theories described previously is that the theories reflect 1950s and 1960s United States culture. When the theories are tested in other cultures, it is clear that they are not applicable.

THE MEANING OF WORK STUDY

One project that examines basic concepts involved with motivation is the meaning of work research by George England and the Meaning of Work (MOW) International Research Team (England 1986; MOW International Research Team 1987). The study, designed and conducted by an international team of behavioral scientists, examines the view of work in eight countries. The results from a sample of approximately 15,000 workers in various occupations strongly support the idea that the meaning of work is different in different countries. England and his colleagues define and assess the meaning of work using three key concepts:

- *Work centrality.* The degree of general importance and value attributed to the role of working in one's life.
- *Societal norms about working.* Normative beliefs and expectations regarding specified rights and duties attached to working.
- *Work goals.* Work goals and values sought and preferred by individuals in their working lives (England 1986).

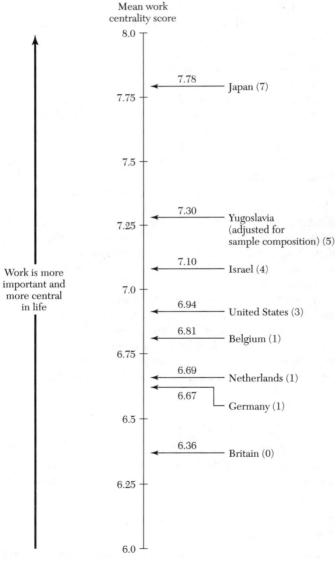

Figure 6-2 **Work Centrality Scores**

Source: MOW International Research Team (1987), *The Meaning of Work: An International Perspective.* London: Academic Press, p. 83.

Work Centrality   Questions on work centrality ask how important work is compared with other parts of a worker's life and the worker's total life. Figure 6-2 presents the results for the eight countries on this measure.

The scores indicate a relatively great variation in the importance of work to people from different countries. The Japanese consider work a very important part of their lives, whereas for the British work has relatively less importance. An interesting finding is that in the eight countries studied, 86.1% of all respondents said they would continue to work even if they no longer had any financial need. Even in Britain, which had the lowest percentage, 68.9% said they would continue to work. In these eight countries with relatively developed economies, work is a major part of the average person's life.

In a study of the meaning of work in Saudi Arabia, 94% of respondents said they would continue to work even if they could live comfortably without doing so (Ali and Al-Shakhis 1989). This illustrates the importance of work in an Arab country, none of which were studied by England.

Societal Norms Toward Working   The second area the MOW Team investigated is societal norms toward working. They defined two norms and measured how people from the eight different countries responded to them. The **entitlement norm** "represents the underlying work rights of individuals and the work-related responsi-

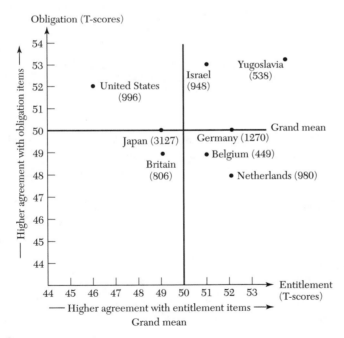

F i g u r e   6 - 3   Societal Norms Scores

Target group data. NOTE: Country results on the two indices are weighted equally regardless of sample size. Country numbers are shown in parentheses. Differences of 1-2 T-scores points between samples compared here can be considered significantly different in a statistical sense which, of course, does not necessarily imply a meaningful difference in practical terms.

Source: MOW International Research Team (1987), *The Meaning of Work: An International Perspective.* London: Academic Press, p. 96.

bility of organizations and society toward individuals. This norm included the notions that all members of society are entitled to meaningful and interesting work, proper training to obtain and continue in such work, and the right to participate in work/method decisions" (MOW International Research Team 1987, p. 94).

The **obligation norm** "represents the underlying duties of all individuals to society with respect to working. This norm included the notions that everyone has a duty to contribute to society by working, a duty to save for their own future, and the duty to value one's work, whatever its nature" (MOW International Research Team 1987, p. 94). Figure 6-3 presents the scores of the eight countries on the two types of norms.

Table 6-1 Importance of Work Goals

	Countries							
Work goals	Belgium (N = 446)	Germany (N = 1248)	Israel (N = 772)	Japan (N = 2897)	Netherlands (N = 967)	United States (N = 988)	Yugoslavia (N = 512)*	Britain (N = 742)
Interesting work	8.25 — 1	7.26 — 3	6.75 — 1	7.38 — 2	7.59 — 2	7.41 — 1	7.47 — 2	8.02 — 1
Good pay	7.13 — 2	7.73 — 1	6.60 — 3	6.56 — 5	6.27 — 5	6.82 — 2	6.73 — 3	7.80 — 2
Good interpersonal relations	6.34 — 5	6.43 — 4	6.67 — 2	6.39 — 6	7.19 — 3	6.08 — 7	7.52 — 1	6.33 — 4
Good job security	6.80 — 3	7.57 — 2	5.22 — 10	6.71 — 4	5.68 — 7	6.30 — 3	5.21 — 9	7.12 — 3
A good match between you and your job	5.77 — 8	6.09 — 5	5.61 — 6	7.83 — 1	6.17 — 6	6.19 — 4	6.49 — 5	5.63 — 6
A lot of autonomy	6.56 — 4	5.66 — 8	6.00 — 4	6.89 — 3	7.61 — 1	5.79 — 8	5.42 — 8	4.69 — 10
Opportunity to learn	5.80 — 7	4.97 — 9	5.83 — 5	6.26 — 7	5.38 — 9	6.16 — 5	6.61 — 4	5.55 — 8
A lot of variety	5.96 — 6	5.71 — 6	4.89 — 11	5.05 — 9	6.86 — 4	6.10 — 6	5.62 — 7	5.62 — 7
Convenient work hours	4.71 — 9	5.71 — 6	5.53 — 7	5.46 — 8	5.59 — 8	5.25 — 9	5.01 — 10	6.11 — 5
Good physical working conditions	4.19 — 11	4.39 — 11	5.28 — 9	4.18 — 10	5.03 — 10	4.84 — 11	5.94 — 6	4.87 — 9
Good opportunity for upgrading or promotion	4.49 — 10	4.48 — 10	5.29 — 8	3.33 — 11	3.31 — 11	5.08 — 10	4.00 — 11	4.27 — 11

Left: Mean ranks.

Right: The rank of each work goal within a given country. Rank 1 is the *most* important work goal for a country and rank 11 is the *least* important work goal for a country.

*Combined target group data were used for Yugoslavia.

Source: MOW International Research Team (1987), *The Meaning of Work: An International Perspective.* London: Academic Press, p. 122.

A country with a higher obligation score supports the traditional work ethic more, whereas a country with a higher entitlement score is moving away from the traditional ethic. At the extremes, the United States and Netherlands show the least balanced positions. The Netherlands has one of the highest entitlement scores and the lowest obligation score. This suggests that the Dutch put more emphasis on individual worker rights and agree less with the idea that everyone has a duty to work. In the United States, societal norms were opposite: Americans had one of the highest obligation scores but the lowest entitlement score. The traditional work ethic, at least as an ideal, is still strong in the United States.

Work Goals   The last area is the relative importance of work goals. Table 6-1 shows the importance of different work goals in the eight countries. None of the eight countries has the same relative ranking of work goals. However, for all countries, "Interesting Work" is ranked in the first, second, or third position, and "Good Pay" ranks first, second, or third for six out of the eight. At the opposite end, "Good Opportunity for Upgrading or Promotion" and "Good Physical Working Conditions" are among the three least important goals for most countries.

Applying the Meaning of Work Research   The meaning of work research can help managers better understand work motivation by providing knowledge of the relative importance and meaning of work in different countries. For example, looking at the work centrality scores, because of the greater importance of work to people in Japan compared with Germany, work itself may be more of a motivating factor in Japan. Therefore, it is not surprising that Germans work fewer hours than do the Japanese. In developing reward systems, managers should consider the importance of various work goals. For example, good interpersonal relations are more important in Israel and the former Yugoslavia than they are in the United States and Japan.

Convergence or Divergence?

▌▌▐ FORCES FOR CONVERGENCE

With the popularity of U.S. business education among international managers throughout the world, there is a tendency to consider U.S. motivation theories as the best or only means for understanding motivational processes (Adler 1991). In addition, global corporations often try to develop consistent policies and practices across their subsidiaries for administrative efficiency and fairness to employees. Therefore, many of these organizations have motivational practices based on U.S. models. These two trends suggest a move toward convergence.

▌▌▐ FORCES FOR DIVERGENCE

However, as pointed out previously, the application of U.S. motivation theories is not effective across all cultures. Managers must develop organizational systems that are flexible enough to take into account the meaning of work and the relative value of rewards within the range of cultures where they operate. By developing an organizationwide approach that is adaptable, an organization should simultaneously be able to maintain consistency across locations and provide programs and rewards that motivate employees from many different cultural backgrounds.

Implications for Managers

With the uncertainty surrounding the application of motivation theories in the United States and other countries, managers might find it difficult to choose an approach to motivating their subordinates. On the basis of current knowledge, the use of process theories appears to be more promising than content theories. The meaning of work and what people find rewarding varies on the basis of culture. In designing approaches to motivation, it is important for managers to consider the cultural frameworks presented in Chapter 2.

When developing a motivational system, managers should consider whether a culture is collective or individualistic to determine if rewards should be on a group or individual basis. Another factor, time orientation, influences whether setting deadlines would influence performance.

These examples suggest a few differences in how culture affects approaches to motivation. Overall, managers need an understanding of the people who work for them to select an appropriate motivation system.

> Managers need an understanding of the people who work for them to select an appropriate motivation system.

Summary

Motivation is effort an individual puts into doing something. To understand motivation in an international context, it is important to learn about American theories and how they might be useful both in the United States and in other countries. Content theories of motivation such as Maslow's Hierarchy of Needs, Herzberg's Motivation-Hygiene Theory, and McClelland's Learned Needs Theory describe the factors that cause people to put effort into their work. Although the precise factors suggested by the theories might not be correct across all societies, their basic frameworks serve as a starting point for understanding needs.

The process theories, including Reinforcement Theory, Goal Setting Theory, Expectancy Theory, and Equity Theory, focus on how someone becomes motivated. These theories, which aim at a deeper level of analysis than content theories, appear to be more promising both for the United States and other countries. However, cultural variables such as individualism or ascription could limit the applicability of some of the theories.

Because rewards are important in many theories and companies generally see rewards as motivating employees, it is important to select rewards that are culturally appropriate. Examples of trends in employee rewards and benefits in Asia and the United States indicate employers are giving a wide range of novel rewards to motivate workers.

Research on the meaning of work in different countries provides further understanding of how to motivate people in different cultures. With insight into the meaning of work, managers can better understand work behaviors and attitudes in different cultures. Because of reliance on U.S. motivational approaches and global corporations' desires for consistent worldwide systems, there are trends toward convergence. However, because managers have difficulty applying U.S. models in other cultures, more local approaches to motivation could develop. Managers therefore must develop flexible motivational systems that can be effective across different cultures.

■ Discussion Questions

1. Why are content theories of motivation less likely to be applicable outside of the United States?

2. Select a country of your choice. What factors should a manager consider in developing a motivational system for this country?

3. What motivates you to work? How do your responses compare with examples of motivational preferences in other countries presented in the chapter?

4. What do you think about some of the new approaches to reward systems? What are some rewards that might be attractive for your culture in the future?

5. How does research on the meaning of work in different countries relate to the question of motivation?

6. If you had to design a global system of motivation for a large corporation, what would be some of your major concerns?

References

ADAMS, J. (1963), "Toward an Understanding of Inequity," *Journal of Abnormal and Social Psychology*, 67, 422–36.

ADLER, N.J. (1991), *International Dimensions of Organizational Behavior*, 2d Ed. Boston: PWS-Kent.

———. (1997), *International Dimensions of Organizational Behavior*, 3d Ed. Cincinnati, OH: South-Western College Publishing.

ALDERFER, C.P. (1969), "An Empirical Test of a New Theory of Human Needs," *Organizational Behavior and Human Performance* (May), 142–175.

ALI, A. and AL-SHAKHIS, M. (1989) "The Meaning of Work in Saudi Arabia," *International Journal of Manpower*, 10(1), 26–32.

BROOKE, J. (1995), "Who Braves Piranha Waters? Your Avon Lady!" *The New York Times* (July 7), A4.

BUERA, A. and GLUECK, W.F. (1979), "The Need Satisfaction of Managers in Libya," *Management International Review*, 19 (1), 113–21.

CHARLES, K.R. and MARSHALL, L.H. (1992), "Motivational Preferences of Caribbean Hotel Workers: An Exploratory Study," *International Journal of Contemporary Hospitality Management*, 4(3), 25–29.

CHEN, C.C. (1995), "New Trends in Rewards Allocation Preferences: A Sino-U.S. Comparison," *The Academy of Management Journal*, 38(2), 408–28.

DESKER-SHAW, S. (1996), "Revving Up Asia's Workers," *Asian Business*, 32(2), 41–44.

DOLAN, K.A. (1996), "When Money Isn't Enough," *Forbes* (November 18), 164–70.

EARLEY, P.C. (1986), "Supervisors and Shop Stewards as Sources of Contextual Information in Goal Setting: A Comparison of the U.S. with England," *Journal of Applied Psychology*, 71, 111–18.

ENGLAND, G.W. (1986), "National Work Meanings and Patterns—Constraints on Management Action," *European Management Journal*, 4, 176–84.

EREZ, M. (1986), "The Congruence of Goal Setting Strategies with Socio-Cultural Values, and Its Effect on Performance," *Journal of Management*, 12, 585–92.

———. and EARLEY, P.C. (1987), "Comparative Analysis of Goal-Setting Strategies Across Cultures," *Journal of Applied Psychology*, 72, 658–65.

GIBSON, J.L., IVANCEVICH, J.M., and DONNELLY, J.H. Jr. (1994), *Organizations: Behavior, Structure, Processes*. Boston: Irwin.

HERZBERG, F. (1968), "One More Time: How Do You Motivate Employees?" *Harvard Business Review* (January/February), 53–62.

———., MAUSNER, B. and SNYDERMAN, B. (1959), *The Motivation to Work*. New York: John Wiley & Sons.

HINES, G.H. (1973), "Cross-Cultural Differences in Two-Factor Motivation Theory," *Journal of Applied Psychology*, 58(3), 375–77.

HOFSTEDE, G. (1980), "Motivation, Leadership, and Organization: Do American Theories Apply Abroad?" *Organizational Dynamics*, 9, 42–62.

HONG, J.C., YANG, S.D., WANG, L.J., CHIOU, E.F., et al. (1995), "Impact of Employee Benefits on Work Motivation and Productivity," *International Journal of Career Management*, 7(6), 10–14.

KANUNGO, R.N. and MENDONCA, M. (1994), "Introduction: Motivational Models for Developing Societies," in Kanungo, R.N. and Mendonca, M., (eds.) *Work Motivation: Models for Developing Countries*. New Delhi: Sage Publications.

KOMAKI, J.L., COOMBS, T., and SCHEPMAN, S. (1996), "Motivational Implications of Reinforcement Theory," in Steers, R.M., Porter, L.W., and Bigley, G.A., (eds.) *Motivation and Leadership at Work*, 6th Ed. New York: McGraw-Hill.

LOCKE, E.A. (1968). "Toward a Theory of Task Motivation and Incentives," *Organizational Behavior and Human Performance*, 3, 157–89.

———. and LATHAM, G.P. (1990), *A Theory of Goal Setting and Task Performance*. Upper Saddle River, NJ: Prentice-Hall.

MASLOW, A. (1954), *Motivation and Personality*. New York: Harper & Row.

MCCARTHY, D.J., PUFFER, S.M., and SHEKSHNIA, S.V. (1993), "The Resurgence of an Entrepreneurial Class in Russia," *Journal of Management Inquiry*, 2(2), 125–37.

MCCLELLAND, D.C. (1966), "That Urge to Achieve," *THINK Magazine*.

———. (1985), *Human Motivation*. Glenview, IL: Scott, Foresman.

———. and BURNHAM, D.H. (1986), "Power Is the Great Motivator," *Harvard Business Review* (March/April), 100–110.

MISRA, S. and KANUNGO, R.N. (1994), "Bases of Work Motivation in Developing Societies: A Framework for Performance Management," in Kanungo, R.N. and Mendonca, M., (eds.) *Work Motivation: Models for Developing Countries*. New Delhi: Sage Publications.

MOW International Research Team (1987), *The Meaning of Work: An International Perspective*. London: Academic Press.

NADLER, D.A. and LAWLER, E.E. (1977), "Motivation: A Diagnostic Approach," in Hackman, J.R., Lawler, E.E., and Porter, L.W., (eds.) *Perspectives on Behavior in Organizations*. New York: McGraw-Hill.

PINDER, C.C. (1984), *Work Motivation*. Glenview, IL: Scott, Foresman.

PORTER, L.W. and LAWLER, E.E.III (1968), *Managerial Attitudes and Performance*. Homewood, IL: Richard D. Irwin.

PUFFER, S.M. (1993), "A Riddle Wrapped in an Enigma: Demystifying Russian Managerial Motivation," *European Management Journal*, 11(4), 473–80.

PUNNETT, B.J. (1995), "Preliminary Considerations of Confucianism and Needs in the PRC," *Journal of Asia-Pacific Business*, 1, 25–42.

ROBBINS, S.P. (1996), *Organizational Behavior: Concepts, Controversies, and Applications*, 7th Ed. Upper Saddle River, NJ: Prentice Hall.

SKINNER, B.F. (1971), *Contingencies of Reinforcement*. East Norwalk, CT: Appleton-Century-Crofts.

STANLEY, A. (1996), "New Face of Russian Capitalism: Avon and Mary Kay Create Opportunities for Women," *The New York Times* (August 14), D1, D16.

STEERS, R.M. and BRAUNSTEIN, D.N. (1976), "Behaviorally Based Measure of Manifest Needs in Work Settings," *Journal of Vocational Behavior*, 9, 251–66.

———., PORTER, L.W. and BIGLEY, G.A., (eds.) (1996), *Motivation and Leadership at Work*, 6th Ed. New York: McGraw-Hill.

TROMPENAARS, F. (1993), *Riding the Waves of Culture: Understanding Diversity in Global Business*. London: The Economist Books.

TULLAR, W.L. (1992), "Cultural Transformation: Democratization and Russian Entrepreneurial Motives," Paper presented at the Academy of Management meetings, Las Vegas, cited in Puffer, S.M. (1993), "A Riddle Wrapped in an Enigma: Demystifying Russian Managerial Motivation," *European Management Journal*, 11(4), 473–80.

WELSH, D.H.B., LUTHANS, F., and SOMMER, S.M. (1993), "Organizational Behavior Modification Goes to Russia: Replicating an Experimental Analysis Across Cultures and Tasks," *Journal of Organizational Behavior Management*, 13, 15–35.

VROOM, V.H. (1964), *Work and Motivation*. New York: John Wiley & Sons.

Groups and Teams

Are We Members?

Sally Barlow earned her MBA in 1996 and started working for the U.S. headquarters of a Japanese bank in New York City. She analyzed the financial statements of large international corporations for the commercial loan department. Sally's opinions greatly influenced the bank's decisions, which often involved loans of several hundred million dollars.

Sally's coworkers were Yoshi Kagami, a male Japanese analyst with the bank for five years in Japan and three years in the United States and Sandra Marcus, an American MBA who had worked for the bank for almost three years. Although they never socialized after work, Sally and Sandra became friendly and often ate lunch together. Yoshi always ate with male Japanese employees.

One day at lunch, Sally told Sandra that she felt distrusted and regarded as a social inferior by her Japanese coworkers. "Sometimes I think even Yoshi looks at us that way," Sally said somewhat uncomfortably. Sandra responded, "Yes, I agree. In fact, I have a job interview at an American bank next week."

Source: B.A. Gold

After reading this chapter, you should be able to:

1. Define groups and teams.
2. Understand the elements of group structure.
3. Know two models of group development.
4. Discuss group processes, including decision making and social loafing.
5. Explain the differences between groups and teams.
6. Appreciate the influences of differences in group and team composition on organizational behavior.
7. Know how groups function in different cultures.

Cultures view groups differently. For the Japanese, group orientation is an important part of national culture. In Japanese organizations participation in group decision making, *ringisei,* is a common practice. In the United States, which emphasizes individual achievement, corporations encourage participation in groups, but teamwork often conflicts with the ethic of individualism. In Israel, which has a socialist political tradition, cooperative work groups are sociopolitical statements embodied in the egalitarianism of the Kibbutz (Bar-Hayim and Berman 1991).

> The cultural dimension of individualism-collectivism is important for explaining behavior in organizations, particularly the use of individuals and groups.

The cultural dimension of individualism-collectivism is important for explaining behavior in organizations, particularly the use of individuals and groups (Hofstede 1980; Trompenaars 1994). Individualism, a tendency for people to look primarily after their own interests rather than those of others, is characteristic of North American, Australian, and Western European societies. A collectivist value orientation, common in Asian, Eastern European, African, and Latin American cultures, emphasizes group welfare instead of individual self interests. The orientation of the national culture—individualistic or collectivistic—affects the way groups function in organizations.

Understanding how groups work is important because they are central to managing organizational behavior effectively. Groups are part of all organizations and a primary tool for achieving an organization's goals. A central managerial task is to improve group and team performance.

What Is a Group?

A **group** is "a plurality of individuals who are in contact with one another who take one another into account, and who are aware of some significant commonality" (Olmsted and Hare 1978, p. 11). Groups form as a result of mutual attraction or interests or because management assigns people to a group.

Group **size,** the number of individuals, is important because it influences communication and group dynamics. Groups range between 2 and approximately 20 members. Communication between 2 people in face-to-face contact is different from communication among 20 people, which is more like a mass audience than a small group. Regarding group dynamics, whereas two people constitute a group, the addition of a third member creates opportunities for more complex interaction—for example, coalition formation.

Groups have common **goals** toward which their members work. Typically, groups work under conditions of a specific time frame and limited resources—for example, a two week period and a budget for gathering and processing information to make a decision. Because of time constraints, resource scarcity, underdeveloped social skills, and other reasons, many groups are ineffective and some fail to achieve their intended goals.

A **team,** which is a type of group, uses self-management techniques to achieve goals to which its members express high commitment. Teams and groups have a structure, a pattern of development, processes, and decision making styles. National and corporate cultures affect these to some extent.

Group Structure

Group structure creates patterns of interaction among members. Elements that compose structure are rules, norms, roles, and status. These are analytic concepts useful for understanding groups in all cultures. For example, all groups, regardless of cultural values, develop and maintain social norms. Similarly, most groups differentiate member status; typically, few members occupy high-status positions. Even groups designed to eliminate status eventually develop leadership positions.

▌▌▌ ELEMENTS OF STRUCTURE

Group structures form through administrative policies and rules or emerge during member interaction. Often, structure is a product of the interaction of management assignment and member preferences.

Rules and Norms   **Rules** specify expected behavior that the organization imposes on group members and can formally sanction disobedience. **Norms** differ from rules because they are informal, usually unstated, and taken for granted by group members. Norms are often more effective for regulating group behavior than rules are because the group generates its own norms, making administrative rules appear irrelevant. For example, a group can develop norms regarding punctuality that are different from the formal rules of the organization. A group could decide that punctuality is not important despite organizational rules that require it. However, the presence of group norms does not remove administrative constraints.

Roles and Status   **Roles** are sets of norms that define behavior appropriate for and expected of various positions within a group. Every role in a group has a status. **Status** is the rank of the role in the hierarchy of the group. **Social power**—authority—is the ability to have others follow directives without question. There is a connection between status and social power. A person who occupies a high-status position and performs the role in a way that the group approves establishes power. It is possible, however, that inadequate role performance can fail to establish the voluntary approval of the group. This decreases or eliminates the power of the role occupant and requires reestablishment of the legitimacy of the role.

Within an organization, group members often occupy multiple roles with different statuses. This creates **role conflict** because the demands of the various roles are incompatible. An example is conflict that managers experience between the roles of friend/colleague and supervisor/evaluator of subordinates.

Leaders and Followers   Two important roles are group leader and follower. Research on groups distinguishes between two types of leaders: task leaders and socio-emotional leaders. The **task leader,** also labeled the *initiating leader*, focuses the group on goal achievement. Task leaders clarify the goals, present information, ask other members for information, and evaluate the group's progress toward making a decision. In other words, the task leader's efforts aim directly toward specific outcomes.

The **socio-emotional leader**, also known as the *relationship or maintenance* leader, focuses on the emotional and social aspects of a group. Socio-emotional leaders encourage and praise others, resolve conflicts, and engage in behavior that facilitates the group's work. Overall, this leader role focuses on constructing and maintaining group cohesion.

The two leader roles are complimentary in effective groups. Without a task leader a work group risks evolving into a social club; the group focus becomes its members' sentiments and interpersonal relations instead of task achievement. Overemphasis on task leadership—when the leader makes important decisions without the participation of other members—results in members losing their sense of purpose. It is widely accepted that a balance between the two leadership styles is the most effective way to manage a group. However, it is likely that the emphasis on leadership type varies with national culture. For example, some cultures prefer autocratic leadership—an emphasis on task accomplishment and low participation in decision making—whereas others focus on group leaders as facilitators.

Followers, group members who do not have leadership roles, are important to understand. Although research either ignores followers or assumes they support the leader and the group's goals, it is probable that the amount of subordinate participation and leader support varies with national and organizational culture. Hofstede's (1980) **power distance** variable suggests that national cultures low on power distance—those most likely to question the leader's actions—would be the least supportive followers, whereas cultures high on power distance would be the most supportive of a group leader's efforts.

Group roles often rotate among members. For example, the task leader role can shift when issues require a particular group member's expertise. However, for groups in cultures that prefer autocratic leadership, it is unlikely that a significant amount of leadership movement would occur. In groups that prefer democratic styles of leadership, the opportunities for various group members to occupy leadership roles is greater.

Similarly, members share or rotate the socio-emotional leader role depending on the type of support behavior required. Autocratic group leadership reduces the visible function of the support leader role. This does not mean, however, that the leader fails to support the group but instead acts alone to achieve what he or she perceives are its members' interests; support roles increase in groups with democratic leadership and norms.

Formal and Informal Groups **Formal groups** accomplish a particular goal or serve a specific purpose. In most instances management appoints a leader, membership is mandatory, and rules govern behavior. This type of group reflects the idea that pooling resources for decision making is superior to individual effort.

Informal groups evolve naturally in organizations, often without the awareness of management. People who work together in a functional area, across specializations, or as a result of frequent contact can form relationships based on similar experiences, common interests, and friendship. Informal groups vary in their contribution to an organization's goals. In some cases, informal groups contribute to goal achievement because their members cooperate on recognized tasks—for example, when they complete a committee assignment. In other cases, the group can undermine the achievement of official goals they view as invalid—for example, by sabotaging production output. In either situation, the norms that develop are powerful, and informal groups exert significant social control.

Informal subgroups often develop within a formal group and can exert considerable power. For example, they can form a voting block or, less overtly, influence a group's efforts by supporting its members for various roles. In addition, informal groups help their members make sense of the actions of management and protect member interests against what they perceive as unreasonable management demands.

A hypothesis is that culture contributes to managerial preferences for using either formal or informal groups. Cultures with high power distance are likely to use formal groups more than are cultures with low power distance. High–power distance cultures often create barriers to informal group formation because the enforcement of rules and regulations prohibits interpersonal interaction. Low–power distance cultures develop norms and have values that permit the development of informal groups but do not necessarily encourage their formation.

The situation is more complex in some cultures. High–power distance collective societies like China and Hong Kong have many informal groups within organizations. Organizations achieve goals as a result of organization members having membership in powerful informal groups. In other words, despite the stated intention of formal decision making groups, action occurs through the use of "connections."

> **High–power distance collective societies like China and Hong Kong have many informal groups within organizations.**

GROUP DEVELOPMENT: TWO MODELS

The Five Stage and Punctuated Equilibrium models of group development, like most research on groups, are from the United States. How culture might affect the models follows.

The Five-Stage Model   The **Five-Stage perspective** is the most well known and widely used theory of group development. In this view, groups experience five distinct phases (Tuckman and Jensen 1977):

- *Forming.* The initial phase of group development involves group members getting acquainted. This involves learning the traits, strengths, and behaviors of other members. Members also decide at this time whether participation in the group meets their needs. Finally, they also begin to identify group leadership.

- *Storming.* After forming, several important issues must be confronted. First, the group must establish its goals and priorities. The second issue involves structuring interaction among the members. A central concern is, Who will fulfill which roles?

- *Norming.* During the norming stage, the group develops a set of rules and roles—implicitly or explicitly—that coordinate the group's activities and facilitate the accomplishment of its goals.

- *Performing.* This stage is reached when the group understands its goals and roles and has developed rules that guide its performance. The group does most of its substantive work during this stage.

- *Adjourning.* Once a group makes its decision, it often adjourns or disbands. Adjournment can occur because the allotted time for the group to make a decision expires, the issue the group was intended to address changed radically, the group failed to operate effectively or lost key members, or the group achieved its purpose and is no longer needed.

Groups often move back and forth among these stages as a result of conflict. With resolution of the conflict, sequential movement resumes. In other cases, an event such as a new member or a crisis can return the group to an earlier stage. Also, the demarcation of stages is not clear or necessarily noticeable to group participants.

The Punctuated Equilibrium Model   Another theory of group development is the **punctuated equilibrium model** (Gersick 1988). Instead of a steady progression of stages, as in the Five-Stage model, the punctuated equilibrium model identifies two distinctly different modes of group functioning. In this model, which is supported by research studies conducted in the United States, the first meeting is important because it sets the climate for the group and establishes its leadership. This is followed by a period of equilibrium—routine group functioning—that changes abruptly at the **midpoint** of the group's allotted time. The equilibrium is disrupted by recognition that the task must be completed and creates a **revolutionary** change in the group's arrangements. The new arrangements shift, in effect, to a task orientation that results in project completion.

Culture and Group Development   Three variables that could affect these models in different cultures are the power-distance dimension, the individual-collective dimension, and cultural variations in the orientation to time.

Power-distance can influence the level of participation in groups. In high–power-distance cultures, there would be less follower participation than in low–power-distance cultures. This could reduce interaction between group leaders and followers and alter the developmental sequence by compressing the stages or eliminating the punctuation between periods of equilibrium and revolution because the leader has centralized power throughout the group's existence.

The individual-collective variable affects group development because of the relationships it creates among group members. The individual orientation encourages competition and conflict among members, whereas the collective orientation facilitates collaboration. For example, in the Five-Stage Model the storming stage would probably develop differently if group members willingly modify their opinions to conform to the group or aggressively defend individual positions. An extreme individual orientation could prevent a group from developing an effective work pattern.

If a culture views time as a scarce resource and sets rigorous deadlines, groups will probably develop differently than in cultures where time pressures are absent. For example, cultures less concerned with time might not set deadlines; the absence of time pressure could eliminate the midpoint and maintain equilibrium.

Group Processes

A variety of social processes characterizes behavior in groups. Groups continuously experience some type of change as a result of member interaction. These processes sometimes transform group functioning as the punctuated equilibrium model suggests, or their cumulative effect could produce minor but meaningful changes.

COMMUNICATION

Communication is central to groups because it is the major mechanism for achieving their goals. Culture affects **communication** in groups by shaping roles and statuses and the interactions among them. For example, culture influences group norms that govern who is permitted to talk, how much a member can talk, who can interrupt a conversation, and whether factual or emotional communication is viewed as persuasive. Communication in groups with low power-distance differs from that in groups with high power-distance values. Low power-distance creates informal communication structures compared with formal communication structures in high power-distance cultures. Finally, in high-context cultures, rules specify how members should communicate, which affects group interaction.

GROUP CULTURE

A group develops its own culture (Trice and Beyer 1993). The basis for **group culture** can be membership in a formal or informal group, and occupation, union membership, ethnic or religious background, or membership in a department that provides common experiences. The distinctive cultures of groups form **subcultures**. Group culture and subcultures form and maintain themselves through shared symbols, ceremonies, rituals, and values. These become a means for establishing a group's identity that differentiates it from other groups.

Strong group culture can effect groups two ways: First, it can produce a highly cohesive group that works well together, either to achieve organizational goals or to establish goals that regulate the group output below the level expected by management (Mayo 1945), and second, strong group culture can result in conflict between groups over organizational resources such as personnel, technology, finances, and prestige. Some level of intergroup conflict is typical in organizations and can be a source of innovation; the absence of conflict among groups is often an indication that work groups have low levels of cohesiveness and competitiveness and are indifferent to organizational goals.

The culture of groups can change. New leadership, innovative technology, organization restructuring, and task reassignment can produce interpersonal tensions that change group culture. For example, introducing new technology challenges group member expertise, producing changes in member status. New group norms and culture develop to realign group members with the new technology (Barley 1986).

DECISION MAKING

A key function of groups is making decisions. **Group decisions** are useful for technical and organizational reasons. From a technical perspective, groups pool the skills, talents, and experiences of many people instead of relying on one decision maker. From an organizational perspective, group decision making—the active participation of many people—increases the likelihood of decision implementation.

Individual Versus Group Decision Making   Groups do not perform all decision making. In many situations in organizations, individual managers or other employees make decisions by themselves. They then inform group members of the decision and expect them to implement it.

National and organizational cultures vary in the amount of **decision making participation** that organization members require. In cultures with low expectations for influencing decision making, individual managerial decisions are effective; subordinates expect to "take orders" and implement them without question. However, in cultures that value the opinions of individuals—those with individualistic

> National and organizational cultures vary in the amount of decision making participation that organization members require.

and democratic values—this type of individual decision making is not any less effective technically but could encounter resistance because group members feel as though they should influence all phases of management, including decision making, instead of being restricted to implementation. An example is **co-determination** in Germany, in which worker representatives hold decision-making roles on corporate boards. Co-determination has permitted German industry to adjust effectively and peacefully to economic change (Thelen 1987).

But not all group decision making works as intended. Some group processes that appear desirable actually create conditions that result in misguided actions.

Groupthink **Groupthink** is a group decision-making process that occurs when members of a highly cohesive group are unable to evaluate each other's inputs critically (Janis 1982). Groupthink often results in less than optimal decisions, including decisions that lead to disasters. According to Janis (1982), symptoms of groupthink are as follows.

- *Illusions of invulnerability.* Members of the group overemphasize the strength of the group and believe that they are beyond criticism or attack. This symptom leads the group to approve risky actions about which individual members might have serious concerns.
- *Illusions of unanimity.* Group members accept consensus prematurely, without testing whether all members *truly* agree. Silence is often taken for agreement.
- *Illusions of group morality.* Members of the group believe that the group is "right" and above reproach by outside critics. Therefore, members feel no need to debate ethical issues.
- *Stereotyping of the "enemy" as weak, evil, or stupid.* Members do not realistically examine their competitors and oversimplify their motives. They do not consider the stated aims of outside groups or anticipated reactions of outsiders.
- *Self-censorship by members.* Members refuse to communicate concerns to others because of fear of disturbing the consensus.
- *Mind-guarding.* Some members take responsibility to ensure that negative feedback does not reach influential group members.
- *Direct pressure.* In the unlikely event that a note of caution or concern is interjected, other members quickly respond with pressure to bring the deviant back into line.

Groupthink might be more prevalent in Southeast Asia than in other cultures (Kwok 1992). Collective oriented cultures place group interests ahead of individual interests, and the influence of leaders on groups is stronger than in the West, as is obedience to hierarchical authority. As a result, it is difficult for individuals to express opposing views, and they readily conform to group standards. From the Asian point of view, this is not necessarily an undesirable process. In individualistic societies, however, groupthink is viewed as an organizational pathology.

Finally, "multicultural [groups and] teams find themselves less susceptible to groupthink because they are less likely to subconsciously limit their perspectives, ideas, conclusions, and decisions to that of the majority or team leadership" (Adler 1997, p. 137).

PARTICIPATION AND SOCIAL LOAFING

Another process is member involvement in groups. Studies of social loafing are one way to understand the effect of culture on group involvement. Social loafing "occurs when individuals decrease the amount of effort they put into a task—loaf—while doing that task with other people" (Northcraft and Neale 1994, p. 302).

Research has compared the effect of collective-individualistic orientations on the presence and extent of social loafing (Earley 1989, 1993; Gabrenya, Latane, and Wang 1983). One study hypothesizes that the composition of the group that a manager was in would affect the manager's level of participation (Earley 1993). If managers with collectivist orientations worked in groups that shared their orientations, they would feel more efficacious—able to work well—alone and as a group member, than if they worked in a group with an individualist orientation. Managers with individualist orientations "will anticipate more rewards and feel more efficacious, and thus perform better, while working alone than while working in an ingroup [people with the same values] or an outgroup [people with different values] context" (Earley 1993, pp. 324–25). In other words, in addition to an individual's cultural orientation, the value orientation of the workgroup they are part of effects social loafing.

This hypothesis was tested on data collected in the United States, which is a highly individualistic culture; the People's Republic of China, which emphasizes a collective orientation; and Israel, which also has a collectivist value system. The results support the hypothesis. According to Earley (1993, p. 341) "collectivists have lower performance working alone or in an outgroup than they do working in an ingroup." Collectivists—the Israeli and Chinese workers—will not work hard in all group contexts, "only those contexts for which performance has implications for his or her ingroup seem to stimulate performance" (Earley 1993, p. 341). The performance of individualists who thought they were working in an ingroup or an outgroup was lower than was the performance of individualists working alone.

In summary, a person's collective-individualistic orientation affects group participation modified by his or her understanding of the group's values.

Teams

Teams are designed to meet the demands of new types of organizations that require creativity, flexibility, and high levels of performance. Teams are similar to groups because they experience developmental stages, differentiate into roles, create norms, establish a culture, and have a communication structure.

HOW TEAMS DIFFER FROM GROUPS

Technically, a **team** is different from a group because it is "a small number of people with complementary skills who are committed to a common purpose, set of performance goals, and approach for which they hold themselves mutually accountable" (Katzenbach and Smith 1993, p. 112). Teams have more cohesiveness and more responsibility and use member talents more effectively than do other groups. Weiss (1996, pp. 142–43) notes these specific differences:

- *Shared leadership.* Teams have shared leadership roles, whereas groups usually have a strong, focused leader.
- *Accountability.* Teams have individual and mutual accountability, whereas groups are based mostly on individual accountability.

- *Purpose.* Teams work toward a specific purpose, whereas a group's purpose is usually identical to the organization's mission.
- *Work products.* Teams deliver collective work products, whereas groups have individual work products.
- *Communication.* Teams encourage open-ended discussion and active problem-solving meetings, whereas groups attempt to run meetings that are efficient.
- *Effectiveness.* Teams measure performance by direct assessment of their collective work products, whereas groups measure effectiveness indirectly by their influence on others.
- *Work style.* Teams discuss, decide, and delegate but do the work together, whereas groups discuss, decide, and delegate and then do the work individually.

In addition to the differences between teams and groups, there are also issues involving the function of teams in organizations and their composition. For example, teams can operate at various levels within an organization, including the executive, middle management, and operations levels. An example of an operations level team is a total quality team that uses a team approach to quality that emphasizes continuous improvement instead of traditional bureaucratic post-production inspection.

Group and Team Composition

The composition of groups and teams within organizations depends on the diversity of the national population. Multinational corporations are an important exception, however, because they consist of employees from countries with many different types of populations.

▌▌▌ TYPES OF GROUPS

Homogeneous cultures such as Japan and South Korea have little concern with group diversity. In Germany, where there is increasing **heterogeneity** in the workforce, diversity is becoming an issue because guest workers are displacing native workers. The United States has a heterogeneous population that will become more diverse in the future, creating more demand for multicultural work groups. (We discuss these trends further in Chapter 13.)

In the global business environment, the types of groups are homogeneous groups, token groups, bicultural groups, and multicultural groups (Adler 1991, p. 127). A **homogeneous group** contains members who have the same backgrounds and generally understand events and the world in general more similarly than other types. A **token group** consists of members with the same background with the exception of one member who is different in some significant way. The token member probably interprets things differently from the other group members. **Bicultural groups** are those in which "two or more members represent each of two distinct cultures; for example, a fifty-fifty partnership between Peruvians and Bolivians, or a task force composed of Saudi Arabians and Jordanians, or a committee with seven Spanish and three Portuguese executives" (Adler 1991, p. 127).

Finally, **multicultural groups** have members of three or more ethnic backgrounds. An example is a United Nations agency composed of representatives of as many as 15–20 cultures.

The composition of teams and groups—regardless of level within an organization—can range from monocultural to multicultural (Cox 1991). The managerial argument for using multicultural teams is that they are more innovative than are monocultural teams because they incorporate diverse viewpoints into decision making (see Table 7-1). Also, because they reflect the composition of a society, rather than the preferences of a single group or a minority elite, they are more effective at understanding the needs and desires of customers. Finally, multicultural teams advance the social responsibility of firms by creating equal opportunity for all social groups.

However, there are also disadvantages to diversity in groups and teams within organizations (see Table 7-1). As noted previously, one possible advantage of diversity is that people with different value systems bring novel perspectives to a group, fostering creative problem solving. At the same time, however, the disadvantage is that group members might not trust each other and therefore fail to collaborate fully. Further, distrust can result in poor communication across subgroups that compose the group and create conflict or disorganization.

Table 7-1   Advantages and Disadvantages of Group Diversity

Advantages	*Disadvantages*
Diversity Permits Increased Creativity	*Diversity Causes Lack of Cohesion*
Wide range of perspectives	Mistrust
More and better ideas	Lower interpersonal attractiveness
Less "groupthink"	Stereotyping
Diversity Forces Enhanced	More within-culture conversations
Concentration to Understand Others'	Miscommunication
Ideas	Slower speech: Non-native speakers and translation problems
Meanings	Less accurate communication
Arguments	Stress
	More counterproductive behavior
	Less agreement on content
	Tension
Increased Creativity Can Lead to	*Lack of Cohesion Causes Inability to*
Better problem definitions	Validate ideas and people
More alternatives	Agree when agreement is needed
Better solutions	Gain consensus on decisions
Better decisions	Take concerted action
Groups Can Become	*Groups Can Become*
More effective	Less efficient
More productive	Less effective
	Less productive

Source: Table from "Advantages and Disadvantages of Group Diversity" by Nancy J. Adler from *International Dimensions of Organizational Behavior*, 3/e. Copyright (©) 1997 SWCP. Reprinted by permission of South-Western College Publishing, a division of International Thomson Publishing Inc., Cincinnati, Ohio 45227.

▌▌▌ RESEARCH ON GROUP DIVERSITY

Research on diversity in organizations distinguishes between variables that are directly **observable attributes** of diversity—such as race, ethnic background, age, and gender—and less visible or **underlying attributes**—such as education, technical abilities, functional background, tenure in the organization, socioeconomic background, personality characteristics, and values (Milliken and Martins 1996).

The results of research on observable attributes—conducted mainly in the United States—are fairly consistent:

> In general, the more diverse a group is with respect to gender, race, or age, the higher its turnover rate (people leaving the group) and the more likely it is that dissimilar individuals will turn over and be absent. . . . Diversity may lead to discomfort for all members of a group, leading to lower integration within the group and a higher likelihood of turnover. There is also some evidence of negative affective reactions to observable differences on the part of supervisors—in that supervisors tend to perceive dissimilar subordinates less positively and tend to give them lower performance ratings (Milliken and Martins 1996, p. 408).[1]

Several studies suggest that diverse groups generate more alternatives in decision making and cooperation within the group. Research also finds that these benefits occur only when a diverse group has been intact for a period of time. However, member turnover could occur before groups reach a stage that takes advantage of diversity.

Research on groups composed of diverse nationalities in the Netherlands similarly found that individuals not of the majority nationality were less satisfied with their jobs than were majority members (Verkuyten, de Jong, and Masson 1993). In a study conducted in Australia (Bochner and Hesketh 1994), minority members perceived more discrimination in the workplace but valued cultural diversity more highly than did majority members.

Research on underlying attributes differs from studies of observable attributes because it usually focuses on top management teams rather than on lower-level participants. The research findings are as follows:

> Diversity along skill- or knowledge-based dimensions seems to have some positive cognitive outcomes for top management groups and project teams. One reason may be that diversity along these skill-based dimensions translates into a greater variety of perspectives being brought to bear on decisions and, thereby, increases the likelihood of creative and innovative solutions to problems. Also, problems such as those that a top management group deals with often require information input from a variety of functional areas within the organization (Milliken and Martins 1996, p. 412).[2]

There are also difficulties integrating diverse members into management groups, similar to those of lower-level groups, including the possibility of minority member turnover.

In summary, although research has not entirely supported the managerial rationale for the use of teams, there is evidence that teams provide benefits in certain circumstances. Research also indicates that the disadvantages of teams have been exaggerated in the management literature. When a team has functioned for a period of time beyond initial member turnover and still retains a diverse composition, conflict and other disadvantages fail to emerge. But how do teams and groups actually work in different cultures?

---

[1]Excerpts from "Searching for Common Threads: Understanding the Multiple Effects of Diversity in Organizational Groups" by F. Milliken and L. Martins from *Academy of Management Review*, 21, 2, 1996: 406–33. Reprinted by permission of Academy of Management.

[2]Ibid.

Groups at Work in Four Cultures

Cultures structure and use groups and teams in different ways. In South Africa group composition is a mechanism for social change. Groups in Japan reflect Japanese culture's collectivist values. Korea is an example of an Asian culture that does not rely on group or team participation in organizations. Finally, in Israel democratic work groups function like teams and reflect the dominant values of the society.

> **Cultures structure and use groups and teams in different ways.**

SOUTH AFRICA: MULTICULTURAL GROUPS

In South Africa, new types of groups emerge as social, economic, and political processes evolve. Frequently, groups with novel compositions implement social goals. An example is the South African Broadcasting Corporation's attempt to reflect the composition of the nation's population in the post-Apartheid era.

> It is 6 A.M. on Nelson Mandela's birthday, and "Good Morning South Africa" is on the air. The hosts—two men, one black, one white—wear ties bearing the President's smiling face and take turns greeting the audience in English and Afrikaans.
>
> Over on the news desk, a black woman and a white man deliver the day's top story, again switching in and out of the two languages. Taped interviews take place in a variety of languages. Later two more news anchors reintroduce the same stories, this time in Sotho and Zulu.
>
> This type of multilingual program, officials say, is the future of the reborn South African Broadcasting Corporation. And if it is expensive and confusing, well, that is the price of atoning for the sins of the past.
>
> While America struggles with the concepts of affirmative action and cultural diversity, South Africa is rushing to embrace them. In education, in business and in government, the country is scrambling to reverse decades of racial discrimination by infusing blacks into society's top institutions (McLarin 1995, p. 2).[3]

It is too early to evaluate the success of multicultural groups in South Africa. It is also premature to know if in addition to implementing national social policy, diverse group composition will create innovations and improve the quality of decisions.

JAPAN: GROUP DECISION MAKING

In Japan, the decision-making process most frequently used in organizations is *ringisei*, decision making by consensus. Most widely used by lower and middle level managers, *ringisei* requires the circulation of documents to organization members to gain their approval for a proposal before it is implemented. This process ensures that subordinates have the opportunity to voice their views and possibly influence the final decision, which is made by a manager.

Because of the large number of people involved, this procedure is relatively slow. However, in addition to better decisions, because of collective commitment to the action, it reduces resistance to change and improves implementation quality and speed. Finally, "as with all other characteristics of the Japanese management system, decision making is embedded in a complex of parts that hang together and rely upon trust and subtlety developed through intimacy (Ouchi 1981, p. 40).

---

[3]Excerpt from "The Voice of Apartheid Goes Multicultural" by Kimberly J. McClarin from *The New York Times*, July 25, 1995. Copyright © 1995 by The New York Times Co. Reprinted by permission.

▌▌▌ KOREA: DECISION MAKING AT THE TOP

Not all Asian cultures use groups for decision making in organizations. Korean corporations—large family conglomerates known as *chaebols*—seldom use groups to make decisions. Family members who own and manage the business make all decisions, and employees who occupy positions in elaborate bureaucratic structures implement them.

Some Korean organizations, however, use a process similar to the Japanese consensus decision making system. But it is "nothing but a formal process to rationalize and formalize the decisions made by the top executives" (Chang and Chang 1994, p. 135). In reality, then, there are few opportunities for employees to participate in group decisions, and the communication structure is highly formal, a legacy of "the military-dominated government in the past decades, which guided the private sector of the economy" (Chung and Lee 1989, p. 177).

▌▌▌ ISRAEL: DEMOCRATIC DECISION MAKING

The Israeli kibbutz, a collective farm or industry, uses democratic participation in all aspects of its operations and reflects the core Israeli social values of democracy, egalitarianism, and collectivism. The principles of a kibbutz are "community ownership of all property, absolute equality of members, democratic decision making, the value of work as both end and means, communal responsibility for child care, and primacy of the group over individuals" (Gannon 1994, p. 215). In recent years, there have been pressures to permit some private property and more individual freedom. The egalitarian character of group-oriented life is expressed in these social arrangements:

> Members of the kibbutz receive no pay for their work. All of their essential needs—food, shelter, clothing, medical care, and education—are provided by the community. Children are raised with their peers, meals are usually eaten in the kibbutz dining hall, and members convene regularly to discuss and vote on issues. Many jobs rotate among members. All positions of authority—such as those of kibbutz chief executive, plant managers, and supervisors—change every two or three years. Power is not permitted to accumulate in the hands of individuals. The kibbutzim range in size from 100 to 2,000 members and are small enough so that the individual's role in the community is visible and tangible (Gannon 1994, p. 215).[4]

Democratic ideology permeates the kibbutz involving all members in major decisions. In a sense, the entire kibbutz is the decision-making unit, enforcing the ideal of the primacy of the group. The kibbutz functions like a team.

⬤onvergence or Divergence?

▌▌▌ FORCES FOR CONVERGENCE

An important trend over the past 20 years is that societies that have traditionally emphasized individualism are borrowing collectivist, group-oriented management techniques, primarily from Japan. In the United States, for example, there is an emphasis on using groups for continuous improvement programs and in promoting autonomous work groups. One argument is that highly effective organizations in the United States blend individual and group orientations (Ouchi 1981).

---

[4]Excerpt from *Understanding Global Cultures: Metaphorical Journeys through 17 Countries* by M.J. Gannon and Associates. Copyright © 1994 by Sage Publications, Inc. Reprinted by permission of Sage Publications, Inc.

Former collectivist societies—for example, China—have become more individualistic by selectively introducing capitalist principles such as markets and profit. Although it is unlikely that East and West will produce a seamless blend, as complex cultural, political, social, and economic changes unfold, the result could be creative mixtures of individualism and collectivism.

❚❚❚ FORCES FOR DIVERGENCE

As the Culture at Work vignette suggests, creating effective multicultural teams requires more than combining people from different cultures in a group and expecting them to develop collaborative work styles by themselves. A force for divergence is that tensions among cultures could continue despite attempts to constructively manage them.

Another issue is that in organizations in heterogeneous societies, the perception could be that the use of multicultural teams is a threat to dominant groups. Because of reluctance to redistribute power, it might be difficult to move beyond tokenism and minimum compliance with legal requirements to creative use of diverse teams. Of course, for similar reasons, homogeneous societies with autocratic leadership have no reason to use teams of any type.

Implications for Managers

As new types of organizations emerge, groups and teams will become more important, particularly in organizations that operate in different cultures. Because of this, managers should become skilled at diagnosing, managing, and maintaining group performance.

❚❚❚ MANAGING GROUPS

There are differences in managing monocultural and culturally diverse groups and teams. As groups become more diverse, managers should avoid replacing nonfunctional performance criteria—such as religion or ethnic identity—with traits, skills, and talents that are important for a position. In other words, the objectives of the organization take precedence over multicultural considerations (Adler 1997).

To accomplish this, managers should emphasize a clear vision or superordinate goal, in an attempt to form a cohesive group. Without a clear, strong goal, the diversity of the group will produce multiple goals and evolve into competing subgroups.

Managers should attempt to create equal power among the members of a diverse group. If one subgroup gains more power through cultural dominance, the results could be nonparticipation by other members and destructive conflict. One way to manage this is to distribute authority according to ability to accomplish a task, rather than non–performance-related criteria.

It is also important to avoid ethnocentrism—the assumption that one's own culture is superior to other cultures. Viewing one culture, particularly the manager's, as superior to other cultures, reduces the benefits of multicultural interaction. Group members should establish mutual respect for one another's cultures and recognize contributions of individual people on the basis of expertise. Finally, because of group diversity, a manager must provide more opportunities for feed-back. According to Adler (1991, p. 141):

> Given the different perspectives present, culturally diverse teams have more trouble than homo-geneous teams in collectively agreeing on what constitutes a good or bad idea or decision. . . . External feedback helps the group see itself as a team and serves the function of teaching the team to value its diversity, recognize the contributions made by each member, and trust its collec-tive judgment.

In summary, as with the other topics in this book, it is important for managers to recognize the limits their own culture imposes for understanding the nature of groups in other cultures. Two important implications are that managers must learn how to diagnose group behavior that occurs in another culture and find ways to manage a group without unintentionally creating conditions that cause the group to develop norms that produce behavior contrary to the manager's intended results.

These implications for managers reflect the North American cultural prefer-ence for the rational, universalistic use of human resources to achieve organiza-tional goals. Of course, there are other ways to use human resources that are valid from other cultural perspectives. For example, a manager could decide that only his blood relatives should make decisions because he distrusts nonkin experts. In a va-riety of cultures, a manager might believe that groups should not make decisions because they threaten her power; it is preferable to accumulate and maintain power, even if the decisions are inferior.

▌▌▌ NEW USES OF GROUPS AND TEAMS

One view of the role of groups and teams in the global context is that they will re-place traditional organizational structures. Instead of hierarchies and corporations rooted in specific geographic locations, loosely knit, flexible groups and teams will achieve an important place in capital intensive, high value-added, high-technology companies (Reich 1991). These groups will work on projects that require ideas, fi-nancing, and new combinations of people for specific short term purposes. After project completion, the group disbands, and its members reform into other teams.

The use of teams will probably increase in cross-cultural negotiations. As is-sues facing organizations become more complex, teams of negotiators will be nec-essary because they can combine a variety of skills, exercise independent judgment, and self-manage. It is likely that these teams will be multicultural and serve as coor-dinating mechanisms for negotiating cultural and technical issues.

▌ Summary

Groups and teams are an important part of organizations. Whether the values of a culture are individualist or collectivist affects the role of teams in organizations. Groups have different functions in collective cultures than they do in individualistic cultures. For example, in Japan and Israel, groups are more important than individ-uals. In the United States, individuals are more important than groups. Another im-portant variable is the composition of groups and teams. They can be either ho-mogenous or heterogeneous; this creates different patterns of interaction among members.

Key elements of group structure are rules, norms, roles, and statuses. A cen-tral role in groups and teams is that of the leader, which is characterized by either a task or socio-emotional emphasis. The roles of followers are also important in groups.

Groups develop over time following either a rational linear progression or a punctuated equilibrium model of two distinct and almost unrelated phases. Another aspect of groups and teams is the processes that occur in them including communication, culture formation, social loafing, and decision making. Groupthink, a complex social process that affects decision making, is viewed by some cultures as a pathology and by others as desirable.

Teams differ from groups because they share leadership, have more acceptance of goals, and are more accountable for their actions. An important issue is the composition of teams and groups and whether membership diversity is beneficial for performance. As globalization increases, it is likely that groups will become more multicultural.

Managers must understand how to diagnose a group to be able to manage and improve its performance. Although there are not many systematic studies of cross-cultural groups and how they differ, the key cultural variables, particularly individualism-collectivism orientation, suggest that behavior in groups varies as a result of culture.

■ Discussion Questions

1. What are the characteristics of a group?
2. How does the concept of individualism-collectivism contribute to understanding the way that culture affects the use of groups and teams?
3. Discuss the meaning of roles and status in groups. How are status and power related?
4. What is an informal group? Why is it important for managers to understand informal groups?
5. From your participation in groups, which model of group development—the Five-Stage perspective or the Punctuated Equilibrium Theory—explains the way that groups evolve over time in your country?
6. What are some techniques that can reduce the likelihood of a decision-making group experiencing groupthink?
7. How do groups differ from teams?
8. In your view, do the advantages outweigh the disadvantages of member diversity in groups and teams?
9. Examine the view that small groups of highly talented people acting as temporary systems will replace current pyramidal organizational structures. How probable is this scenario?
10. As the leader of a multicultural group, what actions could you take when the group forms to improve its long-term performance?

References

ADLER, N. (1991), *International Dimensions of Organizational Behavior*, 2d Ed. Boston: PWS-Kent.
——— (1997), *International Dimensions of Organizational Behavior*, 3d Ed. Cincinnati, OH: South-Western Publishing Co.
BAR-HAYIM, A. and BERMAN, G. (1991), "Ideology, Solidarity, and Work Values: The Case of the Histadrut Enterprises," *Human Relations*, 44 (4), 357–70.
BARLEY, S. (1986), "Technology as an Occasion for Structuring: Evidence from Observations of CT Scanners and the Social Order of Radiology Departments," *Administrative Science Quarterly*, 78–108.

BOCHNER, S. and HESKETH, B. (1994), "Power Distance, Individualism/Collectivism, and Job-Related Attitudes in a Culturally Diverse Work Group," *Journal of Cross-Cultural Psychology*, 25, 233–57.

CHANG, C. and CHANG, N. (1994), *The Korean Management System: Cultural, Political, Economic Foundations*. Westport, CT: Quorum.

CHUNG, K. and LEE, H. (1989), "National Differences in Managerial Practices," in K. Chung and H. Lee, (eds.) *Korean Managerial Dynamics*. New York: Praeger.

COX, T. (1991), "The Multicultural Organization," *Academy of Management Executive* (May), 34–47.

EARLEY, P. (1989), "Social Loafing and Collectivism: A Comparison of the United States and the People's Republic of China," *Administrative Science Quarterly*, 34, 565–81.

———(1993), "East Meets West Meets Mideast: Further Explorations of Collectivistic and Individualistic Work Groups," *Academy of Management Journal*, 36 (2), 319–48.

GABRENYA, W., LATANE, B. and WANG, Y. (1983), "Social Loafing in Cross-Cultural Perspective," *Journal of Cross-Cultural Psychology*, 14(3), 368–84.

GANNON, M. (1994), *Understanding Global Cultures: Metaphorical Journeys Through 17 Countries*. Thousand Oaks, CA: Sage Publications.

GERSICK, C. (1988), "Time and Transition in Work Teams: Toward a New Model of Group Development," *Academy of Management Journal*, 31, 9–41.

HOFSTEDE, G. (1980), *Culture's Consequences: International Differences in Work-Related Values*. Beverly Hills, CA: Sage Publications.

JANIS, I. (1982), *Groupthink*, 2d Ed. Boston: Houghton-Mifflin.

KATZENBACH, J. and SMITH, D. (1993), "The Discipline of Teams," *Harvard Business Review*. (March–April), 110–25.

KWOK, K. (1992), "Groups and Social Relationships," in R. Westwood, *Organisational Behaviour: Southeast Asian Perspectives*. Hong Kong: Longman.

MAYO, E. (1945), *The Problems of an Industrial Civilization*. New York: Arno Press.

McLARIN, K. (1995), "The Voice of Apartheid Goes Multicultural," *The New York Times* (July 25), 2.

MILLIKEN, F. and MARTINS, L. (1996), "Searching for Common Threads: Understanding the Multiple Effects of Diversity in Organizational Groups," *Academy of Management Review*, 21(2), 402–33.

NORTHCRAFT, G. and NEALE, M. (1994), *Organizational Behavior: A Management Challenge*. Fort Worth, TX: Dryden Press.

OLMSTED, M. and HARE, A. (1978), *The Small Group*, 2d Ed. New York: Random House.

OUCHI, W. (1981), *Theory Z: How American Business Can Meet the Japanese Challenge*. New York: Avon.

REICH, R. (1991), *The Work of Nations: Preparing Ourselves for 21st-Century Capitalism*. New York: Alfred A. Knopf.

THELEN, K. (1987), "Codetermination and Industrial Adjustment in the German Steel Industry: A Comparative Interpretation," *California Management Review*, 3, 134–45.

TROMPENAARS, F. (1994), *Riding the Waves of Culture: Understanding Diversity in Global Business*. New York: Irwin.

TRICE, H. and BEYER, J. (1993), *The Cultures of Work Organizations*. Upper Saddle River, NJ: Prentice Hall.

TUCKMAN, B. and JENSEN M. (1977), "Stages of Small Group Development Revisited," *Group and Organization Studies*, 2, 419–27.

VERKUYTEN, M, DE JONG, W. and MASSON, C. (1993), "Job Satisfaction Among Ethnic Minorities in the Netherlands," *Applied Psychology: An International Review*, 42, 171–89.

WEISS, J. (1996), *Managing Diversity, Cross-Cultural Dynamics, and Ethics*. Minneapolis/St. Paul: West Publishing.

Organizational Culture

Old Age Benefits

The server took our order for two shrimp tempura and one assorted sushi. The conversation turned to our experiences as university professors. Our lunch guest, a professor from a German university, started the conversation: "I have been in the School of Business Administration, Department of Public Administration at the University of Mannheim for eight years. Before that I was an Associate Professor at the Free University of Berlin. I received my doctorate from the University of Erlangen—Nurnberg in 1967. I'm fifty-seven years old. My research interests are how public bureaucracies can become more efficient."

My American colleague asked, "Why did you tell us your age? In the United States we would never tell people how old we are."

The German professor explained, "In Germany age determines seniority. As I get older I get more benefits: a larger office, more administrative support, and more research assistants. This way the distribution of resources is very clear and done fairly."

Source: B.A. Gold

1. Define organizational culture and know why it is important.

2. Distinguish among organizational, national, and global culture and understand the relationships among them.

3. Evaluate the culture-free approach to understanding organizational culture.

4. Identify levels of organizational culture.

5. Know what organizational culture does.

6. Discuss the cultural dimensions and typology approaches to understanding organizational culture.

7. Understand how organizational culture can be managed.

Organizations, like nations, have cultures. Different organizations may have the same objectives—to make VCRs or to provide financial services, for example—

> **Research into how organizational culture influences organizational behavior has increased dramatically.**

but variations in organizational culture differentiate how they pursue these goals. For example, the culture of one financial services company promotes innovation and risk taking, whereas another firm's culture emphasizes reliability and customer service.

Research into how organizational culture influences organizational behavior has increased dramatically. The primary reason for renewed interest in organizational culture is that the success of many companies can be attributed to their work cultures. For example, in the automobile industry, Japanese organizational culture, which reflects major themes from Japanese national culture, became an important factor for explaining the superior workmanship in Japanese cars compared with American cars (Cole 1990).

What Is Organizational Culture?

Organizational culture is a pattern of basic assumptions—invented, discovered, or developed by a given group as it learns to cope with its problems of external adaptation and internal integration—that has worked well enough to be considered valid and, therefore, to be taught to new members as the correct way to perceive, think, and feel in relation to those problems (Schein 1985, p. 9).

Like the culture of a society, organizational culture, a product of secondary socialization, is taken for granted by members of an organization (see Schutz 1967). It is the "natural" way of understanding the business world and taking action. Because of this, it is difficult for members of an organization to appreciate the impact of corporate culture on their behavior. Similarly, an outsider—such as a foreign businessperson, consultant, or researcher—usually experiences difficulty discovering the basic assumptions that form an unfamiliar organization's culture.

National and Global Culture

NATIONAL CULTURE

National culture, like organizational culture, provides basic assumptions that legitimate and guide behavior. Although they operate in similar ways, many management researchers view the relationship between national and corporate culture as complex (Trice and Beyer 1993).

Some theorists see little, if any, relationship between national and corporate culture and argue that a "logic of industrialization" (Harbison and Myers 1959, p. 117) affects all organizations the same way. In this view, one outcome of economic development, along with modern technology, is to produce organizational cultures and structures that are similar and independent of national culture.

Although the argument is different from the industrialization theory, a recent study demonstrates that Japanese automobile companies successfully transplanted their organizational cultures and structures to the United States (Florida and Kenney 1991). The environment—national and corporate culture in the U.S.—did not affect Japanese firms' ability to establish their business practices in a different culture. This study provides support for the view that organizational culture and structure form and operate independently of local or national culture.

An alternative perspective is that national culture and other elements in an organization's environment determine, to some extent, internal organizational culture. For example, Martin writes,

> It is misleading to deny the influence of the environment on the content of cultures in organizations. The implication, of course, is that *we cannot understand what goes on inside an organizational culture without understanding what exists outside the boundary* (1992, p. 113).

Precisely how national culture affects organizational culture is not yet clear. It is possible that in some cultures—for example, theocracies, which intertwine religion, politics, and culture—the influence on organizational cultures is substantial. In contrast, in secular cultures, which separate religion from other spheres of life, it is possible that the effect on organizational culture is less or takes a different form.

▌▌▌ GLOBAL CULTURE

Globalization, increasing awareness of activities in other parts of the world, also affects organizational culture. First, in the global economy many competitors are no longer local or national but global; shoe manufacturers in São Paulo and New York City compete with those in Shanghai for sales worldwide. The extension of the organization's environment creates heightened awareness, cost competition, and thus a need to respond to organizational practices of international competitors. For example, American industries have borrowed practices, such as just-in-time and quality circles, that are part of Japanese corporate culture.

> Globalization, increasing awareness of activities in other parts of the world, also affects organizational culture.

A second global cultural force is communication. Mass media, particularly global advertising and news broadcasts, are mechanisms for the diffusion of deep rooted social values and practices such as democratic institutions, along with transient consumer preferences. Modern communication also connects manufacturers, merchants, financiers, and consumers more than ever.

A third element of globalization is the educational systems of economically advanced countries. Higher education and research transfer management ideas and business values globally. Elementary and secondary education are also influential because advanced industrial countries monitor the education their students receive in comparison to other nations (Bracey 1996). This often affects curricular reforms, particularly in mathematics, technology, and science education.

Finally, multinational corporations contribute to shaping organizational culture on a global basis through the development of specific corporate cultures. The management philosophy of McDonald's restaurants in Russia, discussed in the next section, illustrates this process.

Understanding Organizational Culture

One way to understand an organization's culture is to ask people how they get work done in an organization. Moscow State University Professor Oleg Vikhanskii interviewed Glen Steeves, the manager of the first McDonald's to open in Moscow, to discover how McDonald's adjusted to Russian society, which had never experienced a fast-food restaurant (Puffer 1992).

Vikhanskii asked: "Do you use the same systems and procedures as in other McDonald's restaurants around the world?" Steeves replied:

Absolutely. The training systems and all the procedures used here are exactly the same as what we use in Canada, Japan, England, or Spain. The procedures are the same as the ones we use everywhere around the world.

Vikhanskii: But Russians' behavior is different from Americans', isn't it?

Steeves: I disagree with that. I remember the orientation sessions. People ranged from eighteen to fifty-five years old. Until they started talking, I thought I was back in Canada: they looked the same, they interacted the same, they were smiling, and they had a good time. Our employees take to McDonald's with a passion. They're very proud of what they're doing. What's more, they're very proud of the exciting opportunities.

Have we had to do anything different here because of different attitudes and behavior? No. We applied the same principles here in Moscow as we would in Canada. We have the same training program, and we evaluate employees the same way. We use the same motivational techniques to make it interesting for them. For example, we have crew meetings every three months. This creates a sense of family, a sense of belonging to a specific company. Last summer, for example, we rented one of the large liners on the Moscow River and took them for a cruise. We had a big party with dinner, dancing, and entertainment, and George Cohan [Vice Chairman of Moscow McDonald's and President and founder of McDonald's Restaurants of Canada] came and talked with the crew members.

Vikhanskii: Can you mention some differences in Russians' attitudes and behaviors?

Steeves: We do a great deal of job screening as well as intensive interviewing. We believe we get the best people. Moreover, the training process, motivational system, and reward system certainly prevent attitude and behavior problems from arising in the restaurant. Employees' performance is reviewed every three months in terms of what they do well and how they can improve their performance.

Every month we have some sort of activity going on that makes working here different and special. For instance, we have large parties and dances on a regular basis. We also had a Halloween dance, even though it is not typically practiced in Moscow. The Canadians and the Russian crew members decorated the restaurant, and we all wore costumes and danced. It was just as we would have done in Canada. As George Cohan likes to say, it was a form of cultural exchange between Canadians and Russians.

I have nothing but great respect for the employees. What they do is tremendous. They are working in the busiest restaurant in the world in which there is no end to the line of customers. One of the things that customers mention is not only the quality of the food, but also the quality of the service. On opening day one of our Soviet partners turned to George Cohan and asked, 'Where did you get those people?' George Cohan answered, 'We got them right here.' (Puffer 1992, pp. 279–80).[1]

This interview demonstrates that McDonald's has a strong organizational culture—a particular way of doing things—that it takes for granted is the correct and perhaps, only way, to run a business. It applies its organizational culture throughout the world with great success. Indeed, it appears never to cross Steeves' mind that Russians may be different from Canadian, Japanese, or English workers. To him, all national cultures fit McDonald's work culture.

> The McDonald's philosophy illustrates the culture-free approach to global management and organizational behavior.

The McDonald's philosophy illustrates the **culture-free approach** to global management and organizational behavior. Basically, it states that because of technology, policies, rules, organizational structure, and other variables that contribute to efficiency and effectiveness, the role of national culture in shaping organizational behavior, and therefore the need to understand it, is irrelevant for managing.

---

[1]Excerpt from *The Russian Revolution: Preparing Managers for the Market Economy, 1992* by Sheila M. Puffer. Reprinted by permission of M.E. Sharpe, Inc., Armonk, NY 10504.

An interview with Pavel Ivanov, an assistant manager of the Moscow McDonald's when it opened, suggests, however, that national culture does affect the behavior of McDonald's Russian employees. According to Ivanov, who is now a U.S. citizen, there are distinct differences between McDonald's in Russia and in the United States. For Russians employment at McDonald's is a high-status job because it offers steady work, comparatively high wages, opportunity for promotion, and free meals. In Russia, even people with university degrees want these jobs. These features not only make a job at McDonald's attractive but difficult to obtain and keep.

In contrast, in the United States, McDonald's is an employer of last resort. Students and senior citizens take part-time positions and earn minimum wage until a job with better opportunity is available. American culture denigrates employment in fast-food restaurants, with the result that many such restaurants perpetually search for employees.

According to Ivanov, the result of these different cultural orientations is that the service, cleanliness, and quality of food are superior in the Moscow McDonald's compared with those in the United States. This suggests that national culture does affect organizational culture.

Yet another view of cross-cultural research designed to help us understand the relationship between national and corporate culture is the following:

> It seems fair to summarize the findings on cross-national comparisons by concluding that there are cross-cultural differences among nations that undoubtedly affect organizations in some ways, but that the full range of these differences has not yet been well documented. Neither managers nor researchers can assume that practices from one country will be automatically acceptable in another; at the same time, there are powerful forces within organizations emanating from the logic of organizing and the technologies employed to produce goods and services that undoubtedly pattern behaviors and perhaps some values and beliefs in similar ways across nations and geographical regions. In effect, organizations are culture free in some respects, but culture bound in many others (Trice and Beyer 1993, p. 339).

Culture—national and organizational—is only one variable for explaining behavior in organizations. Other variables are strategy, size, power, technology, and the noncultural elements of the external environment—for example, political and economic events (see Hodge, Anthony, and Gales 1996). From the cultural perspective, national and organizational cultures distinguish a McDonald's in Moscow from one in Bombay or Brooklyn, even though the technology, roles, rules, and other aspects of the organization are similar.

To explore the role of organizational culture further, in the next section, we discuss levels of culture.

Levels of Organizational Culture

An image of organizational culture, like national culture, is an iceberg, with some elements above water and others submerged. Elements above water are not only more visible, but easier to understand. Elements below water are difficult to observe and more important for understanding culture because they are foundations of the culture. In addition, elements above water are amenable to change; submerged elements are either resistant or slow to change.

Several differences between national and organizational culture modify the iceberg metaphor. First, organizational culture is less comprehensive than national culture; the range of values and underlying assumptions of organizations are narrower. Second, organizational culture is more self-contained than national culture; management philosophy, strategy, and goals provide organizational boundaries even though elements of national culture influence it. Finally, organizational culture is more manageable than national culture. For example, the selection, training, socialization, and reward structure for employees restricts the variability of its members and constructs a comprehensive set of values and norms that management controls.

As a result, the submerged and visible elements of organizational culture are less likely to be unknown or in conflict than they would be in national culture. This does not mean, however, that no submerged elements exist, but rather that the line between the submerged and visible elements is extremely porous.

For analytical purposes, however, organizational culture is separated into four levels: artifacts, espoused values, actual values, and basic underlying assumptions (Schein 1990).

▌▌▊ ARTIFACTS

Artifacts, the most visible and observable elements of organizational culture, are the concrete aspects of an organization that symbolize its culture. These include material aspects of the organization such as its architecture, physical layout, and decoration.

A second type of artifact is slogans, organizational stories, myths, corporate heroes, rites, rituals, and ceremonies. The organization's members, clients, and general public construct and interpret them. Often, these groups interpret artifacts differently, and multiple meanings of them arise within and outside the organization (Martin 1992).

Many theorists view artifacts as the least representative of the actual culture of an organization. Because it is not difficult to interpret them—although some may be intentionally false or misleading—they are shallow compared with actual values and basic assumptions. Another perspective, however, is that artifacts interact with "deeper" cultural traits in complex ways.

The Culture at Work vignette illustrates an organization ritual—enacted by a rule—and the difficulty interpreting it. Age determines a professor's resources in German universities. Older academics receive larger offices, additional research assistants, and a more generous budget than do their younger colleagues. What does this mean? Do the infirmities of old age suggest that older faculty members need more assistance? Does advanced age indicate wisdom and that older faculty use resources more wisely than their younger colleagues? Is it a reward for longevity? Or, is it a bureaucratic device that bypasses the sometimes nasty politics of resource allocation?

▌▌▊ ESPOUSED VALUES

Espoused values are the public values and principles that the organization's leaders announce it intends to achieve. They include mission statements, goals, and ideals. It is possible, of course, that espoused values are not the actual values manifested in organizational behavior. For example, most government officials espouse the value of service to the people who put them in office. Occasionally, however, political figures act on a different set of values and use the government agencies they control to enrich themselves or advance the agenda of interest groups, rather than benefit their constituents.

ACTUAL VALUES

To be considered the **actual values** of an organization, espoused values require independent, observable behavior to validate them. If an organization espouses high levels of worker participation in decision making, it should demonstrate that workers actually contribute to decisions. Enacted espoused values reflect the basic underlying assumptions—the deepest level of culture—and also contribute, to some extent, to the construction of artifacts.

BASIC UNDERLYING ASSUMPTIONS

Basic underlying assumptions are unconscious beliefs and values that structure feelings, perceptions, thoughts, and actions that members of a culture view as the only correct understanding of life. As discussed in Chapter 2, basic assumptions are constructed through a complex process involving primary and secondary socialization and orientations toward diverse social conventions such as time, space, nature, and human relations. Unlike espoused values, the basic assumptions do not require validation; they are articles of faith.

Generally, although an organization may have basic assumptions and values that are different from the national culture, the deep structure of national culture makes it unlikely that the organization modifies them extensively. In most instances, corporate culture emphasizes or exaggerates major national cultural themes. Therefore, within a society, basic underlying organizational assumptions and values are relatively similar. An example is that in Japan a fundamental assumption of most corporate cultures is group allegiance. In comparison, in the United States the values that support an ethic of individual achievement are usually unquestioned.

Identifying and understanding basic assumptions is difficult. Ironically, foreign observers often generate insights into the meaning of the assumptions and values of a culture that are more insightful than native participants. For example, de Tocqueville (1840) and Varenne (1977), both French intellectuals, are considered the most astute observers of the basic values and behaviors of Americans. This may be due, in part, to the sensitivity of outsiders to cultural differences and the inability of insiders to recognize and question their assumptions systematically.

Similarly regarding organizations, an independent consultant or researcher—an outsider—who does not share the basic assumptions of the organization is likely to understand its value system more accurately than do its members. However, outsiders whose national culture is the same as the organization's experience limitations; they share the assumptions of the national culture in which the organization functions.

Identifying and understanding basic assumptions is difficult.

During periods of organizational change, however, underlying assumptions become more problematic and visible even to the organization's members. In the organizational change process—particularly a response to external forces—the new values are often the subject of debate and conflict before they become part of a new organizational culture.

SUBCULTURES

The cultures of organizations are not unitary. Whereas basic assumptions permeate an organization, alternative assumptions that either supplement or replace some common assumptions form organizational subcultures. **Subcultures**, shared meanings created and maintained by groups within an organization, reflect the division of labor, including departments, professional expertise, union membership, and position status. Also contributing to subculture formation are age, gender, race, ethnic background, religion, and national culture.

Subcultures contain their own rituals and ceremonies that have distinct meaning for their members and create ingroup identification. As informal groups within an organization, subcultures often challenge and conflict with the organizationwide culture. An example is workers who identify with their department or occupation rather than with the entire organization and act to enhance their department at the expense of others.

What Organizational Culture Does

▎▎▊ THE FUNCTIONS OF CULTURE

Organizational culture produces functional behaviors that contribute to organizational goal achievement. It also is a source of dysfunctional behaviors that have adverse effects on organizational success (Robbins 1996).

An important **function of organizational culture** is to distinguish an organization from other organizations and its general environment by providing it with an **external identity**. In a similar way, culture provides an identity for organization members; it locates them within an organizational and occupational structure that is recognizable to themselves and others. Culture also creates a **sense of commitment** to a social entity greater than one's self-interest.

Culture is also a source of **high reliability** in organizations. According to Weick (1987, p. 113):

> A system which values stories, storytellers, and storytelling will be more reliable than a system that derogates these substitutes for trial and error. A system that values stories and storytelling is potentially more reliable because people know more about their system, know more of the potential errors that might occur, and they are more confident that they can handle those errors that do occur because they know that other people have already handled similar errors.

Culture also provides members with an **interpretive scheme** or way to make sense of the arrangements of positions and activities in an organization (Weick 1995). It acts as a perceptual filter, embodied in stories and myths, that creates meaning out of routine, frequently experienced events, as well as unique situations.

Finally, culture is a **social control mechanism**. Through culture—particularly a strong, effective culture—the organization defines the reality that organization members experience. It socializes new members into a particular way of doing things and periodically resocializes its long-term members. For example, organizational rites and ceremonies reward and reinforce desired behavior as well as demonstrate and legitimate the organizational power structure.

▎▎▊ THE DYSFUNCTIONS OF CULTURE

The major **dysfunction**—negative outcome—of organizational culture is that it can create **barriers to change**. A strong organizational culture provides members with an explicit set of behaviors that have worked well in the past. Of course, the expectation is that these behaviors will be effective in the future. Paradoxically, a strong culture can produce rigidity in the organization, preventing appropriate modifications to new conditions.

For example, the International Business Machine Corporation (IBM), which developed a strong corporate culture, became hostage to it. IBM had specially designed notebooks for "taking notes at IBM meetings, with spaces at the bottom of each page for two witnesses to sign off" (Hays 1995, p. 1). This practice grew out of the culture of efficiency but symbolizes the extent to which IBM's culture became absorbed in trivial rules instead of change.

Of course, an organizational culture that resists change is not a problem in national cultures that value a time orientation toward the past and seek stability rather than change. A strong, change-resistant culture is also not a central issue for organizations that operate in stable environments that require repetitive, predictable, reliable performance.

Another dysfunction of culture is that it can create **conflict within the organization**. As noted previously, subcultures often emerge in organizations. Subcultures may become so cohesive that they develop values that are distinctive enough to separate the subgroup from the rest of the organization. For example, a research and development department may be oriented toward conducting basic research, a professional value orientation, ignoring the development of new products the organization can manufacture.

> Of course, an organizational culture that resists change is not a problem in national cultures that value a time orientation toward the past and seek stability rather than change.

Another type of dysfunctional behavior is that subcultures can change at different rates than do other units in the organization. This results in reduced internal coordination that adversely affects external relations. For instance, an information technologies department can introduce computer systems that are beyond the skills of average employees. Even with training, workers can resist the new technology or experience a long learning period. Related to this, change-oriented subcultures can experience conflict with subcultures that do not value change. This prevents them from exploring novel solutions for organizational problems.

Analyzing Organizational Culture

Two methods for analyzing organizational culture are to examine the dimensions of an organization's culture within the context of the general culture and to develop an organizational culture typology.

▌▌ DIMENSIONS OF ORGANIZATIONAL CULTURE

Dimensions of national culture are also useful for analyzing organizational culture. Adapting Kluckhohn and Strodtbeck's framework to organizational culture, Schein (1990) identifies the following dimensions: (1) the organization's relationship to its environment, (2) the nature of human activity, (3) the nature of reality and truth, (4) the nature of time, (5) the nature of human nature, (6) the nature of human relationships, and (7) homogeneity versus diversity.

Each dimension has associated questions (see Table 8-1). For example, the relationship of the organization to its environment is explored by asking if the organization perceives itself as dominant, submissive, or harmonizing in relation to its environment. Similarly, for the dimension of time, relevant questions are organizational orientation toward the past, present, and future.

The dimensions have different values because answers to the questions vary within and across cultures. Organizational cultures within a country are likely to vary

Table 8-1 Some Underlying Dimensions of Organizational Culture

Dimension	Questions to be answered
1. The organization's relationship to its environment	Does the organization perceive itself to be dominant, submissive, harmonizing, searching out a niche?
2. The nature of human activity	Is the "correct" way for humans to behave to be dominant/proactive, harmonizing, or passive/fatalistic?
3. The nature of reality and truth	How do we define what is true and what is not true; and how is truth ultimately determined both in the physical and social world?
4. The nature of time	What is our basic orientation in terms of past, present, and future, and what kinds of time units are most relevant for the conduct of daily affairs?
5. The nature of human nature	Are humans basically good, neutral, or evil, and is human nature perfectible or fixed?
6. The nature of human relationships	What is the "correct" way for people to relate to each other, to distribute power and affection? Is life competitive or cooperative? Is the best way to organize society on the basis of individualism or groupism? Is the best authority system autocratic/paternalistic or collegial/participative?
7. Homogeneity versus diversity	Is the group best off if it is highly diverse or if it is highly homogeneous, and should individuals in a group be encouraged to innovate or conform?

Source: Table adapted from *Organizational Culture and Leadership*, p. 86 by Edgar H. Schein. Copyright © 1985 by Jossey-Bass Inc., Publishers. Reprinted by permission of Jossey-Bass Inc., Publishers.

less than do those across countries. Subsidiaries of multinational and global corporations experience variation based on the culture of countries where they operate.

The result is a paradigm or configuration that specifies patterns among the dimensions and explains how the organization's culture affects behavior in the organization. It also provides a way to understand the influences of the organization on its external environment and the environment's influences on the organizational culture.

▌▌▌ A CROSS-CULTURAL TYPOLOGY

Another approach to understanding organizational culture is to identify specific types of organizational cultures in different countries. This strategy assumes that "differences between national cultures help determine the type of corporate culture 'chosen' " (Trompenaars 1994, p. 152), rather than variations in technology, economic systems, or other factors. It differs from Schein's approach in that it (1) focuses more on internal organizational variables—for example, the authority system; (2) develops only four organizational culture types; and (3) links the types to specific national cultures.

According to Trompenaars (1994), organizational cultures are one of four analytical types: family, Eiffel Tower, guided missile, and incubator. Table 8-2 presents the variables and characteristics of each type.

Family Culture   Family organizational culture emphasizes personal, face-to-face relationships. It is hierarchical with an authority structure based on power differentials commonly experienced between parents and children. According to Trompenaars:

> The result is a power-oriented corporate culture in which the leader is regarded as a caring parent who knows better than his subordinates what should be done and what is good for them. Rather than being threatening, this type of power is essentially intimate and benign. The work of the corporation in this type of culture is usually carried forward in an atmosphere that in many respects mimics the home. (1994, p. 154).

The Japanese create a family organizational culture in many of their corporations. Other cultures with similar arrangements are nations that industrialized relatively late, creating a rapid transition from feudalism to industrialism. France, Belgium, India, Greece, Italy, Singapore, South Korea, Japan, and Spain are examples of nations that prefer family corporate cultures (Trompenaars 1994).

T a b l e   8 - 2   **Characteristics of Trompenaars' Four Corporate Cultures**

Variables	Family	Eiffel Tower	Guided Missile	Incubator
Relationships between employees	Diffuse relationships to organic whole to which one is bonded	Specific role in mechanical system of required interactions	Specific tasks in cybernetic system targeted upon shared objectives	Diffuse, spontaneous relationships growing out of shared creative process
Attitude toward authority	Status is ascribed to parent figures who are close and powerful	Status is ascribed to superior roles, which are distant yet powerful	Status is achieved by project group members who contribute to targeted goal	Status is achieved by individuals exemplifying creativity and growth
Ways of thinking and learning	Intuitive, holistic, lateral, and error-correcting	Logical, analytical, vertical, and rationally efficient	Problem centered, professional, practical, cross-disciplinary	Process oriented, creative, ad hoc, inspirational
Attitudes toward people	Family members	Human resources	Specialists and experts	Co-creators
Ways of changing	"Father" changes course	Change rules and procedures	Shift aim as target moves	Improvise and attune
Ways of motivating and rewarding	Intrinsic satisfaction in being loved and respected	Promotion to greater position, larger role	Pay or credit for performance and problems solved	Participating in the process of creating new realities
Management style	Management by subjectives	Management by job description	Management by objectives	Management by enthusiasm
Criticism and conflict resolution	Turn other cheek, save others' faces, do not lose power game	Criticism is accusation of irrationalism unless there are procedures to arbitrate conflicts	Constructive task-related only, then admit error fast and correct	Must improve creative idea, not negate it

Eiffel Tower Culture   **Eiffel Tower culture** is a classic bureaucratic structure. It emphasizes a division of labor and coordination through a hierarchy of authority and relies on planning to accomplish its goals. Trompenaars distinguishes it from the family culture, where the authority structure is diffuse, based on the following observation:

> Each higher level has a clear and demonstrable function holding together the levels beneath it. You obey the boss because it is his or her role to instruct you. The rational purpose of the corporation is conveyed to you through him. He has legal authority to tell you what to do, and your contract of service, overtly or implicitly, obliges you to work according to his instructions. If you and other subordinates did not do so, the system could not function (1994, p. 160).

A central characteristic of this organization is replacement of individual human qualities with the idea of a **social role**, a position governed by impersonal rules and norms. The source of status is the role, not personal attributes. Change in a bureaucratic organization occurs with changes in the roles and rules. Because reorganization threatens the established culture, change usually meets with resistance. Employees become comfortable with the roles they occupy and the authority of their position. New roles and norms create the possibility of reduced status and norms that circumscribe behavior in unwelcome ways—for example, by increasing accountability for performance by readjusting hierarchical relations. In Trompenaars' view, the Eiffel Tower type is characteristic of corporate cultures in Denmark, the Netherlands, and Germany.

Guided Missile Culture   **Guided missile culture** differs from the family and Eiffel Tower cultures because it is egalitarian. However, it is impersonal and task oriented, resembling the Eiffel Tower culture. "Indeed," writes Trompenaars,

> . . . the guided missile culture is rather like the Eiffel Tower in flight. But while the rationale of the Eiffel Tower culture is means, the guided missile has a rationale of ends. Everything must be done to persevere in your strategic intent and reach your target.
>
> The guided missile culture is oriented to tasks, typically undertaken by teams or project groups. It differs from the role culture in that the jobs of members are not fixed in advance. They must do whatever it takes to complete a task, and what is needed is often unclear and may have to be discovered (Trompenaars 1994, p. 170).

This culture is egalitarian because it employs experts in technical fields. Experts work on projects together rather than take directives from superiors. Technical expertise reduces emotional elements in the culture, producing a bureaucratic culture based on knowledge rather than position, as in the Eiffel Tower, or on emotional ties, as in the family culture. Guided missile culture flourishes in the United States, Canada, and the United Kingdom.

Incubator Culture   The **incubator culture** is radically different from the other cultures; it attempts to minimize organizational structure and culture. It develops with this mind-set: "If organizations are to be tolerated at all, they should be there to serve as incubators for self-expression and self-fulfillment" (Trompenaars 1994, p. 173). Minimal organizational structure facilitates a culture that is egalitarian, personal, and highly creative. In most cases, incubator cultures are in knowledge and science industries such as computer software development firms. This type of organizational culture is prevalent in Silicon Valley, California and Route 128 near Boston in the United States and in Sweden, where automobile manufacturing systems create a culture to enhance the intellectual and physical conditions of work.

These four cultures are ideal types—mental constructs that represent "pure" organizational cultures. In reality, most societies contain mixtures of them. For example, in Canada, the United Kingdom, and the United States, which Trompenaars characterizes as guided missile types, many organizations have family or incubator cultures. In addition, many organizations contain multiple culture types within them—for example, a guided missile and an incubator culture. Usually, however, one type characterizes the entire organization more than the others.

Managing and Changing Organizational Culture

LEADERSHIP AND ORGANIZATIONAL CULTURE

Can leaders manage organizational culture? The answer depends on whom you ask. Edgar Schein, an influential theorist of organizational culture, maintains that the central role of an organizational leader is to create, manage, and, when necessary, destroy an organization's culture (Schein 1985). The destruction of culture is necessary to create organizational change by establishing a new culture. This suggests that organizational cultures are rational, manageable entities.

> Can leaders manage organizational culture? The answer depends on whom you ask.

Another answer is that "the part that leadership plays in organizational cultures has not been systematically explored" (Trice and Beyer 1993, p. 255). Many models of organizational culture and the role of leadership in managing are anecdotal and prescriptive instead of being based on scientific investigation. Consequently, it is not known if organizational culture can be managed effectively.

A third response is that organizational cultures contain significant amounts of **nonrational elements**, behavior not grounded in empirical data or distorted to serve a particular group's interests. These include destructive or negative emotions, erroneous beliefs, and idiosyncratic interpretations of the organization's past, present, and future. They often result in smoldering resentments and prolonged overt conflicts at the individual, group, and organizational levels.

Nonrational elements of organizational culture can be dysfunctional by impeding goal attainment. For example, during periods of organizational innovation they are often barriers to change. Leaders are frequently unable to shape or otherwise control nonrational and other aspects of organizational culture.

ELEMENTS OF CULTURE LEADERS CAN CHANGE

Even if the leader is not central to creating and managing organizational culture, a leader can affect organizational culture in a variety of ways. For example, a leader can change the selection criteria for people to become organization members. This could involve raising the educational level of new entrants, selecting people more or less representative of the population in terms of race, ethnicity, age, and gender, or hiring only the leader's friends and relatives.

Similarly, a leader can change the socialization of organizational members by reformulating training programs and introducing new managerial philosophies and values. For example, in industrialized countries in recent years, new hires and existing employees attend workshops to improve their contributions to quality.

The current movement toward decentralized organizations that emphasize worker empowerment represents a shift in managerial philosophy.

Leaders can also change the meaning of work in an organizational culture. Their interpretations of ceremonies, rituals, stories, and organizational heroes can fit new circumstances and provide new meanings to adapt an organization to changing external environments. An example is IBM's dress code change. IBM built a reputation of corporate efficiency symbolized by its employees' dark, three-piece business suits. This image became dysfunctional in the early 1990s when it became apparent that IBM had failed to adapt to a rapidly changing global business environment. It symbolized rigidity and inability to change rather than its intended message. In an attempt to change the corporate culture, IBM introduced more casual dress for its employees, symbolizing its desire to be flexible and in touch with the times.

Even by using sophisticated managerial tools, a leader may not be able to change the underlying assumptions of an organization. Most organizational theorists conclude that it is difficult to change the deeper levels of organizational culture (Hofstede et al. 1990). For example, changing from a risk-averse to a risk-seeking organizational culture is extremely difficult, particularly if the national culture is not supportive. Similarly, in an ascriptive national culture with hiring and promotion based on close interpersonal relationships, it would be difficult to change to an achievement-based organizational culture.

It is clear, however, that leaders can change the artifacts or surface manifestations of organizational culture. Changes range from developing new corporate images to the elimination of corporate status symbols and renewed attention to customers.

International managers can manage foreign subsidiaries to accommodate local organizational cultures or change them by attempting to establish the headquarters' organizational culture. As noted previously, Japanese automobile companies have successfully transplanted their organizational culture to manufacturing facilities in the United States (Florida and Kenney 1991).

Instead of directly changing organizational culture, an alternative approach is to create culture change by altering organizational structure as discussed in Chapters 11 and 12. By rearranging positions within an organization, for example, increasing or decreasing the levels in a hierarchy, elements of organizational culture change. However, change often occurs in an organization's structural arrangements but fails to change its culture or individual worker behavior (Elmore, Peterson, and McCarthey 1996).

In summary, managers can change organizational culture by using an array of techniques along with general secondary socialization processes. But planned organizational culture change—like any type of change—can encounter resistance and implementation difficulties and often produces unintended consequences.

Convergence or Divergence?

▌▌▌ FORCES FOR CONVERGENCE

There are social, economic, and technological forces that have been present for decades that tend to produce similar organizational cultures throughout the world. The most powerful factor is industrialization. Along with technological innovations, bureaucratic administration usually accompanies industrialization. Bureaucratization creates a distinctive organizational culture characterized by an emphasis on standardization of performance. It also contains several dysfunctions, however, including inability to adapt to changing conditions and an inflexible hierarchy. But some theorists argue that the hierarchic structure of bureaucracy is not dysfunctional (Jaques 1990).

Another factor contributing to convergence is organizational strategies for managing culture. Hoecklin (1995) identified four ways multinational corporations can manage cultural differences: (1) build a strong corporate culture internationally, (2) develop a common technical or professional culture worldwide, (3) rely on strong financial or planning systems, and (4) leave each corporate culture alone.

Of the four strategies, the first two are likely to produce policies and rules encouraging uniform cultures. The third one, strong financial or planning systems, could also affect culture if these systems extend beyond the organization's technical production. In summary, with the growth of multinational corporations it is likely that organizations themselves will produce pressures toward the convergence of organizational cultures.

▌▌▌ FORCES FOR DIVERGENCE

One force for divergence is the use of organizational culture as a competitive tool. Many companies attempt to create unique cultures that foster innovation, competitiveness, or a relationship with customers that distinguishes them from their competitors.

A second force creating divergence is national culture. This manifests itself in the emergence of preferences for doing things in specific, culturally expressive ways. An example is the collectivist culture of the Israeli kibbutz, which attempts to create an egalitarian work environment (Bar-Hayim and Berman 1991). Another example is the Japanese cultural preference for group orientation that Western cultures experience difficulty adapting (Ouchi 1981). A final example is experimentation with humanistic work designs in the Swedish automobile industry that have not diffused to other cultures (Ellegard et al. 1992).

Implications for Managers

International managers should be as familiar with different organizational cultures as they are with differences in national cultures. They cannot assume that organizational cultures in other countries are the same as the culture of their organization. Consequently, they must analyze organizational cultures to be able to coordinate activities with them or change them.

Managers must understand what levels of organizational culture they can influence. For example, it is unlikely that international managers can change the basic assumptions of an organizational culture in a national culture that is significantly different from their own. However, it is possible that they can change and manage culture at the artifact level.

Managers also must know how an organization's culture can influence them. For example, organizational culture can affect managers by either supporting or undermining management initiatives. Cultures with values different from a manager's are unlikely to be supportive and require appropriate adjustments.

> International managers should be as familiar with different organizational cultures as they are with differences in national cultures.

■ Summary

Organizational culture is an important factor shaping behavior in organizations. One viewpoint is that culture plays a small role in determining the functioning of an organization and that processes such as industrialization are universal and cut across cultures. An alternative viewpoint is that organizational culture is related to national culture because organizational boundaries do not prevent the values and behavior of the surrounding culture from influencing it.

Organizational culture exists on several levels in organizations, ranging from observable artifacts to difficult-to-detect basic assumptions. These features construct a culture that can either be functional or dysfunctional for the organization.

One approach to understanding organizational culture is to develop a typology. Trompenaars distinguishes among several types of organizational cultures and suggests that certain types are found more predominantly in different cultures. Trompenaars' types of organizational culture are family, Eiffel Tower, guided missile, and incubator.

Although there is little agreement as to what extent culture is manageable, organizational leaders can influence the entrance and socialization of new members and interpret stories and rituals important to the organization. These are key components of culture creation and maintenance. The leader can also change the organization's culture by attempting to reframe the underlying assumptions.

The prospect of organizational cultures becoming more alike or dissimilar depends on the evolution of national cultures. Movement toward more homogeneous national cultures will probably result in similar organizational cultures.

It is important for mangers to understand organizational culture in order to coordinate activities within the organization. Managers also should know how organizational culture influences them.

■ Discussion Questions

1. Define organizational culture.
2. What is the relationship among organizational, national, and global cultures?
3. Why are basic assumptions considered by many theorists to be the deepest level of organizational culture?
4. Discuss the argument that organizations are culture free.
5. Could you use Trompenaars' typology of organizational cultures to analyze organizations in your country?
6. Is it possible to prevent some of the dysfunctional aspects of organizational culture, such as resistance to change, from occurring?
7. What are some of the elements of organizational culture that a leader can change?
8. In your view, are the cultures of organizations becoming more alike, staying about the same, or under pressure to become distinctive from one another?

References

Bar-Hayim, A. and Berman, G. (1991), "Ideology, Solidarity, and Work Values: The Case of the Histadrut Enterprises," *Human Relations*, 44, 4, 357–70.

Bracey, G. (1996), "International Comparisons and the Condition of American Education," *Educational Researcher*, 25, 1, 5–11.

Cole, R. (1990), "U.S. Quality Improvement in the Auto Industry: Close but No Cigar," *California Management Review*, 32, 4.

DE TOCQUEVILLE, A. (1961), *Democracy in America*. New York: Schocken.

ELLEGARD, K., JONSSON, D., ENSTROM, T., JOHANSSON, M., MEDBO, L., and JOHANSSON, B. (1992), "Reflective Production in the Final Assembly of Motor Vehicles—An Emerging Swedish Challenge," *International Journal of Operations & Production Management*, 12 (⅞), 117–33.

ELMORE, R., PETERSON, P., and McCARTHEY, S. (1996), *Restructuring in the Classroom: Teaching, Learning and School Organization*. San Francisco: Jossey-Bass.

FLORIDA, R. and KENNEY, M. (1991), "Transplanted Organizations: The Transfer of Japanese Industrial Organization to the U.S," *American Sociological Review*, 56, 381–98.

HAYS, L. (1995), "Manzi Quits at IBM and His Many Critics Are Not at All Surprised," *The Wall Street Journal*, (October 12), 1.

HARBISON, F. and MYERS, C. (1959), *Management in the Industrial World: An International Study*. New York: McGraw-Hill.

HODGE, B., ANTHONY, W. and GALES, L. (1996), *Organization Theory: A Strategy Approach*. Upper Saddle River, NJ: Prentice Hall.

HOECKLIN, L. (1995), *Managing Cultural Difference: Strategies for Competitive Advantage*. Reading, MA: Addison-Wesley.

HOFSTEDE, G., NEUIJEN, B., OHAYV, D., and SANDERS, G. (1990), "Measuring Organizational Cultures: A Qualitative and Quantitative Study Across Twenty Cases," *Administrative Science Quarterly*, 35, 286–316.

JAQUES, E. (1990), "In Praise of Hierarchy," *Harvard Business Review*, January–February.

MARTIN, J. (1992), *Cultures in Organizations: Three Perspectives*. New York: Oxford.

OUCHI, W. (1981), *Theory Z: How American Business Can Meet the Japanese Challenge*. New York: Avon.

PUFFER, S. (ed.) (1992), *The Russian Management Revolution: Preparing Managers for the Market Economy*. Armonk, NY: Sharpe.

SCHEIN, E. (1985), *Organizational Culture and Leadership*. San Francisco: Jossey-Bass.

———. (1990), "Organizational Culture," *American Psychologist*, 45 (2), 109–19.

SCHUTZ, A. (1967), *The Problem of Social Reality*. The Hague: Martinus Nijhoff.

TRICE, H. and BEYER, J. (1993), *The Cultures of Work Organizations*. Upper Saddle River, NJ: Prentice Hall.

TROMPENAARS, F. (1994), *Riding the Waves of Culture: Understanding Diversity in Global Business*. New York: Irwin.

VARENNE, H. (1977), *Americans Together: Structured Diversity in a Midwestern Town*. New York: Teachers College Press.

WEICK, K. (1987), "Organizational Culture as a Source of High Reliability," *California Management Review*, 29 (2), 112–27.

———. (1995), *Sensemaking in Organizations*. Thousand Oaks, CA: Sage Publications.

Leadership

Machismo!

Working in the banana plantations in Central America is difficult. The scorching sun and oppressive humidity make the ten hour days seem endless. Pay is low and the food is terrible. Sanitation is inadequate; diarrhea is common. Yet the men who harvest the banana crop each cut tons of bananas every day.

Ernesto was a field foreman. His job was to make the men work hard—he "pushed" them to keep production high. To make money, labor costs had to be kept low and productivity high. Often the men would gripe among themselves that Ernesto was too demanding.

One day, Manuel, a new, young, hard-working field hand, complained to Ernesto that he was pushing him too hard. The older workers looked on in silence. Ernesto told Manuel that if he wanted to keep his job he should do as told.

Later that day, Manuel again complained to Ernesto. Ernesto told Manuel that if he complained again he would be fired.

Manuel swung his machete at Ernesto. Instead of ducking, Ernesto blocked the blow with his hand. With blood gushing from a deep wound, Ernesto pinned Manuel to the ground. Two workers helped subdue and remove Manuel.

At his retirement party, 21 years later, Ernesto's long time co-foreman, Armando, recounted this story to the assembled friends. He told them—suppressing a tense laugh—that after that incident Ernesto's authority was never challenged.

Source: B.A. Gold

Learning Objectives

After reading this chapter, you should be able to:

1. Define leadership.
2. Understand the relationship between culture and leadership.
3. Discuss the theory of leader legitimacy and a cross-cultural contingency model of leadership.
4. Describe typical leadership patterns in two cultures.
5. Identify issues that affect women becoming leaders in various cultures.
6. Consider ways that leadership is becoming more similar or different because of changes in organizations worldwide.

Cultural values and norms shape and support organizational leadership. Without the compliance of organizational members—their acceptance of socially constructed assumptions, values and behaviors—leaders cannot maintain their authority. With the support of followers, leaders can manage the resources required for the achievement of organizational and societal goals.

While social values support a particular style of leadership, a successful leader interprets and translates the culture's value system, in the process modifying it, to achieve organizational efficiency and effectiveness. For example, formulating corporate strategies, the development of new products and markets, managing the organization's culture, and managing organizational change engage leaders in simultaneous support from and change of the culture. National and organizational cultures affect the leader, and the leader affects the cultures.

What Is Leadership?

Defining leadership is not straightforward, especially in a cross-cultural context. One difficulty is that not all cultures have the term *leader*. The closest equivalent in Japanese, Chinese, and Korean to leader is similar to *coach* in English (Trice and Beyer 1993). *Headship* captures the nature of the authority role in familial organizations, which are prevalent in Asian cultures (Westwood and Chan 1992). In the German language, there is "no word exactly corresponding to the meaning of the term *manager* in English. Present-day Germans also avoid using the German word for leader (*führer*) because of its association with Hitler" (Trice and Beyer 1993, p. 254). Of course, the variety of terms used in different cultures does not mean leadership is absent, but rather that the nuances indicate that different cultures vary in their understandings of and expectations for authority roles.

Another difficulty is that in cultures in which the leader is an important role in organizations, it has multiple scientific definitions (Bass 1990) and diverse meanings in everyday life. Consider the subtle differences used in the United States to distinguish leadership roles and responsibilities. Terms for leader include *boss*, *administrator*, *head honcho*, *supervisor*, *director*, *manager*, *mentor*, *coach*, *executive*, *head*, *chief*, *master*, and *chairperson*. In addition, in the United States, distinctions in titles such as *assistant vice president*, *vice president*, *executive vice president*, *senior vice president*, and *president* have a great deal of meaning. Not all cultures recognize such fine distinctions or view leadership as so important.

The concept of power distance (Hofstede 1984) captures an important element of "leadership." **Power distance** is the willingness of less powerful members of organizations to accept unequal distribution of power. A central characteristic of modern organizations is separation of roles and responsibilities between leaders and followers. However, some cultures emphasize power differences more than others.

A definition of **leadership** is "the influential increment over and above mechanical compliance with the routine directives of the organization" (Katz and Kahn 1978, p. 528). This definition captures the essence of the distinction between the leader and other organizational roles. Without an increment over mechanical compliance, instead of leadership, administrative or management functions occur. Leadership focuses on creativity, vision, and long-term organizational development, whereas management deals with routine operations. Before discussing leadership theories, we present variables that affect cross-cultural leadership.

Culture and Leadership

NATIONAL CULTURE

National culture influences leadership. Deeply held values regarding the rights and duties of citizens form the core of national culture and constitute a worldview. These values, codified in documents such as constitutions, laws, and ethical codes, proscribe and control behavior. Like other aspects of culture, they are taken for granted by the members of a society as the correct, and perhaps only, way to act.

> National culture influences leadership.

A worldview expresses ideals that are often not attained and, on occasion, violated. Most societies have mechanisms for identifying and punishing deviation. In the case of leadership, if the leader violates core values—for example, engaging in immoral or illegal activities—he can lose authority over subordinates and be removed from the leadership position. Leadership derives from and represents socially constructed legal, moral, and ethical obligations.

The relationship between national cultural values and actual behavior in organizations is complex. For example, in many Western cultures women are increasingly encouraged to become organizational leaders and managers, and the concept of equal pay for equal work receives wide support. However, even in the United States, where employment laws mandate equal treatment for men and women, a "glass ceiling" effect exists. This is a set of subtle barriers that conflict with cultural ideals and often function to prevent women from achieving the highest levels of management (Northcraft and Neale 1994). In Japanese companies located in the United States the glass ceiling takes a different form; non-Japanese workers often experience barriers to promotion.

POLITICAL CULTURE

The values of the political system of a country affect organizational leadership. Political structures usually reflect central national culture values, including ideas about the most appropriate and effective type of leadership. Countries with democratic political values and systems of government, such as the United Kingdom and United States, prefer participative leadership in the workplace, a key element in the human relations school of management theory (Guillén 1994). Countries that have had autocratic political regimes and limited experience with democracy, such as Spain, have low expectations for worker participation in organizational decision making and use nonparticipatory management philosophies, typically some form of scientific management (Guillén 1994).

ORGANIZATIONAL CULTURE

Leaders influence organizational culture and often attempt to create, maintain, or change it to improve the performance of an organization (Trice and Beyer 1993). One view is that managing organizational culture is a leader's major contribution to an organization (Schein 1985). Whether this is true or not, the relationship between leadership and organizational culture is the focus of much recent research.

Not only do leaders create, maintain, and on occasion change organizational culture, but at the same time culture places constraints on leaders and shapes their behavior. For example, in an organization with a culture that values participatory decision making, a leader who prefers centralized decision making has difficulty being effective. Similarly, an organizational culture that values stability and continuity resists attempts to change it unless there is a prolonged deterioration in performance. (Chapter 8 discusses organizational culture in detail.)

In summary, national, political, and organizational cultures vary across societies and affect leadership styles to some extent. Management scholars are in the early stages of constructing theories and conducting research into the influence that these variables have on leadership behavior. Consequently, precisely which leadership behaviors are universal and which are products of a specific culture remains unknown (see Dorfman 1996).

▌▓ LEADERSHIP, CULTURE, AND ORGANIZATIONAL CHANGE

Recent actions of Daimler-Benz AG, a major German corporation, demonstrate the interaction of leadership and national, political, and organizational culture. In 1993 Daimler-Benz, which manufactures luxury automobiles, lost money for the first time since World War II. Part of the reason for the loss was a recession in 1992–93 and a belated response to increased global competition.

To return to profitability, Edzard Reuter, Chief Executive of Daimler-Benz, initiated major changes at the company. Significant union concessions included reducing the workforce by 20%. The company also disposed of unprofitable businesses and old-line managers. In addition, management decided that Mercedes Benz would manufacture automobiles outside Germany to develop a global presence. The scope of the changes was so significant that "from the shop floor to the boardroom, it imposed an unfamiliar new creed: Change or die" (Gumbel and Choi 1995, p. A10). These rapid changes occurred despite difficulty firing workers, labor representation on the board of directors, and the glacial speed of change in Germany. Explaining the changes, a senior executive observed, "We simply want to become less German" (Gumbel and Choi 1995, p. A10).

These changes required the corporation's leaders to specify a new vision for the organization's future, restructure the organization, and create a new organizational culture within a national and organizational culture that resisted change. As a result of the changes, Daimler-Benz was profitable by early 1995.

The experience at Daimler-Benz illustrates the complexities of effective leadership. The changes at Daimler were not proactive but implemented after the organization experienced intense competition from Japanese automobile manufacturers. But even under conditions of duress—a threat to long-term survival—change was not easy. For example, Reuter had to circumvent long-established national and corporate culture to create a new corporate culture oriented toward the demands of the global economy. In implementing innovations, Reuter had the difficult job of changing the culture that supported his authority without alienating customary sources of support.

Organizational leadership is a difficult, demanding set of behaviors.

Organizational leadership is a difficult, demanding set of behaviors. It is a cultural product that challenges the culture by exploring and implementing new management methods to make organizations responsive to changing economic and social conditions.

Leadership Theories

▐▐▐ THEORIES DEVELOPED IN THE UNITED STATES

Since World War II, there have been more than 3,500 studies of leadership, the majority conducted by social scientists working in the United States (Bass 1990). Important leadership theories formulated in the United States are trait theory, Theory X and Y, the Ohio State and University of Michigan behavioral theories, Managerial Grid theory, situational, contingency, and the Path Goal theory. Although the details of each theory vary, the major emphasis is on participation as a means for establishing follower motivation to achieve specific goals. The newer theories recognize that in certain situations, increasing leader use of power over subordinates may be necessary to improve their effort when participation is not effective.

Limitations of U.S. Theories   Despite their intuitive appeal, widespread dissemination by consultants, and use by businesspeople, U.S. theories have received either very little or inconclusive support from research with data collected in the United States (Yukl 1994). Lack of support in the culture that produced a theory reduces the probability that the theory explains behavior in other cultures. There are several reasons for this. First, it is difficult to demonstrate empirical support for most social science theory. Second, these theories and the studies designed to test them, reflect American values and the context of American business for the half century following World War II. For instance, only recently have American businesses had to contend with issues such as a diverse domestic workforce and the need to manage in a global economy. Therefore it is premature to assume that American leadership theories have universal application.

Theory X and Y   Rather than discuss the strengths and weaknesses of each leadership theory mentioned previously, Douglas McGregor's Theory X and Y illustrates some of the limitations of American theories, particularly their culture boundedness.

McGregor's thesis is that leadership and management styles vary according to assumptions about human nature. McGregor's theory is based on the insight that leadership is

> the result of management's conception of the nature of its task and all the policies and practices which are constructed to implement this conception. The way a business is managed determines to a very large extent what people are perceived to have "potential" and how they develop. . . . The blunt fact is that we are a long way from realizing the potential represented by the human resources we now recruit into industry (1960, p. iv).

According to McGregor, Theory X is a set of assumptions that people prefer to avoid hard work and therefore require constant direction and supervision. Theory Y assumptions are more optimistic and view workers as self-motivated and capable of undertaking complex work with little direct supervision under the proper conditions. The task of management under these assumptions is to trust workers more and provide opportunities for workers to flourish.

The assumptions of Theory X and Y correspond to Kluckhohn and Strodtbeck's basic human nature dimension. Theory X managers believe people are primarily evil, and Theory Y managers view people as basically good.

Although McGregor's theory is a seminal contribution to management theory, it is unclear that it accurately explains leader behavior in the United States or other cultures. For instance, not all cultures view human nature as consisting of either exclusively positive or negative qualities. The Kluckhohn and Strodtbeck framework suggests that some cultures have a more complex or mixed view of human nature. People exhibit a variety of work characteristics, some consistent with Theory X and others similar to Theory Y assumptions. This complexity of human nature and orientation toward work is apparent even in the United States and will increase as its population becomes more diverse.

One leadership style that a culture with contradictory norms and values produces is **ambivalent leadership** (Merton 1970). Ambivalence—alternating between opposite values and behaviors—is not the product of inadequate understanding of human nature, but rather consists of difficulty acting in a consistent, coherent way in response to the diverse, sometimes conflicting, values of a complex, heterogeneous, society.

With minor modification, McGregor's theory reflects the ambivalence of modern societies and organizations. Instead of viewing Theory X and Y as mutually exclusive, human behavior and organizations are now understood as being composed of elements of both X and Y. Leaders experience inconsistent sets of organizational norms producing contradictory behavior.

McGregor's Theory Y also assumes that collaboration between leaders and followers is more productive than an adversarial, controlling relationship. This leadership style is consistent with a low–power distance orientation. In high–power distance cultures, however, a participative leader may appear incompetent because he or she is expected to lead by displaying expertise, power, or other dominating behaviors rather than including subordinates in decision making. In addition, collaboration and cooperation are components of a distinctly American ideology that fits the requirements of an industrialized democratic society, rather than an inherent aspect of human nature. Similarly, not all societies value achievement and self-development.

▍▍▍ CULTURAL ASSUMPTIONS OF LEADERS ABOUT WORKERS

One way to view the consequences of assumptions leaders and workers develop is to examine labor relations in various countries. Labor relations reflect key assumptions about human nature—for example, whether workers are lazy and untrustworthy or able to take initiative and work autonomously.

Labor relations in Europe are substantially different than they are in the United States. In most European countries labor relations are political and based on greater social class distinctions between workers and management or ownership. Also, the government takes a more direct role in regulating labor and management and in responsibility for worker social security concerns. Finally, because of the long history of unions there is a higher degree of acceptance and integration of them into the economy than in the United States (Briscoe 1995).

In Japan labor relations are different from those in the United States and Europe. Each firm organizes and usually controls a union. For example, the head of the union could be a middle manager appointed by the company. Other labor management practices, including lifetime employment, seniority-based promotions, and firm performance–based bonuses, "were developed as a response to a very militant union action after the end of World War II. Largely because of their successes, today's Japanese unions tend to be quite responsible in negotiations, they abide by their contracts, and strikes are quite rare" (Briscoe 1995, p. 163).

In South America there is yet another relationship between management and labor. Basically, there is a "close relationship between the unions and government, with the result that many rights and benefits for workers have been codified in law" (Briscoe 1995, p. 163). Codification reduces the potential for adversarial relationships between the parties and provides a framework for cooperation.

This brief survey of labor relations demonstrates that assumptions that govern interaction between management and lower level participants vary considerably in different cultures. The presence of unions and laws governing labor relations is consistent with Theory X assumptions that workers require close monitoring and strict enforcement of rules. It also reflects worker wariness of management that requires institutionalized arrangements to control the power of organizations.

Although McGregor and other American theorists have identified important issues, there are serious limitations in American leadership theories, particularly when applied to other cultures (Bass 1990; Yukl 1994). A more useful approach is comparative leadership frameworks.

Types of Leadership Legitimacy

▌▌▌ WEBER'S THEORY OF LEADERSHIP

Max Weber, a German sociologist, developed a comparative framework for understanding the legitimacy of leaders. Weber wanted to understand what conditions were required for people to obey authority. In historical and cross-cultural investigations, Weber identified three social bases of leader legitimacy: traditional, rational, and charismatic authority.

- **Traditional authority** "rests on an established belief in the sanctity of immemorial traditions and the legitimacy of the status of those exercising authority under them" (Weber 1947, p. 328).

- **Rational authority** "rests on a belief in the legality of patterns of normative rules and the right of those elevated to authority under such rules to issue commands" (Weber 1947, p. 328).

- **Charismatic authority** is based "on devotion to the specific and exceptional sanctity, heroism or exemplary character of an individual person, and of the normative patterns or order revealed or ordained by him" (Weber 1947, p. 328).

These types of authority exist in cultures throughout the world. Often, however, one type is more prevalent in a society than others. For example, traditional authority patterns are characteristic of Asian societies, in which senior males, a patriarchy, provide organizational leadership.

Rational authority underpins bureaucratic organizations (Weber 1947). Bureaucracy, discussed in Chapter 11, is the administrative structure of government agencies, schools, businesses, and other organizations throughout the world. Despite the negative connotations of bureaucracy, for example, red tape, unnecessarily elaborate hierarchy, and lack of creativity, it is the model of modern rational organizations. Bureaucracy is very efficient and effective when used in organizations that perform predictable, routine tasks (Perrow 1986).

Charismatic authority, which according to Weber occurs infrequently, can erupt in all societies, regardless of the dominant type of authority. The intense conviction of followers that the leader possesses special gifts or talents supports the charismatic leader. Charismatic authority creates radical change in a society or organization. The type of change can be positive or in some cases—for example, authoritarian political figures such as Hitler—extremely negative.

Charismatic leadership is the most appropriate type for leaders in developing countries because their primary need is social change (Kanungo and Mendonca 1996). Other types of leadership—for example, those that encourage employee participation—seek to maintain society and organizations or help them adjust gradually to changing circumstances. These types of leadership are more appropriate for developed nations with established institutions and organizations.

> **Charismatic leadership is the most appropriate type for leaders in developing countries because their primary need is social change.**

Although it is possible to characterize a society as having a predominant type of authority structure, there are often multiple sources of leadership legitimacy. For example, in the United States and other societies with advanced economies, it is common practice that an organization's leaders, along with all other employees, are subject to rationally constructed rules. These include codified personnel policies, financial practices, and organizational structure. But, at the same time, in the United States as in developing countries, many family-owned and-operated businesses use a form of traditional authority. For example, in a family business, instead of selecting personnel on qualifications—a rational method—personal characteristics such as family membership are more important. In Trompenaars' cultural framework this is the difference between achievement and ascription.

Finally, charismatic leaders emerge periodically in both rational and traditional organizational settings. Charismatic leaders break established patterns, creating dramatic departures from "business as usual." For example, according to many observers, Lee Iacocca rescued the Chrysler Corporation from bankruptcy by persuading the United States government to guarantee loans to the failing corporation. This was a radical departure from past practice as was Iacocca's close identification with the fate of Chrysler.

▌▌▌ LEADERSHIP AND ETHICS

Legitimate leadership is moral. Leaders, like occupants of other social roles, represent themselves to others as being sincere. In modern societies, of course, leaders often use impression management to present themselves in a more positive way than might actually be the reality.

> **Legitimate leadership is moral.**

Leaders set the moral and ethical standards for an organization. If they are not what they claim and discrepancies between their intentions and actions are substantial, organization members are likely to challenge their authority. Because this has become fairly common, many leaders find their legitimacy challenged and need to reestablish their authority continually. Being elected Prime Minister of England is one thing; maintaining the authority to exercise power in the role is another.

Rational authority has less of an ethical obligation than does traditional and charismatic authority, but leadership based on rational authority nonetheless has legal and ethical requirements to meet. Unlike traditional and charismatic authority, it does not uphold long-established traditions that preserve a culture's way of life or provoke social change that creates significant uncertainty. Rational authority derives legitimacy from efficient administration that distills ethical and moral issues into rules. It is ethical when it enforces rules and does not disobey laws. (In Chapter 3 we discuss ethics in detail.)

▮▮▮ TRANSFORMATIONAL LEADERSHIP

A concept related to charismatic authority is **transformational leadership** (Burns 1978). Transformational leadership is a type of leadership more commonly found than charisma, especially in contemporary business organizations. The transformational leader acts as a teacher, role model, and inspirational figure to create conditions under which subordinates enthusiastically contribute to the organization (Bass 1985). In addition, transformational leaders focus on the nonroutine aspects of an organization, including establishing a vision for the organization's future, making decisions with long-term consequences, creating an organizational culture, and initiating and managing change (Kotter 1990).

In societies in which there is high power distance between authority figures and subordinates, the use of transformational leadership faces limitations. Leader and follower expectations and behaviors are different. The assumptions of these cultures do not promote intermingling of leadership and subordinate roles. Under such circumstances, a leader empowering subordinates, rather than directing them, is unlikely.

▮▮▮ LEADERSHIP AND MEANING

An important element of leadership, particularly charismatic and transformational, is that leaders create **symbolic meaning systems** for organizational participants (Trice and Beyer 1993). A meaning system is constructed of selective interpretations of societal and organization traditions, customs, rituals, and artifacts that contribute to organizational culture. The leader interprets and shapes the larger culture to the needs of the organization. Its products are particular ways of doing things in organizations in different cultures and a distinctive organizational identity.

A meaning system creates *the* Japanese, *the* British, and *the* South African way of doing things. It also produces the specific identity of a corporation within a national culture. For example, the meaning system embodied in organizational culture distinguishes NEC from Sony in Japan, IBM from Apple in the United States, and BMW from Daimler-Benz in Germany.

The Culture at Work vignette is an example of a single act that captures the meaning of leadership in a particular culture and organizational setting. Agricultural labor in Central America requires toughness and courage. The leader created legitimacy by confronting worker disobedience directly with the possibility of physical harm. A single act symbolized the qualities of a leader and core value of the organizational culture. Even in a culture that views leadership as a display of machismo, not everyone is willing to risk bodily harm to establish his credentials. But a successful leader does and reinforces the values of the larger culture and the organization.

▮▮▮ A CONTINGENCY APPROACH TO CROSS-CULTURAL LEADERSHIP

Another way to understand leadership is the contingency approach. Contingency theory posits that there are multiple leadership styles that depend on variables such as follower characteristics, the position power of the leader, and the type of task to be accomplished. This differs from a strategy identifying "one best way" for leading an organization or group, the objective of early leadership research such as

McGregor's Theory X and Theory Y and, to some extent, Weber's legitimacy typology and the transformational approach.

The **international contingency model of leadership** (Kreitner 1995) uses national culture as the contingent variable. The reasoning supporting the model, which provides general guidelines for international managers, not a scientific theory, is that different leadership styles fit various national cultures.

This model incorporates the **path-goal** model of leadership. The path-goal model attempts to explain how the behavior of a leader influences the satisfaction and performance of subordinates dependent on aspects of a situation. The task of leadership is to strengthen subordinates' perception of the ties among effort, performance, and desired outcomes. To do this a leader should adapt her style to various situations. The four leadership behaviors follow (House and Mitchell 1974):

1. **Directive leadership**: Letting subordinates know what they are expected to do, giving specific guidance, asking subordinates to follow rules and procedures, scheduling and coordinating work;

2. **Supportive leadership**: Giving consideration to the needs of subordinates, displaying concern for their welfare, and creating a friendly climate in the work unit;

3. **Participative leadership**: Consulting with subordinates and taking their opinions and suggestions into account;

4. **Achievement-oriented leadership**: Setting challenging goals, seeking performance improvements, emphasizing excellence in performance, and showing confidence that subordinates will attain high standards.

In the international contingency model (Table 9-1), participative leadership is the most broadly applicable style because it is the most culturally acceptable

T a b l e 9 - 1   International Contingency Model of Leadership: Culturally Appropriate Path-Goal Leadership Styles

Country	Directive	Supportive	Participative	Achievement-Oriented
Australia		x	x	x
Brazil	x		x	
Canada		x	x	x
France	x		x	
Germany		x	x	x
Great Britain		x	x	x
Hong Kong	x	x	x	x
India	x		x	x
Italy	x	x	x	
Philippines	x	x	x	x
Sweden			x	x
Taiwan	x	x	x	x
United States		x	x	x

Source: Kreitner, R. (1995), *Management*, 6th Ed. Boston: Houghton Mifflin, pp. 613–14. Kreitner's sources are Rodrigues, C.A. (1990), "The Situation and National Culture as Contingencies for Leadership Behavior: Two Conceptual Models," in Prasad S.B. (ed.) *Advances in International Comparative Management*. (Greenwich, CJ: JAI Press pp. 51–68; and Hofstede, G. and Bond, M.H. (1988), "The Confucius Connection: From Cultural Roots to Economic Growth," *Organizational Dynamics* (Spring), pp. 4–21.

style in the countries listed. Directive leadership is the least appropriate leadership style.

One criticism of the model is that it "underestimates the appropriateness of the directive leadership style in many situations in certain countries" and that "many directive (authoritarian) leaders achieve good result without damaging morale" (DuBrin 1995, p. 292).

According to the model, "Hong Kong and the Philippines, probably because of their rich cultural diversity, are unique in their receptiveness to all four leadership styles" (Kreitner 1995, p. 613). A counter argument is that Hong Kong accepts diversity not because of its cultural composition but because of the pragmatism of its dynamic capitalist economy.

Despite limitations, this model is a beginning for understanding the influence of culture on leadership. A more comprehensive contingency theory would account for additional factors such as the political culture of a society, the relationship between labor and management, and different production technologies. It would also rely more on empirical studies of levels of worker participation in different cultures (see Pavett and Morris 1995). To illustrate further the importance of culture as a variable affecting leadership, in the next section we describe typical leadership patterns in two cultures.

Leadership in Two Cultures

Overseas Chinese cultures, in which age and family relationships are of central importance for leadership, illustrate leadership and organization based on a mixture of cultural traditions and contemporary business practices. Leadership in France provides a portrait of a culture in which there is interaction between traditional and rational authority.

OVERSEAS CHINESE LEADERSHIP

In Chinese culture, the legitimacy of a leader is patrimonial loyalty. According to Weber's typology, this is a traditional form of authority. Peter Drucker (1994, p. 20), writing about the business activities of overseas Chinese (ethnic Chinese living outside Mainland China), captures the essence of this leadership style:

> Outwardly, these new multinational groups look exactly like other businesses. But they function drastically differently, as a clan. The Japanese, it has often been said, owe their success to their ability to run the modern corporation as a family. The overseas Chinese owe their success to their ability to run their family as a modern corporation.
>
> All the plant managers in the Manila group [a branch of a multinational corporation], for example, are related to the founder—and to each other—by blood or marriage. "We wouldn't dream of going into a new business," the chief operating officer told me, "if we did not have a relative available to run it." He, himself, is Dutch, but he is married to the founder's niece. When he joined the group the founder said to him: "I don't care how many concubines or mistresses you have. But on the day on which my niece and you separate or file for divorce you can look for another job."
>
> The word of the founder-CEO is law. But his authority far more resembles that of a Confucian head of the house (or Scottish Highland chieftain of yore) than that of the head of a business. He is expected to base his decisions on the best interests of the clan and to manage so as to guarantee the clan's survival and prosperity. What holds the multinationals together is neither ownership nor legal contract. It is mutual trust and the mutual obligations inherent in clan membership.

Traditional cultures are slow to change, and continuity with the past is a central value. The overseas Chinese leadership style reflects this in the form of patriarchy in modern global organizations.

▌▌▌ FRENCH ADMINISTRATIVE LEADERSHIP

The French, like the overseas Chinese, accept unequal distribution of power and centralization of decision making. Another theme in French organizational life is an emphasis on uncertainty avoidance. The general setting of business is one in which "familial relationships are . . . very much in evidence, specifically paternalistic ones" (Sorge 1993, p. 69). At the same time, another element found in France is a fairly strong belief in individualism that creates a "constant tension between the demand for strong authority, and individualistic assertion against it" (Sorge 1993, p. 71).

Embedded in formal organizations are characteristics that protect individuality through conformity with rules and regulations. "Whereas the Anglo-Saxon individualist tries to do his or her 'own thing' and considers hierarchy a dirty word, the French individualist tries to achieve a perfection within a protective niche provided by a stable organization" (Sorge 1993, p. 72). In other words, French culture, which highly values equality, is consistent with bureaucratic rationality.

Comparative studies of European organizations have found that French organizations usually have more levels of hierarchy, along with more lateral segmentation into departments and work groups. Also, staff and line responsibilities are clearer in France than they are in Britain or Germany. Directly concerning leadership,

> the hierarchy is more top-heavy in France, with between 1½ and 2 times as many supervisors and managers as in German organizations. The lowest level of the industrial production hierarchy is more separate from the workers, enjoys more disciplinary authority, and is counted among the white-collar employees, whereas the equivalent in Germany has blue-collar status and less disciplinary authority. Spans of control at different levels in France are usually smaller, indicating the possibility of tighter supervision (Sorge 1993, p. 75).

Compared with German organizations, there are also more nonmanagerial white-collar specialists in either administrative or technical functions. This proliferation of roles, along with written rules, instructions, and communications, is the result of the high uncertainty avoidance orientation of the French.

At the top of the hierarchy is the chairman of the board. The chairman's leadership style is typically "paternalistic and charismatic, in the manner of the great generals and field marshals" (Sorge 1993, p. 78). Between the top leaders and the workers is a large group of managers or *cadres*. Although this system does result in certain inefficiencies, it provides reliable uniformity of operation, not a pathological bureaucracy.

▌▌▌ OBSERVATIONS ON TWO CULTURES

The overseas Chinese and French, as with most cultures, are not easy to compare. Nevertheless, they both have a paternalistic form of leadership, a traditional basis of legitimacy found in many societies.

There is a significant difference, however. Whereas Chinese culture retains traditional male forms of leadership coupled with familialism, the French have developed a merit system for employment within bureaucracies, rather than relying on age or kinship.

This variation reflects a different cultural heritage. The French pattern develops from the nation-building, revolutionary ideas of the eighteenth century, particularly the ideals of fraternity and equality. The overseas Chinese leadership style retains traditional male control over institutions that characterized the dynastic regimes throughout China's history.

Women as Leaders

The role of women in various societies forcefully illustrates cultural differences in leadership. Cultures vary in their encouragement of women's participation in the workplace and particularly willingness to have women in authority positions. Of course, attitudes toward women and the opportunities provided them, are complementary to the role of men and the type of leadership they prefer. The leadership roles of women—or lack thereof—also illustrate problems encountered in the transition from traditional to rational leadership.

In this discussion we present women's managerial status in Japan, Poland, and Tanzania. These countries present issues of particular interest in the current global context. Japan is an industrialized nation with a capitalistic economy that retains traditional views toward women. Poland exemplifies issues facing former communist countries, particularly their attempts to develop new ideologies, values, attitudes, and behaviors. Finally, Tanzania is representative of the struggles developing nations confront in the modernization process, including extreme forms of institutionalized gender inequality.

> **C**ultures vary in their encouragement of women's participation in the workplace and particularly willingness to have women in authority positions.

▌▌▌ JAPAN

Japanese managerial techniques have become an area of intense scrutiny by American (Ouchi 1981) and British (Oliver and Wilkinson 1992) businesspeople and management scholars. This interest arose because of Japan's success in the production of high-quality manufactured goods—notably consumer electronics and automobiles—that have severely challenged American and British products. What role have women played in the emergence of Japan as an industrial power?

Until recently, women played almost no role in the management of Japanese companies. Although highly educated, the expectation was that they would work for a few years after high school, then marry, raise a family, and return to the labor force as part-time workers. Among the cultural factors that created this pattern is that women did not attend elite universities or major in disciplines such as engineering, law, or business and the permanent employment system in large firms favored investment in the training of men. Also, Japanese men view a nonworking wife as a status symbol, and large corporations require long work hours and participation in business-related social activities after work, making it difficult for women to have both management careers and fulfill traditional family obligations successfully.

There are few women managers in large Japanese corporations and the public sector. Data suggest, however, that, "the smaller the firm, the greater the presence of women in management" (Steinhoff and Tanaka 1994, p. 87). In Japan only 1% of businesses are classified as large, whereas 99% are medium or small and employ 81% of the private sector employees. Many of these firms have women presidents, including women's and children's clothing stores, real estate rental agencies, retail kimono stores, road construction firms, and restaurants. This suggests that there is a dual economy: a large-scale industrial and service sector dominated by men and a small-scale personal service sector managed by women. Japanese women managers are also successful in foreign corporations located in Japan, where there are different views on gender equality.

The prospects for women managers in large companies appear to be increasing but not rapidly. Attitudes toward the hiring and promotion of women are improving, and it appears that male employees in large companies are becoming more accepting of women managers. More important, however, for accelerating women into major companies, is a projected labor shortage due to low birthrates. In other words, perhaps more than cultural change, the educational requirements of workers in an advanced economy, coupled with population decline, could open managerial positions in large corporations to women.

▐▌▌ POLAND

An important issue for Poland is the changes in its economy and society in the postcommunist era. Under communism, women experienced significant barriers to advancement into management. After World War II, a primary consideration for leadership within the communist party was loyalty rather than education or skills. Because they had not been members of the communist party, fought in the war, or participated in the resistance movement, few women qualified for leadership positions. When the political situation stabilized in the late 1940s, leader selection criteria shifted to professional qualifications. Women were vastly underrepresented again because the pool of leaders came from those already selected—loyal communists—who had the opportunity to acquire the new skills needed for advancement.

From 1950 to 1955, during Stalin's regime, there were more favorable conditions for women, particularly an ideological emphasis on social equality, communist control of politics, and a shortage of male labor. During this time, 22% of the total leaders promoted were women. Fewer women became leaders in the 1960s because of economic stagnation, and in the 1970s female leadership declined further and continued to decline in the 1980s. Siemienska (1994, p. 245) writes:

> In other words, at any given time the political and economic interests of the Communist party, in large measure, determined the vicissitudes of women's promotion opportunities. In practice, Poles had no commitment to gender equality; and, as resistance to the party grew, women's opportunities declined. At times of political struggle, the number of women in local leadership decreased. Party survival, and not representation, was the key concern of politicians. The lowest number of women (3 percent) promoted to managerial and supervisory positions at local levels was in 1982, the first year after the imposition of martial law.[1]

In addition, the occupational structure that communism produced was highly gender segregated. In 1989, women accounted for between 71% and 84% of finance, insurance, education, culture, art, and trade positions. Also, during the communist period, women were essentially absent at the highest administrative levels of government but were well represented in managerial positions in the judiciary and education, despite communist gender-neutral ideology.

In the early 1980s, there was a political crisis in Poland and lack of faith in existing institutions. Martial law, instituted in 1981, further increased discontent. The independent trade union, Solidarity, had about 10 million members at this time. By the end of the 1980s, Poland's economic system was in disarray, and there were widespread strikes. Lech Walesa, the leader of the illegal Solidarity Union, and the Catholic church intervened. Solidarity was legalized in 1989 and partially free elec-

---

[1]Excerpt from "Women Managers in Poland: In Transition from Communism to Democracy" from *Competitive Frontiers: Women Managers in a Global Economy*, p. 245 by R. Siemienska. Reprinted by permission of Blackwell Publishers.

tions for Parliament took place in June 1989. The election was a victory for Solidarity's candidates and led to the creation of a coalition government.

The Communist party dissolved, and in May 1990 Poland experienced its first free elections in the postwar era. These events increased political and economic reforms intended to change from totalitarianism to democracy and from a centrally planned economy to a market oriented economy.

However, "the change in the political system did not improve the political status of women" (Siemienska 1994, p. 225). In addition, "the Catholic church, which has always played a powerful role in Poland and which emerged from Communist rule as a central power, is a major force in the current move to return women to more traditional roles as full-time homemakers and mothers" (Siemienska 1994, p. 256).

In terms of employment, after communism, women confronted a job market that mainly required manual labor. Women were roughly 52% of the unemployed in the early 1990s. Siemienska (1994, p. 256) concludes, "the new period of greater political democracy and the move to a freer market economy struck a damaging blow to women's political and economic positions."

TANZANIA

Tanzania, a former British colony, is on the coast of East Africa. It is a predominately agricultural society, with 86% of the population employed in agriculture in 1980. Of the population of 23 million, 51% are women, and there are more than 120 ethnic groups with one national language. With an annual per capita income of approximately US$280, Tanzania is among the poorest countries in the world.

There is substantial inequality between men and women with regard to education and employment. Considerably more women than men are illiterate and are more likely to drop out of school because of family demands for their labor.

Since 1967, the socialist government has attempted several times to modernize the industrial base of the country but failed. For example, the government enacted legislation aimed at eliminating discrimination against women in employment. However, these programs and policies have had little impact on the structure of employment for women.

There have been recent efforts to identify and develop women managers. A government-sponsored institute, which covers southern Africa, organized workshops, research, and training for women managers. Women who become managers after graduation from a university usually enter the public sector in education, health, or personnel management. In Tanzania, senior civil service posts require presidential appointment, and "very few women surmount this barrier. The few who qualify are rarely selected" (Hollway and Mukurasi 1994, p. 346).

In Tanzania the relationship between marriage partners is one of extreme inequality; men have nearly total control over their wives' domestic and occupational roles. The relationship between spouses is based on

> patriarchal authority [that] is a complex product of cultural practices that predate colonial domination and the effect of first Muslim and then Christian influences. It seems that the strong patriarchal tradition which gives men control over their wives and daughters transcends the effects of religious differences on gender relations in Tanzania (Hollway and Mukurasi 1994, p. 348).

Sexual harassment in the workplace is common in Tanzania. This puts women in a double bind. On one hand, their husbands are extremely possessive, jealous, and powerful. On the other hand, male superiors routinely engage in sexual harassment. Moreover, success in the workplace provokes rumors that a woman slept with a man in a powerful position. There is some evidence that if a woman is married to a high-status male, there is less sexual harassment. But generally,

> women have authority within the organization, based on expertise and position; men, however, still tend to relate to women first as women—that is, as inferior. This dilemma produces the common situation in which women managers find their formal authority undermined (Hollway and Mukurasi 1994, p. 350).

Convergence or Divergence?

Are there cultural trends and business issues common among nations creating pressures for one style of leadership in organizations? Or will various types of leadership continue and multiply as more cultures participate in global commerce? Will global organizations impose their leadership style throughout their operations, adapt to local preferences, or develop new styles of leadership?

FORCES FOR CONVERGENCE

The primary force for change toward a universal leader style is global corporations. General Electric (GE) illustrates the impact that a global organization can have on changing leadership in other cultures.

To restructure from an international to a global corporation, GE's Chairman, Jack Welch, a transformational leader, initiated an extensive organizational change process to revolutionize the way GE does business. "A primary motivation for GE's transformation is the need for speed" (Tichy and Sherman 1993, p. 20–21) which requires new types of leadership based on this philosophy:

> Until employees accept personal responsibility for their work, they need supervision, which Welch regards as a waste of time. So whenever possible, GE tries to eliminate supervisory positions, giving people more power to control their own work. Such responsibility can transform the relationship of workers to their employer: Instead of behaving like children who follow their parents' orders, employees interact with their bosses as adults and peers (Tichy and Sherman 1993, p. 21).

For leadership of its global operations, GE's strategy is to develop executives with "global brains" who have "the ability to understand and respect the national and ethnic biases of others, and to feel comfortable anywhere in the world" (Tichy and Sherman 1993, p. 227). Because of its success, the GE philosophy of leadership is likely to diffuse to other global corporations.

FORCES FOR DIVERGENCE

A force for divergence is resistance of national cultures to new styles of leadership. An example is Bernard Liautaud, a 34-year-old French entrepreneur with an MBA from Stanford University, who started a software company modeled after the Silicon Valley, California way of running a business. In 1990 the company began with $1 million venture capital and by late 1996 the company was worth almost $1 billion. This extraordinary growth was uncharacteristic in France.

Liautaud, who became a highly visible businessman, told the president of France that the key to business success was to "promote a shareholding culture: Think global, think marketing, reduce taxes" (Cohen 1997, p. 1). But the president made no changes to the heavily regulated economy. When Liautaud's company's "shares fell recently because of delays in a new software program, there were some smug 'I told you so's' from the Paris establishment" (Cohen 1997, p. 1).

Liautaud transplanted a new leadership style to his own company, but to many in France, global entrepreneurship is a threat to the economy and national identity of France, and the French are seeking to retain traditional leadership styles.

Implications for Managers

Understanding leadership is important for managers, even if not at the executive level, because managers perform leadership functions (Sayles 1993). Culture influences the legitimacy of a leader or manager. Certain types of cultures accept a particular leadership style—for example, paternalism—that other cultures either reject or accept with difficulty. In a cross-cultural situation, a manager has the choice of either imposing a leadership style on subordinates with different cultures or adapting her leadership style to the expectations of the culture. It is possible that the culture of a country is so different from a leader's own culture that neither option is viable. Under conditions in which cultural differences are extensive, it may be more effective to use indigenous managers rather than those from a corporate headquarters whose culture does not fit the situation. It is important for managers to assess cultures other than their own carefully to determine those aspects they can change in a particular situation and which are immutable.

A final implication is that when a considerable amount of organizational change is desirable, either a charismatic or transformational leadership style is appropriate. This type of leadership is useful in developing countries, even if inconsistent with cultural preferences.

Summary

The role of leadership in an organization is complex. *Leadership* has many definitions because it has multiple meanings to members of organizations. Also, the meaning of leadership varies across cultures. Basically, however, leadership involves power distance that varies with national culture and political culture.

Most leadership theories developed in the United States have limitations when applied to other cultures. McGregor's Theory X and Theory Y illustrate these limitations but also suggest that the research questions asked by American scholars have applicability to various cultures. Weber's typology of traditional, charismatic, and rational authority provides a set of concepts for examining leadership across cultures, as does contingency theory.

The major patterns of leadership in two societies illustrate Weber's typology and contingency theory. In overseas Chinese societies traditional patriarchal leadership patterns combine with familialism. French leadership is also patriarchal but relies less on kin relations and extensively on bureaucratic principles.

The situation of women as leaders in three societies illustrates the role of culture on leadership. In Japan, few women occupy leadership positions in major companies, but women do run many small companies. In Poland, women face obstacles to leadership even after the demise of communism because of the ideological position of the Catholic church and a major need for manual labor in the current labor market. Finally, in Tanzania, women confront the dual cultural issues of husbands who would prefer to have their wives at home and institutionalized sexual harassment at work.

Forces for convergence are the spread of leadership styles of multinational and global organizations. Forces for divergence include attempts to preserve culturally specific leadership styles. International managers must understand leadership because they often perform leadership functions, even at nonexecutive levels. Knowing which leadership approaches are appropriate in different situations helps a manager to become more effective.

■ Discussion Questions

1. Why is leadership important for organizations?
2. In what ways does culture affect leadership?
3. What are some of the limitations of American leadership theories for understanding cross-cultural leadership?
4. Why is the concept of legitimacy important for understanding leadership?
5. What are some of the contributions of charismatic and transformational leaders to organizations?
6. What are the main components of a contingency approach to leadership? What are its weaknesses?
7. What role does ethics play in effective leadership?
8. What leadership behavior should an international manager use in a culture different than her own?
9. Discuss leaders with whom you are familiar from two different cultures. How does culture effect their leadership style?

References

BASS, B. (1990), *Bass & Stogdill's Handbook of Leadership: Theory, Research, and Managerial Application*, 3rd Ed. New York: The Free Press.

——. (1985), *Leadership and Performance Beyond Expectations*. New York: The Free Press.

BLUNT, P., JONES, M., and RICHARDS, D. (eds.) (1993), *Managing Organisations in Africa: Readings, Cases, and Exercises*. New York: Walter de Gruyter.

BRISCOE, D. (1995), *International Human Resource Management*. Upper Saddle River, NJ: Prentice Hall.

BURNS, (1978), *Leadership*. New York: Harper & Row.

COHEN, R. (1997), "For France, Sagging Self-Image and Esprit," *The New York Times* (February 11), 1 & 6.

DORFMAN, P. (1996), "International and Cross-Cultural Leadership," in Punnett, B. and Shenkar, O. (eds.) *Handbook for International Management Research*. Cambridge, MA: Blackwell Publishers.

DRUCKER, P. (1994), "The New Superpower: The Overseas Chinese," *The Wall Street Journal* (December 20), 17.

DUBRIN, A. (1995), *Leadership: Research Findings, Practice, and Skills*. Boston: Houghton Mifflin.

GUILLEN, M. (1994), *Models of Management: Work, Authority, and Organization in a Comparative Perspective*. Chicago: University of Chicago Press.

GUMBEL, P. and CHOI, A. (1995), "Germany Making Comeback, with Daimler in the Lead," *The Wall Street Journal* (April 7), A10.

HOFSTEDE, G. (1984), *Culture's Consequences: International Differences in Work-Related Values*. Newbury Park, CA: Sage Publications.

HOLLWAY, W. and MUKURASI, L. (1994), "Women Managers in the Tanzanian Civil Service," in Adler, N. and Izraeli, D., (eds.), *Competitive Frontiers: Women Managers in a Global Economy*. Cambridge, MA: Blackwell.

HOUSE, R.J. and MITCHELL, T.R. (1974), "Path-Goal Theory of Leadership," *Contemporary Business*, 3 (Fall), 81–98.

KANONJO, K. and MENDONCA, M. (1996), "Cultural Contingencies and Leadership in Developing Countries," in Bamberger, P. and Erez, M. (eds.), *Research in the Sociology of Organizations: Cross-Cultural Analysis of Organization.* Greenwich, CT: JAI Press.

KATZ, D. and KAHN, R. (1978), *The Social Psychology of Organizations,* 2d. Ed. New York: John Wiley & Sons.

KOTTER, J. (1990), *A Force For Change: How Leadership Differs From Management.* New York: The Free Press.

KREITNER, R. (1995) *Management,* 6th Ed. Boston: Houghton Mifflin.

MCGREGOR, D. (1960), *The Human Side of Enterprise.* New York: McGraw-Hill.

MERTON, R. (1970), "The Ambivalence of Organizational Leaders," in Oates, J., Jr. (ed.) *The Contradictions of Leadership.* New York: Appleton-Crofts.

NORTHCRAFT, G. and NEALE, M. (1994), *Organizational Behavior: A Management Challenge,* 2d Ed. Fort Worth, TX: The Dryden Press.

OLIVER, N. and WILKINSON, B. (1992), *The Japanization of British Industry: New Developments in the 1990s,* 2d Ed. Oxford: Blackwell.

OUCHI, W. (1981), *Theory Z: How American Business Can Meet The Japanese Challenge.* New York: Avon Books.

PAVETT, C. and MORRIS, T. (1995), "Management Styles Within a Multinational Corporation: A Five Country Comparative Study," *Human Relations,* 48(10), 1171–190.

PERROW, C. (1986), *Complex Organizations: A Critical Essay,* 3rd Ed. New York: Random House.

SAYLES, L. (1993), *The Working Leader: The Triumph of High Performance Over Conventional Management Principles.* New York: The Free Press.

SCHEIN, E. (1985), *Organizational Culture and Leadership.* San Francisco: Jossey-Bass.

SIEMIENSKA, R. (1994), "Women Managers in Poland: In Transition from Communism to Democracy," in Adler, N. and Izraeli, D. (eds.), *Competitive Frontiers: Women Managers in a Global Economy.* Cambridge, MA: Blackwell.

SORGE, A. (1993), "Management in France," in Hickson, D. (ed.), *Management in Western Europe: Society, Culture, and Organization in Twelve Nations.* New York: Walter de Gruyter, 65–87.

STEINHOFF, P. and TANAKA, K. (1994), "Women Managers in Japan," in Adler, N. and Izraeli, D. (eds.), *Competitive Frontiers: Women Managers in a Global Economy.* Cambridge, MA: Blackwell.

TICHY, N. and SHERMAN, S. (1993), *Control Your Destiny or Someone Else Will: Lessons in Mastering Change—The Principles Jack Welch is Using to Revolutionize General Electric.* New York: Harper Collins.

TRICE, H. and BEYER, J. (1993), *The Cultures of Work Organizations.* Upper Saddle River, NJ: Prentice Hall.

WEBER, M. (1947), *The Theory of Social and Economic Organization.* New York: The Free Press.

WESTWOOD, R. and CHAN, A. (1992), "Headship and Leadership," in Westwood, R. (ed.), *Organisational Behavior: Southeast Asian Perspectives.* Hong Kong: Longman.

YUKL, G. (1994), *Leadership in Organizations,* 3d Ed. Upper Saddle River, NJ: Prentice Hall.

International Human Resource Management

HRM Japanese Style

Large Japanese companies—Sony, Hitachi, Sumitomo—hire a group of new employees each year. These employees, blue-collar recruits from high schools and managers from universities, form a cohort in the company for 15 years. Many even live together in a company dormitory. To further intensify the meaning of the company and its role in their lives, managers encourage employees to marry co-workers.

Employees view their jobs as supporting their managers and work groups. To encourage this, workers rotate among departments to learn overall company operations. This increases loyalty to the organization. These human resource practices occur in an environment where career development is long term and employees spend their entire lives working for one employer.

Source: Dillon, L.S. (1990), "The Occidental Tourist," *Training and Development Journal*, 44, 72–80.

After reading this chapter, you should be able to:

1. Define international human resource management (IHRM).

2. Understand how corporate strategy influences IHRM.

3. Explain the major IHRM functions: recruitment and selection, training and development, performance evaluation, compensation and benefits, and labor relations.

4. Discuss additional concerns of managing expatriate employees.

Organizations have different approaches to managing employees. How they find employees, pay, train, and promote them varies with culture. These issues are more complex when companies are global because they usually attempt to treat their employees equitably, yet in a culturally appropriate manner. In addition, organizations often send employees to assignments outside their home countries, creating special concerns for the organization and employee.

The Culture at Work vignette describes a culture that values close links between the lives of employees and employer. Employees enter as a group, remain together, often marry each other, and spend entire careers in the same organization. These practices, which create loyalty and stability, reflect the collective, strong uncertainty avoidance, future-oriented Japanese culture. Of course, not all cultures and organizations use these same practices. How cultures and organizations in them treat employees is the focus of international human resource management.

What Is International Human Resource Management?

The field of **international human resource management (IHRM)** includes three major areas:

1. the management of human resources in global corporations
2. the management of expatriate employees
3. the comparison of human resource management (HRM) practices in a variety of different countries.

HRM is responsible for all aspects of employee administration. This includes recruiting and selecting employees, providing orientation and training, evaluating performance, administering a compensation system, and handling other aspects of labor relations. IHRM takes care of these functions as well as additional ones. When an organization operates in different countries, employing citizens of different nationalities, there are greater complexities involved (Dowling, Schuler, and Welch 1994).

A major part of IHRM is managing **expatriates**, employees who work outside their home countries. The company takes greater responsibility for expatriates than it does for domestic workers because it asks them to work outside their home countries. International human resource (IHR) managers might help prepare expatriates to live in another country, find them housing, or arrange for the company to pay their taxes.

In the Netherlands, companies must pay employees who lose their jobs unemployment benefits equal to 70 percent of their salaries for up to two and one half years.

When managing human resources, a global organization considers whether to take a consistent approach across countries, to handle each country as unique, or something in between. Factors influencing this decision are corporate strategy, the mix of countries where subsidiaries are located, and laws affecting HRM practices in these countries. The IHR manager must be familiar with local HRM laws and practices in order to make the correct decision.

HRM laws, regulations, and practices can influence a company's decision on where to locate a subsidiary. Prevailing wage rates, employee benefits required by law, and ease of dismissing employees can make one country more attractive than another. For example, in the

Netherlands, companies must pay employees who lose their jobs unemployment benefits equal to 70 percent of their salaries for up to two and one half years (Wiersma 1996). These are very generous benefits—and expensive for multinational corporations—compared with unemployment benefits in other countries.

International Corporate Strategy and IHRM

The approach to IHRM often reflects an organization's international corporate strategy. IHR managers participate in the international strategic planning process, but usually in a limited way (Bird and Beechler 1995; Briscoe 1995; Miller et al. 1986). However, "HR managers can and should provide essential advice and input at every step of the traditional strategic management process" (Briscoe 1995, p. 33). A more effective strategy results if a broader range of organizational units participates in its development. Regardless of the extent of their involvement in developing international corporate strategy, IHR managers are influenced by it. An organization's overall corporate strategy usually determines the approach to managing and staffing subsidiaries.

APPROACHES TO MANAGING AND STAFFING SUBSIDIARIES

There are four major approaches to managing and staffing subsidiaries (Dowling, Schuler, and Welch 1994; Phatak 1995). These reflect how the organization develops its human resource policies and the preferred type of employee for different positions. They are as follows:

1. **Ethnocentric.** The home country approach prevails. Headquarters makes key decisions, employees from the home country hold important jobs, and the subsidiaries follow home country HRM practices.

2. **Polycentric.** Each subsidiary manages on a local basis. A local employee heads a subsidiary, because headquarters managers are not considered to have adequate local knowledge, but promotion from a foreign subsidiary to headquarters is rare. Subsidiaries usually develop HRM practices locally.

3. **Regiocentric.** This is similar to the polycentric approach, but regional groups of subsidiaries reflecting the organization's strategy and structure function as a unit. There is some degree of autonomy in regional decision making, and promotions are possible within the region but rare from the region to headquarters. Subsidiaries within a region develop a common set of HRM practices.

4. **Geocentric or global.** Using a worldwide integrated business strategy, the organization manages and staffs on a global basis. Nationality is not a major factor in promotion decisions. HRM practices develop with input from headquarters and subsidiaries and are generally consistent across locations.

In the ethnocentric approach, the cultural values and business practices of the home country are predominant. Headquarters develops a managing and staffing approach and consistently applies it throughout the world. Companies following the ethnocentric approach assume the home country approach is best and that employees from other parts of the world can and should follow it. Managers from headquarters develop practices and hold key positions in the subsidiaries to ensure consistency.

The polycentric approach is in direct opposition. The assumption is that each country is different and that the subsidiaries in each country should develop locally appropriate practices under the supervision of local managers. The regiocentric approach is similar except that the "local" unit is a region rather than a country.

With the geocentric approach, organizations try to combine the best from headquarters and the subsidiaries to develop consistent worldwide practices. Manager selection is based on competency rather than nationality.

Organizations taking either an ethnocentric or geocentric approach have fairly consistent practices worldwide. Those taking a polycentric or regiocentric approach have variation in practice based on location.

CHOOSING AN APPROACH TO IHRM

Overall international corporate strategy determines the choice of the four approaches to IHRM. However, the following five factors also influence the approach to IHRM (Fisher, Schoenfeldt, and Shaw 1993):

1. **Political and legal concerns.** A subsidiary in a foreign country is subject to local law. Some laws directly affect HRM policy. For example, some countries limit the number of expatriates a foreign company may employ, precluding an ethnocentric approach. In other countries, foreign companies qualify for tax incentives if they hire and provide training for locals. This may predispose the company towards a polycentric approach.

2. **Level of development in foreign locations.** Some locations may lack adequate numbers of local people with appropriate levels of managerial and technical skills, requiring an organization to bring in expatriates. This makes an ethnocentric approach more likely. The availability of a talented workforce enables a company to select any approach.

3. **Technology and the nature of the product.** This factor relates to the two previous items. With the use of highly sophisticated manufacturing technology or the need for high-quality standards, headquarters employees help ensure consistency, thereby necessitating an ethnocentric approach. Modifying the basic product to appeal to local or regional markets calls for managers who know the local situation. Here, a polycentric or regiocentric approach makes more sense.

4. **Organizational life cycle.** The organization's stage of internationalization or the product's stage in the life cycle can influence the approach to IHRM. For example, when an organization first ventures into international business, if often takes an ethnocentric approach. As the organization expands internationally, subsidiaries could be treated as additions to the corporation and managed by locals, a polycentric approach. As the firm continues to grow, increased productivity and cost control become more important. At this stage, the company could take a regiocentric or geocentric approach. In the final stage, the company views its operations as global. At this point, the approach to HRM should be global as well.

5. **Cultural differences.** The cultures of the headquarters and subsidiaries influence the approach. In some countries the locals prefer the ethnocentric approach. For example, the Japanese are more likely than either Americans or Europeans to use headquarters managers in subsidiaries (Tung 1988). A second issue is the number and makeup of cultures in foreign subsidiaries. If the number and extent of cultural differences among the subsidiaries become too great, instituting a geocentric policy may be difficult.

Choosing an approach to IHRM is complex. If an organization integrates human resources practices into its overall strategy, it is likely to be more successful. However, "previous empirical research has tended to show that of all functions, human resource management tends more closely to adhere to local practices." (Rosenzweig and Nohria 1994, p. 231). American management researchers consider consistency between corporate level strategy and the HR practices of subsidiaries to be important (Bird and Beechler 1995). In contrast, Europeans emphasize the strategic role of HRM less. European HR managers may have to follow the dictates of top management, giving them less control and autonomy than their American counterparts. However, there is usually more government support for the labor market, giving the manager more choices (Fisher, Schoenfeldt, and Shaw 1993).

Major IHRM Functions

IHRM has responsibility for the five functional areas discussed in this section: recruitment and selection, training and development, performance evaluation, compensation and benefits, and labor relations. Because expatriate employees are often treated differently than other employees, a discussion of additional issues involved in managing expatriates follows this section.

▌▌▌ RECRUITMENT AND SELECTION

Recruitment and selection are the processes through which an organization takes in new members. **Recruitment** involves attracting a pool of qualified applicants for the positions available. **Selection** requires choosing from this pool the candidate whose qualifications most closely match the job requirements.

Classifying Employees   Traditionally, employees in international organizations are classified as one of three types:

1. **Parent Country National (PCN).** The employee's nationality is the same as the organization's—for example, a French citizen working for a French company in Algeria.

2. **Host Country National (HCN).** The employee's nationality is the same as the location of the subsidiary—for example, an Algerian citizen working for a French company in Algeria.

3. **Third Country National (TCN).** The employee's nationality is neither that of the organization nor that of the location of the subsidiary—for example, an Italian citizen working for a French company in Algeria.

However, as IHRM staffing becomes increasingly more complex, these classifications do not cover all employees (Briscoe 1995). For example, within the European Union (EU), citizens of member countries can work in other member countries without a work permit. Therefore, how to classify a German citizen working for a Spanish company in Spain is not clear. Is this person a PCN, HCN, or TCN?

Classification might seem unimportant. But in many organizations, an employee's classification is tied to compensation, benefits, and opportunities for promotion.

How Managing and Staffing Approaches Influence Recruitment and Selection In an international organization, the managing and staffing approach strongly affects the type of employee the company prefers. In a company with an ethnocentric approach, PCNs usually staff important positions at headquarters and subsidiaries. With a polycentric approach, HCNs generally work in foreign subsidiaries while PCNs manage headquarters positions. In the regiocentric approach, both PCNs and managers from the region—either HCNs or TCNs—staff regional headquarters positions while local subsidiaries are mostly staffed by HCNs. Finally, an organization with a geocentric approach chooses the most suitable person for a position, regardless of type.

In its approach to recruitment and selection, an organization considers both headquarters practices and those prevalent in the countries of its subsidiaries. Local culture always influences recruitment and selection practices, and in some countries, local laws require a specific approach. For example, in international manufacturing and processing facilities in Mexico, known as **maquiladoras**, companies recruit with a sign announcing job openings outside the facility or by employees introducing family members who are looking for jobs (Teagarden et al. 1995). Another example is Hungary, where government attempts to combat unemployment have led to the requirement that an organization must get permission from the Local Labor Center of the Ministry of Labor before hiring an expatriate (Bangert and Poor 1995).

Selecting the Right Candidate In choosing the right candidate, a balance between internal corporate consistency and sensitivity to local labor practices is a goal. Different cultures emphasize different attributes in the selection process depending on whether they use achievement or ascriptive criteria. When making a hiring decision, people in an achievement-oriented country consider skills, knowledge, and talents. Although "connections" can help, companies generally only hire those with the required qualifications. In an ascriptive culture, age, gender, and family background are important. An organization selects someone whose personal characteristics fit the job.

Some countries have laws prohibiting discrimination against certain groups in hiring, promotion, and compensation. In the United States, for example, it is illegal to make hiring decisions on the basis of race, gender, color, national origin, religion, age (older than 40 years), disability, pregnancy, and in some locales, sexual orientation. In choosing a candidate to hire, employers cannot ask questions relating to these personal characteristics; the expectation is that hiring decisions are based purely on qualifications.

In countries where there are no laws regarding hiring practices, an employer may ask any questions or seek candidates with certain personal characteristics. For example, in Japan, some large companies looking for new management trainees only consider current year male graduates from elite universities.

Companies taking a global approach to strategy may have difficulty integrating subsidiary practices that vary from heavy regulation to none. One global approach, developed by Artise (1995), begins with a basic selection system appropriate for the company's operating system. Using the basic system, the organization then makes modifications to adapt it to the various cultures in which the company does business. Artise suggests choosing applicants on the basis of competency, motivation, and fit with the company. He recommends a Job Model to characterize a position on five aspects: results achievable, priorities, obstacles, environment, and management style. The goal is to find the optimum match between the Job Model and applicant qualifications.

Artise also suggests modifying the basic process of selection for cultural differences. For example, after a Korean applicant responds, "the interviewer should allow for a three-to-four-second silent gap to take place, remaining focused on the applicant and displaying a subtle pleasant smile. [This is to allow] a nonverbal *reading* of the other's intentions" [known as *nunchi*] (Artise 1995, p. 92).

Artise's proposal for a global system is based on an achievement orientation. Matching applicant qualifications with the needs of the job is the classic approach to selection developed in North America. A North American company's managers might consider this system sufficiently global to implement worldwide. A Japanese company's managers, conversely, might feel it places too much stress on qualifications and not enough on personal characteristics. Because the Japanese recruit for a general position within the company rather than a specific job, the Job Model aspect of the approach might also be irrelevant.

▌▌▌ TRAINING AND DEVELOPMENT

The **training and development** function includes planned individual learning, organization development, and career development. It is a recognized professional field known as **human resource development (HRD).** At the international level, HRD professionals are responsible for training and development of employees located in subsidiaries around the world, specialized training to prepare expatriates for assignments abroad, and development of a special group of globally minded managers.

Delivery of Programs Worldwide   The delivery of international HRD programs is either centralized or decentralized (Marquardt and Engel 1993). With a centralized approach, training originates at headquarters and corporate trainers travel to subsidiaries, often adapting to local situations. This fits the ethnocentric model. A geocentric approach is also centralized, but the training develops through input from both headquarters and subsidiary staff. Trainers could be sent from various positions in either the headquarters or subsidiaries to any other location in the corporation. In a decentralized approach, training is on a local or regional basis, following a polycentric or regiocentric model.

When training is decentralized, the cultural backgrounds of the trainers and trainees are usually similar. Local people develop training materials and techniques for use in their own area. If the organization takes a centralized approach, the trainers still need to make appropriate adaptations to the local culture, and the cultures of both the trainers and the trainees must be considered.

To maximize training effectiveness, it is important to consider how trainees learn most effectively. Cultural factors have a strong impact on training practices in different parts of the world. For example, in North America, where power distance is small, the relationship between the trainer and trainees tends toward equality. The trainer and trainees use first names, and the trainees feel free to challenge or question what the trainer says. In Malaysia, where power distance is large, a trainer receives greater respect. Students use his surname and title, and he is an expert that students rarely challenge.

> In North America, where power distance is small, the relationship between the trainer and trainees tends toward equality.

In Table 10-1 we outline the effect of culture on training practices in four parts of the world: the United States and Canada, East Asia, the Middle East and North Africa, and Latin America. Although the table describes the regions in broad, general terms, it provides insight into the major differences. However, an effective trainer must learn the specifics of the country and culture of the trainees to select the best approach.

Developing Globally Minded Managers   As global competition increases, it is increasingly important for successful companies to have a group of managers with a global perspective. Companies must identify managers with global potential and

T a b l e 1 0 - 1   The Impact of Culture on Training and Development Practices

	United States/ Canada	East Asia	Middle East/ North Africa	Latin America
HRD Roles	Trainer and trainee as equals; trainees can and do challenge trainer, trainer can be informal and casual.	Trainees have great respect for trainer who should behave, dress, and relate in a highly professional, formal manner.	Trainer highly respected, trainees want respect and friendly relationship, formality is important.	Preference for a decisive, clear, charismatic leader as trainer, trainees like to be identified with and loyal to a successful leader.
Analysis and Design	Trainer determines objectives with input from trainees and their managers, trainees openly state needs and want to achieve success through learning.	Trainer should know what trainees need, admitting needs might represent loss of face to trainees.	Difficult to identify needs because it is improper to speak of others' faults, design must include time for socializing, relationship building, and prayers.	Difficult to get trainees to expose weaknesses and faults, design should include time for socializing.
Development and Delivery	Programs should be practical and relevant, using a variety of methodologies with lecturing time limited.	Materials should be orderly, well organized and unambiguous, trainees most accustomed to lecture, note taking, and limited questioning.	Need adequate opportunity for trainer and trainees to interact, rely on verbal rather than written demonstrations of knowledge acquired, avoid paper exercises and role playing.	Educational system relies on lecture and has more theoretical emphasis, training should be delivered in local language.
Administration and Environment	Hold training in comfortable, economical location, trainee selection based on perceived needs of organization and individual.	Quality of program may be judged on the basis of quality of location and training materials, ceremonies with dignitaries, certificates, plaques, and speeches taken as signs of value of program.	The learning process should be permeated with flourishes and ceremonies, program should not be scheduled during Ramadan, the month of fasting.	Value and importance judged by location, which dignitaries invited for the ceremonies, and academic affiliation of trainer, time is flexible: beginning or ending at a certain time not important.

Source: Adapted from Marquardt, M. and Engel, D.W. (1993), *Global Human Resource Development*. Upper Saddle River, NJ: Prentice Hall, 25–32.

provide them various training and development opportunities. For example, having one or more international assignments, working on cross-national teams and projects, and learning other languages and cultures contribute to making a manager more globally minded. In addition, an organization should include not only PCNs but also HCNs and TCNs in this group.

PERFORMANCE EVALUATION

Performance evaluation is the systematic appraisal of employees' performance within the organization. In Western multinational corporations, performance appraisals are usually done yearly and use a standardized evaluation form. Sometimes, the organization also requires supervisors to discuss the results of the appraisals with each employee.

Performance evaluation is challenging for any organization. This is because its purposes are to provide information for organizational decisions such as promotions and salary increases and to give feedback to employees to help them develop and improve. These two purposes are in conflict: The first is evaluative while the second is developmental.

At the international level, the complexity is greater because the organization must evaluate employees from different countries working in different subsidiaries. The need for consistency across subsidiaries for performance comparisons conflicts with the need to consider the cultural background of employees to make the evaluation meaningful. For example, in Mexico an individual's public image is important, and public criticism of an employee might be justification for leaving a company (de Forest 1994). Consequently, the delivery of a balanced performance review, including both strengths and weaknesses, requires tact and delicacy.

As with other functions, the approach to performance evaluation depends on the organization's overall HRM strategy. A company with an ethnocentric approach is likely to use the same performance evaluation process used at headquarters for its subsidiaries. Some companies translate evaluation forms into local languages, whereas others use the original language everywhere. An enterprise with a polycentric or regiocentric approach develops local procedures within each country or region. Finally, a company with a geocentric approach uses the same performance evaluation system worldwide, but it has universal applicability. Developing a global system is the most challenging.

One example of a global approach is the strategic performance measurement and management system developed by Pepsi-Cola International (PCI) (Schuler, Fulkerson, and Dowling 1991). PCI initiated development of the system by determining individual performance success factors common to its many markets and countries. It then developed common values and a multinational vocabulary to link employees from the more than 150 countries where PCI brands are sold. The resulting performance appraisal system recognizes market conditions and level of economic development that affect employee performance. PCI's system simultaneously functions as a means for obtaining strategic objectives of the global business and the needs of the local environment and manager.

COMPENSATION AND BENEFITS

The **compensation and benefits** function develops and administers the salary system and other forms of remuneration such as vacation and sick pay, health insurance, and pension funds. In developing an international system of compensation and benefits, an organization has two primary concerns. The first is comparability (Briscoe 1995). A good compensation system assigns salaries to employees that are internally comparable and competitive within the marketplace. For example, the salary of a senior manager is usually higher than that of a supervisor, and each position should receive an amount within the local market range. The international organization must also consider the salaries of people who may transfer from other locations.

The second major concern is cost (Dowling, Schuler, and Welch 1994). Organizations strive to minimize all expenses, and payroll is one of the largest.

Setting Compensation and Benefit Levels   Compensation and benefits are closely tied to local labor market conditions, even when an organization takes an ethnocentric or geocentric approach. The availability of qualified local people to fill positions, prevailing wage rates, the use of expatriates, and local laws interact to influence the level of compensation and benefits. For example, if there are few applicants available for positions, the remuneration for those positions generally increases. To reduce expenses, the IHR manager might then consider bringing in an expatriate.

A company usually develops a policy, which could apply globally, to offer salaries and benefits representing a specific market level. For example, a large successful multinational company that emphasizes the quality of its products and employees could have a global policy to pay the highest wages everywhere it operates. Another company could offer top salaries in the country where it does research and development yet pay average wages in the country where it manufactures.

▌▌▌ LABOR RELATIONS

The **labor relations function** identifies and defines the roles of management and workers in the workplace. The concept of labor relations varies greatly in different parts of the world. In the United States, for example, labor relations are often a formal relationship, sometimes antagonistic, between labor and management defined by a union contract. In Japan, the relationship between management and unions is cooperative, and management often appoints union leaders (Hodgetts and Luthans 1994).

In many countries the government regulates labor relations practices. Consequently, in this function more than other HRM functions, an organization may have to be polycentric. However, even though labor relations are local level issues, it is good corporate strategy to coordinate labor relations policy across subsidiaries (Dowling, Schuler, and Welch 1994).

Union Organization   Although some unions are "international," in fact, most unions are organized at the local, company, regional (within country), or national level. There is no multinational union that would allow a global corporation to negotiate terms for its employees worldwide. However, some unions are developing regional offices that include several countries. These will handle issues that arise as a result of regional trading blocs such as the European Union. For example, in Europe, there are approximately 50 industry-based continentwide committees; however, companies have not yet begun to meet with them (Briscoe 1995).

Union Membership   The number of workers within a country who are union members varies dramatically around the world (see Table 10-2). In addition, the relative power of these unions is not represented by union membership figures. For

Table 10-2   **Union Density Figures for a Selected Group of Countries**

Country	Percentage of Union Membership	Year
Argentina	28%	1993
Brazil	13–30% (estimated)	1993
Canada	29.5%	1993
Chile	12.3%	1993
China	92%	1993
Costa Rica	15%	1993
Egypt	50%	1992
France	8–10%	1993
Germany	39.5%	1992
Greece	30%	1993
Italy	15%	1992
Japan	24.2%	1993
Malaysia	9.1%	1992
Mexico	25–30%	1991
New Zealand	34.3%	1993
Spain	11%	1992
United States	15.8%	1992
Zimbabwe	17%	1993

Source: U.S. Department of Labor, Bureau of International Labor Affairs, Foreign Labor Trends and Bureau of Labor Statistics. Dates as indicated in table.

example, in France, although only 12% of workers belong to a union, contracts negotiated by them affect about 85% of workers (Briscoe 1995).

Managing Expatriates

Organizations that employ PCNs and TCNs must deal with the complexities of employing and moving people outside of their home countries. Employing expatriates, although it may be a good business decision, is expensive. Because of the additional compensation required, an expatriate stationed in an expensive city—Tokyo, London, or Paris—could cost a company up to US$350,000 in the first year (Briscoe 1995). Consequently, successfully handling all aspects of expatriate HRM is extremely important.

EXPATRIATE FAILURE RATES

Because of the great expense involved in employing expatriates, it is important that they be successful when in the foreign assignment. Researchers define **failures** as expatriates who do not remain abroad for the duration of their assignment. Managers who finish their assignments but do so ineffectively are called **"brownouts."** An expatriate returning early could cost a company $50,000 to $200,000. There are also additional costs to the organization such as damaged reputation or lost business (Black and Gregersen 1991).

Differences in Failure Rates   The success rates of expatriates from different countries varies. In a large-scale comparative study of companies from the United States, Western Europe, and Japan, human resource administrators reported the expatriate failure rates in their organizations, including those who had to be recalled to the home country or dismissed because they could not function in the foreign assignment (Tung 1988). For U.S. companies, the percentage rates varied from less than 10% to as high as 40% with most companies responding in the 10%–20% range. For Western European companies, the majority were less than 5%, with very few companies reaching as high as 15%. The Japanese had the lowest failure rates, with a large majority at less than 5%, and no company reporting higher than 15%.

For all three groups, the rigor of selection and training procedures was strongly related to the failure rate. However, the reasons for failure varied in the three groups. American and Western European expatriates generally failed because of lack of social abilities or problems with their families. The number one reason was failure of the spouse to adjust. For the Japanese, the major reason for failure was the expatriate's failure to handle larger responsibilities.

> American and Western European expatriates generally failed because of lack of social abilities or problems with their families. The number one reason was failure of the spouse to adjust.

A recent study of Japanese expatriates living in Hong Kong and Taiwan concluded that Japanese failure rates may be as high as those found in the U.S. companies. The number one reason for failure was family-related problems caused by the children's education or the spouse's social life (Fukuda and Chu 1994).

These two studies collected information on the failure rates from HR managers within the companies. Self-reports indicate that Japanese expatriates experience greater difficulty adjusting and consider themselves less effective than do American expatriates (Stening and Hammer 1992).

Men and women also have different failure rates. Of the 686 major North American multinationals surveyed recently, only 3% had female expatriates, but 97% of the women reported a successful assignment (Adler 1994).

These studies suggest that companies must improve their approach to selection and training. Ways to do this include more attention to selection, training, assistance in cultural adjustment, evaluation, compensation, and cultural reentry for expatriates.

SELECTION OF EXPATRIATES

A successful expatriate must be able to both do the job and handle a new cultural environment; therefore, he requires both technical/managerial skills and social/coping skills. Ultimately, the expatriate must do his job competently, learn to live comfortably in a new culture, and ensure that his family adapt as well.

Western European and Japanese multinationals emphasize the need for two types of skills, looking for managers who have both technical competence and the ability to handle a new cultural environment. In North American corporations, in spite of research showing the importance of both types of skills, technical competence is often the only criterion for an expatriate position (Dowling, Schuler, and Welch 1994; Mendenhall, Dunbar, and Oddou 1987; Tung 1988).

Unfortunately, behaviors that are successful at home may not work abroad. American managers working in Hong Kong exhibited the same behaviors that were successful in the United States. However, these behaviors did not match those of successful Hong Kong Chinese managers. For the Hong Kong Chinese managers, there was no relation between successful job performance and any of the behaviors on a standard U.S. measure of managerial behavior. For the American managers in Hong Kong, only "integration," maintaining a closely knit organization and resolving intermember conflicts, related to success (Black and Porter 1991).

▌▌▌ EXPATRIATE TRAINING

As discussed earlier, expatriates are more successful when their organizations train them to prepare for their life and work abroad. In spite of that, many expatriates, particularly those from North America, receive little or no training prior to their new assignments (Briscoe 1995; Dowling, Schuler, and Welch 1994; Tung 1988). Lack of training is a major cause of expatriate failure.

The most important aspect of expatriate training is cross-cultural training. **Cross-cultural training (CCT)** prepares an expatriate to live and work in a different culture because coping with a new environment is much more challenging than dealing with a new job. A variety of training methodologies is available for CCT. In Table 10-3 we outline some of the popular ones and give a brief description of each.

An organization can choose an appropriate CCT method using three situational factors of the expatriate's assignment: culture novelty, degree of interaction with host country nationals, and job novelty (Black and Mendenhall 1989).

Culture novelty is the degree of difference between the new culture and the expatriate's home culture. This can be measured by comparing the two cultures on a cultural framework such as Hofstede's or Trompenaars'. Differences in language represent another aspect of culture novelty. The need to speak a language that is very different from the expatriate's native language is indicative of higher culture novelty. Finally, the expatriate's previous experience with the culture is important. For example, a Chinese-American being assigned to Taiwan might experience less culture novelty than an Italian-American.

Table 10-3   Cross-Cultural Training (CCT) Methods

■ Cultural Briefings	Explain the major aspects of the host country culture, including customs, traditions, everyday behaviors.
■ Area Briefings	Explain the history, geography, economy, politics, and other general information about the host country and region.
■ Cases	Portray a real-life situation in business or personal life to illustrate some aspect of living or working in the host culture.
■ Role Playing	Allows the trainee to act out a situation that he or she might face in living or working in the host country.
■ Culture Assimilator	Provides a written set of situations that the trainee might encounter in living or working in the host country. Trainee selects one from a set of responses to the situation and is given feedback as to whether it is appropriate and why.
■ Field Experiences	Provide an opportunity for the trainee to go to the host country or another unfamiliar culture to experience living and working for a short time.

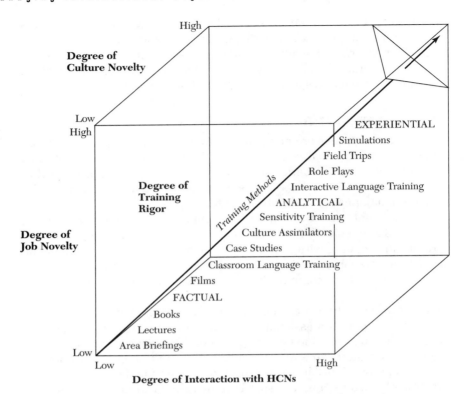

Figure 10-1 **How Situational Factors Influence the Selection of a CCT Method**

Source: Adapted from Black, J.S. and Mendenhall, M. (1989), "A Practical but Theory-based Framework for Selecting Cross-Cultural Training Methods" *Human Resource Management*, 28(4), 511–539.

The degree of interaction with host country nationals refers to how often and at what level the expatriate communicates with locals. The frequency, importance, and nature of communications are of concern. Finally, job novelty involves the new job demands, including expectations, job constraints, and job choices, particularly the degree of autonomy.

Culture novelty is the most strongly weighted, as adjusting to a new culture is more challenging than adjustments to the other two factors. With greater culture novelty, more need to interact with host country nationals, and greater job novelty, the need to have more rigorous CCT increases. Figure 10-1 illustrates how the situational factors effect the selection of a CCT method.

CROSS-CULTURAL ADJUSTMENT

Expatriates and their families need time to become familiar with their new environment and to become comfortable living there. When they arrive, the newness of the experience is exciting. A few months later, when they have had more experience with the culture, expatriates might begin to feel frustrated or confused as they try to make sense of their new living situation. This feeling is "culture shock." As expatriates get comfortable and understand more about the culture, usually three to six months after arrival, the culture shock will wear off, and they will experience a more normal feeling (Adler 1997). Figure 10-2 diagrams the culture shock cycle.

Figure 10-2 **Culture Shock Cycle**

Source: Figure 8.2 "Culture Shock Cycle" from *International Dimensions of Organizational Behavior*, 3e by N.J. Adler. Copyright © 1997. Reprinted by permission of South-Western College Publishing, a division of International Thomson Publishing Inc., Cincinnati, Ohio 45227.

Expatriates must adjust to a new work situation, interactions with locals, and a new general environment (Black and Gregersen 1991). A company can facilitate the adjustment by providing training for the expatriate and his or her family before and during the assignment (Black and Mendenhall 1989), making job requirements clear, and having a predecessor orient the expatriate (Black and Gregersen 1991).

EXPATRIATE EVALUATION

The performance evaluation of expatriate managers is particularly difficult. The job a person does abroad can include much more than what she does at home. A manager often steps into the role of counselor, trainer, troubleshooter, or diplomat in addition to her assigned job responsibilities. With the need for adapting to a new culture, a different way of doing business, and often a new language, many factors influence expatriate performance.

For senior expatriate managers, part of the evaluation often includes the financial performance of the subsidiary. Although it seems to be objective, many factors outside the manager's control affect this result. Local tax rates, currency rate fluctuations, or local labor laws make it more or less difficult to be profitable in a certain location. For example, an American expatriate working in Chile was able to stop a strike that would have closed down his plant for months. At the same time, due to exchange rate fluctuations, the subsidiary experienced a significant downturn in sales. When evaluating this manager, headquarters mostly ignored his achievement of averting the strike and instead focused on the sales data, giving him a slightly better than average rating (Oddou and Mendenhall 1995). In this situation the home office did not fairly consider all the external factors.

EXPATRIATE COMPENSATION

When companies employ a large number of expatriates, the cost of relocating and compensating them for living outside their home countries can be three to five times their domestic salaries (Dowling, Schuler, and Welch 1994). Consequently, these compensation costs greatly influence an organization's use of expatriates.

Compensation Approaches   An organization's general policy influences expatriate compensation. Three common approaches are a home-based policy, a host-based policy, and a region-based policy (Dowling, Schuler, and Welch 1994). With a home-based policy, employees' compensation follows the scale of their home countries. Thus, a German and a Canadian working in the same position in Thailand receive a salary based on their pay in Germany and Canada. Although the result is salary inequity, if the length of the assignment abroad is not long, the expatriate may still use colleagues at home for comparison. With longer assignments, however, an expatriate from a country with a lower pay scale may feel she is being treated unfairly.

The host-based policy sets salaries at the level of the host country with benefits usually tied to the home country. This is attractive to employees relocated to an area with higher salaries than their home countries offer. However, if the assignment is short term, returning home to a lower salary could be difficult.

Finally, region determines the third approach. Compensation for employees working outside their home countries reflects whether their relocation is within their home region or in another region. With this approach, an assignment closer to home (within the region) receives compensation at a lower rate than one further away (outside the region).

Special Compensation and Benefits   Expatriates usually receive extra compensation for the inconvenience of living abroad. Also, large companies often pay additional benefits to their expatriate employees to motivate and provide a comfortable life for them abroad. These benefits can include an overseas premium, housing allowance, cost of living allowance, moving expenses, tuition for dependent education, home leave, and tax reimbursement payments. In Table 10-4 we describe these.

The amount paid depends on the company, employee nationality, and location of the assignment. Established policies for expatriate compensation exist in many large multinational corporations. In other companies, expatriate compensation and benefits are ad hoc and dependent on the negotiating ability of the expatriate.

An example of the variety is the compensation packages offered by 36 major multinationals to Hong Kong expatriates working in the People's Republic of China (Stewart and DeLisle 1994). More than 90% of the companies provided a

Table 10-4   Typical Expatriate Benefits

■ Overseas Premium	Additional percentage of base salary (usually 10%) paid to compensate for inconvenience of living abroad
■ Housing Allowance	Provision of comfortable housing for free or at a rate similar to what the expatriate would incur at home
■ Cost of Living Allowance (COLA)	Payment of additional amount to cover extra costs to allow expatriate to live in the same way as at home—for example, to buy home country foods and other products
■ Moving Expenses	Expatriate and family transportation and goods shipment to and from assignment location
■ Tuition for Dependent Education	Reimbursement for expatriate's children to receive a home country education, for example, private school in the assignment location or boarding school back home
■ Home Leave	Expatriate and family transportation and time off to return home
■ Tax Reimbursement Payments	Reimbursement for any additional taxes payable by expatriate as a result of living abroad

hardship allowance as a percentage of base pay (averaging 36%) or as a daily fixed allowance (approximately US$50 per day). More than 90% of the companies also paid for tax liability over the Hong Kong level. In addition, many companies paid meal allowances (36%), laundry allowances (69%), and family allowances (25%).

EXPATRIATE REENTRY

After the expatriate completes her assignment and returns home, she must adjust in the same way as when going abroad. The work, people, and general environment are no longer familiar. The expatriate and her company are usually unprepared to deal with this situation. The disorientation experienced by a returning expatriate is known as **reverse culture shock**.

The expatriate gains valuable information and experience from an international assignment, but for many organizations this is lost because of failure to manage expatriate reentry successfully. By one estimate, about 25% of returning expatriates leaves the company within a year after returning (Black, Gregersen, and Mendenhall 1992).

Organizations can ease the transition of returning expatriates by planning the reentry before the assignment begins (Chowanec and Newstrom 1991). The organization can assign a mentor who will maintain contact with the expatriate throughout the assignment, keeping him up to date on what is going on within the company at home. As the return date gets closer, the mentor can look for a suitable reentry position for the expatriate. The company can also plan to include the expatriate in short-term projects at headquarters during his home leave. Finally, the organization can provide some of the same daily life supports that it supplied upon going abroad—for example, help with moving or children's education.

> By one estimate, about 25% of returning expatriates leaves the company within a year after returning.

Convergence or Divergence?

FORCES FOR CONVERGENCE

Are IHRM practices across countries converging or diverging? Large global companies are striving to develop international human resource management systems that have consistent applicability in a wide variety of countries. Organizations of every nationality face similar problems in trying to manage a work force spanning many countries and cultures. As HRM becomes increasingly recognized as a field that can affect profits, even smaller companies try to take a more professional approach to managing their human resources. These systems have similar goals and often share similar principles.

FORCES FOR DIVERGENCE

However, even in this move toward more consistency and professionalism, there is increasing sensitivity to local cultural and legal differences. Although many companies would like to follow "cutting edge" HRM practices, there is a growing recognition that these practices cannot be imported wholesale into a country. Consequently, unique techniques and practices are being developed to suit different areas.

Implications for Managers

Every international manager has responsibility for effectively managing human resources. Although an organization might employ professional HR managers, the line manager is ultimately responsible for selecting competent people, training them, assessing their performance, and compensating them fairly. The discussion in this chapter provides some insight into the complexities of these issues.

From another perspective, it is also helpful to understand IHRM because it potentially has a personal impact on every international manager. If you aspire to this type of position, or even if you already hold an international management position, knowing what influences IHR decisions can help your career.

■ Summary

International human resource management focuses on the management of human resources on a global basis. An organization's corporate strategy on globalization strongly affects the approach it takes to IHRM. The approach to IHRM in turn influences implementation of the major IHRM functions of recruitment and selection, training and development, performance evaluation, compensation and benefits, and labor relations. Companies taking an ethnocentric approach attempt to impose their home country methods on their subsidiaries. Polycentric or regiocentric approaches follow local practices. Finally, a geocentric or global approach develops practices for worldwide use.

One of the major concerns of IHR managers is managing expatriate employees. Because they must function effectively in a foreign work and living situation, they receive different treatment than do other employees. In choosing expatriates, a company must consider both technical and interpersonal abilities. Successful expatriates receive appropriate training to prepare them to live and work abroad. To motivate them in their assignment, compensation and benefits to expatriates must also be attractive.

In considering whether approaches to IHRM are converging or diverging worldwide, there was evidence of both. Large global corporations would prefer consistent worldwide systems, and smaller companies would like to have more professional IHRM. However, with the variety of local cultures and laws that exist across subsidiaries, the IHR manager must be ready to adapt.

Finally, because international managers have the ultimate responsibility for managing their human resources, they must be aware of the complexities involved. It is also useful to understand IHRM for personal career development.

■ Discussion Questions

1. Why is international human resource management more complex than managing human resources in one country?
2. What is an expatriate? Why is employing an expatriate different from employing an HCN?
3. How does the overall strategy an organization takes to managing international business affect its human resource strategy?

4. What are some of the differences in training practices in different parts of the world? Explain these differences using one or more of the cultural frameworks from Chapter 2.

5. How does culture influence the performance evaluation process? How can companies ensure that their employees are fairly evaluated?

6. How do you feel about an international career? Would you like to work as an expatriate? Why or why not?

References

ADLER, N.J. (1994), "Competitive Frontiers: Women Managing Across Borders," in Adler, N.J. and Izraeli, D.N. (eds.) *Competitive Frontiers: Women Managers in a Global Economy.* Cambridge, MA: Blackwell.

———. (1997), *International Dimensions of Organizational Behavior*, 3rd Ed. Cincinnati, OH: South-Western College Publishing.

ARTISE, J. (1995), "Selection, Coaching, and Evaluation of Employees in International Subsidiaries," in Shenkar, O. (ed.) *Global Perspectives of Human Resource Management.* Upper Saddle River, NJ: Prentice Hall.

BANGERT, D.C. and POOR, J. (1995), "Human Resource Management in Foreign Affiliates in Hungary," in Shenkar, O. (ed.) *Global Perspectives of Human Resource Management.* Upper Saddle River, NJ: Prentice Hall.

BIRD, A. and BEECHLER, S. (1995), "The Link Between Business Strategy and International Human Resource Management Practices," in Mendenhall, M. and Oddou, G. (eds.) *Readings and Cases in International Human Resource Management*, 2nd Ed. Cincinnati, OH: South-Western.

BLACK, J.S. and GREGERSEN, H.B, (1991), "Antecedents to Cross-Cultural Adjustment for Expatriates in Pacific Rim Assignments," *Human Relations*, 44, 497–515.

———.,———., and MENDENHALL, M.E. (1992), "Toward a Theoretical Framework of Repatriation Adjustment," *Journal of International Business Studies*, 23, 737–60.

———. and MENDENHALL, M. (1989), "A Practical but Theory-Based Framework for Selecting Cross-Cultural Training Methods," *Human Resource Management*, 28, 511–39.

———. and PORTER, L.W. (1991), "Managerial Behaviors and Job Performance: A Successful Manager in Los Angeles May not Succeed in Hong Kong," *Journal of International Business Studies*, 22, 99–113.

BRISCOE, D.R. (1995), *International Human Resource Management.* Upper Saddle River, NJ: Prentice Hall.

CHOWANEC, G.D. and NEWSTROM, C.N. (1991), "The Strategic Management of International Human Resources," *Business Quarterly*, 56, 65–70.

de FOREST, M.E. (1994), "Thinking of a Plant in Mexico?" *Academy of Management Executive*, 8, 33–40.

DILLON, L.S. (1990), "The Occidental Tourist," *Training and Development Journal*, 44, 72–80.

DOWLING, P.J. (1988), "International and Domestic Personnel/Human Resource Management: Similarities and Differences," in Schuler, R.A., Youngblood, S.A., and HUBER, V.L. (eds.) *Readings in Personnel and Human Resource Management*, 3rd Ed. St Paul, MN: West.

———. SCHULER, R.S., and WELCH, D.E. (1994), *International Dimensions of Human Resource Management*, 2d Ed. Belmont, CA: Wadsworth.

FISHER, C.D., SCHOENFELDT, L.F., and SHAW, J.B. (1993), *Human Resource Management*, 2d Ed. Boston: Houghton-Mifflin.

FUKUDA, K.J. and CHU, P. (1994), "Wrestling with Expatriate Family Problems: Japanese Experience in East Asia," *International Studies of Management and Organization*, 24, 36–47.

HODGETTS, R.M. and LUTHANS, F. (1994), *International Management*, 2d Ed. New York: McGraw-Hill.

MARQUARDT, M. and ENGEL, D.W. (1993), *Global Human Resource Development.* Upper Saddle River, NJ: Prentice Hall.

MENDENHALL, M.E., DUNBAR, E., and ODDOU, G. (1987), "Expatriate Selection, Training and Career-Pathing: A Review and a Critique," *Human Resource Planning*, 26, 331–45.

MILLER, E.L., BEECHLER, S., BHATT, B., and NATH, R., (1991), "The Relationship Between the Global Strategic Planning Process and the Human Resource Management Function," in Mendenhall,

M. and Oddou, G. eds., *Readings and Cases in International Human Resource Management*. Boston: PWS-Kent.

ODDOU, G. and MENDENHALL, M. (1995), "Expatriate Performance Appraisal: Problems and Solutions," in Mendenhall, M. and Oddou, G., (eds.) *Readings and Cases in International Human Resource Management*, 2d Ed. Cincinnati, OH: South-Western.

PHATAK, A.V. (1995), *International Dimensions of Management*, 4th Ed. Cincinnati, OH: South-Western.

ROSENZWEIG, P.M. and NOHRIA, N. (1994), "Influences on Human Resource Management Practices in Multinational Corporations," *Journal of International Business Studies*, 25, 229–51.

SCHULER, R.S., FULKERSON, J.R., and DOWLING, P.J. (1991), "Strategic Performance Measurement and Management in Multinational Corporations," *Human Resource Management*, 30, 365–392.

STENING, B.W. and HAMMER, M.R. (1992), "Cultural Baggage and the Adaptation of Expatriate American and Japanese Managers," *Management International Review*, 32, 77–89.

STEWART, S. and DeLISLE, P. (1994), "Hong Kong Expatriates in the People's Republic of China," *International Studies of Management and Organization*, 24, 105–18.

TEAGARDEN, M.B., VON GLINOW, M.A., BUTLER, M.C., and DROST, E. (1995), "The Best Practices Learning Curve: Human Resource Management in Mexico's Maquiladora Industry," in Shenkar, O. (ed.) *Global Perspectives of Human Resource Management*. Upper Saddle River NJ: Prentice Hall.

TUNG, R.L. (1988), *The New Expatriates: Managing Human Resources Abroad*. Cambridge, MA: Ballinger.

WIERSMA, U.J. (1996), "Human Resource Management Practices in the Netherlands: An Exploratory Study," BRC Papers on Cross-Cultural Management, Hong Kong Baptist University, Series no. CCMP 96006, April.

Organizational Structure

To Restructure or Not To Restructure? That Is the Question

In March 1994 four MBA students in New York City made a class presentation on corporate downsizing. Wall Street, where many in the class worked, was consolidating its operations departments with firings, and major corporations were laying off people.

In a class of 30, four students had been "rightsized," and seven others worked in firms that either had or were going to restructure by eliminating middle managers. Downsizing affected their employment opportunities, job security, career paths, and, to some extent, their confidence in the future.

During the presentation the students expressed some personal anxiety but accepted periodic restructuring as part of corporate America. To them it was necessary to have "lean and mean" management and a proactive approach to change to survive increasing domestic and global competition.

In the discussion after the presentation, a student from Germany said, "We have similar problems with excess workers in Germany." The class looked in his direction, and there was mild irritation that he had repeated what had already been discussed.

"But," he continued, "we deal with it somewhat differently. Instead of laying people off we share work so that people don't suffer as much. Also it's done with the long-term view that the economy will improve in a few months or years. They will be hired back at some point, anyway. We don't understand why you Americans are so short-term oriented and ready to fire people."

The Americans questioned the German student about the strength of unions in Germany and their role in advocating work sharing. After heated discussion, they concluded that unions and socialist political parties influenced avoiding layoffs and convinced themselves that an impersonal organizational logic dictated the restructuring of U.S. corporations. It was, they decided, a question of good business practice, and social welfare policy should not influence business decisions.

Source: B.A. Gold

Organizational structures vary considerably. Some multinational corporations have hundreds of thousands of employees dispersed throughout the world, dozens of managerial levels, independent business units, and extensive research and development departments. Other multinational corporations have only several thousand employees, few managerial levels, no independent business units, and minimal research and development. There are also family-owned businesses in most societies that vary in their organization structure, ranging from small corner grocery stores to billion-dollar transnational conglomerates.

Culture influences organizational structure in many ways. Because of different social values, the structure of a Korean multinational corporation, which has many of the characteristics of a family business, is different from those found in Japan, Greece, Argentina, South Africa, or the United States. The Culture at Work vignette demonstrates that culture affects how people think about organizational structure and, consequently, their actions: One culture views structure as determined by impersonal, rational market forces, whereas the other culture views structure as directly linked to the fates of individuals and the product of social policy choices.

> **Culture influences organizational structure in many ways.**

What Is Organizational Structure?

Organizational structure is the arrangement of positions in an organization. Positions, or roles, are intentionally structured to accomplish the goals of the organization. The basic components of structure are **complexity, centralization**, and **formalization**. Before discussing them, we present the open systems perspective of organizations, because properties in an organization's environment influence the components of structure.

▌▌▌ THE SYSTEMS PERSPECTIVE OF ORGANIZATIONS

Organizations are **open systems** that interact with their environment rather than exist independently of surrounding influences. Organizations continuously require inputs from the environment in the form of raw materials, human resources, finance, and ideas. After inputs are transformed through a variety of processes, an organization returns output to the environment in the form of products, services, and knowledge (Katz and Kahn 1978).

One important element in an organization's environment is the values of the national culture. Values influence a wide array of behaviors in organizations—for example, what is moral or legal, who should be hired, and whether authority should be centralized.

Another key component of an organization's environment is other organizations. These include raw material suppliers, competitors, regulatory agencies, and customers. An important aspect of the relationships among organizations that affects structure is the diffusion of management theories and practices. Contact with other organizations—usually in the same industry—influences organization structure because of a desire to emulate successful management theories and practices (Abrahamson 1996).

Another feature of structure is that management can change it to adapt to an organization's environment. An example is a recent change in the structure of the Coca-Cola Company. Because it sells products around the world, Coke is often cited as an example of a global company. It was not until January 1996, however, that Coke changed its organizational structure to reflect its global presence.

> Now, the Coca-Cola Company could adopt the song "We Are the World" as its corporate motto.
>
> The $10 billion company announced a basic shift in its world view yesterday, eliminating the very concept of a "domestic" and "international" Coca-Cola beverage business in the administrative structure of its worldwide operations.
>
> Coca-Cola downgraded its United States business to be just part of one business unit among the six Coke has for its global regions. Analysts said that move was a first for any major consumer products company, but agreed that it could be imitated (Collins 1996, p. 35).[1]

In the discussion of multinational organizational structures later in this chapter, we present the various types of organizational structures from which companies like Coke can select.

Elements of Structure

One approach to understanding organizational structure is to examine variables that compose it. The extent of complexity, formalization, and centralization of every organization reflects its structure.

Complexity **Complexity** is the extent to which an organization has subparts. Three important components of complexity are horizontal differentiation; vertical or hierarchical differentiation; and spatial dispersion.

Horizontal differentiation is the way that tasks performed by the organization are subdivided (Hall 1996). Organizational tasks can be divided in two ways. The first type of job specialization is the **micro division of tasks**, breaking jobs into their smallest components that individuals can perform well with low levels of education and training. An example is automobile assembly lines, which fragment and simplify work. The second is division of labor using highly trained specialists who have extensive responsibilities in performing a complex task—for example, medical

---

[1]Excerpt from "Coke Drops 'Domestic' and Goes One World" by Glenn Collins from *The New York Times*, January 13, 1996. Copyright (©) 1996 by The New York Times. Reprinted by permission of The New York Times.

doctors who do open heart surgery. The larger the number of different positions across the organization, the higher the level of horizontal differentiation.

Vertical or hierarchical differentiation is the number of levels in an organization. A measure of vertical differentiation is the number of levels between the highest and lowest position in an organization. The assumption is that the higher the level, the greater the authority of the position. Some organizations have few levels and others have dozens; more levels indicate greater differentiation.

The final component of complexity is **spatial dispersion**, a form of horizontal and vertical differentiation. The activities of an organization can be in one place or in different locations on either the basis of power centers, that is, hierarchy, or specialization. An example of spatial dispersion based on specialization is a corporation headquartered in Mexico with factories in Honduras, Brazil, and Canada that manufacture products customized for local markets. Regarding the location of authority, management can decide to replicate the power structure at each location or concentrate it at headquarters.

Centralization   Centralization focuses on the decision-making authority of members of an organization. When decisions are made by a few people—usually those at the top—an organization is centralized. When decisions are delegated to lower-level participants, an organization is decentralized. The larger the percentage of important decisions made by lower level members, the more the organization is decentralized.

Formalization   Formalization is the extent that rules, policies, and procedures govern organization members' behavior. The more extensive the documentation of appropriate behavior, the more formalized the organization. Theoretically, rules can specify all actions in an organization. It is also possible that an organization has no formal rules or policies. Typically, organizations operate between these extremes.

Patterns   These variables often form specific patterns. Typically, centralized organizations are highly formalized and specialized with a micro division of labor. This is characteristic of **mechanistic** or bureaucratic organizations. Decentralized organizations often have low formalization and specialization based on depth of knowledge. This is an **organic structure** (Burns and Stalker 1961).

▌▌▌ EXPLAINING STRUCTURE: THE CONTINGENCY PERSPECTIVE

Through logical argument, inductive and deductive theories, and empirical research, management scholars and sociologists have argued that one variable explains more of the structural aspects of organizations than others. These explanations—**determinist theories**—range from technology as the primary causal variable of structure (Perrow 1967) to strategy (Chandler 1962) and size (Blau and Schoenherr 1971).

Most organizational studies conducted in the United States identify one best way to structure organizations and manage them. Even **contingency theories**, with the view that there are multiple causes or types of structure, limit variables that affect structure to a small number that are controllable by management such as types of coordination (Lawrence and Lorsch 1967) or the task structure of the organization (Thompson 1967).

In addition, most research in the United States and Western Europe views organizational structure as **culture-free**—that is, consisting of universal causes (Child 1974; Hickson et al. 1974). In this view, the logic of formal organization is independent of values found in different cultures. It does not deny variations in values but views them as irrelevant because technology, strategy, size, and other variables apply across cultures as explanations for organization structure.

An alternative argument is that culture is the major determinant of whether a specific management philosophy and organizational structure will be prevalent in a society (Trompenaars 1993). The values and assumptions of a culture determine preferences for the way that positions are arranged in organizations. Proponents of this view argue that cultural and managerial choices influence organization structures rather than deterministic processes such as industrialization, mechanization, and bureaucratization.

The position taken here is that culture is an important variable but not the only explanation of organization structure. Multiple factors create organizational structure. However, the focus will be on the contribution of culture to structure.

▌▌▌ CULTURE AND ORGANIZATIONAL STRUCTURE

A study of Japanese automobile plants in the United States tested the prediction of organizational theory that the environment of the United States would make Japanese practices such as team-based management and just-in-time supplier relationships difficult to transfer (Florida and Kenney 1991). The research found that transplanted Japanese factories successfully implemented these practices. This suggests that cultural values—ways of structuring work—are strong enough to persist in the value system of another society.

A study that compared 14 matched English and Indian manufacturing firms in a variety of industries (Tayeb 1987) explored the contingency and universal—that is, culture free—approach to explaining organization structure. The English and Indian organizations were similar in terms of centralization, joint decision making, specialization, and number of hierarchical levels. Key areas in which there were differences were delegation, formalization, use of job descriptions, and the direction of communication.

The universalistic theory explains the similarities in the organizations. However, different *means* achieved the similarities. For example, both groups of organizations had centralized decisions. In the English sample, however, managers consulted with lower-level employees and delegated to them before making a final decision. In the Indian sample, there was comparatively little discussion of decisions with lower-level workers. Tayeb (1987, p. 257) concludes:

> Contingency theory and the culture-free thesis gained moderate support . . . but the model they suggest is inadequate and cannot explain the many differences between the Indian and English organizations which were also found. These differences appear to be more consistent with the general characteristics of the societies in which these organizations operate, and their employees' cultural traits.

An interesting example of the effects of culture on organization structure is the Swedish automobile industry. Instead of the assembly line production made famous by Henry Ford and refined by U.S. automobile companies, the Swedish automotive industry has experimented with a variety of structures largely determined by their value system, not the requirements of efficient production.

The latest version of Swedish automobile production is "reflective production" (Ellegard et al. 1992). Some characteristics of reflective production that differ from assembly line production structures follow:

- The assembly work has to be viewed in a wide context on the shopfloor. It must include not only the assembly itself, but also the preceding phases, i.e., controlling the materials, structuring the materials and tools, and the subsequent phases, i.e., final inspection, and if necessary, adjustment and further inspection. The vertical division of labor is also affected in that assembly workers take over certain administrative tasks. This new concept of assembly work calls for the workers' own reflections.
- In reflective production, the assembly work itself becomes intellectualized and thereby meaningful. The work teams are able to rebalance their own work.
- Established empirical knowledge of grouping and restructuring work tasks is also a basic precondition for the realization of efficient and humane production systems (Ellegard et al. 1992, pp. 121–22).[2]

From the perspective of organizational structure, reflective production blurs traditional distinctions of horizontal and vertical differentiation and adds an intellectual, or "reflective," component to assembly work. Workers understand the entire manufacturing process and contribute to its structure. Swedish culture values work as an intellectual, humane activity, and the structure of reflective production fulfills these values more than does standard assembly line structures that predetermine micro-tasks and reduce workers to appendages of machines.

Finally, conducting an historical study of the management philosophies and practices of the United States, Great Britain, Germany, and Spain, Guillén (1994) discovered variation according to each nation's value system. Cultural values—including religion—influence the way that organizations in these countries are managed and structured.

In summary, these and other empirical studies suggest that differences in cultural values contribute to variation in organizational structure.

ORGANIZATIONAL STRUCTURE, CULTURE, AND ORGANIZATIONAL BEHAVIOR REVISITED

There are three views of how organizational structure affects organizational behavior. The first view, which is consistent with the studies discussed previously, is that cultural values affect organization structure, which then influences organizational behavior.

An alternative view, structuralism, is that organization structure influences— even determines—values. Proponents of this position claim that, "The structures of objective social positions among which people are distributed exert more fundamental influences on social life than do cultural values and norms, including ultimately the prevailing values and norms" (Blau 1977, p. x).

A third view is that organizational behavior is the product of the interaction of structure and values. National cultural values and corporate culture interact with structural variables. In other words, a dialectical process among national culture, organizational culture, and structure produces organizational behavior by creating constraints on behavior.

---

[2]Excerpt from "Reflective Production in the Final Assembly of Motor Vehicles—An Emerging Swedish Challenge" by K. Ellegard, D. Jonsson, T. Enstrom, M. Johansson, L. Medbo and B. Johansson from *International Journal of Operations & Production Management*, 12 7/8. 1992. Copyright © 1992 by *International Journal of Operations & Production Management*. Reprinted by permission.

Types of Organizational Structure

Another approach to understanding organizational structure is to construct models of different types of organizations instead of isolating specific variables such as complexity, centralization, and formalization.

||| BUREAUCRACY

In a classic typology, Weber (1946) identifies the following characteristics of **bureaucracy**:

- *Each position has fixed official duties.* Job descriptions exist for each position that create a high degree of specialization in a small number of comparatively routine tasks.
- *Conduct is governed by impersonal rules and regulations.* Impersonal—not intentionally abrasive behavior—ensures that each case that the bureaucracy deals with is treated in the same way.
- *Effort is coordinated through a hierarchy of levels of authority.* The assumption of this arrangement is that the higher the position, the more expertise the position holder possesses.
- *Order and reliability are maintained through written communication and files.* In a bureaucracy all transactions are documented; this establishes records that create accountability.
- *Employment is a full-time occupation for members of the organization.* Members of the organization are "professionals"; their primary occupational focus is the tasks of their position.
- *Appointment to office is made by superiors.* The heads of bureaucratic organizations are appointed on the basis of their technical skill.
- *Promotion is based upon merit.* Those most qualified—as demonstrated through a written examination or other method—are promoted.

Weber views bureaucracy as the product of historical progression toward rational administration because, compared with other ways of organizing, bureaucracy is efficient and effective. For example, in patrimonial administration, legitimate authority is derived from a male leader. Only members of the patriarch's clan, regardless of knowledge or ability, were permitted to occupy positions. In many contemporary societies, some variations of this type of organization still exist, usually in family businesses as discussed subsequently.

Because it is a major form of organization, there are many studies of bureaucracy. One approach examines the extent to which bureaucracy actually achieves rational administration. Researchers found many departures from rationality or **dysfunctions** of bureaucracy. A central insight is that the strict adherence to rules for situations that are not standard or "typical" cases—the bureaucratic personality—often produces results that are contrary to the goals of the organization (Merton 1968).

Other studies focus on the relationship of elements such as hierarchy and centralization of power, the effects of size on organizations, and how bureaucracies develop and change. Many of these research findings are counterintuitive. For example, after a review of studies of the relationship between size and centralization, Blau and Meyer (1987, p. 100) conclude:

> Almost all the empirical research on organizations . . . suggests that stereotypes of large organizations as excessively bureaucratic are misleading. To be sure, structural differentiation increases with size, but the rate of increase in numbers of organizational units and in levels of hierarchy actually decreases with size. Administrative overhead, measured by ratios of either administrators to production workers or supervisory to nonsupervisory personnel, also decreases with size. And large, multitier organizations, particularly those whose personnel rules are most formalized, tend to be the most decentralized, in that decisions are delegated to levels below top management. Altogether, bureaucratic controls seem to be less intensive in large organizations than in small ones.

Not all cultures or subcultures view rational administration as desirable. For example, one objective of family businesses is intergenerational control of the business. Whether this behavior is rational or not depends on cultural assumptions and values. Most societies, regardless of their values, have some form of bureaucratic organization in business and the public sector because it is efficient and effective for administering routine, repetitive tasks. For example, McDonald's, a major global company, is a highly effective bureaucracy.

SIMPLE STRUCTURE

Simple structure is characteristic of new or small organizations. There is little need for elaborate coordination because the organization is not complex; top management supervises through direct supervision. There is also centralization in top management with employees exerting little independent decision making or influence. The organization's goals are those of its top manager, who is frequently also its owner. This type of organization is typical of entrepreneurial activity in its early stages and of small family businesses.

ORGANIC STRUCTURE

Organic structure is the opposite of bureaucracy. Bureaucracy is a rigid, often dysfunctional type of organization, whereas organic structures are flexible and change oriented and foster creativity. The following are features of organic structures:

- Knowledge and ability determine participation in decision making and problem solving rather than position titles.
- Decision making is decentralized, and there is an attempt to involve lower-level participants in decision making whenever possible.
- Communication channels operate vertically and horizontally. In other words, information is shared throughout the organization including across areas of expertise and status.

One type of organic structure is the **matrix**. In matrix structures, instead of a bureaucratic authority structure with employees accountable to a supervisor, an employee reports to more than one supervisor. For example, an engineer can report to the head of a functional area and a project manager when developing a product or project. Of course, it is more complex than either a simple structure or a bureaucracy and has the potential for creating conflict among the supervisors. Nevertheless, many cultures use matrix structures, including the United Kingdom, the United States, and Germany. Other cultures prefer the principle of a single supervisor—unitary chain of command—particularly the French.

▌▌▐ MULTIPLE STRUCTURES

Many organizations have **multiple structures** (Hall 1996). Hospitals and universities are complex structures that contain both bureaucratic administration and more organic professional structures. In addition to requiring more coordination, these types of organizations often experience conflict as a result of the coexistence of different structures. For example, doctors, who work in a professional bureaucracy with some of the characteristics of organic structures, are often in conflict with nurses, who work in a fairly bureaucratic mode.

Structural Variations

Although bureaucracy and organic structures are common organizational types throughout the world, some organizations modify them by incorporating selected elements of each. One widespread type of organization, family business, takes a variety of forms and demonstrates the impact of culture on organizational structure.

▌▌▐ FAMILY BUSINESS

Family business is a major form of organizational structure throughout the world. Even in economically advanced societies, family businesses make up a large segment of the economy. Features of family businesses that distinguish them from non–family-owned-and-operated corporate structures follow:

> Family business is a major form of organizational structure throughout the world.

- The composition of the governance and management structures—the organizational elite—are primarily family members. In other words, ascription is a more important criterion for employment than is achievement.
- There is usually distrust of nonkin employees and outsiders. However, it is possible that nonkin employees can become trusted, particularly when they demonstrate long-term loyalty.
- There are often difficulties with leadership succession. The issue is usually conflict over selecting a child or other relative to succeed the founder or current head. This illustrates one of the nonrational aspects and weaknesses of family businesses.
- The business can suffer from family member lack of expertise; for example, no family member is an attorney or accountant, and the advice of outsiders is considered untrustworthy.
- Business decision making is often on the basis of kin requirements, not done "rationally." There is a preference for affective relationships, characterized by personal obligations, over calculated, nonpersonal decision making.
- In family firms, paternalism is the typical management style. This creates centralization of authority in the male leader. Family respect for the patriarch often creates conservative, risk-averse behavior, including reluctance to use external financing as a source for expansion.

The following example illustrates conditions typical of family businesses:

[Corporate] growth strategies in India also relate to family structure. There, family objectives such as creating employment for family members are a strong impetus for forming a business. Recently, an American businessman suggested to his Indian joint venture partner that the latter use a standard market-portfolio model (á la Boston Consulting Group) to plan his business expansion. His partner refused to invest unequally in the five existing businesses because each business was managed by a son. Unequal investment would cause family discord. Even in firms where some of the board of directors are not family members, the norm of family consensus can be very strong. Family owner-managers often hold private council before submitting plans to the Board (Terpstra and David 1991, p. 172).

Within the constraints of these characteristics, family businesses take various forms. Some are small and local, whereas others develop into dispersed multinational conglomerates. For example, the Garza Sada family of Mexico controls Grupo Industrial Alfa, Mexico's largest conglomerate, with interests in steel, petrochemicals, and food (Carroll 1995).

CHINESE FAMILY BUSINESS

Chinese family businesses (CFBs) are an interesting example of family business structure. The structure of overseas Chinese businesses is usually one of two types. The first is small businesses that include only family members. The second type is controlled by family members but also employs nonfamily members and operates as a clan or extended family, which permits it to grow considerably larger than businesses that restrict themselves to family members.

The ideology of CFBs centers on patrimonialism, which, in practice means paternalism, hierarchy, mutual obligation, responsibility, familialism, personalism, and connections (Chen 1995). Related to this—as in family businesses in other cultures—is a close relationship between power and ownership. The product of this combination is autocratic leadership and a personalistic style of management. These features result in organizations that include a key role for the owners in management, keep the organization small, and promote factionalism.

According to Chen (1995), the small size of CFBs limits them to simple structures that restrict them to focusing on only one aspect of a business—for example, production, sales, or service. This creates a situation in which "all employees are expected to be involved in the main products or the services of the company, which directly create profits" (Chen 1995, p. 87).

Another feature is that CFBs do not have systematic sets of rules, systems, or roles. This also creates a low level of specialization, and workers can be assigned to any task "at the whim of the business owners" (Chen 1995, p. 87). The result is an informal organization in which the owner has extensive power that he often uses arbitrarily and abusively.

Within this framework—a lack of formal structure and rules—personal relationships and "feelings about other people are likely to take precedence over more objectively defined concerns such as organizational efficiency" (Chen 1995, p. 87). This creates a situation in which cliques form as a substitute for formal structure. One consequence of clique formation based on personal loyalties is that intergroup contests frequently escalate into disruptive conflicts.

Many features of CFBs are also present in family businesses in other cultures. A recurring theme in the CFB is factionalism and conflict. Writing about family businesses in the United States, Levinson (1971) titled an article "Conflicts that Plague Family Businesses." Conflict occurs over issues such as ownership, control, career development, and particularly, over succession. These conflicts occur between parents and children, among children, between nuclear and extended family members, and between family members and nonfamily members.

In the next section we discuss structures that are family businesses at their core but develop into enormous conglomerates as the result of government intervention and values different from those typically found in family businesses.

NATIONAL STRUCTURAL VARIATIONS

In addition to family businesses and their diverse structures, there are cultural variations in the governance of business that affect organizational structure. Two forms that are substantially different from corporate governance in the West are the Japanese *keiretsu* and the Korean *chaebol*. They have origins in, and still have characteristics of, family firms, which not only affect their governance, but to some extent, also influence the micro-structure of work and interpersonal relationships. They are of additional importance because they have played a critical role in the rapid economic development of Japan and Korea (Lincoln, Gerlach, and Ahmadjian 1996).

Japanese *Keiretsu* The origins of the Japanese *keiretsu* are family-owned federations of firms, *zaibatsu*, that existed prior to World War II. After the war, they were reorganized into the looser *keirestu*, which are complex interfirm networks that combine market exchange and noneconomic social relations. To facilitate control and coordination, each member firm of a *keiretsu* owns a small—up to 20%—part of the stock of the other firms in the group. "The group is usually in a large number of industries, and at the core of the group is often a bank. Very few shares of the firm trade on open equity markets. Since investment is internally generated, it is usually oriented to long-run gains and holding market share" (Fligstein and Freeland 1995, p. 38).

In addition to a bank, *keiretsu* usually include a *soga shosha*, a general trading company that supports the *keiretsu* by coordinating the companies within the group by buying and selling services, providing information, and maintaining information networks within the *keiretsu*. This aspect of Japanese business structure seems to be unique to Asian culture. Other countries, including Korea, Mexico, and Brazil, have started organizations similar to *soga shosha*, with only Korea experiencing success.

The effect of *keiretsu* on the performance of Japanese firms is considerable. According to Lincoln, Gerlach, and Takahashi (1992, p. 561):

> Once castigated as atavistic "feudal" structures imperiling the full modernization of an ascendant economy, *keiretsu* networks, like other institutions in Japanese economic life, are increasingly credited with conferring a key competitive advantage on Japan. For their member firms, *keiretsu* networks reduce costs and risk, facilitate communication, ensure trust and reliability, and provide insulation from outside competition.

Korean *Chaebols* Large conglomerates or financial cliques known as *chaebols* dominate the South Korean economy. The definition of *chaebol* is "a business group consisting of large companies which are owned and managed by family members or relatives in many diversified business areas" (Yoo and Lee 1987, p. 97). Examples of *chaebols* are corporations such as Hyundai, Samsung, Lucky-Goldstar, Hanjin, and Daewoo.

Since the end of the Korean War, the government has played a large and active role in the investment patterns of the *chaebols*. As a result, unlike in the United States and other countries, private financial markets play almost no role in the growth of the South Korean economy. Most financing comes from government-controlled banks, enabling the government to decide which *chaebols* receive money for expansion. In return for favorable treatment, the *chaebols* make large contributions to politicians.

The family ownership and diversified business operations of *chaebols* are similar to the former Japanese *zaibatsus*. An important feature of *chaebols* that differs from Japanese *keiretsu* is that founders are more active in management; in Japan there are more nonfamily managers. As a result, the founder's business philosophy influences the management style of *chaebols*.

In summary, "Korean firms are large, integrated, and diversified, yet under the control of a small number of families with strong ties to government" (Fligstein and Freeland 1995, p. 39).

Emerging Structures in the Global Economy

The globalization of the economy has created new types of organizational structures that involve using human resources more efficiently, managing increasing levels of complexity, and becoming more responsive to changes in their environment.

▌▌▌ BOUNDARYLESS ORGANIZATIONS

One new structure, the **boundaryless organization**, breaks the traditional demarcations of authority, political, communication, and task specialization found in bureaucracies and other organizational structures. Features of a boundaryless organization include a widespread use of project teams, interfunctional teams, networks, and similar structural mechanisms, thus reducing boundaries that typically separate organizational functions and hierarchical levels. In addition, boundaryless organizations form strategic alliances with suppliers, customers, and in some cases, competitors (Hirschhorn and Gilmore 1992). The purpose of the blurring of internal and external boundaries is to be more responsive to changes in a dynamic global economy.

Of course, even in a boundaryless corporation, there is an authority structure as well as task and political boundaries. However, these boundaries are flexible and have no resemblance to the rigid horizontal and vertical dimensions of traditional organizations. In its extreme form, the boundaryless organization is a horizontal organization organized around basic processes such as new product development, sales, and customer support instead of traditional functional areas.

In boundaryless organizations, a key management challenge is to socialize and train organization members to encourage new forms of behavior and prevent returning to the segmenting effects of the bureaucratic mentality.

▌▌▌ MULTINATIONAL, GLOBAL, INTERNATIONAL, AND TRANSNATIONAL STRUCTURES

A characteristic of many corporations is that they are not located within the geographical boundaries of one country. In addition, these corporate structures are complex because they usually produce multiple products and services.

Multinational firms focus on a strategy that is primarily country oriented and locally responsive. Their structures are decentralized. In contrast, **global** companies are centralized and follow a strategy built on global-scale cost advantage. **In-**

T a b l e   1 1 - 1   **Organizational Characteristics of Multinational, Global, International, and Transnational Firms**

Organizational Characteristics	*Multinational*	*Global*	*International*	*Transnational*
Configuration of assets and capabilities	Decentralized and nationally self-sufficient	Centralized and globally scaled	Sources of core competencies centralized, others decentralized	Dispersed, interdependent, and specialized
Role of overseas operations	Sensing and exploiting local opportunities	Implementing parent company strategies	Adapting and leveraging parent company competencies	Differentiated contributions by national units to integrated worldwide operations
Development and diffusion of knowledge	Knowledge developed and retained within each unit	Knowledge developed and retained at the center	Knowledge developed at the center and transferred to overseas units	Knowledge developed jointly and shared worldwide

Source: From *Managing Across Borders: The Transnational Solution* by A. Bartlett and S. Ghosal. Copyright © 1989, 1991 by Harvard Business School Press. Reprinted by permission of Harvard Business School Press.

ternational firms develop products and innovations in their domestic market and then transport them to foreign affiliates, where the products and technologies are adapted to local needs. These companies are centralized and sequential. Table 11-1 presents the organizational characteristics of these types of firms.

The **transnational** firm differs from these types in that it avoids dichotomous structures such as product or geography-based, centralized or decentralized, independent or dependent (Bartlett and Ghosal 1989). Alternatively, it attempts to achieve solutions tailored to specific situations, and differentiated structures replace systemwide structures. For example, some businesses within a corporation might be appropriately organized in a worldwide centralized structure, whereas others should be adapted to local conditions and decentralized to take advantage of local manufacturing and marketing.

This type of organizational structure creates high levels of interdependence among countries and cultures. Bartlett and Ghoshal (1989, p. 60) write:

> The transnational centralizes some resources at home, some abroad, and distributes yet others among its many national operations. The result is a complex configuration of assets and capabilities that are distributed, yet specialized. Furthermore, the company integrates the dispersed resources through strong interdependencies. . . . The British subsidiary may depend on France for one range of products, while the French depend on the British for others. Some of these interdependencies are automatic outcomes of the configuration of assets and resources. Frequently, however, they are specifically designed to build self-enforcing cooperation among interdependent units.

> A characteristic of many corporations is that they are not located within the geographical boundaries of one country.

HETERARCHY

Heterarchy is a form of multinational organization that utilizes aspects of markets and hierarchies. Market principles are situations in which economic activities are conducted between unrelated parties who use explicit contracts or prices as the primary mechanism to coordinate their activities. Each party does what is in their best interest for each transaction.

Hierarchy involves transactions between parties related to one another—for example, through ownership or through implicit contracts such as between employers and employees and when coordination exists through vertical authority relations.

According to Hedlund (1986, p. 20),

> The heterarchical MNC [multinational corporation] differs from the standard geocentric [a single headquarters] one in terms of strategy and in terms of [the direction of the relationship between strategy and] structure. *Strategically*, the main dividing line is between exploiting competitive advantages derived from a home country base on the one hand, and actively seeking advantages originating in the global spread of the firm. . . . When it comes to the *structure* of the enterprise and the process of managing it . . . the idea of structure determining strategy [rather than the other way around] . . . is a fundamental one for the heterarchical MNC. Rather than identifying properties of the industry in which it competes and then adapting its structure to the demands thus established, the [heterarchical] MNC first defines its structural properties and then looks for strategic options following from these properties [italics in original].[3]

In this type of organizational structure, instead of reliance on traditional hierarchy—where ideas, technology, and people originate from the geographical center of the organization—managers design the multinational structure so that ideas, products, technology, and other functions and processes can originate from any element in the system. Hedlund (1986) identifies the following other features of this new type of MNC:

- The heterarchical multinational enterprise has multiple centers, each with competence in one or another business, product, or function. Resources are diffused within the network of affiliates, and it is implicitly assumed that ideas can come from any country.
- Subsidiary managers play strategic roles within not just their own units but the enterprise as a whole. The notion of "headquarters" is diluted.
- Thinking and decision making are not restricted to the center; every part of the enterprise can participate. In this manner, the feedback loop between action and thought is tightened.
- Integration is achieved primarily through normative control and only secondarily through coercive or bureaucratic means. Socialization and "corporate culture" become more important.
- In contrast to a matrix, a heterarchy recognizes that organizations can be built along more than two dimensions. Thus, research and development could be organized one way, production a second, and marketing a third.
- Finally, managers have flexibility in the selection of governance modes. A subsidiary could purchase components from it or sell its production externally. Similarly, coalitions with other firms and actors can be frequent in the heterarchical multinational enterprise (Vernon, Wells, and Rangan 1996, pp. 78–79).

This model of organization is only beginning to emerge in practice. From the perspective of culture, a heterarchy treats each culture on an equal basis: There is no headquarters, ideas flow from all divisions, and corporate culture replaces national culture as a control mechanism. In a sense, a hetrarchy transcends specific cultures.

---

[3]Excerpt and description of MNC from "The Hypermodern MNC-A Hetarchy?" by G. Hedlund from *Human Resource Management*, 25, (1), 1986, 9–25. Reprinted by permission of John Wiley & Sons, Inc.

Convergence or Divergence?

FORCES FOR CONVERGENCE

Two organizational structures that exist in most societies are bureaucracy and patrimony. Most societies have government agencies and private corporations that are bureaucratic in principle, if not in practice. Hierarchy, a micro-division of labor, the concept of position or office, and appointment and promotion on merit are widely accepted principles. Of course, these principles can be compromised with nepotism and various practices that are based on custom rather than rational economic calculation.

Similarly, the presence in most societies of family ownership and management of business organizations suggests that patrimony is still widespread. It is likely that these organizational arrangements persist because they are effective in achieving valued outputs and are consistent with cultural values and practices in many societies. It could be argued then that, to a certain extent, there is and will remain similarities in organizational structures across societies.

At the same time, traditional organizational structures are either being replaced or supplemented with networks that require flexibility and innovation. Usually these are organizations that are capital intensive, knowledge based, and technology driven. These new types of organization create pressures toward convergence, as do traditional multinational organizations.

FORCES FOR DIVERGENCE

Factors producing divergence are the stage of economic development of a country, variations in relationships between political and industrial sectors, cultural values, and competitive pressures that result in new forms of organization. Regarding competitive pressures, organizational structure—such as the use of teams, relations with suppliers, the use of technology—are important ingredients in gaining strategic advantage. In other words, there are important strategic reasons for the development and maintenance of distinctive organizational structures.

Implications for Managers

Interest in organizational structure is increasing. Downsizing, the reduction in the number of middle level managers, one of several adjustments to global competitive pressures, has created the possibility that elaborate hierarchies are no longer necessary. But at the same time that U.S. corporations are reducing the scale of organizations, although it might be a limited phenomenon, the Chinese and Koreans are creating large, complex organizations.

As noted previously, not all corporations have impersonal rules and professional relationships—bureaucratic principles—but often rely on the insights of strong authority figures and affective relationships. A key issue for global managers is the ability to understand and, in some cases, manage unfamiliar structures in unfamiliar cultures.

An alternative approach is to manage as though structure is irrelevant. This is similar to the culture-free or universalistic perspective; all that matters is individual relationships. The limitation of this approach is that organizational structures shape employee behavior. To understand their behavior a manager must understand the structure they work in.

Yet another objective for managers is to learn how to operate in network organizations. These either have no hierarchies or minimal vertical differentiation and patterns substantially different than traditional vertical differentiation into a micro division of labor. In addition, network organizations are usually spatially dispersed and are temporary systems.

■ Summary

Organizational structures vary within industries, between industries, and across cultures. One of the determinants of organization structure is culture, particularly social values regarding the nature of work, the rational use of resources, the desired quality of interpersonal relationships, and the social welfare of a society. A counter argument is that there are universal organizational structures that are determined by noncultural variables such as technology, size, strategy, and the organization's competitive environment. In this view, culture plays little, if any, role in determining organization structure.

Key variables for understanding organizational structures are complexity, centralization, and formalization. Depending on their arrangement, these variables produce various forms of organization. Some commonly found types of organization structures are bureaucracy, simple structure, matrix, and family businesses. Culturally distinct structures are Japanese *keiretsu* and Korean *chaebols*. In recent years, new forms of global structures have emerged, including boundaryless organizations, networks, and heterarchies.

Some factors—for example, transnational corporations—are creating similar organization structures throughout the globe. At the same time, other factors such as national culture produce distinctive structural arrangements. An example is the Swedish automotive industry, which over many years has attempted to find ways to assemble high-quality cars without sacrificing the human aspects of work to the technical efficiency requirements of the traditional assembly line.

Finally, managers can choose to manage in a way that is sensitive to variations in organizational structure or to approach every organization as though structural variations do not affect interpersonal relationships. In some instances, such as the family business structure, it is difficult to avoid the implications of culture on structural arrangements.

■ Discussion Questions

1. What is organizational structure?
2. What variables contribute to creating organizational structure?
3. Discuss the rationale for including culture as a determinant of organizational structure.
4. How does a matrix organization differ from a bureaucracy? When would it be appropriate to use a matrix structure?
5. What are the characteristics of a family business?
6. In what way does the *keiretsu* form of organization differ from the governance structures of business found in the United States?

7. What feature distinguishes new and emerging organizational structures from established ones?

8. Why should a manager have a knowledge of organizational structures in different cultures?

References

ABRAHAMSON, E. (1996), "Management Fashion," *Academy of Management Review*, 21 (1), 254–85.

BARTLETT, C. and GHOSAL, S. (1989), *Managing Across Borders: The Transnational Solution*. Boston: Harvard Business School Press.

BLAU, P. (1977), *Inequality and Heterogeneity: A Primitive Theory of Social Structure*. New York: The Free Press.

———. and SCHOENHERR, R. (1971), *The Structure of Organizations*. New York: Basic Books.

———. and MEYER, M. (1987), *Bureaucracy in Modern Society*. New York: Random House.

BURNS, T. and STALKER, G. (1961), *The Management of Innovation*. London: Tavistock Publications.

CARROLL, P. (1995), "Garza Sadas Build an Unrivaled Latin Empire," *The Wall Street Journal* (December 11), A9.

CHANDLER, A. (1962), *Strategy and Structure*. Cambridge, MA: MIT Press.

CHEN, M. (1995), *Asian Management Systems: Chinese, Japanese and Korean Styles of Business*. New York: Routledge.

CHILD, J. (1974), "What Determines Organizational Performance? The Universals vs. the It-All-Depends," *Organizational Dynamics* (Summer), 2–18.

COLLINS, G. (1996), "Coke Drops 'Domestic' and Goes One World," *The New York Times* (January 13), 35.

ELLEGARD, K., JONSSON, D., ENSTROM, T., JOHANSSON, M., MEDBO, L. and JOHANSSON, B. (1992), "Reflective Production in the Final Assembly of Motor Vehicles—An Emerging Swedish Challenge," *International Journal of Operations & Production Management*, 12 (7/8), 117–33.

FLIGSTEIN, N. and FREELAND, R. (1995), "Theoretical and Comparative Perspectives on Corporate Organization," *Annual Review of Sociology*, 21–43.

FLORIDA, R. and KENNEY, M. (1991), "Transplanted Organizations: The Transfer of Japanese Industrial Organization to the U.S," *American Sociological Review*, 56, 381–98.

GUILLÉN, M. (1994), *Models of Management: Work, Authority, and Organization in a Comparative Perspective*. Chicago: University of Chicago Press.

HALL, R. (1996), *Organizations: Structures, Processes, and Outcomes*. Upper Saddle River, NJ: Prentice Hall.

HEDLUND, G. (1986), "The Hypermodern MNC—A Heterarchy?" *Human Resource Management*, 25 (1), 9–25.

HICKSON, D., HININGS, C., McMILLAN, D., and SCHWITTER, J. (1974), "The Culture-Free Context of Organization Structure: A Tri-National Comparison," *Sociology*, 8, 59–80.

HIRSCHHORN, L. and GILMORE, T. (1992), "The New Boundaries of the 'Boundaryless' Company," *Harvard Business Review* (May/June), 96–109.

KATZ, D. and KAHN, R. (1978), *The Social Psychology of Organizations*, rev. ed. New York: John Wiley & Sons.

LAWRENCE, P. and LORSCH, J. (1967), *Organization and Environment*. Cambridge, MA: Harvard University Press.

LEVINSON, H. (1971), "Conflicts that Plague Family Businesses," *Harvard Business Review* (March/April), 90–98.

———, GERLACH, M., and AHMADJIAN, C. (1996), "*Keiretsu* Networks and Corporate Performance in Japan," *American Sociological Review*, 61 (1), 67–88.

———., ———, and TAKAHASHI, P. (1992), "*Keiretsu* Networks in the Japanese Economy: A Dyad Analysis of Intercorporate Ties," *American Sociological Review*, 57 (5), 561–85.

MERTON, R. (1968), *Social Theory and Social Structure*, Enlarged Ed. New York: The Free Press.

PERROW, C. (1967), "A Framework for the Comparative Analysis of Organizations," *American Sociological Review*, 26, 688–99.

TAYEB, M. (1987), "Contingency Theory and Culture: A study of Matched English and Indian Manufacturing Firms," *Organization Studies*, 8 (3), 241–61.

TERPSTRA, V. and DAVID, K. (1991), *The Cultural Environment of International Business*, 3d Ed. Cincinnati: South-Western.

THOMPSON, J. (1967), *Organizations in Action*. New York: McGraw-Hill.

TROMPENAARS, F. (1993), *Riding the Waves of Culture: Understanding Diversity in Global Business*. London: The Economist Books.

VERNON, R., WELLS, L., and RANGAN, S. (1996), *The Manager in the International Economy*. Upper Saddle River, NJ: Prentice Hall.

WEBER, M. (1946), *Essays in Sociology*. New York: Oxford University Press.

YOO, S., and LEE, S. (1987), "Management Style and Practice of Korean Chaebols," *California Management Review*, 24 (4), 95–109.

Organizational Change

Another Change?

In November 1995, the 33 members of Jani Hanson's contract compliance department at AT&T had to fill out a form asking them to supply their individual job history, current job responsibilities, and a justification for retaining their job. For Jani and her coworkers—along with other AT&T workers across the United States—it was the first step in the planned reduction of 40,000 employees. A few months earlier, Robert Allen, AT&T's chief executive officer, had announced one of the largest corporate restructurings in history. In the next year, AT&T would split into three separate companies to become more competitive in the global economy.

For Jani it was a stressful time. When she graduated from college six years earlier, she considered herself extremely lucky to get a job at AT&T. It was a cutting-edge company with a sophisticated corporate culture, and she expected long-term employment there. But as she filled out the employment history form—after eight different jobs within the company in six years—she found herself becoming anxious. Jani enjoyed her job and considered AT&T a good employer. She wanted to stay with the company in New Jersey. Also, she and her boyfriend were thinking about getting married and buying a condominium.

In January 1996 Jani's supervisor told her that she still had a job with AT&T—in Chicago. Relocating was difficult but better than un-

After reading this chapter, you should be able to:

1. Define organizational change and understand why managing organizational change is an important part of international management.

2. Understand the individual, group, and structural levels of change.

3. Know what internal and external factors influence organizational change.

4. Explain the role of national and organizational culture on organizational stability and change.

5. Understand the processes involved in planned organizational change, including sources of resistance to change and ways to overcome them.

6. Understand how macro level theories of organizational change influence the management of change.

> employment; the restructuring terminated one-third of her depart-
> ment. Jani, reflecting on her experience, concluded, "I have a job—at
> least until the next restructuring."
>
> *Source*: B.A. Gold

Organizations throughout the world are undergoing rapid changes. Recent large-scale changes are the globalization of corporations and privatization of industries in former Communist countries. Less dramatic changes that nonetheless have significant implications are e-mail, computerization, and international quality standards. Change is so prevalent that the management of change has become a major part of an international manager's responsibilities.

To manage change effectively, it is necessary to understand the influences of societal and organizational culture on organizations. Some cultures and organizations have an orientation toward the future and embrace change and others preserve traditional behavior.

Other issues also affect organizational change. Do organizations change as a result of changes in their environments? Does change occur because organizations have life-cycles? Or, do they change in rationally planned ways under the guidance of managers?

What Is Organizational Change?

Organizational change reconfigures components of an organization to increase efficiency and effectiveness. Change can occur at the level of the individual, group, or organizational structure. Because organizations are systems, change in one area affects other areas to some extent. However, organizational structure change influences group and individual change more than changes in individuals and groups affect the organization.

INDIVIDUAL CHANGE

Individual change occurs when the behavior of a person is different as a result of new information, training, experience, or rearrangement of an organization's structure. The Culture at Work vignette illustrates individual change created by structural change. AT&T changed frequently, creating continuous uncertainty for employees. As a result, Jani's attitude toward the corporation changed, and she felt less secure in her job and less company loyalty. In addition, Jani and other AT&T employees experienced change as individuals because their roles were different after the organization restructured.

GROUP CHANGE

Group change can take several forms, including new leadership, increased or diminished cohesiveness, and transition into a team. One type of group change is development through either a series of rational stages—for example, forming, storming, norming, performing, and adjourning (Tuckman and Jensen 1977) or one rapid, dramatic change or punctuation (Gersick 1988). An example of planned group change is the introduction of total quality management (TQM). To implement TQM—

continuous quality improvements—successfully, a group changes into a team, shares responsibility and accountability, and learns how to change itself when necessary.

▌▌▌ STRUCTURAL CHANGE

Organization structure change is the deliberate rearrangement of the positions, departments, or other major units of an organization. For example, many firms in the People's Republic of China plan to become multinational conglomerates. To accomplish this, private firms and large state-owned monopolies are forming groups that share senior management. These large groups, often headed by former government officials, receive preferential access to financing, stock-market listings, and government-regulated areas of industry and trade (Kahn 1995). Large organizational size increases power.

> Organization structure change is the deliberate rearrangement of the positions, departments, or other major units of an organization.

Senior Chinese managers believe that these changes will enable them to compete more effectively in the global marketplace. At the same time the Chinese initiated these structural changes, many Western companies are restructuring through downsizing and decentralization to become more competitive.

The German telephone company is another example of organizational level change. Germany is renowned for its manufacturing excellence but never developed responsiveness to customers. Deutsche Telekom AG, the German telephone monopoly, keeps people waiting for years to have a phone installed, and its customers have learned to accept inferior service (Steinmetz 1995).

To change this situation, the German government plans to privatize the phone company and improve it through competition. To create change the company hired an outsider, Ron Sommer, formerly of the Sony Corporation. In addition to upgrading the system's equipment, Sommer plans to eliminate one-quarter of the workforce and, through improved training, refocus the remaining employees more directly on customers (Steinmetz 1995).

The changes will not be easy. In addition to extensive government regulations—telephone lines must be laid underground, not hung from poles—the employees are government workers. This means that each employee is entitled to a $35\frac{1}{2}$-hour work week and a six-week annual vacation. These and other employment conditions make it difficult to increase worker productivity and control costs.

As these examples demonstrate, not only does change occur in various organizational levels, but a variety of factors initiates and influences the change process.

Sources of Organizational Change

Two sources of organizational change are internal and external factors. They interact with the national culture, organizational culture, management philosophy, and organizational structure to produce either minor adjustments or major changes in individual roles, group performance, or the entire organization.

▌▌▌ INTERNAL CHANGE FACTORS

Internal change factors are an organization's technical production system, political processes, and culture (Tichy 1983). At times these factors exert strong and direct pressures for change. At other times, when the organization is in equilibrium, internal factors maintain organizational stability but retain the potential for creating change.

Technical Production Processes Sources of change in the **technical production system**, which involves core transformation processes, include the following:

- *Production.* These include problems such as high personnel turnover, inadequate training, coordination difficulties between organizational units, high rates of waste, and downtime because of machinery malfunctions.
- *New technologies.* The introduction of a new technology can change patterns of behavior within an organization. In addition to displacing workers and requiring retraining, a new technology can rearrange the organization's power structure. For example, workers skilled in a new technology often acquire higher status.
- *Quality.* Many variables contribute to the quality of a product—including materials, design, assembly—making quality problems difficult to detect and possibly located throughout the organization.

Political Processes Sources of change in the organization's **political processes**, the distribution of power, include the following:

- *New organizational goals.* New goals realign the organization's resources and produce a series of changes throughout the organization, including increasing the power of groups whose interests the new goals represent.
- *Conflict.* Interpersonal and intergroup conflict either results in diversion of energy from organizational goals or creates pressure for change.
- *New leadership.* The primary purpose of a new leader is to create change (Gersick 1991). This is more likely when the organization is confronting crises or severe problems and when the new leader is from outside the organization.

Organizational Culture In the organization's symbolic system, or **culture,** sources of change include the following:

- *Values.* The organization's values—a central element in its culture—can become a source of strain and conflict if they are no longer appropriate for the organization's goals.
- *Norms.* The unwritten but widely understood and powerful informal "rules" of the organization become a source of change if they are inconsistent with the organization's goals.
- *New member socialization.* New members are a source of change because they create departures from past practice. Organizations are not able to reproduce themselves without some unintended change because of imperfect socialization that results in deviations from desired behavior.

▋▋▋ THE ROLE OF INTERNAL CHANGE VARIABLES

Some internal change factors produce incremental pressures for change that are not apparent until they accumulate into significant problems. Contributing to this is the tendency to avoid or delay change on the basis of the belief that problems will self-correct. The result is that change often occurs under urgent conditions.

   In other instances, the diagnosis of a problem is correct and timely, but a solution is not apparent or available. Also, a problem could be unique, the organization could be unable to formulate a solution, or multiple variables could interact, creating unmanageable complexity.

   An example of the complexity of internal change is the adoption of new technologies. Although it appears that new technology is a neutral element that should not significantly affect an organization beyond improving efficiency, many studies demonstrate that it can affect the nature of work (Zuboff 1985) and the social relations among workers (Barley 1986).

▌▌▌ EXTERNAL CHANGE VARIABLES

External sources of change are events in the environment that are usually beyond the organization's control. They can affect the organization immediately, influence other elements in its environment that then affect it, or make their impact in the future. With increased awareness of events in other countries and the globalization of the economy, even external events far removed from an organization's immediate environment are important sources of change. The distinction between immediate and general environments is becoming difficult to maintain as globalization increases.

> **E**xternal sources of change are events in the environment that are usually beyond the organization's control.

The Immediate Environment   Some important external forces in an organization's **immediate environment**, influences with which it is continually in contact, that create pressures for change are the following:

- *Domestic competition.* Most organizations have competitors that require some form of monitoring and response.
- *Population trends.* Demographic factors that affect the workforce include birth rate, age, gender, race, ethnicity, religion, and culture. To some extent, immigration and population control policies affect how these variables create change.
- *Social trends.* Consumer preferences, increases in two–wage earner families, divorce rates, crime rates, education levels, and urbanization are some social trends that affect organizations.
- *Government actions.* National and local governments affect organizations by either reducing or increasing their regulation of areas such as taxation, labor laws, and the environment.

The General Environment   Sources of change in an organization's general environment, which extends beyond its immediate environment and expands as globalization progresses, are the following:

- *Foreign competition.* The globalization of business intensifies the nature of competition; competitors can be located anywhere in the world. This is also true of the flow of capital, information, and knowledge.
- *Social movements.* Recent examples of social movements—organized citizen protest groups—intended to exert influence on governments and organizations are campaigns to end child and prison labor, feminism, and the environmental or "green" movement.
- *Political-economic movements.* These are organized attempts to influence the distribution of economic resources through legislation or other forms

of regulation. Recent examples are the North American Free Trade Agreement, the European Union, and the World Trade Organization. Agreements such as these formulate policies that reduce trade barriers and can result in the relocation of factories across national borders.

- *Technology.* New technologies that affect business organizations include improvements in communication, computerization, and automation. These can be developed in one country but in a relatively short time affect businesses everywhere.

- *Professionalization.* The growth of expertise influences organizational change because as occupations' knowledge bases improve, they become more influential in the way organizations operate. Increasingly, knowledge workers such as computer programmers and investment bankers are becoming transnational.

- *Culture contact.* Globalization has increased familiarity with other cultures' management techniques—for example, the influence of Japanese management practices on non-Japanese corporations.

▌▌▊ THE ROLE OF EXTERNAL CHANGE VARIABLES

Organizational theories such as **population ecology** (Hannan and Freeman 1989) and to some extent, **institutional theory** (Scott 1995), view the primary source of change as external and beyond the control of management. For example, similar to natural selection in biology, population ecology views the environment as selecting those types of organizational forms that survive. From this perspective, organizations do not adapt; instead, certain types fail and are replaced with different types. An implication for the management of organizations is that instead of being proactive through attempts to change the organization's environment, management is reactive and, in most instances, finds it difficult to adapt to the new environment. An example of this perspective is Carroll and Hannan's (1995, p. xi) observation:

> When the ecological perspective on organizations initially appeared in the mid-1970s, critics . . . were quick to claim that it was a theory applicable only to small organizations. Large and powerful organizations such as General Motors, IBM, and the Bank of America could control their environments and therefore were immune from selection processes. . . . Less than twenty years later, the speciousness of these claims jumps off the page, as many previously dominant firms have failed or are in the process of doing so. History abounds with examples of fallen organizations that once seemed unassailable.

As the globalization of the economy progresses, the environments in which organizations exist will become increasingly more complex and difficult to understand, let alone control. Demands on management to adapt or radically change organizations to new circumstances will probably increase as well.

▌▌▊ CHANGE VARIABLES AND CULTURE

Internal and external variables exist in the context of national and organizational culture. They simultaneously influence culture and are influenced by it; their impact on organizations could be direct but is more often mediated by culture. Important issues are how national cultures respond to change and what change strategies can be used in particular cultures. In the next section we discuss some ways that national culture influences the change process.

National Culture and Organizational Change

Cultures vary in their receptivity to change. Some cultures change slowly and actively resist change—even to the point of attempting to prevent outside influences—because they value traditional behavior. Other cultures embrace change but, on occasion, significant segments of their population attempt to reestablish traditional values and behavior and view progress as a threat (Hunter 1996). Yet other cultures are ambivalent toward change and simultaneously embrace, resist, and fear it.

▌▌▌ TIME ORIENTATION

One way to understand a culture's relationship to change is its orientation toward time (Trompenaars 1993). Some cultures are **past oriented**, view tradition and history as important, and interpret the present through the lens of ancient principles, customs, and texts. Other cultures are **present oriented** and focus on the moment. For these societies, history is relatively unimportant and the future is not of great concern. Finally, some cultures are **future oriented** and emphasize planning and future achievements. In these societies, progress is a central theme, the fate of future generations is a concern, and there is belief that rational thought can guide human action (Nisbet 1980).

Traditional cultures with a past orientation resist change, whereas cultures with a present-orientation display either ambivalence or reluctant acceptance of the new. Cultures with a future orientation tend to view change as desirable and, to some extent, inevitable.

▌▌▌ RESISTANCE TO CHANGE

Even present, and future-oriented societies experience resistance to change. To some extent, for all cultures, resistance to change is attributable to the uncertainty associated with change, including the awareness that change is not always improvement and can produce unintended consequences (Merton 1936) or reverse results with negative outcomes (Sieber 1981).

It is important for managers to understand sources of resistance to change so they can anticipate and reduce them. Tradition, habit, resource limitations, threats to power and influence, and fear of the unknown, are forms of resistance to change found in all societies.

> Even present- and future-oriented societies experience resistance to change.

Tradition   **Tradition** is a preference for acting based on custom and precedent. The most compelling reason for adherence to tradition—including religion—is that the practices it prescribes have worked sufficiently well to warrant continuing them. Changes in the organization's external environment can create problems if the organization persists with its traditions. If the environment changes very little over long periods of time, tradition might not be an impediment to change. However, in the last decades of the 20th century, little has remained unchanged, creating pressures on tradition-bound organizations.

Habit   **Habit** differs from tradition, because all organizations, whether they revere traditions or not, engage in habitual behaviors. Much of what an organization does is habitual because it forms regular, stable patterns of events over time that are taken for granted and become mindless actions, "overlearned routines triggered by simple categories and coarse attributions of causality" (Weick 1987, p. 8).

Resource Limitations   Another barrier to change is **resource limitations**. Societies and organizations within them have varying levels of resources—human, financial, intellectual. From a comparative perspective, organizations in advanced industrial economies generally have more resources for supporting change than do organizations in developing countries. Of course, within countries the availability of resources varies with the history and success of an individual organization. For example, in the United States, AT&T has more ability to finance change than does a small family owned company.

Power and Influence   Threats to **power** and **influence** are frequently barriers to change. Change in an organization can involve both anticipated and unanticipated alterations in the power and influence structure. Those with power could inadvertently find that they have participated in a change that decreases their power and increases the power of others. For example, the introduction of a new technology—for example, computers—could shift power toward computer programmers and away from senior executives who are unfamiliar with modern technology.

Fear of the Unknown   Another barrier to change is **fear of the unknown**. Even if the proposed change has clear benefits, participants in the change can experience concern over not knowing their future situation. An example is a promotion that brings more responsibility and compensation. Although it is positive, the person receiving the promotion could experience uncertainty over his or her ability to achieve a high level of performance with new coworkers, an increased number of subordinates, and more demanding work. Potentially harmful change increases reasons to fear the unknown.

Values   Cultures can be categorized by level of resistance to change using the dimensions of culture identified by Hofstede (1980). In Table 12-1 countries with the strongest resistance to change, as measured by high power distance, low individualism, and high uncertainty avoidance, include most of Latin America, Portugal, and the former Yugoslavia. Countries most accepting of change have low power distance, high individualism, and low uncertainty avoidance. These are the United Kingdom, the United States, Sweden, Finland, Norway, and the Netherlands. Harzing and Hofstede (1996, p. 315) write:

> Summarizing the assumed influence of the various cultural dimensions on resistance to change we suggest that both power distance and uncertainty avoidance increase the resistance to change, while individualism reduced it. We did not find clear indications for a relationship with masculinity.

Regarding Korea, Japan, and Taiwan, Harzing and Hofstede (1996, p. 316) note that their location on the values dimensions is counterintuitive. They write:

> These three countries are very innovative, and innovation certainly requires change. So one would expect these countries to show up in the weak resistance-to-change clusters. . . . A partial explanation for this contradiction can be found by introducing the . . . fifth dimension, long-term orientation.

Long-term orientation includes values such as persistence that explain the growth of these economies.

Table 12-1   Resistance to Change in Different Clusters of Countries

Resistance level	Dimension Scores			Country Clusters
	PD	**ID**	**UA**	
4 (strongest)	high	low	high	most of Latin America, Portugal, Korea, the former Yugoslavia
3 (strong)	med	med	high	Japan
	high	high	high	Belgium, France
	high	med	high	Spain, Argentina, Brazil, Greece, Turkey, Arab countries
	high	low	med	Indonesia, Thailand, Taiwan, Iran, Pakistan, African countries
2 (medium)	high	low	low	Philippines, Malaysia, India, Austria, Israel
	low	med	high	
	med	high	med	Italy, Germany, Switzerland, South Africa
1 (weak)	med	high	low	Singapore, Hong Kong, Jamaica
0 (weakest)	low	high	low	Anglo countries, Nordic countries, Netherlands

PD-power distance; ID-individualism; UA-uncertainty avoidance

Source: Excerpts and table from *Research in the Sociology of Organizations: Cross Cultural Analysis of Organizations*, pp. 315, 316 and 327 by Anne-Wil Harzing and Geert Hofstede. Copyright © 1996 by JAI Press Inc. Reprinted by permission of JAI Press Inc.

Organizational Culture and Change

The resistance to change of national culture is not identical with resistance to change in organizations. Although Harzing and Hofstede's schema is useful for explaining resistance to change at the societal level, it neglects the possibility that within a society, diverse industries and different types of organizations experience more or less resistance. In other words, even though the values of a society appear to be uniform, subsystems within a society often have different values. For example, a technology firm in a high resistance to change society is unlikely to have the same level of resistance as the society. However, it might not be as change oriented as a similar firm in a society that is receptive to change.

Another limitation to focusing exclusively on values is that, as discussed previously, a wide array of internal and external factors interacts with culture to create organizational change. Managing change involves more than understanding values.

MANAGING CHANGE

There are many approaches to managing organizational change. For example, one view is that the leadership of an organization should initiate change (Tichy and Sherman 1993). An alternative view is that top-down change fails because lower-level employees, who are closest to customers, are the most knowledgeable about what requires change (Beer, Eisenstat, and Spector 1990). There is also disagreement about which components of an organization should be changed and in what ways. For example, to improve efficiency, should a company increase or decrease the number of job specializations? Or should management invest in new technology and employee training?

Organization Development   Planned organizational change, **organization development (OD)**, is an attempt to apply social science research and theories to create more "rational" organizations (Burke 1982). OD involves attempting to improve organizational efficiency and effectiveness, create organizational "health," and build capacity to change continuously. Through the use of interventions designed to improve team functioning, decision making, communication, and empowerment, OD improves organizational processes, the causes and structure of behavior, rather than content, and the tasks of an organization. Although top management usually initiates an OD project, OD practitioners often attempt to use collaborative strategies involving the various groups and individuals that are part of the change.

OD interventions have been successful in a variety of cultures, including developing nations with comparatively little adjustment to the specific culture where the intervention occurs (Golembiewski 1987). However, there is growing data suggesting that the assumptions and values of OD are specific to the United States and not congruent with values in other advanced economies such as France (Amado, Faucheux, and Laurent 1991).

Lewin's Model of Change   A widely used model of planned organizational change is Lewin's (1951) three-stage process of unfreezing, movement, and refreezing. In the version presented here, we add a diagnosis phase to the beginning and renewal as the last phase.

- *Phase 1: Diagnosis.* At the beginning of planned organizational change, it is essential to understand accurately what requires change. During diagnosis and other phases of change, two possible approaches are (1) a doctor–patient relationship in which the patient—the organization—provides information for the doctor—an OD consultant or other expert—who alone determines the type of illness and its cure and (2) a collaboration involving as many participants as possible throughout the change process. Diagnosis involves identifying the problem, isolating its primary causes, and developing an appropriate and effective solution (Northcraft and Neale 1994). Not all problems are self-evident. For example, the cause of employee discontent can be extremely difficult for management to unearth; an outside consultant might have to survey groups of employees, analyze the data, and then work with groups to understand it. Similarly, locating the major cause of a problem is also difficult. There are often multiple causes, some "hidden" deep within the organization's history or culture. Finally, there are many potential solutions to a problem. Are dissatisfied employees motivated by more money, better working conditions, or increased responsibility? Or should highly motivated individuals replace workers performing poorly? Organizational problems typically exist in the organization's purpose, structure, reward system, technology, interpersonal relationships, leadership, and environment. Problems causing pressures for change can exist in several areas simultaneously. Because organizations are complex systems, a problem in one area usually affects other areas—but sometimes indirectly.
- *Phase 2: Unfreezing.* This phase is preparation for change. Recognition of the need for change develops along with the definition of organizational problems. The objectives are to overcome resistance to change, formulate

an implementation plan, and identify ways to measure the outcomes of the change. For OD to succeed, the diagnosis must be understood and accepted by individuals and groups involved in the change.

- *Phase 3: Movement.* The task of this phase is implementing recommendations for change. Managers often believe if the diagnosis was correct and the unfreezing phase was successful, implementation should be comparatively easy because organization members simply must follow plans. In many instances, however, even well-developed plans are not easy to execute (Gold and Miles 1981) and fail either temporarily or permanently (Gold 1995).

  A **change agent** often facilitates the movement phase. A change agent is usually an outside expert, but can be an employee, who consults with an organization for a specific change project. Change agents assist with all phases of the change process, particularly in the overall strategy and the resolution of conflicts.

- *Phase 4: Refreezing.* Refreezing is the institutionalization of changes implemented in the movement phase. The changes are now part of everyday life in the organization. An aspect of institutionalization is measuring the effects of the changes. Some key questions follow: Did the changes accomplish the goals identified in the diagnosis phase? As a result of the change, were there any unanticipated outcomes?

- *Phase 5: Renewal.* The final stage, organizational renewal, includes processes in which management and other members engage after refreezing to determine if and when the organization requires additional planned change. After an organization has successfully changed, it is likely that either its environment or internal conditions will change again. Instead of waiting for a crisis to develop, producing the need for major change, an organization can change incrementally.

Managing Resistance to Change   Resistance to change in organizations is similar to resistance in cultures. As discussed previously, tradition, habit, limited resources, shifts in power and influence, fear of the unknown, and values affect receptivity to change. With few exceptions, some form of resistance to change is common in organizations because groups in an organization have different interests. One group could perceive certain actions as benefiting it and the organization, whereas another group can interpret those same actions as ill conceived.

To overcome resistance to change, Lewin's theory suggests that it is more effective for change agents to remove barriers than to emphasize reasons supporting change. Kotter and Schlesinger (1979, pp. 106–14) identify five ways to manage resistance to planned organizational change:

- *Education and communication.* Organization members often fail to understand the type and benefits of change and resist what they do not understand. Communication explaining the nature of anticipated change often reduces resistance or at least notifies people what to expect.

- *Participation and involvement.* Consultation, collaboration, and other forms of joint decision making in the design of change increase understanding, support, and enthusiasm for the change. This strategy reduces resistance, increases commitment, and improves the likelihood of implementation.

> To overcome resistance to change, Lewin's theory suggests that it is more effective for change agents to remove barriers than to emphasize reasons supporting change.

- *Negotiation and agreement.* Organization members who support the change and those who oppose it negotiate various aspects of the change to achieve an acceptable change program and workable implementation plan. There is an exchange of concessions for cooperation.
- *Manipulation and co-optation.* When the initiators of change have more power than those who oppose the change do and the opponents have little bargaining power, the use of formal authority and power can gain compliance. Changes in policies and rules and, if necessary, personnel transfers or terminations remove barriers and induce others to change.
- *Coercion.* When the need for change is urgent—that is, the organization is in crisis—opposition becomes irrelevant, and formal power and authority unilaterally implement the change.

▎▎▎ THE INTERACTION OF NATIONAL AND ORGANIZATIONAL CULTURES

The success of a change program, as well as approaches to overcoming resistance, vary with the complexity and scope of behavior an organization attempts to change, the change techniques it uses, as well as national and organizational culture.

National Culture   One approach to selecting change strategies for different cultures is the extent to which values resist change and fitting a change strategy to them. Harzing and Hofstede (1996) propose some change strategies based on Kotter and Schlesinger's models for the groups of countries, which we present in Table 12-2.

Table 12-2   Change Strategies for Different Groups of Countries

Change Strategy	PD	ID	MA	UA	Country Clusters
	Dimension Scores				
5 (power)	high	low	high	high	Colombia, Equador, Venezuela, Mexico
4 (power, manipulation/ persuasion)	high	low	med	high	rest of Latin America, Spain, Portugal, former Yugoslavia, Greece, Turkey, Arab countries, Korea
3 (manipulation/ persuasion)	med	med	high	high	Japan
	high	high	med	high	Belgium, France
	high	low	med	low	Indonesia, Thailand, Taiwan, Iran, Pakistan, African countries
	high	low	med	low	Philippines, Malaysia, India
	med	low	high	low	Singapore, Hong Kong, Jamaica
2 (manipulation/ persuasion, consultation)	low	med	med	high	Austria, Israel
	med	high	high	med	Italy, Germany, Switzerland, South Africa
1 (consultation, participation)	low	high	high	low	Anglo countries
	low	high	low	low	Nordic countries, Netherlands

PD-power distance; ID-individualism; MA-masculinity; UA-uncertainty avoidance

Source: Adapted from Harzing A.W., and Hofstede, G. (1996), "Planned Change in Organizations: The Influence of National Culture," in Bamberger, P. and Erez, M., (eds.) *Research in The Sociology of Organizations: Cross-Cultural Analysis of Organizations.* Greenwich, JAI Press, 327.

Countries with high power distance, low individualism, high masculinity, and high uncertainty avoidance require a change strategy that emphasizes power or coercion. Countries in this category are Colombia, Equador, Venezuela, and Mexico. At the other end of the scale, countries with low power distance, high individualism, and low uncertainty avoidance need consultative, participative change strategies. These countries include the United Kingdom, the United States, Australia, Sweden, Denmark, Finland, and the Netherlands.

Organizational Culture   But not all organizations have the same values as the national culture. It seems likely, therefore, that certain organizational cultures will be more receptive to change. A hypothesis is that the more technologically and knowledge-oriented an organization, the less likely it is to resist change despite existing in and possessing change-resistant national culture variables. This does not suggest that national culture plays no role in change, but rather that specific corporate cultures modify it.

From another perspective, although in the Harzing and Hofstede (1996) model, the culture of the United States is very low on resistance to change and the change strategy inferred is a mixture of consultation and participation, there are organizational cultures in American industries that would not be responsive to these techniques. For these companies, manipulation, persuasion, and possibly coercion would be more effective change strategies. Examples are retail outlets, fast-food restaurants, and other bureaucratically organized industries. There is also substantial evidence that large segments of American public education have organizational cultures resistant to change (Sarason 1996), although it is unlikely that manipulation or coercion would be effective change strategies for schools.

Another issue is that certain types of studies produce more detail and nuance in describing and analyzing an organization's culture. For example, Kim (1992, p. 217), who conducted an ethnographic study of a Korean company, writes:

> My study has led me to conclude that the culture of Poongsan [the company's name] cannot be dichotomized in terms of polar concepts, as if they were mutually exclusive and exhaustive. Rather, the traditional and modern cultures coexist in Poongsan's organizational culture. For the present, at least, the behavior patterns of Poongsan industrial workers seem to be marked not by convergence but by contrasting dual ethics, the traditional and the modern.
>
> As for the precise balance between tradition and modernity in the organizational culture of Poongsan, it is difficult to discern or assess the ranges of the two cultures for each employee and manager. The balance differs from issue to issue, and from one individual to another. The self-interest of managers and workers leads them to respond to each situation selectively, choosing between two contrasting ethics at each time.[1]

Dichotomies present in organizational culture that affect the acceptance of change often escape detection in large-scale survey research. The detailed study of a single organization reveals the complexity of organizational culture and suggests that it is not fully congruent with a particular national culture. To manage change successfully, those implementing it must thoroughly understand the richness and complexity of cultures—national and organizational.

---

[1]Excerpt from *The Culture of Korean Industry: An Ethnography of Poongsan Corporation* by Choong Sam Kim. Copyright © 1992 by The University of Arizona Press. Reprinted by permission of The University of Arizona Press.

Macro-Organizational Change Theories

Macro-level theories identify processes that create change independent of national culture and, to some extent, managerial action.

A **macro-level typology** of organizational change provides a larger framework for understanding the processes of organizational change described previously. For example, although culture plays a significant role in reactions toward and the management of change, macro-level theories identify processes that create change independent of national culture and, to some extent, managerial action. We describe four macro-organizational change theories, life-cycle, teleological, dialectical, and evolutionary theory (Van de Ven and Poole 1995), in the following sections.

LIFE-CYCLE THEORY

Life-cycle theory borrows concepts from fields as diverse as biology, child development, and moral development. The central view of life-cycle theory is that

the developing entity has within it an underlying form, logic, program, or code that regulates the process of change and moves the entity from a given point of departure toward a subsequent end that is prefigured in the present state (Van de Ven and Poole 1995, p. 515).[2]

A form that is originally primitive becomes more developed and complex over the course of the life cycle. In addition, the progression over the life cycle follows a single sequence of stages, is cumulative, and "each stage of development is seen as a necessary precursor of succeeding stages" (Van de Ven and Poole 1995, p. 515). Life-cycle theory views organizational development as driven by something similar to a genetic code within the developing organization. The implication of this theory for the management of change is that organizations have developmental patterns that managers must recognize and adapt to.

TELEOLOGICAL THEORY

Teleological theory relies on the philosophical doctrine that a purpose or goal is the final cause for guiding the movement of an organization. It involves assuming that "the entity is purposeful and adaptive; by itself or in interaction with others, the entity constructs an envisioned end state, takes action to reach it, and monitors the progress" (Van de Ven and Poole 1995, p. 516).

Teleological theory differs from life-cycle theory because it does not prescribe a sequence of stages of organizational development. With its emphasis on goal achievement, this theory underlies much managerial and organizational behavior theory. Also in this theory management is proactive and exerts considerable control through strategy, planning, and decision making.

DIALECTICAL THEORY

Another approach to understanding development and change in organizations is **dialectical theory**. In dialectical theory,

---

[2]Excerpt from "Explaining Development and Change in Organizations" by A. Van de Ven and M. Poole from *Academy of Management Review*, 1995, 20: 510–40. Reprinted by permission of Academy of Management.

stability and change are explained by reference to the balance of power between opposing entities. Struggles and accommodations that maintain the status quo between oppositions produce
stability. Change occurs when these opposing values, forces, or events gain sufficient power to
confront and engage the status quo (Van de Ven and Poole 1995, p. 517).[3]

The product of conflict—the struggle between thesis and antithesis—is a
synthesis. The synthesis can become the thesis of a new conflict that starts the dialectical process again. Change is the product of conflict in historical forces.
These forces are beyond managerial control—for example, the dynamics of capitalist economies. In this sense, dialectical theory is similar to population ecology
theory because both view external variables as major determinants of organizational behavior.

▌▐▌ EVOLUTIONARY THEORY

Evolutionary theory borrows key ideas from biological evolutionary theory and
views change as proceeding

through a continuous cycle of variation, selection, and retention. Variations, the creations of
novel forms of organizations, are often viewed to emerge by blind or random change; they just
happen. Selection of organizations occurs principally through the competition for scarce resources, and the environment selects entities that best fit the resource base of an environmental
niche (Van de Ven and Poole 1995, p. 518).[4]

Two types of evolution are continuous or **gradual evolution** and **punctuated equilibrium**. Punctuated equilibrium is the argument that evolution is not
gradual but instead characterized by long periods of organizational stability or equilibrium punctuated by short periods of intense, fundamental change that create discontinuities (Romanelli and Tushman 1995). It is possible to manage transitions
from one stage to another—for example, by creating a punctuation that transforms
the organization.

▌▐▌ CULTURAL IMPLICATIONS
OF MACRO CHANGE THEORIES

From the cultural perspective, these theories are useful for analyzing organizational change in societies with different cultural orientations. Life-cycle theory
can describe the organizational change processes of past-oriented societies, because even tradition-bound organizations experience birth, growth, and decline.
For example, family businesses are often traditional in their outlook toward
change but nonetheless experience change as a result of maturational processes.

Punctuated equilibrium theory can explain the type of change experienced
by organizations in present- and future-oriented societies that produce turbulent
environments resulting in evolutionary discontinuities. An example is the change
organizations are experiencing in former communist countries. Instead of being
run by the Soviet government, many Russian corporations are suddenly privately
owned and expected to operate efficiently enough to generate profits. Another
example is the computer industry, which periodically experiences revolution-

---

[3]Ibid.
[4]Ibid.

ary change because of new technology and the development of path-breaking software.

Convergence or Divergence?

▌▌▌ FORCES FOR CONVERGENCE

The major forces for organizational change throughout the world are pressures on nations and corporations to be competitive. The limitations of pyramidal organizations—with chains of command, rules, and regulations—that focus on producing large quantities of standardized products, are increasingly evident as national economies and geographic boundaries become less important (Reich 1991). Replacing rigid structures are flexible, temporary teams of knowledge workers who act as free-floating quasi-entrepreneurs whose mission is to create change.

Even if organizations fail to transform into flexible forms such as networks or webs, other pressures for change include attempts to standardize product quality across nations, the diffusion of advanced management techniques, and the transfer of technological innovations.

▌▌▌ FORCES FOR DIVERGENCE

Casting doubt on convergence, emerging nations often have difficulty eliminating stages of development and instead evolve gradually through economic and organizational stages. Even though acculturation, the transfer of elements of one culture to another, has probably accelerated, problems remain with diffusion of organizational innovations. For example, Japanese quality control techniques transferred imperfectly to the automobile industry in the United States (Cole 1990).

In addition, culture and local conditions can act as barriers to change and continue to influence management and organizational behavior. The appeal of national, regional, religious, ethnic, and other variables that provide distinct cultural identities could increase, fragmenting the global economy in significant ways and creating resistance to change rather than propelling organizations toward similar changes. From this perspective, the global economy could become integrated because of trade interdependencies but is unlikely to change toward a unitary corporate culture and structure.

Implications for Managers

The primary implication for managers is that culture influences organizational change. National and organizational cultures play a role in determining when management perceives a need for change, what change is appropriate, the nature of resistance to change, and the success of planned change.

An international manager must assess each of these areas when formulating a change program. Although all cultures resist change to some extent, it is likely that cultures with reverence for tradition will either not perceive the need for change or strenuously resist it. One strategy under these conditions is to replace local managers with local or expatriate managers who accept the rationale for change. Another option is to implement extensive retraining programs for indigenous managers and lower level employees. Yet another approach is a combination of structural rearrangements and new technology that requires minimal voluntary value change but alters roles, interaction, and ultimately worker behavior and values.

Along with the influence of culture, the international manager must be aware of internal and external forces for change and how specific cultures respond to them. Finally, it is also important for managers to understand the larger processes that affect organizational change, such as social evolution, and the limitations they impose on planned change.

■ Summary

Organizational change is an important topic for managers because a substantial part of their jobs requires the formulation and implementation of planned organizational change. Affecting all managers and workers is the increasing amount of change produced by the internationalization and globalization of organizations. Instead of managing local external and internal pressures for change, managers now must contend with changes and pressures for change in many parts of the world that have the potential to change their organization.

Organizational change occurs at the level of roles, groups, and organizational structure. The most significant change is structural because it affects the other levels. Sources of change are internal and external variables. Internal variables include the technical production process, political processes, and the organization's culture. External forces are population and social trends, political-economic movements, social movements, technology, competition, professionalization, and culture contact.

National culture influences organizational change because cultures respond differently to change. The time orientation of cultures can be past, present, or future oriented. In addition, various factors create resistance to change such as tradition, habit, resource limitations, power and influence, fear of the unknown, and values.

Lewin's three-phase theory for managing change, organization development, and macro change theories are useful for managers to understand the dynamics of change. It is also important for managers to know how to overcome resistance to change, including education and communication, participation and involvement, negotiation and agreement, manipulation and co-optation, and the use of coercion.

Finally, managers must be aware that some theories of change—for example, organizational ecology, life-cycle theory, dialectical theory, and evolutionary theory—limit the role of managers in initiating and controlling the change processes of organizations.

■ Discussion Questions

1. Why is organizational change so prevalent throughout the world? What has caused the rate of change to accelerate in the past two decades?
2. What role does culture play in either promoting or creating barriers to change?
3. Why is it important for managers to understand and apply sophisticated theories of change?
4. Do you think resistance to change is as prevalent as the authors claim it is? If so, based on your experience, why do people respond to change the way they do?
5. What can a manager do if the ways to overcome resistance to change fail to work?

6. In your view, is it possible for managers to succeed in implementing planned organizational change?

7. What are some of the unanticipated outcomes of planned change? How can they be managed?

8. In your view, are organizations changing in ways that will reduce the contribution of specific national cultures in shaping their organizations?

9. Describe a planned change in an organization in which you participate. What is the change? How was it implemented? What were the results?

References

AMADO, G., FAUCHEUX, C., and LAURENT, A. (1991), "Organizational Change and Cultural Realities: Franco-American Contrasts," *International Studies of Management and Organization*, 21, 3, 62–95.

BARLEY, S. (1986), "Technology as an Occasion for Structuring: Evidence from Observations of CT Scanners and the Social Order of Radiology Departments," *Administrative Science Quarterly*, 31, 78–108.

BEER, M., EISENSTAT, R., and SPECTOR, B. (1990), "Why Change Programs Don't Produce Change," *Harvard Business Review* (November/December), 158–66.

BURKE, W. (1982), *Organization Development: Principles and Practices*. Boston: Little, Brown.

CARROLL, G., and HANNAN, M. (eds.) (1995), *Organizations in Industry: Strategy, Structure and Selection*. New York: Oxford University Press.

COLE, R. (1990), "U.S. Quality Improvement in the Auto Industry: Close But No Cigar," *California Management Review* 32, 4, 43–67.

GERSICK, C. (1988), "Time and Transition in Work Teams: Toward a New Model of Group Development," *Academy of Management Journal*, 31, 9–41.

———. (1991), "Revolutionary Change Theories: A Multilevel Exploration of the Punctuated Equilibrium Paradigm," *Academy of Management Journal*, 31, 9–41.

GOLD, B. (1995), "Explaining Educational Change: A New Paradigm," Paper presented at the Annual Meeting of the American Sociological Association, Washington, DC.

———, and MILES, M. (1981), *Whose School Is It, Anyway?* New York: Praeger.

GOLEMBIEWSKI, R. (1987), "Is OD Narrowly Culture-bound? Prominent Features of 100 Third-World Applications," *Organization Development Journal*, 5, 20–29.

HANNAN, J. and FREEMAN, J. (1989), *Organizational Ecology*. Cambridge, MA: Harvard University Press.

HARZING, A. and HOFSTEDE, G. (1996), "Planned Change in Organizations: The Influence of National Culture," in Bamberger, P. and Erez, M., (eds.), *Research in The Sociology of Organizations: Cross-Cultural Analysis of Organizations*. Greenwich, CT: JAI Press.

HOFSTEDE, G., (1980), *Culture's Consequences: International Differences in Work-Related Values*. Newbury Park, CA: Sage Publications.

HUNTER, M. (1996), "Europe's Reborn Right," *New York Times Magazine* (April 21), 38–43.

KAHN, J. (1995), "Chinese Corporations Bulk Up to Take On the World: Business Giants Believe Their Great Size Is the Key to Competing," *Wall Street Journal* (July 5), A6.

KIM, C. (1992), *The Culture of Korean Industry: An Ethnography of Poongsan Corporation*. Tucson, AZ: University of Arizona Press.

KOTTER, J. and SCHLESINGER, L. (1979), "Choosing Strategies for Change," *Harvard Business Review*, 57, 106–14.

LEWIN, K. (1951), *Field Theory in Social Science*. New York: Harper and Row.

MERTON, R. (1936), "The Unanticipated Consequences of Purposive Social Action," *American Sociological Review*, 1, 894–904.

NISBET, R. (1980), *History of the Idea of Progress*. New York: Basic.

NORTHCRAFT, G. and NEALE, M. (1994), *Organizational Behavior: A Management Challenge*. Fort Worth, TX: Dryden Press.

REICH, R. (1991), *The Work of Nations: Preparing Ourselves for 21st-Century Capitalism*. New York: Alfred A. Knopf.

ROMANELLI, E. and TUSHMAN, M. (1994), "Organizational Transformation as Punctuated Equilibrium: An Empirical Test," *Academy of Management Journal*, 37, 1141–66.

SARASON, S. (1996), *Revisiting "The Culture of the School and the Problem of Change."* New York: Teachers College Press.

Scott, R. (1995), *Institutions and Organizations*. Newbury Park, CA: Sage Publications.

Sieber, S. (1981), *Fatal Remedies*. New York: Plenum.

Steinmetz, G. (1995), "Customer-Service Era Is Reaching Germany Late, Hurting Business," *Wall Street Journal* (June 1), 1, A8.

Tichy, N. (1983), *Managing Strategic Change: Technical, Political and Cultural Dynamics*. New York: John Wiley & Sons.

———. and Sherman, S. (1993), *Control Your Own Destiny or Someone Else Will: How Jack Welch is Making General Electric the World's Most Competitive Company*. New York: Doubleday.

Trompenaars, F. (1993), *Riding the Waves of Culture: Understanding Diversity in Global Business*. New York: Irwin.

Tuckman, B. and Jensen, M. (1977), "Stages of Small Group Development Revisited," *Group and Organization Studies*, 2, 419–27.

Van de Ven, A., and Poole, M. (1995), "Explaining Development and Change in Organizations," *Academy of Management Review*, 20, 510–40.

Weick, K. (1987), "Perspectives on Action in Organizations," in J. Lorsch (ed.), *Handbook of Organizational Behavior*. Upper Saddle River, NJ: Prentice Hall.

Zuboff, S. (1985), "Automate/Informate: The Two Faces of Intelligent Technology," *Organization Dynamics*, 39–54.

Part III

EMERGING ISSUES IN INTERNATIONAL ORGANIZATIONAL BEHAVIOR

Managing Diversity

Learning Diversity from a Foreign Acquisition

In the late 1980s, to cut costs in its battle against a hostile takeover, U.S.-based Pillsbury closed its Affirmative Action Department. A short time later, Grand Metropolitan, a British firm, acquired Pillsbury, including its well-known brands Burger King, Green Giant, and Häagen Dazs.

The new owners believed that in the United States multiculturalism could benefit Pillsbury. Grand Metropolitan reinstated the Affirmative Action Department, renaming it the "culture diversity" function. *Diversity* was defined as meeting the needs of women and Afro-Americans.

After reinstituting the department, top management attended a series of lectures emphasizing the business value of diversity. As a result, Pillsbury introduced a reward structure that awarded bonuses to senior managers for encouraging diversity. Within six months there was a serious commitment to diversity by Pillsbury. In fact, the definition of diversity expanded to include working style, age, education, and sexual preference.

The commitment to diversity in the United States and the program's success encouraged Grand Metropolitan's headquarters in the United Kingdom to implement similar programs. Eventually, the company made managing diversity a priority throughout its global operations.

Source: Herriot, P. and Pemberton, C. (1995), *Competitive Advantage Through Diversity: Organizational Learning from Difference*. London: Sage. Copyright (c) 1995 by P. Herriot and C. Pemberton. Reprinted by permission of Sage Publications Ltd. and the authors.

Learning Objectives

After reading this chapter, you should be able to:

1. Define *diversity*.
2. Understand how different cultures view diversity.
3. Explain Cox's model of the multicultural organization.
4. Discuss various ways of managing diversity in organizations.
5. Describe unintended results of managing diversity.
6. Consider how managing diversity can be a competitive advantage.
7. Debate whether approaches to managing diversity are converging or diverging worldwide.

Organizations in many countries are experiencing increased diversity in their domestic employees. Labor forces are becoming more diverse as a result of immigration, social movements, political events, and population trends. At the same time, as organizations globalize and employ people in other countries, they search for ways to manage them effectively. The following are examples of these trends:

- Although the United States has always been a country of immigrants, almost half of the new additions to the labor force in the 1990s will be non-Caucasian (Cox 1993).

- Because of population changes and increasing competition for highly skilled, competent people, the number of women in the British workforce has been increasing (Hammond and Holton 1994).

- As a result of the changes in governments in Eastern Europe, many people moved to Western Europe, particularly Germany, to seek greater economic opportunities.

- Hong Kong's rising standard of living has led to the importation of a substantial population of Philippino domestic helpers.

- Japanese companies in the United States find managing their diverse American employees to be complex and perplexing.

With increasing diversity across the globe, as well as the greater internationalization of corporations, managers must understand diversity and how to manage it.

What Is Diversity?

Diversity is a range of differences, including gender, race, ethnicity, and age—characteristics that might be apparent from looking at someone. It also includes differences that are not visible, such as education, professional background, functional area of expertise, sexual preference, and religion. All of these differences are important because they affect how individuals behave within an organization. Employees who belong to the same group often have similar patterns of behavior. As an organization becomes more diverse, differences among groups can become more pronounced and lead to questions of how to manage diversity.

Research on managing diversity developed from studies of equal employment and discrimination that focus on assimilating groups into the mainstream. Current research on managing diversity differs because of an emphasis on "celebration," or valuing, of differences.

Researchers have used different definitions of managing diversity. Most of them include three main points (Kandola 1995): First, effective management of diversity and differences among people can add value to a company; second, diversity includes all types of differences, not only the obvious physical differences such as gender or ethnicity; and third, organizational culture and working environment issues are concerns of managing diversity. The contemporary view of diversity is that:

> Managing diversity, if it has an overriding image, is that of an organization as a mosaic. The differences come together to create a whole organization, in much the same way as the single pieces of a mosaic come together to create an image. The differences are acknowledged, accepted and have a place in the whole structure (Kandola 1995, p. 132).

Managing diversity, if it has an overriding image, is that of an organization as a mosaic.

Another metaphor for diversity is the salad bowl: In the same sense as the mosaic, the concept is that each individual has a unique contribution to make in an organization. When diverse backgrounds and talents combine in an organization, they produce a synergistic effect.

The dimensions of diversity and how different nations or organizations identify the different groups represented within them vary significantly. For some, gender and racioethnicity constitute diversity; for others, a greater array of variables is important.

How Different Cultures View Diversity

The way a culture views diversity depends on the cultural values of people in that society. The range of population differences in that culture and attitudes toward them also affect the view of diversity. In the United States, a country of immigrants, there has been a 200-year history of dealing with people who are different. In Japan, historically isolated from other cultures for centuries and today relatively homogeneous, the view of diversity is much different. Germany, with a tradition of guest workers since the end of World War II and an influx of immigrants in the early 1990s, has yet another view. The next section presents views of diversity in the United States, Japan, and Germany.

THE UNITED STATES

In the United States, there is a fundamental tradition valuing equality and equal opportunity. Although relationships among members of different racial and ethnic groups have not always been harmonious—and are not today—law and public and corporate policy over the past 40 years have made numerous attempts to address diversity issues. In the 1990s, multiculturalism and valuing diversity are well established. For example, as Fowers and Richardson (1996, pp. 611–12) wrote:

> The great moral force of the multicultural argument is evident in the influence that it has gained in . . . American society . . . Opposition to racism and oppression has become part of the moral framework of mainstream society in the United States . . . [T]he enduring moral power of the ideal of equality has been articulated and demonstrated in the slow and difficult expansion of basic human rights from the privileged few to include all groups and individuals in the United States, at least in principle. In spite of frequent opposition, we have come to see individual rights as universal and inalienable on the basis of this perspective on human dignity.

> Multiculturalism is, in some respects, the most recent stage of this universalization. It calls on us to recognize the rights of all peoples, and it attempts to ensure the dignity and first-class citizenship of all. Of course, racism and oppression have not been eliminated, but racist and oppressive practices and their legitimating theories of racial superiority or tribalism have become unacceptable to us, at least in our public discourse.

In the United States there are various laws that provide **equal employment opportunity**. These laws prohibit employment discrimination on the basis of race, gender, ethnicity, religion, color, age, disability, pregnancy, national origin, and citizenship status. There are also **Affirmative Action** laws, which are an attempt to make up for past systematic discrimination against women and minorities through a quota system. Table 13-1 lists some of these laws.

With the increasing diversity in the domestic workforce, many companies in the United States have found it necessary to develop initiatives to promote mutual

Table 13-1   **Major U.S. Federal Laws and Regulations Affecting Equal Employment Opportunity**

Law	*Coverage*
Equal Pay Act of 1963	Prohibits gender-based pay differentials for equal work.
Title VII, 1964 Civil Rights Act (as amended in 1972)	Prohibits job discrimination in employment based on race, color, religion, gender, or national origin.
Executive Order 11246 (1965)	Requires contractors and subcontractors performing work on federal or federally assisted projects to prepare and implement affirmative action plans for minorities and women, persons with disabilities, and veterans.
Age Discrimination in Employment Act (1967) ADEA	Prohibits age discrimination in any terms and conditions of employment, including areas such as hiring, promotion, termination, leaves of absence, and compensation. Protects individuals age forty and over.
Rehabilitation Act of 1973	Prohibits contractors and subcontractors of federal projects from discriminating against applicants and/or employees who are physically or mentally disabled, if qualified to perform the job. This statute also requires the contractor to take affirmative action in the employment and advancement of individuals with disabilities.
The Vietnam Era Veterans Readjustment Assistance Act of 1972 and 1974	Requires government contractors and subcontractors to take affirmative action with respect to certain classes of veterans (of the Vietnam Era and Special Disabled Veterans).
The Immigration Reform and Control Act of 1986 (IRCA)	Prohibits employers from discriminating against persons authorized to work in the U.S. with respect to hire or termination from employment because of national origin or citizenship status. IRCA makes it illegal for an employer knowingly to hire an alien who is not authorized to work in the U.S. All new hires must prove their identity and eligibility to work in the U.S.
Americans with Disabilities Act of 1990, Title I (ADA)	Prohibits employers from discriminating against qualified applicants and employees with disabilities in regard to any employment practices or terms, conditions, and privileges of employment
Civil Rights Act of 1991	Focuses on burdens of proof and remedies in cases of discrimination based on race, color, religion, gender, age, disability (under the ADA) and/or national origin. The Act grants to plaintiffs the right to a jury trial and makes available compensatory and punitive damages (capped at $300,000).

Source: Adapted from Fernandez, J.P. (with M. Barr) (1993), *The Diversity Advantage: How American Business Can Out-perform Japanese and European Companies in the Global Marketplace.* New York: Lexington, 314–16.

understanding and cooperation. One example is the Valuing Differences program instituted by the Digital Equipment Corporation (DEC) in the mid-1970s. The program focused on the need for people with different backgrounds to talk about their differences. Discussion groups called Core Groups included men and women of all ethnicities and races, representing all levels of the organization. The program evolved, and in 1985, Digital made Valuing Differences a company function and included it in DEC's written policy. Employees at DEC realized that by recognizing and appreciating one another's differences, they could work most effectively with each other (Mandell and Kohler-Gray 1990).

Not only do large corporations have diversity programs, but small companies find them useful as well. For example, the 11-employee firm Cardiac Concepts, Inc., which specializes in cardiovascular testing, made effective use of a diversity training program. During a four-hour training session, employees gained a better understanding of the values and lifestyles of their colleagues from other cultures and ultimately improved working relationships (Lee 1993).

Another view of diversity in the United States is in management education. The American Assembly of Collegiate Schools of Business (AACSB), the accrediting body for business schools in the United States, has mandated the teaching of diversity issues as part of the undergraduate and graduate curricula. This indicates the importance AACSB believes such issues have for managers now and in the future.

The study, management, and legislation of diversity continues to develop in the United States. In spite of a strong legal basis for equality dating to the U.S. Constitution and more recent equal opportunity legislation, there is overwhelming evidence that within organizations individuals from different groups are not treated the same way (Cox 1993). Although opportunities for women and minorities have improved considerably since the early 1960s, the ideal of equality has yet to be achieved.

JAPAN

The view of diversity in Japan is quite different. Historically, Japan had little contact with the rest of the world until the mid-1800s (Fernandez 1993). A small island nation, it was important for individuals to work together in order to provide the necessities for all to survive. Today the population of Japan is relatively homogeneous, the vast majority of people being ethnic Japanese. There are small numbers of ethnic Koreans and Chinese, some of whom have lived in Japan for generations, as well as tiny populations of expatriates and foreign students.

Japanese culture is extremely group-oriented, and acceptable behavior is clearly defined. In Japanese society, an individual knows how to behave on the basis of age, gender, and position. Behaviors that deviate from appropriate norms are subject to sanction.

Within organizations, the Japanese have a characteristic management style that is credited for the worldwide success of Japanese business and the rapid development of the Japanese economy in the latter part of the twentieth century. The management system is intertwined with Japanese culture. Although some practices were brought from abroad, such as quality circles, the Japanese developed and made them their own.

Characteristics of the Japanese management system include managerial autonomy, rigid hierarchical organizations, consensus decision making, lifetime employment, promotion based on seniority, and relative equity in compensation between management and workers (Chen 1995). However, the recession Japan experienced in the early 1990s and changes occurring in Japanese society may have created the need for new organizational forms and practices that borrow from the West (Abegglen and Stalk 1991; Chen 1995; Durlabhji and Marks 1993; Pascale and Athos 1981; Whitehill 1991).

In large corporations in Japan the level of position is related to the age and gender of the incumbent, with older males holding the most senior positions. Retirement has generally been around age 55 to 60 years, and the number of women in managerial positions has been extremely limited.

In 1990, women made up 41% of the labor force in Japan. Almost all women work after they complete school and then "retire" when they marry or get pregnant. Many women rejoin the workforce when their children are older. In large companies and government, women occupy only 2–3% of managerial positions. However, smaller firms have more women managers. A 1989 study found companies employing fewer than 100 people had more than 20% women managers. Throughout the workforce, the largest numbers of women managers are at the lowest level of management, in charge of a subsection (*kakaricho* position) (Steinhoff and Tanaka 1994). Japanese women also find greater opportunity in foreign companies that are generally not attractive to top male university graduates. However, the number of these companies is relatively small (Lansing and Ready 1988; Steinhoff and Tanaka 1994).

In 1986 an equal opportunity law went into effect throughout Japan prohibiting discrimination against women in new employee training, retirement, and dismissal. It also lifted some restrictions against night work and overtime for women. However, the new law merely *encourages* equal opportunity in recruiting, hiring, and promoting (Fernandez 1993), and the sole enforcement mechanism is "administrative guidance" (Steinhoff and Tanaka 1994).

After the law went into effect companies developed a two-track system. At the time of initial hiring, women choose between a traditional woman's job and a career position supposedly equivalent to those offered permanent male employees (Steinhoff and Tanaka 1994). With the economic recession in Japan in the early 1990s came limited career opportunities for both men and women, but the impact on females was greater.

The Japanese maintain a highly restrictive immigration policy, and in 1990 had an average of 1.53 children per family (Steinhoff and Tanaka 1994). Although at present diversity in domestic organizations is unimportant or even irrelevant, these factors combined with a long-term labor shortage, suggest that the Japanese may need a more diversified workforce with respect to age, gender, and possibly foreign workers. Outside Japan, Japanese companies constitute some of the major forces in global markets. As their experience with subsidiaries outside of Japan shows, the Japanese need to consider managing diversity on a worldwide basis.

▌▌▌ GERMANY

Diversity in Germany is somewhere between the United States and Japan. Although the majority of German residents is ethnically German, there is a history of "**guest workers**" from abroad in the former West Germany dating to after World War II, when there was a shortage of men to rebuild the war-devastated economy. German industries recruited workers primarily from southern Europe and northern Africa, including Turkey, Greece, Yugoslavia, Italy, Spain, Portugal, Morocco, and Tunisia. The intention was that guest workers would eventually return to their home countries. The foreign worker population in Germany increased tremendously over a 40-

year period, from 80,000 in the mid-1950s to 2.6 million in the mid-1990s. In 1992, guest workers constituted almost 12% of all wage and salary workers (Fernandez 1993).

As the economic and political situation in Europe changed, so did the attitude toward foreign workers. "Foreigners at first were not considered threatening but somewhat magical and very exotic. By 1964, however, an anti-Turkish image emerged ... Resentment and prejudices against Turks have increased since then, leading to violent and even deadly attacks" (Fernandez 1993, p. 167).

With the change of governments throughout Eastern Europe and the reunification of East and West Germany in October 1990, the situation for guest workers grew more complex. Germany's liberal asylum laws and generous provisions for social services made the country a magnet for many from the former Communist states of Eastern Europe. The number of asylum seekers increased rapidly in the early 1990s to half a million in 1992. By the end of that year, Germany changed its asylum laws. Asylum seekers from bordering countries and countries that did not practice political persecution were not allowed to enter Germany and could only appeal from abroad (Fernandez 1993).

In addition, the high wages and benefits guaranteed to German workers are making them noncompetitive, even in Germany. For example, the national unemployment rate in Germany in 1996 was 10.3% with 14% in the former East Germany. In spite of 200,000 German construction workers being out of work, the industry employs 500,000 foreigners. The European Union allows workers from member countries to work in any other member country without a permit. Because these workers do not receive the same benefits and work more flexible hours than German workers, they are cheaper to hire (Andrews 1996).

The enormous costs of integrating the former East Germany and the influx of asylum seekers coupled with the lackluster economy of the early 1990s created a climate of resentment against foreign workers. Although many Germans would prefer guest workers be sent home, they are essential in jobs in garbage collection, janitorial services, and the hospitality industry, which the Germans avoid (Fernandez (1993).

The treatment of working women is also evolving. In the former West Germany approximately half of working-aged women were in the labor force, compared with more than 80% in the former East Germany. With the change in the economic system in East Germany in the early 1990s came massive unemployment. Women, who made up more than 60% of the unemployed, felt the impact of unemployment more strongly (Berthoin Antal and Krebsbach-Gnath 1994; Wiedemeyer, Beywl, and Helmstadter 1993).

Although women were widely present in the labor force in the former East and West Germanys, they received on average one-third less pay than men, were concentrated in relatively few industries, and were far less likely than men to be managers, particularly at a senior level. The constitution of the Federal Republic of Germany recognizes the equal rights of men and women. Additional laws requiring equal opportunity and the development of equal opportunity positions throughout public administration came into effect in the 1980s. Similar recommendations and voluntary guidelines were suggested to the private sector (Berthoin Antal and Krebsbach-Gnath 1994).

Although the government was required by law to take measures to increase the recruitment, promotion, and training of women, there were no sanctions for failure to comply. During the reunification process, both in the public and private sectors, the equal opportunity guidelines and standard practices that had been used in

West Germany were not applied in East Germany, resulting in "significant gender bias in the decisions to keep, fire, or recruit staff in both the public and private sectors, and that bias [was expected to] have far-reaching consequences" (Berthoin Antal and Krebsbach-Gnath 1994, p. 218).

To summarize, the situation in Germany with respect to organizational diversity lies somewhere between that in the United States and Japan. Many women work, and some equal opportunity legislation exists, yet differences in the treatment of men and women persist. A sizable population of guest workers also continues to be an important part of the German workforce. Although guest workers make an important contribution to the German economy, they are concentrated in lower-level jobs and receive lower pay than Germans. Since the reunification of Germany in 1990, the dynamics of diversity have changed and continue to evolve. With a low birthrate, it is likely that in the future Germany will have to make continued and, most likely, greater utilization of women and foreign workers to sustain the needs of the economy.

> As the millennium approaches, the U.S. workforce continues to increase in diversity, and more businesses are going into international markets, creating the need to manage a wider variety of employees, customers, and suppliers.

The examples of the United States, Japan, and Germany illustrate that different cultures view diversity in different ways. Because of the American view of diversity, there is a large amount of research on differential treatment of individuals of different races, ethnic groups, genders, ages, education levels, professional backgrounds, and other factors. As the millennium approaches, the U.S. workforce continues to increase in diversity, and more businesses are going into international markets, creating the need to manage a wider variety of employees, customers, and suppliers. The result is both academic research on questions related to diversity and organizational action in developing programs and practices to deal with diversity.

Cox's Model of the Multicultural Organization

A model of diversity developed by Cox (1991, 1993) identifies six dimensions to analyze an organization's capability for effectively integrating culturally diverse employees. Table 13-2 presents these dimensions and their definitions.

On the basis of how an organization treats these six dimensions, Cox classifies it as one of three organizational types; monolithic, plural, or multicultural. Table 13-3 gives the characteristics of these three organizational types.

The Monolithic Organization The **monolithic** organization includes predominately the same type of people. People who are different from the majority often work only in a limited number of positions or departments. Because people with different backgrounds do not hold positions throughout the organization, minority group members usually follow the organizational norms set by the majority to survive. Members of the minority culture usually do not participate in many informal activities, and the majority group is unlikely to adopt minority-culture norms. Intergroup conflict is relatively low because the organization is so homogeneous; however, discrimination and prejudice are common.

Most Japanese companies would be classified as monolithic. The majority of people working in them are Japanese men, and the few women are primarily con-

Table 13-2 **Six Dimensions to Analyze Organizational Capability for Effective Integration of Culturally Diverse Employees**

Dimension	Definition
1. Acculturation	Modes by which two groups adapt to each other and resolve cultural differences
2. Structural Integration	Cultural profiles of organization members including hiring, job-placement, and job status profiles
3. Informal Integration	Inclusion of minority-culture members in informal networks and activities outside of normal working hours
4. Cultural Bias	Prejudice and discrimination
5. Organizational Identification	Feelings of belonging, loyalty, and commitment to the organization
6. Inter-group Conflict	Friction, tension, and power struggles between cultural groups

Source: From "Multicultural Organization" by T. Cox from *Academy of Management Executive*, May 1991, 35. Reprinted by permission of Academy of Management.

centrated in lower level and part-time positions. An important part of Japanese work culture involves socializing with coworkers after work, usually at male-oriented bars and small restaurants. Although it is increasingly becoming more acceptable for women to join these informal after-work activities, married women with home and family responsibilities do not have adequate time, and many are uncomfortable participating in such activities (Steinhoff and Tanaka 1994).

Because of the dominance of men, conflict between men and women in Japanese organizations is low. As a result of their low status, women receive less favorable treatment than men but, in complying with organization norms and cultural values, do little to change their treatment.

Table 13-3 **Characteristics of Cox's Three Organizational Types**

Dimension of Integration	Monolithic	Plural	Multicultural
Form of Acculturation	Assimilation	Assimilation	Pluralism
Degree of Structural Integration	Minimal	Partial	Full
Integration into Informal Organization	Virtually none	Limited	Full
Degree of Cultural Bias	Both prejudice and discrimination against minority-culture groups are prevalent	Progress on both prejudice and discrimination but both continue to exist, especially institutional discrimination	Both prejudice and discrimination are eliminated
Levels of Organizational Identification*	Large majority-minority gap	Medium to large majority-minority gap	No majority-minority gap
Degree of Intergroup Conflict	Low	High	Low

*Defined as difference between organizational identification levels between minorities and majorities.

Source: From "Multicultural Organization" by T. Cox from *Academy of Management Executive*, May 1991, 35. Reprinted by permission of Academy of Management.

The Plural Organization   The **plural organization** is the second type. It includes a wider variety of people, and management makes a greater effort to include people who differ from the majority. Structural integration is more extensive than in the monolithic organization because the number of minority group members is usually greater. However, minority group members may not be equally represented at different levels or in different functions. Minority group members are more involved in informal activities, and prejudice and discrimination are less than in the monolithic organization. However, the level of conflict among different groups tends to be high.

Cox (1991) categorizes the typical large firm of the 1990s in the United States as plural. These companies emphasize "an affirmative action approach to managing diversity." They have programs to promote equal opportunity or affirmative action—for example, recruitment and selection procedures to assure equal access to jobs or special training programs to benefit women and minority members. As a result, many large American companies have the same proportion of minority employees as in the population, but there are few women and minority managers. Because of special programs, and in some cases preference for hiring and promoting women and minority group members, some Caucasian men in the United States feel they are treated unfairly. This is one reason for conflict between groups.

The Multicultural Organization   The third type of organization is **multicultural**. The multicultural organization overcomes the problems of the plural organization, and rather than just having a diverse set of employees, diversity is valued. One characteristic of the multicultural organization is pluralism, meaning both majority and minority group members adopt some of the norms of the other. In addition, in the multicultural organization members of different groups hold positions throughout the organization and participate fully in informal activities. There is no prejudice or discrimination, all employees identify equally with the organization, and conflicts between groups are minimal. In 1991, Cox felt that few, if any, organizations could be classified as multicultural; but in his view, this type should be the model for the future.

Interest in managing diversity is a result of the changing nature of the workforce in several countries (Davidson 1991; Johnston and Packer 1987, Rajan 1990). Researchers have focused on the expected benefits an organization could gain if diversity is properly managed (Cox and Blake 1991; Kandola 1995). Benefits include the ability to attract and retain talented people from a broader range of groups, more flexible working practices that allow more immediate response to changing conditions, and potentially greater effectiveness from work teams. We discuss diversity as a competitive advantage subsequently.

How Organizations Manage Diversity

Organizations manage diversity in a variety of ways. This section presents a comprehensive model for an organizational level approach and several examples of actual techniques.

■■■ AN ORGANIZATIONAL LEVEL APPROACH

Contemporary organizational structures may not be appropriate for managing diversity (Kandola 1995). Eight factors are important for creating a new type of organization that can manage diversity:

1. **Organizational vision** refers to an organizational statement of why diversity is important, a general policy on diversity and how to use it, and the expected benefits to be gained.

2. **Top management commitment** is the support given to the diversity vision by senior executives. Top management must set an example for others to follow and allocate the necessary resources to implement the vision.

3. **Auditing and assessment of needs** means the organization collects data to ensure that different groups receive the same treatment. For example, an organization could determine the number of minority group employees at various levels and in different areas of the company or administer an attitude survey to collect information on how members of different groups feel they are being treated. A firm can discover potential problem areas with these techniques.

4. **Clarity of objectives:** Based on the results of the audit and assessment, management can set clear objectives relating to diversity and tie these to overall business objectives. It is important that managing diversity be seen as essential to the overall success of the business.

5. **Clear accountability:** Members of the organization should be responsible for carrying out diversity objectives. Allowing employees to participate in objective setting is one way of ensuring an understanding of and commitment to the goals. All involved should have an understanding of the policies and strategies.

6. **Effective communication** must also be maintained within and outside the organization; everyone needs to know the organization's diversity initiatives.

7. **Coordination of activity:** An individual or group coordinates the implementation of the diversity strategy. Part of this coordinating effort involves seeking information about new diversity initiatives from all sources.

8. **Evaluation:** The overall diversity strategy, as well as individual actions, must be evaluated. Data collected in the auditing and assessment of needs are helpful in providing a starting point against which to compare the program outcomes.

By following this strategy, an organization can be more successful in implementing diversity initiatives (Kandola 1995).

TECHNIQUES FOR MANAGING DIVERSITY

In addition to the organizational level approach, companies also undertake specific activities to manage diversity. The examples of DEC's Valuing Differences program and the diversity training program at Cardiac Concepts, Inc. presented earlier in the chapter are two techniques. Other successful approaches are training programs, core groups, multicultural teams, and using senior managers to oversee diversity programs.

Managing Diversity Training Programs   A very popular technique is the **managing diversity training program.** The time required for the program varies from a few hours to a few days. The major focus of training is raising levels of awareness and sensitivity to diversity issues. An example is the program of the Anti-Defamation League (ADL) of B'nai B'rith—a Jewish organization in the United States—in which the management of diversity is approached as a job skill. It begins with participants in small groups talking about their own ethnic identity and how it influences their behavior. In the next part, trainees consider the ways they could be identified and the commonalities and differences that exist among themselves.

Another activity is a test of cultural knowledge to see how much people know about other cultures. Games, exercises, and videos stimulate discussion, and the program concludes with a discussion about diversity efforts in the participants' own organizations (Castelli 1990).

Core Groups   **Core groups** consist of several employees from different cultural backgrounds who meet regularly. The group members discuss their attitudes, feelings, and beliefs about cultural differences and how they influence work behavior. The group provides an opportunity for individuals to speak frankly about their differences, and over time, they usually become more comfortable in dealing with diversity issues. Cox believes that the core group "is one of the most powerful tools available for organization change work related to managing diversity" (1993, p. 260). The DEC program discussed earlier is an example of this type.

Multicultural Teams   **Multicultural teams** contain workers from different cultural groups who learn how to maximize their effectiveness by taking full advantage of their differences. An example of this approach is British Petroleum's European finance center in Brussels, Belgium, where the staff members come from more than a dozen countries. The objectives of the program include (1) making team members aware of cultural differences and how they influence various aspects of the organization; (2) assisting members in becoming more aware of their own differences and how they can work with other team members; (3) improving communication among team members and with others at the finance center; (4) creating a set of work rules for the team; and (5) developing a shared team vision (Fernandez 1993).

Senior Managers of Diversity   In some organizations, the management of diversity is so important that the corporation creates a senior management position responsible for all diversity initiatives. This position demonstrates the company's commitment and ensures that its efforts are genuine. For example, at BankAmerica, which employs 85,000 people worldwide, the creation of the director of diversity position was a recommendation of an organization wide diversity task force formed in 1994 (Deutsch 1996).

Other Approaches   Other approaches used by corporations include recruitment and selection programs that focus on hiring individuals who value diversity, compensation and reward programs tied to achieving diversity goals, language training, mentoring programs, cultural advisory groups, and corporate social activities that celebrate diversity (Cox 1993; Fernandez 1993).

Unintended Results of Managing Diversity

So far, this chapter presents a positive view of managing diversity, suggesting that organizations of the future must be multicultural and that including all leads to more positive organizational outcomes. Evidence indicates, however, that in some situations, managing diversity has had unintended negative consequences (Nemetz and Christensen 1996; Thomas and Ely 1996). For example, when organizations develop special programs to encourage women and minorities, majority males often feel they are left out or treated unfairly. Affirmative action programs that give preferential treatment to certain groups may stigmatize individuals from those groups if others feel their qualifications are substandard. Management that brings in increased numbers of women and minorities, yet fails to appreciate and reward their contributions, engenders tension throughout the organization.

Organizations that make a commitment to managing diversity must also realize the effect of other influences on employees' attitudes and behavior (Nemetz and Christensen 1996). People's views on managing diversity are shaped by their family and friends, religion, education, profession, and other factors. Therefore, an organization must recognize that the impact of managing diversity programs may be limited because of competing influences.

> Management that brings in increased numbers of women and minorities, yet fails to appreciate and reward their contributions, engenders tension throughout the organization.

Managing Diversity for Competitive Advantage

As the workforce becomes increasingly more diverse worldwide, organizations that manage diversity well may have a competitive advantage (Cox and Blake 1991; Mandell and Kohler-Gray 1990). In addition to social responsibility benefits, there are six areas in which companies can gain competitive advantage from managing diversity well: (1) cost, (2) resource acquisition, (3) marketing, (4) creativity, (5) problem solving, and (6) organizational flexibility (Cox and Blake 1991).

Managing diversity well can create cost savings for organizations. People who are dissatisfied with their jobs are more likely to be absent or leave the organization. In the United States, women and minorities are likely to have higher absenteeism and turnover rates than White males (Cox 1996; Cox and Blake 1991). Higher rates of absenteeism and turnover might result because of dissatisfaction with a firm's treatment. On the positive side, pregnant workers in the United States have greater organizational commitment to organizations judged to be "family friendly" (Francesco and Thompson 1996). There is a cost associated with absenteeism and turnover, so reducing them translates into a cost savings for the employer.

Failure to manage diversity well in countries that have equal employment opportunity laws can also be expensive. For example, in 1993, Shoney's, a family-style restaurant chain in the United States, paid US$134.5 million to settle a class action suit claiming that the company had discriminated against Afro-Americans (Gaiter 1996).

The resource acquisition benefit comes when an organization has a reputation as a good place for all kinds of people to work. As women and minorities make up a larger percentage of the workforce in many countries, being able to attract the best of these groups is becoming increasingly more important.

Managing diversity well also improves a corporation's marketing. As organizations market their products and services to an increasingly more diversified domestic or global market, a well-managed diverse set of employees can help provide insight into the best approaches to these markets. Consumers from diverse groups might also prefer to buy from companies that value diversity.

Creativity and innovation is another potential result of having diverse groups and teams in an organization: The presence of a variety of viewpoints stimulates creativity. Along with this come higher-quality solutions to problems. As discussed in Chapter 7, a heterogeneous group can produce more creative solutions to complex or innovative problems. Positive outcomes result when the group is able to manage its differences. Understanding the background of each member and giving each an equal opportunity to participate can help facilitate the process.

The final potential advantage is organizational flexibility. As the organization welcomes a diverse set of individuals and the different viewpoints they bring, it potentially becomes more open and adaptable to new ideas and changing environments.

To summarize, managing diversity well potentially benefits an organization in the areas of social responsibility, cost, resource acquisition, marketing, creativity, problem solving, and organizational flexibility. To gain these benefits, however, the organization must create a climate that values diversity and where each employee has an equal chance to contribute and succeed.

Convergence or Divergence?

FORCES FOR CONVERGENCE

Managing diversity in organizations is a domestic concern for companies in North America and Europe. With the increased multiculturalism in these regions as well as more involvement in international markets, there is a strong need to better manage diversity. Outside of North America and Europe, the populations of many other countries are also extremely diverse.

Organizations have a wide variety of approaches to managing diversity domestically, and in some cases these extend to global operations. For example, in the Culture at Work vignette at the beginning of this chapter, when Grand Metropolitan, a British company, acquired the American food company Pillsbury, it reinstated and expanded the former Affirmative Action Department and made it into the "culture diversity" function. Later, Grand Metropolitan's management brought this concept back to its headquarters in the United Kingdom, and the company made the decision to manage diversity from a corporate multinational perspective.

As companies continue to internationalize and populations become more mobile, it is possible that a wider variety of groups will be represented in the workforce of countries such as Japan. As diversity within organizations worldwide increases, approaches to managing diversity could become similar.

FORCES FOR DIVERGENCE

Outside North America and Europe, there is less interest in managing diversity. In some countries, the idea might seem unimportant or irrelevant. For example, in Japan, where the workforce is relatively homogeneous, the need to manage diversity is far less important than in the United States. Even today, though Japanese companies expand worldwide, in many cases they either fail to recognize or make no attempt to manage the diversity in some of their subsidiaries.

Implications for Managers

With the simultaneous trends toward globalization and domestic multiculturalism, an important part of an international manager's job is managing a diverse work-force. Understanding the impact of diversity within an organization and knowing how to utilize the diversity efficiently are needed skills.

It is also important for the international manager to realize that different cultures view diversity differently. Countries with diverse populations have different approaches to the diversity. In some, members of diverse groups maintain a degree of separation, whereas in others, they freely interact. In countries where diversity is limited, there may be no societal guidelines for working with people who are different. Effective international managers must understand how the cultures they work in treat diversity and the potential impact this can have for them.

> Effective international managers must understand how the cultures they work in treat diversity and the potential impact this can have for them.

■ Summary

The concept of managing diversity has been developed and applied primarily in North America and Europe. As a result of changing demographics in these two areas, domestic labor forces are increasingly more diverse. There are also increasingly greater numbers of businesses entering international markets. The result is a strong need to manage the ensuing diversity to increase organizational effectiveness.

Cox's (1993) model of the multicultural organization analyzes an organization's capability for effectively integrating culturally diverse employees. There are three organizational types: the monolithic, plural, and multicultural. Although most organizations of the 1990s throughout the world fit the monolithic or plural type, in the future there will be greater need for companies, particularly those that are global, to be multicultural. To manage diversity in organizations, it is possible to take an organization-level approach to move a company toward the multicultural organizational type, or companies can use different activities to manage diversity.

Managing diversity can sometimes have unintended results. An organization might create negative feelings in the majority if it is seen as unfairly accommodating minorities. Organizations must also realize the multiple influences on employees' attitudes and behaviors as they establish diversity programs.

Managing diversity well can be a competitive advantage for organizations. An organization can benefit in the areas of social responsibility, cost, resource acquisition, marketing, creativity, problem solving, and organizational flexibility.

In the late 1990s, the managing diversity concept is common in North America and Europe. In other parts of the world, the issue of diversity might seem unimportant or irrelevant. However, with changing demographics and greater internationalization of business, the need for managing diversity will spread and could lead to greater convergence.

An effective international manager needs to develop skills in understanding and managing diversity. Because different cultures have various approaches to diversity, it is important to understand these approaches and the potential impact they could have on the manager.

■ Discussion Questions

1. How does your community define diversity? Your country? How are people who differ from the majority treated at work?

2. Select an organization with which you are familiar. (If you do not work, it could be your school, church, student, or community organization.) Using Cox's organizational types, how would you classify this organization? What do you think would be the most effective type for this organization now? In the future? Why?

3. What approaches do organizations use to manage diversity? Give an example from your personal experience or one that you have read about in another source. How effective is the approach taken in your example?

4. As a manager of a work group that has members from different backgrounds, what can you do to maximize the team's effectiveness?

5. Select a country of the world (your own or another). How does this country's view of diversity compare with those of the United States, Japan, and Germany?

References

ABEGGLEN, J. and STALK, G., Jr. (1991), *Kaisha, the Japanese Corporation*. New York: Basic Books.

ANDREWS, E.L. (1996), "The Upper Tier of Migrant Labor: German Builders Cut Costs Importing Eager Europeans," *The New York Times* (December 11), D1, D4.

BERTHOIN ANTAL, A. and KREBSBACH-GNATH, C. (1994), "Women in Management in Germany: East, West, and Reunited," in Adler, N.J. and Izraeli, D.N., (eds.) *Competitive Frontiers: Women Managers in a Global Economy*. Cambridge: Blackwell Publishers, 206–23.

CASTELLI, J. (1990), "Education Forms Common Bond," *HRMagazine* (June), 46–49.

CHEN, M. (1995), *Asian Management Systems: Chinese, Japanese and Korean Styles of Business*. New York: Routledge.

COX, T. JR. (1991), "The Multicultural Organization," *Academy of Management Executive* (May) 34–47.

———. (1993), *Cultural Diversity in Organizations: Theory, Research & Practice*. San Francisco: Berrett-Koehler.

———. and BLAKE, S. (1991), "Managing Cultural Diversity: Implications for Organizational Competitiveness," *Academy of Management Executive*, 5(3), 45–56.

DAVIDSON, M.J. (1991), "Women Managers in Britain—Issues for the 1990s," *Women in Management Review*, 6, 5–10.

DEUTSCH, C.H. (1996), "Corporate Diversity, in Practice," *The New York Times* (November 20), D1, D19.

DURLABHJI, S. and MARKS, N.E., (eds.) (1993), *Japanese Business: Cultural Perspective*. Albany, NY: SUNY Press.

ELEGANT, R. (1990), *Pacific Destiny: Inside Asia Today*. New York: Crown.

FERNANDEZ, J.P. (with M. BARR) (1993), *The Diversity Advantage: How American Business Can Out-perform Japanese and European Companies in the Global Marketplace*. New York: Lexington.

FOWERS, B.J. and RICHARDSON, F.C. (1996), "Why Is Multiculturalism Good?" *American Psychologist*, 51, 609–21.

FRANCESCO, A.M. and THOMPSON, C.A. (1996), "Pregnant Working Women: An Unrecognized Diversity Challenge," Presented at the Annual Meeting of the American Psychological Association Toronto, Canada, August.

GAITER, D.J. (1996), "Eating Crow: How Shoney's, Belted by a Lawsuit, Found the Path to Diversity," *Wall Street Journal* (April 16), A1, A6.

HAMMOND, V. and HOLTON, V. (1994), "Great Britain: The Scenario for Women Managers in Britain in the 1990's," in Adler, N.J. and Izraeli, D.N. (eds.) *Competitive Frontiers: Women Managers in a Global Economy*. Cambridge: Blackwell Publishers, 224–42.

HARMON, M.V. (1996), "Building a Shared Understanding and Commitment to Managing Diversity," *Journal of Business Communication*, 33(4), 427–42.

HERRIOT, P. and PEMBERTON, C. (1995), *Competitive Advantage through Diversity: Organizational Learning from Difference*. London: Sage.

ILES, P.A. (1994), "Developing Learning Environments: Challenges for Theory, Research and Practice," *Journal of European Industrial Training*, 18(3), 3–9.

JOHNSTON, W.B. and PACKER, A.E. (1987). *Workforce 2000: Work and Workers for the 21st Century*. Indianapolis; Hudson Institute.

KANDOLA, R. (1995), "Managing Diversity: New Broom or Old Hat?" *International Review of Industrial and Organizational Psychology*, 10, 131–67.

———. and FULLERTON, J. (1994), "Diversity: More Than Just an Empty Slogan," *Personnel Management*, 26(11), 46–50.

LANSING, P. and READY, K. (1988), "Hiring Women Managers in Japan: An Alternative for Foreign Employers," *California Management Review* (Spring), 112–27.

LEE, M. (1993), "Diversity Training Grows at Small Firms," *Wall Street Journal* (September 2), B2.

MANDELL, B. and KOHLER-GRAY, S. (1990), "Management Development that Values Diversity," *Personnel* (March) 41–47.

NEMETZ, P.L. and CHRISTENSEN, S.L. (1996), "The Challenge of Cultural Diversity: Harnessing a Diversity of Views to Understand Multiculturalism," *The Academy of Management Review*, 21, 434–62.

PASCALE, R. and ATHOS, A. (1981), *The Art of Japanese Management*. New York: Warner Books.

RAJAN, A. (1990), *1992 A Zero Sum Game: Business Know-how and Training Challenges in an Integrated Europe*. London: Industrial Society.

STEINHOFF, P.G. and TANAKA, K. (1994), "Women Managers in Japan," in Adler, N.J. and Izraeli, D.N. (eds.), *Competitive Frontiers: Women Managers in a Global Economy*. Cambridge: Blackwell Publishers, 79–100.

THOMAS, D.A. and ELY, R.J. (1996), "Making Differences Matter: A New Paradigm for Managing Diversity," *Harvard Business Review* (September–October) 79–90.

WIEDEMEYER, M., BEYWL, W., and HELMSTADTER, W. (1993), "Employment Promotion Companies in Eastern Germany: Emergency Measures or a Basis for Structural Reform?" *International Labour Review*, 132, 605–21.

WHITEHILL, A.M. (1991), *Japanese Management: Tradition and Transition*. New York: Routledge.

The Globalization of Organizational Behavior: Future Trends

 at Work

Virtual Learning

"Here we are teaming with engine, airframe, electronics makers and suppliers, customers, even competitors . . . spread all over the place. . . . We're trying to learn how to work together under these conditions: to share design and management information, to develop and sustain parallel engineering efforts across distances and between organizations. . . . We need to figure out how to manage our functional, philosophical, and cultural differences—to share just enough of our design and manufacturing processes to get the work done faster without giving away the store."

—Senior Executive, Aerospace Industry

Source: Excerpt from *Going Virtual: Moving Your Organization into the 21st Century* by Ray Grenier and George Metes. Copyright (©) 1995 by Prentice Hall. Reprinted by permission of Prentice Hall, Inc.

Learning Objectives

After reading this chapter, you should be able to:

1. Evaluate the prospects for human progress.

2. Understand forces that affect the future of the nation-state.

3. Describe issues involved in maintaining cultural identities as globalization increases.

4. Explain the impact of technology on the future of organizations and work.

5. Understand emerging types of organization structures.

6. Reflect on future changes in work.

7. Discuss the role of organizations in preserving the natural environment.

8. Summarize anticipated changes for managing organizational behavior in the future.

Organizations are complex social constructions. Rationally designed, they often act differently from their designers' intentions and occasionally create reverse consequences. One reason organizations develop in unpredictable ways is that to survive, they adapt to complex internal and external circumstances. Another reason is that their environments create uncertainty.

In both cases, managers make decisions with incomplete information. If the rate of change continues at the current pace or accelerates, the complexity and uncertainty organizations confront in the millennium will increase. Forecasting will become more difficult, creating less control and more unanticipated consequences.

Although it is difficult and risky to predict changes in organizations and national cultures, it is necessary to explore possible futures. Will the environments in which organizations exist remain the same, deteriorate, improve, or change in unexpected ways?

What Is the Future of Progress?

Organizations have a stake in progress. Products of human progress, organizations attempt to use human and material resources rationally. Organizations measure their ability to attain goals in terms of growth, including increased size, improved revenues, and greater profits. Customers demand better products, more responsive service, and innovation. In addition, employees expect to experience career advancement and accumulation of personal assets. The expectation of progress—movement to an improved state of affairs—is part of modern organizations.

SKEPTICISM IN PROGRESS

In *History of the Idea of Progress*, Nisbet (1980, p. 317) writes: "While the twentieth century is far from barren of faith in progress, there is nevertheless good ground for supposing that when the identity of our century is eventually fixed by historians, not faith but abandonment of faith in the idea of progress will be one of the major attributes." Does Nisbet's prediction stand up almost 20 years later?

Indicators for skepticism in progress are abundant. There are approximately 40 wars at all times in the world. In the mid-1990s, Central Europe and parts of Africa experienced the horror of ethnic cleansing. Economic development in many parts of the world is progressing haltingly, if at all. Race relations and the state of inner cities in the United States are eroding further. Sweatshops operate throughout the world. In summary there are many economic, social, and political problems throughout the world that appear to be intractable.

OPTIMISM IN PROGRESS

Indicators of progress are also numerous. Atomic bombs dropped in the 20th century, but have not since World War II. Communist regimes challenged the West but now embrace capitalism. The Asian rim experienced unprecedented economic growth and influenced and improved Western business practices. In South Africa a multi-racial society replaced apartheid.

Some observers of economic trends and organizations view the present as an era of significant change and opportunity for progress. Mitroff, Mason, and Pearson (1994, p. 11) write:

> The world is going through a transition—many would say a fundamental revolution—that is as profound as that from the Agrarian to the Industrial Age. Indeed, we have already moved from the Industrial to the Information/Knowledge/Systems Age. One sure sign of revolution is the inability of old institutions, old functions, and core competencies to adapt and cope with new problems.

Important questions are: What impact does globalization have on national cultures? How does globalization affect organizations? What types of organizations will emerge in the change from the Industrial to the Information Age?

> **Some observers of economic trends and organizations view the present as an era of significant change and opportunity for progress.**

What Is the Future of the Nation-State?

The future of the nation-state is uncertain (Ohmae 1995; Sassen 1996). A country with a single culture, economy, and political agenda is increasingly difficult to find. As immigration increases worldwide, the populations of countries are becoming more heterogeneous, and their cultures are changing rapidly with the influx of new ideas. At the same time, however, there is a powerful trend to retain native culture, which, in a return to tribalism, often results in the establishment of separate nation-states (Drucker 1993; Naisbitt 1994).

▋▋ THE BREAK-UP OF THE STATE

A notable example of this trend in the 1990s is the horrific war in the former Yugoslavia that resulted in the formation of new nation-states based on ethnic identity. Other recent examples of countries being divided include Czechoslovakia, which became Slovakia and the Czech Republic; the Soviet Union's breakdown into 15 independent countries; and the establishment of an Arab governed Palestinian state (Naisbitt 1994).

This type of change also occurs in less violent ways. Quebec's referendum to secede from Canada, based on the struggle for French-Canadian identity, almost passed in 1996. In New York City, the borough of Staten Island proposed secession to pursue its own economic, political, and cultural agenda.

At the same time that nations are becoming smaller, there is also a trend toward regional integration and alliance. For example, the European Union (EU) is a regional alliance that began with an economic mission and evolved into a political structure. The goal of the EU is for goods, services, and people to move freely across national borders by the standardization of goods and services, plans for a central bank and European currency, and the right of EU citizens to work in any member country without a work permit. When the EU integrated in 1992, it became the world's largest economic market (Thurow 1992).

The North American Free Trade Agreement (NAFTA) of 1994 is another example of regional integration and alliance. NAFTA establishes the framework for the free trade of goods and services among Canada, Mexico, and the United States.

There is discussion that NAFTA expand to AFTA (Americas Free Trade Agreement) to include all of the Americas. Other economic alliances exist in Latin America and Asia, with more expected.

These two trends are a simultaneous movement toward smaller and larger political units—a need to belong to a "cultural tribe" but, at the same time, a desire to unite into larger units through which tribes can derive the benefits of large size. How do trends influencing the nation-state affect the future of cultures?

What Is the Future of Cultures?

Sophisticated communications technology enables people to know instantaneously what is happening around the globe. Also, the proliferation of mass-produced consumer products, entertainment created and distributed by global conglomerates, and the expansion of multinational organizations affects all cultures. Under these conditions, will nations and groups within them be able to maintain their cultural identities?

THE PERSISTENCE OF CULTURAL IDENTITY

Ninety percent of countries have culturally diverse populations. For example, in Indonesia, 300 different ethnic groups speak a variety of languages and practice many different religions on the nation's 3,000 islands. The People's Republic of China includes 56 different nationalities, and the majority Han speak various dialects. Kenya, Uganda, and Gabon each have about 40 different ethnic groups (Naisbitt 1994). These groups maintain distinct histories and cultural identities.

Cultural identity is also likely to persist because of the importance of tourism—which relies on distinct customs and traditions—for the economy of many nations. In the early 1990s, 10.6 % of the world's workforce was employed in the tourism industry and produced 10.2% of the world gross national product (Naisbitt 1994). Predictions are that global tourism will grow faster than the world economy.

The strongest factor in the retention of cultural identity is that humans strive to maintain a sense of local community even when social institutions—mass communications, multinational corporations—evolve that eclipse them and threaten deterioration of traditional social arrangements (Gehlen 1980). Upholding tradition and group cultural identity and community provide a balance to the movement toward a global way of life.

Culture Blending At the same time, a significant amount of cultural blending is occurring. The jeans, T-shirt, and sneakers uniform of American teenagers has become casual dress around the world. Food from various cultures has been transplanted and adapted to the palates of other cultures. Common also is "fusion" cuisine, which mixes different cultural ingredients and styles.

In management, there is interest in adopting successful techniques from abroad. Quality circles, which originated in the United States and developed into an effective technique throughout Japan, are being readopted into the United States. In addition, sophisticated U.S. human resource management systems are being modified to fit local laws and practice in countries around the world.

In summary, there is a simultaneous movement toward greater cultural identity for individual groups and a trend toward increasing similarity and even blending across cultures. The result will either be cultural isolation or, more likely, cultural synergy.

What Is the Future of Technology?

The rapid pace of change is most noticeable in technology. Improvements in telecommunications, computers, consumer electronics, and televisions have had a major impact on much of the world's population, although many developing nations are still unaffected.

NEW COMMUNICATION TECHNOLOGIES

Organizations of all types and sizes rely extensively on advanced communication technology for a variety of functions. For example, communication occurs through a wider variety of media than it did a few years ago, including electronic mail (e-mail), facsimile (fax), audio or visual conferencing facilities, and voice mail. Because of new communication devices, people thousands of miles apart can work together efficiently without traveling.

Communication technologies also permit employees in many organizations to work from home—telecommuting—rather than physically going to the office. Benefits for the employee are greater flexibility for scheduling work and personal activities and less time and travel expense. The company benefits from reduced overhead expense because telecommuting requires less work space.

Prototypes for an automatic interpreting telephone were developed in the early 1990s. With these phones, a person will be able to call anywhere and have the message interpreted instantaneously. By 2000, interpreter phone technology will probably handle transactions as complex as making a hotel or airline reservation. Predictions are that a decade later, even more complex and widespread use of interpreter telephones will be available (Naisbitt 1994).

TECHNOLOGY AND OPERATIONS

New technologies have changed all aspects of an organization's operation. In manufacturing, robots and computer systems that operate less expensively and with less error have replaced large numbers of workers. In the steel industry, for example, the most cost-effective operations employ a few highly skilled workers, not large numbers of unskilled workers as in the past. Computer-assisted design (CAD) and manufacturing (CAM) systems give manufacturers greater flexibility in what they produce. With these technologies, economies of scale are obtainable by producing small quantities of a single product, enabling a company to meet the needs of different markets.

> New technologies have changed all aspects of an organization's operation.

Technology has also produced extensive changes for ordering and delivery. Computerized systems track inventory from raw material throughout production until it becomes a finished product and delivered to the end user. As materials are needed, automated systems order the exact quantity for delivery at a specified time. This allows raw material suppliers, the manufacturer, and the distributor to reduce or eliminate inventory and prevent human error. However, a recent study (Upton and McAfee 1996, p. 123) found:

> Even highly sophisticated companies have found—and continue to find—the task of creating seamless electronic networks of lean, computer-integrated manufacturing operations to be frustrating and difficult. Managers at most of these companies are still struggling to make their information systems more flexible. They are perplexed about why so much paper is still being shuffled around. They are desperate to figure out how to extend the network to more of their partners without causing costs and overhead to balloon. And they do not understand why their heavy investments in IT [information technology] have not radically changed the way their companies work.[1]

In recruitment and selection, some organizations use the Internet as an additional method to access a global labor market. An applicant can "advertise" with a resume on the Internet, have copies of relevant work available for a prospective employer to review, or give a short presentation online. For example, an artist could include copies of her work on a World Wide Web home page in either still, video, or three-dimensional formats. In the United States, many job applications use fax and e-mail instead of traditional mail.

▌▌▌ UNINTENDED BY-PRODUCTS

In addition to intended benefits, technology often has negative social costs. Faxes, e-mail messages, and phone conversations are almost instantaneous, saving time but creating pressure for much faster responses than traditional communication demands. One result is less time to make decisions, possibly reducing their quality. Another unintended outcome is severe information overload.

Finally, technology reduces interpersonal interaction. For example, telecommuting can result in isolation and stress. Robots and other computer systems often eliminate jobs or reduce the remaining work to merely tending machinery. Similarly, the use of technology often results in work becoming so simplified that it "deskills" work, creating employee alienation.

What Organizational Structures Will Emerge?

Organizational structures of the future are already developing. The rapid pace of change makes it imperative that organizations develop flexibility and replace rigid hierarchies with team-oriented forms of organization. In addition, multiple layers of middle management are being replaced by horizontal, process-oriented forms in which empowered workers make decisions. Contact with customers and suppliers is more frequent and responsive. Finally, performance evaluation focuses directly on work outcomes.

▌▌▌ VIRTUAL ORGANIZATIONS

Strategic alliances, often involving organizations from more than one country, are forming to undertake specific projects. For example, the Safari notebook computer was produced by an alliance of American Telephone & Telegraph Company,

---

[1]Excerpt from "The Real Virtual Factory" by David M. Upton and Andrew McAfee from *Harvard Business Review* (July–August 1996). Copyright© 1996 by the President and Fellows of Harvard College. All rights reserved.

Marubeni Trading Co., Matsushita Electric Industrial Co., and Henry Dreyfuss Associates. Apple Computer collaborated with Sony to manufacture the least expensive version of its PowerBook notebook computer in 1991 (Byrne, Brandt, and Port 1993). Strategic alliances, often among competitors, usually form to meet a specific project objective and then disband.

Organizations of the future are likely to be "virtual organizations." Although this idea is similar to *virtual reality*, its origin is the term *virtual memory*, which refers to a computer's capability to act as if it has more memory than it actually does. It suggests that an organization can be more than a static entity; it can act as though it were larger and more effective than the sum of its resources.

Flexibility is a key feature of virtual organizations. Reassigning of full-time workers to projects as needed reduces costs and uses expertise more effectively. Also, using temporary contract workers for a variety of schedules and tasks gives organizations additional flexibility.

> Flexibility is a key feature of virtual organizations.

Another aspect of flexibility is that small organizations and large organizations that "act small" will succeed. An organization that requires a long time to make decisions—a characteristic of many bureaucracies—will be unable to compete with a company that has small teams of people making decisions and solving problems quickly.

Strategic alliances are also a feature of virtual organizations. Partnering, either long or short term, with other organizations increases the capacity and efficiency of a single firm and results in greater synergy of ideas.

But as the Culture at Work vignette that opens this chapter illustrates, becoming a virtual organization is not an easy transition for many organizations. It requires learning a new way of thinking about the nature of organization. Overcoming habits, traditions, and organizational learning disabilities requires effort and a long period of change (Argyris and Schon 1996, Senge 1990).

NEW TYPES OF GLOBAL ORGANIZATIONS

In addition to becoming virtual, increasing numbers of organizations will expand beyond their geographical boundaries either internationally or globally. Although the characteristics of global structures are still evolving, they operate in different cultures, use virtual organizing principles, collaborate with other global or international organizations, and are not headquartered in a specific place.

Alternatively, organizations in the future will be radically different because even modern global organizations are variations on old themes: "The fundamental problem is that the basic structure of . . . business is outmoded and has outlived its usefulness" (Mitroff, Mason, and Pearson 1994; p. 12).

One version is that new organizational arrangements will contain six core functions around which the structural features evolve (Mitroff, Mason, and Pearson 1994): crisis management, issues management, total quality management, environmentalism, globalism, and ethics. These functions are coordinated and influenced by four centers: knowledge/learning; recovery/development; world service/spiritual, and a world-class operations center. A leadership institute integrates the four centers into a whole.

The recovery/development center illustrates the new emphasis. The key issue for the center is: How can organizations help employees recover from whatever personal, emotional dysfunctions or problems they bring to the organization and develop new positive ways of existing? In addition, how can the center help the organization as a whole recover from systemic dysfunctions and develop into a healthy system?

What Is the Future of Work?

From a concentration of workers in manufacturing jobs, there is movement toward a global workforce of knowledge and service workers. As developments in technology continue to bring mechanization and computerization to the workplace, demand grows for skilled workers to create and operate technology. It will be possible to do more work with fewer people, but the knowledge requirements for each person will increase.

TEAMS

One change in organizational structure created by new technology's need for flexibility is the use of teams. Teams have a spectrum of responsibilities, and members work effectively together because of cross-training. Teams also function on a project basis—working for a limited time on a specific task—giving organizations greater flexibility. In the future, individuals will probably belong to several teams simultaneously.

LEADERSHIP

The roles of leader and manager will change. As organizations move toward flatter structures, composed of constantly evolving teams, individuals within teams will assume leader roles, probably on a temporary basis. In addition to the technical knowledge necessary to accomplish the team's task, it will also be important to acquire specific leadership skills to manage members as equals. Traditional hierarchical authority structures will change, and self-managing teams will be common.

TOTAL QUALITY

With the growth of the global economy, there will be more emphasis on international quality control standards. These standards—for example, ISO 9000—focus on the process of work to regulate quality. This will require extensive training in techniques that stress quality throughout the manufacturing process instead of current methods of inspection after manufacture. Training in effective teamwork is also part of total quality programs.

THE MOBILITY OF WORK

Globalization of work means reduction of the importance of geography. This affects some industries and professions more than others. For example, personal services—restaurants, health care, and retail stores—are location bound. Other industries—such as computer software development—are free of the restrictions of geography. A computer programmer can be anywhere and be in continuous contact with his customers and employer.

> Globalization of work means reduction of the importance of geography.

One negative consequence of high mobility in the workplace is that family life could suffer. Children and spouses can experience social maladjustments because of frequent relocation. Another potential problem is that communities can deteriorate into collections of rootless workers with no expectations of establishing social bonds with their neighbors.

WORKER MOTIVATION

Worker motivation could be different in the future because of the new types of organizations. As more workers perform knowledge work, it is likely that expectations for interesting work will increase along with symbolic forms of reward such as working on worthwhile, innovative projects rather than performing routine technical tasks.

Motivation could become a problem because of the temporary and rapidly shifting nature of team-based knowledge work. Certain personality types might find the new work arrangements rewarding, whereas others will find them anxiety provoking. In addition, work arrangements that require self-motivation such as telecommuting could create the need for new control structures or novel forms of reward that recognize the ability to work independently.

THE ROLE OF WOMEN

The role of women in the workplace of the future is complex. In some cultures—for example, Japan—because of changing values and demographics, the number of women workers will increase. In many cultures, however, religious fundamentalist movements oppose women entering the workforce. In still other societies, attitudes toward women are resistant to change although their ideology espouses gender equality. For example, even after recent economic, social, and political reforms,

> Russia remains a highly sexist society, where women, regardless of marital or professional status, are rarely allowed a prominent public role. Despite, or perhaps because of, 70 years of Soviet lip service to female equality, women distrust feminism. The few who can afford the luxury of not working often find that option irresistible—particularly when their husbands insist (Stanley 1997, p. 1).

Finally, it is likely that the role of women in North America and Western Europe will continue to improve faster than in other cultures, not only because of legislated equality but as a result of the centrality of creativity, knowledge, and interpersonal skills necessary to manage sophisticated organizations.

What Is the Future of the Natural Environment?

Organizations are becoming aware of their impact on the environment (Shrivastava 1995). These concerns are a response to environmental protection legislation in Western countries, consumer activism for environmentally friendly products, and opportunities for cost savings. They are also responses to environmental catastrophes such as the Union Carbide disaster in Bhopal, India; the meltdown of the nuclear reactor in Chernobyl; and the destruction of the Brazilian rain forest.

CORPORATE RESPONSES

Recycled waste products from industrial processes can make useful products. For example, instead of venting gas created in refining into the atmosphere, Mobil Oil Company captures it to produce lightweight packaging material. Greater use of recycled materials reduces the amount of waste produced by companies.

A corporate leader in environmentalism is The Body Shop, the British cosmetics retailer. The company uses recycled paper for its letterhead and toilet paper and offers a refill service for customers who return used bottles. The Body Shop also searches worldwide for natural, renewable ingredients to manufacture cosmetics and aggressively promotes environmental causes (Roddick 1991).

▌▌▌ SUSTAINING THE ENVIRONMENT

A key issue is how to protect the environment in the future. The earth's resources are finite and require management. A major political issue affecting natural resource management is the disparity between advanced and developing societies. Are the expenses of clean manufacturing technologies and other costs of environmentalism too onerous for developing nations? Has the exploitation of the world's resources by Western societies—for example, oil, gold, and uranium—resulted in political and cultural imperialism? These are difficult questions that remain unresolved.

What Is the Future of Management?

As organizations and their environments change, future managers will need new skills and knowledge. How will the changes discussed previously influence the management of global organizational behavior in the future?

▌▌▌ SUBCULTURES

If cultural subgroups within countries continue to seek autonomy, the result could eventually be hundreds of countries. If each develops its own laws and business practices, global business will be more complex; organizations will have to understand the environment of each country to sell to that market or establish a business. As a result, an effective manager will need to understand culture and how it affects organizational behavior.

▌▌▌ TECHNOLOGICAL ADVANCES

Skills for managing technological change will become more important for managers. Understanding how various cultures respond to technology and being prepared to deal with them will make the change process easier. A manager also needs to prepare personally for change by constantly keeping up to date with professional, organizational, and industry developments. Because of the enormous amount of information available and training requirements, this is not an easy task. For example, how many managers use the newest hardware and software in production, finance, and human resource management?

▌▌▌ MANAGING NEW ORGANIZATIONAL STRUCTURES

Organizations worldwide will move toward more flexible forms, with strategic alliances across borders common, and people's participation limited to specific short-term tasks. An effective managerial behavior is the capacity to quickly adjust to and influence people from diverse cultures and backgrounds working on a short-term team.

Will Organizations Change?

Organizational culture often resists change. In addition, in some instances, managerial actions intended to create improvements contribute to the creation of new problems in organizations. What then is the prospect for significant change in organizations?

▌▌▌ UNANTICIPATED OUTCOMES

Reverse outcomes are already present as a result of the globalization of organizations. Recent research indicates that social problems in American cities are, to some extent, the result of new global economic arrangements. Wilson (1996, p. 54) wrote:

> The disappearance of work in many inner-city neighborhoods is in part related to the nationwide decline in the fortunes of low-skilled workers. Fundamental structural changes in the new global economy, including changes in the distribution of jobs and in the level of education required to obtain employment, resulted in the simultaneous occurrence of increasing joblessness, and declining real wages for low-skilled workers.

According to Wilson, this process has more than changed the nature of work in American cities; it has eliminated it. This has created a situation of severely disadvantaged citizens and affected race relations in the United States. To some extent, it has influenced the culture of all Americans.

Of course, the exodus of jobs from American inner-city neighborhoods is a benefit to the economies of developing nations. But this is a temporary situation because manufacturers are eager to move to the next low-wage labor market.

As a result of globalization, American work organizations changed, but in ways that adversely affected a large segment of the population. The organizations that remain have also changed; they require higher levels of education and skills for service and knowledge work. It is possible, however, that solutions to these social problems may be innovative and eventually improve American society—for example, reform of inner-city education, the construction of adequate housing, and universal health care.

With the creation of new types of service and knowledge organizations that have consequences beyond the workplace, will traditional bureaucracies survive?

▌▌▌ THE RESILIENCE OF BUREAUCRACY

Predictions in the 1960s were that the end of bureaucracy was eminent (Bennis 1966). It was said that as a type of organizational structure, bureaucracy was defective and would wither away because of the following:

- It was incapable of adjusting to the accelerated pace of change.
- It was not capable of administering large, complex organizations because of its tendency to simplify the division of labor, hierarchy, standardization, and roles.
- Its tendency toward simplification would not be useful in coping with increasingly more complex environments.
- The increasing specialization of organizational tasks required skills that were not compatible with bureaucratic administration.

■ Managerial behavior was changing from impersonality in human relations to a concern with new conceptions of human beings that emphasized collaboration and other humanistic and democratic ideals.

The prediction was correct to some extent. New forms of organization such as networks, teams, and the virtual workplace, which are possible because of advances in computers, technology, and telecommunications and sophisticated management techniques, have produced decentralization and flexibility. But the idea that geographic dispersion of organizations will reduce bureaucratic forms of control might not occur "precisely because of the territorial dispersal facilitated by telecommunication. . . . Agglomeration of certain centralizing activities has sharply increased" (Sassen 1991 p. 5).

More important, bureaucracy continues to exist in all societies because, despite dysfunctions, it is basically efficient and effective for administration and social control. Bureaucracy is the organizational form of diverse businesses—including banks, insurance firms, restaurants, factories, and retail stores—as well the administrative apparatus of the state.

The persistence of bureaucracy may also be a product of culture. Crozier, in his classic work *The Bureaucratic Phenomenon* (1964, p. 54), writes:

> **The persistence of bureaucracy may also be a product of culture.**

Why do people build organizations where impersonal rules and routine will bind individual behavior to such an extent? Why do they build bureaucracies? . . . They are trying to evade face-to-face relationships and situations of personal dependency whose authoritarian tone they cannot bear.

Do the people who work in organizations—bureaucratic, virtual, matrix, and boundaryless—fear each other because of a basic human cultural value such as aversion to domination? Or is technology changing faster than our ability to redesign human relations and organizations? Is globalization occurring at a rate beyond our ability to absorb its implications and create new institutions? Or are these reservations and concerns merely ill-founded second thoughts and reluctance to accept the benefits of progress?

Convergence or Divergence?

It is difficult to assess the extent to which cultures and organizations are becoming more alike, maintaining their differences, or becoming increasingly dissimilar. Macro trends that characterize the global economy create pressures for convergence through globalization. These include deregulation, the opening of markets, and economic regionalization. At the same time, other macro trends suggest forces for divergence, including the resurgence of national and regional cultures, religious revivalism, and disparities between economically advanced and developing nations.

Organizational, or micro-level, behavior also contains elements that could result in either convergence or divergence. The diffusion of new technologies is a force for convergence, but the way a specific culture modifies technology to fit its values maintains differentiation. Similarly, implementation of a transplanted management practice—for example, group decision making—is likely to undergo alterations that harmonize with the culture adapting it.

The assessment of whether there is a global trend toward convergence of organizational behavior and management also depends on the phenomena selected and their interpretation. One example is that "China's legislature unveiled a major revision of its criminal law today, introducing new offenses like money laundering and insider trading, and eliminating the overtly political category of 'counterrevolutionary' crimes" (Faison 1997, p. 1). Does this reflect deep changes in Chinese culture, an adaptation to the selected elements of capitalism introduced into the Chinese economy, or a way to confront illegalities committed by foreign business people?

Another example involves recent attempts to standardize management principles through the use of international quality standards. If an organization implements these principles, does it affect the organization in a significant way—for example, by redesigning its processes and structures to resemble organizations in other cultures? Does quality standardization create standardization of behavior? Or does the national and organizational culture remain unaffected?

A final example is cultural value conflict over the adoption of new technologies. Iran, an Islamic theocracy, views the Internet as a way to extend its culture worldwide by using it as a source for information about Islamic law and religion (MacFarquahar 1996). It also wants to use the Internet to modernize communication for its businesses and universities. The Internet, however, carries information that is counter to Iran's fundamentalist view of Islam, including pornographic magazines, political tracts that support the deposed Shah, and Western propaganda. The new technology fits the needs of the national and organizational cultures but also threatens to destroy them. The problem is finding ways to use the Internet to spread Islamic culture and modernize Iran's organizations without contaminating either the national or organizational cultures.

These examples capture some of the issues in the debate over whether industrialization or culture is a more influential source in determining management practices and behavior in organizations. It could be that the debate has no resolution or, more likely, that industrialization and culture both play significant roles for understanding and managing organizations. Even if the industrialization process is the major cause of organizational behavior, it is inherently worthwhile to learn about other cultures.

Implications for Managers

Assuming that the trends outlined previously continue or accelerate, the major implication for managers—domestic and international—is that more than ever, change in all its forms, is a factor that managers must confront. Successful change management requires the ability to identify variables and trends that affect an organization and the acquisition of skills necessary to plan and implement new ideas, technologies, and processes.

Related to the necessity to understand and manage change, managers must increase the scope of their interests and improve their knowledge base. Knowledge of local issues and problems is no longer adequate; global issues have intruded on organizations more extensively than ever before and in ways that will potentially produce fundamental change. As a result, managers must develop personal and organizational systems for continuous learning accompanied by methods for translating new ideas into practical applications.

Also implied by current trends is that accelerated change and more complex organizational environments increase the possibility of a rise in negative unanticipated consequences. For example, causality is more difficult to attribute because the global economy is more elaborate and dynamic with sources of change more numerous and difficult to anticipate. In addition, as a result of the diversity of participants in the economy, preferences shift frequently and abruptly, often turning a good idea into a bad one.

Another implication is that instead of being passive actors in the globalization process, managers have opportunities to shape the emerging global economy by influencing the design of new types of organizations. To do this managers must construct new organizational types informed by augmented knowledge and the enhanced skills that effective management requires.

A final implication is the possibility that the social power of managers may expand significantly. As central participants in the decision making and control structure of organizations, managers influence the creation of organizational outputs; managers contribute to the success or failure of organizations and the reproduction of society. Consequently, if new forms of organization emerge that rely more on managerial expertise, power may become more centralized in organizations. In the future, managerial decisions and actions may determine the decline or advancement of society—human progress—more than they do today.

■ Summary

The future is not knowable. An important issue, however, is whether there is belief in human progress. At the present time, some societies are experiencing progress in some areas but not in others. Other societies are in turmoil and are not enjoying economic advances. However, optimism abounds during periods of major psychological shifts, and the new millenium inspires optimism.

An important issue is the future of the nation-state. Recent events suggest the possibility of the creation of more nation-states and the continuation of distinct cultures. A key question is whether mass communication and cross-cultural commerce will transform distinctive cultures into uniform cultures.

Another issue is the impact of technology on society and organizations. Technology has influenced organizations and the nature of work and will continue to, particularly as the use of new forms of communication and computerization spreads. One result of technological change, along with acceleration in the rate of change, is the redesign of organizations into flexible, team oriented structures.

Preservation of the natural environment also shapes organizational behavior. Finding ways to create sustainable organizations without endangering the environment are important concerns. All of these changes will influence the nature of work. Will work be more or less challenging in the future?

All of these changes will increase the demands on managers in the global economy. Effective managers will continuously improve their technical skills and ability to interact with people from a variety of cultures as members of teams in virtual organizations.

■ Discussion Questions

1. What is your perspective on the nature of human progress? Has the 20th century been one of progress or skepticism in progress? Will the next century be the same or different than the 20th century regarding the prospects for progress?

2. In your view, what are the major changes that will affect global management and organizational behavior during the next decade? The next two decades?

3. What is the future of the nation-state in which you live?

4. How has technology affected your life? Have the ways you learn and work been affected by technology? Will technology affect your career choice?

5. In what ways, if any, has the organization structure of your school or workplace changed in recent years?

6. What issues involving the natural environment are important in your community and nation? How are they being addressed?

7. In your opinion, will it become more or less important to understand regional and national cultures to conduct business during the next decade?

8. If work changes in some of the ways mentioned in the text, do you think that it will become more interesting and meaningful or more routine and boring for the majority of workers?

9. What personal attributes will successful managers of the future possess?

References

ARGYRIS, C. and SCHON, D. (1996), *Organizational Learning II: Theory, Method, and Practice.* Reading, MA: Addison-Wesley.

BENNIS, W. (1968), "The Coming Death of Bureaucracy," *Think* (November–December), 30–35.

BYRNE, J., BRANDT, R., and PORT, O. (1993), "The Virtual Corporation," *Business Week* (February 8), 98–103.

CROZIER, M. (1964), *The Bureaucratic Phenomenon.* Chicago: University of Chicago Press.

DRUCKER, P. (1993), *Post-Capitalist Society.* New York: HarperCollins.

FAISON, S. (1997), "Chinese Revise Criminal Code, Not Its Essence," *The New York Times* (March, 7), 1.

GEHLEN, A. (1980), *Man in the Age of Technology.* New York: Columbia University Press.

MacFARQUHAR, N. (1996), "With Mixed Feelings, Iran Tiptoes to the Internet," *The New York Times* (October 8), A3.

MITROFF, I., MASON, R., and PEARSON, C. (1994), "Radical Surgery: What Will Tomorrow's Organizations Look Like?" *Academy of Management Executive*, 8 (2), 11–21.

NAISBITT, J. (1994), *Global Paradox*, New York: William Morrow.

NISBET, R. (1980), *History of the Idea of Progress.* New York, Basic Books.

OHMAE, K. (1995), *The End of the Nation State: The Rise of Regional Economies.* New York: The Free Press.

RODDICK, A. (1991), *Body and Soul.* New York: Crown.

SASSEN, S. (1991), *The Global City: New York, London, Tokyo.* Princeton, NJ: Princeton University Press.

———. (1996), *Losing Control? Sovereignty in an Age of Globalization.* New York: Columbia University Press.

SENGE, P. (1990), *The Fifth Discipline: The Art & Practice of The Learning Organization.* New York: Doubleday.

SHRIVASTAVA, P. (1995), "The Role of Corporations in Achieving Ecological Sustainability," *Academy of Management Review*, 20 (4), 936–60.

Stanley, A. (1997), "Russian Wives Learn What Money Can't Buy," *The New York Times* (March 11), 1.

THUROW, L.C. (1992), "Who Owns the Twenty-First Century?" *Sloan Management Review* (Spring) 5–16.

UPTON, D. and McAFEE, A. (1996), "The Real Virtual Factory," *Harvard Business Review* (July–August), 123–33.

WILSON, W. (1996), *When Work Disappears: The World of the New Urban Poor.* New York: Alfred A. Knopf.

Part IV
READINGS IN INTERNATIONAL ORGANIZATIONAL BEHAVIOR

Cultural Constraints in Management Theories

Geert Hofstede

IN MY VIEW

Lewis Carroll's *Alice in Wonderland* contains the famous story of Alice's croquet game with the Queen of Hearts.

> Alice thought she had never seen such a curious croquet-ground in all her life; it was all ridges and furrows; the balls were live hedgehogs, the mallets live flamingoes, and the soldiers had to double themselves up and to stand on their hands and feet, to make the arches.

You probably know how the story goes: Alice's flamingo mallet turns its head whenever she wants to strike with it; her hedgehog ball runs away; and the doubled-up soldier arches walk around all the time. The only rule seems to be that the Queen of Hearts always wins.

Alice's croquet playing problems are good analogies to attempts to build culture-free theories of management. Concepts available for this purpose are themselves alive with culture, having been developed within a particular cultural context. They have a tendency to guide our thinking toward our desired conclusion.

As the same reasoning may also be applied to the arguments in this article, I better tell you my conclusion before I continue—so that the rules of my game are understood. In this article we take a trip around the world to demonstrate that there are no such things as universal management theories.

Diversity in management *practices* as we go around the world has been recognized in U.S. management literature for more than thirty years. The term "comparative management" has been used since the 1960s. However, it has taken much longer for the U.S. academic community to accept that not only practices but also the validity of *theories* may stop at national borders, and I wonder whether even today everybody would agree with this statement.

"Cultural constraints in management theories" by Geert Hofstede. Reprinted by permission of the author.

The issues explored here were presented by Dr. Hofstede, the Foundation for Administrative Research Distinguished International Scholar, at the 1992 Annual Meeting of the Academy of Management, Las Vegas, Nevada, August 11, 1992.

An article I published in *Organizational Dynamics* in 1980 entitled "Do American Theories Apply Abroad?" created more controversy than I expected. The article argued, with empirical support, that generally accepted U.S. theories like those of Maslow, Herzberg, McClelland, Vroom, McGregor, Likert, Blake, and Mouton may not or only very partly apply outside the borders of their country of origin—assuming they do apply within those borders. Among the requests for reprints, a larger number were from Canada than from the United States.

Management Theorists are Human

Employees and managers are human. Employees as humans was "discovered" in the 1930s, with the Human Relations school. Managers as humans was introduced in the late 1940s by Herbert Simon's "bounded rationality" and elaborated in Richard Cyert and James March's *Behavioral Theory of the Firm* (1963, and recently re-published in a second edition). My argument is that management scientists, theorists, and writers are human too: They grew up in a particular society in a particular period, and their ideas cannot help but reflect the constraints of their environment.

The idea that the validity of a theory is constrained by national borders is more obvious in Europe, with all its borders, than in a huge borderless country like the United States. Already in the sixteenth century Michel de Montaigne, a Frenchman, wrote a statement which was made famous by Blaise Pascal about a century later: "*Vérite en-deça des Pyrenées, erreur au-delà*"—There are truths on this side of the Pyrenées which are falsehoods on the other.

From Don Armado's Love to Taylor's Science

According to the comprehensive ten-volume Oxford English Dictionary (1971), the words "manage," "management," and "manager" appeared in the English language in the sixteenth century. The oldest recorded use of the word "manager" is in Shakespeare's "Love's Labour's Lost," dating from 1588, in which Don Adriano de Armado, "a fantastical Spaniard," exclaims (Act I, scene ii, 188):

"Adieu, valour! rust, rapier! be still, drum! for your manager is in love; yea, he loveth".

The linguistic origin of the word is from Latin *manus*, hand, via the Italian *maneggiare*, which is the training of horses in the *manege*; subsequently its meaning was extended to skillful handling in general, like of arms and musical instruments, as Don Armado illustrates. However, the word also became associated with the French *menage*, household, as an equivalent of "husbandry" in its sense of the art of running a household. The theatre of present-day management contains elements of both *manege* and *menage* and different managers and cultures may use different accents.

The founder of the science of economics, the Scot Adam Smith, in his 1776 book *The Wealth of Nations*, used "manage," "management" (even "bad management") and "manager" when dealing with the process and the persons involved in operating joint stock companies (Smith, V.i.e.). British economist John Stuart Mill (1806–1873) followed Smith in this use and clearly expressed his distrust of such hired people who were not driven by ownership. Since the 1880s the word "management" appeared occasionally in writings by American engineers, until it was canonized as a modern science by Frederick W. Taylor in *Shop Management* in 1903 and in *The Principles of Scientific Management* in 1911.

While Smith and Mill used "management" to describe a process and "managers" for the persons involved, "management" in the American sense—which has since been taken back by the British—refers not only to the process but also to the managers as a class of people. This class (1) does not own a business but sells its skills to act on behalf of the owners and (2) does not produce personally but is indispensable for making others produce, through motivation. Members of this class carry a high status and many American boys and girls aspire to the role. In the United States, the manager is a cultural hero.

Let us now turn to other parts of the world. We will look at management in its context in other successful modern economies: Germany, Japan, France, Holland, and among the Overseas Chinese. Then we will examine management in the much larger part of the world that is still poor, especially South-East Asia and Africa, and in the new political configurations of Eastern Europe, and Russia in particular. We will then return to the United States via mainland China.

Germany   The manager is not a cultural hero in Germany. If anybody, it is the engineer who fills the hero role. Frederick Taylor's *Scientific Management* was conceived in a society of immigrants—where large numbers of workers with diverse backgrounds and skills had to work together. In Germany this heterogeneity never existed.

Elements of the mediaeval guild system have survived in historical continuity in Germany until the present day. In particular, a very effective apprenticeship system exists both on the shop floor and in the office, which alternates practical work and classroom courses. At the end of the apprenticeship the worker receives a certificate, the *Facharbeiterbrief*, which is recognized throughout the country. About two thirds of the German worker population holds such a certificate and a corresponding occupational pride. In fact, quite a few German company presidents have worked their way up from the ranks through an apprenticeship. In comparison, two thirds of the worker population in Britain have no occupational qualification at all.

The highly skilled and responsible German workers do not necessarily need a manager, American-style, to "motivate" them. They expect their boss or *Meister* to assign their tasks and to be the expert in resolving technical problems. Comparisons of similar German, British, and French organizations show the Germans as having the highest rate of personnel in productive roles and the lowest both in leadership and staff roles.

Business schools are virtually unknown in Germany. Native German management theories concentrate on formal systems. The inapplicability of American concepts of management was quite apparent in 1973 when the U.S. consulting firm of Booz, Allen, and Hamilton, commissioned by the German Ministry of Economic Affairs, wrote a study of German management from an American view point. The report is highly critical and writes among other things that "Germans simply do not have a very strong concept of management." Since 1973, from my personal experience, the situation has not changed much. However, during this period the German economy has performed in a superior fashion to the United States in virtually all respects, so a strong concept of management might have been a liability rather than an asset.

Japan   The American type of manager is also missing in Japan. In the United States, the core of the enterprise is the managerial class. The core of the Japanese enterprise is the permanent worker group; workers who for all practical purposes are tenured and who aspire at life-long employment. They are distinct from the non-permanent employees—most women and subcontracted teams led by gang bosses, to be laid off in slack periods. University graduates in Japan first join the permanent worker group and subsequently fill various positions, moving from line to staff as the need occurs while paid according to seniority rather than position. They take part in Japanese-style group consultation sessions for important decisions, which extend the decision-making period but guarantee fast implementation afterwards. Japanese are to a large extent controlled by their peer group rather than by their manager.

Three researchers from the East-West Center of the University of Hawaii, Joseph Tobin, David Wu, and Dana Danielson, did an observation study of typical preschools in three countries: China, Japan, and the United States. Their results have been published both as a book and as a video. In the Japanese preschool, one teacher handled twenty-eight four-year-olds. The video shows one particularly ob-noxious boy, Hiroki, who fights with other children and throws teaching materials down from the balcony. When a little girl tries to alarm the teacher, the latter an-swers "What are you calling me for? Do something about it!" In the U.S. preschool, there is one adult for every nine children. This class has its problem child too, Glen, who refuses to clear away his toys. One of the teachers has a long talk with him and isolates him in a corner, until he changes his mind. It doesn't take much imagination to realize that managing Hiroki thirty years later will be a different process from managing Glen.

American theories of leadership are ill-suited for the Japanese group-con-trolled situation. During the past two decades, the Japanese have developed their own "PM" theory of leadership, in which P stands for performance and M for main-tenance. The latter is less a concern for individual employees than for maintaining social stability. In view of the amazing success of the Japanese economy in the past thirty years, many Americans have sought the secrets of Japanese management hop-ing to copy them.

> There are no secrets of Japanese management, however; it is even doubtful whether there is such a thing as management, in the American sense, in Japan at all. The secret is in Japanese society; and if any group in society should be singled out as carriers of the secret, it is the workers, not the managers.

France   The manager, U.S. style, does not exist in France either. In a very enlight-ening book, unfortunately not yet translated into English, the French researcher Philippe d'Iribarne (1989) describes the results of in-depth observation and inter-view studies of management methods in three subsidiary plants of the same French multinational: in France, the United States, and Holland. He relates what he finds to information about the three societies in general. Where necessary, he goes back in history to trace the roots of the strikingly different behaviors in the completion of the same tasks. He identifies three kinds of basic principles (*logiques*) of manage-ment. In the U.S., the principle is the *fair contract* between employer and em-ployee, which gives the manager considerable prerogatives, but within its limits. This is really a labor *market* in which the worker sells his or her labor for a price. In France, the principle is the *honor* of each class in a society which has always been and remains extremely stratified, in which superiors behave as superior beings and subordinates accept and expect this, conscious of their own lower level in the na-tional hierarchy but also of the honor of their own class. The French do not think in terms of managers versus nonmanagers but in terms of *cadres* versus *non-cadres*; one becomes cadre by attending the proper schools and one remains it forever; regardless of their actual task, cadres have the privileges of a higher social class, and it is very rare for a non-cadre to cross the ranks.

The conflict between French and American theories of management became apparent in the beginning of the twentieth century, in a criticism by the great French management pioneer Henri Fayol (1841–1925) on his U.S. colleague and contemporary Frederick W. Taylor (1856–1915). The difference in career paths of the two men is striking. Fayol was a French engineer whose career as a *cadre supérieur* culminated in the position of Président-Directeur-Général of a mining company. After his retirement he formulated his experiences in a pathbreaking text on organization: *Administration industrielle et générale*, in which he focused on the sources of authority. Taylor was an American engineer who started his career in industry as a worker and attained his academic qualifications through evening studies. From chief engineer in a steel company he became one of the first management consultants. Taylor was not really concerned with the issue of authority at all; his focus was on efficiency. He proposed to split the task of the first-line boss into eight specialisms, each exercised by a different person; an idea which eventually led to the idea of a matrix organization.

Taylor's work appeared in a French translation in 1913, and Fayol read it and showed himself generally impressed but shocked by Taylor's "denial of the principle of the Unity of Command" in the case of the eight-boss-system.

Seventy years later André Laurent, another of Fayol's compatriots, found that French managers in a survey reacted very strongly against a suggestion that one employee could report to two different bosses, while U.S. managers in the same survey showed fewer misgivings. Matrix organization has never become popular in France as it has in the United States.

Holland   In my own country, Holland or as it is officially called, the Netherlands, the study by Philippe d'Iribarne found the management principle to be a need for consensus among all parties, neither predetermined by a contractual relationship nor by class distinctions, but based on an open-ended exchange of views and a balancing of interests. In terms of the different origins of the word "manager," the organization in Holland is more *menage* (household) while in the United States it is more *manege* (horse drill).

At my university, the University of Limburg at Maastricht, every semester we receive a class of American business students who take a program in European Studies. We asked both the Americans and a matched group of Dutch students to describe their ideal job after graduation, using a list of twenty-two job characteristics. The Americans attached significantly more importance than the Dutch to earnings, advancement, benefits, a good working relationship with their boss, and security of employment. The Dutch attached more importance to freedom to adopt their own approach to the job, being consulted by their boss in his or her decisions, training opportunities, contributing to the success of their organization, fully using their skills and abilities, and helping others. This list confirms d'Iribarne's findings of a contractual employment relationship in the United States, based on earnings and career opportunities, against a consensual relationship in Holland. The latter has centuries-old roots; the Netherlands were the first republic in Western Europe (1609–1810), and a model for the American republic. The country has been and still is governed by a careful balancing of interests in a multi-party system.

In terms of management theories, both motivation and leadership in Holland are different from what they are in the United States. Leadership in Holland presupposes modesty, as opposed to assertiveness in the United States. No U.S.

leadership theory has room for that. Working in Holland is not a constant feast, however. There is a built-in premium on mediocrity and jealousy, as well as time-consuming ritual consultations to maintain the appearance of consensus and the pretense of modesty. There is unfortunately another side to every coin.

The Overseas Chinese   Among the champions of economic development in the past thirty years we find three countries mainly populated by Chinese living outside the Chinese mainland: Taiwan, Hong Kong, and Singapore. Moreover, Overseas Chinese play a very important role in the economies of Indonesia, Malaysia, the Philippines, and Thailand, where they form an ethnic minority. If anything, the little dragons—Taiwan, Hong Kong, and Singapore—have been more economically successful than Japan, moving from rags to riches and now counted among the world's wealthy industrial countries. Yet very little attention has been paid to the way in which their enterprises have been managed. *The Spirit of Chinese Capitalism* by Gordon Redding (1990), the British dean of the Hong Kong Business School, is an excellent book about Chinese business. He bases his insights on personal acquaintance and in-depth discussions with a large number of Overseas Chinese businesspeople.

Overseas Chinese American enterprises lack almost all characteristics of modern management. They tend to be small, cooperating for essential functions with other small organizations through networks based on personal relations. They are family-owned, without the separation between ownership and management typical in the West, or even in Japan and Korea. They normally focus on one product or market, with growth by opportunistic diversification; in this, they are extremely flexible. Decision making is centralized in the hands of one dominant family member, but other family members may be given new ventures to try their skills on. They are low-profile and extremely cost-conscious, applying Confucian virtues of thrift and persistence. Their size is kept small by the assumed lack of loyalty of non-family employees, who, if they are any good, will just wait and save until they can start their own family business.

Overseas Chinese prefer economic activities in which great gains can be made with little manpower, like commodity trading and real estate. They employ few professional managers, except their sons and sometimes daughters who have been sent to prestigious business schools abroad, but who upon return continue to run the family business the Chinese way.

The origin of this system, or—in the Western view—this lack of system, is found in the history of Chinese society, in which there were no formal laws, only formal networks of powerful people guided by general principles of Confucian virtue. The favors of the authorities could change daily, so nobody could be trusted except one's kinfolk—of whom, fortunately, there used to be many, in an extended family structure. The Overseas Chinese way of doing business is also very well adapted to their position in the countries in which they form ethnic minorities, often envied and threatened by ethnic violence.

Overseas Chinese businesses following this unprofessional approach command a collective gross national product of some 200 to 300 billion US dollars, exceeding the GNP of Australia. There is no denying that it works.

Management Transfer to Poor Countries

Four-fifths of the world population live in countries that are not rich but poor. After World War II and decolonization, the stated purpose of the United Nations and the World Bank has been to promote the development of all the world's countries in a war on poverty. After forty years it looks very much like we are losing this war. If one thing has become clear, it is that the export of Western—mostly American—management practices *and* theories to poor countries has contributed little to nothing to their development. There has been no lack of effort and money spent for this purpose: students from poor countries have been trained in this country, and teachers and Peace Corps workers have been sent to the poor countries. If nothing else, the general lack of success in economic development of other countries should be sufficient argument to doubt the validity of Western management theories in non-Western environments.

If we examine different parts of the world, the development picture is not equally bleak, and history is often a better predictor than economic factors for what happens today. There is a broad regional pecking order with East Asia leading. The little dragons have passed into the camp of the wealthy; then follow South-East Asia (with its Overseas Chinese minorities), Latin American (in spite of the debt crisis), South Asia, and Africa always trails behind. Several African countries have only become poorer since decolonization.

Regions of the world with a history of large-scale political integration and civilization generally have done better than regions in which no large-scale political and cultural infrastructure existed, even if the old civilizations had decayed or been suppressed by colonizers. It has become painfully clear that development cannot be pressure-cooked; it presumes a cultural infrastructure that takes time to grow. Local management is part of this infrastructure; it cannot be imported in package form. Assuming that with so-called modern management techniques and theories outsiders can develop a country has proven a deplorable arrogance. At best, one can hope for a dialogue between equals with the locals, in which the Western partner acts as the expert in Western technology and the local partner as the expert in local culture, habits, and feelings.

Russia and China   The crumbling of the former Eastern bloc has left us with a scattering of states and would-be states of which the political and economic future is extremely uncertain. The best predictions are those based on a knowledge of history, because historical trends have taken revenge on the arrogance of the Soviet rulers who believed they could turn them around by brute power. One obvious fact is that the former bloc is extremely heterogeneous, including countries traditionally closely linked with the West by trade and travel, like Czechia, Hungary, Slovenia, and the Baltic states, as well as others with a Byzantine or Turkish past; some having been prosperous, others always extremely poor.

> The industrialized Western world and the World Bank seem committed to helping the ex-Eastern bloc countries develop, but with the same technocratic neglect for local cultural factors that proved so unsuccessful in the development assistance to other poor countries. Free market capitalism, introduced by Western-style management, is supposed to be the answer from Albania to Russia.

Let me limit myself to the Russian republic, a huge territory with some 140 million inhabitants, mainly Russians. We know quite a bit about the Russians as their country was a world power for several hundreds of years before communism, and in the nineteenth century it has produced some of the greatest writers in world literature. If I want to understand the Russians—including how they could so long support the Soviet regime—I tend to re-read Lev Nikolayevich Tolstoy. In his most famous novel *Anna Karenina* (1876) one of the main characters is a landowner, Levin, whom Tolstoy uses to express his own views and convictions about his people. Russian peasants used to be serfs; serfdom had been abolished in 1861, but the peasants, now tenants, remained as passive as before. Levin wanted to break this passivity by dividing the land among his peasants in exchange for a share of the crops; but the peasants only let the land deteriorate further. Here follows a quote:

> (Levin) read political economy and socialistic works . . . but, as he had expected, found nothing in them related to his undertaking. In the political economy books—in (John Stuart) Mill, for instance, whom he studied first and with great ardour, hoping every minute to find an answer to the questions that were engrossing him—he found only certain laws deduced from the state of agriculture in Europe; but he could not for the life of him see why these laws, which did not apply to Russia, should be considered universal. . . . Political economy told him that the laws by which Europe had developed and was developing her wealth were universal and absolute. Socialist teaching told him that development along those lines leads to ruin. And neither of them offered the smallest enlightenment as to what he, Levin, and all the Russian peasants and landowners were to do with their millions of hands and millions of acres, to make them as productive as possible for the common good.

In the summer of 1991, the Russian lands yielded a record harvest, but a large share of it rotted in the fields because no people were to be found for harvesting. The passivity is still there, and not only among the peasants. And the heirs of John Stuart Mill (whom we met before as one of the early analysts of "management") again present their universal recipes which simply do not apply.

Citing Tolstoy, I implicitly suggest that management theorists cannot neglect the great literature of the countries they want their ideas to apply to. The greatest novel in the Chinese literature is considered Cao Xueqin's *The Story of the Stone*, also known as *The Dream of the Red Chamber* which appeared around 1760. It describes the rise and fall of two branches of an aristocratic family in Beijing, who live in adjacent plots in the capital. Their plots are joined by a magnificent garden with several pavillions in it, and the young, mostly female members of both families are allowed to live in them. One day the management of the garden is taken over by a young woman, Tan-Chun, who states:

> I think we ought to pick out a few experienced trust-worthy old women from among the ones who work in the Garden—women who know something about gardening already—and put the upkeep of the Garden into their hands. We needn't ask them to pay us rent; all we need ask them for is an annual share of the produce. There would be four advantages in this arrangement. In the first place, if we have people whose sole occupation is to look after trees and flowers and so on, the condition of the Garden will improve gradually year after year and there will be no more of those long periods of neglect followed by bursts of feverish activity when things have been allowed to get out of hand. Secondly there won't be the spoiling and wastage we get at present. Thirdly the women themselves will gain a little extra to add to their incomes which will compensate them for the hard work they put in throughout the year. And fourthly, there's no reason why we shouldn't use the money we should otherwise have spent on nurserymen, rockery specialists, horticultural cleaners and so on for other purposes.

As the story goes on, the capitalist privatization—because that is what it is—of the Garden is carried through, and it works. When in the 1980s Deng Xiaoping allowed privatization in the Chinese villages, it also worked. It worked so well that its effects started to be felt in politics and threatened the existing political order; hence the knockdown at Tienanmen Square of June 1989. But it seems that the forces of privatization are getting the upper hand again in China. If we remember what Chinese entrepreneurs are able to do once they have become Overseas Chinese, we shouldn't be too surprised. But what works in China—and worked two centuries ago—does not have to work in Russia, not in Tolstoy's days and not today. I am not offering a solution; I only protest against a naive universalism that knows only one recipe for development, the one supposed to have worked in the United States.

A Theory of Culture in Management

Our trip around the world is over and we are back in the United States. What have we learned? There is something in all countries called "management," but its meaning differs to a larger or smaller extent from one country to the other, and it takes considerable historical and cultural insight into local conditions to understand its processes, philosophies, and problems. If already the word may mean so many different things, how can we expect one country's theories of management to apply abroad? One should be extremely careful in making this assumption, and test it before considering it proven. Management is not a phenomenon that can be isolated from other processes taking place in a society. During our trip around the world we saw that it interacts with what happens in the family, at school, in politics, and government. It is obviously also related to religion and to beliefs about science. Theories of management always had to be interdisciplinary, but if we cross national borders they should become more interdisciplinary than ever.

Cultural differences between nations can be, to some extent, described using first four, and now five, bipolar *dimensions*. The position of a country on these dimensions allows us to make some predictions on the way their society operates, including their management processes and the kind of theories applicable to their management.

As the word culture plays such an important role in my theory, let me give you my definition, which differs from some other very respectable definitions. Culture to me is *the collective programming of the mind which distinguishes one group or category of people from another*. In the part of my work I am referring to now, the category of people is the nation.

Culture is a *construct*, that means it is "not directly accessible to observation but inferable from verbal statements and other behaviors and useful in predicting still other observable and measurable verbal and nonverbal behavior." It should not be reified; it is an auxiliary concept that should be used as long as it proves useful but bypassed where we can predict behaviors without it.

The same applies to the *dimensions* I introduced. They are constructs too that should not be reified. They do not "exist"; they are tools for analysis which may or may not clarify a situation. In my statistical analysis of empirical data the first four dimensions together explain 49% of the variance in the data. The other 51% remain specific to individual countries.

The first four dimensions were initially detected through a comparison of the values of similar people (employees and managers) in sixty-four national subsidiaries of the IBM Corporation. People working for the same multinational, but in different countries, represent very well-matched samples from the populations of their countries, similar in all respects except nationality.

The first dimension is labelled *Power Distance*, and it can be defined as the degree of inequality among people which the population of a country considers as normal: from relatively equal (that is, small power distance) to extremely unequal (large power distance). All societies are unequal, but some are more unequal than others.

The second dimension is labelled *Individualism*, and it is the degree to which people in a country prefer to act as individuals rather than as members of groups. The opposite of individualism can be called *Collectivism*, so collectivism is low individualism. The way I use the word it has no political connotations. In collectivist societies a child learns to respect the group to which it belongs, usually the family, and to differentiate between in-group members and out-group members (that is, all other people). When children grow up they remain members of their group, and they expect the group to protect them when they are in trouble. In return, they have to remain loyal to their group throughout life. In individualist societies, a child learns very early to think of itself as "I" instead of as part of "we". It expects one day to have to stand on its own feet and not to get protection from its group any more; and therefore it also does not feel a need for strong loyalty.

The third dimension is called *Masculinity* and its opposite pole *Femininity*. It is the degree to which tough values like assertiveness, performance, success, and competition, which in nearly all societies are associated with the role of men, prevail over tender values like the quality of life, maintaining warm personal relationships, service, care for the weak, and solidarity, which in nearly all societies are more associated with women's roles. Women's roles differ from men's roles in all countries; but in tough societies, the differences are larger than in tender ones.

The fourth dimension is labelled *Uncertainty Avoidance*, and it can be defined as the degree to which people in a country prefer structured over unstructured situations. Structured situations are those in which there are clear rules as to how one should behave. These rules can be written down, but they can also be unwritten and imposed by tradition. In countries which score high on uncertainty avoidance, people tend to show more nervous energy, while in countries which score low, people are more easy-going. A (national) society with strong uncertainty avoidance can be called rigid; one with weak uncertainty avoidance, flexible. In countries where uncertainty avoidance is strong a feeling prevails of "what is different, is dangerous." In weak uncertainty avoidance societies, the feeling would rather be "what is different, is curious."

The fifth dimension was added on the basis of a study of the values of students in twenty-three countries carried out by Michael Harris Bond, a Canadian working in Hong Kong. He and I had cooperated in another study of students' values which had yielded the same four dimensions as the IBM data. However, we wondered to what extent our common findings in two studies could be the effect of a Western bias introduced by the common Western background of the researchers: remember Alice's croquet game. Michael Bond resolved this dilemma by deliberately introducing an Eastern bias. He used a questionnaire prepared at his request by his Chinese colleagues, the *Chinese Value Survey* (CVS), which was translated from Chinese into different languages and answered by fifty male and fifty female students in each of twenty-three countries in all five continents. Analysis of the CVS data produced three dimensions significantly correlated with the three IBM dimensions of power distance, individualism, and masculinity. There was also a fourth dimension, but it did not resemble uncertainty avoidance. It was composed, both on the positive and on the negative side, from items that had not been included in the IBM studies but were present in the Chinese Value Survey because they were rooted in the teachings of Confucius. I labelled this dimension: *Long-term* versus *Short-term Orientation*. On the long-term side one finds values oriented towards the future, like thrift (saving) and persistence. On the short-term side one finds values rather oriented towards the past and present, like respect for tradition and fulfilling social obligations.

Table R1-1 Cultural Dimension Scores for Ten Countries

	PD	*ID*	*MA*	*UA*	*LT*
United States	40L	91H	62H	46L	29L
Germany	35L	67H	66H	65M	31M
Japan	54M	46M	95H	92H	80H
France	68H	71H	43M	86H	30*L
Netherlands	38L	80H	14L	53M	44M
Hong Kong	68H	25L	57H	29L	96H
Indonesia	78H	14L	46M	48L	25*L
West Africa	77H	20L	46M	54M	16L
Russia	95*H	50*M	40*L	90*H	10*L
China	80*H	20*L	50*M	60*M	118H

PD=Power Distance; ID=Individualism; MA=Masculinity; UA=Uncertainty Avoidance;
LT=Long-Term Orientation; H=top third, M=medium third, L=bottom third (among 53
countries and regions for the first four dimensions; among 23 countries for the fifth)
*estimated

Table R1-1 lists the scores on all five dimensions for the United States and for the other countries we just discussed. The table shows that each country has its own configuration on the four dimensions. Some of the values in the table have been estimated based on imperfect replications or personal impressions. The different dimension scores do not "explain" all the differences in management I described earlier. To understand management in a country, one should have both knowledge of and empathy with the entire local scene. However, the scores should make us aware that people in other countries may think, feel, and act very differently from us when confronted with basic problems of society.

Idiosyncracies of American Management Theories

In comparison to other countries, the U.S. culture profile presents itself as below average on power distance and uncertainty avoidance, highly individualistic, fairly masculine, and short-term oriented. The Germans show a stronger uncertainty avoidance and less extreme individualism; the Japanese are different on all dimensions, least on power distance; the French show larger power distance and uncertainty avoidance, but are less individualistic and somewhat feminine; the Dutch resemble the Americans on the first three dimensions, but score extremely feminine and relatively long-term oriented; Hong Kong Chinese combine large power distance with weak uncertainty avoidance, collectivism, and are very long-term oriented; and so on.

The American culture profile is reflected in American management theories. I will just mention three elements not necessarily present in other countries: the stress on market processes, the stress on the individual, and the focus on managers rather than on workers.

The Stress on Market Processes   During the 1970s and 1980s it has become fashionable in the United States to look at organizations from a "transaction costs" viewpoint. Economist Oliver Williamson has opposed "hierarchies" to "markets." The reasoning is that human social life consists of economic transactions between individuals. We found the same in d'Iribarne's description of the U.S. principle of the contract between employer and employee, the labor market in which the worker sells his or her labor for a price. These individuals will form hierarchical organizations when the cost of the economic transactions (such as getting information, finding out whom to trust etc.) is lower in a hierarchy than when all transactions would take place on a free market.

From a cultural perspective the important point is that *the "market" is the point of departure or base model*, and the organization is explained from market failure. A culture that produces such a theory is likely to prefer organizations that internally resemble markets to organizations that internally resemble more structured models, like those in Germany of France. The ideal principle of control in organizations in the market philosophy is *competition* between individuals. This philosophy fits a society that combines a not-too-large power distance with a not-too-strong uncertainty avoidance and individualism; besides the United States, it will fit all other Anglo countries.

The Stress on the Individual   I find this constantly in the design of research projects and hypotheses; also in the fact that in the U.S., psychology is clearly a more respectable discipline in management circles than sociology. Culture however is a collective phenomenon. Although we may get our information about culture from individuals, we have to interpret it at the level of collectivities. There are snags here known as the "ecological fallacy" and the "reverse ecological fallacy." None of the U.S. college textbooks on methodology I know deals sufficiently with the problem of multilevel analysis.

> Culture can be compared to a forest, while individuals are trees. A forest is not just a bunch of trees: it is a symbiosis of different trees, bushes, plants, insects, animals, and micro-organisms, and we miss the essence of the forest if we only describe its most typical trees. In the same way, a culture cannot be satisfactorily described in terms of the characteristics of a typical individual. There is a tendency in the U.S. management literature to overlook the forest for the trees and to ascribe cultural differences to interactions among individuals.

A striking example is found in the otherwise excellent book *Organizational Culture and Leadership* by Edgar H. Schein (1985). On the basis of his consulting experience he compares two large companies, nicknamed "Action" and "Multi." He explains the differences in culture between these companies by the group dynamics in their respective boardrooms. Nowhere in the book are any conclusions drawn from the fact that the first company is an American-based computer firm, and the second a Swiss-based pharmaceutics firm. This information is not even mentioned. A stress on interactions among individuals obviously fits a culture identified as the most individualistic in the world, but it will not be so well understood by the four-fifths of the world population for whom the group prevails over the individual.

One of the conclusions of my own multilevel research has been that culture at the national level and culture at the organizational level—corporate culture—are two very different phenomena and that the use of a common term for both is confusing. If we do use the common term, we should also pay attention to the occupational and the gender level of culture. National cultures differ primarily in the fundamental, invisible values held by a majority of their members, acquired in early childhood, whereas organizational cultures are a much more superficial phenomenon residing mainly in the visible practices of the organization, acquired by socialization of the new members who join as young adults. National cultures change only very slowly if at all; organizational cultures may be consciously changed, although this isn't necessarily easy. This difference between the two types of culture is the secret of the existence of multinational corporations that employ, as I showed in the IBM case, employees with extremely different national cultural values. What keeps them together is a corporate culture based on common practices.

The Stress on Managers Rather than Workers   The core element of a work organization around the world is the people who do the work. All the rest is superstructure, and I hope to have demonstrated to you that it may take many different shapes. In the U.S. literature on work organization, however, the core element, if not explicitly then implicitly, is considered the manager. This may well be the result of the combination of extreme individualism with fairly strong masculinity, which has turned the manager into a culture hero of almost mythical proportions. For example, he—not really she—is supposed to make decisions all the time. Those of you who are or have been managers must know that this is a fable. Very few management decisions are just "made" as the myth suggests it. Managers are much more involved in maintaining networks; if anything, it is the rank-and-file worker who can really make decisions on his or her own, albeit on a relatively simple level.

An amusing effect of the U.S. focus on managers is that in at least ten American books and articles on management I have been misquoted as having studied IBM *managers* in my research, whereas the book clearly describes that the answers were from IBM *employees*. My observation may be biased, but I get the impression that compared to twenty or thirty years ago less research in this country is done among employees and more on managers. But managers derive their *raison d'être* from the people managed: Culturally, they are the followers of the people they lead, and their effectiveness depends on the latter. In other parts of the world, this exclusive focus on the manager is less strong, with Japan as the supreme example.

Conclusion

This article started with *Alice in Wonderland*. In fact, the management theorist who ventures outside his or her own country into other parts of the world is like Alice in Wonderland. He or she will meet strange beings, customs, ways of organizing or disorganizing and theories that are clearly stupid, oldfashioned or even immoral—yet they may work, or at least they may not fail more frequently than corresponding theories do at home. Then, after the first culture shock, the traveller to Wonderland will feel enlightened, and may be able to take his or her experiences home and use them advantageously. All great ideas in science, politics, and management have travelled from one country to another, and been enriched by foreign influences. The roots of American management theories are mainly in Europe: with Adam Smith, John Stuart Mill, Lev Tolstoy, Max Weber, Henri Fayol, Sigmund Freud, Kurt Lewin and many others. These theories were re-planted here and they developed and bore fruit. The same may happen again. The last thing we need is a Monroe doctrine for management ideas.

Reading 2

The Globalization of Business Ethics: Why America Remains Distinctive

David Vogel

In a number of important respects, the increased globalization of the economies of the United States, Western Europe, and Japan is making business practices more uniform. The structure and organization of firms, manufacturing technologies, the social organization of production, customer relations, product development, and marketing—are all becoming increasingly similar throughout the advanced industrial economies. One might logically think that a similar trend would be taking place with respect to the principles and practices of business ethics.

This is occurring, but only very slowly. Business ethics has not yet globalized; the norms of ethical behavior continue to vary widely in different capitalist nations. During the last decade, highly publicized incidents of misconduct on the part of business managers have occurred in virtually every major industrial economy. These scandals have played an important role in increasing public, business, and academic awareness of issues of business ethics in the United States, Western Europe, and Japan. Yet the extent of both public and academic interest in business ethics remains substantially greater in the United States than in other advanced capitalist nations. While interest in business ethics has substantially increased in a number of countries in Europe, and to a lesser extent in Japan, no other capitalist nation approaches the United States in the persistence and intensity of public concern with the morality of business conduct.

The unusual visibility of issues of business ethics in the United States lies in the distinctive institutional, legal, social, and cultural context of the American business system. Moreover the American approach to business ethics is also unique: it is more individualistic, legalistic, and universalistic than in other capitalist societies.

RECENT BUSINESS SCANDALS

Much of the current surge in public, business, and academic interest in business ethics in the United States can be traced to the scandals associated with Wall Street during the 1980s. Characterized by one journalist as "the most serious corporate crime wave since the foreign bribery cases of the mid-1970s," these abuses began with money-laundering by the Bank of Boston in 1986 and check-kiting by E.F. Hutton in 1987. They went on to include: violations of insider-trading regulations by Paul Thayer, who received a five-year jail term; Dennis Levine and the so-called "yuppie Five"; and Ivan Boesky, who was fined $100 million and sentenced to prison for three years. Half of all the cases brought by the SEC alleging illegal use of stock market information since 1949 were filed during a five-year period in the middle of the 1980s.

In 1988, "junk-bond king" Michael Milken and his firm, Drexel Burnham, were indicted for violating federal securities laws and regulations. Both subsequently paid large fines and Milken was sentenced to prison for ten years, subsequently reduced to two. At about the same time, the public became aware of widespread evidence of fraud in the savings and loan industry. A number of bankers were indicted and convicted, including Charles Keating Jr., head of one of the nation's largest savings and loan associations. In 1991, Salomon Brothers admitted that it had committed, "irregularities and rule violations in connection with its submission of bids in certain auctions of Treasury securities" (*Business Week* 1991b). Two managing directors were suspended and the investment bank's Chairman and Chief Executive, John Gutfreund, was forced to resign after admitting that he had known of the firm's misconduct, but had neglected to report it.

Much of the recent increase in interest in business ethics outside the United States can also be attributed to various business scandals that came to light in Europe and Japan during roughly the same timeperiod. In 1982, an American company that had acquired a leading British member of Lloyd's found "undisclosed financial commitments and funds missing from the firm's reinsurance subsidiaries" (Feder 1984 p. 6). In 1985, another major scandal struck London's insurance market: 450 individual members of Lloyd's lost $180 million underwriting policies organized by agents who were alleged to have stolen some of the funds. At about the same time in London, "a wave of suspicious price movements in advance of takeover bids . . . prompted concern that insider trading is spreading" (Putka 1985). In 1987, Geoffrey Collier, a top trader at Morgan Grenfell Group PLC, was indicted for illegally earning more than $20,000 on two mergers involving his prestigious investment banking firm.

The same year, Ernest Saunders, the chief executive of Guinness, a major British-based alcohol beverages company, was accused of attempting to illegally prop up the price of his company's shares in order to help support its bid for the Distillers beverages group. Saunders was arrested and spent a night in jail. He was subsequently forced to sell many of his possessions, including his spacious home in Buckinghamshire, to meet legal costs, and all of his remaining assets were frozen. Saunders' trial did not begin for another three and half years, making the "Guinness Affair," the most prolonged financial scandal in the history of the City of London. In 1990, Saunders was found guilty of having helped engineer the stock's "fortuitous rise" and was sentenced to five years in prison. Three other prominent executives were also found guilty in what has been described as the "financial trial of the century" (Rice and Waters 1992). *The Guardian* (1990, p. 1) noted, "The six-month trial has lifted the lid on the seamy side of the City exposing a sordid story of greed, manipulation and total disregard for takeover regulations."

In 1991, another prominent British businessman, Robert Maxwell, was implicated in a number of wide-ranging abuses, including the looting of a large pension fund and deceptive record-keeping designed to conceal the insolvency of various firms that he controlled. Maxwell died under mysterious circumstances shortly before his "massive international confidence game"—involving large numbers of respectable British and American banks and accounting firms—became public (*The Economist* 1991c). It was subsequently revealed that Maxwell had plundered a total of £450 million from various pension funds he controlled.

In the fall of 1991, the Irish press reported that "four times in the [space of] 16 months, major Irish companies have been hit by crises over secret deals, alleged cover-ups and hidden conflicts of interest." These "crises" included the falsification of company records by Aer Lingus Holidays and Goodman International, the purchase by Irish Sugar of a firm in which the company's chief executive was a part owner, and the "questionable purchase" of a piece of property by Telecom Eireann which had been previously owned by the firm's chairman, Michael Smurfit. Smurfit, the wealthiest businessman in Ireland, was forced to resign his position following press disclosure of this apparent conflict of interest.

In 1989, the French stock market experienced two "blockbuster scandals" that "hinted of insider trading before takeovers" (Greenhouse 1991). In the most celebrated case, investors in France, Luxembourg and Switzerland bought more than 200,000 shares in the Triangle Corporation, shortly before the firm was acquired by Pechiney, the state-owned aluminum company. The stock purchases had been made in the United States and had been brought to the French Government's attention by the Securities and Exchange Commission. While the accusations were "modest by American standards," they "ballooned into a huge scandal" that dominated the front pages of the French press for more than a week (Greenhouse 1989).

In 1990, an official at Deutsche Bank, Germany's largest commercial bank and a major participant in Frankfurt's bank-dominated securities market, was implicated in tax evasion linked to insider trading (Protzman 1991). By the summer of 1991, "the number of people under investigation in Germany for insider trading and/or related tax evasion [had] . . . risen to 25" (*Economist* 1991b). The following year, billionaire financier Carlo De Beneditti, Olivetti's Chief Executive Officer, was sentenced to six years in prison for having been an accessory to the 1982 collapse of Banco Ambrosiano. Thirty-two co-defendants were also convicted (Riding 1992).

Japan, too, has recently experienced a considerable number of business-related scandals. In the spring of 1987, one of the subsidiaries of the Toshiba Corporation was discovered to have sold advanced milling equipment to the Soviet navy to be used for making submarine propellers, in violation of both Japanese law and an international treaty restricting the export of military-related technology to Communist-bloc countries. Both the Chairman and President of the company were forced to resign. Shortly thereafter numerous cases of influence-peddling by the Recruit Company became public: a press report revealed that the firm had given shares at below-market prices to a number of prominent politicians in the ruling Liberal Democratic Party in exchange for various political favors. A number of politicians were forced to resign and the chairman of Recruit, Hisashi Shinto, along with several of his fellow executives, were indicted on bribery charges. On October 9, 1990, Shinto was convicted: he was fined $170,000 and given a two-year prison term, which was suspended due to his age.

In 1991, another major scandal surfaced in Japan. Nomura Securities and Nikko Securities, two of Japan's major brokerage firms, admitted to having lent more than $250 million to a well-known underworld organization. Tax authorities revealed that the same two firms had been secretly reimbursing large clients for stock market losses; other firms were subsequently implicated in this practice as well. In addition, the Sumitomo Bank, Japan's second largest, had lent more than $1 billion to an Osaka trading company headed by a former official of the bank, who then squandered nearly $2 billion in "shady deals." In another major banking scandal, a number of Japan's most prestigious financial institutions, including the Industrial Bank of Japan Ltd., were linked to a scheme involving $2.5 billion in fraudulently obtained loans. In the Spring of 1992, former Chisan Co. Chairman Hirotomo Takai was sentenced to four years in prison and fined $3.8 million for evading $25.6 million in taxes, "the largest-ever tax fraud by an individual" (Japan Times Weekly International Edition 1992). And in 1992, Sagawa Kyubin, a mob-related company, was revealed to have donated more than $17 million to a number of prominent Japanese politicians, including three former prime ministers and two current cabinet members.

Three important business-related scandals have also occurred in Australia. In July 1989, five prominent businessmen, including Ian Johns, the former managing director of an Australian merchant bank, were arrested and charged with insider trading. The following month, Laurie Connell, a prominent Perth financier, was charged with making statements in the annual report of Rothwells, the merchant bank that collapsed in 1988. In 1990, George Herscu, the bankrupt Australian property magnate, was sentenced to five years in jail for bribing a state government minister. Two years later, Alan Bond, one of Australia's most successful entrepreneurs—his fortune is estimated at $7.6 billion—was sentenced to two and one-half years in prison for fraud.

THE RESPONSE

As a response, in part, to these numerous cases of business misconduct, the level of public, business, and academic interest in issues of business ethics increased throughout much of the industrialized world. While interest in this subject was largely confined to the United States during the 1970s, during the 1980s it spread to a number of other capitalist nations as well. In 1983, the first chair in business ethics was established in Europe at the Netherlands School of Business; a second was established at another Dutch university three years later and four more have been founded subsequently in other European countries. In 1986, the Lord Mayor of London organized a formal conference on company philosophy and codes of business ethics for 100 representatives from industry and the professions. The following year, a group of 75 European business managers and academics established the European Business Ethics Network (EBEN); its first conference was held in 1987, and four more have been held since, most recently in Paris in 1992. In 1987, the first European business ethics journal, *Ethica Degli Affari*, was published, in Italy.

Since the mid-1980s, two ethics research centers have been established in Great Britain, in addition to one each in Belgium, Spain, Germany, and Switzerland. A survey of developments in European business ethics published in 1990 reported that, "since three or four years ago the stream of publications (on business ethics) has been rapidly growing," with a disproportionate amount coming from Great Britain, Germany, Austria, and Switzerland (van Luijk 1990). In addition to the EBEN, business ethics networks have been established and national conferences held in Italy (1988), France (1989), and the Netherlands (1990).

Three leading European business schools—INSEAD in France, the London Business School, and Italy's Bocconni—have established elective courses in business ethics and several others have held public conferences on this topic; some have also begun to include sessions on ethics in their executive educational programs. The first European business ethics casebook was published in 1991 and the first issue of a management-oriented publication, *Business Ethics: A European Review*, appeared in the winter of 1992 (Donaldson 1991). Interest in business ethics is also increasing in Japan, though on a much smaller scale. In 1989 and 1991, the Institute of Moralogy sponsored international ethics conferences in Kashiwa City, Chiba Ken, Japan.

THE "ETHICS GAP"

Notwithstanding these initiatives, the "ethics gap," between the United States and the rest of the developed world remains substantial. By any available measure, the level of public, business, and academic interest in issues of business ethics in the United States far exceeds that in any other capitalist country. Nor does this gap show any sign of diminishing: while interest in the subject in Europe has increased in recent years, its visibility in America has increased even more.

In America, each new disclosure of business misconduct prompts a new wave of public indignation, accompanied by numerous articles in the business and popular press which bemoan the general decline in the ethical conduct of managers and seek to explain "what went wrong" in the most recent case. This is frequently followed by Congressional hearings featuring politicians demanding more vigilant prosecution of white-collar criminals; shortly thereafter, regulatory standards are tightened, penalties are increased, and enforcement efforts are strengthened. Executives, in turn, make speeches emphasizing the importance of good ethical behavior for business success, using the most recent round of indictments and associated business failures to demonstrate the "wages of sin." Business educators then re-emphasize the need for additional instruction in ethics, often receiving substantial sums of money from various businessmen to support new educational programs. The most recent scandal then becomes the subject of a case, to be taught in an ever increasing number of business ethics courses designed to assist the next generation of managers in avoiding the pitfalls of their predecessors. When a new scandal occurs—as it invariably does—the cycle begins anew.

No comparable dynamic has occurred in other capitalist nations, where public interest in business ethics tends to be episodic rather than cumulative: thus, only in America are the 1980s referred to as a "decade of greed." As the *Financial Times* (1992) noted in the summer of 1992, "Despite the all-pervasive scandals of the 1980s, there is a tendency in Europe to regard the study of business ethics as faddish." To be sure, the level of public concern with the morality of business does vary in other capitalist nations. For example, it has been much higher in Great Britain and the Netherlands than in Japan. But no other nation has approached the United States in the intensity and duration of public interest in business misconduct. Why? Why are Americans so outraged? How can one account for the distinctive importance of issues of business ethics in American society?

The most obvious explanation is that the conduct of American business has in fact been less ethical. Thus, Americans may be more preoccupied with the ethics of business because there is more misconduct to worry about. Not surprisingly, this explanation is favored by many European managers. However it is not persuasive. Certainly Japan has experienced at least as many major business scandals, and yet there is less interest in business ethics in Japan than in any other major capitalist nation. Moreover, when one compares the relative size of the American economy to that of other capitalist nations, it is not true that either more, or more important, cases of misconduct by businessmen have surfaced in the United States during the last decade.

Rather the importance of issues of business ethics in the United States lies in the distinctive institutional, legal, social, and cultural context of the American business system. In brief, Americans are more concerned with the ethics of business because they have higher expectations of business conduct. Not only is more business conduct considered unethical in the United States, but unethical behavior is more likely to be exposed, punished, and therefore become a "scandal" in America than in other capitalist nations.

MORE REGULATION

The most important reason why there appears to be so much more white-collar crime in the United States is that there are so many more laws regulating business in the United States to be broken. Moreover, regulations governing business tend to be more strictly enforced in the United States than in other capitalist nations. In addition, thanks to more aggressive journalism, as well as to government disclosure requirements, business misdeeds are more likely to be exposed in the United States.

One British journalist commented following the "Maxwell mess," that, "unlike in America, there is no vigorous probing process that names and uncovers embarrassments. Regulators here are invariably shy about using their powers and often are unable to do so" (Fashi and Fronal 1991). The situation in Britain is in striking contrast to the resources the American federal government devoted to investigating and prosecuting Michael Milken. Moreover, British libel laws also make it more difficult for journalists to disclose the abuses they do uncover. Some observers have suggested that the French insider-trading scandal of 1989 would have been buried, "as previous French governments . . . have buried previous scandals, were it not for the SEC's involvement" (Greenhouse 1989). One Japanese journalist recently observed, "In Japan today, if you have the word 'Inc.' attached to your name, you can commit crimes with little risk and only minor penalties" (Sterngold 1992). In fact, the only reason why the "dubious behavior" of Japan's brokerage firms in reimbursing clients for losses became a major financial scandal in 1991 was due to the involvement of organized crime; otherwise the government would have been unlikely to investigate.

By contrast, with the active help of an unrestricted and uninhibited media that places a high priority on investigative reporting, Congressional committees with substantial resources to conduct investigations, and ninety-five entrepreneurial United States Attorneys, America appears to have developed a "great . . . scandal machine [that is] running with ferocious momentum."[1] The chances that business misdeeds will escape exposure and prosecution are fewer in the United States than in any other capitalist nation.

Moreover, many activities for which American managers and corporations have pleaded guilty or have been convicted—most notably making campaign contributions from company funds and providing gifts to foreign government officials to secure contracts—are not illegal in other capitalist nations. This is also the case with respect to the violations of American securities laws to which Michael Milken pleaded guilty, as well as for Salomon Brothers' violations of the Treasury Department's bond trading rules (in fact, the rule that Salomon broke only came into existence in the United States some months earlier). With the exception of France, insider trading was legal throughout Europe until the early 1980s. It is still not against the law in Germany—although there is a voluntary code prohibiting it—and was only banned in Japan in 1989.

The issue of sexual harassment also illustrates the contrast between the standards of business conduct in America and other capitalist nations. Americans in general and American women in particular have higher standards for the conduct of male managers and more reason to expect that their complaints will be taken seriously by both the press and by government officials than in most other capitalist nations. While sexual harassment has been considered a form of sex discrimination in the United States since 1979, it only became illegal in France in 1992, while the concept itself was translated into Japanese for the first time in 1989. The first successful legal action against sexual harassment in Japan took place in April 1992. Moreover, American laws and regulations governing workplace discrimination on the basis of sex are both stricter—and better enforced—than in most other capitalist nations.

LEGAL VULNERABILITY

Another distinctive feature of the contemporary legal environment of business in the United States is the relatively large exposure of both individual executives and corporations to legal prosecution. As recently as two decades ago, the prosecution of individuals for white-collar crime in the United States was relatively rare. On occasion, high-status individuals were sentenced to prison; for example, in 1938, Richard Whitney, who had been president of the New York Stock Exchange, was found guilty of embezzlement and sentenced to five years in federal prison. In the early 1960s, a handful of senior managers from General Electric and Westinghouse received light prison sentences after they were found guilty of price-fixing.

However, this began to change in the early 1970s when, in connection with Watergate, a number of high-status individuals were sentenced to prison. By the end of the decade, what began as a trickle had become a flood: "Businessmen spent more time in jail for price-fixing in 1978 than in all the 89 years since the passage of the Sherman Antitrust Act" (Galluccio 1979, p. 61). Sixty-five percent of the individuals convicted of security law violations during the 1980s received jail sentences.

While the Federal Corrupt Practices Act made senior managers personally liable for monitoring its enforcement, the most important increase in the exposure of individual managers for corporate compliance took place in the area of environmental law. As recently as 1983, "jail sentences for polluters were unheard of" (Ferrey 1988, p. 12). In 1984, Federal courts handed out prison terms totaling two years and individual fines totaling $198,000. But five years later they handed out prison terms totaling 37 years and fines totaling $11.1 million. The number of individuals indicted increased from 40 in 1983 to 134 in 1990. Between 1986 and 1991, a total of 90 individuals were jailed for Federal environmental crimes. Of those sentenced to prison for environmental violations through 1988, one-third were corporate presidents while less than one-quarter were workers who had actually released the pollution.

During the 1980s Congress added tougher criminal penalties to a number of environmental statutes while Federal sentencing guidelines issued in 1987 increased penalties for a number of environmental violations, putting them on a par with drug-related felonies. "As a result, jail has become much more likely for defendants in environmental cases, even for first-time offenders" (Gold 1991, p. B10). The Clean Air Act Amendments of 1990 not only expanded the number of violations that can be treated as criminal, but subjected to criminal prosecution any executive who had knowledge that a particular violation had taken place. According to a government official, now senior executives "realize that there is a real risk" of a prison term when environmental damage can be traced specifically to a company's acts. He added, "the word has really gotten out because of the increased level of enforcement." A corporate lawyer commented, "[Prosecutors] don't have much flexibility. If [the company] make[s] a mistake, the guy's going to jail" (Gold 1991, p. B10).

The *Economist* observed, "Polluters . . . have replaced drug-money launderers as the favorite target of government prosecutors out to make a name for themselves" (*Economist* 1991b). The number of lawyers employed by the environmental crimes section of the Justice Department increased from 3 in 1982 to 25 in 1991, while the criminal enforcement program of the Environmental Protection Agency grew from 23 investigators in 1982 to 60 in 1991. Similar expansions took place in a number of states.

A growing number of executives also have been indicted on criminal charges for violations of workplace health and safety regulations. In one "landmark" case, Film Recovery Inc., three corporate officials were, for the first time in American history, found guilty of murder in connection with the death of an employee. The owner and executives were jailed for 25 years each and fined for murder, involuntary manslaughter, and reckless conduct for knowingly exposing their employees to workplace hazards. Nearly one-half of American states now have legislation providing for corporate criminal liability for the death of employees. "Los Angeles County law-enforcement officers have been requested to treat every workplace fatality as a potential homicide" (Kahn 1987, p. 48).

Not only has there been a steady increase in the number of corporate law violations classified as criminal, but the federal government also has become much more aggressive in seeking large financial penalties against corporations. The average corporate fine increased eight-fold between 1988 and 1990. Prominent corporations fined substantial sums from the mid-1980s to 1992 include the Bank of Boston ($500,000 for violating the Bank Secrecy Act of 1970); Exxon ($100 million for the Exxon Valdez disaster); Chrysler ($7.5 million for rolling back odometers in more than 60,000 vehicles); General Electric ($10 million for overbilling the government for computers); Northrop ($17 million for weapons test fraud); Salomon Inc. ($200 million in penalities); and Drexel Burnham ($650 million in fines and restitution for violations of federal securities laws). The penalty imposed on Drexel was the largest in the history of capitalism and helped force the firm into bankruptcy—a fate that has not befallen any large firm subject to government prosecution in either Europe or Japan.

One important reason why so many American corporations have established ethics codes and training programs has to do with federal sentencing guidelines that went in effect on November 1, 1991, but which had been made public much earlier. These guidelines not only double the median fine for corporations found guilty of crimes such as fraud, but state that companies convicted of various crimes will receive more lenient treatment if they have previously demonstrated good faith efforts to "be a good corporate citizen." For example, "a fine of $1 million to $2 million could be knocked down to as low as $50,000 for a company with a comprehensive program, including a code of conduct, an ombudsman, a hotline, and mandatory training programs for executives" (Kahn 1987, p. 48).

ENFORCEMENT IN EUROPE AND JAPAN

It is true that regulation has been strengthened and penalties increased in other capitalist nations as well. For example, in response to the deregulation of London's capital markets that took place in the mid-1980s, the British Government moved to better protect the interest of investors. Britain now has unlimited fines and up to two years of imprisonment for insider-trading violations. However, the British have emphasized the streamlining of industry self-regulation, not the establishment of a government oversight body similar to the American Securities and Exchange Commission. Notwithstanding the Saunders case, enforcement, while it has increased, still "remains infrequent" in Britain (*New York Times* 1991).

In response to the insider-trading scandals that occurred in France during the late 1980s, the French Government expanded the size and power of the Commission des Operations de Bourse, its principal stock market oversight agency. Previously known as a "small and toothless watchdog," its budget was increased fourfold and its staff size doubled—making it comparable in resources to the S.E.C. (Greenhouse 1991, p. C6). It also was empowered to impose fines of up to 10 million francs (approximately $2 million) or up to ten times the illegal profits in cases involving insider trading. Insider trading in France is also punishable by up to two years in prison. However, France's regulatory agency has yet to use its new authority to impose civil fines for insider trading, although through the summer of 1991, it had conducted 79 investigations and turned 15 of them over to prosecutors.

Following a highly publicized number of financial scandals in Japan, four prominent businessmen—the president and chairman of Nomura, the chairman of Sumitomo Bank, and the president of Nikko Securities—were forced to resign in the fall of 1991. But only one individual was arrested. The Ministry of Finance subsequently imposed suspensions of up to six weeks on Japan's four leading stockbrokers. Although this represented "some of the stiffest sentences ever meted out by ministerial order," unlike in the case of Drexel, the penalty did not affect the four companies' dominance of Japanese stock trading. Nor has the Ministry of Finance made a serious effort to strengthen its regulation of Japan's financial markets. The maximum fine for violating the recently enacted ban on brokers for paying compensation for losses is only ¥500,000 (approximately $3,760). There has been only one prosecution for insider trading, and only one for share-price manipulation, "even though market professionals consider this to be a chronic problem" (Sterngold 1991, p. c6).

The prosecution of violators of environmental regulations has increased in a number of European countries. For example, the German penal code was recently amended to provide for the increased use of criminal penalties. "The German criminal law system is considered to be one of the best legal systems for the protection of the environment" (Vercher 1990, p. 448). The number of criminal proceedings nearly doubled between 1980 and 1985, while the rate of convictions is among the highest in Europe.

Criminal law has also begun to be used to enforce environmental regulations in Spain, Sweden, Holland, and Finland. However, criminal penalties are still not imposed on polluters in France, Italy, and Britain. Historically, the British have been reluctant to impose any form of judicial penalties against violators of environmental regulations. This has recently begun to change; for example, the number of successful civil prosecutions against companies and individuals initiated by the newly established National Rivers Authority increased from 334 in 1989 to 574 in 1990. But fines remain modest: only two have been for more than £200,000, with the average less than £10,000. Moreover, the individuals who have been prosecuted have been small businessmen and farmers, not corporate executives. Even in Germany it remains highly unusual for senior managers to be held personally responsible for environmental violations committed by their subordinates.

On balance during the last 15 years, more corporate officers and prominent businessmen have been jailed or fined in the United States than in all other capitalist nations combined. Likewise, the fines imposed on corporations in the United States have been substantially greater than in other capitalist nations. While the penalties for white-collar crime also have increased outside the United States, over the last decade the magnitude of the difference between the legal vulnerability of corporations and individual managers in the United States and those in other capitalist nations has increased. This development both reflects the high standards that exist in corporate conduct in the United States and also serves to re-enforce the perception that business misconduct is more pervasive in the United States.

PUBLIC EXPECTATIONS

The high expectations of business conduct in the United States are not confined to the legal system. They also are reflected in the way many Americans invest and consume. For example, "ethical investment" funds in the United States enable individuals and institutions to make their investment strategy consistent with their political/social values either by avoiding investments in firms they judge to be behaving irresponsibly or by increasing their holdings of the stocks and bonds of firms that are acting "socially responsibly." While such funds exist in a number of European countries—including Britain and the Netherlands—they both originated and remain much larger in the United States. The same is true of the use of various social criteria to screen investments by institutional investors. For example, in no other capitalist nation have so many institutional investors divested themselves of shares of firms with investments in South Africa.

The American penchant for evaluating and comparing corporate social and ethical performance extends beyond capital markets; it also informs consumer judgments of business. Various private non-profit organizations in America regularly "rank" corporations in terms of their behavior on such dimensions as women and minority employment, military contracting, concern about the environment, and animal testing; one such guide, published by the Council on Economic Priorities, has sold more than 350,000 copies (Corson et al. 1989). Such rankings are virtually unknown outside the United States, as are awards for "excellence in ethics." The Japanese may be obsessed with ranking corporations, but they appear to have overlooked this particular dimension of corporate performance.

Similarly, the number of companies that have been subject to consumer boycotts on the basis of their social policies has increased substantially in the United States in recent years. By contrast, consumer boycotts are much less common in Europe and virtually unknown in Japan (the most recent took place in the early 1970s and it involved the prices of televisions). A number of consumer boycotts have taken place in Great Britain, but far fewer than in the United States—even after taking into account the relative sizes of the two economies.

Once again, the contrast in public expectations of business behavior in the United States and other capitalist nations is marked: relatively few consumers or investors outside the United States appear to pay much attention to the political and social behavior of the firms whose products they consume or whose stocks and bonds they purchase. Indeed, what is striking is how little writing on business ethics in continental Europe actually mentions individual corporations at all; rather it tends to focus on more abstract concerns having to do with the relationship between ethics and economics. This is also true of the numerous statements of the Papacy on the "moral philosophy of business," which focus on the justice or lack thereof of the economic system, not on the ethics of particular corporations (De Woot 1990). More generally, the debate over the role of business in Europe has focused on how to organize the economy, while in the United States it has emphasized standards of conduct for companies whose private ownership is assumed.

This in turn may be due to another distinctive characteristic of American society, namely, the considerable emphasis that has historically been placed on the social obligations of business. Because business corporations played a critical role in the development of cities and the shaping of communities in the United States, they have long been perceived as social institutions with substantial responsibility for the moral and physical character of the communities in which they have invested. Both the doctrine of corporate social responsibility and the practice of corporate philanthropy date back more than a century in the United States. By contrast, in both Europe and Japan, the responsibility of business has historically been defined more narrowly. Since all these economies, with the exception of Britain, industrialized later, it was government rather than corporations that both set the terms of economic development and assumed responsibility for various civic functions. Even today, corporate philanthropy remains primarily an American phenomenon.

BUSINESS VALUES

Ironically, it may be precisely because the values of "business civilization" are so deeply ingrained in American society that Americans tend to become so upset when the institutions and individuals whom they have looked up to—and whose values and success they have identified with—betray their trust. More generally: "In the United States . . . the single all-pervasive 'ought' rampages widely beyond the control of the 'is.' The result is a unique and ever-present challenge . . . posed by the gap between the ideals by which the society lives and the institutions by which it functions" (Huntington 1981, p. 60). Because the public's expectations of business conduct are so high, the invariable result is a consistently high level of public dissatisfaction with the actual ethical performance of business.

An important key to understanding the unique interest of Americans in the subject of business ethics lies in America's Protestant heritage: "The United States is the only country in the world in which a majority of the population has belonged to dissenting Protestant sects" (Huntington 1981, p. 60). This has important implications for the way in which Americans approach the subject of business ethics. By arguing that one can and should do "God's work" by creating wealth, Protestantism raised the public's expectations of the moral behavior of business managers. Thus, thanks in part to the role played by Reformed Protestantism in defining American values, America remains a highly moralistic society. Compared to the citizens of other capitalist nations, Americans are more likely to believe that business and morality are, and should be, related to each other, that good ethics is good business, and that business activity both can and should be consistent with high personal moral values.

While the high expectations of business conduct shared by Americans has a strong populist dimension, this particular understanding of the proper relationship between business and morality is not in any sense anti-business. It is also shared by much of the American business community. Indeed, the latter appear as concerned about the ethical lapses of their colleagues as is the American public. A survey of key business leaders conducted by Touche Ross in 1987 reported that more than two-thirds believe "that the issue of ethics in business has not been overblown in the current public debate" (Ross 1987, p. 2). Admittedly, some of these expressions of concern about business ethics amount to little more than public relations. But it is impossible to read through the reports on business ethics in the United States is-sued by such organizations as the Business Roundtable, Touche Ross, or the Con-ference Board without being struck by the sincerity of the concerns of the execu-tives whose views they report.

Where else but in the United States would a group of nationally prominent ex-ecutives establish and fund an organization such as the Business Enterprise Trust in order to offer annual awards for outstanding ethical behavior by corporations and individual managers? (O'Toole 1991). While the belief that good ethics and high profits go hand in hand is certainly not confined to American businessmen, they seem to articulate it more frequently than do their counterparts in other capitalist nations. One senses that many of the latter are a bit more cynical about the relation-ship. For example, in Germany, "Insider trading doesn't have much of a stigma. Tax evasion is a gentleman's sport" (*Business Week* 1987).

Because the moral status of capitalism in Europe has traditionally been prob-lematic, there appears to be much more cynicism about the ethics of business in Eu-rope and Japan. Europeans, in part due to the legacy of aristocratic and pre-capital-ist values, have always tended to view the pursuit of profit and wealth as somewhat morally dubious, making them less likely to be surprised—let alone outraged—when companies and managers are discovered to have been "greedy." For their part, the "Japanese seem almost inured to the kind of under-the-table favors whose disclosure sparked the [1991] scandal." As one Japanese investor put it, "It's so much a part of Japanese culture and tradition that the people don't think they're doing anything wrong" (*Business Week* 1991).

One Japanese political consultant recently mused: "I wonder sometimes when the Japanese people will rise up and say, 'We've had enough.'" But the only answer I can give for sure is 'Not in this century, at least'" (Reid 1991, p. 18).

Not surprisingly, many Europeans regard the current level of interest of Amer-icans in the ethics and morality of business conduct—to say nothing of other as-pects of American society—as somewhat excessive. Corporate codes of conduct, ethics training programs, lists of "ethical" and "unethical" firms—are all seen as signs of an "unusually moralizing society," one that "people in old and cynical Eu-rope often find difficult to take . . . seriously" (Reid 1991, p. 18). The extent of moral scrutiny and self-criticism that pervades contemporary American society prompted the *Economist* to publish an editorial entitled, "Hey, America, Lighten Up A Little." (*Economist* 1990).

KEY DIFFERENCES IN BUSINESS ETHICS

The United States is distinctive not only in the intensity of public concern with the ethical behavior of business, but also in the way in which business ethics are de-fined. Americans tend to emphasize the role of the individual as the most critical source of ethical values, while in other capitalist nations relatively more emphasis is placed on the corporation as the locus of ethical guidance. Second, business ethics tends to be much more legalistic and rule-oriented in the United States. Finally, Americans are more likely to consider their own ethical rules and standards to be universally applicable.

Business ethics in the United States has been strongly affected by the "tradi-tion of liberal individualism that . . . is typical of American culture" (van Luijk, p. 542). Not surprisingly, a frequent characteristic of business ethics cases devel-oped in the United States is that they require the individual to decide what is right on the basis of his or her own values. While the company's goals and objectives or the views of the individual's fellow employees are not irrelevant, in the final analysis they are not intended to be decisive. Indeed, they may often be in conflict.

By contrast, "in European circumstances it is not at all evident that managers, when facing a moral dilemma, will navigate first and foremost on their personal moral compass" (van Luijk, p. 542). Rather managers are more likely to make decisions based on their shared understanding of the nature and scope of the company's responsibilities. The legitimate moral expectations of a company are shaped by the norms of the community, not the personal values or reflections of the individual. The latter has been labeled "communicative" or "consensual business ethics" (van Luijk, pp. 543–44).

One possible outcome of the tension between the interests and values of the company and those of the individual employee is whistle-blowing. Critics of business in the United States have urged increased legal protection for whistle-blowers—and, in fact, some regulatory statutes in the United States explicitly protect those who publicly expose violations of various company policies.

By contrast, the idea that there could even be such a tension between the individual and the organization is thoroughly alien to Japanese business culture, where whistle-blowers would be regarded more as traitors than heroes. Only a handful of European countries have laws protecting whistle-blowers. And few non-American firms have established formal mechanisms, such as the appointment of ombudsmen, to enable employees to voice their moral concerns about particular corporate policies. Workers in many other capitalist nations may well feel a greater sense of loyalty toward the firms for which they work, and a greater respect for those in authority.

A second critical difference between business ethics in America and other capitalist countries has to do with the role of law and formal rules. Notwithstanding—or perhaps because of—its traditions of individualism, Americans tend to define business ethics in terms of rules; the writing on business ethics by Americans is replete with checklists, principles, and guidelines for individual managers to follow in distinguishing right from wrong.

Americans' tendency to think of ethics in terms of rules is reflected in the widespread use of corporate codes among U.S.-based companies. Such codes are much less common in Europe, although their use has recently increased in Britain. One French observer notes:

> The popularity of codes of ethics in the United States meets with little response in Europe, America's individualism does not correspond to the social traditions of Europe. These large differences make fruitless all desire to imitate the other's steps.[2]

One French manager, whose firm had recently been acquired by an American company, stated:

> I resent having notions of right and wrong boiled down to a checklist. I come from a nation whose ethical traditions date back hundreds of years. Its values have been transmitted to me by my church and through my family. I don't need to be told by some American lawyers how I should conduct myself in my business activities.[3]

Henri-Claude de Bettignies, who teaches business ethics at INSEAD, adds:

> Some European leaders perceive corporate codes of conduct as a device which deresponsibilizes the individual, i.e., he does not have to think for himself, he just needs to apply the codes of conduct which he has learnt and which—through training—have programmed him to respond in a certain "corporate" way (de Bettignies 1991, p. 11).

By contrast, European firms appear to place greater emphasis on informal mechanisms of social control within the firm. Indeed, European managers frequently profess astonishment at the apparent belief of many American executives, as well as government officials, that a company's adoption of a code can actually alter the behavior of its employees.

There is a third critical difference between business ethics in the United States and other capitalist nations. Americans not only tend to define business ethics in terms of rules and procedures; they also tend to believe that American rules and procedures should be applied universally. For example, no other nation requires the foreign subsidiaries of its multinational corporations to follow the laws of their home country as frequently as does the United States. Thus the United States is the only nation that restricts its firms from making payments to secure contracts or other benefits outside its borders. A survey of European executives reported that, "nearly 40 percent would never complain about bribery by a business rival—or answer charges of bribery against themselves." (Lewis 1978, p. 2). Similarly, in no other nation have corporations been so frequently criticized for exporting products that do not conform to the health and safety standards of their "home" country.

Universalism also has a second dimension having to do with the importance of the distinction between "us" and "them." American business culture—and American society—attaches considerable importance to treating everyone in the same arm's-length manner. By contrast, the Japanese—and, to a lesser extent, the citizens of Latin Europe—define their responsibilities in more particularistic terms: managers, as well as government officials, in these countries place less value on treating everyone equally and attach much more importance to fulfilling their obligations to those individuals and institutions with whom they have developed long-standing and long-term relationships. (Significantly, it is very difficult to translate the phrases "equal opportunity" and "level playing field" into Japanese.) On this dimension, Britain and much of northern Europe is much closer to the United States.

All these dimensions are, in fact, inter-related. To summarize the American approach: business ethics is about individuals making moral judgments based on general rules that treat everyone the same. By contrast, business ethics in Europe and Japan has more to do with managers arriving at decisions based on shared values, often rooted in a particular corporate culture, applied according to specific circumstances and strongly affected by the nature of one's social ties and obligations.

CONCLUSION

Regulatory rules and standards, especially with the European Community and between the United States and Western Europe, are certainly becoming more similar. For example, a strengthening of environmental regulation has occurred in virtually all capitalist nations, while legal restrictions on insider trading—a decade ago, largely confined to the United States—are now the norm in Europe. Similarly, a number of European nations have recently enacted legislation banning sexual harassment. The prosecution of white-collar criminals has also recently increased in Europe. In 1989, the first Swede to be found guilty of insider trading was sentenced to five years in prison. Not only are many American legal norms and standards of corporate conduct being adopted in other capitalist nations, but as globalization proceeds and world commerce is increasingly driven by multinational firms, these firms may well come to adopt common ethical standards. These developments are important. But they continue to be overshadowed by the persistence of fundamental national differences in the ways in which business ethics is defined, debated, and judged.

While much has been written on differences in the laws and business norms of developed and less-developed nations, the equally important contrasts in the way in which ethical issues are discussed and defined *among* the developed nations has been all but ignored.[4] Significantly, among the hundreds of ethics cases developed for use in management education in the United States and Europe, only *one*— Toshiba Machine Company—contrasts differences in ethical norms between two advanced industrial nations. We need a better appreciation of the differences in the legal and cultural context of business ethics between the United States and other capitalist nations, and between Western and Asian economies as well, if managers are to work effectively in an increasingly integrated global economy.

References

Business Week (1987), "The Insider-Trading Dragnet Is Stretching Across the Globe" (March 23), 51.

Business Week (1991a), "Hidden Japan," (August 26), 18.

Business Week (1991b), "The Salomon Shocker: How Bad Will It Get?" (August 26), 36.

CORSON, B. et al., (1989), *Shopping for A Better World*. New York: Ballantine Books.

DE BETTIGNIES, H. (1991), "Ethics and International Business: A European Perspective." Paper presented at the Tokyo Conference on the Ethics of Business in a Global Economy, Kashiwashi, Japan, (September 10–12), 11.

DE WOOT, P. (1990), "The Ethical Challenge To The Corporations: Meaningful Progress Individual Development," in Enderle, G. et al., eds., *People In Corporations*. Boston: Kluwer Academic Publishers, 79.

DONALDSON, J. (1991), *Ethics in European Business—A Casebook*. London: Academic Press Ltd.

Economist (1990), "Hey America, Lighten Up A Little," (July 28).

Economist (1991a), "Dishing the Dirt" (February 9), 70.

Economist (1991b), "Sweeping out the Stables" (August 31), 15.

Economist (1991c), "An Honor System Without Honor," (December 14), 81.

Ethics in American Business, (1987), Touche Ross, (December), 2.

FARHI, P. and FRANKEL, G. (1991), "Pardon Me, Old Bean, But Aren't Your Pants on Fire?" *Washington Post National Weekly Edition* (December 23–29), 20.

FEDER, B. (1984), "Overseeing Insurance Reform at London's Venerable Mart," *The New York Times* (January 8), 6.

FERREY, S. (1988), "Hard Time," *The Amicus Journal* (Fall) 12.

Financial Times (1992), "Ethics and Worse" (July 3), 12.

GALLUCCIO, N. (1979), "The Boss in the Slammer," *Forbes* (February 5), 61.

GOLD, A. (1991), "Increasingly, A Prison Term Is the Price Paid by Polluters," *The New York Times* (February 15), B10.

GREENHOUSE, S. (1989), "Modest Insider-Trading Stir Is a Huge Scandal in France," *The New York Times* (January 30), D1.

GREENHOUSE, S. (1991), "An Old Club Transformed," *The New York Times* (July 23), C6.

The Guardian (1990), (August 28), 1.

HUNTINGTON, S.P. (1981), *American Politics: The Promise of Disharmony*. Cambridge, MA: Harvard University Press, 60.

Japan Times Weekly International Edition (1992), "Top Tax-Evader Gets Four-Year Sentence," (May 11–17), 2.

KAHN, J. (1987), "When Bad Management Becomes Criminal," *INC.* (March), 48.

LEWIS, P. (1978), "European Businessmen Don't Take Their Morality So Seriously," *The New York Times* (March 3), Section 4, 2.

MILOTTE, M. and NALLY, D. (1991), "A Season of Scandals," *The Sunday Tribune*, (September 22), 6; see also Clarke, P. and Tierney, E., (1992), "Business Troubles in the Republic of Ireland," *Business Ethics; A European Review* (April), 134–38.

New York Times (1991), "Investors Beware: Stock Market Rules Vary Considerably," (July 23), C7.

O'TOOLE, J. (1991), "Doing Good by Doing Well," *California Management Review*, 33/3 (Spring), 9–24.

PROTZMAN, F. (1991), "Insider Trading Scandal Grows," *New York Times* (July 23), C6.

PUTKA, G. (1985), "British Face Finance-Industry Scandals Just as They Move to Deregulate Markets," *The Wall Street Journal* (August 12), 20.

REID, T.R. (1991), "In Japan, Too, Money Is The Mother's Milk of Politics," *Washington Post National Weekly Edition* (September 14–29), 18.

RICE, R. and WATERS, R. (1992), "Fraud Office Drops Charges in Third Guinness Case," *Financial Times* (February 9), 1.

RIDING, A. (1992), "Olivetti's Chairman Is Convicted in Bank Fraud that Shocks Italy," *The New York Times* (April 17).

STERNGOLD, J. (1991), "Informal Code Rules Markets," *The New York Times* (July 23), C6.

——— (1992), "Japan's Rigged Casino," *New York Times Magazine* (April 26), 48.

VAN LUIJK, H.J.L. "Recent Developments in European Business Ethics," *Journal of Business Ethics*, 9, 538.

VERCHER, A. (1990), "The Use of Criminal Law for the Protection of the Environment in Europe: Council of Europe Resolution (77)28," *Northwestern Journal of International Law Business*, 10, 448.

Endnotes

1. The quotation is from *Scandal* by Suzanne Garment. Quoted in Jonathan Yardley, "The Truly Corrupt Vs. the Merely Sleazy," *Washington Post National Weekly Edition*, October 7–23, 1991, p. 35. While Garment's book is about political scandals, her analysis can be applied to scandals involving the private sector as well.

2. Kerhuel, A. "De Part et D'Autre De L'Atlantique" [David Vogel translation].

3. This statement was made at an executive training session at IMD in the fall of 1991 that the author taught.

4. The handful of exceptions includes: Catherine Langlois and Bodo Schegelmilch, "Do Corporate Codes of Ethics Reflect National Character? Evidence from Europe and the United States," *Journal of International Business Studies* (Fourth Quarter 1990), pp. 519–39; van Luijk, op. cit., pp. 537–44; Ernest Gundling, "Ethics and Working with the Japanese: The Entrepreneur and the 'Elite Course,'" *California Management Review*, 33/3 (Spring 1991): 25–39; Joanne Ciulla, "Why Is Business Talking about Ethics?" *California Management Review*, 34/1 (Fall 1991): 67–86.

Negotiating with Romans—Part I

Stephen E. Weiss

"Smith," an American, arrived at the French attorney's Paris office for their first meeting. Their phone conversations had been in French, and Smith, whose experience with the language included ten years of education in the United States, a year of residence in France with a French family and annual trips to Paris for the previous seven years, expected to use French at this meeting. "Dupont," the Frenchman, introduced himself in French. His demeanor was poised and dignified; his language, deliberate and precise. Smith followed Dupont's lead, and they went on to talk about a mutual acquaintance. After ten minutes, Dupont shifted the topic by inquiring about

Smith's previous work in international negotiations. One of Dupont's words—"operations"—surprised Smith, and he hesitated to respond. In a split second, Dupont, in fluent English, asked: "Would you like to speak in English?"[1]

Smith used the approach to cross-cultural interaction most widely advocated in the West, with a history dating back to St. Augustine: "When in Rome, do as the Romans do." It had seemed to be a reasonable way to convey cooperativeness, sensitivity to French culture, and respect for Dupont as an individual. But Smith overlooked important considerations, as have many other people who continue to recommend or follow this approach.[2]

The need for guidance for cross-cultural negotiators is clear. Every negotiator belongs to a group or society with its own system of knowledge about social interaction—its own "script" for behavior.[3] Whether the boundaries of the group are ethnic, organizational, ideological, or national, its culture influences members' negotiations—through their conceptualizations of the process, the ends they target, the means they use, and the expectations they hold of counterparts' behavior. There is ample evidence that such negotiation rules and practices vary across cultures.[4] Thus cross-cultural negotiators bring into contact unfamiliar and potentially conflicting sets of categories, rules, plans, and behaviors.

Doing as "Romans" do has not usually resolved this conflict effectively. (Throughout this article, the terms "Romans" and "non-Romans" are used as shorthand for "other-culture negotiators" and "own-culture negotiators," respectively.) "Fitting in" requires capabilities that relatively few non-Romans possess; most cultures involve much more than greeting protocols.[5] The approach takes for granted that Romans accept a non-Roman's behaving like a Roman when, actually, many Romans believe in at least some limits for outsiders.[6] Also, the approach presumes, misleadingly, that a Roman will always act Roman with a non-Roman in Rome.

Today's challenges should motivate a cross-cultural negotiator to search for additional approaches or strategies. An American negotiator may meet on Tuesday with a group of Japanese who speak through an interpreter and meet on Thursday one-on-one with a Japanese who is fluent in English and a long-time personal friend. In addition, geographical referents are blurring: just off of Paris's Boulevard St. Germain, an American can go to a Japanese restaurant in search of Japanese food and customs, yet find there Chinese waiters who speak Chinese to each other and French to their customers. Indeed, Americans negotiate with Japanese not only in Tokyo and Los Angles but at third sites such as London. They may forgo face-to-face meetings to communicate by fax, E-mail, telephone, or video conference. Some of these negotiators have one day to finalize a sale; others have fourteen months to formulate a joint venture agreement. This variety of people and circumstances calls for more than one strategic approach.

What are the options for conducting negotiations in culturally sensitive ways? What should non-Roman negotiators do, especially when they lack the time and skills available to long-time expatriates?[7] How should the non-Roman businessperson prepare to use a culturally responsive strategy for negotiation with a particular Roman individual or group in a particular set of circumstances?

This article presents a range of eight culturally responsive strategies for Americans and other groups involved in cross-cultural negotiations at home and abroad. The corresponding framework takes into account the varying capabilities of different negotiators across different circumstances and thus provides options for *every* cross-cultural negotiator. Among other benefits, it enables a negotiator to move beyond the popular, one-size-fits-all lists of "dos and don'ts" for negotiating in a particular culture to see that what is appropriate really depends on the negotiating strategy. In short, this article offers the manager a broadened, realistic view of strategies for effective cross-cultural negotiation.

EIGHT CULTURALLY RESPONSIVE STRATEGIES

Stories of cross-cultural conflict—faux pas and "blunders"—abound.[8] They highlight feelings of anxiety, disorientation, misunderstanding, and frustration, and they tempt negotiators to try to minimize apparent behavioral differences by "matching" or "imitating" their counterparts' ways. But there are more fundamental goals for a cross-cultural negotiator.

> Consider what often happens when Americans negotiate with Japanese. Viewing negotiation as a process of exchange involving several proposal-counterproposal iterations, Americans inflate their demands in initial proposals and expect later to give and receive concessions. Their Japanese counterparts often do not promptly reciprocate with a counterproposal. Thus the Americans offer concessions, hoping that they will kick the exchange model—"the negotiations"—into gear. The Japanese, however, ask many questions. By the end of the talks, the Americans feel frustrated, with the extent of their concessions and conclude that Japanese do not negotiate. Although the Americans may believe that the Japanese are shrewdly trying to determine how much their American counterparts will concede, it is quite likely that these Japanese are operating from a different model of negotiation: negotiation as a process of gathering information, which, when consistent and complete, will reveal a "correct, proper, and reasonable" solution (Blaker 1977, p. 50).

Research on communication suggests that the minimal, fundamental goal for non-Romans is to ensure that both sides perceive that the pattern of interaction makes sense.[9] For negotiation to occur, non-Romans must at least recognize those ideas and behaviors that Romans intentionally put forward as part of the negotiation process (and Romans must do the same for non-Romans). Parties must also be able to interpret these behaviors well enough to distinguish common from conflicting positions, to detect movement from positions, and to respond in ways that maintain communication. Yet a non-Roman's own script for negotiation rarely entails the knowledge or skills to make such interpretations and responses.

Figure R3-1 shows the range of negotiation characteristics that may vary across cultures. The basic concept of the process, for instance, may be one of distributive bargaining, joint problem solving, debate, contingency bargaining, or nondirective discussion. Groups and organizations may select negotiators for their knowledge, experience, personal attributes, or status. Protocol may range from informal to formal; the desired outcome may range from a contract to an implicit understanding.

A culturally responsive strategy, therefore, should be designed to align the parties' negotiating scripts or otherwise bring about a mutually coherent form of negotiator interaction. This definition does *not* assume that the course of action is entirely premeditated; it can emerge over time. But a culturally responsive strategy does involve a clear goal and does consist of means by which to attain it. Effectively implemented, such a strategy enables the negotiators to convey their respective concerns and to respond to each other's concerns as they attempt to reach agreement.

By contrast, strategies that do not consider cultural factors are naive or misconceived. They may sometimes be successful for non-Romans, but they are hardly a reliable course of action. One such strategy is to deliberately ignore ethnic or

General Model

1. Basic Concept of Process

Distributive bargaining / Joint problem-solving / Debate / Contingency bargaining / Nondirective discussion

2. Most Significant Type of Issue

Substantive / Relationship-based / Procedural / Personal-internal

Role of the Individual

3. Selection of Negotiators

Knowledge / Negotiating experience / Personal attributes / Status

4. Individuals' Aspirations

Individual ⟵――――――――――⟶ Community

5. Decision Making in Groups

Authoritative ⟵――――――――――⟶ Consensual

Interaction: Dispositions

6. Orientation toward Time

Monochronic ⟵――――――――――⟶ Polychronic

7. Risk-Taking Propensity

High ⟵――――――――――⟶ Low

8. Bases of Trust

External sanctions / Other's reputation / Intuition / Shared experiences

Interaction: Process

9. Concern with Protocol

Informal ⟵――――――――――⟶ Formal

10. Communication Complexity

Low ⟵――――――――――⟶ High

11. Nature of Persuasion

Direct experience / Logic / Tradition / Dogma / Emotion / Intuition

Outcome

12. Form of Agreement

Contractual ⟵――――――――――⟶ Implicit

Figure R3-1   Cultural Characteristics of Negotiation

Source: Adapted from S.E. Weiss with W. Stripp. *Negotiating with Foreign Business Persons* (New York: New York University Graduate School of Business Administration, Working Paper # 85–6, 1985), p. 10.

other group based differences and operate as if "business is business anywhere in the world." A "business is business" approach does not avoid culture; it actually represents a culture, one usually associated with U.S. businesspeople or a cosmopolitan elite: Negotiators cannot blithely assume the predominance of this particular business culture amid the multiple cultures represented in their negotiations.

The framework shown in Figure R3-2 organizes eight culturally responsive strategies according to the negotiator's level of familiarity with the counterpart's culture; the counterpart's familiarity with the negotiator's culture; and the possibility for explicit coordination of approaches.[10] For the sake of clarity, it focuses on negotiations between two parties, each belonging to one predominant culture.

"Familiarity" is a gauge of a party's current knowledge of a culture (in particular, its negotiation scripts) *and* ability to use that knowledge competently in social

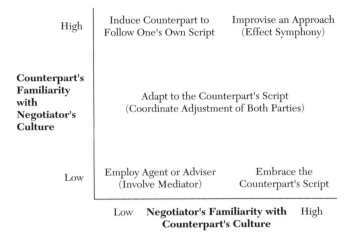

| | Low | Negotiator's Familiarity with
Counterpart's Culture | High |

(Figure matrix:)

High — Induce Counterpart to Follow One's Own Script   Improvise an Approach (Effect Symphony)

Counterpart's Familiarity with Negotiator's Culture — Adapt to the Counterpart's Script (Coordinate Adjustment of Both Parties)

Low — Employ Agent or Adviser (Involve Mediator)   Embrace the Counterpart's Script

F i g u r e   R 3 - 2   Culturally Responsive Strategies and Their Feasibility

Brackets indicate a joint strategy, which requires deliberate consultation with counterpart. At each level of familiarity, a negotiator can consider feasible the strategies designated at that level and any lower level.

interactions.[11] Operationally, high familiarity denotes fluency in a predominant Roman language, extensive prior exposure to the culture, and a good track record in previous social interactions with Romans (which includes making correct attributions of their behavior).[12] This is no mean accomplishment; it takes some twenty-four to thirty-six months of gradual adaptation and learning for expatriates to "master" how to behave appropriately (Black and Mendenhall 1991). Note that negotiators can consider using the strategies feasible at their level of familiarity and *any* strategies corresponding to lower levels of familiarity.

The strategies in brackets in the figure are those that require coordination between parties. Although all negotiators must ultimately coordinate their approaches with counterparts during the talks, if only tacitly, sometimes parties can explicitly address coordination and coherence issues.

LOW FAMILIARITY WITH COUNTERPART'S CULTURE

The negotiator who has had little experience with a counterpart's culture has a choice of two culturally responsive strategies and, depending on the counterpart's familiarity with the negotiator's culture, a possible third. If the counterpart's familiarity level is low, neither party is well equipped cross-culturally; their interaction can be facilitated by changing the people involved.[13] That is, the negotiator can employ an agent or adviser or involve a mediator. If the counterpart's familiarity level is high, a third strategy becomes feasible: inducing the Roman to follow the negotiating script of one's own cultural group.

Employ Agent or Adviser   To augment his or her own capabilities, a business negotiator can employ cultural experts, translators, outside attorneys, financial advisers, or technical experts who have at least moderate and preferably high familiarity with both the counterpart's and the negotiator's cultures. These experts serve two distinguishable roles, as "agents" who replace the negotiator at the negotiating table or as "advisers" who provide information and recommend courses of action to the negotiator.

In 1986, a U.S. chemical company that had bartered chemicals for tobacco from Zimbabwe hired an American commodities trader in London to negotiate the sale of the tobacco and some chemicals to Egyptian officials and executives. The Egyptians were offering payment in commodities; the U.S. company sought $20 million cash. As an agent, the American trader engaged in lengthy meetings, rounds of thick coffee, and late-night talks with the Egyptians and succeeded in arranging cash sales of the Egyptian commodities to the United Kingdom, Bangladesh, and other countries. (Lohr 1988, pp. 32–88).

The value of this strategy depends on the agent's attributes. Skilled, reputable agents can interact very effectively with a negotiator's counterpart. However, their employment may give rise to issues of increased structural complexity, trust, and ownership of the process, not to mention possible cultural tensions between principal and agent.[14] Clearly decipherable by a counterpart, this strategy works well when the counterpart accepts it and the particular agent involved.

Employing an adviser involves other actions and effects.

Between 1983 and 1986, IBM prepared proposals for a personal computer plant for approval by Mexico's National Commission on Foreign Investment. The company hired Mexican attorneys, consulted local experts such as the American Chamber of Commerce and U.S. embassy staff, and met with high-level Mexican government officials. These advisers provided information about political and social cultures and the foreign investment review process, access to influential individuals, and assessments of the leanings of key decision makers on the commission (Weiss 1990).

A negotiator can select this strategy unilaterally and completely control its implementation. Of all eight strategies, this one is the least decipherable, sometimes even undetectable, by the counterpart. It is also uniquely incomplete in that it does not directly provide a script for negotiating. The negotiator must go on to select, with or without the adviser's assistance, a complementary strategy.

Involve a Mediator   The use of go-betweens, middlemen, brokers, and other intermediaries is a common practice within many cultures and represents a potentially effective approach to cross-cultural negotiation as well. It is a joint strategy; both negotiator and counterpart rely on a mutually acceptable third party to facilitate their interaction. In its most obvious form, the strategy involves contacting a mediator prior to negotiations and deliberately bringing him or her into the talks. A mediator may also emerge, as happens when the "introducer" (*shokaisha* in Japanese [Graham and Sono 1989]) who first brought the negotiator to the counterpart continues to play a role or, in team-on-team negotiations, when an individual involved in the talks who does not initially have authority as a mediator, such as an interpreter, becomes a de facto mediator in the course of the negotiation. Such cross-cultural mediators should be at least moderately and preferably highly familiar with the cultures of both parties.

In the 1950s, an American truck manufacturer negotiated a deal to sell trucks to a Saudi contractor because of the intermediation of Adnan Khashoggi. Khashoggi, the son of the personal physician of the founder of Saudi Arabia, had met the manufacturer while in college in the United States and learned about the contractor's needs upon returning to Saudi Arabia. This was his first "deal," long before his involvement with Lockheed and Northrop. By the 1970s, each of his private jets reportedly contained two wardrobes: "one of three-piece suits, shirts, and ties; . . . the other of white cotton thobes [and] headdresses, . . . the full traditional Arabian regalia" (Lacey 1981; Tyler 1992).

With this strategy, a negotiator faces some uncertainty about the negotiation process: Will the mediator use one side's negotiation script at the expense of the other's? If the mediator is from a third culture, will he or she use that culture's ways—or introduce something else?[15] In relying on a mediator, the negotiator relinquishes some control of the negotiation. Then again, the mediator can educate the negotiator about the counterpart's culture and bring out ideas and behavior from each side that make the interaction coherent. It is important to find an individual who is not only appropriately skilled but who will also maintain the respect and trust of both parties.[16]

Induce the Counterpart to Follow One's Own Script   Deliberately inducing the counterpart to negotiate according to the model common in one's own culture is feasible when the counterpart is highly familiar with one's culture. Possibilities for inducement range from verbal persuasion to simply acting as if the counterpart will "come along"—as happens when Americans speak English to non-American counterparts known to speak English as a second language.

> When U.S.-based ITT and CGE of France conducted merger talks in the mid-1980s, negotiators used "an American business—American M&A [merger and acquisition]" approach, according to French participants. The French went along with it (despite their unfavorable impressions that it consisted of a "vague" general concept of the deal, emphasis on speed, and formulation of long contracts), because only U.S. law and investment firms had the capacity to carry out this highly complex negotiation. Although their motivations are not exactly known, ITT lawyers have stated that their chief negotiator followed their own methodical style, one developed within ITT (Weiss 1991).

The pros and cons of this strategy hinge on the counterpart's perception of the negotiator's motivations for pursuing it. The counterpart may conclude that the negotiator is naive or deliberately ignorant of cultural differences; arrogant; culturally proud but not antagonistic; or merely using an expedient strategy.[17] It is reported that IBM's Thomas Watson, Sr., once said: "It's easier to teach IBM to a Netherlander than to teach Holland to an American" (IBM World Trade Corporation 1979). Using one's own ways could also be the result of mistakenly concluding that the two parties share one culture (e.g., Americans and English-speaking Canadians).

For this strategy to work most effectively, the negotiator should convey that it is not based on a lack of respect for the counterpart or for the counterpart's culture. It is the counterpart, after all, who is being called on to make an extra effort; even with a high level of familiarity with the negotiator's culture, a counterpart usually feels more skilled and at ease with his or her own ways. (Were the counterpart to *offer* to follow the negotiator's script, we would be talking about an embrace strategy by the counterpart, which is described below.)

Moderate Familiarity with Counterpart's Culture

The negotiator who already has had some successful experience with a counterpart's culture gains two more strategic options, provided that the counterpart is at least moderately familiar with the negotiator's culture. The unilateral strategy is to adapt one's usual approach to the counterpart's. The joint version is to coordinate adjustment between the two cultures.

Adapt to the Counterpart's Script   Negotiators often modify their customary behavior by not expressing it to its usual degree, omitting some actions altogether, and following some of the counterpart's ways. The adapt strategy refers to more than this behavior, however; it refers to a broad course of action usually prompted by a deliberate decision to make these modifications.[18]

> In the early 1980s, American negotiators in the Toyota-Ford and GM-Toyota talks over car assembly joint ventures prepared by reading books such as James Clavell's *Shogun* and Edwin Reischauer's *The Japanese*, watching classic Japanese films (e.g., "Kagemusha"), and frequenting Japanese restaurants. Then they modified their usual negotiating behavior by: (1) paying extra attention to comportment and protocol, (2) reducing their expectations about substantive progress in the first few meetings, (3) providing Japanese counterparts with extensive, upfront information about their company and the U.S. business environment, and (4) trying "not to change positions too much once they had been voiced" (Weiss 1987, 1988).

A major challenge for the negotiator considering this strategy is to decide which aspects of his or her customary negotiating script to alter or set aside. The aspects most seriously in conflict with the counterpart's may not be easily changed or even readily apparent, and those most obviously in conflict or easily changed may not, once changed, markedly enhance the interaction. Marketing specialists have distinguished between customs to which non-Romans must conform, those to which non-Romans may but need not conform, and those from which non-Romans are excluded (Lateora and Hess 1971). Although a marketing specialist has a fixed, one-sided target in seeking entry into the counterpart's arena, these distinctions may also guide some of the cross-cultural negotiator's deliberations.

A counterpart usually notices at least some evidence of a negotiator's use of the adapt strategy. Deciphering all of the modifications is difficult. It may also be difficult for a counterpart to distinguish an adapt strategy from a badly implemented embrace strategy (described below). Further, if both the negotiator and the counterpart pursue this strategy on their own initiative, their modifications may confuse rather than smooth the interaction. Still, a negotiator can independently make the choice to adapt and usually finds at least some areas within his or her capacity to do so.

Coordinate Adjustment of Both Parties   The parties may develop, subtly or overtly, a joint approach for their discussions; they may negotiate the process of negotiation. The jointly developed script is usually a blend of elements from the two parties' cultures; it is not totally distinct from them yet not wholly of one or the other. It may take various forms.

> At the outset of a 1988 meeting to discuss the telecommunications policies of France's Ministry of Industry and Tourism, the minister's chief of staff and his American visitor each voiced concern about speaking in the other's native language. They expressed confidence in their listening capabilities and lacked immediate access to an interpreter, so they agreed to proceed by each speaking in his own language. Their discussion went on for an hour that way, the American speaking in English to the Frenchman, and the Frenchman speaking in French to the American.

In a special case of this strategy, the parties "bypass" their respective home cultures' practices to follow the negotiating script of an already existing, third culture with which both have at least moderate familiarity. The parties know enough about the other's culture to recognize the limits of their capabilities in it and the desirability of additional guidance for their interaction.

> Negotiations over MCA's acquisition by Matsushita Electric Industrial Company in 1990 were conducted largely via interpreters. At one dinner, MCA's senior American investment banker and Matsushita's Japanese head of international affairs were stymied in their effort to communicate with each other until they discovered their fluency in the same second language. They conversed in French for the rest of the evening (Bruck 1991).

Professional societies, trade groups, educational programs and institutions, and various other associations can similarly provide members with third scripts for conduct. This phenomenon is dramatically illustrated, within and between teams, when people who do not share a language play volleyball or soccer socially. The sport provides a script for behavior.

Overall, this strategy has the benefits of the adapt strategy while minimizing the likelihood of incompatible "adjustments." For some Roman counterparts (e.g., Arabs and Chinese), verbally explicit implementation of this strategy for interaction will be awkward—even unacceptable (See Thubron 1987). Other groups' members will appreciate its decipherability and the shared burden of effort that it implies. Since both parties must go along with it, the negotiator's opportunity to "veto" also preserves some control over its implementation.

High Familiarity with Counterpart's Culture

Finally, the negotiator highly familiar with a counterpart's culture can realistically contemplate, not only the five aforementioned strategies, but at least one and possibly two more. If the counterpart is not familiar with the negotiator's culture, the negotiator can unilaterally embrace the other's negotiating script (i.e., "do as the Romans do"). If both parties are highly familiar with each other's cultures, they can jointly or unilaterally search for or formulate a negotiating script that focuses more on the individuals and circumstances involved than on the broader cultures. Such strategies may radically change the process.

Embrace the Counterpart's Script   The embrace strategy calls for the negotiator to use the negotiation approach typical of the counterpart's culture.

> In the 1970s, Coca-Cola undertook negotiations with a state-run, foreign trade organization in the People's Republic of China in order to produce and sell cola drinks there. The company sent one of its research chemists, a China-born man with no business background, to Cambridge University to study Chinese language and culture studies for a full year. Later acclaimed to be highly knowledgeable about China, this chemist was the most active negotiator for Coca-Cola in what became a ten-year endeavor (Sloane 1974 p. D2).

Relatively few individuals should attempt this strategy. It demands a great deal of the negotiator, especially when the cultures involved differ greatly. In general, it requires bilingual, bicultural individuals—those who have generally enjoyed long-term overseas residence.

When implemented well, especially when very different cultures are involved, this strategy is clearly decipherable by a counterpart. (When it is not, a counterpart may confuse it with an adapt strategy.) Furthermore, the embrace strategy can make the interaction relatively easy and comfortable for the counterpart. The strategy requires considerable effort by the negotiator, and its implementation remains largely—but not completely—within the negotiator's control.

Improvise an Approach   To improvise is to create a negotiation script as one negotiates, focusing foremost on the counterpart's particular attributes and capabilities and on the circumstances. Although all negotiators should pay some attention to the Roman counterpart as an individual, not all can or should improvise. The term is used here as it is used in music, not in the colloquial sense of "winging it" or of anyone being able to do it. Musical improvisation requires some preconception or point of departure and a model (e.g., a melody, basic chord structure) that sets the scope for performance. Similarly, the negotiator who improvises knows the parties' home cultures and is fully prepared for their influence but can put them in the background or highlight them as negotiation proceeds.

> In the early 1990s, Northern Telecom, a Canadian-owned telecommunications equipment supplier with many Americans in its executive ranks and headquarters in both Mississauga, Ontario, and McLean, Virginia, maintained a "dual identity." Its personnel dealt with each other on either an American or a Canadian basis. On the outside, the company played up its Canadian identity with some governments (those unenthusiastic about big American firms, or perhaps not highly familiar with American ways), and played up its American identity with others (Symonds et al. 1992).

This strategy is feasible only when both parties are highly familiar with the other's culture. Without that level of familiarity, the negotiator would not know what the counterpart is accustomed to or how he or she is affected, and would not be able to invoke or create ways to relate to the counterpart effectively; nor would the counterpart recognize or respond to these efforts appropriately. At the same time, since the counterpart is highly skilled in at least two cultures and may introduce practices from both or either one of them, it is extremely important to consider the counterpart as an individual, not just as a member of a culture. High familiarity enables the negotiator to do just that, because he or she does not need to devote as much effort to learning about the counterpart's culture as other negotiators do.

> During the Camp David "peace" talks between Egypt, Israel, and the United States in the late 1970s, then President Jimmy Carter set up a one-on-one meeting with Prime Minister Menachem Begin to try to break an impasse. Carter took along photos of Begin's eight grandchildren, on the backs of which he had handwritten their names. Showing these photos to Begin led the two leaders into talking about their families and personal expectations and revitalized the intergovernmental negotiations.[19]

This strategy is often used at high levels, especially at critical junctures, but it need not be limited to that. It can counteract the treatment of a counterpart as an abstraction (e.g., stereotype) and can facilitate the development of empathy. It also seems particularly efficacious with counterparts from cultures that emphasize affective, relationship factors over task accomplishment and creativity of presence over convention.

On the down side, the cultural responsiveness of the improvise strategy is not always decipherable by the counterpart. When a top-level negotiator is involved, the counterpart may assume that the negotiator's strategy is to appeal to status or authority rather than to recognize cultural issues. If the strategy overly "personalizes" negotiation, its implementation can lead to the kinds of problems once pointed out in former U.S. Secretary of State Henry Kissinger's "personal diplomacy": becoming too emotionally involved, failing to delegate, undercutting the status of other possible representatives, and ignoring those one does not meet or know.[20] The strategy may not be appropriate for all cultures and may be difficult to orchestrate by a team of negotiators. It also offers fewer concrete prescriptions for action and greater uncertainty than the four other unilateral strategies. Nevertheless, its malleability should continue to be regarded as a major attribute.

Effect Symphony   This strategy represents an effort by the negotiator to get both parties to transcend exclusive use of either home culture by exploiting their high familiarity capabilities. They may improvise an approach, create and use a new script, or follow some other approach not typical of their home cultures. One form of coordination feasible at this level of familiarity draws on both home cultures.

> For their negotiations over construction of the tunnel under the English Channel, British and French representatives agreed to partition talks and alternate the site between Paris and London. At each site, the negotiators were to use established, local ways, including the language. The two approaches were thus clearly punctuated by time and space. Although each side was able to use its customary approach some of the time, it used the script of the other culture the rest of the time (Dupont 1990).

Effecting symphony differs from coordinating adjustment, which implies some modification of a culture's script, in that both culture's scripts may be used in their entirety. It is also one resolution of a situation where both parties start out independently pursuing induce or embrace strategies. Perhaps the most common form of effecting symphony is using a third culture, such as a negotiator subculture.

> Many United Nations ambassadors, who tend to be multilingual and world-traveled interact more comfortably with each other than with their compatriots (see, for example, Alger 1983). Similarly, a distinct culture can be observed in the café and recreation area at INSEAD, the European Institute of Business Administration, which attracts students from thirty countries for ten intensive months.

Overall, the effect symphony strategy allows parties to draw on special capabilities that may be accessible only by going outside the full-time use of their home cultures' conventions. Venturing into these uncharted areas introduces some risk. Furthermore, this strategy, like other joint strategies, requires the counterpart's cooperation; it cannot be unilaterally effected. But then, as former U.S. Ambassador to Japan Edwin Reischauer suggested about diplomatic protocol, a jointly established culture—the "score" of a symphony—makes behavior predictable (Reischaur 1986). It can also make it comprehensible and coherent.

IMPLICATIONS

A cross-cultural negotiator is thus not limited to doing as the Romans do or even doing it "our way" or "their way." There are eight culturally responsive strategies. They differ in their degree of reliance on existing scripts and conventions, in the amount of extra effort required of each party, and in their decipherability by the counterpart. As a range of options, these strategies offer the negotiator flexibility and a greater opportunity to act effectively.

Because the strategies entail different scripts and approaches, they also allow the negotiator to move beyond the simplistic lists of behavioral tips favored to date in American writings. For example, an American working with Japanese counterparts is usually advised to behave in a reserved manner, learn some Japanese words, and exercise patience (Thayer and Weiss 1987). Such behavior applies primarily to an adapt strategy, however, and different strategies call for different concepts and behaviors. Table R3-1 gives some examples of how an American might behave with Japanese counterparts, depending on the unilateral strategy employed.

Similarly, for his meeting with Dupont in Paris, Smith could have considered strategies other than "embrace" and its associated script. An adapt strategy may not have necessitated speaking exclusively in French. Table R3-2 suggests some ways he might have behaved, given each unilateral strategy. Smith might also have contemplated using strategies in combination (e.g., "adapt," then "embrace"), especially if meetings had been scheduled to take place over a number of months.

At the same time, only the negotiator highly familiar with the counterpart's culture can realistically consider using all eight strategies. The value of high famil-

Table R3-1   **Recommended Behavior for Americans Negotiating with the Japanese* (by type of culturally responsive strategy)**

Employ
- Use "introducer" for initial contacts (e.g., general trading company).
- Employ an agent the counterpart knows and respects.
- Ensure that the agent/adviser speaks fluent Japanese.

Induce
- Be open to social interaction and communicate directly.
- Make an extreme initial proposal, expecting to make concessions later.
- Work efficiently to "get the job done."

Adapt
- Follow some Japanese protocol (reserved behavior, name cards, gifts).
- Provide a lot of information (by American standards) up front to influence the counterpart's decision making early.
- Slow down your usual timetable.
- Make informed interpretations (e.g., the meaning of "it is difficult").
- Present positions later in the process, more firmly and more consistently.

Embrace
- Proceed according to an information-gathering, *nemawashi* (not exchange) model.
- "Know your stuff" cold.
- Assemble a team (group) for formal negotiations.
- Speak in Japanese.
- Develop personal relationships, respond to obligations within them.

Improvise
- Do homework on the individual counterpart(s) and circumstances.
- Be attentive and nimble (improvising entails different behaviors for different Japanese).
- Invite the counterpart to participate in mutually enjoyed activities or interests. (e.g., golf).

*These are examples, not a complete listing, of attitudes and behaviors implied by a negotiator's use of each strategy.

iarity, as a current capability or as an aspiration to achieve, should be clear. The value of the cultural focus should also be clear, notwithstanding the importance of also focusing on the individual counterpart. Culture provides a broad context for understanding the ideas and behavior of new counterparts as well as established acquaintances. It also enables the negotiator to notice commonalities in the expectations and behavior of individual members of a team of counterparts, to appreciate how the team works as a whole, and to anticipate what representatives and constituents will do when they meet away from the cross-cultural negotiation. As long as the negotiator intends to go on negotiating with other Romans, it behooves him or her to pay attention to commonalities across negotiation experiences with individual Romans—to focus on cultural aspects—in order to draw lessons that enhance effectiveness in future negotiations.

As presented here, the eight culturally responsive negotiation strategies reflect one perspective: feasibility in light of the negotiator's and counterpart's familiarity with each other's cultures. That is a major basis for selecting a strategy, but it is not sufficient. This framework maps what is doable; it should not be interpreted as recommending that the best strategies for every negotiation are those at the highest levels of familiarity—that improvising is always better than employing advisers. The

Table R3-2   **Recommended Behavior for Americans Negotiating with the French* (by type of culturally responsive strategy)**

Employ

■ Employ an agent well-connected in business and government circles.

■ Ensure that the agent/adviser speaks fluent French.

Induce

■ Be open to social interaction and communicate directly.

■ Make an extreme initial proposal, expecting to make concessions later.

■ Work efficiently to "get the job done."

Adapt

■ Follow some French protocol (greetings and leave-takings, formal speech).

■ Demonstrate an awareness of French culture and business environment.

■ Be consistent between actual and stated goals and between attitudes and behavior.

■ Defend views vigorously.

Embrace

■ Approach negotiation as a debate involving reasoned argument.

■ Know the subject of negotiation *and* broad environmental issues (economic, political, social).

■ Make intellectually elegant, persuasive yet creative presentations (logically sound, verbally precise).

■ Speak in French.

■ Show interest in the counterpart as an individual but remain aware of the strictures of social and organizational hierarchies.

Improvise

■ Do homework on the individual counterpart(s) and circumstances.

■ Be attentive and nimble (improvising entails different behaviors for different French individuals).

■ Invite counterpart to participate in mutually enjoyed activities or interests (e.g., dining out, tennis).

*These are examples, not a complete listing of attitudes and behaviors implied by a negotiator's use of each strategy.

best strategy depends on additional factors that will be discussed in Part 2. In its own right, the framework represents a marked shift from prevailing wisdom and a good point of departure for today's cross-cultural negotiators.

References

ADLER, N.J. and BARTHOLOMEW, S. (1992), "Managing Globally Competent People," *The Executive*, 6, 58.

ALGER, C.F. (1983), "United Nations Participation as a Learning Experience," *Public Opinion Quarterly* (Summer), 411–26.

BESCHLOSS, M.R. and TALBOTT, S. (1993), *At the Highest Levels*. Boston: Little, Brown.

BLACK, S. and MENDENHALL, M. (1990), "Cross-Cultural Training Effectiveness: A Review and Theoretical Framework for Future Research," *Academy of Management Review*, 15, 113–36.

———and———(1991), "The U-Curve Adjustment Hypothesis Revisited: A Review and Theoretical Framework," *Journal of International Business Studies*, 22, 225–47.

BLAKER, M. (1977), *Japanese International Negotiating Style*. New York: Columbia University Press.

BOCHNER, S. (1982), "The Social Psychology of Cross-Cultural Relations," in Bochner, S. ed., *Cultures in Contact*. Oxford: Pergamon, 5–44.

BRISLIN, R.W. et al. (1986), *Intercultural Interactions*. Beverly Hills, CA: Sage Publications.

BRUCK, C. (1991), "Leap of Faith," *The New Yorker* (September 9), 38–74.

CAMPBELL, N.C.G. et al. (1988), "Marketing Negotiations in France, Germany, the United Kingdom, and the United States," *Journal of Marketing*, 52, 49–62.

CARNEVALE, P.J.D. (1986), "Strategic Choice in Mediation," *Negotiation Journal*, 2, 41–56.

CATEORA, P.R. and HESS, J.M. (1971), *International Marketing*. Homewood, IL: Irwin.

CAVUSGIL, S.T. and GHAURI, P.N. (1990), *Doing Business in Developing Countries*. London: Routledge.

CHURCH, A.T. (1982), "Sojourner Adjustment," *Psychological Bulletin*, 91, 545–49.

COHEN, R. (1991), *Negotiating Across Cultures*. Washington, DC: U.S. Institute of Peace Press.

COOLEY, R.E. and ROACH, D.A. (1984), "A Conceptual Framework," in Bostrom, R.N. ed., *Competence in Communication*. Beverly Hills, CA: Sage Publications, 11–32.

CRONEN, V.E. and SHUTER, R. (1983), "Forming Intercultural Bonds," in Gudykunst, W.B. ed., *Intercultural Communication Theory: Current Perspectives*. Beverly Hills, CA: Sage Publications.

DUPONT, C. (1990), "The Channel Tunnel Negotiations, 1984–1986: Some Aspects of the Process and Its Outcome," *Negotiation Journal*, 6, 71–80.

EARLEY, P.C. (1987), "Intercultural Training for Managers," *Academy of Management Review*, 30, 685–98.

FISHER, G. (1980), *International Negotiation: A Cross-Cultural Perspective*. Yarmouth, ME: Intercultural Press.

FISHER, R. (1981), "Playing the Wrong Game?" in Rubin, J.Z. ed., *Dynamics of Third Party Intervention*. New York: Praeger, 98–99, 105–6.

———and URY, W. (1981), *Getting to Yes*. Boston: Houghton-Mifflin.

FRANCIS, J.N.P. (1991), "When in Rome? The Effects of Cultural Adaptation on Intercultural Business Negotiations," *Journal of International Business Studies*, 22, 403–28.

GRAHAM, J.L. and ADLER, N.J. (1989), "Cross-Cultural Interaction: The International Comparison Fallacy," *Journal of International Business Studies*, 20, 515–37.

———and HERBERGER, Jr., R.A. (1983), "Negotiators Abroad—Don't Shoot from the Hip," *Harvard Business Review* (July/August), 166.

———and SANO, Y. (1989), *Smart Bargaining: Doing Business with the Japanese*. New York: Ballinger, 30.

———et al. (1988), "Buyer-Seller Negotiations Around the Pacific Rim: Differences in Fundamental Exchange Processes," *Journal of Consumer Research*, 15, 48–54.

GUDYKUNST, W.B. and TING-TOOMEY, S. (1988), *Culture and Interpersonal Communication*. Newbury Park, CA: Sage Publications.

"IBM World Trade Corporation" (1979), Harvard Business School. Reprinted in Davis, S.M. *Managing and Organizing Multinational Corporations*. New York: Pergamon Press.

LACEY, R. (1981), *The Kingdom: Arabia and the House of Sa'ud*. New York: Avon Books.

LOHR, S. (1988), "Barter Is His Stock in Trade," *New York Times Business World* (September 25), 32–36.

POSSES, F. (1978), *The Art of International Negotiation*. London: Business Books.

PRUITT, D.G. (1981), *Negotiation Behavior*. New York: Academic Press, 41–44, 195–97.

———and RUBIN. J.Z. (1986), *Social Conflict Escalation, Stalemate, and Settlement*. New York: Random House.

REISCHAUER, E.O. (1986), *My Life Between Japan and America*. New York: Harper and Row.

RICKS, D. and MAHAJAN, V. (1984), "Blunders in International Marketing: Fact or Fiction?" *Long Range Planning*, 17, 78–83.

RUBIN, J.Z. (1981), "Introduction," in Rubin, J.Z. ed., *Dynamics of Third Party Intervention*. New York: Praeger, 3–43.

———and SANDER, F.E.A. (1988), "When Should We Use Agents? Direct vs. Representative Negotiation," *Negotiation Journal* (October), 395–401.

SLOANE, L. (1979), "Lee, Coke's Man in China," *The New York Times* (February 5), D2.

SYMONDS, W.C. et al. (1992), "High-Tech Star," *Business Week* (July 27), 55–56.

THAYER, N.B. and WEISS, S.E. (1987), "Japan: The Changing Logic of a Former Minor Power," in Binnendijk, H. ed., *National Negotiating Styles*. Washington, DC: Foreign Service Institute, U.S. Department of State, 69–72.

THOMAS, K.W. and KILMANN, R.H. (1974), *Thomas-Kilmann Conflict Mode Instrument*. Tuxedo, NY: Xicom, Inc.

THUBRON, C. (1987), *Behind the Wall*. London: Penguin.

TOUVAL, S. and ZARTMAN, I.W. (1989), "Mediation in International Conflicts," in Kressel, K. and Pruitt, D.G. eds., *Mediation Research*. San Francisco: Jossey-Bass, 115–37.

TYLER, P.E. (1992), "Double Exposure: Saudi Arabia's Middleman in Washington," *The New York Times Magazine* (June 7), 34ff.

WEISS, S.E. (1987), "Creating the GM–Toyota Joint Venture: A Case in Complex Negotiation," *Columbia Journal of World Business* (Summer), 23–37.

———(1988), "One Impasse, One Agreement Explaining the Outcomes of Toyota's Negotiations with Ford and GM," paper presented at the Academy of International Business Annual Meeting.

———(1990), "The Long Path to the IBM–Mexico Agreement: An Analysis of the Microcomputer Investment Negotiations, 1983–1986," *Journal of International Business Studies*, 21, 565–96.

———(1991), "Negotiating the CGE–ITT Telecommunications Merger, 1985–1986: A Framework-then-Details Process," paper presented at the Academy of International Business Annual Meeting (November).

Endnotes

1. All examples that are not referenced come from personal communication or the author's experiences.

2. Contemporary academic advocates of this approach for negotiators include Covusgil and Ghauri 1990; Graham and Herberger 1983; and Posses 1978.

3. The concept of a script has been applied by: Gudykunst and Ting-Toomey 1988.

4. See, for example, N.C.G. Campbell et al. 1988 and J.L. Graham et al. 1988. For evidence from diplomacy, see Cohen 1991 and Fisher 1980.

5. See Graham and Adler 1989. The authors conclude that their subjects adapted to some extent, but a lack of adaptability could also be convincingly argued from their data.

6. For an experimental study showing that moderate adaptation by Asians in the United States was more effective than substantial adaptation, see Francis 1991.

7. The majority of leaders of North American firms still lack any expatriate experience and foreign language ability, according to Adler and Bartholomew 1992.

8. See, for example, Ricks and Mahajan 1984. Note that the impact of faux pas may vary in magnitude across cultures. In some cultures, inappropriate behavior constitutes an unforgivable transgression, not a "slip-up."

9. See Cronen and Shuter 1983. Their concept of "coherence" neither presumes that the interactants make the same sense of the interaction nor depends always on mutual understanding.

10. Although similar in form, this plot differs in theme from the "model of conflict-handling responses" developed by Thomas and Kilmann 1974. It also differs in key variables from the "Dual Concerns" model of Pruitt and Rubin 1986. Moreover, neither of these models appears to have yet been applied cross-culturally.

11. This notion of familiarity draws on Dell Hymes's concept of communicative competence. See Cooley and Roach 1984.

12. See, for example, Brislin et al. 1986; Church 1982; Earley 1987; and Black and Mendenhall 1990.

13. Changing the parties involved is commonly mentioned in dispute resolution literature. See, for example Fisher and Ury 1981.

14. For empirical research on negotiating representatives and their boundary role, constituents, and accountability within a culture, see Pruitt 1981. With respect to agents, see Rubin and Sander 1988.

15. For additional ideas about what a mediator may do, see Carnevale 1986.

16. See Rubin 1981; and Touval and Zartman 1989.

17. Such positions have been associated with people in nations with long-established cultures, such as China, France, and India. For instance, some Mexican high officials who speak English fluently have insisted on speaking Spanish in their meetings with Americans. While this position could be influenced by the historical antipathy in the U.S.-Mexico relationship and the officials' concern for the status of their office, it also evinces cultural pride.

18. Adapting has been widely discussed in the literature. See, for example Bochner 1982.

19. Found among the exhibits at the Carter Center Library and Museum, Atlanta, Georgia.

20. Fisher 1981. On the additional problem of losing touch with constituencies, see the 1989–1991 Bush-Gorbachev talks described in Beschloss and Talbott 1993.

Chinese Employees' Perceptions of Distributive Fairness

YU Kaicheng

Fairness or justice, as an indicator of social ethics and values, has long been pursued by people as a lofty ideal. People everywhere have traditionally been interested in the fair distribution of social and organizational resources and wealth—the product of collective efforts. Fairness, in essence, relates to the issue of entitlement—that is, who ought to be allocated how much? Justice in general is a core value holding together societies and organizations. It has attracted much attention in various fields, including political economics, ethics, law, religion, sociology, and psychology. Organizational behavior, as an applied science, focuses on the rules that govern the forming, generation, and functioning of employees' perceptions of fair distribution of rewards in business administration.

The negative impact of perceived unfairness on employees' motivation has been widely recognized, but the pursuit of fairness has not been considered a very powerful motive in the West. That may be why the equity theory has been less basic in Western social and behavioral science than have need and expectancy theories.

In China, however, things are different. Fairness may be one of the most influential and sensitive sociopolitical issues in Chinese society that relates not only to employees' morale in industries but also to the stability of the society. Perceptions of unfairness have, in the past, triggered several peasant uprisings, and the matter remains significant today. This can be attributed to two kinds of facts: First, objectively, there is a considerable amount of unfair distribution in China, especially the corruption of officials; and second, subjectively, Chinese people are said to have high sensitivity and low tolerance toward income differentiation. As a result, fairness has been a major focus of people's attention in China. Many Chinese scholars in recent years have tried to specify the traditional, cultural, ideological, and situational factors that affect the formation of distinctive Chinese concepts of fairness. They have also identified some of its social psychological implications.

This is, however, a very difficult and complicated task. The first reason is that the formation of one's perception of fairness is a subjective process that includes

Source: YU Kaicheng, Dalian University of Technology. This reading is original to this text.

judgments against certain criteria or norms. No objective criteria or norms have been universally recognized and accepted. People tend to have different reference and selection criteria and norms when making their judgments while the pattern of selection per se is very complicated. For example, a person may select and apply different norms to judge fairness when different types of rewards are distributed (Foa and Foa 1974, 1980). Even when the same types of rewards are allocated, a person may apply multiple norms simultaneously but assign a different weight to each to form an intricate combination and sequence of fairness norms (Yu, Bunker, and Wilderom 1989; Yu, Wilderom, and Hunt 1989).

The second reason lies in the relativity that exists in people's fairness judgment. This means that people often make this judgment through social comparison. As a result, one's perception of fairness relies heavily on which targeted individual or group he or she selects as the reference in the comparison (Adams 1965). In addition, it also relies on the person's feeling about the referent target. For example, research has found that Chinese people, who are supposed to be more collective-oriented than Westerners, are more tolerant of the "in group" when reward allocation deviates from accepted fairness norms (Yang and Hui 1986; Chiu 1988). This implies that social contracts play a significant role in one's fairness judgment (Resoher 1986). Bles and Moag (1986) point out that one's perception of fairness is affected by the nature of the interactional relation between the reward distributor and its receiver. They suggested a new term for this concept, *interactional justice*, to distinguish it from the conventional concept of fairness that mainly focuses on resource distribution. The study of fairness has thus become more complicated.

The third factor concerning the difficulty and complexity of studying fairness is the asymmetry of fairness perception, another derivative of the first factor, the subjectivity of the perception. This means that people tend to be much more sensitive to unfair distribution when they feel that they are underpaid than overpaid. Yu (1991) found, when identifying people's unfairness sensitivity thresholds, that the sensitivity threshold for the underpaid situation is much lower than that for the overpaid situation. Wu (1991) refers to these characteristics as "being hygienical," borrowing from Herzberg's Motivation-Hygiene Theory (Herzberg, Mausner, and Snyderman 1959). This can be readily explained by the fact that, although some people form their perception of fairness on the basis of a certain ideal or moral value, that of many others is on the grounds of protecting or securing their self interests. Therefore, it is quite easy for them to readjust their perceptions to reduce the sense of feeling guilty when they believe they are overpaid, given that the judgment is purely subjective.

Despite the difficulty and complexity of fairness studies, the issues can be approached by narrowing the scope of interest to a specific aspect. In this paper, I focus on the basic norms that Chinese people tend to use in judging fairness of reward allocation and the cultural and ideological sources of those references.

BASIC FAIR DISTRIBUTIVE NORMS

Deutsch (1975) identifies a series of internal values or norms concerning distribution fairness: (1) outcome should be gained proportional to each one's input; (2) treat everyone equally; (3) to each according to one's need; (4) to each according to one's ability; (5) to each according to one's effort; (6) to each according to one's achievements; (7) to give each one equal opportunities for completion, free of any bias or discrimination; (8) based on market supply and demand; (9) based on common interests; (10) based on the principle of mutual interests; and (11) to make no one's gain lower than a preset bottom line.

Deutsch believes that there has never been an absolutely objective sequence of these norms that inherently fits human nature in terms of its significance. This is understandable when the subjectivity and complexity of the formation of fairness perceptions are considered. He pointed out that only the top three norms in the list are the most basic and ones that people of any society could follow. Each of them has a certain specific function and thus would be perceived as being fair in a corresponding situation. They are:

1. *Equity norm:* One's gain (outcome) is proportional to his or her contribution (input). This is variously labeled as the norm of contribution, performance, merit, or proportion. It is best manifested by Adam's formulation (1965): $Op/Ip = Oa/Ia$; that is, one's perception of fairness or equity is not determined by a comparison of the absolute amount of his or her gain with that of a referent target, but rather by the comparison of outcomes to inputs.

2. *Equality norm:* Everyone should be allocated an equal amount of resources without considering any other factors, so the corresponding formulation should be $Op = Oa$.

3. *Need norm:* The share of resources one gains should be based on his or her need, and the formulation now becomes $Op/Np = Oa/Na$.

As far as the specific function of each basic norm is concerned, the *equity norm* is supposed to produce high average group productivity, because the distribution based on this norm is most beneficial to high performers who have been motivated to perform even better. This results in the maximization of the productivity of the whole group. The *equality norm* is expected to lead to the best group harmony and stability: Now it is the poor performers who benefit the most and are happiest, though they are the minority. Average performers, who tend to be the majority, could live with the norm with few complaints because they are distributed equally anyway, either in the equity or the equality norm. Better performers, though angry and dissatisfied, have little voice in the distribution decisions because they are the minority. The *need norm* is said to be the most humanistic and most helpful to individual well-being and personal development. On the other hand, each basic norm tends to have certain negative effects: The *equity norm* tends to produce conflicts, especially when income differences are large and people's equality orientation is serious. The *equality norm* tends to turn out low group productivity. As for the *need norm*, it sounds perfect and ideal but is not realistic to operate under current conditions.

Each of the three basic formulations mentioned previously covers only one norm. The following general formulation is supposed to consider the three basic norms: $Op/IpNp = Oa/IaNa$.

When the equity norm is preferred, it implies that differences in needs make no sense and could be neglected; thus, in fact, $Np = Na$. So the formulation returns to Adam's formulation $Op/Ip = Oa/Ia$. With the same logic, the formulation returns to $Op/Np = Oa/Na$ when the need norm comes into operation and the input gap is neglected, and it returns to Op/Oa when the equality norm dominates the situation while both the input and need gaps are ignored.

THE MARXIAN PERSPECTIVE ON SOCIAL FAIRNESS

A full appreciation of the unprecedented changes in the perceptions of distributive fairness of Chinese employees in current-day China requires an accurate understanding of the Marxian perspective on social fairness.

There is, however, a popular bias in the West that because the Communist Party always claims that the Party, on behalf of the laboring classes, has been striving for the goal of social equality, the norm that naturally fits socialism is equality. In this view, because the norm of equity tends to encourage a gap between the rich and the poor, it must fit only capitalism. Even many people who live in socialist countries but have never been exposed to the classical works of Marxism may have this kind of naive understanding. It clearly is a misunderstanding of Marxist doctrine. In classical Marxism, egalitarianism has never been advocated; instead, its extreme form—absolute egalitarianism—is customarily criticized in socialist politics as being "reactionary" because it does not promote but hinders the growth of productivity in society. This is an important criterion to test the appropriateness of concepts and theories.

In Marxism the need norm is regarded as an ideal. It is an ultimate goal that the distributive norm should be promoted and pursued because of its humanistic nature. It is also recognized as unrealistic to implement in the current situation because there are several preconditions it requires, including a tremendous abundance of material wealth in the society, which is almost impossible in the near future, let alone at present. In fact, the key tenet of Marxism, the principle of distribution appropriate to the "primary phase of communism"—that is, socialism (China is now so underdeveloped that the Chinese Communist party (CCP) claims that China is now still in the "primary phase of socialism")—is "from each according to his ability, to each according to his work," the latter part of which is a statement of the equity norm. For a country as poor and backward as China, the implementation of the norm is likely the only way to promote the growth of productivity, a basic objective of the socialist revolution.

As for the need norm, Marx (1875) had a famous remark in his "Critique of the Gotha Program":

> In a higher phase of communist society, after the enslaving subordination of the individual to the division of labor, and therewith also the antithesis between mental and physical labor, has vanished; after labor has become not only a means of life but life's prime want; after the productive forces [have] also increased with the all-round development of the individual, and all the springs of cooperative wealth flow more abundantly—only then can the narrow horizon of bourgeois right be crossed in its entirety and society inscribe on its banner: From each according to his ability; to each according to his need!

Two points in the quotation need further analysis; first, the former part of the principle of distribution, "from each according to his ability"; second, the preconditions Marx has set up for the implementation of it and the phrase "the narrow horizon of bourgeois right."

When an individual contributes all he can to society, but his performance, given the same working conditions and training, is still poorer than that of others because of poorer ability, why should this person, as an individual of equal status with all the others, be given less "cooperative wealth"? He really needs more, because he should not be responsible for his poorer ability or physical and mental defects that are givens endowed by nature. It is clearly unfair! The equal right—of receiving a distribution according to one's work—as Marx argues, is really equal when one accepts the fact that unequal talent and hence unequal abilities are natural rights. Therefore, that equal right, in terms of its content, is not equal. Marx labeled it a "bourgeois right." In this sense, only fairness based on the need norm is authentic.

However, Marx is a historical materialist who knows quite well that the development of society cannot get rid of the constraints of historical conditions. An underdeveloped socialist country—current-day China—has inevitably brought up vestiges of the old society from the womb, and its wealth is far from being abundant, so the contribution norm is probably the only option to be chosen.

THE EGALITARIANISM ORIENTATION IN CHINA AND ITS CULTURAL SOURCES

Since Deng Xiaoping initiated reforms in the late 1970s, Chinese leaders began to call for the elimination of egalitarianism and reestablishment of the socialist principle of distribution—that is, from each according to his ability, to each according to his work. They also claim the necessity of breaking down the "Three Iron Systems"—the Iron Rice Bowl, the Iron Chair, and the Iron Salary (lifelong employment, stable position, and rigid compensation)—and to enlarge reasonable income gaps between people by allowing part of the people to become wealthier first. Some Western observers believe that this is evidence that the CCP is going to give up socialist revolutionary principles and to implement some capitalist ones. This is a misunderstanding based on the wrong assumption that the equity norm is appropriate to capitalism only.

As a matter of fact, Chinese leaders have never advocated or supported egalitarian distribution. Instead, they have consistently and clearly held the opposite position. For example, Mao (1963) criticized this principle, as early as 1929, when he was leading his Red Army to carry on a life-and-death military struggle with Chiang Kaichek, by pointing out that "absolute egalitarianism beyond reason must be opposed because it is not required by the struggle; on the contrary, it hinders the struggle."

Nobody, however, could deny the fact that the most noteworthy characteristic of the Chinese perspective on distributive fairness is one of egalitarianism. Chinese people are said to be very sensitive and of low tolerance toward income gaps between people that are regarded as potentially disruptive in collective social systems that put group harmony and social integration as the top priority. The egalitarian orientation is variously labeled by Chinese people as "Red Eye Disease," "Comparison Disease," or "Oriental Jealousy." When diagnosing the pathology of the "disease," the collective effects of a series of historical, cultural, ideological, and situational factors would be found, two of which are likely the major causes.

First, the traditional feudalistic culture, especially the mentality of peasants could be a cause. Mao (1929) has sharply pointed out that egalitarianism is "the product of a handicraft and small peasant economy" and is "a mere illusion of peasants and small proprietors."

Being "temperate, kind, courteous, restrained, and magnanimous" have traditionally been regarded as the "Five Basic Virtues" in China. The danger of unequal distribution has long been the focus of attention of scholars and politicians. As early as around 2,500 years ago, Confucius in his well-known quotation claimed that "no worry about scarcity but unevenness; no worry about poverty but instability." In the past, perceptions of unfairness have triggered hundreds of peasants' uprisings. As early as the 10th century, Li Shun and Wang Xiaobo, the two peasant leaders of a well-known uprising during the North Song Dynasty, wrote a slogan of "to equalize the poor and rich; to even the noble and humble" on their banners, probably the first time in history for Chinese peasants to express their ideals in such a clear-cut and bold manner. The major characters in the great Chinese classical novel *Shui Hu* were Robin Hood style heroes who equally allocated what they gained among themselves, also reflecting the same naive ideals of the peasants. Peasants, linking closely to the primitive and individual laboring pattern with very small production capacity, could not imagine the huge production capacity of contemporary societies. When the wealth and resources of a society available to people are so little, one has no choice but to be very calculative. Under such a condition, equal distribution seems to be the only feasible or even desirable option.

Unfortunately, and almost without exception, leaders of all the previous peasant uprisings, having overthrown the old and corrupt feudal dynasty, would soon establish their own on the same basis as the old one. They themselves soon became the new emperors, enjoying enormous prerogatives and large fortunes. That is why when Mao (1929) points out that egalitarianism is but "a mere illusion of peasants and small proprietors," he also asserted that "even under socialism there can be no absolute equality, for material things will then be distributed on the principle of 'from each according to his ability, to each according to his work,' as well as on that of meeting needs of the workers." In addition, the notion that peasants have no independent ideology but must attach themselves to that of their opposite class—landlords and their representatives, the emperors—has also been implied.

The second major cause of egalitarianism lies in the distribution practices implemented in the military and administrative system of the CCP since the Red Army was formed in 1927 until the early 1950s, the beginning days of the People's Republic: the "Supply System," a system of payment in kind providing working personnel and their dependents with equal amounts of the primary necessities of life. Mao (1964) gives a specific description about that:

> So far the Red Army has no system of regular pay, but issues grain, money for cooking oil, salt, firewood and vegetables, and a little pocket money. . . . In addition to grain, each man receives only five cents a day for cooking oil, salt, firewood and vegetables, and even this is hard to keep up. . . . Fortunately, we are inured to hardships. What is more, all of us share the same hardships, from the commander of the army to the cook, everyone lives on the daily allowance of five cents, apart from grain. As for pocket money, everybody gets the same amount, either it is twenty cents or forty cents. Consequently, the soldiers have no complaints against anyone.

Mao was certainly aware that the system was not an ideal but rather a temporary measure about which he had little choice; it was determined by the extreme scarcity of materials as well as by what was required by the circumstances of the struggle they were facing. The policy of unity and equality between cadres and soldiers was an important distinction between the Red and White army; this made the Red Army able to endure the extreme hardship and fight bravely, although many of them were captured from the White Army but were from poor peasant families.

The Supply System, at first glance, looks like one based on the equality norm. In essence, however, it is based on the need norm but at a very low supply level that can only maintain people's survival while taking a form of equal distribution. This is understandable and justified, because it fits the basic assumptions of historical materialism: that there is not any innate value of fairness that is naturally universal to any person in any society at any time. Instead, the prevailing value of fairness in a society is always determined by the physical living conditions of the society, and it consistently changes both in terms of its content and form with the change of the society's economic relationships (Li 1984). For example, in the diary of his round-the-world tour on the Beagle, Charles R. Darwin observed and recorded an interesting event: When the most senior man of a primitive tribe on Tierra del Fuego of Argentina was given a blanket by a visitor, he looked very pleased. But then he gathered all the members of his tribe, old and young, male and female, and tore the gift into strips of equal width and allocated to each member a strip without considering for what it could be used (Lin and Zhao 1986). This story also serves evidence that proves that "it is man's social being that determines his thinking" (Mao 1963). In a society with such a low level of productivity and scarcity of material supply, one could not imagine any deviation from the distribution practice based on the need norm. In the final analysis, the value of fairness as a part of the societal superstructure, like all the other values, is determined by its economic basis—the level of production capability of the productive force.

Since the People's Republic was founded in 1949, the country's economy has continuously improved. Leaders began to give up the supply system and gradually substitute a regular pay system, first in the governmental system and enterprises in 1952 and then in the military system in 1955. Various incentive systems, including the piece rate, were introduced into industries in the mid-1950s as well. The socialist principle of distribution was advocated and officially recognized.

The CCP, however, does not exist in a vacuum; it inherits a heavy load of tradition and a huge population, of which peasants constitute 80%. Since the revolution, China took peasants as its principal force, so peasants have made up a majority of the Party's cadre team. This team's belief that the major objective of revolution is to equalize all members of society, both in terms of their status and wealth, was strengthened by the egalitarian distribution practiced for decades in the revolutionary team, a fact that then formed a basis for the ultra-left ideology. In 1958, Zhang Chunqiao, a careerist and middle-rank cadre and later the chief theorist among the Gang of Four, began to whip up the ultra-left ideology by publishing a notorious article, "Do away with the Bourgeois Right Ideology" (Zhang 1958). He attacked the then-prevailing compensation system by asserting that the system had corroded the minds of cadres and workers, made them think of nothing but their personal interests and caused them to be preoccupied with their personal gains and losses. He insisted that the abandonment of the supply system was a serious regression.

During the Cultural Revolution, the ultra-left ideology was heatedly debated. This time, the ultra-leftists attacked even more fiercely, insisting that any kind of material incentive was poison for all working people (Zhang 1975). They deliberately depreciated the value of mental labor and sent hundreds of thousands of intellectuals to do physical labor. They took the average of the total fund for bonuses as a fixed additional component of compensation and labeled it as "additional salary." Everyone was then given fixed pay unrelated to performance, and thus any material incentive was eliminated. The masses satirically called the fixed pay system, which was not adjusted for 13 years, plus the lifelong employment the "Iron Bowl System" and "Eating meals from a shared pot." This system led the country to the verge of economic collapse.

When Deng Xiaoping took control in the 1970s, he brought order out of chaos by issuing a series of right-oriented policies. He soon rehabilitated the socialist principle of distribution and called for smashing the "Iron Bowl" and the "Big Pot." He also increased interactions with the outside world, which has changed the values of Chinese people accordingly. The norm of contribution has struck root in the heart of the people, including managers, to such an extent that a comparative empirical study found the preference of Chinese managers for highly differentiated distributive patterns consistent with an equity-based logic to be even stronger than that of their U.S. counterparts (Meindl, Yu, and Lu 1989).

A document recently issued by the Central Committee (CC) of the CCP titled "A Resolution of the CC of the CCP about a Number of Issues in Establishing the Socialist Market Economy" proclaims that it is necessary "to insist the system of taking 'to each according to his work' in individual income distribution as the main body, while coexisting with multiple distribution patterns to reflect the principle of giving priority to efficiency and at the same time giving consideration to justice" (CC of the CCP 1993). The statement does not give a clear-cut definition for the term *justice* but implies that justice is the opposite of efficiency and virtually implies that *equality* is the only synonym of justice without awareness that efficiency, or its basis equity, is also another kind of justice.

What is the distribution practice in China today? In recent years, a so-called Structural Pay System has become popular in many administrative and public institutions as well as business organizations. In this system, one's pay is composed of three major components: First, the *basic pay* is universally the same for every working person with a function of maintaining and assuring one's basic level of living, similar to that of the supply system. Second, the *position pay* is a reward for fulfilling the major responsibilities of a job as required by the job description. This component is relatively stable, so a distinction should be made between it and the bonus that is contingent on current performance in a recent period of time—for example, a month, six months, or a year. Third, the *seniority pay* increases a definite amount with the completion of another work year counted from whenever the person began working. This component, at first glance, seems to be based on the equality norm, because everyone enjoys the same amount of increase for the same period of work, no matter what job he holds. But that is not the case, for the equality norm requires that everyone receive the same amount of pay; here the pay for those with more seniority is higher than that for those with less seniority. On further analysis, the seniority component, in essence, is pay for the additional work experience accumulated in the past work year. It is still based on the contribution norm, because work experience, like one's education, reflects one's potential to make more contribution and thus should be rewarded. Now, however, with more joint ventures and subsidiaries of international corporations established in China, the structural pay system has been fading out, and the concept of a contemporary compensation system has been introduced into China.

EMPLOYEES' SPECIAL CONCERNS IN PERCEPTIONS OF FAIRNESS IN MAINLAND CHINA

Although the norm of contribution has become the prevailing and dominant one in China, the impact of traditional culture and practices in the minds of Chinese employees should by no means be undervalued. Chinese social scientists began to study the unique perception of distributive fairness in the mid-1980s (Han 1987; Jin 1986; Lan 1987; Xin 1988; Xu and Sun 1987; Zhou and Lu 1985), but few studies were empirical. I began to try this in the field in cooperation with a few Western colleagues (Yu, Bunker, and Wilderom 1989; Yu, Wilderom, and Hunt 1989), some findings from which are enlightening to the understanding of Chinese employees' perceptions of fairness.

The relationship between relevant variables in the norm of contribution or equity is clearly depicted by Adams' (1965) formulation: $Op/Ip = Oa/Ia$. However, because one's perception of distributive fairness is formed in a purely subjective judgment process, different people would have different understanding and cognizance about the variables concerned, which can lead to quite different conclusions and consequences.

Let us first look at the variable O—that is, the outcome or reward one gains in a distribution. Because Adams' (1965) theory is based on the concept of social exchange in a business organization setting, *reward* can be defined as resources allocated to employees by an organization in exchange for certain contributions made by them. Traditionally, people tended to focus on merely economic rewards that were known as *hygiene factors*, such things as physical work conditions, relations with superiors and peers, and others that satisfy mainly lower order needs and are mediated externally (Herzberg, Mausner and Snyderman 1959). Then scholars of the humanistic school of thought began to emphasize rewards that satisfy higher-order needs by providing nonfinancial rewards (Likert 1967; McGregor 1960), or by mediating these rewards through employees themselves (Deci 1972). With this expansive view of rewards, a variety of resources can be identified and added to the reward inventory—from those hard, economic, and tangible ones (e.g., pay, bonus, fringe benefits,) to those intangible and symbolic ones (e.g., raise recognition, honorable titles, trust, respect, as well as enriched job characteristics such as skill variety, task significance and identity, access to feedback, participation in decision making, opportunities to be trained and to self actualize). Resources have now been so broadly defined as "anything that can be transmitted from one person to another," a definition "broad enough to include things as different as a smile, a check, a haircut, a newspaper, a reproachful glance, and a loaf of bread" (Foa and Foa 1980).

Increasingly, it has been recognized that distributive norms vary in accordance with types of resources to be distributed (Deutsch 1985). Therefore, people became more interested in figuring out reasonable, meaningful, and systematic classifications of resource and reward types. As a result, a variety of ways of differentiating rewards has been created, but one factor that underlies these various classifications is the material/socioemotional dimension. The previously mentioned lower-order need satisfiers are material in nature, providing for the physiological well-being of employees, whereas the higher order need satisfiers are socio-emotional resources that mainly enhance the psychological well-being of employees. In fact, there is certain overlapping between the two types of rewards. For example, a promotion that enhances one's status and prestige should be regarded as a socio-emotional and nonfinancial reward, but it also tends to bring a simultaneous pay rise; though, in essence, the former is the cause whereas the latter is an effect.

According to Maslow's Need Hierarchy Theory (1943), a higher-order need begins to function only when its adjacent lower need is satisfied; therefore, material rewards are effective in motivating employees in China because the country is still poor and underdeveloped. For example, housing is universally a basic necessity for people's survival. In the West, what sort of housing a person prefers is merely his personal business; in China, however, housing has traditionally been a significant benefit provided by one's organization, and employees only pay a symbolic amount of rent. This kind of housing policy is probably due to the Supply System, and to the fact that Chinese employees have been paid with a particularly low compensation and cannot afford their own houses. The system consumes a huge portion of the government budget annually; people are now striving to reform it, but it is a very tough and complicated job and will take time. Hence, providing adequate housing is the number one concern in the reward package of organizations and is crucial to employees' morale and commitment.

Another interesting aspect of housing as a reward is that, as a practice, the average area occupied by a household member of an employee's house is generally taken into account in the decision of housing distribution. The data, in essence, represents the degree of crowding in one's house, so it implies that the need norm is widely recognized as an important or even top consideration for housing distribution that does not occur in the distribution of any other type of resources (Yu, Wilderom, and Hunt 1989). This again proves the notion that a resource, when in serious scarcity and involving the basic living condition, tends to be distributed on the basis of the need norm. In this case, it means every employee's area per member is given the same consideration no matter what status and seniority he has.

Noneconomic rewards should also be given attention in China. Respect, trust, opportunities to be trained abroad, and conditions for self-actualization, among others, are of particular significance, especially for white-collar workers and managers.

As far as the input or contribution—the variable I in Adams' (1965) formulation—is concerned, from the view of a Western employee, his contribution to the organization (which is also the justification or "capital" with which he can ask for a reward from the organization as a requital) is very simple: work performance—that is, the quantity and quality of work and the value created for the organization. However, from the view of Chinese employees, the contribution one makes to his organization has multiple components. They can be roughly categorized into two groups: personal, such as one's job performance and the merit one wins; and environmental, including work conditions, responsibilities, risks, and level of work required. In fact, the judgment is very subjective, so whatever one regards as a reward is a reward indeed. The same is true of the significance assigned to a reward. In this respect, Chinese employees brought up in the same cultural settings tend to have some common features, discussed subsequently.

First, there is a very popular saying in China that "if I have no merits, I do have hardship; or at least I have exhaustion." This implies that Chinese employees tend to assign a big weight to one's work attitude and the effort one has made in his work—no matter what the results. This, which I call an *effort norm*, can be attributed to two sources: the impact of the egalitarian orientation and the traditional value and practice that a steady and dependable work attitude, being content with an ordinary status, and not being concerned about rewards (usually labeled as the "Spirit of An Old Yellow Ox") has been traditionally regarded as a virtue and encouraged vigorously.

The second input, assigned a bigger weight, is a distinctive feature in China— morality, which is a concept of multiple components including one's political integrity, consisting of patriotism and loyalty to socialist ideals and the reform policy; honesty; dependability; justice; and diligence in both one's work and social life. In China, one's morality not only plays a key role in the promotion decision but is also significant in the distribution of other kinds of rewards, such as pay, prestige, housing, and even opportunities for training, because the policies of the CCP have traditionally been to put a priority on morality. It means that one would be placed at the end of the waiting list for distribution of many kind of rewards after he commits a certain misdeed in terms of morality, no matter how good his job performance is.

Third, seniority is an input that must be seriously considered in reward distribution. In other counties, organizations also pay attention to seniority in reward distribution, but in China morality, ability, and seniority have traditionally been juxtaposed as the three key determinants, especially for promotion consideration. This policy reflects not only an acknowledgment of one's past contributions and respect and recognition of accumulated work experiences (which are supposed to be help-ful to future work), but also the influence of the egalitarian tradition.

Some unique factors in current China regarding reward allocation are situa-tional in nature. For example, the CCP began to reform its cadre system in the mid-1980s through a Four "-ize" policy—that is, to make the cadre force revolutionized (in political harmony with the Party), intellectualized (better educated), profession-alized (qualified to act as leaders and managers in the new economic system), and "youngerized" (if a few candidates for promotion are almost equal in aspects other than their ages, the younger would be given more priority). This "youth norm" on the surface looks contradictory to the seniority norm, but in fact each of them gov-erns different aspects of the promotion decision.

Because China is now in a period of transition, it has not completely gotten rid of the rigidity of its original centrally planned economic system, and its newborn market economy is still far from being mature and perfect, especially its labor mar-ket. The so-called system of organizational ownership of employees has just begun to unfreeze. Workers' mobility is limited; this creates a special problem concerning fairness: that of equal outcomes versus equal opportunities. Some Chinese scholars question the validity of Adams' (1965) theory in current China by arguing that it is in fact unfair to emphasize equal ratios of employees' outcomes to their inputs while equal opportunities are not available to all of them, just like a race with different starting points (Bi 1988). Maybe it is useful to introduce a new variable C (chance) into Adams' (1965) equation to revise it to: $OpCp/Ip = OaCa/Ia$, so fairness is real-ized only when those with a bigger chance (favorable opportunities) are allocated less rewards to balance those of the referent person. When equal opportunities are available to everyone in the society—that is, $Cp = Ca$—the equation would return to its normal form.

I describe my understanding of the distinctive features of employees' percep-tions of distributive fairness. One can see the basic conflict between the tradition-ally egalitarian values and the value of performance-contingent rewards that exists between the classical Marxism and the practices recently introduced from abroad. Obviously, the basic issues of fairness are closely related to the struggle between those who would like to preserve the status quo and those who seek to change it. Even under the most stable social conditions, flaws in the basic values of fairness are revealed by unfairness, which remains unsolved, and at least part of the tradi-tional values that have served in the past require revision and reinterpretation so as to redress new needs and newly aroused consciousness. The issues of fairness are even more complicated by the broad, profound, and radical reform currently hap-pening in China. Fortunately, it seems that the major trends for changes in values concerning distributive fairness are moving towards the acceptance of international values, and we expect an acceleration of the changes.

References

ADAMS, J.S. (1965), "Inequity in Social Exchange," in Berkowitz, L., ed., *Advances in Experimental Social Psychology*, Vol. 2. New York: Academic Press.

BI, X. (1988), "The Comparison Mechanism and the Perspective of Fairness," *Brightness Daily* (February 11).

BLES, R.J. and MOAG, J.S. (1986), "International Justice: Communication Criteria of Fairness," in Lewicki, R.J., Seppand, B.H., and Bazerman, M.H. eds., *Research on Denotation in Organi-zations*. Greenwich, CT: JAI Press.

Central Committee of the Chinese Communist Party (1993), "The Resolution on Several Issues About the Establishment of Socialist Market Economic System," *Quishi*, No. 23.

CHIU, C. (1988), *"The Notion of Justice and Pattern of Justice Behavior in Chinese Culture,"* master's thesis, unpublished, Hong Kong University.

DECI, E.L. (1972), "The Effects of Contingent and Noncontingent Rewards and Controls on Extrinsic Motivation," *Organizational Behavior and Human Performance*, No. 8.

DECI, E.L. (1971), "Effects of Externally Mediated Rewards on Intrinsic Motivation," *Journal of Personality and Social Psychology*, No. 18.

DENG, X. (1980), "Reply to Inquiries of Italian Reporter O. Falach," *Selected Works of Deng Xiaoping* (Chinese version), 1st Ed. Beijing: People's Press.

DEUTSCH, M. (1975), "Equity, Equality and Need: What Determines Which Values Will Be Used as the Basis of Distributive Justice?" *Journal of Social Issues*, Vol. 31.

FOA, E.B. and FOA, U.G. (1974), *Social Structures of the Mind*. Springfield, IL: Charles C. Thomas.

———and——— (1980), "Resource Theory of Social Exchange," in Gergen, K.J., Greenberg, M.S., and Willis, R.H. eds., *Social Exchange: Advances in Theory and Research*. New York: Plenum.

HAN, Z. (1987), "On the Perspectives of Fairness and Efficiency in a Commodity Economy," *Brightness Daily* (December 14).

HERZBERG, F., MAUSNER, B. and SNYDERMAN, B. (1959), *The Motivation to Work*, 2d Ed. New York: John Wiley & Sons.

JIN, P. (1986), "To Promote Productivity via Fairness and to Realize Fairness via Efficiency," *Economic Studies*, No. 7.

LAN, X. (1987), "The Guiding Principle on Adjusting the Values of the Relationship Between Fairness and Efficiency," *Brightness Daily* (May 21).

LI, C. (1984), *Popular Ethics*. Changchun, Jilin, China: Jilin People's Press.

LIKERT, R. (1967), *New Pattern of Management*, 2d. Ed. New York: McGraw-Hill.

LIN, J. and ZHAO, C. (1986), *A Course in Ethics*. Changchun, Jilin, China: Jilin People's Press.

MASLOW, A.H. (1943), "A Theory of Human Motivation," *Psychological Review*, Vol. 80.

MAO, Z. (1928), "Struggle in the Chingkang Mountains," *Selected Works of Mao Zedong*. Vol. 1, 1st Ed. Beijing: Foreign Language Press.

———(1929), "On Correcting Mistaken Ideas in the Party," *Selected Works of Mao Zedong*. Vol. 1, 1st Ed. Beijing: Foreign Language Press.

———(1963), *Where Do Correct Ideas Come From?* First Pocket Ed. Beijing: People's Press.

MARX, K. (1875), "Critique of the Gotha program—Marginal Notes to the Program of the German Worker's Party," in Padovov, S.K. ed., *Karl Marx on Revolution*, Vol. 1. New York: McGraw-Hill.

McGREGOR, D. (1967), *The Human Side of Enterprise*. New York: McGraw-Hill.

MEINDL, J.R., YU, K.C. and LU, J. (1987), "Distributive Justice in the Workplace: Preliminary Data on Managerial Preferences in the PRC," in Beak, J.B. ed., *Proceedings of the International Conference on Personnel and Human Resources Management*. Hong Kong.

SHI, J. (1993), "The Analects of Confucius," *Annotation on the Analects of Confucius*. Chengdu, Sichuan, China: Bashu Press.

WU, L. (1991), "New Exploration on Equity Theory," *Behavioral Sciences*, No. 3.

XIN, C. (1987), "Problems of Fairness and Efficiency in the Reform of the Distribution System," *Brightness Daily*.

XU, C. and SUN, W. (1987), "Why People Still Complain When Meat in their Bowl Has Been Becoming More?" *People's Daily* (August 16).

YANG, C.F. and HUI, C.H. (1986), "Equal Distribution and Sense of Unfairness," *Journal of Chinese Psychology*, 28 (2).

YU, K.C., WILDEROM, C.P.M. and HUNT, R.G. (1989), "Reward Allocation Norm of Employees in the People's Republic of China," *Proceedings of the Third International Conference of Management*. Eastern Academy of Management.

YU, K.C., BUNKER, D.R. and WILDEROM, C.P.M. (1989), "Employee Values Related to Rewards and the Operation of Reward System in Contemporary Chinese Enterprises." Eastern Academy of Management.

YU, W. (1991), "Threshold of Fairness Gaps and Fair Distribution," *Behavioral Sciences*, 1.

ZHANG, C. (1958), "Do Away with Bourgeois Right Ideology," *People's Daily* (October 13).

———(1975), "On the All-Round Dictatorship over Bourgeois," *People's Daily* (April 1).

ZHOU, W. and LU, Z. (1985), "Give Priority to Efficiency While Paying Consideration to Justice—A Trade-off for Forwarding Towards Prosperity," *Economic Studies*, No. 2.

Reading 5

The Tyranny of a Team Ideology

Amanda Sinclair

Teams in various forms have become ubiquitous ways of working. As task forces, committees, work groups, and quality circles, they are used to provide leadership, accomplish research, maximize creativity, and operationalize structural flexibility (Peters and Waterman 1982; Payne 1988).

The prescriptions of much contemporary management thinking are based on a dominant ideology of teamwork. While teams have been narrowly construed as a tool of the Organization Development Model, the ideology is much more pervasive. Teams are embraced as tools of diverse models of organizational reform from organization development (Dunphy 1976) to work restructuring (Poza and Markus 1980), from quality management to industrial democracy and from corporate culture and Japanese management approaches to complex contingency prescriptions. Beliefs about the benefits of teams occupy a central and unquestioned place in organizational reform. It is all the more surprising that, despite some differences in context, the team ideology has been espoused with such consistency.

The hegemony of this ideology has been supported by researchers who offer the "team" as a tantalizingly simple solution to some of the intractable problems of organizational life. Teams appear to satisfy everything at once: individual needs (for sociability, self-actualization, participative management), organizational needs (for productivity, organizational development, effectiveness) and even society's needs for alleviating the malaise of alienation and other by-products of modern industrial society (Johnson and Johnson 1987).

However, do work groups deserve the status they have acquired as multi-purpose panaceas for organizational problems? As has been powerfully argued in organizational analysis (Burrell and Morgan 1979; Astley and Van de Ven 1983; Reed 1985; Alvesson 1987), the dominance of a particular paradigm has substantial costs in the institutionalization of mechanisms of control. The purpose of this article is to scrutinize the ideological basis of the prevailing team paradigm. Four sets of assumptions which underpin the ideology are identified:

1. Narrowly conceived definitions of work groups and group work are based on the assumption that mature teams are task-oriented, and have successfully minimized corruption by other group impulses.

2. It is an individual motivation formula and a "unitary view" of organizations which assumes confluence, not conflict, between individual, group and organizational goals (Burrell and Morgan 1979, p. 204).

3. Simplistic views of the superiority of participative leaders are held.

4. The views are also held that power, conflict, and emotion are subversive forces that divert groups from work.

Research from some alternative critical, psychoanalytic, and other perspectives is used to suggest some areas in which the paradigm requires overhaul.

A premise of this paper is that teams can contribute to getting work of all kinds done, but not when their application is informed by a narrow framework that nurtures inappropriate expectations. Further, and more critically, the team ideology embraced by these assumptions tyrannizes because, under the banner of benefits to all, teams are frequently used to camouflage coercion under the pretence of maintaining cohesion; conceal conflict under the guise of concensus; convert conformity into a semblance of creativity; give unilateral decisions a co-determinist seal of approval; delay action in the supposed interests of consultation; legitimize lack of leadership; and disguise expedient arguments and personal agendas.

DEFINITIONS OF TEAMS AND GROUP WORK

Management theorists have defined a "team" as a distinctive class of group, which is more task-oriented than other groups, and which has a set of obvious rules and rewards for its members (Adair 1986). According to this view, high-performing teams substitute collective goals and an interest in the task at hand for individual agendas and inter-personal conflicts.

Group theorists have noted the parallels between therapeutic groups and other types of work groups (Foulkes 1964, p. 110). However, the emphasis of team ideology on the task-orientation of teams has tended to idealize and resist recognizing that groups with a task still experience anti-task behavior, and indeed have much in common with other types of groups.

Seeking to understand both individual and group work, researchers have, on the whole, been dogged by the search for discrete or measurable outputs of work. Work has many forms. Some definitions of individual work contrast "performance" and "effectiveness" in administrative and managerial contexts (Likert 1967; Sorenson 1971) with creativity and innovation in research or scientific contexts (Gordon 1961; Schön 1963), yet such experimental measures often seem to bear little resemblance to individual experiences of work (Terkel 1974).

Efforts to define group work by researchers in the team ideology tradition have produced a range of measures referring either to the output or to the quality of group process. In the former category are group work as productivity and drive (Stogdill 1972), decision-making (Klein 1961) and problem-solving (Vroom 1969). In the latter category are group work as compatibility (Schultz 1955), cohesiveness (Argyle 1969) and effectiveness—a combined measure of task interdependence, outcome interdependence, and potency (Shea and Guzzo 1987). Work is assumed to have occurred if there is output (products assembled, agenda items canvassed, responsibilities allocated) and the process is variably operationalized by measures such as cohesiveness (Mudrack 1989).

However, none of these measures provide a simple means of diagnosing when and what work occurs in groups or what group work looks like when it does occur. For example, what kind of exchange is a working one and does all decision-making constitute evidence of group work? Further, groups, even more often than individuals, are appointed to ill-defined and even unachievable tasks such as ensuring communication or coordinating activities (Kanter 1983). How are these tasks to be evaluated and monitored? When has sufficient communication occurred to qualify as task accomplishment? In many work groups there is considerable scope for the group to define its own task, and there is evidence that definitions are never permanently resolved—while it suits one individual to view the task as completed, another will see it differently.

A number of researchers have endeavoured to refine our understanding of what work takes place when, from the suggestion that "the talk" itself is work (Weick 1979; Gronn 1983), to the argument that the presence of work is signalled by identifiable items of behavioral interaction (Klein 1961; Bales 1970; Jacques 1970).

Despite this encouraging agreement that work in groups can take various forms, team theorists almost inexorably end up looking for decision-making as the predominant group work indicator. Yet historians, public policy analysts and clinicians, amongst others, provide evidence that decision-making is a poor indicator of work and our focus should be the process by which the decision is reached rather than simply the decision itself (Bion 1961; Allison 1971; Janis 1972; Tuchman 1984; Turk 1988). Thus, meetings which rate high on number of decisions are often characterized by low participation rates, a dictatorial leadership style and a dejected and withdrawn group mood. In contrast, meetings which may be evaluated by members as "hard working" can be full of flight reactions—extended and collaborative exchanges, where a metaphor or fantasy captures the group's imagination. This suggests that a complex and perhaps team-specific definition of group work is required, with varied blends of decision-making and fantasy.

It has often been assumed as part of the team ideology that work and fantasy are exclusive, as if groups and organizations are only capable of a fixed sum of emotional impetus which either gets vested in the task, or is swept away by fantasy (Kets de Vries and Miller 1984b). Accompanying this assumption is the view that groups need ways to resist fantasy (Janis 1972). On the contrary, observations suggest that for some groups, fantasy and accompanying emotions positively assist work and the creative process. Indeed, if we take one definition of fantasy we can see components which could also be interpreted as evidence of creative group work: elements are selected for extended discussion; actions are taken advantage of for the creation of symbolic meaning; the selected elements and chance combinations are elaborated; the elaboration is performed cooperatively as an inter-personal process; and the group process has the qualities of a "chain reaction"—a process which reinforces itself increasingly in an accelerated curve of interest, excitement and involvement (Bales 1970).

By their emphasis on the measurable performance outcomes of teams such as decision-making, researchers have constructed standards for teams which tell only half the story, and perhaps tell the wrong half. Because work groups have such diverse tasks, environments and compositions, teams require context-specific definitions of group work (Payne 1988). For example, reporting on agenda items may signify work in one context and an escape from work in another. Flight reactions may indicate work for one group and escape for another. The work of any group is likely to be a unique and changing blend of decision-making, exchange of information, conflict, fantasy, participativeness and other group behaviors.

THE CONFLUENCE OF INDIVIDUAL, GROUP AND ORGANIZATIONAL INTERESTS

Organization Development (OD) is constructed on the assumptions that work groups have positive consequences for the worker's self-development, for individual satisfaction and performance in the workplace, and consequently for organizational productivity (Gulowsen 1972). While the OD model has been qualified and superseded in many contexts, these assumptions have persisted in more recent models of organizational effectiveness.

The first component of this formula is individual motivation. Our suspicions might be aroused by the turnover in the make-up of work motivation which teams so obligingly satisfy. With the earliest Human Relations theorists, workers' needs were for sociability (Mayo 1945; Lewin 1947). Then, following Maslow's postulation of a hierarchy of needs, attention focused on responsibility and autonomy, the opportunity to self-direct, self-reward, and self-actualize (Herzberg et al. 1959; MacGregor 1960). Later, work motivation was closely tied to workers' needs for participative or democratic leadership style supported by a flat organizational structure (Likert 1976).

Work groups are a structural solution which suits all these views of work motivation. Yet their turnover underlines the inconclusiveness of efforts to test them. Carey (1981), for example, cites the findings of studies which have been ignored because they found no obvious change in workers' behavior as a result of "democratic consultation". Despite this absence of evidence and other cross-cultural research which contradicts such assumptions about motivation, the basic tenets of this model have been very hard to shift (Faucheux et al. 1982). In the wider psychological debate little support has been found for Maslow's hypothesis (Hofstede 1980; Sievers 1986; Landy and Becker 1987). However, it has provided a convenient and, at the time, eminently defensible justification for a whole range of Organization Development techniques, including teams, in which both researchers and management had a strongly vested interest (Baritz 1960; Anthony 1977; Thompson 1983; Alvesson 1987).

Despite the evidence that people are not so simply motivated by the sociability and self-actualization supposedly offered in work groups, much of management theory still prescribes teams as if they are a haven for the alienated employee. Behavior which does not conform to the ideology is dismissed as idiosyncratic aberration by organization theorists:

> The quality of interpersonal relationships among group members often leaves much to be desired. People fall too readily into patterns of competitiveness, conflict, and hostility, only rarely do group members support and help one another as difficult ideas and issues are worked through. (Nadler, Hackman, and Lawler 1979)

The authors of this masterly understatement cite the research findings that groups containing people trained in inter-personal skills do not show improved task effectiveness, often alarmingly the reverse.

Does work in groups generate heightened job satisfaction? The popular wisdom of management theory is that every individual can find, or be helped to find, a "role" in groups (Benne and Sheats 1948). This article suggests the opposite, that individuals experience substantial and continuing internal tensions as group members, and that participation in groups is usually stressful and only occasionally, for some, satisfying.

There is evidence from several quite different perspectives that being in teams is stressful. Because group work involves ambiguous performance standards, often based on the judgements of peers, additional sources of uncertainty and tension are introduced. Work groups evoke emotions for individuals in situations where "feeling rules" are more negotiable with a consequent increase in "emotional labor" (Van Maanen and Kunda 1989, p. 56). Psychoanalytic research indicates that in becoming organizational group members, individuals "often lose their problem-solving facilities, become emotionally segregated, and blame others for their failure" (Wells 1980, p. 170). Evidence from industrial democracy programs reveals that participation in work groups can often be a source of stress rather than satisfaction (Rothschild-Whitt 1986). Indeed, certain types of workers and certain types of work seem better suited to solitary work environments, and individuals with particular work styles will never perform well in the team (Handy 1978; Belbin 1981).

Even for those who thrive on the group experience and perhaps enjoy their job more, is there necessarily any improvement in task performance? A strong link between satisfaction and performance in the workplace has not been finally established (Perrow 1986). If we challenge Herzberg's starting point that individuals basically want to work, can it not be that group members use their groups to escape work? Observations of work groups reveal behavior which is anti-task, designed to avoid work and, in some cases, this behavior predominates.

Finally, does improved individual performance necessarily lead to organizational effectiveness? The prevailing paradigm of organizational theory—that of structural functionalism—asserts that the basic movement of both groups and organizations is toward an operating equilibrium, upheld by a consensus between members which serves both organizational and individual interests (Burrell and Morgan 1979; Keeley 1983; Smircich 1983; Morgan 1986). Conflict in the group is seen as a treatable aberration rather than an endemic affliction. The paradigm assumes that individual goals can be catered for by organizational goals.

In the more recent corporate culture recipes for excellent, integrative, and clannish organizations, teams are a basic building block (Ouchi 1981; Peters and Waterman 1982; Kanter 1983). According to the theorists, there is a direct link between the team's capacity to provide a sense of meaning, an empowering or "power tool," a route to creativity, flexibility and "cheap learning," and effective organizational performance (Peters and Waterman 1982). Assumptions of the confluence of individual and organizational interests and the consequent benefits of teams are evident in other recipes for organizational reform. The quality circles and "ringi" system of decision-making are well-known, though misunderstood, features of Japanese management.

There is increasing evidence that teamwork does not always produce the anticipated benefits. The cult of the "team player" in corporate cultures is more likely to produce frustration and stress in those outside the power elite, such as the middle and lower-level employee, whose experience bears no resemblance to the mythology (Zaleznik 1989, p. 268). The "groupism" which was lauded as the basis of Japanese management's success has been revealed by Clegg et al. as "ideological wish-fulfillment" (1989).

Yet, hardly surprising, the implications for teams of more critical research about organizational life have not been considered by the team builders. Alternative perspectives suggest an altogether different understanding of the relationships between individuals, work groups, and organizations. Instead of believing that individual power needs can be accommodated within groups, which are then liberated to deal with the task, an alternative view regards all group activity as the consuming and irresolvable struggle for power. Instead of expecting a group's impetus to be towards work, behavior is seen as being fundamentally political. In the place of the worker as a natural group member is an individual possessed with idiosyncratic and uncompromising needs, for whom group life is only attractive if it promises power, not subordination.

Teams do not necessarily provide fulfillment of individual needs, nor do they necessarily contribute to individual satisfaction and performance or organizational effectiveness. On the contrary, it is likely that the infatuation with teams and the consequent requirement for individuals to work in meetings means that, quite simply, organizations are not getting the best performance from many of their members.

REQUIREMENTS OF GROUP LEADERS

One of the virtues of work groups lauded by organizational theorists is their capacity for self-management (Manz and Sims 1987). In a somewhat excessive reaction against the traditional autocratic styles of leadership in organizations, democratic and participative style management through work groups was uncritically embraced as the way to motivate workers (Zaleznik 1977). It is argued that, in the flat organization, decision-making is delegated to groups, and workers are able to assume responsibility, take initiatives, and participate in decision-making, rather than look to others to do so. It is further argued that because workers have participated in these processes, they will be more committed to, and keen to implement, group decisions. The ideal leadership style of "Delegation" suits mature teams and liberates leaders, so we are to believe, from having to worry at all about "task" or "relationship" behavior (Hersey, Blanchard, and Hambleton 1980).

In oversimplifying the requirement for leadership as one of learning a more participative style, the team ideology has ensured that many work groups have suffered from being encouraged to dispense with, or ignore, leadership concerns. Psychoanalytic and socioanalytic research has demonstrated the centrality of leadership to group behavior (Rice 1965). Both the group as a whole and the individual members are dependent on leadership being exercised. Group process theorists are unanimous that all groups will experience phases of identifying with, rejecting, and working through relations with authority (Bennis and Shepard 1956; Mills 1964; Slater 1966). This process cannot be eliminated simply by eliminating leaders from groups. Kets de Vries and Miller (1984a) argue that the main determinant of a group's capacity to manage its work and fantasy life is the insight, judgment, and self-knowledge of the leader. Other recent research confirms that the most critical ingredients of team success is its leadership, and refusal to recognize its importance is a sure recipe for producing a group obsessed by authority relations. The abdication of leadership can, in effect, paralyze groups.

Just what is effective team leadership? Reviews and findings have substantially qualified the conditions under which participative leadership is desirable and effective (Locke and Schweiger 1979). It is now recognized that teams are not substitutes for strong, visionary leadership by one individual (Bower and Weinberg 1988). Weick (1978) has proposed the term "medium" as a metaphor for leader, to help one understand the effect and effectiveness of leaders in groups. The leader's prime function in a group is to filter and enact environmental complexity in a way which the group finds comprehensible. Denhardt has explored the unconscious dynamic of leadership suggesting that "every act of leadership is oriented towards some alteration in the 'consciousness' of the group. . . . The leader expresses not what the group is but what it might be . . . one version of the group's potential" (Denhardt 1981, p. 130). Inevitably, any subsequent leader actions provide the seeds of his or her demise, but such leadership initiatives are essential to group creativity. Accompanying renewed attention to leadership should be a new perception about how the leader should operate within the team which goes beyond the narrow managerial perspective of the team ideology (Fisher 1986; Kets de Vries 1988).

POWER, CONFLICT, AND EMOTIONS AS SUBVERSIVE FORCES IN WORK GROUPS

Organization theory recipes for good groups and winning teams rate groups on the "quality of decision-making", "communications," "cohesion," "clarity and acceptance of goals," "acceptance of minority views" and other criteria (Schein 1969). Such recipes betray a simplistic expectation of group "maturity" and "effectiveness", down-playing the endemic forces of power, conflict and emotion in groups. How, for example, is "acceptance of minority views" to be indicated?

Within groups, power has been treated as a regrettable and regressive tendency exercised by individuals who fail to identify with the collective task. While even the most fervent team proponents recognize that political pressures exist in groups, the response of the ideology is to minimize the impact of power, through training and containing or banishing power-seekers or by creating an organizational environment in which a spirit of egalitarianism renders power and conflict irrelevant. An alternative view is that power-seeking to advance individual ends is endemic in groups. This view recognizes that neither training nor organizational actions will alter the intrinsically political nature of teams. Further, it recognizes that the team ideology's distaste for power has diverted attention from the way power works in groups, in interaction with task and other behaviors, toward constructive as well as destructive ends. According to this view, individuals use a variety of political tactics in teams, some of which don't look like the conventional exercise of power (Kets de Vries 1980). For example, Fiorelli finds that power within clinical and health treatment groups "was not equally distributed since an overwhelming majority of treatment decisions was influenced by one discipline" (i.e. medicine) and concludes that "autocratic decision-making was . . . more prevalent than consensual decision-making" (1988, p. 9).

Similarly, Janis records a high incidence of error in group decision-making arising from political factors such as a group "composed of hostile factions engaged in internecine warfare" and the "familiar" scenario "when a powerful autocratic leader induces conformity to his or her idiosyncratic position, stifling all dissent, skepticism, and cautionary information from the members . . . out of fear of recrimination" (Janis 1985, pp. 165–69).

Rather than viewing the urges to exercise power as a threat to teams, group behavior could be analyzed as conflict between individuals seeking to exercise power in different ways. "Task-oriented" behavior could be recast as a particular type of power-seeking by some individuals, and desirable outcomes of groups (in "decisions," "productivity," "creativity") could be comprehended as the successful assertion of some individuals' power-seeking efforts over others.

The view that "consensus is vital" is also prevalent among management theorists advising on the operation of teams. "Insist on consensus" Hardaker and Ward

(1987) exhort, paying no attention to the implications of such an imposed "consensus" or to what conflicts and power discrepancies are superficially concealed. Unanimous decisions and easily won "consensus" inevitably betray a condition of group powerlessness rather than effectiveness.

Since Janis (1972) recognized the phenomena of "groupthink," team builders have acknowledged that groups generate pressures to conform, and that they can impede rather than encourage "the healthy exchange of views." Instead of an effort to understand the basis of conflict and conformity in groups, this important insight has prompted a flurry of predictable recipes for creativity which include generating commitment, developing roles, and morale.

According to this recipe, the creative process boils down to the team simply looking "beyond" what it's doing now to new possibilities (Hare 1982; Hardaker and Ward 1987).

Despite the conflict-laden experience most people encounter in groups, relatively little attention has been given to the phenomenon of intra-group conflict (Smith and Berg 1988). Only now are we beginning to come to grips with the inevitability of conflict, the nature of conflict as basic incompatibility rather than just surface disagreement (Putman 1986), and the limits on our skills and scope to manage conflict in groups.

The structural-functional or functionalist paradigm has upheld consensus and individual rationality as the basis on which groups should operate. Since the backlash against T-groups and Sensitivity Training as tools of organizational development, theorists have attempted to separate emotion-laden encounter or "growth groups" from task-oriented teams. Like power, emotion has been regarded as a disruptive, rather than productive force in work groups, and its expression has been discouraged.

In contrast, Bion (1961) argues that emotion is a mobilizing force of all groups and for all individuals, and group life creates conflict between the need for belonging and a sense of frustration at having to conform. A central dilemma for the individual in the work group rests in his or her ability to maintain individuality while achieving the satisfaction of belonging to the group. It is a dilemma devoid of permanent resolution, condemning the group member to ongoing management of the "anxiety provoked by perceived annihilation in membership on the one hand and separation and loss of affiliation on the other" (Diamond and Allcorn 1987, p. 526).

Despite varying opinions on the interrelatedness of conflict, emotion and a group's capacity to work, there is agreement that a group's confrontation and comprehension of conflict and its emotional responses to it, liberates or "releases" the group (Diamond and Allcorn 1987; Schneider and Shrivastava 1988; Smith and Berg 1988). Releases the group to what? Does greater effectiveness, adaptiveness, or work, however defined, necessarily follow? Or is the network of interdependencies that generate conflicting emotion simply temporarily reorganized—perhaps generating an appearance of work? Groups expressing emotion have typically been treated by management theorists as escaping work. My observations suggest, to the contrary, that the expression of some group emotion may be an essential ingredient in the work formula of some groups.

Intra-personal and inter-personal conflict are endemic and inevitable in work group life. Conflict and work, for some groups, go hand in hand. Simply focusing on the eventual "consensus", "decisions", or outcomes of groups only acknowledges the final prevailing distribution of power, rather than the way the group progresses through alternative distributions. Alternatively, groups could be encouraged to recognize conflict as "an index of vitality" (Smith and Berg 1987; p. 648).

An analysis of who holds power in groups provides a yardstick to predict how behavior is likely to be perceived in a group—as work or as non-work. Behavior which recognizes and defers to the dominant power-holders in the group is likely to be labelled constructive or task-oriented, while behavior which challenges that power is labelled disruptive and counter-productive. It follows that groups with a clear and accepted distribution of power are most likely to be judged productive because decisions have arisen (albeit unilaterally) and actions arise. That a team has a reputation for decision-making and hence for productivity might say much more about the mechanisms of power and control in the group than the level of information exchanged, quality of interaction, level of creativity or other indices of group behavior. An alternative view might require that group work cannot occur without a basic redistribution of power.

CONCLUSION

There are signs that the team ideology might be in decline. Some organization theorists and some organization members seem relieved to admit the difficulties of getting groups to work. While Drucker (1988) forecasts that the "New Organization" will be flatter, with "decentralized and autonomous units" and extensive use of "task forces", he recognizes that these structures create problems—how, for instance, are they to be led? How are the ambitions of professional specialists to be reconciled with those of managers? Other management commentators advocate a return to one-to-one leadership with leaders making clear individual decisions without recourse to management teams and to more individualistic organizational cultures (Handy 1978; Bennis and Nanus 1985).

A vast amount of research and theory-building about teamwork has been undertaken. Yet the rich and complex understanding emerging from many disciplinary fronts is not reflected in the team ideology which prevails among managerially oriented consultants and experts, proselytizing trainers and educators. To witness an infatuation that "the group is good" is disturbing when it is the rationale for organizational upheaval, but even more so when there is little acknowledgement of the inequities, costs, and risks that often accompany team structures.

The hegemony of the ideology has created a tyranny of oppressive stereotypes fed by a team-building industry. The framework of organization theory, in which teams have been located, has underplayed some of the vital ingredients of groups, while the mutually beneficial characteristics of groups have been widely overstated. The advocates of the team ideology have avoided the analysis of power and conflict by the imposition of an artificial consensus.

How should we determine whether or when teams have a place in organizations? A popular way to anticipate whether or not a team-based organizational structure will be appropriate is to adopt a contingency approach. Contingency models match the appropriate structure to the context—the technology, the environment and level of turbulence, the managerial style and degree of differentiation within the organization. Clearly, creative or capable teams are a fragile phenomena in which a combination of circumstances culminate in an experience that is as rewarding as it is effective.

The argument here does not dispute that teams can be satisfying, productive, and creative contexts. What is suggested is that whether they are, will not be a product of cultural, organizational, or environmental characteristics. Rather, the effectiveness of teams depends on the extent to which their application is informed by ideology, on the one hand, or careful and critical appraisal, on the other. The extent to which the team ideology is unquestioningly embraced will determine how fruitful is the experience of participation with groups. It is the ideology, rather than the team itself, which tyrannizes, because it encourages teams to be used for inappropriate tasks and to fulfill unrealistic objectives. By developing a more critical appreciation of the costs and limitations of teams, they will be put to better use.

This article identifies some assumptions about teams which have become so entrenched as to disguise their ideological basis. Some valuable alternative research, largely neglected by the mainstream team ideology, is recollected to restore recognition of the complex ways in which teams work and the ways in which their use can be ill-informed. By documenting the case for those who choose to work alone, by encouraging a greater awareness of the inevitable ambivalence of individuals in groups and an understanding of the flow and force of group emotions, conflict and requirements for leadership, individuals and groups are more likely to operate in a more individually satisfying and work-directed way. These and other alternative ways of thinking about the dynamics of work groups should alleviate the tyrannical tendencies created by the ideology.

References

ADAIR, J. (1986), *Effective Team Building.* London: Pan.

ALLISON, G.T. (1971), *The Essence of Decision: Explaining the Cuban Missile Crisis.* Boston: Little, Brown.

ALVESSON, M. (1987), *Organization Theory and Technocratic Consciousness: Rationality, Ideology and Quality of Work.* Berlin: Walter de Gruyter.

ANTHONY, P.D. (1977), *The Ideology of Work.* London: Tavistock.

ARGYLE, M. (1969), *Social Interaction.* London: Methuen.

ASTLEY, W.G. and VAN DE VEN, A.H. (1983), "Central Perspectives and Debates in Organisational Theory," *Administrative Science Quarterly* 28, 245–75.

BALES, R.F. (1970), *Personality and Interpersonal Behaviour.* New York: Holt, Rinehart and Winston.

BARITZ, L. (1960), *The Servants of Power.* Connecticut: Wesleyan University Press.

BELBIN, R.M. (1981), *Management Teams: Why They Succeed or Fail.* London: Heinemann.

BENNE, K.D. and SHEATS, P. (1948), "Functional Roles of Group Members," *Journal of Social Issues* 42, 41–49.

BENNIS, W.G. and NANUS, B. (1985), *Leaders: The Strategies for Taking Charge.* New York: Harper and Row.

BENNIS, W.G. and SHEPARD, H.A. (1956), "A Theory of Group Development," *Human Relations* 9, 415–37.

BION, W.R. (1961), *Experience in Groups.* London: Tavistock.

BOWER, J.L. and WEINBERG, M.W. (1988), "Statecraft, Strategy and Corporate Leadership," *California Management Review* 30/2, 39–56.

BREHMER, B. (1986), "The Role of Judgement in Small Group Conflict and Decision-making," Arkes, H.R. and Hammond, K.R. eds. *Judgement and Decision-making: An Interdisciplinary Reader.* Cambridge: Cambridge University Press, 293–310.

BUCKLOW, M. (1966), "A New Role for the Work Group," *Administrative Science Quarterly* 11, 59–78.

BURRELL, G. and MORGAN, G. (1979), *Sociological Paradigms and Organizational Analysis.* London: Heinemann.

CAREY, A. (1981), "The Lysenko Syndrome in Western Social Science," in Ainsworth, W.M. and WILLIS, Q.F. eds. *Australian Organisational Behavior.* South Melborne: Macmillan, 212–24.

CLEGG, S., HIGGINS, W. and SPYBEY, T. (1989), " 'Post Confucianism,' " Social Democracy and Economic Culture" in Clegg, S.R. and Redding, S.G. eds., *Capitalism in Contrasting Cultures.* Berlin: Walter de Gruyter, 31–78.

DENHARDT, R.B. (1981), *In the Shadow of Organization.* Lawrence, Kansas: The Regents Press.

DIAMOND, M.A. and ALLCORN, S. (1987), "The Psychodynamics of Regression in Work Groups," *Human Relations* 40/8, 525–43.

DRUCKER, P.F. (1988), "The Coming of the New Organisation," *Harvard Business Review* (Jan.–Feb.), 45–53.

DUNPHY, D. (1976), "The Behavioural Scientists: The Role of the Consultant," *Australian Journal of Public Administration* 35/1, 9–24.

FAUCHEUX, C., AMADO, G. and LAURENT, A. (1982), "Organizational Development and Change," *Annual Review of Psychology* 33, 343–70.

FIORELLI, J. (1988), "Power in Work Groups: Team Members' Perspectives," *Human Relations* 41/1, 1–12.

FISHER, B.A. (1986), "Leadership: When Does the Difference Make a Difference" in Hirokawa, R.Y. and Poole, M.S. eds. *Communication and Group Decision-making*. Beverly Hills, Cal.: Sage, 197–215.

FOULKES, S.H. (1964), *Therapeutic Group Analysis*. London: Allen and Unwin.

GORDON, W.J.J. (1961), *Synectics. The Development of Creative Capacity*. New York: Harper.

GRONN, P. (1983), "Talk as the Work: The Accomplishment of School Administration," *Administrative Science Quarterly* 28/1, 1–21.

GULOWSEN, J. (1971), "A Measure of Work Group Autonomy" in Davis, L.E. and Taylor, J.C. eds. *Design of Jobs*. Harmondsworth: Penguin, 374–90.

HANDY, C.B. (1978), *Gods of Management*. London: Souvenir Press.

HARDAKER, M. and WARD, B.K. (1987), "Getting Things Done: How to Make Team Work," *Harvard Business Review* (Nov.–Dec.), 112–20.

HARE, A.P. (1982), *Creativity in Small Groups*. Berkeley, Cal.: Sage.

HERSEY, P., BLANCHARD, K. and HAMBLETON, R.K. (1980), "Contracting for Leadership Style: A Process and Instrumentation for Building Effective Work Relationships" in Hersey, P. and Stinson, J. eds. *Perspectives in Leadership Effectiveness*, Ohio: Ohio University Press, 95–120.

HERZBERG, F., MAUSNER, B. and SNYDERMAN, B. (1959), *The Motivation to Work*. New York: Wiley.

HOFSTEDE, G. (1980), "Motivation, Leadership and Organization: Do American Theories Apply Abroad?" *Organizational Dynamics* (Summer), 42–63.

JACQUES, E. (1970), *Work Creativity and Social Justice*. London: Heinemann.

JANIS, I. (1972), *Victims of Groupthink*. Boston: Houghton-Mifflin.

JANIS, I. (1985), "Sources of Error in Strategic Decision-making" in Pennings, J.M. ed., *Organizational Strategy and Change*, San Francisco: Jossey-Bass, 157–97.

JOHNSON, D.W. and JOHNSON, F.P. (1987), *Joining Together: Group Theory and Group Skills*. New Jersey: Prentice-Hall.

KANTER, R.M. (1983), *The Change Masters*. New York: Simon and Schuster.

KEELEY, M. (1983), "Values in Organisational Theory and Management Education," *Academy of Management Review* 8/3, 376–86.

KETS DE VRIES, M.F.R. (1980), *Organisational Paradoxes: Clinical Approaches to Management*. London: Tavistock.

——— (1988), "Prisoners of Leadership," *Human Relations* 41/3, 261–80.

——— and MILLER, D. (1984a), *The Neurotic Organization*. San Francisco: Jossey-Bass.

——— and MILLER, D. (1984b), "Group Fantasies and Organisational Functioning," *Human Relations* 37/2, 111–34.

KLEIN, J. (1961), *Working with Groups*. London: Hutchinson.

LANDY, F. and BECKER, W.S. (1987), "Motivation Theory Reconsidered" in Staw, B. ed., *Research in Organizational Behavior* Vol. 9. Connecticut: JAI Press, 1–38.

LEWIN, K. (1947), "Frontiers in Group Dynamics, Concept, Method and Reality in Social Science," *Human Relations* 1, 5–41.

LIKERT, R. (1967), *The Human Organization: Its Management and Value*. New York: McGraw-Hill.

LOCKE, E.A. and SCHWEIGER, D.M. (1979), "Participation in Decision-making: One More Look" in Staw, B. ed., *Research in Organizational Behaviour*, Vol. 1. Connecticut: JAI Press, 265–339.

MACGREGOR, D. (1960), *The Human Side of Enterprise*. New York: McGraw-Hill.

MANZ, C.C. and SIMS, H.P. (1987), "Leading Workers to Lead Themselves: The External Leadership of Self-managing Work Teams," *Administrative Science Quarterly* 32/1, 106–29.

MASLOW, A.H. (1954), *Motivation and Personality*. New York: Harper.

MAYO, E. (1945), *The Social Problems of an Industrial Civilisation*. Boston: Harvard Graduate School of Business Administration.

MILLS, T.M. (1964), *Group Transformation*. Englewood Cliffs, NJ: Prentice-Hall.

MORGAN, G. (1986), *Images of Organization*. California: Sage.

MUDRACK, P.E. (1989), "Group Cohesiveness and Productivity: A Closer Look," *Human Relations* 42/9, 771–85.

NADLER, D., HACKMAN, J. and LAWLER, E. (1979), *Managing Organisational Behaviour.* Boston: Little, Brown.

OUCHI, W. (1981), *Theory Z.* New York: Addison-Wesley.

PAYNE, R. (1988), *The Effectiveness of Research Teams: A Review* (Working Paper No. 169). Manchester: Manchester Business School.

PERROW, C. (1986), *Complex Organizations*, 3rd Ed. New York: Random House.

PETERS, T.J. and WATERMAN, R.H. (1982), *In Search of Excellence.* New York: Harper and Row.

POZA, E. and MARKUS, M. (1980), "Success Story: The Team Approach to Work Restructuring." *Organizational Dynamics* (Winter), 2–25.

PUTNAM, L.A. (1986), "Conflict in Group Decision-making" in Hirokawa, R.Y. and Poole, M.S. eds., *Communication and Group Decision-making*, 175–96.

REED, M. (1985), *Redirections in Organisational Analysis.* London: Tavistock.

RICE, A.K. (1965), *Learning for Leadership: Interpersonal and Intergroup Relations.* London: Tavistock.

ROTHSCHILD, J. and WHITT, J.A. (1986), *The Co-operative Workplace: Potential and Dilemmas of Organisational Democracy and Participation.* Cambridge: Cambridge University Press.

SCHEIN, E.H. (1969), *Process Consultation.* Reading, Mass.: Addison-Wesley.

——— (1972), *Organisational Psychology*, 2nd Ed. Englewood Cliffs, NJ: Prentice-Hall.

SCHNEIDER, S.C. and SHRIVASTAVA, P. (1988), "Basic Themes in Organizations," *Human Relations* 41/7, 493–515.

SCHÖN, D.A. (1963), *Displacement of Concepts.* London: Tavistock.

SCHUTZ, W.C. (1955), "What Makes Groups Productive?" *Human Relations* 8/4, 429–65.

SHEA, G. and GUZZO, R. (1987), "Group Effectiveness: What Really Matters?" *Sloan Management Review* 28/3, 25–31.

SIEVERS, B. (1986), "Beyond the Surrogate of Motivation," *Organization Studies* 7/4, 335–51.

SLATER, P.E. (1966), *Microcosm.* New York: Wiley.

SMIRCICH, L. (1983), "Concepts of Culture and Organisational Analysis," *Administrative Science Quarterly* 28, 339–58.

SMITH, K.K. and BERG, D. (1987), "A Paradoxical Conception of Group Dynamics," *Human Relations* 40/10, 633–58.

SMITH, K.K. and BERG, D. (1988), *Paradoxes of Group Life.* San Francisco: Jossey-Bass.

SORENSON, J.R. (1971), "Task Demands, Group Interaction and Group Performance," *Sociometry* 34, 413–95.

STOGDILL, R.M. (1972), "Group Productivity, Drive and Cohesiveness," *Organisational Behavior and Human Performance* 8, 26–43.

TERKEL, S. (1974), *Working: People Talk about What They Do All Day and How They Feel About What They Do.* New York: Pantheon Books.

TJOSVOLD, D. (1987), "Participation: A Close Look at its Dynamics," *Journal of Management* 13/4, 739–50.

THOMPSON, P. (1983), *The Nature of Work.* London: Macmillan.

TUCHMAN, B.W. (1984), *The March of Folly: From Troy to Vietnam.* New York: Alfred A. Knopf.

TURK, D.C. and SALOVEY, P. (eds.). (1988), *Reasoning, Inference and Judgement in Clinical Psychology.* New York: The Free Press.

VAN MAANEN, J. and KUNDA, G. (1989), " 'Real Feelings': Emotional Expression and Organizational Culture" in Cummings, L.L. and Staw, B. eds., *Research in Organizational Behaviour*, Vol. II. Greenwich, Conn.: JAI Press, 43–103.

VROOM, V.H. (1969), *The Handbook of Social Psychology*, 2nd Ed. Reading, Mass.: Addison-Wesley.

WEICK, K. (1978), "The Spines of Leaders" in McCall, M. and Lombardo, M. eds., *Leadership: Where Else Can We Go?* Durham: Duke University Press, 37–81.

——— (1979), *The Social Psychology of Organising.* New York: Random House.

WELLS, L. (1980), "The Group as a Whole: A Systematic Socio-analytic Perspective on Interpersonal and Group Relations" in Alderfer, C.P. and Cooper, C.L. eds., *Advances in Experiential Social Processes*, Vol. 2. New York: Wiley, 165–99.

ZALEZNIK, A. (1977), "Managers and Leaders: Are They Different?" *Harvard Business Review* 55/2, 67–78.

ZALEZNIK, A. (1989), "The Mythological Structure of Organizations and its Impact," *Human Resource Management* 28/2, 267–77.

Reading

Managerial Leadership in Chinese Industrial Enterprises: Legacies of Complex Structures and Communist Party Involvement

John R. Schermerhorn, Jr.
Mee-Kau Nyaw

The management literature is now replete with observations, commentary, and empirical research on continuing reforms of state-owned industrial enterprises in the People's Republic of China. The foundation work of Tung (1982) is complemented by an increasing number and variety of responsible contributions whose predominant concerns include management development (Warner 1985), value comparisons (Lai and Lam 1985; Shenkar and Ronen 1987), structural arrangements (Warner and Nyaw 1986), negotiating patterns and business style (Frankenstein 1986), and broader political-economic perspectives (Bachman 1988; Petras 1988).

Among these books and articles, however, there is some inclination to focus attention on changes occurring in Chinese institutions as a result of recent reforms. This is the case even though Chinese society retains an underlying conservatism resulting in a pattern of "ups *and* downs" or "speed-ups *and* slow-downs" as it adjusts and readjusts on the political, economic, and business scenes (Henley and Nyaw 1986b; Petras 1988). The massacre in Beijing at Tiananmen Square on June 4, 1989, and subsequent reactionary treatment of student leaders and sympathizers of the "democracy" movement, are dramatic and most unfortunate cases-in-point.

Facing sanctions and criticisms from other nations of the world for its handling of this internal turmoil, China's communist leadership has had to reassess the country's economic reforms in the context of emerging sociopolitical developments. But even as another period of adjustment unfolds, the continuing strength and enduring influence of China's politically-based institutions and infrastructure remains apparent. There is a need, accordingly, for organization theorists to give increased attention to the historical aspects of institutional change and political control as they affect the management of industrial enterprises in China. Schermerhorn (1987) identifies three paradoxes that deserve special consideration in this regard.

"Managerial Leadership in Chinese Educational Industrial Enterprises: Legacies of Complex Structures and Communist Party Involvement" by J.R. Schermerhorn, Jr. and M.K. Nyaw from *International Studies of Management and Organization*, 1990, Vol. 20, 9–21. Reprinted by permission of M.E. Sharpe, Inc., Armonk, NY 10504.

1. *The paradox of the enterprise operating environment.* Chinese industrial enterprises operate in a reform environment that seeks greater economic growth and offers new market freedoms, yet the enterprises are still influenced by central planning tendencies that constrain them.

2. *The paradox of the enterprise organization structure.* Chinese industrial enterprises face pressures to increase productivity and business performance, yet they must simultaneously support multiple systems that serve political and social objectives.

3. *The paradox of the enterprise power structure.* Factory directors and the management cadre in Chinese industrial enterprises are assuming greater responsibilities for performance results, but internal checks and balances in parallel authority structures remain strongly influenced by the Chinese Communist Party.

Paradoxes such as these have important implications for the emergence of managerial leadership in Chinese firms. Many (if not most) enterprises have struggled over the past several years to respond to "new" administrative initiatives encouraged under the reforms (Burton 1987). But the pace of truly transformational change is hampered by an entrenched state bureaucracy with strong roots to the past (Henley and Nyaw 1986a), the failure of many managers to assume authority commensurate with their performance responsibilities (Boisot and Child 1988), and political risk tracing to the continued influence and self-interests of the Chinese Communist Party (Bachman 1988; Petras 1988). As highlighted once again by the 1989 Tiananmen events, forty-plus years of socialism and a strong party presence in all aspects of Chinese society are proving to be conservative forces even in a reform environment.

At a minimum, therefore, what can be expected of this historical context for present-day action in Chinese enterprise is organizational change that will remain inherently incremental. The core nature of the contemporary Chinese sociopolitical milieu may constrain future developments to those which, as Cyert and March (1963) would suggest, fall "in the neighborhood" of past operations. Thus, the remainder of this paper examines the traditions established by complex enterprise structures and Communist Party involvement, with special interest in their implications for managerial leadership.

THE COMPLEX ORGANIZATION OF CHINESE INDUSTRIAL ENTERPRISE

State-owned Chinese industrial enterprises, as described by Henley and Nyaw (1986a), are structured quite differently from their typical Western counterparts. Many of their characteristic features are byproducts of China's socialist environment, and they are quite enduring. Even as the reforms continue to evolve, the presence of simultaneous systems and parallel authority structures lend a unique "Chinese" character to any firm (Schermerhorn 1987).

Simultaneous Systems

Figure R6-1 portrays three systems that operate "simultaneously" to create the typical Chinese industrial enterprise: the life support, sociopolitical support, and business and operations systems. Of these, only the last is shared in common with most Western commercial enterprises. The other two systems are "ancillary" and have no direct relationship to the production of goods or services. They achieve meaning

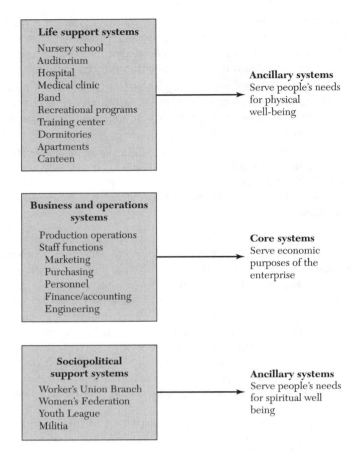

Figure R6-1   Simultaneous Systems within the Traditional Chinese Industrial Enterprise

only in the broader setting of China's socialist society, which views all organizations as instruments of the state.

Components of the *enterprise life-support system* assist workers to fulfill such necessities of everyday life as housing, health care, child-care and education, and even recreation and entertainment. They involve the employing firm in assisting a worker's entire family in meeting their daily needs, and they represent a large proportion of any enterprise's day-to-day operating concerns (Ignatius 1989b). The extent of this commitment is illustrated at the First Automobile Works in Changchun, where some 80% of 60,000 total workers are employed in ways totally unrelated to car production—everything from barbering to police work. The factory director is quoted as saying: "Each year, I have to worry about housing for 2,000 couples getting married, nurseries for 2,000 newborn babies, and jobs for 2,500 school-leavers. I am mayor as well as factory head. Of course I have a bigger burden than my counterparts in the U.S." (Leung 1989, p. A14).

Components of the *enterprise sociopolitical support system*, by contrast, are designed to advance socialist ideology. To this extent, Redding and Wong (1986) consider Chinese organizations as "politically dominated" and designed in part with ideological purposes in mind. The enterprise branch of the Chinese Communist

Party is the center point for this ideology. Sociopolitical support systems such as the following exist within the firm and allow the party to exert a "political" presence:

Worker's Union: An enterprise branch of a national trade union with the objective of advancing worker welfare within the firm.

Women's Federation: An enterprise unit with the primary objective of safeguarding female rights.

Communist Youth League: An enterprise branch of a national youth league with the primary objective of helping the party express itself to young workers and young members of workers' families.

Militia: An enterprise unit with the primary objective of creating a paramilitary self-defense capability among workers.

Both the life-support and sociopolitical-support systems complicate the operating structures of Chinese organizations. They also extend managerial responsibilities into a far broader arena than is typical to most western organizations. The "Chinese" firm is, therefore, quite distinctive in the internal complications that result from its simultaneous systems.

Parallel Authority Structures

As shown in Figure R6-2 "administrative" and "party" authority co-exist within the Chinese industrial enterprise. Although reforms have sought broader roles for factory directors and administrative cadre, enterprise party secretaries and the party cadre remain formally vested in the organization structure (Jiang 1980; Tung 1982; Zhu 1985; Henley and Nyaw 1986a; Petras 1988). Through its presence in a "parallel"

F i g u r e   R 6 - 2   **Parallel Internal Authority Structures in the Traditional Chinese Industrial Enterprise**

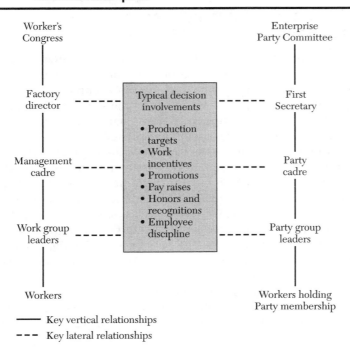

Worker's Congress

Enterprise Party Committee

Factory director

Typical decision involvements

- Production targets
- Work incentives
- Promotions
- Pay raises
- Honors and recognitions
- Employee discipline

First Secretary

Management cadre

Party cadre

Work group leaders

Party group leaders

Workers

Workers holding Party membership

—— Key vertical relationships
- - - Key lateral relationships

authority structure, the party reserves a potentially active and influential role in most enterprise decisions.

The party's authority within the enterprise has traditionally led to involvement in matters of managerial *control*—making sure that the factory director and other administrators work according to state and party plans and policies, and managerial *motivation*—stepping in to encourage people to work hard on behalf of the socialist state. At the Xian Department Store, for example, a policy to identify publicly the "Forty Worst Shop Assistants" was initiated to correct poor customer service. The store's Communist Party secretary was quoted as saying (Ignatius 1989, p. 1): "It's the only system we've found to pressure workers to do better. Those designated the 'worst' feel embarrassed. Otherwise, our efforts would have no effect." A contrite salesclerk whose name appeared on the list was quoted as lamenting: "I accept my punishment. . . . I view my little three-foot shop counter as a window of socialist civilization."

In this and many other ways, Chinese institutions thus operate in the boundaries of the parallel authority structure depicted in Figure R6-2. Within any individual enterprise, it is not uncommon for the party cadre to be involved in appointing the factory director and other high-level officials at one decision-making extreme, and in making employee compensation and discipline decisions at the other. Furthermore, this party involvement stands in addition to its active role in such ancillary units as the enterprise workers union and workers congress (Henley and Nyaw 1986a)—many high-ranking trade unionists and representatives of workers congresses are themselves party members. This means that the party's influence in each firm is very highly integrated. In many cases, it is the party structure that serves as final arbiter of disputes arising within or among the many disparate internal units of the enterprise (Henley and Nyaw 1987). In all cases, the existence of party influence through the parallel authority structures complicates management and administrative processes in Chinese industrial enterprises.

PERSPECTIVES ON THE EMERGENCE OF MANAGERIAL LEADERSHIP

China's management reform program since 1979 has pressured enterprise administrators to think strategically, to be business oriented rather than production oriented, to take greater risks, and to be more entrepreneurial (Ma 1980; Kasper 1982; Byrd and Tydrick 1984). Yet, when viewed from the structural perspective just presented, it is clear that the emergence of new "managerial leadership" in Chinese firms is constrained by forces of contemporary history.

At a most fundamental level, the traditional management functions have each been to some extent accomplished in the past by persons or groups other than a firm's administrative officials. *Planning* was largely done according to the mandates of state plans and by local government and ministerial interpretations of these plans into enterprise objectives. *Organizing* was minimized, since the complex internal organization of simultaneous systems and parallel authority structures permeated and restricted the very essence of Chinese industrial enterprise. *Leading* was constrained by a lack of managerial authority singularly to direct worker performance as the party cadre often assumed dominant roles in "encouraging" and "disciplining" workers in job performance. *Controlling* was largely an issue of ensuring conformity with the targets and budgets established by state-mandated plans, and was accomplished with the direct involvement of the party cadre on all matters of operating consequence.

Such historical legacies can make it difficult for true managerial leadership to emerge within a firm. Subtle suggestions of this conclusion are found in Burton's (1987) observation that the current reforms are designed to protect the status quo of the Chinese Communist Party. The forces of stability, even in times of change, therefore, run deep in this setting. They are found in an entrenched state bureaucracy whose officials have tendencies toward retaining central control (Henley and Nyaw 1986b; Boisot and Child 1988). They also exist in the failures of some, perhaps most, factory directors to assume the authority commensurate with the responsibility made available to them under the reforms (Petras 1988; Boisot and Child 1988).

This inherently conservative side of Chinese enterprises must be better understood—both to broaden the understandings of "outsiders" who seek to better understand these enterprises and even conduct business with them, and to help "insiders" establish an agenda for the development of enterprise managerial leadership that is more realistic, given the prevailing conditions in China. Two organizational phenomena of specific relevance here are the "substitutes for leadership" and "learned helplessness" effects.

Substitutes for Leadership

Kerr and Jermier (1978) originally identified *substitutes for leadership* as the situation where organizational, individual, and/or task variables substitute for direct managerial leadership in work situations. They point out, for example, the formalization (of rules, roles, plans, and goals), inflexibility (rigidity in operating protocols and in applying rules and procedures), and well-developed staff functions (serving in advisory and directive roles) can all provide task direction for individual workers as a substitute for direct leader initiatives. In leadership theory, this concept is important because it offers a way for managers to avoid "redundant" leadership behaviors—that is, attempting to do something already provided for in the situation. Instead, it encourages them to provide "complementary" leadership behaviors that fill needs otherwise unmet by situational and individual variables. For the short run at least, past legacies may make this difficult to accomplish in Chinese enterprises.

> Observation: The contemporary history of Chinese organizations includes many substitutes for leadership whose legacies continue to make it difficult to satisfy reform expectations for the development of more personal managerial leadership among members of the administrative cadre.

Because substitutes for leadership have operated in the past—based on the external state bureaucracy, the enterprise party structure, and the historical lack of managerial authority—many of China's present administrative cadre may have a "trained incapacity" for personal managerial leadership. Because such leadership substitutes continue to exist, it can and should be expected that Chinese institutions are by their very natures still "training" many of the cadre to be "incapable" of personal managerial leadership in the future. Chinese socialist traditions, for example, include an important place for "emulation campaigns" designed to increase workforce motivation. Whereas the administrative cadre are involved in these campaigns, "leadership" of them has largely rested with enterprise party officials serving the important party role of raising political consciousness and commitment among workers (Henley and Nyaw 1987).

If and where the party proves willing to extricate itself from providing "substitutes" for managerial leadership, one has to inquire whether or not members of the administrative cadre have the expertise and/or willingness to fill the void. *If* and where the party is *un*willing to extricate itself from such leadership, one has to wonder what implications this holds for the ultimate assumption of complementary leadership roles by the administrative cadre. Past leadership substitutes in Chinese firms have the potential to constrain managerial development in the present and future, even under the most progressive of conditions.

Learned Helplessness

"Alienation," "aimlessness," and "powerlessness" can develop among people who feel a lack of control over events shaping their lives. Social psychologists recognize that such feelings can arise in the workplace from a condition called *learned helplessness*. This is the tendency of persons who have been subject to tight controls, punishment for any misbehaviors, and repeated failures, to lose confidence that they have the skills required to succeed in their jobs (Martinko and Gardner 1982, 1987). Learned helplessness occurs when a person learns from an experience of past inadequacies to feel incapable of future success.

Too many "signals" in the current Chinese economic and political environment foster learned helplessness and discourage personal leadership development among members of China's administrative cadre. In particular, the external state and party supervising external control over internal enterprise affairs has historically discouraged leadership initiatives by the administrative structure. Factory director Wu Changhai, for example, helped "turn around" the ailing Xian Food Machinery Factory (Clark 1988). But he got into trouble with his superiors in the state bureaucracy after refusing their demands for what he considered an excessive share of his factory's new profits. They, in turn, harassed him by sending in state inspection teams and encouraging workers to denounce him. Wu was taken off his job for more than a year. Instead of a "success" experience based on his managerial leadership initiatives, Wu experienced a "failure." For Wu and others like him, who now have the added experience of the 1989 Tiananmen events to consider, future reticence to display personal leadership initiatives is even more likely.

The organizational structures and policies, evaluation and reward systems, and goals typical to Chinese enterprises further establish learned helplessness conditions. In China, bureaucratic *structures and policies* in the past have led to tight external state controls and ever-present internal supervision by the party cadre. Organizational *evaluation and reward systems* in the past have not discriminated among workers on a true performance basis, and were often tied to issues of good "citizenship" behavior as interpreted by the party cadre. Enterprise *goals* in the past have been set by state plans and supervised through the external state bureaucracy and internal party cadre. Learned helplessness in these and other aspects of management can create frustration and passivity within the administrative cadre, even to the point where managers are unable to respond to new expectations and opportunities made available to them.

> Observation: The contemporary history of Chinese organizations displays a tendency toward learned helplessness among members of the administrative cadre. This, in turn, makes it difficult for them to satisfy reform expectations for the expression of more personal managerial leadership.

Unfortunately, learned helplessness effects will most likely prove insidious and longlasting as they continue to "trickle down" throughout the management levels of any Chinese enterprise. Someone who is expected *not* to exercise initiative at one level of managerial responsibility is *not* likely to encourage it on the part of lower-level personnel, or to view it with much favor if so exercised by them. As a result of this self-reinforcing cycle of learned helplessness in the administrative ranks, Chinese firms can be expected to struggle for some time to come with performance limitations founded more on a lack of managerial leadership than on actual industrial potential.

IMPLICATIONS FOR RESEARCH AND LEADERSHIP DEVELOPMENT

In order to better understand what is taking place within the Chinese industrial enterprises of today, one has to be aware of the historical and complex structural foundations from which Chinese firms are incrementally evolving. Substitutes for leadership and learned helplessness, both influenced by the role of the Chinese Communist Party in internal enterprise affairs, exemplify lingering constraints on the development of more truly personal managerial leadership by members of the administrative cadre.

Research Implications

Management theorists should be cautious when framing their research questions and conceptualizations on Chinese organization and management practices. They should view the present aspects of Chinese industrial enterprises in the context of the past, and they should avoid premature conclusions based more on the allure of future possibilities than on current realities. A research agenda sensitive to such issues might address questions such as these.

1. *What is the current role of the Chinese Communist Party as part of the parallel authority structure of enterprise decision making?* In various industries and in organizations of various types, how is authority distributed between party and administrative cadre for managerial decisions? In what ways and under what conditions is the party role changing in respect to these decisions? In what ways is it remaining stable? What are the implications of the party's enterprise presence for organizational design and managerial leadership in the future?

2. *Is there a difference between the managerial "leadership" required to achieve organizational effectiveness in each of the multiple and simultaneous systems of the Chinese industrial enterprise?* If the typical Chinese factory director assumes a broader role than his or her Western counterparts, one that is more of the "mayoral" role described by Schermerhorn (1987), can the director provide effective leadership to both ancillary and business systems of the enterprise? Or, does the Chinese firm operate with a group form of "executive office" responsible for ancillary as well as core business and commercial systems? If so, what are the consequences of this office and its political aspects to enterprise management and performance?

3. *Which structures within Chinese industrial enterprises provide appropriate and inappropriate "substitutes for leadership"?* What is known about past and present substitutes for leadership in Chinese organizations? What, if anything, can be done to maximize their advantages and minimize their disadvantages in the future? How is leadership responsibility in Chinese firms vested in people as opposed to structures, and to what extent is this investiture capable of changing in the present sociopolitical context of the economic reform environment?

4. *What practices and conditions within Chinese industrial enterprises are still fostering the development of "learned helplessness" among the administrative cadre?* How have the complex structures of the past and the traditional role of the party contributed to the emergence of learned helplessness? How pervasive is learned helplessness, and is there any "pattern" to its occurrence? What, if anything, can be done to overcome learned helplessness and establish true managerial leadership and confidence among China's administrative cadre?

Leadership Development Implications

To the extent that historical constraints on the development of managerial leadership are recognized in China, appropriate leadership development initiatives can and should be pursued. At the policy level, of course, the implications for change are complex and fundamental, especially in respect to the country's present political environment. Extreme limits on managerial leadership development seem indigenous to the prevailing system, especially now that the 1989 Tiananmen events have reconfirmed the strength of political influences over day-to-day affairs in all aspects of Chinese life. Yet at the level of enterprise operations, particularly in individual firms where special attention is given to improved management, modest initiatives of a leadership development nature may be possible.

Four training strategies identified by Martinko and Gardner (1982) for dealing more generally with learned helplessness may offer some potential short-run and local benefits. These strategies are:

1. *Immunization training:* Recognize that new entrants to the administrative cadre are likely to find that past legacies within the firm constrain leadership initiatives. Prepare them through training to expect these difficulties and to understand their personal reactions. Provide them with first-job managerial assignments that assure reasonable amounts of early success. This will help build their confidence for later dealings with more formidable leadership constraints at higher levels of managerial responsibility.

2. *Discrimination training:* Recognize that existing members of the administrative cadre will have special difficulty adapting to any changing expectations associated with management reforms. Increase their self-confidence by training them to better understand differences between past and present situations in the firm. Train and counsel them to understand how the future is expected to be even more different from the past and present, and to recognize the personal skills required to achieve managerial success in the future.

3. *Attributional training:* Recognize that the administrative cadre, already experiencing a sense of learned helplessness, is likely to view past leadership failures and difficulties as being caused by external forces beyond its control. Train them to better understand their individual strengths and weaknesses as managers, and to recognize personal avenues for change and development. Train them to better understand new opportunities, even very small ones, that exist within the firm, and which allow them to further develop their leadership abilities.

4. *Modeling training:* Recognize that members of the administrative cadre can benefit from "role models" who demonstrate the desired managerial

leadership and offer day-to-day reinforcement for the leadership development efforts of others. Train "high-potential" managers to become more confident and capable leaders by assigning them to work with and for others in the firm who already display the desired leadership qualities. Make sure such role models are available at all levels of managerial responsibility in the firm.

CONCLUSION

Given the continuing novelty to the Western eye of reforms in the Chinese economic and political scenes, it has been tempting to interpret developments in enterprise management from a narrow perspective dominated by prospects for change. Yet there can be little doubt that the managerial leadership in state-owned Chinese industrial enterprises is limited by complex historical legacies of a structural and political nature. And while there certainly is some manifestation of personal managerial leadership among the administrative cadre in today's enterprises, it is unlikely that dramatic improvements in this important dimension of organizational life will occur either quickly or smoothly. China's past, simply put, holds too great a grasp on its present and future affairs—something demonstrated all too well in the 1989 Tiananmen massacre and party crack-down on the student-led "democracy movement." Management researchers and observers, accordingly, should give all due attention to the constraining legacies of traditional organizational practices and the role of the Communist Party on the emergence of managerial leadership in Chinese industrial enterprises.

POSTSCRIPT

It is now July 1990. For all practical purposes, China's management and organizational reforms are still severely constrained in the aftermath of the June 4, 1989, Tiananmen disaster. The party is asserting control over the country's institutions, and most enterprises seem to be taking "two steps back" on their difficult path to true industrial progress. Once again, it seems, enterprise managers must live with the "down-side" of yet another of China's "speed-up and slow-down" cycles.

The difficulties of developing managerial leadership under such conditions are even more evident today than when our article was first drafted. After the turmoil and trauma of the past year, one has to wonder how members of the administrative cadre can sustain commitments to management and leadership development when their roles in enterprise affairs are subject to such externally-induced change and uncertainty.

By the time this postscript is read, some major transformation may have occurred to unlock the full productive potential of China's industries. It is more likely that social, political, and economic conditions will continue to limit both industrial development and the emergence of true managerial leadership in Chinese enterprises. As long as this continues to be the case, a great national resource—the managers of China's organizations—will remain largely underutilized.

References

BACHMAN, D. (1988), "Politics and Political Reform in China," *Current History*, 87, 249–56.

BOISOT, M. and CHILD, J. (1988), "The Iron Law of Fiefs: Bureaucratic Failure and the Problem of Governance in the Chinese Economic Reforms," *Administrative Science Quarterly*, 33, 507–27.

BURTON, C. (1987), "China's Post-Mao Transition: The Role of the Party and Ideology in the 'New Period,'" *Pacific Affairs*, 60, 431–46.

BYRD, W. and TIDRICK, G. (1984), *Recent Chinese Economic Reforms: Studies of Two Industrial Enterprises*. Washington: The World Bank.

CLARK, L.H., Jr. (1988), "China Must Avoid the 'Marble-boat' Syndrome," *The Wall Street Journal*, (June 9), 28.

CYERT, R.M. and MARCH, J.G. (1963), *A Behavioral Theory of the Firm*. Englewood Cliffs. NJ: Prentice Hall.

FRANKENSTEIN, J. (1986), "Trends in Chinese Business Practice: Changes in the Beijing Wind," *California Management Review*, 39, 148–60.

HENLEY, J.S. and NYAW, M.K. (1986a), "Introducing Market Forces into Managerial Decision-making in Chinese Industrial Enterprises," *Journal of Management Studies*, 23, 635–56.

―――― (1986b), "Reforming Chinese Industrial Management," *Euro-Asia Business Review*, 5, 10–15.

―――― (1987), "The Development of Work Incentives in Chinese Industrial Enterprises—Material versus Non-Material Incentives," Chapter 9 in Warner, M. ed., *Management Reforms in China*. London: Frances Pinter Publishers.

IGNATIUS, A. (1989a), "Now if Ms. Wong Insults a Customer, She Gets an Award," *The Wall Street Journal*, (January 24), 1.

―――― (1989b), "In this Factory Town, China's Welfare State Is Still Alive and Well," *The Wall Street Journal*, (October 17), 1, 23.

JIANG, Y. (1980), "On the Leadership System of Socialist Enterprises," *Hongqi* [Red Flag], 21, 9–13. (in Chinese)

KASPER, W. (1982), "Note on Sichuan Experiment," *The Australia Journal of Chinese Affairs*, 7, 163–72.

KERR, S. and JERMIER, J. (1978), "Substitutes for Leadership: Their Meaning and Measurement," *Organizational Behavior and Human Performance*, 22, 375–403.

LAI, G.T. and LAM, C.Y. (1985), "A Study on Work-Related Values of Managers in the People's Republic of China (Part II)," *Hong Kong Manager*, 22, 23–59.

LEUNG, J. (1989), "Socialism Burdens a Chinese Car Venture," *The Wall Street Journal*, (April 13), A14.

MA, H. (1980), "On the Reform of Industrial Enterprise Leadership System," *Jinqji Quanli* [Economic Management], 12, 14–22. (in Chinese)

MARTINKO, M.J. and GARDNER, W.L. (1982), "Learned Helplessness: An Alternative Explanation for Performance Deficits," *Academy of Management Review*, 7, 195–204.

―――― (1987), "The Leader/Member Attribution Process," *Academy of Management Review*, 12, 235–49.

PETRAS, J. (1988), "Contradictions of Market Socialism in China (Part I)," *Journal of Contemporary Asia*, 18, 3–23.

REDDING, S.G. and WONG, G.Y.Y. (1986), "The Psychology of Chinese Organizational Behavior," Chapter 7 in Bond, M. ed., *The Psychology of the Chinese People*. Hong Kong: Oxford University Press.

SCHERMERHORN, J.R., Jr. (1987), "Organizational Features of Chinese Industrial Enterprise: Paradoxes of Stability in Times of Change," *Academy of Management Executive*, 1, 345–49.

SHENKAR, O. and RONEN, S. (1987), "Structure and Importance of Work Goals Among Managers in the People's Republic of China," *Academy of Management Journal*, 30, 564–75.

TUNG, R. (1982), *Chinese Industrial Society Post Mao*. New York: Lexington Books.

WARNER, M. (1985), "Training China's Managers," *Journal of General Management*, 11, 12–26.

―――― (1987), *Management Reforms in China*. London: Frances Pinter Publishers.

ZHU, Y. (ed.) (1985), *Contemporary China Economic Management*. Beijing: China Shehui Kexue Chubanshe. (in Chinese)

Understanding the Bear: A Portrait of Russian Business Leaders

Reading

Sheila Puffer

Consider the following descriptions of individuals who made *Moscow Magazine*'s (1991/1992) list of the Top 50 business people in Russia:

> Evgenii Alekseevich Brakov—Fifty-four years old, married with one daughter and a granddaughter. General Director of the huge ZIL Automobile Factory. Rags-to-riches story: Brakov began as a humble mechanic at ZIL (top-of-the-line Russian limousine) and worked his way to the top. No time for hobbies, he is utterly devoted to turning ZIL into a successful company.
>
> Dmitrii Vladimirovich Liubomudrov—Financial director of the industrial finance firm Profiko, founded in August 1990. Thirty years old, married with one child. Hobbies include horseback riding and Amateur Song Club. One of the founders of MosInkomBank. Director of brokers office of Moscow Central Stock Exchange and the Russian Commodity Exchange. Among Soviet and foreign bankers is well-known for being meticulous and hard working. An outstanding horseman, at one time he even trained horses for professional competition. He is also an excellent electrician; a large part of the everyday appliances in his home were made with his own hands (*Moscow Magazine* 1991/92).

In some ways North Americans may feel they already know such people. They possess the same hard-driving ambition, boundless energy, and keen ability that are associated with successful business leaders in the United States. Yet, by probing a little deeper, some important differences emerge that, if not well understood, could interfere with Russian and U.S. managers' efforts to work effectively together.

This article draws upon interviews and surveys of Russian managers that I have conducted since 1979 while living and working periodically in Russia and collaborating with a number of Russian and American colleagues. In part, we will explore how the traits that made managers successful under communism compare with those that are needed in the nascent market economy.[1] The framework for this portrait of Russian business leaders will consist of four leadership traits that researchers have identified in effective leaders in the United States: (1) leadership motivation; (2) drive; (3) honesty and integrity; and (4) self-confidence (Kirkpatrick and Locke 1991). I will first describe how historical influences in traditional Russian society have shaped these traits, and then discuss how these traits apply to Russian managers in two eras: the "Red Executive"[2] of the communist regime which prevailed from 1917 to 1991,[3] and the market-oriented manager who has emerged in the market economy which began to develop after the breakup of the Soviet Union at the end of 1991.[4]

Leadership Motivation

Leadership requires first and foremost the strong desire to lead. Leadership motivation includes: (1) the desire to exercise power and be recognized as influential and occupying a position superior to others; and (2) the willingness to assume responsibility.

Traditional Russian Society   The image of Russian leaders as powerful autocrats is legendary (Mead 1955). Centralization of authority and responsibility in Russia has a long history. In the peasant village communes of medieval Russia, the board of village elders was entrusted to "find the common will" (Vakar 1962). Villagers would discuss issues in an open forum in such a way that suggestions and criticisms were lost in the din and could not be pinned on any individual. According to a proverb, "No one is responsible for the *mir*" (village commune) (Vakar 1962). It was the elders' task to sort through the comments, define the consensus of the group, and make recommendations to the chief elder (*starosta*). Group members believed that it was not possible to anticipate the elders' wishes, and would wait to be told what to do rather than initiate action themselves. In sum, the village elders who were the leaders in traditional Russian society wielded unchallenged power and bore full responsibility for the welfare of the group. In addition, they behaved paternalistically toward the members of the community, and were addressed as *batiushka* (little father).

> One-person leadership, which denoted the unquestioned authority of the leader, had predominated in the army and in public administration under Emperor Paul I in the late eighteenth century, and was legalized under Lenin in 1923 as the basic management tenet of Soviet enterprises.

The Red Executive   Traditional Russian attitudes toward power and responsibility found their way into work organizations in the communist period and resulted in practices that hampered the effectiveness of enterprise managers and their subordinates. According to communist principles, managers were supposed to balance two types of leadership reminiscent of the village commune and the board of elders: one-person leadership (*edinonachalie*) and collective leadership (*kollegial'nost'*). One-person leadership, which denoted the unquestioned authority of the leader, had predominated in the army and in public administration under Emperor Paul I in the late eighteenth century, and was legalized under Lenin in 1923 as the basic management tenet of Soviet enterprises (Kuromiya 1984). A few years later, managers were instructed by the party to combine one-person leadership with collective leadership. The leader's task was to identify issues and set goals. The collective was then expected to discuss the issues and submit a proposal to the leader, who in turn made the decision and instructed the collective to implement it. This alternating wave pattern, that our research team labelled "centralized leadership/grass-roots democracy," was short-lived (Vlachoutsicos 1990 p. 76). Stalin's totalitarian oppression and managers' critical roles in the rapid industrialization of the country in the 1930s resulted in centralized leadership stifling grass-roots democracy as enterprise managers became more autocratic. During *perestroika*, the 1987 Law on the Soviet State Enterprise was intended to redress the imbalance of power and improve economic performance by granting greater participation in decision making to the collective. The law mandated the election of line managers by the workers and the creation of an elected council of the workers' collective in each enterprise to oversee organizational decision making. However, neither initiative had a lasting effect. In 1989, the Soviet government abolished the election of managers in response to protests by influential enterprise managers who argued that the policy was undermining organizational effectiveness. Managers cited instances in which workers elected bosses who made life easy for them rather than those who made tough decisions in the interests of productivity and efficiency. Furthermore, the workers' council was essentially an advisory body to top management who retained final decision-making authority in enterprises.

Wielding virtually all the power within their enterprises, heads of enterprises also bore all the responsibility. They became thoroughly overburdened, and enterprises became paralyzed because no one took action without authorization from their superior as a way of avoiding blame if something went wrong. In fact, Russian executives have marvelled at the way Western executives delegate many tasks, freeing themselves to concentrate on strategic decision making (Karniskin 1992). In contrast, Russian executives were micro managers and macro puppets.

The Market-Oriented Manager   Many enterprise managers have endeavored to retain the autocratic grip on power that they have enjoyed for decades. Now, however, in an attempt to save their enterprises from bankruptcy, they are forced to share power with employees who have become owners, as well as with outside investors and stockholders. These established managers, therefore, must learn to use their power in a more collegial way in order to survive in the new economic environment.

The urgent requirements for restructuring state enterprises and creating new business ventures in Russia call for individuals who have a high need for power and who are willing to assume a high level of responsibility for their work. Some promising signs come from surveys that my colleagues and I have conducted. Many of the forty Moscow entrepreneurs we surveyed in 1992 had created their businesses in order to be their own boss, and were willing to share power and create an atmosphere of participation in their organizations, particularly in small firms staffed by talented professionals (McCarthy, Puffer, and Shekshnia 1993). We also found that 120 managers at all hierarchical levels of state-owned enterprises felt considerable responsibility for their work (McCarthy and Puffer 1992), attitudes that were confirmed by government economic officials (Gregory 1989). Yet, managers must continue to push responsibility down the hierarchy and teach subordinates to solve problems themselves (Shaw, Fisher, and Randolph 1991). Besides delegating routine tasks, senior executives need to learn and practice strategic decision making to make their enterprises competitive and economically viable.

Drive

The second cluster of leadership traits is drive, a set of the following five characteristics associated with expending a high level of effort: (1) achievement motivation, (2) ambition, (3) initiative, (4) energy, and (5) tenacity. High achievers gain satisfaction from performing challenging tasks, meeting high standards, and finding better ways of doing things. Ambitious people have a strong desire to advance in their careers and to demonstrate their abilities. Having initiative means being proactive in making choices and pressing for change. Energetic leaders have great physical, mental, and emotional vitality and stamina. Lastly, tenacity refers to persevering under adversity and pursuing goals that may take many years to accomplish.

> **According to egalitarian principles, no one was supposed to sink too low, nor was anyone to rise too high. People who strived to be better than others were seen as taking away the rightful share of others.**

Traditional Russian Society   In the communal living and farming conditions of traditional Russian society, the well-being of the collective was highly valued, and individuals who showed signs of making themselves better than the group were viewed with suspicion and contempt. Consequently, such individualistic traits as achievement striving, ambition, and initiative were considered to be socially undesirable and destructive for group harmony. The norm was to blend into the group and avoid challenging the standard way of doing things. In fact, farming techniques in Russia remained primitive for so long that grain yields were the lowest in all the long-settled countries, including India (Maynard 1948). There was an anti-achievement attitude that could be summarized as, "Don't rock the boat."

In a similar vein, ambitious people have long been viewed with resentment, suspicion, and envy, feelings that stem from the deeply rooted view that social justice consists of everyone subsisting at the same level. According to egalitarian principles, no one was supposed to sink too low, nor was anyone to rise too high. People who strived to be better than others were seen as taking away the rightful share of others. (Connor 1991). One anecdote about Russians' preoccupation with envy involves a peasant to whom God would grant any wish, but would also give his neighbor twice as much. After much thought, the peasant asked God to strike out one of his eyes along with both of his neighbor's eyes (Sobchak 1990). In place of ambition, then, Russians substituted envy, creating "the syndrome of equal poverty for all" (Shmelev 1990).

> **Russians are a tenacious people. Their ability to endure hardship and survive under adverse conditions is a hallmark of their character.**

Another characteristic often associated with Russians is caution. The peasant admonition dating from the fifteenth century, "to look both ways," is thought to be associated with the rough terrain and harsh environment (Kliuchevskii 1987). With such a high value placed on cautious behavior, it is little wonder that initiative was not a common feature of traditional Russian society.

The last two elements of drive, energy and tenacity, also bear a unique Russian stamp. Russians are notorious for their bursts of energy, followed by long periods of lethargy. Historians have traced this behavior to peasants who would work feverishly during the spring and summer to bring in the harvest, and then lie idle throughout the long, cold winter months. A nineteenth-century Russian historian boldly concluded: "No other nation in Europe can put forward such concentrated spasms of labor as the Russian" (Kliuchevskii 1987, p. 315).

Russians are a tenacious people. Their ability to endure hardship and survive under adverse conditions is a hallmark of their character. They have persevered through brutally harsh winters, the ravages of war, and severe shortages of basic material goods and comforts that the Western world takes for granted. Many believe that their destiny, reinforced by the teachings of the Russian Orthodox Church, is to endure suffering as a means to a brighter future. Two often-heard refrains are that life is a struggle, and that one must be patient.

The Red Executive   Conditions in most enterprises during the communist period were frustrating for managers who had high levels of drive. For instance, their achievement strivings were channelled toward meeting unrealistic deadlines and manufacturing products specified in the plan using insufficient or inferior raw materials, unsuitable equipment, and unmotivated workers. While standards for production volume were often unrealistically high, quality standards were often abysmally low or easily subverted (Forker 1991). In short, achievement-oriented managers were frustrated pawns of the central planning authorities.

> **During the communist regime initiative was not only discouraged, but was often punished.**

To be successful, upwardly striving managers had to direct their ambition toward service to the party and advancement of their enterprise's collective good. Their success depended on both talent and political factors, including party membership, protection, connections, and loyalty to superiors (Gregory 1987). In addition, it was common for managers advancing to top management ranks in enterprises to spend several years on leave working in a communist party organization before returning to a line management position in their enterprise.

During the communist regime initiative was not only discouraged, but was often punished. Officially, managers were rewarded for meticulously following rules and demonstrating loyalty to communist party principles. However, behind the scenes, many managers showed exceptional initiative and creativity by finessing problems in order to meet planned targets. For example, at an electric motor manufacturing plant we studied in 1988, a multimillion-dollar computerized machine tool ordered from Europe by ministry officials turned out to be incompatible with the existing machine tools on the assembly line. Several dozen workers were assigned to perform the operation by hand using outmoded tools—an expensive and labor-intensive process. (Puffer and Ozira 1990).

During the communist period, conscientious managers had to have the energy to work long hours and be all things to all people. Managers whom our team interviewed in 1988 would joke that they worked an "eight-hour day"—from 8 a.m. to 8 p.m., that is (Lawrence and Vlachoutsicos 1990). Heads of enterprises spent most of their time "fighting fires." They were "hands-on" managers who would tour their plants once or twice a day and become involved in operational problems. Unfortunately, the amount of energy required to be successful took its toll on the health of many Russian managers. Heads of Soviet enterprises have been diagnosed as experiencing more stress and health problems than managers in the United States, Japan, and India (Ivancevich, De Frank, and Gregory 1992).

Managers during the communist period struggled tenaciously to accomplish routine tasks. Effective managers persevered under adversity and fulfilled their enterprise's plans in spite of shortages and bureaucratic obstacles. For example, a successful materials manager we interviewed in 1988 had chronic problems getting a supplier to provide copper wire for a new model of motor. First, the manager went several hundred miles to see the supplier. When this attempt failed, the plant used economic sanctions against the supplier who paid them several thousand rubles in fines, yet still sent no wire. Finally, the manager had higher authorities force his counterpart to meet with him at the ministry in charge of wire production. The motor plant finally began receiving the wire, but shipments were consistently at least 5% short (Puffer 1990).

> **Although there is no longer any legal restriction on realizing one's personal ambition by starting a private enterprise, there is still tremendous social pressure against ambitious entrepreneurs.**

The Market-Oriented Manager   A growing number of managers and entrepreneurs are exhibiting the five elements of drive that are associated with success in a market economy. For example, according to one recent study, Russian entrepreneurs have as much achievement motivation as their American counterparts (Tullar 1992). My colleagues and I also found that entrepreneurs sought challenging tasks and had high standards. Many in our study had left the security of the state sector to start new businesses that would allow their scientific and technical expertise to flourish. Moreover, they rated the high quality of their products and services as the number one factor contributing to their firms' success. (McCarthy, Puffer, Shekshnia 1993). The spirit of these achievement-oriented individuals is that the sky's the limit.

Although there is no longer any legal restriction on realizing one's personal ambition by starting a private enterprise, there is still tremendous social pressure against ambitious entrepreneurs. As one American journalist observed: "In America, it's a sin to be a loser, but if there's one sin in Soviet society, it's being a winner" (Barringer 1989). In essence, "blind, burning envy of a neighbor's success . . . has become (virtually at all levels) a most powerful brake on the ideas and practice of restructuring [the economy] (Shmelev 1991, p. 34). Ambitious business people, therefore, must deal with the problem of overcoming the sin of being a winner, and being the object of envy and resentment. The new economic conditions have also sparked a heated debate about social justice in the press, including the legitimacy and morality of private enterprise. In some articles entrepreneurs have been portrayed as latter-day *Nepmen* (entrepreneurs encouraged for a few short years during Lenin's New Economic Plan) and *kulaks* (prosperous peasants who were often accused of exploiting other peasants). Many entrepreneurs recall how such people were persecuted in earlier times, and fear they will suffer the same fate. According to Oleg Smirnov, a Russian representative of Pepsi-Cola: "There is no tradition of law in this country, so some powerful official can strangle a cooperative [private business] in five minutes—there are sixty-four thousand ways to do it" (Smirnov 1990, p. 285).

Many new Russian entrepreneurs are also demonstrating a great deal of initiative, although one study has found them to be more risk averse and less innovative than Americans (Tullar 1992). Nevertheless, hordes of entrepreneurs, brimming with initiative, have been unleashed in Russia. Their attitude is, "Let's do business." Claimed Herman Sterligov, president of the computerized commodity exchange, The Alysa System, in Moscow: "Every day we have a thousand people who come to our Moscow office saying, 'Please privatize us' or 'I have this idea and I need funding'" (Sterligov 1992, p. 79).

The new entrepreneurs must also possess energy and stamina to start their own businesses and foster their growth. Some people are pursuing so many opportunities that they seem to work eight days a week. An outstanding example is Sviatoslav Fedorov, who was named Businessman of the Year in 1991 by *Moscow Magazine* in recognition of his ventures that include eye surgery clinics, medical manufacturing plants, and hotels and casinos (Hofheinz 1991/92; Kirkland 1990). Among the most energetic entrepreneurs are young people who have little experience with the communist regime. In Moscow, for example, teenagers could be found recently washing cars and fetching hamburgers for customers unwilling to wait in line. The most enterprising were earning as much as 300,000 rubles a month when the average monthly wage was less than 10,000. Such individuals "were not tainted by all those years of 'Glory to the Communists' " and they represent "the first generation that will have no doubts about the need for a market economy" (Lasov 1993, pp. 20, 21).

Whereas communist managers struggled tenaciously to accomplish the routine, market-oriented managers, who face immense obstacles, struggle to accomplish the new. There is virtually no legal or economic infrastructure to support private enterprise, and venture capital is extremely limited. The Moscow entrepreneurs my colleagues and I queried in 1992 cited the unstable political situation and government regulation as the biggest obstacles to doing business (McCarthy, Puffer, and Shekshnia 1993). For example, some laws are so ambiguous or rewritten so frequently that it is difficult for firms to develop long-term business strategies.

Honesty and Integrity

Effective leaders are viewed as credible and trustworthy because they behave ethically and exhibit honesty and integrity. Honesty means telling the truth, and integrity refers to being consistent in words and actions.

Traditonal Russian Society   While there are many basic similarities in the ethical and value systems of Western and Russian people, two important differences stand out. The first one, the dual ethical standard, refers to the way ethics is construed in different situations. In the West, particularly in America, people are expected to employ the same set of ethical standards regardless of the situation. In contrast, in Slavic cultures two sets of ethical standards have developed—one for impersonal or official relationships, and one for personal relationships (Lefebvre 1982). In short, there is deception in business dealings, but fealty in friendship. Thus, in Russia, while it would not necessarily be considered unethical to deceive someone in a business transaction to achieve a worthy goal, it would be considered unethical to deceive a friend or trusted colleague. In contrast, in the United States, deception would be considered unethical in both business and personal relationships.

The second feature of the Russian ethical system is the use of *blat*, informal influence or connections to obtain favors. This practice probably stems from the era of serfdom and bondage that began under Ivan III in 1440 and lasted until The Emancipation Act of 1861. Peasants worked land they did not own, and would curry favor with landowners by bringing them food they had grown.

The Red Executive   The dual ethical standard was evident in the distinction made between personal and professional honesty by the managers with whom I studied in Moscow in 1979. They contended that honesty was essential in personal conduct, such as keeping one's word, but that honesty in terms of managing by the rules was considered unrealistic, and even undesirable. The managers agreed that if they tried to abide by all of the 80,000 rules and regulations in an average enterprise, they would not accomplish much and would not be successful in their jobs (Puffer 1981). This duality of ethics helps explain why, under communism, a great many people routinely engaged in behavior that was in violation of the 1961 twelve-point moral code of the communist party (DeGeorge 1969). For instance, the relatively common practice of stealing state property from the workplace was certainly not condoned, but it was viewed by most people as less serious than stealing possessions from an individual. Moreover, workers and professionals would deceive managers about production quality and output, and the managers in turn would deceive ministry officials. Enterprises typically would keep two sets of books, one containing actual results for their own records, the other containing information prepared for the ministry. In this way the enterprise would receive its bonuses, while protecting itself from receiving a tight plan or fewer resources. It was a game in which virtually everyone tacitly participated. Such deception was often a matter of survival, and was viewed as a necessary evil.

Another questionable practice stemmed from the use of *blat* to break through bureaucratic bottlenecks and grease the wheels of the state. Managers would make informal deals to get things done, such as obtain scarce spare parts or obtain authorization for an activity. Personal gifts or needed goods or services produced by the enterprise were the customary methods. Good managers knew the boundary between using *blat* for the legitimate benefit of the organization as opposed to abusing it for personal gain or other corrupt purposes.

In the communist system, then, a good manager was skilled in manipulating the truth as well as in using *blat* for the benefit of the enterprise and the individuals who worked in it. At the same time, a good manager did not betray employees and developed a relationship based on personal trust and honesty with them. Managers and employees were like a family with mutually dependent members whose personal and professional lives were intertwined.

The Market-Oriented Manager   Ethics and morality have come under much public scrutiny since *perestroika* and the disintegration of the Soviet Union. People have expressed their dismay at the decline in moral values which occurred under the communist regime. Professor Dmitrii Likhachev, considered by many to be the spiritual and moral leader of *perestroika*, said that a fundamental failing of the Soviet people is "we became used to a double life: we say one thing, but we do the other. We have unlearned how to tell the truth, the full truth" (Likhachev 1987a). Professor Likhachev attributes this society of deception to the fact that traditional Russian culture was shown disrespect and even destroyed by the communists (Likhachev 1987b).

Corruption and unethical behavior are rampant in both business and government. Some entrepreneurs are tenaciously trying to hold onto their businesses and keep them from being overtaken by the criminal element. For instance, some private business owners have formed associations to find ways to deal with threats by organized crime. Similarly, a few years ago, one thousand taxi drivers staged a meeting at Vnukovo Airport to discuss how to avoid paying protection money. (Roberts and LaFollette 1990). Still other entrepreneurs have rebuilt their businesses that were sabotaged or closed down by government officials (Jones and Moskoff 1991). Yet, most businesses are at the mercy of the mafia, and murders of business people have been reported in the press. (Volokhov 1993).

> **To run their businesses, people are forced to grease the palms of government officials to obtain licenses and permits, as well as of criminal figures who threaten violence if they do not receive a portion of the profits.**

The pervasiveness of corruption associated with "wild capitalism" in Russia makes it extremely difficult for ethically-minded business people to function. To run their businesses, people are forced to grease the palms of government officials to obtain licenses and permits, as well as of criminal figures who threaten violence if they do not receive a portion of the profits. Furthermore, ethical business people frequently endure unfounded criticism from the general public, many of whom hold the stereotype that all entrepreneurs are dishonest and exploitative. Finally, some people who want to conduct business in an ethical manner are prisoners of their experience in the communist period. According to Ira Tatelbaum, an American partner in a Moscow clothing factory, some of his Russian employees still want to do business the old convoluted, underhanded way. Out of habit they use *blat*, but are learning to appreciate the relative simplicity and straightforwardness associated with standard Western business practices. (Tatelbaum 1992).

Self-Confidence

The many demands placed upon leaders require them to have self-confidence in making decisions under uncertainty, directing the work of others, overcoming obstacles, taking risks, and accepting responsibility for mistakes.

Traditional Russian Society   Throughout their history, Russians have been portrayed as having self-confidence that ranged from helplessness to bravado. At one extreme, writers such as Dostoevskii and Gogol' have depicted Russians as a pessimistic people who see life as gloomy and hopeless and beyond their control. Some scholars believe this mentality has its origins in religious beliefs that a savior will deliver the people from their plight. At the other extreme are writers who portray Russians as highly confident and adept at outsmarting others. For example, in the nineteenth-century short story by Leskov, *The Left-Handed Man*, a cross-eyed left-handed Russian craftsman outdid British metalworkers by making shoes for a steel flea they had made for the Tsar.

The Red Executive   As in literature and folklore, extremes of self-confidence can also be found among Russian business leaders. During the communist period managers' self-confidence took a blow from the inferior quality of products they produced, yet they took pride in the "big is beautiful" phenomenon of running some of the biggest factories in the world. Russian managers were also the target of sharp criticism by the public. One frustrated citizen even proposed that the entire power structure be replaced by foreigners in the following letter to the editor of a popular magazine:

"Where, for heaven's sake, is there a sensible distribution? When are we going to be well off? With bosses like we've got now—never. I therefore propose that we sack all the apparatchiks from leading posts, all the various factory managers, and all the sundry farm chairmen . . . and invite managers and administrators from West Germany, asking them to take over. I figure the situation would improve immediately. If we don't, it's no use anticipating any improvements in three years or even ten. If you remember, in Peter the Great's time we invited plenty of foreigners to Russia to serve and work, and they successfully replaced the arrogant grandees and bureaucrats. It worked great" (Kononov 1990).

The Market-Oriented Manager   Among market-oriented managers self-confidence ranges from cynicism about their ability to solve problems, to over-promising what they ~an actually deliver to their business partners and clients. Low self-confidence may account for the wish that some managers have for others, particularly foreigners, to solve their problems for them. As Vladimir Kachenuyk, a Russian executive, explained:

> [T]he people in the Soviet Union in general have an almost fanatic belief in the United States . . . All the American goods, American experience and ideas, American organization and production management, American technology—outstanding! All of these are being perceived as a panacea which will prove to be the salvation of the Soviet Union. (Kachenuyk 1992).

> **Low self-confidence may account for the wish that some managers have for others, particularly foreigners, to solve their problems for them.**

A call for help from foreigners was expressed more seriously by Eduard Shevardnadze, former Soviet foreign minister, in an appeal for Western investment following the dissolution of the Soviet Union: "We are sure that Russia can be saved by foreign business" (Shevardnadze 1992).

In contrast, the power that high self-confidence has in improving managerial performance is illustrated by the success story of the Cheremushkii Sewing Factory. In the late 1980s, with a boost of self-confidence derived from increased pride in their product, enterprise officials succeeded in having Russian women actually purchase some of the 22 million brassieres they manufactured annually, rather than continue to produce them "for the warehouse." The brassieres had been of high quality, but women refused to wear them because of the stigma of Russian-made goods. A retired American businessperson, Harold Willens, conducted an experiment in Moscow whereby he had 50 identical brassieres made in the United States, and then switched half the labels. Those with Russian labels were disparaged by consumers. When the factory managers and ministry officials realized that they offered a high-quality product, they launched a marketing campaign about their "world-class bras" and received an increase in orders as a result (Parker 1990).

Despite such successes, some highly ambitious entrepreneurs need to guard against becoming overly confident. With many attractive opportunities to explore, and few laws and regulations to control their business dealings, a number of entrepreneurs have adopted a "Wild West" attitude toward doing business. By cutting corners and acting unscrupulously for quick gains, they tarnish the reputation of private enterprise for everyone.

> **The music of the market is playing, and many North Americans may find themselves dancing with the bear.**

No More Dancing in the Dark: Some Guidelines

The fall of communism and the reconfiguration of the Russian political and economic system have created many promising opportunities for doing business with Russians. This trend is likely to continue. The music of the market is playing, and many North Americans may find themselves dancing with the bear. Whether Russian partners come from established state enterprises or from fledgling entrepreneurial firms, I hope this portrait describes them sufficiently to avoid the feeling of dancing in the dark. However, for those still unsure about taking the first step, let us look at ways that this portrait of Russian leaders can help Western firms build effective business partnerships. The following guidelines should help create a favorable impression on Russians by showing sensitivity to the way Russians perceive themselves and do business. In addition, these guidelines should enable Westerners to develop the appropriate responses and behaviors to make interactions with Russian business leaders go smoothly.

First, relieve Russians of responsibility for unforeseen negative consequences. Power, responsibility, and decision making are typically centralized in Russian organizations, and many executives have difficulty delegating authority. Russian managers at all levels are accustomed to exercising power without being challenged by subordinates, but they hesitate to act, even on trivial matters, if they fear being held responsible for decisions that have not been explicitly approved by the head of the organization or not been prescribed in standard procedures. Consequently, it is easier for Russians to take action if their partners relieve them of responsibility for unforeseen negative consequences. They should be assured that someone else will bear the responsibility. This unconventional approach is part of the risk associated with doing business with Russian partners, and it is important to exercise judgment about the particular situations in which it is appropriate.

Second, avoid appearing exploitative, and respect collectivistic attitudes. Russian business leaders have had much of their drive suppressed by communal traditions and attitudes passed on from peasant society, as well as by the egalitarian principles of communist ideology and the stultifying bureaucracy of the centrally planned economic system. Three of the five components of drive—achievement, ambition, and initiative—have been denigrated in Russia. People with a high need for achievement have been condemned for being individualistic, antisocial, and enemies of the people. Personal ambition has been met with envy, vindictiveness, and derision. And initiative has usually been received with indifference, at best, and punishment, at worst. Negative attitudes towards these characteristics are so deeply ingrained in the Russian psyche that many Russians who want to realize their ambitions feel pressure from two sources—public scorn and their own guilt from violating the values they were raised with.

Foreign joint ventures have also been the target of such criticism. Some Russians view them as "a convenient front for those trying to make money . . . as fast as possible" (Alekseyev 1991, p. 41). Therefore, when working with Russians, foreign firms should avoid presenting an image that could be construed as exploitative of individual Russians or of their society. In addition, foreign firms should respect their Russian colleagues' requests to avoid publicizing their achievements, material possessions, or privileges. They simply don't want to arouse feelings of envy or guilt, since the egalitarian norm of social justice is still strong. However, Western firms should take their cues from their Russian colleagues, because some of them may be more open about their accomplishments and may want recognition and approval.

Third, stress the importance and urgency of taking action. Russian leaders have two components of drive in abundance: energy and tenacity. They are used to hard work, can call upon large reserves of energy when required, and they are capable of persevering in spite of immense obstacles. In the words of Sviatoslav Fedorov, the highly successful surgeon-*cum*-entrepreneur: "The notion that all Russian workers are stupid or lazy is nonsense. But what can you expect if the government takes away property and forces them to live like domestic animals?" (Fedorov 1990, p. 67).

To spur Russian partners to action, then, Westerners should emphasize the importance and urgency of the situation, and stress that the Russians' utmost effort is needed to ensure success. This appeal should also be accompanied by valuable material rewards. The noted Russian economist, Pavel Bunich, commented that Russians who work in Western joint ventures will work hard as long as they are rewarded sufficiently to compensate for the absence of security and benefits they had enjoyed without exerting much effort in state-owned enterprises. Says Bunich, "Who would otherwise want to lose benefits more or less guaranteed by the state?" (Bunich 1991, p. 41).

> **Westerners should consider it their duty to uphold the highest standards of business practice as a service to Russians who are learning the ways of the world economy.**

Fourth, forge personal relationships. As in any interpersonal interaction, integrity and honesty are crucial for developing a lasting and rewarding relationship with Russian business colleagues. Developing mutual trust and respect with them presents special challenges in light of some Russian practices that violate Western ethical sensibilities. One way to shape ethical behavior is by effectively using the Russian concept of dual ethics. This involves making a genuine and serious effort to forge a strong personal relationship with Russian colleagues, rather than maintaining an arms-length, formal business relationship. An approach of strengthening personal ties is more likely to trigger the ethical behavior, loyalty, and trust that Russians show their closest friends, family members, and colleagues. The tendency, if it existed at all, for Russians to see foreigners as simply impersonal business contacts to be duped and exploited, should be greatly reduced.

Fifth, uphold the highest standards of business practice. Another approach to developing an ethically sound business relationship with your Russian counterparts is to instill respect for business ethics, protocol, and accepted business practices. The market economy is such a new phenomenon in Russia that few people have a complete understanding of its complexities. Furthermore, many otherwise sophisticated Russians are unaware of the official legislation, as well as the unofficial accepted business practices, that keep a potentially destructive free market in check. Westerners should consider it their duty to uphold the highest standards of business practice as a service to Russians who are learning the ways of the world economy. For example, it would be useful to demonstrate how standard Western business procedures eliminate the need to use connections (*blat*) and underhanded methods of doing business.

Sixth, encourage joint problem solving. It is important to have an awareness of the two extremes of self-confidence that Russian colleagues might exhibit. In some cases, low self-confidence may lead them to look to their Western partners to solve problems and provide needed resources. To develop a mutually beneficial long-term relationship, however, it is better for all concerned to take the time to make decisions and resolve issues together. Such an approach, while time consuming, provides a stronger foundation for developing expertise and commitment of both sides.

Seventh, develop a concrete action plan. On some occasions Russians may engage in seemingly impulsive or reckless behavior resulting from over-confidence or bravado. Because of inexperience, they may not fully understand the complexities of a situation, and may overestimate their ability to deal with it successfully, or overlook the steps involved in putting an idea into practice. In such cases it would be helpful to develop a concrete action plan with them to ascertain the feasibility of their ideas.

References

ALEXSEYEV, B. (1991), "Joint Ventures: Is the Formula Right?" *Soviet Life* (October), 41.

BARRINGER, F. (1989), "Comment at the conference, Chautauqua at Pitt: The Fifth General Chautauqua Conference on U.S. and Soviet Relations," (October 30). Cited in Smith, H. (1990), *The New Russians*. New York: Random House, 203.

BUNICH, P. (1991), cited in Alexseyev, B. "Joint Ventures: Is the Formula Right?" *Soviet Life* (October), 41.

CONNOR, W.D. (1991), "Equality of Opportunity," in Jones, A. Connor, W.D. and Powell, D.E. eds., *Soviet Social Problems*. Boulder, CO: Westview, 137–53.

DeGEORGE, R.T. (1969), *Soviet Ethics and Morality*. Ann Arbor, MI: The University of Michigan Press.

FEDOROV, S. (1990), cited in Kirkland, R.I. "Curing Communism," *Moscow Magazine* (October), 64–68.

FORKER, L.B. (1991), "Quality: American, Japanese, and Soviet Perspectives," *The Academy of Management Executive*, 5(4), 63–74.

GORER, G. and RICKMAN, J. (1949/1962), *The People of Great Russia: A Psychological Study*. New York, NY: Norton.

GREGORY, P.R. (1987), "Productivity, Slack, and Time Theft in the Soviet Economy," in Millar, J.R. ed., *Politics, Work, and Daily Life in the USSR: A Survey of Former Soviet Citizens*. Cambridge: Cambridge University Press, 241–75.

GREGORY, P.R. (1989), "Soviet Bureaucratic Behavior: *Khozyaistvenniki* and *Apparatchiki*," *Soviet Studies*, (October), 511–25.

HOFHEINZ, P. (1991/92), "The Pied Piper of Capitalism," *Moscow Magazine* (December/January), 50, 51.

IVANCEVICH, J.M., DeFRANK, R.S. and GREGORY, P.R. (1992), "The Soviet Enterprise Director: An Important Resource Before and After the Coup," *The Academy of Management Executive*, 6(1), 42–55.

JONES, A. and MOSKOFF, W. (1991), *Ko-ops: The Rebirth of Entrepreneurship in the Soviet Union*. Bloomington, IN: Indiana University Press, 66–70.

KACHENUYK, V.A. (1992), cited in Vance, C.M. and Zhuplev, A.V. "Myths About Doing Business in the Soviet Union: An Interview with Vladimir A. Kachenuyk, Deputy Director, Moscow Personnel Center," *Journal of Management Inquiry*, 1(1), 66–9.

KANISKIN, N.A. (1992), "The Western Executive and the Soviet Executive: A Talk With Nikolai A. Kaniskin," in Puffer, S.M. ed., *The Russian Management Revolution: Preparing Managers for the Market Economy*, Armonk, NY: M.E. Sharpe, 41–51.

KIRKPATRICK, S.A. and LOCKE, E.A. (1991), "Leadership: Do Traits Matter?" *The Academy of Management Executive*, 5(2), 48–60. Two cognitive traits identified by these researchers, cognitive ability and knowledge of the business, are not discussed in this article, which focuses on motivational traits.

KLIUCHEVSKII, V.O. (1987), *Collected Works*. Vol. 1. Moscow: Mysl', 312.

KONONOV, A. (1990), Letter to the editor of *Sobesednik*, 31 August. Translated in Riordan, J. and Bridger, S. eds., (1992), *Dear Comrade Editor: Readers' Letters to the Soviet Press Under Perestroika*, Bloomington, IN: Indiana University Press, 230.

KUROMIYA, H. (1984), "*Edinonachalie* and the Soviet Industrial Manager 1928–1937," *Soviet Studies*, 36(2), 185–204.

LASOV, A. (1993), cited in Auerbach, J. "Coming of Age in Capitalistic Russia," *The Boston Globe* (January 4), 20, 21.

LAWRENCE, P.R. and VLACHOUTSICOS, C.A. (1990), "Managerial Patterns: Differences and Commonalities," in Lawrence, P.R. and Vlachoutsicos, C.A. *Behind the Factory Walls: Decision Making in Soviet and U.S. Enterprises*. Boston: Harvard Business School Press, 271–86.

LEFEBVRE, V.D. (1982), *Algebra of Conscience: A Comparative Analysis of Western and Soviet Ethical Systems*. Boston: D. Reidel Publishing Company.

LIKHACHEV, D.S. (1987a), "*Trevogi Sovesti*" ("Pangs of Conscience"), *Literaturnaia Gazeta* (January 1).

LIKHACHEV, D.S. (1987b), "*Ot Pokaianiia—K Deistviiu*" ("From Repentance—to Action"), *Literaturnaia Gazeta*, September 9. For a summary in English of these two articles by Likhachev, see Krasnov, V. (1991), "Dmitrii Likhachev on Morality, Religion, and Russian

Heritage," *Russia Beyond Communism: A Chronicle of National Rebirth.* Boulder, CO: Westview Press, 81–86.

MAYNARD, J. (1948), *Russia in Flux.* New York: Macmillan, 30.

MCCARTHY, D.J. and PUFFER, S.M. (1992), "Perestroika at the Plant Level: Managers' Job Attitudes and Views of Decision Making in the Former USSR," *Columbia Journal of World Business,* 27(1), 86–99.

MCCARTHY, D.J., PUFFER, S.M. and SHEKSHNIA, S.V. (1993), "The Resurgence of an Entrepreneurial Class in Russia," *Journal of Management Inquiry,* 2(2), 125–37.

MEAD, M. (1955), *Soviet Attitudes Toward Authority.* New York: William Morrow and Company.

Moscow Magazine (1991/92), "Moscow Magazine's Top 50," *Moscow Magazine,* (December/January) 52–57.

PARKER, R. (1990), "Inside the 'Collapsing' Soviet Economy," *The Atlantic Monthly,* (June), 68–76.

PUFFER, S.M. (1990), Unpublished field notes for *Behind the Factory Walls: Decision Making in Soviet and U.S. Enterprises.* Boston, MA: Harvard Business School Press. Notes dated 1988.

———— and OZIRA, V.I. (1990), "Capital Investment Decisions" in Lawrence, P.R. and Vlachoutsicos, C.A. eds. *Behind the Factory Walls: Decision Making in Soviet and U.S. Enterprises.* Boston: Harvard Business School Press, 183–226.

———— (1981), "Inside a Soviet Management Institute," *California Management Review,* 24(1), 90–6.

ROBERTS, P.C. and LAFOLLETTE, K. (1990), *Meltdown: Inside the Soviet Economy.* Washington, DC: Cato Institute, 97.

SHAW, J.B., FISHER, C.D. and RANDOLPH, W.A. (1991), "From Maternalism to Accountability: The Changing Cultures of Ma Bell and Mother Russia," *The Academy of Management Executive,* 5(1), 7–20.

SHEVARDNADZE, E. (1992), cited in "The Dark Forces are Growing Stronger," *Time* (October 5), 64, 65.

SHMELEV, N. (1990), Speech to the Third Congress of People's Deputies, March 12, reported in *Foreign Broadcast Information Service,* (March 14).

———— (1991), "New Anxieties," in Jones, A. and Moskoff, W. eds., *The Great Market Debate in Soviet Economics.* Armonk, NY: M.E. Sharpe, 3–35.

SOBCHAK, A. (1990), cited in Smith, H. *The New Russians.* New York: Random House, 204.

STERLIGOV, H. (1992), cited in Klebnikov, P. "A Market Grows in Russia," *Forbes* (June 8), 79–82.

TATELBAUM, I. (1992), unpublished interview by Kara Danehy, Northeastern University, Boston, August.

TULLAR, W.L. (1992), "Cultural Transformation: Democratization and Russian Entrepreneurial Motives." Paper presented at the Academy of Management meetings, Las Vegas.

VAKAR, N. (1962), *The Taproot of Soviet Society.* New York, NY: Harper, 47.

VLACHOUTSICOS, C.A. (1990), "Key Soviet Management Concepts for the American Reader," in Lawrence, P.R. and Vlachoutsicos, C.A. eds. *Behind the Factory Walls: Decision-Making in Soviet and U.S. Enterprises.* Boston: Harvard Business School Press, 76.

VOLOKHOV, V. (1993), "*Ubivaiut Vsekh Podriad*" ("People Are Being Murdered One After the Other"), *Novoe Russkoe Slovo* (February 13–14), 15.

Endnotes

1. Many Russians believe that there are specific traits characterizing successful women managers. These traits are discussed in S.M. Puffer, "Women Managers in the Former USSR: A Case of Too Much Equality?" in N.J. Adler and D.N. Izraeli, eds., *Competitive Frontiers: Women Managers in a Global Economy* (Cambridge, MA: Blackwell, 1993).

2. This term is taken from D. Granick, *The Red Executive* (Garden City, NY: Doubleday Anchor, 1962).

3. The discussion of the communist period will focus mostly on senior executives in manufacturing organizations, since the industrial sector was the most emphasized and the most prestigious. Conditions in other sectors such as services and R&D were largely comparable.

4. We will look at executives who are transforming their state-owned enterprises into various forms of private and employee ownership, as well as entrepreneurs who have founded start-up businesses. In 1992, 46,000 enterprises were wholly or partially privatized, bringing the total to six percent of Russian industry (*Economic Newsletter,* Russian Research Center, 16(6), February 20, 1993). Despite this small percentage, privatization efforts are expected to increase dramatically over the next few years. For a comparison of managers in the former Soviet Union with Eastern European managers, see A. Shama, "Management Under Fire: The Transformation of Managers in the Soviet Union and Eastern Europe," *The Academy of Management Executive,* 7(1), 1993, 22–35.

Reading

Management Development:
An African Focus

Merrick L. Jones

Anyone interested in issues of Third World development is painfully aware of the complexities, contradictions, and cruel paradoxes involved. Recent events in Africa have thrown the issues into stark focus. Africa is a cockpit of turbulent change, where the transition from traditional societies to modern nation states confronts those involved with painful and complex puzzles. The myriad problems facing the continent are reflected daily in Western newspapers. Great human tragedies unfold as whole nations are devastated by droughts and other natural calamities. Famine, population growth, deforestation, the advancing deserts, civil wars, border disputes, military coups, political intrigues, one-party states, tribalism, guerrilla movements: The catalogue is reported with scant sympathy—indeed, it sometimes seems, with gleeful smugness. Meanwhile, the peoples of Africa struggle with the awful natural and man-made problems that confront them in building nation states within the arbitrary boundaries bequeathed to them by the departed colonial powers. No one can doubt that it will be a long and supremely difficult struggle. There have been, and will be, many failed experiments, many dead ends, many setbacks in the process. But one central reality seems inescapable: In coping with acute scarcity of resources and lack of developed infrastructure, great skills of management and organization will be imperative.

The question is: Will the importation of management concepts and practices from the industrialized West meet Africa's needs? Questions concerning the transferability across nations of management concepts and practices are complex and controversial. There is as yet no consensus about the nature of the arguments involved or about how empirical data can usefully be obtained and compared.

Onyemelukwe (1973) considers the educational implications, asserting that "The belief is that whatever is not going well can always be rectified by training. The result is a staggering investment in foreign-orientated training schemes with little in the way of return in investment." And:

> Looking through courses and lectures on management organised in various parts of Africa by universities and institutes of management, one is faced with a galaxy of do-it-yourself kits and

shorthand prescriptions. . . . it is the refusal of many authors and researchers in the field of management to give a significant place to social and cultural factors that limits the usefulness of their work.

In this paper I consider some of the issues in relation to an investigation of managerial thinking in one African country, Malawi. In particular, I focus on the data concerning the way Malawian managers think about their work, and implications for management education and training. Very briefly, the study involved 105 Malawian senior and middle-level managers from both the private and public sectors in a questionnaire survey designed to elicit their thinking on aspects of their work, especially their satisfactions and their relationships with subordinates. The questionnaire was based on an instrument used originally by Haire, Ghiselli, and Porter (1966) in 14 countries, and subsequently in similar studies in many other parts of the world (including 3 African countries). In addition, 47 managers were involved in a semistructured interviewing survey, which was intended to focus on similar issues and to provide insights on the contextual fabric of the Malawian manager's world. The aims of the study were:

1. to investigate managerial thinking about a limited number of important issues in a national context (Malawi);

2. to compare data from this investigation in a practical way with those produced by similar studies in other countries;

3. to examine factors in the Malawian context that might account for similarities and differences between the thinking of the Malawian managers and that of other managers;

4. to relate these findings to the education and training of managers in Malawi, and to consider their appropriateness; and

5. to consider possible areas for further investigation.

In this paper my intention is to focus mainly on item 4. Before considering the data from the study and their implications for the education and training of Malawian managers, it might be useful to present *very briefly*, some relevant information about the country.

Malawi is located in southern central Africa, bordering Zambia to the west, Tanzania to the north east, and Mozambique. By African standards it is not a big country, its area totaling 118,500 square kilometers, of which about one-fifth comprises the great lake that dominates the country, Lake Malawi. However, Malawi's population density is about four times as high as the African average, at 47 persons per square kilometer overall. At the time of the last population census, in 1982, Malawi's population stood at a little over 6.5 million.

In common with other nations in this part of Africa, Malawi has a turbulent history, experiencing long periods of stability and at other times the eruptions of migratory peoples entering the region from other population centers. Although the details of these movements are still being elaborated, it is clear that the great lake, the third biggest in Africa, has been a focal point for centuries in this part of the continent. In more recent times, the territory that now constitutes Malawi was subjected to the depredations of slave traders operating from the Indian Ocean coast, and to the influx of Ngoni peoples from the south, driven to their northward odyssey by the turmoil, in what is now the Republic of South Africa, caused by the rise of the great Zulu empire. Another powerful influence was the coming of European missionaries and explorers in the latter half of the nineteenth century. As the scramble for Africa divided the continent into spheres of influence for the European powers at the turn of the century, the area of the lake eventually became the British colony of Nyasaland.

Unlike other British colonies in Africa, Nyasaland offered no exploitable natural resources and did not attract large numbers of European settlers. Evidence suggests that Britain's attitude toward its colony of the lake was at least ambivalent, and possibly at times downright unenthusiastic. An attempt in 1953 to form a federation in central Africa consisting of Northern Rhodesia (now Zambia), Southern Rhodesia (now Zimbabwe), and Nyasaland was doomed to failure. The independent nation of Malawi emerged after a long and complex struggle that had its roots early in the present century, but developed as a significant movement during the 1950s.

The "wind of change" was then gathering strength in southern Africa, and the British colonies there were experiencing a common, if individually manifested, movement toward self-government. For Malawi the crucial moment came when Dr. H.K. Banda returned to Nyasaland, in July 1958, after having lived and practiced medicine in the USA, Europe, and Ghana for many years. From that day, events were set in train that led, with historical inevitability, to independence from Britain in July 1964 and, in 1966, to the status of a republic within the Commonwealth. Dr. Banda became President (and in 1971 was made the Life President) of the new Republic of Malawi. The story of Dr. Banda's apparently historic destiny in liberating the country of his birth from its colonial masters is extraordinary, and his continued dominance as leader of Malawi is an overwhelming factor in the nation's development. Since this reality forms a part of the national context in which Malawian organizations function and Malawian managers work, it may be useful to explore briefly the nature of Malawi's political milieu.

Since the 1960s we have observed the achievement of independence by most of Africa's former colonial territories. The dominant picture we in the West receive of Africa through our media is one of a continent in a turbulent transition, with national regimes apparently changing, sometimes violently, with bewildering frequency. Some states seem to have tried almost every conceivable form of government, from multiparty democracy to military dictatorship, in search of a suitable system. Malawi has been notably absent in reports of such developments. The overwhelmingly powerful and pervasive influence of the Life President on all facets of Malawian life is important, because we could expect that the consequences of such a situation would inevitably include the ways in which organizations operate and managers behave.

Turning to Malawi's economic position, the country is, in terms of per capita income, one of the world's poorest nations. At independence the country had a small industrial sector and a rudimentary economic infrastructure. Few exploitable mineral resources have been located in any quantity. The policies of the government since independence therefore have emphasized the development of agricultural, transport, and communications infrastructure. As a landlocked country, Malawi faces problems, sometimes acute, in routing its crucial agricultural exports and its imports. Problems of transporting goods great distances across difficult terrain are frequently aggravated by climatic conditions and guerrilla activity. Since Malawi's independence, the protracted war in Rhodesia (now Zimbabwe) and the continuing civil insurrection in Mozambique have presented intractable difficulties for Malawian administrators and businessmen.

Malawi, by African standards, enjoys a good climate for a variety of agricultural activities and is blessed with relatively productive soils. There has been impressive development in the production of a number of cash crops, including tobacco, tea, coffee, and sugar, which form the bulk of the country's exports. In addition, greater yields of subsistence crops, importantly maize, have been consistently achieved. Malawi is one of the few African countries that are largely self-sufficient in staple foodstuffs.

Although the industrial base remains modest in size, development in this sector also has been impressive. The following figures relating to paid employment in Malawi (1980) are relevant:

- Total in paid employment—294,707
- In professional, technical, and related posts—21,716 (7.4%)
- In managerial/administrative occupations—4,127 (1.5%).

These figures, supplied by the Manpower Planning Unit, Office of the President and Cabinet, relate to December 1980 and are the most recent available in this form. By 1983 (the latest figures available), the number of individuals in paid employment was approximately 387,000, over 50% of whom were engaged in agriculture.

MALAWIAN MANAGERS

It would be neither possible nor relevant to report in this paper the details of findings from the interviewing and questionnaire surveys. My intention is to put forward some fairly direct statements about Malawian managers and the organizations in which they work, and to consider their implications for management development. These statements appear to reflect as directly as possible the data produced by the investigation.

In general terms, management education and training have attracted some rather critical comments, and it may be useful to look very briefly at this wider context before we focus on the Malawian situation.

Safavi (1981), reporting on a project involving the 57 countries and territories of Africa during a 4-year study of management education and development programs, paints a "gloomy picture" of "a number of areas of conflict between classroom and culture, between Western theory and African reality." A number of observers have similar concerns. Nyerere (cited by Onyemelukwe 1973) has observed that the training of African managers appears to have been designed to divorce them from the societies it is supposed to equip them to serve. Hofstede (1980) claims that Western management theories, although widely taught, are not practiced by non-Western managers. Successful managers "perform a cultural transposition of ideas . . . there is no single formula for management development to be used in different cultures" (p. 380); there is a need to ascertain what constitutes "success" in a particular culture. Hyden (1983) comments on the absurdity of what he calls "technique peddling" by Western management consultants in Africa, exemplified by bizarre attempts to undertake Organization Development (OD) consultancies (with their accompanying American individualistic, humanistic values) in African organizations: "The African personality is full and wholesome in a sense that does not tally with the demands of systematic rationality." Yet African managers "have been moulded in a type of management thinking that makes them strangers in their own environment" (p. 159).

It is difficult to dispute the view that strategies and methods used to educate and train African managers have generally been based on Western theories and practices, with little, if any, consideration of the environments in which African organizations function. What can be done to change the situation? Simply asserting, as so many observers do, that management education and training must take cognizance of the environmental realities of Africa does not get us very far. Do the data from this study of Malawian senior and middle managers provide any pointers? It is perhaps appropriate to preface the discussion of the issues with two notes of caution.

First, it is important to avoid the common assumption that education and training can be relied upon to accomplish changes in human behavior and thinking. There is a line of reasoning (or rather, assumption) that:

TRAINING
(usually equated with classroom-based courses)
↓
INDIVIDUAL LEARNING
↓
IMPROVED INDIVIDUAL JOB PERFORMANCE
↓
IMPROVED ORGANIZATIONAL PERFORMANCE

At each level the assumption can be challenged, and experience indicates that, without positive managerial action, the training of individuals rarely leads to improved organizational performance. I am therefore conscious of the need to exercise caution in advancing ideas about the education and training of Malawian managers, especially since I believe that the causes of important aspects of their thinking are to be found in fundamental national sociocultural and political elements.

Second, there is at present no way of judging with any degree of accuracy the extent to which Malawian organizations and management have developed distinctive features. Malawi was a British colony, and is now a member of the Commonwealth. Its systems (for example, in education, communications, industry, commerce, technology, health care, public utility provision, and government organization) would be familiar to British expatriates and visitors. The major language of business and government is English. Most Malawian administrators and executives will have been trained on the Western model, many of them in Britain; and, as the data confirm, most have worked with expatriate (predominantly British) managers, often taking over from an expatriate boss. The study has shown that traditional modes of social and family organization still inhere in contemporary Malawi as fundamental aspects of the life of individuals, even those, such as managers, who have moved out of the rural subsistence economy to paid employment in the expanding urban sector. To ask the question "How Westernized are Malawian organizations and managers?" is not to anticipate a precise answer, but to realize that more research will be necessary before we can even begin to make useful judgments about this important issue.

Using the data from this study, supplemented by those from other relevant studies, I propose the following general statements about Malawian managers and the organizations in which they work, which may serve as a useful base for a discussion of relevant strategies for management education and training:

1. Malawian organizations function in an environment of acute resource scarcity, economic uncertainty, and highly centralized political power.

2. These organizations tend to retain the major characteristics of structures developed in the colonial era, namely, rather rigid bureaucratic, rule-bound hierarchies.

3. Organizations tend to be viewed by society as a whole as having a wider mission than is generally understood in the West, being expected to provide socially desirable benefits such as employment, housing, transport, and assistance with important social rituals and ceremonies; considerations of profit maximization and efficiency may be viewed as secondary or incidental.

4. There is among Malawian workers a generally instrumental orientation toward work, involving high expectations of the benefits, to the worker and his extended family, that employment brings, but less in the way of loyalty and commitment to the organization (or profession) that is said to typify the employer–employee relationship in the West.

5. There is in Malawian society an emphasis on prestige and status differences, creating relationships of dependency, which in organizations finds expression in wide differentials between organizational levels, particularly between managers and workers, extreme deference to and dependence upon one's boss, and a paternal, concerned, but strict style of management.

6. The collectivist values of Malawian society are reflected in organizations in the high regard managers have for their subordinates as people; in a view of workers as a network of people rather than as human resources; in an emphasis on maintaining relationships rather than on providing opportunities for individual development; in an emphasis on "highly ritualised interpersonal interactions which often place greater value on the observance of protocol than the accomplishment of work-related tasks" (Blunt and Popoola 1985, p. 159); in a desire by workers for a close relationship with the boss; and in a reluctance by managers either to accept individual blame for mistakes or to criticize individual subordinates in a direct manner.

7. Malawian managers tend to view their authority, professional competence, and information as personal possessions, rather than impersonal concomitants of their organizational role, and as a source of status and prestige.

8. This, coupled with the emphasis on the wide differential—in status, power, education, experience, and perceived ability—between managers and workers makes Malawian managers very reluctant to delegate authority, to share information, and to involve subordinates (who may be perceived as a potential source of threat) in decision-making processes.

9. Malawian managers regard security as an important factor in their work, to be reinforced by unchanging structures, detailed procedures, and close supervision of subordinates.

10. Malawian managers desire a good relationship with their boss, whom they perceive as a key figure, but frequently find this to be a problematic relationship because the boss manages them in a manner similar to what

they employ with their own subordinates; this may find expression in dissatisfaction with their perceived opportunities for autonomy and self-actualization.

11. Individualistic (as opposed to universalistic) criteria tend to influence organizational behavior; hence, insecurity is increased because decisions cannot be consistently predicted, and blame for mistakes tends to be assigned on a personalized basis.

12. Malawian managers have constantly to be sensitive to political pressures and aware of developments that might affect them as power coalitions change.

13. Malawian managers tend to recognize their role in achieving organizational performance (this, on the basis of our limited data, does not seem to apply to civil servants to the same degree), and to emphasize their individual professional or technical expertise rather than their "managerial" functions.

14. Malawian managers have a keen awareness of the necessity to acknowledge and manage their wider social obligations to extended family and kinship systems, and of the possible conflicts that may thereby exist in relation to their formal organizational roles.

15. Malawian managers often find their relationships with expatriate bosses and colleagues problematic and tend to view expatriate executives as lacking in the sensitivity they view as essential, especially in their dealings with workers.

The data from the study appear to confirm that the demands of formal organizations create tensions and conflicts for Malawian managers. It is well understood that the processes of industrialization on the Western model demand the utilization of technical and scientific knowledge, but it is perhaps less clearly recognized that the use of such knowledge depends somewhat on the acceptance of the values and "world view" that are its sociocultural foundation.

The data from this study provide several examples of the tensions and problems that can occur when Western management ideas and practices are transplanted into a non-Western environment. There is, for instance, the apparent contradiction that Malawi is a newly independent nation in the process of rapid change, a characteristic shared by all African states to a greater or lesser degree and likely to continue. Yet the organizations that are to be instrumental in bringing about and managing change are, as a number of commentators have observed, generally bureaucratic, rigid, and rule-bound. On the level of managerial motivation, there is another apparent contradiction: Malawian managers reflect in many aspects of their thinking African traditional, communalistic values, yet they stress the importance of their needs for autonomy and self-actualization at work (the individualistic focus more characteristic of Western societies).

Jenkins (1982) and Rutherford (1981) in studies of Malawian managers, remark on the strong, expressed need for structure, guidelines, and clear direction (reflecting a preoccupation with security). This apparent acceptance of "universalistic" criteria for behavior in organizations is contrasted with the evidence that managers regularly bypass organizational structures and make decisions on the basis of "particularistic" (i.e., what the managers in the study referred to as "personalized") criteria.

EDUCATION AND TRAINING OF MALAWIAN MANAGERS

Organizational behavior is influenced by a complex set of interrelated factors. The Western notion of "rational" behavior is itself the product of such factors, but it is not automatically applicable in other contexts. What appears to a Western observer of African organizations to be "irrational," on closer examination can be seen to reflect a set of values that are different from, but no less valid than, those of the West. For this reason I take the view, in considering the education and training of Malawian managers, that it would be unrealistic and inappropriate to advance prescriptive proposals for changing the existing realities of Malawian organizational life.

The following propositions are intended rather to accept the sociocultural, economic, and political realities and to suggest how Malawian managers might be assisted to be effective and, if they so desire, to change existing systems and practices:

1. Because the Malawian environment is less stable and predictable than is the case in the industrialized nations, "the probability of planned actions going wrong is high . . . margins of error are likely to be particularly large" (Hyden 1983, p. 157). It is therefore important to recognize that the use of Western planning techniques cannot be assumed to guarantee any anticipated outcome. Malawian managers will need to reflect on experiences, since independence, of planning and its effectiveness, and to identify the particular factors that have influenced success or failure.

2. There is a need to acknowledge the collectivist values that inhere in contemporary Malawian society and to consider which Western management practices and techniques might tend to contradict them. For example, it is not difficult to understand why Western performance appraisal and Management by Objectives schemes may find intellectual acceptance by Malawian managers, yet fail in practice. Seddon (1985) has observed that in many African societies it is a sign of weakness to admit incompetence or ignorance. Mistakes are believed to be beyond the control of individuals, and the maintenance of "face" is of crucial importance. There is a highly developed sensitivity to individual criticism, "the most powerful contingencies determining behavior (informally) are 'social evaluations'— pride and shame." In my study there was considerable evidence of a reluctance by managers to criticize individuals.

   In such circumstances, the use of Western practices for assessing individual performance appears to be inappropriate. For Malawian managers to have to learn such practices without a comprehensive analysis of their chances of success and their consequences in terms of Malawian values seems both impractical and wasteful.

3. Similar considerations apply to teaching Malawian managers about the benefits claimed, in the Western context, for delegation of authority, sharing of information, and a generally more participative management style. In the situation I have described, such practices can be seen to contradict many Malawian social values, and have little chance at present of successful adoption. It is important, however, that Malawian managers clearly understand the consequences of their current management style, which (1) tends to push decisions upward in the organizational hierarchy; (2) involves managers in routine, trivial activities; (3) hinders the sharing of information within the organization, thus possibly reducing its capacity to

anticipate and cope with change; (4) encourages highly dependent subordinate behavior; (5) reduces opportunities for subordinates to engage in more interesting work; and (6) on the evidence of my interview survey, appears to be a source of dissatisfaction for managers in terms of relationships with their bosses.

4. Malawian managers require highly developed political skills, both in monitoring developments that may affect them, as "particularistic" criteria influence decision makers inside and outside their employing organizations, and in their relationships with organizational superiors, colleagues, and subordinates. Such skills are not necessarily a major focus in Western management development strategies.

5. Malawian managers require well-developed diplomatic skills, particularly in two contexts. First, their bosses expect them to behave in a deferential manner, far more than is the case in Western views of such a relationship. It seems important that the implications of this type of relationship should be examined in relation to organizational performance. If managers are to be able to cope with change and to provide solutions to emerging problems, will their extreme deference to, and dependence on, more senior executives not inhibit them? Malawian managers expressed dissatisfaction with this relationship and wanted more opportunities (clearly delineated, nevertheless) for autonomy. They also wanted their bosses to behave in a more predictable (i.e., "universalistic") manner and to give them recognition for good performance. In such circumstances of dependency and unfulfilled expectations, Malawian managers need diplomatic and influencing abilities of a high order. Secondly, as we have seen, Malawian managers are often faced with demands from outside the organization, from extended family and kinship groups and (less frequently) from the Party. Such demands may well conflict with the manager's organizational role, and he will need to be skilled in explaining the demands and limitations under which he operates in the organization.

6. When Malawian managers are taught the paramount Western organizational values of effective and efficient use of scarce resources, it is important that they consciously consider and understand the implications of implementing these values in Malawian society, where there is a greater concern for social relationships than for performance, where there are social expectations about the role of organizations that are greater than is customary in the West, and where the notion of considering the individual as a "resource" is strange.

7. Malawian workers tend to have higher expectations about the organization's ability and willingness to accept a degree of responsibility for their welfare and development than is the case in the industrialized West. At the same time, there is a more instrumental attitude toward work, involving fewer considerations of loyalty to the organization. In these circumstances, managers could well consider the implications in terms of employee motivation. Western assumptions about the desirability of self-expression and fulfillment appear to be inappropriate, and uncritical teaching of Western motivation theories to Malawian managers needs to be challenged.

8. The managers in this study indicated that they derived considerable satisfaction from the use of their professional or technical competence, and

were generally concerned about performance (this was decidedly less so in the case of the Malawian civil servants in the study). These strengths might be used in developing managers' understanding of their more directly managerial functions if it can be shown that job satisfaction can be enhanced when management work is viewed as requiring equally prestigious, admirable skills, and that effective performance is more likely when professional and technical expertise is reinforced by managerial capabilities.

9. Although the presence of expatriate managers will lessen in significance, it is at present an area of concern for many Malawian managers. Since it is not realistic to expect that expatriate executives will be selected primarily on the basis of their cultural sensitivity, it might be useful if Malawian managers were helped to understand more about the backgrounds, perspectives, and values of the expatriates. This may go some way in enabling Malawian managers to handle their relationships with expatriates effectively.

STRATEGIES AND METHODS

Turning to considerations of appropriate methods for education and training of Malawian managers, I suggest that the foregoing discussion indicates that the following *outcomes* are priorities:

- In an environment of turbulent change, learning should become a conscious and continuous process for Malawian managers.
- Malawian managers should develop a profound awareness of, and sensitivity to, the sociocultural context in which they operate.
- They should also have a clear understanding of the implicit demands of Western management ideas and practices, and of the facets of Malawian society that might be congruent and incongruent with such demands (for example, deference and dependent relationships).
- There should be a deliberate and reasoned rejection of the uncritical adoption of Western (or other alien) organization and management theories.
- Managers and educators should acknowledge, analyze, and reflect upon the experience of Malawian organizations and develop from it indigenous explanatory concepts.
- Malawian managers should develop more confidence in the validity of their own experiences and their views on management (rather than deferring to outsiders).

When we consider how such outcomes might be achieved through education and training, several factors have to be borne in mind. First, just as Western management ideas must be critically examined in the light of Malawian sociocultural realities, Western notions concerning the education and training of managers have to be understood in terms of the assumptions they make about people and the values that influence them. Many current Western ideas about management development can be seen clearly to reflect values such as individual responsibility for self-actualization; learning as problem solving, involving puzzlement, perturbation, even discomfort for the learner; the value of self-discovered knowledge as opposed to prescribed knowledge; a view of the teacher–learner relationship as involving interdependence and assumed equality; development as involving risk and change for learners; a view of the professional as an individual of independent judgment, self-confident in his relationship with his employing organization; and an increasing degreee of openness in relationships. Contrasted to this I have detailed Malawian values that might be expected to influence management education and training, including the collectivist (as opposed to Western individualist) nature of social relationships; greater awareness of hierarchical levels and deference to authority, which, according to Clarke (1981, p. 240), is expressed in the teacher–learner relationship by "a greater need (by the learner) for clear and unequivocal direction . . . and regular face-to-face contact"; education seen as a way to enhance status rather than for personal growth; learning viewed as a way of avoiding risk by acquiring additional information, to be hoarded and protected as a source of power; and training viewed as a threat rather than an opportunity for self-actualization if it involves an admission of ignorance or shortcomings.

In addition, managers indicated in the questionnaire survey that the most effective ways in which they had learned their managerial abilities were: by doing, by discussing real problems with colleagues, through training by the boss, by observing effective managers, and by analyzing their successes and failures.

This seems to suggest that approaches to management education and training in Malawi should include the following general criteria:

1. As Hyden (1985) has noted: "For a manager to be effective he needs to be sensitive to and work in response to his proximate environment. Many African managers lack a grasp of how they can combine good management with effective response to their environment" (p. 59). People are intuitively and experientially aware of their environment, but it is suggested that managers need to be helped to develop a fuller understanding of and sensitivity to the sociocultural facets of their environment that affect their roles. This will involve teaching strategies that draw upon the experiences of managers and encourage them to reflect on the implications for future action.

2. It must be made clear in organizational policies that the organization accepts a substantial share of responsibility for the development of individuals, and that further education and training do not imply that a manager is incompetent or lacking in some area. It must be understood that management development does not involve a risk for the individual and that the learning environment will be supportive.

3. Learning strategies and methods should reflect the collectivist nature of Malawian society. This would imply that methods should be avoided that focus on individual performance (especially shortcomings). Small-group methods and other supportive techniques seem to be appropriate.

4. There needs to be an explicit focus on continuous learning from experience. Learning opportunities in the organization (such as deputizing for an absent boss, introduction of structural or technological change, launching of a new product, coping with unanticipated difficulties) should be identified and utilized. This will demand that attention be given to developing skills in analyzing successes and failures in a conscious, structured way.

5. Management education and training should help managers understand the processes of organizational change. As noted earlier, the structures of Malawian organizations tend predominantly to be rigidly bureaucratic (embodying security and stability in an environment of accelerating change). Managers need to understand the implications of such organiza-

tional patterns for the effective performance of the roles Malawian society expects organizations to undertake.

6. Managers should be trained in coaching skills, in order to be fully effective in developing subordinates. Organizations need to ensure that the job descriptions of managers include the coaching of subordinates as a priority function.

7. Management development strategies should include structured, on-the-job developmental activities.

8. The group-oriented methods and problem-solving focus of Action Learning suggest that it might be worthwhile to experiment with this approach to management development. Revan's (1982) notion of "comrades in adversity" may address the needs of Malawian managers for security and social interaction while enabling them to identify real problems and to use their shared experience to develop solutions.

CONCLUSION

In the literature about the transfer of Western management concepts and practices, one can detect a developing dichotomy. Some writers assert that the imperatives of organizational life are so powerful, so pervasive, that the "culture of production" will sweep aside local variations in culture, values, and behavior. Others would claim, on the contrary, that in some countries the culture is so distinctive and so enduring that imported notions about organizations and their management will be radically modified or even rejected. The findings from the study of Malawian managers upon which this paper is based provide evidence that both tendencies are present. The "convergence–divergence" debate will continue as cross-cultural research adds to the stock of data for comparison.

For management educators this is inconvenient. It demands that strategies for management development should recognize the complex and distinctive realities of the contexts in which managers perform. The search for relevance will, I suspect, be a crucial task.

References

BLUNT, P. and POPOOLA, O. (1985), *Personnel Management in Africa*. London: Longmans.

CLARKE, R. (1981), "Independent Learning in an African Country, with Special Reference to the Certificate of Adult Studies in the University of Malawi," Ph.D. thesis, University of Manchester, Department of Adult and Higher Education, 240.

HAIRE, M., GHISELLI, E. and PORTER, L. (1966), *Managerial Thinking: An International Study*. New York: Wiley.

HOFSTEDE, G. (1980), *Culture's Consequences: International Differences in Work-related Values*. London: Sage.

HYDEN, G. (1983), *No Shortcuts to Progress: African Development Management in Perspective*. London: Heinemann.

JENKINS, C. (1982), "Management Problems and Management Education in Developing Economies: A Case Study of Malawi," working paper. University of Aston, Management Centre.

ONYEMELUKWE, C. (1973), *Man and Management in Contemporary Africa*. London: Longmans.

REVANS, R. (1982), *The Origins and Growth of Action Learning*. Bromley: Chartwell-Bratt.

RUTHERFORD, P. (1981), "Attitudes of Malawian Managers: Some Recent Research," unpublished paper, University of Malawi.

SAFAVI, F. (1981), "A Model of Management Education in Africa," *Academy of Management Review*, 6(2), 319–31.

SEDDON, J. (1985), "The Development and Indigenisation of Third World Business: African Values in the Workplace," in Hammond, V., ed. *Current Research in Management*. London: Frances Pinter/ATM.

Employee Relations Issues
for U.S. Companies in Mexico

Charles R. Greer
Gregory K. Stephens

Unions are a major force in the Mexican business environment and U.S. companies and managers must be prepared for cultural differences in managing employee relations south of the border. Levels of union membership are higher in Mexico than in the United States, accounting for at least 25 to 30% of the labor force. As with U.S. unions, the potential impact of Mexican unions may be more far-reaching than membership statistics indicate, since some Mexican unions negotiate agreements at the industry level that cover nonunion employees as well. Furthermore, although Mexico is a low-wage country in which employers currently have a power advantage, unions constitute an important influence in the Mexican managerial environment.[1]

THE MEXICAN LABOR
RELATIONS ENVIRONMENT

Political patronage and union corruption are generally perceived as widespread and entrenched in Mexico's labor environment. The *Confederación de Trabajadores de Mexico* (CTM), the most influential of Mexico's labor federations, has benefitted enormously in the past from a quasi-official relationship with the powerful *Partido Revolucionario Institucional* (PRI), the historically dominant political party in Mexico. As in any symbiotic relationship, the CTM's reliance on a political power base constitutes a two-edged sword; union power and influence suffer if the political party's influence wanes or if it withdraws its support for the union, as recent electoral results suggest may be happening today (Rohter 1988).

Because the CTM's association with the PRI often produces greater allegiances to the interests of the government and business, its affiliates can function virtually as company unions. As a result, many of the individuals we interviewed (both labor and management) felt strongly that the CTM affiliates are unresponsive to the interests and welfare of their members. As one indicated:

> Given the way Mexican unions organize at many companies, it is quite possible that Mexican workers may not feel represented even while the company is being told differently by union and government officials. . . . Be aware that just because it is called a 'union' it doesn't necessarily function the way unions do elsewhere.

In a remarkable example of this kind of disregard for workers, we were told of instances in which CTM-affiliated unions "organized" workers without their knowledge or consent. For example, in describing a recent strike at a maquiladora plant, one interviewee stated that the employees were unaware that they were "represented" by a CTM-affiliated union. Many Mexicans perceive the CTM and its affiliates as vehicles for corruption and repression and, as noted, their primary loyalty may be to the governmental administration, and not to union members. Their perceptions, as Collier stated, reflect

> the role of violence, corruption, and bossism, which perpetuate a nondemocratic, coopted, sometimes state-imposed union leadership that is not responsive to the grass roots but [is] dependent upon the state and in league with it to control the working-class base (Collier 1992).

Such repression was charged in recent complaints that the Sony Corporation's Mexican subsidiary, Magneticos de Mexico, collaborated with CTM officials to suppress employees' efforts in Nuevo Laredo to elect officers of their own choosing who would better represent them than the CTM's slate of officers. Allegations of illegal actions included employee intimidation and reprisals such as suspensions, demotions, and terminations (U.S. National Administrative Office 1995). Similarly, we were told of another recent situation in which workers who were dissatisfied with conditions at a U.S.-owned maquiladora plant formed a committee to present their interests to management. Following a one-week strike, a settlement was eventually negotiated by the workers' committee and the company's management, while the CTM officials from the company's union were essentially by-passed in the negotiations. As a result of these proceedings, some of the CTM union's officials were replaced by members of the committee.

Not all union corruption and misdeeds are outgrowths of political patronage, and numerous examples have been documented in the news media of corrupt and illegal practices by organized labor forces in Mexico. Yet, while both the Salinas and Zedillo administrations have attempted to reduce union corruption, recent events have exposed lingering problems at high levels of the administration, indicating the need for ongoing and significant reform efforts. In the long run, corrupt practices may weaken a union's power and influence. Indeed, anti-union sentiment has increased in Mexico as a consequence of widely perceived corruption coupled with failures to obtain desired benefits for members (Middlebrook 1988). Nevertheless, a number of additional factors have the potential to play pivotal and influential roles in Mexico's unstable and rapidly changing labor environment. Among these are:

- inter-union conflicts and rivalries,
- growing public awareness of the relative deprivation of Mexican versus non-Mexican workers,
- management opposition and resistance to unionization,
- cooperative efforts between Mexican and American unions,
- the North American Free Trade Agreement (NAFTA), and
- the transforming leverage of emerging work technologies.

Inter- and Intra-Union Competition

Union membership is somewhat concentrated, as 80% of union members are accounted for by only nine unions.[2] At present, jurisdictional conflicts are increasing within and between Mexico's competing and powerful unions and within its labor federations. As a result, management-employee relations and negotiations have often become enmeshed in and adversely affected by these conflicts. For example, the Sony case submission to the U.S. National Administrative Office (NAO), referred to earlier, was framed in the context of an intra-union struggle taking place throughout the city of Nuevo Laredo in which maquiladora workers were challenging the CTM leadership for more democratic representation within the union. Much of the inter-union strife is occurring between independent unions affiliated with the *Frente Auténtico del Trabajo* and the more established, but less worker-oriented, unions affiliated with the CTM and other labor federations. Our interviewees indicated that, in the interior of Mexico and especially in Mexico City, workers perceive that the *Frente Auténtico del Trabajo* unions offer better representation of their needs.

While one growing cause of conflict between unions may be grassroots, membership-driven pressures for reform, another may be top-down pressure from the administration. During the Salinas administration, serious conflicts developed between the leaders of organized labor and the administration regarding economic and political reforms that conflicted with programs championed by labor. Further turmoil resulted from the administration's efforts to clean up corruption among the union leadership. Consequently, some disruptive and occasionally violent incidents have occurred. Among the more notable examples have been the strikes over union leadership corruption that erupted at the Modelo brewery and at the Ford plant in Cuautitlán. Since reform efforts are ongoing in the current political administration, labor unrest and destabilization can be expected to continue.

The increasing commitment to privatization of industries owned previously by the government is another factor in the destabilization of the labor environment and the growing tensions between Mexican unions. Privatization is having an impact on employee relations because the role of the government as an employer is declining and the government's efforts to make remaining state-owned industries more efficient has resulted in some downsizing.[3] With greater privatization and less direct governmental involvement in the economy, the long-maintained and strong ties between the CTM and the government may be weakening, providing greater opportunities for unions not affiliated with the CTM. A common theme in many of our interviews was the growing influence of independent unions resulting from workers' perceptions that these unions provide more useful and practical membership services than CTM-affiliated unions. To the extent that independent union memberships continue to increase their size and influence, inter-union competition should persist, fostering and promoting fragmentation of the labor movement.

Another likely source of inter- and intra-union strife is the inevitable awareness of Mexican workers of the disparities in real wages that exist with respect to their counterparts in other countries. Such disparities have elsewhere had the effect of increasing demand for stronger union representation (Kelly and Kelly 1994). Mexican workers have experienced significant declines in their real wages since the devaluation of the Mexican peso, and heavier union infighting and more agitation among Mexican workers may occur in the future.

Relative Deprivation

The economic plight of the average Mexican worker has undoubtedly worsened (Middlebrook 1992; Alvarez Bejar 1991). Most recently, real wages fell precipitously following the massive devaluation of the peso in late 1994 and early 1995 (Golden 1994). Nevertheless, real wages have not shown uniform erosion over this period. Examination of the time series of average manufacturing salaries and benefits for the years 1980 through 1994 reveals that after reaching a peak in 1982, real earnings dropped off precipitously in 1983 and then bottomed out in 1988. Real earnings then rose steadily and had almost returned to 1982 levels by 1994.[4] Interestingly, in Mexico large declines in real wages tend to occur during economic downturns, which unions have been unable to counter regardless of their political connections with the government. Conversely, during periods of prosperity, real wages increase even in the absence of labor shortages, perhaps in part a result of the political alliances of some labor organizations.

While badly needed economic reforms may have a positive impact on the long-term viability of the economy, it is clear that workers' purchasing power has suffered substantially in the short term and, as a result, perceptions of the need for organized labor unions with powerful political alliances may persist. The economic distance between the wealthy and the poor in Mexico, always large, appears to have become even more extreme in recent years (Rosenberg 1995).

Relative deprivation theory predicts that the current vast disparities in wealth between the extremely wealthy and the low wages and difficult working conditions of millions of Mexican workers may serve as incentives for collective action.[5] While there are some weaknesses in the ability of relative deprivation theory to predict the specific circumstances in which people will rebel from their governments or other societal institutions, the insurgence of rebels in 1994 in the state of Chiapas is consistent with its predictions (Wheeler 1985), although the degree of protest clearly went deeper than the industrial relations system.

Because a prime incentive for U.S. firms to move operations south of the border has been low wages, the degree of deprivation and impact on unionism will place increasing pressure on managers attempting to hold down costs. While many U.S.-based firms with business interests in Mexico pay above-average Mexican wages, by comparison with workers performing similar functions in the United States, Mexican workers receive only a fraction of U.S. compensation.[6] The experiences of other formerly low wage countries (such as Japan, Taiwan, Korea, and Singapore) and the growing access to broadcast media and other sources of information that allow for cross-border social comparisons suggest that the current wage differentials between the United States and Mexico should diminish over time. Continued efforts by U.S. firms to hold down wage levels provide unions with the strong argument of worker exploitation in their efforts to organize Mexican workers. As stated in a recent article in the popular business press:

> Across Asia and in developing nations around the world, workers and overseers in government and corporations seem to be entering a new era of tension. As the former cheap-labor havens attract more investment and transform themselves into flourishing economies, traditional, often feudal, labor relations are crumbling. The developing world's workers want more money, better working conditions, and more open societies (Lindorff, Miller, and Smith 1994).

While some have argued that Mexican culture places high value on accepting and enduring one's station in life (deForest 1989), extensive research (such as that by Fons Trompenaars) shows that Mexicans and Americans are similar in their inner-directed, more proactive approach to life (Trompenaars 1994). Additionally, both social comparison theory and equity theory predict that demands for better treatment will result from Mexican perceptions of relative deprivation and should accompany their growing educational and skill attainments (Goodman 1982). As education and skill levels increase and the political system becomes more democratic, Mexican workers will likely become less tolerant of income disparities and their experienced relative deprivation. Nevertheless some Mexican workers have very low expectations or are afraid to unionize because they fear employer retaliation. However, as the need for more highly qualified workers increases and the technical and educational qualifications of the average Mexican worker improve, their expectations should change and their fears diminish.

Management Exploitation and Opposition to Unionization

Recently, it has been alleged that some U.S. companies are discharging Mexican employees for union organizing activities. The International Brotherhood of Teamsters and the United Electrical, Radio, and Machine Workers of America (UE) have charged that Honeywell and General Electric terminated Mexican employees who were involved in organizing efforts for the *Frente Auténtico del Trabajo* in both Juarez and Ciudad Chihuahua. While the National Administrative Office review found that the available information on these cases did not support charges that the Mexican government failed to enforce its own labor law, similar cases are under review,[7] and many previously accepted or ignored business practices in Mexico are being given far greater scrutiny than in the past. Regardless of their legality or illegality, such activities seem short-sighted and carry the potential for significant negative consequences for future employee relations and business success in Mexico. Historically, employee relations experience in the United States indicates that such strategies

> not only limit the parties' ability to compromise in distributive bargaining and to engage each other in integrative bargaining during the forcing episode but also risk leaving a legacy of inter-group hostility after the forcing episode had ended. This residue of bitterness can limit the parties' flexibility to implement fostering activities in the period following the forcing campaign (Walton, Cutcher-Gershenfeld, and McKersie 1994, p. 264).

The relatively recent experience of Volkswagen de Mexico (a company with over 40 years of manufacturing experience in Mexico) provides another example of union and management conflict having the potential for negative impact on future employee relations and cooperation. In this example, conflicts over productivity improvements sought by VW led to a month-long shutdown of its Puebla plant. The decision of a government arbitration board approved VW's request to cancel its contract with its approximately 15,000 workers. In doing so, VW was able to eliminate its problem workers while re-hiring the remaining 90% of its workforce. It then renegotiated its contract with the union providing for the introduction of productivity improvements (Hinkelman 1994). A statement by VW de Mexico president Martin Josephi illustrates the changing face of employee relations in Mexico: "We have to recognize that the collective contract and union statues partly encouraged political problems and polarization in the past. We must avoid those problems in the future" (Watling 1992, p. 8).

Some U.S. companies may have added to perceptions of exploitation in their efforts to reduce labor relations uncertainty by establishing unions, usually affiliated with the CTM. One executive recounted that his firm's joint venture was advised by its Mexican labor lawyers that a union would be necessary for eventual success of the venture. Having recognized the political power of the CTM, the executives wanted to avoid a different union because of its high wage demands and negative reputation. Therefore, the joint venture partners purposely established a CTM-affiliated union, which gave greater assurance of trouble-free employee relations critical to the venture's success.

While managerial actions, as described above, may have substantial short-term benefits, these may be derived at the expense of more supportive and productive long-term relationships. The long-term problems that can result are exemplified in the case of a U.S. automobile manufacturer that negotiated a very favorable contract with its CTM-affiliated union for a new engine plant in a region where unions had not been a major factor. The contract gave the company almost unlimited managerial freedom, with the union's influence restricted to only wages and benefits. With such great managerial freedom, there was abundant opportunity for productivity enhancement through flexible work assignments. The company sought to discourage the adoption of restrictive work attitudes and practices by prohibiting transfers from its Mexico City plant. With only a few exceptions, a new and inexperienced workforce was hired. Unfortunately, the company took advantage of the situation and negotiated wages and benefits at one-half and one-third, respectively, of the levels of its other plants in Mexico and imposed a 45-hour work week. Ultimately, due to these exploitative practices, a five-week strike occurred and turnover reached an annual rate of 30%. Given that this plant required extensive training for its workers, the excessive turnover ultimately had a substantial negative impact on the firm's productivity (Shaiken 1988).

Such experiences in Mexico are not unique. In the past, some U.S. companies have created acrimonious long-term employee relations by their initial actions when operating in other countries. To the extent that organizations operating in Mexico pursue policies and actions inimical to the fundamental interests of labor unions representing Mexican workers—and contrary to culturally-based customs, traditions, and values—they may experience prolonged and unnecessarily poor performance. Indeed, understanding the culturally grounded expectations of the labor force is critical to a successful venture in Mexico (Stephens and Greer 1995).

Mexican-U.S. Union Cooperation

Despite previous opposition to NAFTA, U.S.-based unions have, in some instances, tried to cooperate with and provide support for Mexican unions. Several U.S. unions have provided financial, advisory, and other forms of assistance for negotiations and organizing efforts. Unions providing such support include the Teamsters, United Auto Workers, Communications Workers of America, the Farm Labor Organizing Committee, the Amalgamated Clothing and Textile Workers, International Ladies' Garment Workers Union, and the UE. Attempts at multinational union cooperation have been notoriously ineffective in the past (Northrup and Rowan 1977), and it appears that such problems persist. The experience of one U.S. union official with whom we spoke is illustrative. At the direction of his union, he and his director attempted to forge ties with the CTM some twenty-five years ago, but were told in no uncertain terms that their efforts were not wanted. From time to time, this union made further overtures to the CTM, always with the same results. As a result of this, and similar experiences, all of the U.S. union officials with whom we spoke were in agreement that corruption within the CTM is an important obstacle to cross-border union cooperation and support.

Nevertheless, isolated examples of specific supportive activities of American unions and their members include Teamsters and UE contributions to the salaries of Mexican union organizers, and UE assistance to a Mexican union attempting to organize a General Electric plant (*Compañiá Armadora*) in Juarez.

Similarly, members of a union in Minnesota have contributed financially to support Mexican workers at the Ford plant in Cuautitlán in their dispute over lay-offs and work rules.[8] Further, as shown in the earlier discussion of cases submitted by American unions to the U.S. NAO, NAFTA provisions provide additional stimulus and opportunity for cooperation across the border. A recent article in the popular business press about the shifting role of unions in Mexico noted that "NAFTA has threatened this cozy relationship [between Mexican unions and the government] and has set the stage for an unprecedented level of cooperation between labor groups across national borders." (Lindorff, Miller, and Smith 1994). While it is still too early to know whether the extent of cooperation will match the rhetoric, legal recourse through the provisions of NAFTA offers another avenue for cooperative union efforts. This has been demonstrated by the involvement of the UE and the Teamsters in the NAO submissions regarding General Electric and Honeywell (described earlier).

The North American Free Trade Agreement

 Several specific provisions of NAFTA have the potential to serve as direct sources of change in the Mexican labor relations environment. For example, the labor side agreement to NAFTA, the North American Agreement on Labor Cooperation (NAALC), is an important step toward board international consultation and cooperation on employee relations issues. While each member country retains basic sovereignty over its labor legislation and enforcement, the NAALC will influence interpretation and may perform other, as yet undetermined, roles. (Brill and Oratz 1994).

NAFTA and the NAALC also provide for each member country to establish a National Administrative Office (NAO) with responsibilities to review public communications concerning the other member countries' labor law matters and to consider labor rights issues outside their own national boundaries. (Perez-Lopez 1995). While NAFTA recognizes the sovereign law-making and enforcement rights of each member country, the NAOs are empowered to conduct reviews and report findings and recommendations (which are not legally binding) about the extent to which disputed actions have been consistent with a member country's own labor laws. (Compa 1995). Further, the NAOs are the first level of treatment of labor rights issues under the NAALC and are, therefore, gateways to other avenues of recourse. Early cases that have come before the NAOs—such as those involving Honeywell, General Electric, and Sony—suggest that their influence, while primarily consultative, is yet evolving (Brill and Oratz 1994).

Beyond the NAOs, additional methods of advancing the labor objectives agreed upon by the member countries include the Secretariat of the Free Trade Commission (NAFTA, Article 2002), Evaluation Committees of Experts (which can be recommended by any of the NAOs, as established in Article 23 of the NAALC), the use of experts and scientific review boards (NAFTA, Articles 2014 and 2015), and the Arbitral Panels (NAFTA, Articles 2008-2019). Some of these have enforcement powers and authority beyond those provided the NAOs. As with the NAOs, these organizations and procedures are still in their infancy, and their ultimate impact on cross-border employee relations is as yet unknown. Nevertheless, companies and managers should be aware of their evolving activities and influence in the business and labor environment.

In addition to its explicit administrative and oversight provisions, NAFTA and its accompanying labor accords may also serve as an indirect impetus for change in Mexican employee relations. As noted earlier, while private-sector firms can be expected to attempt to protect their economic advantages of lower wages and favorable work-place rules, the experience of other developing countries suggests that such advantages are unlikely to endure. Economic liberalization and increasing privatization of industries, as noted, is already well underway, in part as a result of NAFTA. Such reforms should also increase employer resistance to unionization due to weakening ties between government and labor organizations, the declining role of the government as an employer, and the greater resolve of independent unions to secure economic gains for their members.

Effects of New Work Methods

Changes in the structure of work may also foster changes in the structure of unions and approaches to employee relations. Recent research indicates that Mexican workers can be very amenable to new work technologies and that state-of-the-art methods of work are often easily introduced into the Mexican workplace (Stephens and Greer 1995). Such new work technologies as employee empowerment, self-managed work teams, cross-training, re-engineering, and total quality management (TQM) programs can have a substantial impact on employee relations. We found wide agreement among the participants of our study that Mexican workers seem to be much more flexible and willing to adapt to emerging technologies than American workers. As a Mexican corporate recruiter explained:

> "It's very easy to mold, to train these people in quality . . . when you have an old crew that you want to train or change to the new mentality of quality, then I think it is more . . . difficult in the States than in Mexico."

Another Mexican respondent who had extensive experience as an executive for an automobile manufacturer indicated the following:

> "What I have found is that the guys here, the elderly worker, is like eager to get, to learn, to have new training and to stay in that job. The American old-timer is very difficult. I guess . . . and it goes together with the quality training and all that . . . the Mexican worker is more flexible to different skills."

As new work technologies become more commonplace in Mexico, some union programs and protections will undoubtedly become redundant and the nature of union-management relationships will change. Further, as one scholar has observed, the structure of unions may also be affected.

> With the introduction of new technologies . . . assembly-line production (has) begun to give way in some sectors to more flexible forms of production. Workforces have been reduced, and in some industries new kinds of subcontracting arrangements are being implemented. Evidence in some countries is beginning to suggest that as this reorganization of work occurs, the system of industrial relations based on nationally organized unions may be superseded. While the introduction of such labor processes has been limited in countries like Mexico, their presence in a few key industries may become influential in setting the tone for the overall orientation of the industrial relations system (Collier 1992, p. 154)

EMPLOYEE RELATIONS GUIDELINES

This study has generated a number of guidelines and insights for improving employee relations that may be useful for U.S. companies developing operations in Mexico (see Table R9-1).

Table R9-1   Ten Guidelines for Improving Employee Relations in Mexico

- Exercise caution in alliances with CTM or other government or management dominated unions. Consider carefully trade-offs between the apparent stability of such relationships and the quality of long-term employee relations.

- Understand that opportunities to operate on a non-union basis, or with representation by CTM affiliates or independent unions vary substantially according to geographic region.

- The interpersonal, "soft" aspects of employee relations may be the most critical and difficult to understand and master.

- Approach negotiations with an integrative, problem-solving, or need-based approach, while being prepared for competitive approaches fostered by past exploitative relationships with U.S. companies.

- Do not place too much emphasis on detailed agreements.

- Be prepared to negotiate extensive, more "intrusive" benefits that extend beyond traditional U.S. views of work relatedness.

- Take advantage of abundant opportunities to preserve management prerogatives and flexibility, while being careful to avoid exploitation.

- Do not use conventional tactics as benchmark practices for dealing with work stoppages.

- Consider bargaining approaches linking increased wages and benefits with productivity gains since general productivity levels in Mexico are still far less than desired.

- Monitor trends in the resolution of NAFTA labor issues submitted to the U.S. National Administrative Office and the evolving influence of the NAALC.

Exercise Caution in Alliances with Government or Management-Dominated Unions

As indicated earlier, U.S. companies are sometimes advised that their joint venture may benefit by bringing in a "tame" CTM-affiliated union to avoid dealing with more worker-oriented or militant unions. The approach of the CTM often seems reasonable. For example, its leaders may relax demands in start-up operations and its contracts are typically very short and less detailed as they focus on only a few critical issues. Furthermore, agreement can often be reached in less time than in the United States, often with just a few short meetings. Consequently, these contracts may be less likely to inhibit productivity than some of the detailed and highly restrictive agreements that can put unionized U.S. companies at a competitive disadvantage. Moreover, from the company's perspective, CTM representation has some positive utility despite pervasive corruption, because it is a known quantity, its behavior is predictable, and it usually provides stable labor conditions. In addition, harmonious labor and management relations are not perceived by Mexican workers as an indicator that the union has been coopted by the employer (de Forrest 1994).

Nonetheless, employers should first understand that while the objectives of many independent unions are more closely aligned with worker representation, the objectives of CTM affiliates are more often subjugated to the interests of the political system. As a result, employers should be fully aware of the potential for exploitation if they pursue a power imbalance to the extreme and negotiate a one-sided agreements[9]. They should also consider whether such actions are consistent with their companies' sense of social responsibility.

Understand That Opportunities to Operate on a Non-Union Basis, or with Representation by CTM Affiliates or Independent Unions, Vary Substantially According to Geographic Region

Companies have excellent opportunities to operate on a non-union basis in maquiladora plants along the U.S. border as the level of unionization is quite low. For example, our sources informed us that in the Juarez area in 1995, only about 20 of over 275 plants were unionized. Despite anecdotal evidence that the level of unionization may be somewhat higher in the Eastern than the Western areas of the border, the level of unionization in maquiladoras along the border is generally low.

Our interviewees reported several reasons for these low levels of unionization. First, maquiladora workers are essentially transient, having come from throughout Mexico to find work. Frequently, they come from agrarian settings, have been educated only through the sixth grade, and lack skills applicable in an industrial setting. They generally want to improve their situation by moving on into the United States or by finding higher paying work elsewhere in Mexico. Thus, maquiladora workers were frequently described by our interviewees as complacent or conformist, and they do not see union representation as instrumental to their goals, since they are transient. Second, maquiladora workers typically have few resources to sustain themselves and their families other than their immediate wages and benefits. While it is difficult to obtain reliable data on the fully loaded hourly wage rate in maquiladoras (reported estimates we obtained ranged from a low of $1.08 to a high of $3.20 per hour), with such low wages any interruption in income flow resulting from the process of unionization represents a potential disaster. Third, because of the CTM's failure to improve the lot of workers, unions and their leaders generally lack credibility with maquiladora workers. Fourth, maquiladora employers, who often compete in product markets sensitive to the slightest world-wide variations in wages for unskilled labor, are necessarily very attuned to labor disruptions and cautious about potential losses of their investments in Mexico.[10] Fifth, the work typically performed in maquiladoras is low-skilled assembly work, which can be learned in a very short period of time in plants utilizing equipment that can be quickly moved to another location with relative ease. As a result, workers are necessarily fearful of employers' responses to unionization.

Beyond the border region, the labor relations environment is substantially different. There was wide agreement among our interviewees on several aspects of this environment. In the interior of Mexico, there is much less likelihood that an employer can operate without a union, although there are major differences in union climates between states. Unionization is more prevalent in the southern regions, particularly in Mexico City, although the northern city of Monterrey and the surrounding state of Nuevo Leon are exceptions in that they are heavily unionized. The independent unions, which provide an opportunity for genuine union representation, have an uphill battle against the CTM and the government. Unsurprisingly, they appear to have had little success in the north and in many industries.

Interestingly, although genuine union representation is somewhat rare in Mexico, some observers note that the right of Mexican workers to unionize is widely perceived as one of their most important legislated guarantees (Smith 1994). Furthermore, the highly collectivistic, group-oriented values of Mexican workers, noted by Trompenaars and others, would suggest that unions occupy a more central position in Mexicans' value systems and may be ingrained as major societal institutions. In fact, one interviewee stated that many Mexican workers are amazed that companies would even attempt to operate without a union. Thus, managers should be aware of the huge regional variations in Mexican perspectives on unionization.

The Interpersonal, "Soft" Aspects of Employee Relations May Be the Most Critical and Difficult to Understand and Master

Establishing an atmosphere of respect and consideration is especially critical for effective employee relations in Mexico. U.S. managers must be prepared for a somewhat lengthy period in which their understanding of Mexican culture will be inadequate and their Mexican employees and union officials will not have fully adjusted to the U.S. manager's style. As one executive explained, he had to be very careful in negotiations so as not to offend the other side with behaviors that are generally accepted in his home country: "In the U.S., I can pound on the table and then go have a drink with the union afterwards, but in Mexico, if I pound on the table, they won't talk to me for a month." The importance of interpersonal relations is revealed in another incident related to us by a different individual in which a U.S. plant manager's abrasive style so offended employees that the Mexican partner terminated the entire joint venture.

The importance of paying attention to seemingly small issues, particularly in maquiladora operations, is revealed in other incidents. In one maquiladora, employees took an issue to the state *Junta de Conciliación y Arbitraje* (the Conciliation and Arbitration Board) involving the company's departure from its past practice of providing Halloween candy. In other actions, employees have taken such matters as the quality of food served in the plant cafeteria, dissatisfaction with company transportation service, and seemingly trivial supervisory problems to the *Junta de Conciliación y Arbitraje*. U.S. managers may not place enough emphasis on disputed issues because they may seem trivial in relation to the problems that typically cause employee relations difficulties in the United States. Nonetheless, in Mexico, such issues can take on great importance. Furthermore, Mexican employees, as well as their union officials, still view the employer as *"el patrón,"* who although their boss, has an obligation to care for them and look out for their welfare. One human resource executive stated that while his function was often afforded low priority in the United States, in Mexico this function has much greater influence because of the importance attributed to it by the Mexican employees and because of his role as *"el patrón."*

Even U.S. managers who are sensitive to these issues are sometimes surprised by labor difficulties because they thought that they understood and had a good relationship with their Mexican employees. These difficulties have occurred even after the manager has done all of the "right" things, such as getting to know employees' families on a personal basis, embracing the Mexican culture, participating in sports activities, and so forth.

Interestingly, one Mexican interviewee placed some of the blame for such problems on the many subtle "double meanings" of the Spanish language as spoken in Mexico. Confusion and misinterpretation attributed to the subtleties of hidden or double meanings in language are certainly not unique to "Mexican Spanish," and culturally-specific, socially determined, or even deliberate double meanings have been well-documented in the literature (Ehrlich and King 1992; Pend, Peterson, and Shyi 1991; Benjamin 1977; Erzinger 1994). Such confusion may often be attributed to context sensitivity. High context cultures are those in which cues based in the socio-cultural environment, the situation, and non-verbal behavior are crucial in creating and interpreting communications. Mexico is a relatively high context culture and the United States is a relatively low context culture (Graham, Mintu and Rogers 1994). In Mexico, the context of interpersonal communication should be a more important influence on interpersonal interactions than in the United States, and meaning that is relatively apparent to a Mexican may appear subtle or hidden to an individual from the less context-sensitive United States (Hall 1981). The same individual who raised the issue of double meaning in Mexican Spanish indicated that fully understanding the Mexican culture is so difficult that interpersonal misunderstandings frequently arise even for Mexican-Americans who might be expected to bridge the two cultures.

Approach Employee Relations from an Integrative, Problem-Solving Perspective, but Be Prepared for Competitive or Uncooperative Responses Prompted by Past Exploitative Relationships with U.S. Companies

Under most circumstances the conventional employee relations wisdom informs us that it is generally a good idea to begin negotiations with an integrative, problem-solving, principled, or need-based approach as opposed to a competitive one. Although negotiations with CTM-affiliated unions are usually not especially difficult, in some situations it may be particularly important to be prepared for more competitive negotiations. Negotiations between U.S. employers and Mexican employees have often been characterized by a power advantage for the former. Consequently, unfavorable perceptions and memories may persist and carry over. Nonetheless, when negotiations take a competitive form, trust must be built into the relationship, and this is especially true in Mexico. Integrative or principled approaches can be effective tools for achieving this end and usually do not detract from the company's ability to pursue more competitive approaches when required. So, in addition to their contributions to negotiations, integrative or principled approaches also serve to build trust and help establish long-term relationships.

One recent study, an empirical analysis of bargaining simulations within ten different countries, seems to counter the foregoing argument (Graham, Mintu, and Rogers 1994). This study found negotiator attractiveness (friendly feelings) to be positively related to satisfaction with the outcome of negotiations. For American-American negotiators, it found problem-solving or integrative bargaining styles to be positively associated with negotiators' profits and satisfaction. In contrast, with Mexican-Mexican negotiations, the study found negative relationships between problem-solving negotiation styles and profitability. This unique negative relationship was not found in any of the other ten countries studied.[11] Nonetheless, the fact that competitive styles may be encountered should not cause U.S. negotiators to disregard integrative or principled negotiation styles as their preferred initial approach. While negotiators can always switch to a competitive approach if difficulties are encountered, it may be almost impossible to switch from an initially competitive approach to an integrative or principled approach. Furthermore, Roger Fisher's and William Ury's well-known treatise on principled negotiations anticipates the use of competitive approaches by the other side and provides tactics for converting competitive tactics to the principled negotiator's advantage (Fisher and Ury 1991).

Avoid Placing Undue Emphasis on Detailed Agreements

There are general differences in the emphasis that Mexican and U.S. negotiators place on contracts, as indicated in the following comments from two of our interviewees:

> Mexican Executive: "Basically, the Mexican companies, the Mexican people, they like more of the personal agreement. If we agree that we are going to do something and you put a contract in front of that agreement, it's like you are insulting me."

American Executive: "In Mexico you shake hands and you agree and then when you are about to start things we say, 'We really do need to put this on paper.' Then we put it on paper . . . that's been a big culture shock for me . . . we are more legalistic, and so . . . every time we had an agreement with someone or we were going to have a letter of intent, I would sometimes say, 'Where's the contract?' It would insult people. So I had to change the way I do things."

Given the Mexican culture's greater emphasis on relationships, Americans must learn not to over-emphasize the importance of labor contracts. Aside from the issue of trust, it may be futile to attempt to codify some work rules or procedures in a labor agreement because Mexican workers may view the agreement as insufficiently flexible. Trompenaars's "elements of cultural differences" provide some insight into this issue, in particular his element of cultural particularism versus universalism. According to Trompenaars, Mexican culture is more particularistic, whereas U.S. culture is more universalistic. In particularistic cultures, rules are less rigid and are interpreted with respect to situational contingencies, whereas in universalistic cultures, like the United States, rules are meant to be followed in all situations. Thus, the situational contingencies in which some rules or procedures should not apply may be too complex to codify. With the particularistic Mexican culture, a detailed contract would be counterproductive because its values dictate that if the situation changes, so does the interpretation of the contract. Thus, a particularistic culture requires a far greater degree of flexibility than is possible with a contract in which every last detail is spelled out.

Alternatives to this culturally based explanation are also possible. In particular, it has been suggested that institutional factors, rather than Mexicans' "traditional" reliance on interpersonal relationships and desire for flexibility, may underlie the Mexican tendency to seek "loose" contractual arrangements. For example, it is possible that the legal enforcement of some contractual provisions is seen as practically impossible through judicial intervention and thus unions may not be concerned with the specificity of contract language.[12] Another institutional argument is that greater contract flexibility is needed in Mexico because of greater uncertainty in the business environment and the greater economic impact of political factors (Wederspahn 1994).

In addition to these differences, negotiations with Mexican unions, particularly the CTM, typically involve fewer issues and less complexity than in the United States. Aside from wages and benefits, the union may have little interest in work rules and issues related to management prerogatives. Consequently, labor contracts (and the time necessary to reach agreement) are typically much shorter in Mexico, often less than 20 to 25 pages, most of which is devoted to specification of benefits. This contrasts with contracts for U.S. industrial unions which are often hundreds of pages long. One executive told us that he could typically reach agreement with the CTM in a few meetings as opposed to the six months he usually needed in the United States.

Be Prepared to Negotiate Benefits That Extend Beyond Traditional U.S. Views of Work Relatedness

Another relevant cultural element from Trompenaars' research deals with the permeability of boundaries between work and non-work domains. In Mexican culture, there is less compartmentalization of work activities and personal life activities than in the United States. Work influence and relationships extend into employees' personal life activities in a variety of ways. Examples include the paternalistic responsibilities of the employer, expectations that managers will know and take into account the personal histories of employees, acceptance of nepotism, and reliance on family and friendship relationships in hiring, promotion, and other organizational activities and decisions. As a result of this cultural attribute, more attention may be needed in labor negotiations and relations to address the company's stewardship over the personal life activities of Mexican workers. Indeed, the inclusiveness of current Mexican labor agreements and legislated benefits might be considered an unnecessary or undesirable invasion of privacy in the United States. As an example of such stewardship, 89% of companies in Mexico give employees scrip that can be used to purchase groceries and other goods (Siegel 1993). Benefits are also important because of workers' low wages. Commonly provided benefits in maquiladoras include (but are not limited to) attendance bonuses, holiday pay, two meals at the workplace, transportation to and from work, on-site medical care, and educational programs. These benefits are in addition to those mandated by Mexican law, such as those noted in Appendix II.

Take Advantage of Opportunities to Preserve Management Prerogatives and Flexibility in Workforce Assignment While Avoiding Exploitation

As noted earlier, CTM-affiliated unions tend to demand less from employers during the start-up years and are usually agreeable to the preservation of management prerogatives and flexibility in workforce assignment. However, because employers in Mexico often face an abundant supply of labor they must be careful not to exploit workers by imposing work rules that ultimately detract from the morale of the workforce or instill feelings of resentment. We were told of a situation in which a U.S. executive recognized this potential problem and took preventative action by unilaterally providing employees additional benefits while attributing the credit to local CTM officials.

Avoid Taking as Benchmarks the Tactics for Dealing with Strikes Used by Major Multinational Corporations

As previously discussed, well-known multinational corporations have sometimes created the potential for long-term employee relations difficulties by their heavy-handed approach to work stoppages. Firing a striking workforce to obtain greater efficiencies and advantages in a new contract, when compared with the alternative of negotiating modifications to existing work rules, is clearly damaging to long-term employee relations effectiveness. Nevertheless, some companies have chosen this and similar short-term oriented courses of action even though they incur significant immediate and long-term human resource, financial, and organizational costs.

Consider Bargaining Approaches That Link Increases in Wages and Benefits to Productivity Gains

Although Mexican productivity has increased as much as 6.5% annually in recent years, a substantial gap remains between the productivity of Mexican and U.S. workers. While productivity differences vary across industries and are affected by the level of capital investment, some observers estimate Mexican productivity, in general, at a fraction of that in the United States. There are obviously variations in productivity estimates. Hinkelman noted the experience of a U.S. company which claims that three times more workers are needed to perform the same work in Mexico. Nevertheless, published reports of improvements related to the implementation of quality programs, pay for performance, and similar innovations show that significant productivity gains can be achieved. Furthermore, as noted earlier, new work technologies like these may be more quickly accepted and implemented in Mexico than in the United States. While the exact productivity-related circumstances of each company will differ, the gap is important because labor costs in Mexico are not nearly as low as popularly believed. Legally mandated benefits, customary benefits, and pay for time off work add tremendously to the cost of labor. In reality, the fully loaded Mexican average hourly wage, is substantially higher than the mythical 55 cents per hour wage, although reliable statistics on this figure are difficult to obtain (Hinkelman 1994). For example, an executive from one company told us that their average (fully loaded) hourly wage in Mexico was $3.20.

In addition to these factors, there are two other incentives for focusing on productivity improvement. The first is found in a unique feature of Mexican labor law. Although the governmental board that authorizes strikes, the *Junta Federal de Conciliación y Arbitraje* (JFCA), approves only a small proportion of such requests each year, the employer's productivity is a factor in the board's considerations. In the past, the board has been less likely to approve strikes in situations where the company's productivity was above average (Hinkelman 1994). Nonetheless, it should be noted that some unions view this criterion as a sham. The second incentive lies in the possibility that pay-for-performance reward systems may become one of the principles of a revamped Mexican labor regime that some political parties, private sector groups, and even union representatives and government officials consider a necessity if Mexico is to fully embrace market economics. In 1993, Mexico created the National Commission on Productivity, which has the responsibility of recommending increases in the minimum wage linked with productivity gains.

Monitor Evolving Trends in the Substance and Resolution of NAFTA Labor Cases Submitted to the U.S. National Administrative Office and the Evolving Influence of the NAALC

NAFTA has provided for a number of entities having oversight, review, or enforcement responsibilities in the area of labor relations. Among these are the NAOs, the Secretariat, the Arbitral Panels, and the Evaluation Committees of Experts. While guidelines for the functioning of these bodies have been established, the interpretation and actual application of their powers and authority are still evolving. It is difficult to predict the future nature of their involvement in Mexican and U.S. employee relations, although possibilities may be identified. For example, although not currently in wide use in Mexico today, arbitration and mediation may increasingly be relied upon to settle cross-border commercial disputes between private parties. Whatever the eventual outcomes, it is clear that U.S. managers and companies must be close observers of the development and evolution of labor standards, and flexible enough to adapt to the eventual requirements that will result.

CONCLUSIONS

Employee relations in Mexico are influenced by many of the same cultural values and environmental uncertainties affecting other aspects of business and society in Mexico. Some of these factors function to effectively maintain or even increase the relative influence of unions in Mexico, while others will foster significant changes in the structure and activities of Mexican labor organizations in ways that may be surprising to unprepared companies. Firms doing business in Mexico will increase their probability of sustainable success to the extent that they anticipate future change, are familiar with current realities, and understand past influences on the Mexican labor relations environment. The likelihood of success will be enhanced if U.S. managers recognize that Mexico is undergoing a significant transitionary period and that the next few years are likely to be marked by substantial learning effects.

APPENDIX 1
DATA COLLECTION

This article is based in large part on data obtained in 40 in-depth interviews of individuals, conducted in two phases. In the first phase, 25 individuals were interviewed in sessions which addressed general cultural differences between Mexican and U.S. business management practices, including employee relations. This first phase included 3 preliminary interviews. Interviews in this phase followed a semi-structured format and were informed by the authors' extensive reviews of the relevant practitioner and academic literatures. In this phase, interviewees were asked to describe the following employee relations issues: nature of the relationship, obtaining flexibility, grievance procedures, work stoppages, and innovative ways of dealing with unions. In the second phase, an additional 15 individuals were interviewed in sessions that focused specifically on employee relations and differences between the two countries. Except for one of the preliminary interviews, all interviews were conducted in 1994 and 1995.

Of the interviews, 27 were conducted in Mexico and 13 in the United States. We interviewed U.S., Mexican, and third-country national executives, managers, and officials who worked for a broad cross-section of companies doing business throughout Mexico, as well as the world, both Mexican and U.S. governments, and both Mexican and U.S. labor unions. Industries represented by interviewees, with frequencies indicated in parentheses, included manufacturing (8), transportation (4), retailing (3), insurance (1), computer services (2), universities (1), management consulting (1), construction engineering (2), Mexican labor unions (2), U.S. labor unions (5), Mexican government (3), U.S. government (2), Mexican non-profit economic development agencies (1), U.S. non-profit economic development agencies (3), and other labor agencies and worker advocacy organizations (2).

While the scope of employers' operations or jurisdictions varied, the location of our interviews provides some indication of the representativeness of our sample. The geographic distribution of our interviews, with frequencies indicated in parentheses, was as follows: Mexico City—central region (17), Chihuahua—northern region (6), Juarez—border region (4), El Paso—border region (8), Dallas-Fort Worth—southwest region (3), and other U.S. (2).

Our analysis of data obtained in interviews most closely followed the "template" approach described by B.F. Crabtree and W.L. Miller. With the template approach, which has similarities with content analysis, text is analyzed through the use of an analytical guide or "codebook" consisting of a number of categories or themes relevant to the research question. Template analysis differs from traditional content analysis in that the codebook, whether implicit or explicit, may be revised many times as a result of exposure to the textual data, and the pattern of themes that appears is subjected to qualitative rather than statistical interpretation (Crabtree and Miller 1992).

Other observations of Mexican managerial and employee relations practices arose from the authors' visits at leading Mexican business schools, and one author's visits to several maquiladora manufacturing plants.

APPENDIX II
MEXICAN LABOR LAW
AND LEGISLATION

There are several important features of the Mexican labor law of which companies operating in Mexico should be aware, especially since Mexican labor law is commonly thought to favor the worker over the employer. Although it is not our intent to provide an exhaustive review of Mexican labor law, we have selected several examples that point out important differences with U.S. law.

Application of Labor Law and Union Forms

Since 1931, labor issues have been subject to the Federal Labor Law (*La Ley Federal del Trabajo*), which was completely revised in 1970. Application of the law occurs at both state and federal levels although federal administrators have substantially more power than state administrators. At the federal level, labor law is administered by the Ministry of Labor and Social Welfare (Franco 1991).

Permissible Types of Unions

A unique feature of Mexican labor law is that unions must be registered with the government, but in order to gain official recognition, a union need only obtain the signatures of twenty workers. In reality, employers sometimes have the unique experience of getting to "choose" which union will represent their employees when they recognize CTM unions. Furthermore, only the following five types of unions are permissible under Article 360 of the federal labor law: *Sindicatos gremiales* (craft unions) are composed of workers of the same profession, trade, or specialization. *Sindicatos de empresa* (same company unions) are composed of workers in the same company. *Sindicatos industriales* (industrial unions) consist of workers from two or more companies participating in the same industry. *Sindicatos nacionales de industria* (national industrial unions) have members from two or more companies in the same industry that also operate in two different states. Finally, *sindicatos de oficios varios* (mixed unions) consist of workers in various occupations who wish to form a union, but cannot enroll a minimum of twenty workers from within a single category (Franco 1991).

Worker Protections and Benefits

Federal Juntas and courts have jurisdiction on all labor relations disputes involving industries federally chartered or those in which the parties to the dispute reside in more than one state. All other disputes come within the jurisdiction of the states. Interestingly, the labor law essentially maintains that permanent employees (those on the payroll for at least one year) can be discharged only for just cause. Thus, employees on the payroll for at least a year can be terminated only for causes stipulated in the law. Furthermore, employees being terminated must be informed of the termination in writing and provided with documentation of the basis for termination. Another interesting feature is that employment contracts, which are required to be in writing, are usually indefinite with respect to duration. Interestingly, even companies operating without unions commonly have formal contracts with their employees in order to provide evidence of their employment practices in the event that disputes are taken to governmental authorities. In reality, since terminations appealed to the labor courts are nearly always decided in the employee's favor, the employer should plan on a settlement of several thousand dollars when terminating an employee even for good cause (Hinkelman 1994; Jarvis 1990). Furthermore, anecdotal evidence indicates that Mexican workers are quick to appeal employers' decisions or disciplinary actions.

The Mexican constitution provides for conciliation and arbitration boards (*Juntas de Conciliación y Arbitraje*) with representation on the boards divided equally between workers and employers (plus one government representative). These boards have full legal jurisdiction to deal with worker grievances and their decisions are binding. At the federal level, there is a Federal Conciliation and Arbitration Board, and a local board has been established for each state. Additionally, *juntas accidentales de conciliación* (conciliation boards) may be created for special circumstances. The mandate of these boards allows for conciliation and arbitration of issues involving a broad range of conflicting parties, including: worker vs. employer; worker vs. worker; union vs. union; union vs. worker (regardless of whether the workers are unionized); employer vs. employer; and union vs. state. Different procedures may be necessary depending on whether the hearing is at the state or federal level, but regardless of the venue, dealings with the *juntas* can be extremely complicated and time consuming, and they may have heavy costs for both the firm and the employee (Franco 1991), not the least of which is a protracted decision-making process.

Numerous benefits standards and practices intended to protect the worker raise the cost of doing business in Mexico. For example, the following benefits are among those mandated by law: the *aguinaldo*, a year-end bonus equal to a minimum of two weeks income, payable to all workers; vacation premiums; profit sharing; and social security benefits (Siegel 1993). Other employer responsibilities covered by the labor law include overtime, work hours, holidays and vacations, dismissal and severance procedures, and fringe benefits.

Infractions of the Law and Strikes

A major difference between U.S. and Mexican labor law is that infractions of some aspects of the Mexican Federal Labor Law are subject to severe penalties (Jarvis 1990), whereas criminal penalties under U.S. labor law are found only for violations of provisions of the Labor Management Reporting and Disclosure Act (Landrum Griffin Act). For example, severe fines and even jail sentences can be imposed on employers who fail to pay the minimum wage. Another difference is that the law's treatment of strikes is very different from U.S. practice:

> If the officially recognized labor union declares a strike, all personnel, including management, must leave the facility. Red and black flags hang at each of the locked entrances. Workers receive pay for all the time they are out on a legal strike (Jarvis 1990, p. 62).

Strikes in Mexico may be legally initiated for any of the following reasons: employer actions that violate the agreement; regular contract renewal, revision, or renegotiation; significant economic changes; to force the employer to implement the contract; to force the employer to engage in mandated profit-sharing; annual renegotiation of salaries; and in support of a legal strike at another company. In stalemates, either side may petition the government for assistance (as described above) in settling the dispute. However, regardless of the labor law's treatment of strikes, the reality is that strikes in Mexico are relatively rare (Millon, Perera, and Lowe 1990; Franco 1991).

References

BEJAR, A. ALVAREZ (1991), "Economic Crisis in the Labor Movement in Mexico," in Middlebrook, K.J. ed., *Unions, Workers, and the State in Mexico*. San Diego, CA: Center for U.S.-Mexican Studies, University of California, San Diego, 27–55.

BENJAMIN, G.R. (1977), "Tone of Voice in Japanese Conversation," *Language in Society*, 6 (April), 1–13.

BRILL, E.A. and ORATZ, S.L. (1994), "Labor Accord Put to the Test: Recent Complaints Have Focused Attention on a Side Agreement to NAFTA; Hearings Are Scheduled," *National Law Journal* (September 19), C1.

COLLIER, R.B. (1992), *The Contradictory Alliance: State-Labor Relations and Regime Change in Mexico*. Berkeley, CA: University of California at Berkeley, International and Area Studies.

COMPA, L. (1995), "The First NAFTA Labor Cases: A New International Labor Rights Regime Takes Shape," *U.S.-Mexico Law Journal*, 3 (Symposium), 159–81.

CRABTREE, B.F. and MILLER, W.L. (1992), "A Template Approach to Text Analysis: Developing and Using Codebooks," in Crabtree, B.F. and Miller, W.L. eds., *Doing Qualitative Research*. Newbury Park, CA: Sage Publications, 93–109.

de FOREST, M.E. (1989), "Managing a Maquiladora," *Automotive Industries*, 169 (May), 72–73.

———(1994), "Thinking of a Plant in Mexico?" *Academy of Management Executive*, 8 (February), 33–40.

DURAND PONTE, V.M. (1991), "The Confederation of Mexican Workers, the Labor Congress, and the Crisis of Mexico's Social Pact," in Middlebrook, K.J. ed., *Unions, Workers, and the State in Mexico*. San Diego, CA: Center for U.S.-Mexican Studies, University of California, San Diego, 85–104.

EHRLICH, S. and KING, R. (1992), "Gender-Based Language Reform and the Social Construction of Meaning," *Discourse and Society*, 3 (April), 151–66.

ERZINGER, S. (1994), "Empowerment in Spanish: Words Can Get in the Way," *Health Education Quarterly*, 21 (Fall), 417–19.

FISHER, R. and URY, W. (1991), *Getting to Yes: Negotiating Agreement Without Giving In*, 2d Ed. Boston: Penguin Books.

FRANCO, J.F. (1991), "Labor Law and the Labor Movement in Mexico," in Middlebrook, K.J. ed., *Unions, Workers, and the State in Mexico*. San Diego, CA: Center for U.S.-Mexican Studies, University of California, San Diego, 105–20.

GOLDEN, T. (1994), "Mexican Currency Resumes Its Fall and Stocks Drop," *The New York Times* (December 28), A1(N)–A1(L).

GOODMAN, P.S. (1982), "Social Comparison Process in Organizations," in Staw, B.M. and Salancik, G.R. eds., *New Directions in Organizational Behavior*. Mallabor, FL: Robert E. Krieger Publishing Company, 97–132.

GRAHAM, J.L., MINTU, A.T. and RODGERS, W. (1994), "Explorations of Negotiation Behaviors in Ten Foreign Cultures Using a Model Developed in the United States," *Management Science* 40 (January), 72–95.

HALL, E.T. (1981), *Beyond Culture*. Garden City, NY: Anchor Books.

HECHT, L. and MORICI, P. (1993), "Managing Risks in Mexico," *Harvard Business Review*, 71/4 (July/August), 32–40.

HINKELMAN, E.G., (ed.) (1994), *Mexico Business: The Portable Encyclopedia for Doing Business with Mexico*. San Rafael, CA: World Trade Press.

JARVIS, S.S. (1990), "Preparing Employees to Work South of the Border," *Personnel*, 67 (June), 59–63.

KELLY, C. and KELLY, J. (1994), "Who Gets Involved in Collective Action? Social Psychological Determinants of Individual Participation in Trade Unions," *Human Relations*, 41/1, 63–88.

LAVELLE, M. (1994), "Labor's Charges Test NAFTA Rules in Mexico," *National Law Journal*, 17 (September 19), A16.

LINDORFF, D., MILLER, K.L. and SMITH, G. (1994), "Raised Fists in the Developing World," *Business Week* (November 18), 130–32.

MIDDLEBROOK, K.J. (1988), "Dilemmas of Change in Mexican Politics," *World Politics*, 41 (October), 120–41.

——— (1991), "State-Labor Relations in Mexico: The Changing Economic Political Context," in Middlebrook, K.J. ed. *Unions, Workers, and the State in Mexico*. San Diego, CA: Center for U.S.-Mexican Studies, University of California, San Diego, 1–25.

MILLAN, J., PERERA, M. and LOWE, J. (1990), "The ABC's of Mexican Labor Relations," *Twin Plant News* (May), 40–41.

MOBERG, D. (1993), "Like Business, Unions Must Go Global," *The New York Times* (December 19), F13.

MYERSON, A.R. (1993), "Big Labor's Strategic Raid in Mexico," *The New York Times* (September 12).

NEWMAN, G. and SZTERENFELD, A. (1993), *Business International's Guide to Doing Business in Mexico*. New York: McGraw-Hill.

NORTHRUP, H.R. and ROWAN, R.L. (1977), "Multinational Union Activity in the 1976 U.S. Rubber Tire Strike," *Sloan Management Review* 18/3 (Spring), 17–28.

PEND, T.K., PETERSON, M.F. and SHYI, Y.P. (1991), "Quantitative Methods in Cross-National Management Research: Trends and Equivalence Issues," *Journal of Organizational Behavior*, 12 (March), 87–107.

PEREZ-LOPEZ, J.F. (1995), "The Institutional Framework of the North American Agreement on Labor Cooperation," *U.S.-Mexico Law Journal*, 3, 133.

REES, A. (1989), *The Economics of Trade Unions*, 3rd Ed. Chicago: University of Chicago Press.

ROHTER, L. (1988), "Stiff Setback Seen for Ruling Party in Mexican Voting," *The New York Times* (July 8), A1–A2.

ROSENBERG, J.M. (1995), *Encyclopedia of the NAFTA, the New American Community, and Latin-American Trade*. Westport, CT: Greenwood Press.

SHAIKEN, H. (1988), "High Tech Goes Third World," *Technology Review*, 91 (January), 39–47.

SHORROCK, T. (1993), "Mexico Firings by U.S. Firms Violated NAFTA, Unions Say," *Journal of Commerce* (December 15), 2A.

———(1994), "Workers at GE Plant in Mexico Reject Union," *Journal of Commerce* (August 29), 3A.

SIEGEL, C. (1993), "Real Wages," *World Trade*, 6 (June), 120–21.

SMITH, G. (1994), "Which Side of the Border Are You On? Well, Both," *Business Week* (April 4), 50.

STEPHENS, G.K. and GREER, C.R. (1995), "Doing Business in Mexico: Understanding Cultural Differences," *Organizational Dynamics*, 24 (Summer), 39–55.

TROMPENAARS, F. (1994), *Riding the Waves of Culture: Understanding Diversity in Global Business*. New York: Irwin.

U.S. National Administrative Office (1995), North American Agreement on Labor Cooperation, Bureau of International Labor Affairs, U.S. Department of Labor, "Public Report of Review, NAO Submission 940003," (April 11).

Wall Street Journal (1993), "Borderless Unions Emerge to Challenge Borderless U.S.-Mexico Companies" (November 16), A1.

WALTON, R.E., CUTCHER-GERSHENFELD, J.E. and MCKERSIE, R.B. (1994), *Strategic Negotiations: A Theory of Change in Labor-Management Relations*. Boston: Harvard Business School Press.

WATLING, J. (1992), "VW Fires, Rehires at Mexico Plant," *Automotive News* (August 24), 8.

WEDERSPAHN, G. (1994), "Making the Best of Negotiations in Mexico," *Maquila Magazine*, 5 (November/December), 26–29.

WHEELER, H.N. (1985), *Industrial Conflict*. Columbia, SC: University of South Carolina Press.

Endnotes

1. Estimates of unionization are from Hinkelman (1994). Hinkelman notes estimates of unionization by other observers as high as 50% and Gary Newman and Anna Szterenfeld report that union members account for slightly more than 50% of the Mexican labor force and even higher proportions in industrial sectors of the economy. See Newman and Szterenfeld 1993.

2. There are three sizeable confederations of unions, including the *Confederación de Trabajadores de Mexico* (CTM—about 6 million members), *Confederación Regional Obrera de México* (CROM—about 350,000 members), and the *Confederación Revolucionaria Obrera y Campesina* (CROC—about 500,000 members). These and other unions form the *Congreso del Trabajo* (CT), the over-arching labor congress that represents about 90% of the unionized Mexican labor force. Numerous independent unions are affiliated with the *Frente Auténtico del Trabajo* (FAT), or Authentic Labor Front, an independent federation of unions. Further information regarding these federations may be found in the following sources: Newman and Szterenfeld 1993; Durand Ponte 1991; Shorrock 1993; Collier 1992.

3. By 1993, economic reforms had resulted in the sale, merger, or closure of over 80% of the 1,155 enterprises run by the state, according to Hecht and Morici 1993.

4. We obtained data for average manufacturing salaries and benefits for the years 1980 through 1994 and adjusted these nominal earnings data with the consumer price index in order to derive average real manufacturing salaries and benefits. The source of these salary and benefits data and price index data is Banco de Mexico. *Indicadore Economicos* (June 1992 and April 1995), based on data from *La Nueva Encuesta Industrial Manual del I.N.E.G.I.*

5. We note that while unionism can narrow the gap in earnings between the wealthy and the highest paid workers, it can also widen the gap between the unionized and the non-unionized, most impoverished workers. See Rees 1989. Furthermore, Middlebrook's analysis indicates that the influence of unions was weakened by declines in Mexico's economy during the 1980s. His conclusion that economic decline negatively affected the influence of Mexican unions is consistent with the predictions one would obtain from economic derivation of the demand for union labor.

6. Hecht and Morici (1993, p. 33) note that "manufacturing compensation in Mexico is currently about 14% of U.S. levels and will probably rise to about 20% by the end of the decade."

7. For a discussion and summary of these cases and similar cases and issues, see Compa 1995. Also, see U.S. National Administrative Office 1995; Myerson 1993.

8. As reported in the following sources, the Mexican union *Stimacs*, which is affiliated with the *Frente Auténtico del Trabajo*, was overwhelmingly defeated in the representation election. The UE has charged that the company acted unfairly by promising higher wages with a union defeat and threatening plant closure for a union victory, although General Electric has denied these charges. (*The Wall Street Journal* 1993, Shorrock 1994; Moberg, 1993; Myerson 1993; Smith, 1994; Lindorff, Miller, and Smith 1994; Moberg 1993.)

9. While the outcome of one-sided contracts negotiated with such unions cannot be predicted with precision, there may be strong potential for spoiling the future employee relations environment. Recent research on U.S. domestic labor relations by Richard Walton, Joel Cutcher-Gershenfeld, and Robert McKersie may provide some guidance on the effects. These researchers found that management relying solely on an unrestrained forcing strategy was unable to "even remotely tap the reservoir of skills, experience, and ingenuity of its workforce. Thus the performance gains these managements achieved in practice were less than would be suggested by the substantive changes they won through forcing." (Walton, Cutcher-Gershenfeld, and McKersie 1994, p. 229.)

10. Maquiladora employers are frequently under attack in the media, often unfairly. While their wages are low, they provide the sole alternative to employment for impoverished individuals having few skills.

11. A limitation of the applicability of the Graham, Mintu, and Rodgers study to the present discussion is that their study employed a single dependent variable, profitability, while integrative or principled approaches to negotiation have many other outcome-related benefits that may be even more important in the long-term in the Mexican culture.

12. If this is a valid hypothesis, Mexican unions would be expected to seek more detailed contracts to the extent that courts or court-like institutions (like the Juntas) begin to obtain greater powers (as in the United States) to adjudicate labor disputes and to compel contractual parties to live up to their respective obligations.

Reading

How Chrysler Created an American Keiretsu

Jeffrey H. Dyer

Borrowing from Japanese practices, U.S. manufacturers have cut their production and component costs dramatically in the last decade by overhauling their supplier bases. They have radically pruned the ranks of their suppliers and given more work to the survivors in return for lower prices. And by getting their remaining suppliers to deliver parts just in time and to take responsibility for quality, they have managed to slash inventories, reduce defects, and greatly improve the efficiency of their own production lines.

Now many manufacturers are striving to wring even greater benefits from their suppliers. They would like to involve suppliers much more deeply in product development and to enlist them in the drive for continual improvements of production processes. The prizes they are seeking: ever more innovative products, ever faster product development, and ever lower costs.

But as many managers now realize, accomplishing the first stage was relatively easy because it did not require altering the nature of their relationship with suppliers. The traditional adversarial relationship remained: Manufacturers continued to design products largely without input from suppliers, to pick suppliers on the basis of price through a competitive bidding process, and to dictate the detailed terms of the contract. They continued to expect suppliers to do as they were told and not much more.

In sharp contrast, the second stage—involving suppliers in product development and process improvement—requires radically changing the nature of the relationship. It requires a bona fide partnership, in which there is an unimpeded two-way flow of ideas. Although many managers now talk about their desire to turn their suppliers into partners, the fact of the matter is that actually doing it—after decades of exploiting suppliers by pitting one against the other—is exceedingly difficult. Indeed, the task is so difficult that some executives wonder whether the Japanese partnership model can or even should be transplanted to the United States, where competitive, contractual, arm's-length relationships between manufacturers and their suppliers have long been the norm. They rightly point out that the partnerships among the members of a Japanese keiretsu grew out of cultural and historical experiences that are very different from those that shaped U.S. industries and companies.

One U.S. manufacturer, however, has shown that it is possible to make the transition. This company is Chrysler Corporation. Its experience demonstrates not only that a modified form of the keiretsu model can work in the United States but also that the benefits can be enormous.

Since 1989, Chrysler has shrunk its production supplier base from 2,500 companies to 1,140 and has fundamentally changed the way it works with those that remain. Instead of forcing suppliers to win its business anew every two years, Chrysler now gives most of them business for the life of a model and beyond; excruciatingly detailed contracts have given way to oral agreements. Instead of relying solely on its own engineers to create the concept for a new car and then to design all the car's components, Chrysler now involves suppliers deeply. And instead of Chrysler dictating prices to suppliers, regardless of whether the prices are realistic or fair, the two sides now strive *together* to find ways to lower the costs of making cars and to share the savings.

The results have been astounding. The time Chrysler needs to develop a new vehicle is approaching 160 weeks, down from an average of 234 weeks during the 1980s. The cost of developing a new vehicle has plunged an estimated 20% to 40% during the last decade to less than $1 billion for the Cirrus/Stratus, introduced this year. And, at the same time, Chrysler has managed to produce one consumer hit after another—including the Neon, the Dodge Ram truck, the Cirrus/Stratus, and the new minivan (sold as the Town & Country, Dodge Caravan, and Plymouth Voyager). As a result, Chrysler's profit per vehicle has jumped from an average of $250 in the 1980s to a record (for all U.S. automakers) of $2,110 in 1994.

Of course, Chrysler's astounding comeback is hardly news anymore. But surprisingly, one crucial aspect of the story has been overlooked: exactly how the company managed to transform its contentious relationships with its suppliers. Believing that Chrysler's turnaround might hold lessons for other U.S. manufacturers, I undertook a three-year study of the company's revival. From 1993 to 1996, I interviewed 13 executives at Chrysler and also 33 of the company's suppliers, and analyzed thousands of pages of Chrysler's documents.

From this work emerged a blueprint of the steps that other companies might take to build their own American keiretsus, providing that those steps are accompanied by the exemplary management—or, more accurately, the exemplary leadership—that Chrysler's executives displayed. Four men in particular—Robert Lutz, Chrysler's president; François Castaing, the head of vehicle engineering; Glenn Gardner, LH program manager; and Thomas Stallkamp, head of purchasing, planted the seeds and then nurtured Chrysler's keiretsu. By benchmarking competitors, listening to suppliers, and experimenting with ideas and programs, they gradually developed a vision of the changes that Chrysler needed to make. They came to realize that those changes required transforming both the process of choosing and working with suppliers and the personal relationships between Chrysler's staff and its suppliers. They came to understand that people—both at Chrysler and in suppliers' organizations—must have a common vision of how to collaborate to create value jointly. They came to recognize that trust in relationships will take root only if both parties share in the rewards and not just the risks. And ultimately they incorporated those realizations into the fabric of the company's management systems.

To be candid, the steps that Chrysler took were not always by design. But through trial and error, the automaker has managed to develop supplier management practices that are a model of cooperation and efficiency.

THE IMPETUS FOR CHANGE

In the mid-1908s, as part of an effort to improve its competitiveness, Chrysler conducted an extensive benchmarking study of product development and manufacturing at Honda Motor Company, which was then expanding its manufacturing and sales presence in the United States faster than either Toyota Motor Corporation or Nissan Motor Company. One factor that Chrysler studied was supplier relations.

Honda was organized into product development teams composed of individuals from all key functions, all of whom had cradle-to-grave responsibility for the development of a vehicle. The teams included suppliers' engineers, who had responsibility for both the design and manufacture of a particular component or system. Executives from Chrysler thought initially that Honda's practices were interesting but completely foreign to Chrysler, which was organized by function and which developed products in a traditional sequential process that did not routinely involve suppliers. Chrysler's engineers designed components, and suppliers built them. Whereas Honda selected suppliers that had a history of good relations with the company and a track record for delivering quality products and meeting cost targets, Chrysler selected suppliers that could build components at the lowest possible cost. (Buyers had to obtain quotations from at least three suppliers.) A supplier's track record for performance and quality was relatively unimportant. As a consequence, the typical relationship between Chrysler and its suppliers was characterized by mutual distrust and suspicion.

Honda's approach suddenly looked less foreign after Chrysler acquired the American Motors Corporation in 1987 for its profitable Jeep operations. AMC had implemented some Honda-like supplier-management and development practices. The reason was necessity. Because AMC had neither the resources to design all its own parts nor the power of larger automakers to dictate the prices it was willing to pay for them, it had learned to rely on suppliers to engineer and design a number of its vehicles' components. Also, the engineering and manufacturing staff in AMC's Jeep and truck group had been operating for several years as an integrated team. With just 1,000 engineering employees, AMC had developed three vehicles between 1980 and 1987—the Cherokee, the Premier, and the Comanche—and was beginning a fourth, the Allure coupe. In comparison, Chrysler's 5,500 engineers and technicians had developed only four all-new vehicles during the 1980s: the K-car, the minivan, the Dakota truck, and the Shadow/Sundance.

AMC's operations suggested to Chrysler's executives that Japanese-style partnerships might be possible in an American context. Equally important, that discovery occurred at a time when Chrysler's leaders had been made keenly aware that their development process was inadequate. The company's newly launched LH program (Chrysler Concord, Eagle Vision, and Dodge Intrepid—Chrysler's answers to Ford Motor Company's popular Taurus) was running a projected $1 billion over budget, and the company was in dire financial straits. It had a $4.5 billion unfunded pension fund. Its losses were deepening: After closing three plants in 18 months during 1988 and 1989, Chrysler hit bottom, reporting a record loss of $664 million in the fourth quarter of 1989. With the exception of the minivan, its boxy cars appealed only to older buyers. Chrysler's executives knew they had to do something fast.

Some changes in top management helped. Lutz, who had become president of operations in 1988, championed the effort to adapt and apply the positive lessons learned from Honda and AMC. When Chrysler's chief engineer retired in 1988, Lutz replaced him with François Castaing, AMC's chief engineer. In one of his first

Table R10-1   Supplier-Management Practices at Chrysler Have Changed

Process Characteristics		Relational Characteristics	
1989	*1994*	*1989*	*1994*
Suppliers chosen by competitive bid —Low price wins —Selection after design	Suppliers presourced —Cost targeted to a set price —Selection before design, based on capabilities	Little recognition or credit for past performace (transaction orientation)	Recognition of past performance and track record (relationship orientation)
Split accountability for design, prototype and production parts	Single supplier accountable for design, prototype and production parts	No responsibility for suppliers' profit margins	Recognition of suppliers' need to make a fair profit
Minimal supplier investment in coordination mechanisms and dedicated assets	Substantial investments in coordination and mechanisms and dedicated assets	Little support for feedback from suppliers	Feedback from suppliers encouraged
Discrete activity focus, no process for soliciting ideas or suggestions	Focus on total value-chain improvement, formal process for soliciting suppliers' suggestions	No guarantee of business relationship beyond the contract	Expectation of business relationship beyond the contract
Simple performance evaluation	Complex performance evaluation	No performance expectations beyond the contract	Considerable performance expectations beyond the contract
Short-term contracts	Long-term contracts	Adversarial, zero-sum game	Cooperative and trusting

moves, Castaing recommended that Chrysler slam the brakes on the LH program, and the company picked Glenn Gardner to rethink and relaunch the program. Gardner had been chairman of Diamond-Star Motors Corporation, Chrysler's joint venture with Mitsubishi Motors Corporation, and was familiar with Mitsubishi's product-development process, which was similar to Honda's.

Lutz, Castaing, and Gardner picked the team to develop the LH, a model code that many at Chrysler darkly joked stood for "last hope." The reborn LH program was to serve as a pilot for redesigning Chrysler's product-development process and supplier relations.

To spur creativity and increase the speed of the product development cycle, the three executives made three important changes that broke with tradition. First, to shield the team from internal bureaucracy, they decided to move it away from Highland Park, Michigan, where most of Chrysler's operations were located. Second, to speed decisions internally and to eliminate sequential decision making, they included on the team individuals from design, engineering, manufacturing, procurement, marketing, and finance. Finally, they decided to experiment with new methods of working with suppliers, drawing on the lessons learned from Honda, AMC, and Mitsubishi.

By 1991, Chrysler's senior managers knew they were onto something. The LH was being developed in record time and below the aggressive cost targets set at the beginning of the program. The new approach to product development and working with suppliers was extended to the rest of the company that year.

CHRYSLER'S NEW MODEL

The model of supplier management that Chrysler now uses reflects several important changes in the company's processes for selecting, working with, and evaluating suppliers.

Cross-Functional Teams

To get its functions to present one face to suppliers and to end the conflicting demands and shifting priorities that had been the hallmark of its sequential development process, the company reorganized into cross-functional vehicle-development teams. It now has five cross-functional platform teams—one for large cars, one for small cars, one for minivans, one for Jeeps, and one for trucks. Cross-functional teams improve continuity, coordination, and trust both within Chrysler and between Chrysler and its suppliers. Suppliers also develop more stable relationships with Chrysler's staff and can count on the company to follow through more effectively on promises and agreements.

Presourcing and Target Costing

Presourcing means choosing suppliers early in the vehicle's concept-development stage and giving them significant, if not total, responsibility for designing a given component or system. The rationale for presourcing is that it permits many engineering tasks to be carried out simultaneously rather than sequentially, thereby speeding up the development process.

In addition to having responsibility for design, most presourced suppliers are responsible for building prototypes during development and for manufacturing the component or system in volume once the vehicle is in commercial production. The new practice means that suppliers of such complex components as the heating and air-conditioning system join the product development effort very early and, as prime contractors, take total responsibility for the cost, quality, and on-time delivery of their systems. Suppliers say this approach gives them more flexibility in developing effective solutions to problems.

In the past, Chrysler had often given responsibility for design, manufacture of prototypes, and volume production of a component to separate companies, with the result being a lack of accountability. When suppliers had problems producing a component at the required cost or quality, they would often blame their troubles on the design—not surprising, given that some studies have found that 70% of quality problems in automotive components are due to poor design. Consequently, Chrysler and its suppliers would waste time trying to assign blame for problems when they could have been trying to solve them.

To overcome that fragmented approach, Chrysler had to move away from competitive bidding. For the LH project, Chrysler's corporate purchasing department gave the project's cross-functional platform team a prequalified list of suppliers considered to have the most advanced engineering and manufacturing capabilities. That team, which included people from engineering, quality control, and purchasing, then selected suppliers on the basis of proven ability to design and manufacture the component or system. Each supplier's success in meeting design, cost, and quality targets and in delivering on time was critical to the success of the presourcing process.

The new process also required Chrysler to decide how to set a fair price for the component. Under the old competitive-bidding process, the price of a component or system was deemed fair because it was market driven. However, under the new system, Chrysler had to choose the supplier even before the component was designed. Chrysler decided to adopt the widely used Japanese practice of *target costing*, which involves determining what price the market, or end customer, will pay for the vehicle and then working backward to calculate the allowable costs for systems, subsystems, and components.

How did the company set the initial target costs in the LH program? "Actually, we set them somewhat unscientifically and then, when necessary, had the suppliers convince us that another number was better," says Barry Price, Chrysler's executive director of platform supply for procurement and supply. "We would involve suppliers and tell them, 'I've got X amount of money.' We would let them know what functions the part or system in question would be required to perform and ask, 'Can you supply it for that cost?' Usually, their response would be no, but they at least came back with some alternatives. The first time through, we had to find our way. The second time, we had the benefit of history and, as a result, we developed better targets at the outset of the program."

Target costing has shifted Chrysler's relationship with suppliers from a zero-sum game to a positive-sum game. Historically, Chrysler had put constant pressure on suppliers to reduce prices, regardless of whether the suppliers had been able to reduce costs; the automaker did not feel responsible for ensuring that suppliers made a reasonable profit. Chrysler's new focus on cost instead of price has created a win-win situation with suppliers because the company works *with* suppliers to meet common cost and functional objectives. Naturally, this process begins to build the trust that is critical if partnerships are to take root.

Total Value-Chain Improvement: The SCORE Program

The next step in building a partnership with suppliers is to figure out how to motivate them to participate in continuous improvement processes for the value chain as a whole. Eliciting the full effort and total resources of suppliers is critical because partnerships work only when both parties try to expand the pie. Such cooperation is possible only when the supplier trusts the buyer and when the two parties *really* communicate.

Chrysler began to build trust and improve communications with a small set of suppliers during the reborn LH program. However, it was another program, one that Chrysler began to develop in 1989, that became, almost by accident, the company's most important method for building trust, lowering costs, and improving communication. The formal name of that program now is the Supplier Cost Reduction Effort (dubbed SCORE).

Asking for Help   The basic purpose of SCORE is to help suppliers and Chrysler reduce systemwide costs without hurting suppliers' profits. The catalyst for the SCORE program was a speech that Lutz gave at the Detroit Athletic Club in August 1989 to executives from 25 of Chrysler's largest suppliers. Lutz told the suppliers that because of Chrysler's desperate situation, he wanted their assistance and ideas on how the company could lower both its own costs and those of its suppliers. The message was, "All I want is your brainpower, not your margins."

The fledgling efforts in the LH program to build tighter relationships with suppliers were bearing fruit, and Chrysler's leaders were eager to maintain the momen-

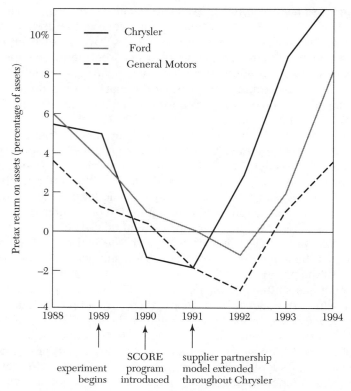

experiment
begins

SCORE
program
introduced

supplier partnership
model extended
throughout Chrysler

Figure R10-1   Chrysler's Profits Overtake Its Rivals'

tum. At the time, General Motors Corporation was increasing its squeeze on suppliers, demanding across-the-board price cuts. In his speech, Lutz wanted to stress that Chrysler was taking a different path.

The suppliers crowded around Lutz after the speech, eager to offer their ideas. Given Chrysler's history of adversarial relationships with suppliers, one might ask why they didn't react cynically to Lutz's request for help. For one thing, they knew that Chrysler was on the ropes. For another, Chrysler had four relatively new leaders who had demonstrated a commitment to radical change: Lutz, Castaing, Gardner, and Stallkamp, the purchasing chief who, in early 1990, had replaced a champion of competitive bidding. There also was hard evidence of Chrysler's sincerity: AMC and the relaunched LH program.

Lutz kept the ball rolling after the speech. He was so impressed with the suppliers' ideas and willingness to share information that he had senior executives schedule follow-up meetings with them. Some ideas were so good that Lutz, Castaing, and Stallkamp decided to establish a formal process for reviewing, approving, and implementing them.

To get advice on how Chrysler could accomplish that task more systematically, Lutz asked a small group of Chrysler's senior executives, including Castaing and Stallkamp, to visit a number of key suppliers. These unusual visits impressed the suppliers, many of whom were upset with GM's heavy-handed treatment. (Chrysler would later strive to contrast its approach with GM's in order to drive home the point that Chrysler's path was different. For example, at a time when GM's purchasing czar, Jose Ignacio Lopez, was prohibiting his buyers from accepting a lunch invitation from a supplier, Stallkamp was instructing his buyers to take suppliers to lunch.)

During these talks, many suppliers complained about how GM was demanding that they reduce prices—a move that would require them to lower their costs—when, from their perspective, GM couldn't even get its own house in order. The suppliers noted that Chrysler, too, was far from perfect. Indeed, Chrysler had long been guilty of turning down or simply ignoring potentially money-saving suggestions from its suppliers—for instance, recommendations that they use a different material in a component—because the suggestions would have required running tests and making other changes in the component or in Chrysler's processes. In many cases, engineers refused even to consider such proposals, because considering them would have increased the engineers' workloads. Others were overly fearful of taking risks.

Unveiling SCORE   It was based on these discussions with suppliers that Chrysler established SCORE as a formal program that committed the automaker to encouraging, reviewing, and acting on suppliers' ideas quickly and fairly, and to sharing the benefits of those ideas with the suppliers. The SCORE program was unveiled in 1990 at a meeting with Chrysler's top 150 suppliers. To emphasize its desire to change, Chrysler specifically asked suppliers to suggest operational changes that it could make in its own organization to reduce both its costs and those of the suppliers. Chrysler soon received a large number of written suggestions.

Chrysler's executives knew that the initiative would fail if the company simply rejected all the ideas or did not respond quickly. So in another display of strong leadership, Chrysler's top managers took personal responsibility for making sure that the company followed through on its promise to review and act on the proposals quickly. Castaing, Stallkamp, and other senior executives met once a month to review the proposals and evaluate Chrysler's responses. Initially, Chrysler's engineers wanted to reject many ideas, and senior managers had to decide when to overrule them. Determined to avoid a not-invented-here syndrome, Castaing forced through some of the ideas, pacifying the engineers by telling them to give the ideas a try simply as an experiment. Enough of the early ideas were accepted to convince suppliers that Chrysler really was open to suggestions. Soon the suggestions were pouring in, and the successes helped break down the engineers' resistance.

To get suppliers to buy into the SCORE program, Chrysler took three steps. First, it focused on what Chrysler itself was doing wrong. Second, it asked suppliers to make suggestions for changes that involved materials or parts provided by lower-tier suppliers—those that provided nonstrategic components or that supplied parts to key suppliers. Only as a third step did it turn to what the key suppliers—the ones that made strategic components or systems—were doing wrong. "The order with which we addressed these issues was important," Chrysler's Barry Price says. "The suppliers never would have gone for self-criticism before we developed a track record of correcting our own problems."

Why were suppliers willing to take the risk of expending resources to offer such ideas? The answer is that Chrysler made it profitable for them to participate in SCORE and demonstrated that it would play fair. "For many, when we fixed our operations, they made huge savings," Price says.

Perhaps even more important, Chrysler offered to share the savings generated by the suppliers' suggestions with the suppliers. Partly because it did not have the resources to audit suppliers and partly to promote trust, Chrysler initially did not quibble when it suspected that a supplier was grabbing more than half. "That first time, we didn't ask for a renegotiation," recalls Price. "We just let them know that we knew. The result: we began to get more and more ideas—sometimes even on products they didn't supply." In one case, a supplier suggested that Chrysler stop making a part out of magnesium and use plastic—an improvement that would cost the supplier the business. That suggestion saved Chrysler more than $100,000 per year.

Beyond the incentive of improving their own profitability and increasing their business with Chrysler, suppliers appreciated being listened to for a change. Under the traditional system, suppliers were rarely asked for their ideas or suggestions for improvement; they were simply given a discrete task and asked to perform that task for a price. Performance expectations were explicitly written in the contract.

Incorporating SCORE   In 1992, Chrysler made SCORE a formal part of its supplier rating system. Chrysler began to *require* suppliers to offer ideas for improvement, to maintain a vehicle system focus, and to make every effort to improve the Chrysler "extended enterprise."

Now Chrysler keeps detailed records of the number of proposals each supplier makes and the dollar savings they generate, and it uses those figures—along with the supplier's performance in the areas of price, quality, delivery, and technology—to grade the supplier's performance. In 1995, a supplier's SCORE rating was 15% of its overall rating, up from 8% in 1994—an indication of how important continual improvement throughout its value chain is to the automaker.

Since February 1994, Chrysler has given suppliers specific annual targets for savings from SCORE ideas. Although Chrysler does not penalize a supplier if it misses a SCORE target, the supplier's performance over time may eventually determine how much business it receives from the automaker. Suppliers are expected to offer suggestions that result in cost reductions equaling 5% of the supplier's sales to Chrysler. The automaker also has expanded the program to enlist suppliers' assistance in reducing vehicle weight, warranty claims, and complexity. (Suppliers receive a $20,000 credit for every part removed from a system.)

Chrysler also tracks the number of proposals awaiting a decision and the amount of time it takes to respond to a proposal. Although the job no longer falls to senior executives, Chrysler's managers continue to review engineers' evaluations of suggestions from suppliers. Managers also help suppliers with the SCORE paperwork and routinely intercede on the suppliers' behalf. In other words, the managers serve as the suppliers' advocates within the company. And to make submitting ideas even easier, SCORE is now an on-line process: a supplier can submit a proposal or check on its status at any time.

When Chrysler accepts a SCORE idea, the supplier has two choices: It can claim its half of the savings or it can share more of the savings with Chrysler in order to boost its performance rating and potentially obtain more business from the automaker.

To understand more clearly how SCORE works, consider the experience of Magna International. One of Chrysler's largest suppliers, Magna provides the automaker with seat systems, interior door and trim panels, engine and transmission systems, and a wide variety of other products. In 1993, Magna made its initial SCORE proposal, suggesting that Chrysler use a different wood-grain material on a decorative exterior molding on its minivan. The material Magna recommended cost less and offered the same quality as the material Magna had been using. Magna documented the proposal on Chrysler's supplier-buyer information form and submitted it to the responsible Chrysler buyer. The buyer then notified engineering and requested its review and consent. The entire process took approximately two weeks. Chrysler approved the proposal, which resulted in annual savings of $250,000. Since then, Magna has submitted 213 additional SCORE proposals, 129 of which Chrysler has approved—for a total cost savings of $75.5 million.

Rather than taking a share of these savings, Magna has opted to give 100% of them to Chrysler in the hopes of boosting its performance rating and winning more business. The result: since 1990, Magna's sales to Chrysler have more than doubled, from $635 million to $1.45 billion. What is more, the greater economies of scale mean that the business with Chrysler is now more profitable, says John Brice, the Magna executive director in charge of the Chrysler account.

SCORE has been astoundingly successful. In its first two years of operation, 1990 and 1991, it generated 875 ideas worth $170.8 million in annual savings to Chrysler. In 1994, suppliers submitted 3,786 ideas, which produced $504 million in annual savings. As of December 1995, Chrysler had implemented 5,300 ideas that have generated more than $1.7 billion in annual savings for the company alone.

Enhanced Communication and Coordination

Chrysler promoted cooperation both among suppliers and between suppliers and Chrysler in several ways. To coordinate communication with and across suppliers more effectively, the automaker has imitated the Japanese practice of employing *resident engineers*—suppliers' engineers who work side by side with Chrysler's employees. The number of resident engineers in Chrysler's facilities has soared from fewer than 30 in 1989 to more than 300 today. Executives at suppliers and at Chrysler claim that this practice has resulted in greater trust and more reliable and timely communication of important information.

To facilitate interaction with suppliers, Chrysler has taken a number of other steps, including the creation of a common E-mail system and the establishment of an advisory board of executives from its top 14 suppliers. In addition, it has instituted an annual meeting of its top 150 strategic suppliers and also holds quarterly meetings with each supplier to discuss strategic and performance issues and to review priorities for the coming year.

For their part, suppliers have demonstrated their trust in Chrysler by increasing their investments in dedicated assets—plant, equipment, systems, processes, and people dedicated exclusively to serving Chrysler's needs. In addition to the resident engineers, nearly all suppliers have purchased Catia (Chrysler's preferred CAD/CAM software), which at $40,000 per engineer (seat) is no small investment. (To help them obtain a lower price for Catia, Chrysler arranged a large-scale group purchase for more than 200 suppliers.)

A number of suppliers also have invested in dedicated facilities to improve their ability to make just-in-time deliveries to Chrysler and to provide it with better service. For example, Textron built a plant dedicated to producing interior trim parts for the LH and located a new design facility less than two miles from the Chrysler Technology Center. Partly as a result of investments such as those, the average distance between Chrysler's assembly plants and its suppliers' facilities has been decreasing. At Chrysler's plant in Belvidere, Illinois, where the Neon is assembled, the number of supplier shipment points has dropped by 43% and the average distance from supplier to assembler plant has shrunk by 26 miles. My previous research has demonstrated that geographic proximity lowers inventory costs and enhances communication. (See my article "Dedicated Assets: Japan's Manufacturing Edge," HBR November-December 1994.)

Long-Term Commitments

To earn suppliers' trust and to encourage them to invest in dedicated assets, Chrysler is giving a growing number of suppliers increasingly longer commitments. The average length of the contracts held by a sample of 48 of Chrysler's suppliers on the LH program in 1994 was 4.4 years. By comparison, Chrysler's supply contracts lasted 2.1 years on average in 1989, according to a 1991 study by Susan Helper titled "How Much Has Really Changed between U.S. Automakers and Their Suppliers?" (Sloan Management Review, Summer 1991).

Today Chrysler has given oral guarantees to more than 90% of its suppliers that they will have the business for the life of the model they are supplying and beyond. Of course, the suppliers must fulfill one condition: They must perform well on the current model and must meet the target cost on the next. "The business is theirs to keep forever or until they elect to lose it," Stallkamp declares.

Suppliers make it clear that Chrysler's longer-term commitments are having the desired effect. "I would certainly say that we are more comfortable making investments and taking risks on behalf of Chrysler than on behalf of our other customers, with whom we have a less secure long-term future," says Ralph Miller, CEO of auto supplier APX International.

Surveys conducted for Ford and Chrysler in 1990, 1992, and 1993 by Planning Perspectives, an independent market-research company, confirm that Chrysler has made tremendous strides in developing cooperative, trusting relationships with its suppliers. In 1990, suppliers rated Chrysler lower than both GM and Ford on five key dimensions, including trust, responsiveness to ideas, and efficiency. By 1993, suppliers rated Chrysler higher than Ford and GM on all five dimensions (significantly higher than GM on all five and significantly higher than Ford on three of the five).

THE AMERICAN KEIRETSU

The American keiretsu that Chrysler has created differs from a Japanese keiretsu in two major respects. First, Japanese manufacturers like Toyota and Nissan typically own 20% to 50% of the equity of their largest suppliers; Chrysler does not and could not take similar stakes. Toyota, for example, has only about 310 suppliers, and those with which it has equity ties, about 50, typically depend on it for two-thirds of their sales. So their destinies are closely intertwined. By comparison, Chrysler still has a much larger group of suppliers, and few of its most important suppliers depend on it for a majority of their sales. Second, approximately 20% of the executives at Toyota's and Nissan's major supplier companies formerly worked for those automakers. This intimacy leads to a high level of understanding and a common culture that Chrysler could never duplicate.

However, Chrysler's arrangement has its advantages. It is much easier for Chrysler to drop underperforming suppliers than it is for Toyota or Nissan. Because those companies cannot drop suppliers so easily, they are under greater pressure to commit resources to help suppliers improve. This assistance almost certainly benefits rivals—including Chrysler—that buy from those suppliers.

Chrysler's formal programs that measure results and offer incentives for improvement ideas are probably more suitable for the U.S. business environment than the Japanese companies' relatively informal approach would be. One could argue that without formal programs such as SCORE, suppliers would not devote the same resources to generating ideas. As Stallkamp observes, "SCORE is a success because it is a communications program, not just a cost-cutting program. By learning how to communicate, we've learned how to help each other." The level of communication needed to make a supplier partnership productive simply may not happen naturally in the U.S. business environment.

On the other hand, Chrysler's policies for building partnerships seem to be too successful in one sense: They appear to be making it harder for the company to continue to shrink its supplier base, which it would like to do to reduce coordination costs, improve quality, achieve even greater economies of scale, and last but not least, strengthen its ties with the suppliers it retains. The shrinkage rate has slowed. Chrysler still has almost four times as many suppliers in the United States as Toyota does in Japan.

In addition, Chrysler still lags far behind its Japanese competitors in converting lower levels of its supply chain to the new supplier-management approach. Its biggest suppliers are only beginning to replicate programs such as presourcing, target costing, and SCORE in their own supply chains.

Even if Chrysler has a long way to go, the progress it has made in the last seven years is nonetheless remarkable. Its success to date in building an American keiretsu—or, as its leaders prefer to call it, Chrysler's "extended enterprise"— proves that decades of adversarial relations can be overcome. As Steve Zimmer, Chrysler's director of operations and strategy for procurement and supply, notes, "We've learned that you don't have to be Japanese to have a keiretsu-like relationship with suppliers." Chrysler has proved that highly productive partnerships with suppliers not only can flourish in the United States but are the wave of the future

Guidelines for Improving the Efficiency of Government in Germany

Reading 11

Peter Eichhorn

TRENDS AND THE NEED FOR REFORM

The Problem

As a result of the unification of East and West Germany, the public sector in Germany needs to straighten out its finances and become more efficient and effective. Public services are operating at a loss, and high tax rates and growing public debt make it necessary to find new ways of managing public institutions more efficiently. Federal, state, and local governments must limit their spending and improve their control over their budgets.

The movement toward modernizing the public sector is fueled by three causes. First, the unification of Germany in 1990 was expensive. The entire infra-

Source: Peter Eichhorn. This reading is original to this text.

structure of East Germany—airports, power stations, the public transport system, public schools, streets, the telephone system, universities, hospitals—must be rebuilt, renewed, and maintained. In addition, the German social security system (health, unemployment and accident insurance, nursing care, pensions) must be financed. Another concern is that formerly socialist plants were not competitive and could not survive under free market conditions. As a result, subsidies are necessary to establish competitive industries.

Second, in 1992 and 1993 Germany was in a recession. The resulting shortfall in tax revenue and increasing expenditures for social programs strangled the budgets of government at all levels. These deficits had to be financed by tax revenue and additional debt.

Third, international developments such as the founding of the European Union in 1993 and competitors in low-wage countries in Eastern Europe and Asia, made it increasingly difficult to maintain a viable economic position. To become competitive, public services must provide an excellent infrastructure for the private sector.

For the federal, state, and local governments, the situation is difficult. There is increasing bureaucracy and frustration among public employees, tall hierarchies and bloated decision making procedures, lack of flexibility, waste, inefficiency, and no strategic plan. Of course, the deteriorating financial situation makes it impossible to reorganize and hire more personnel to initiate needed public programs.

The Aims of Reform

The objective of government is to improve the fulfillment of its duties to the public. In addition to maintaining consistently high legal standards, it is desirable to have more efficient administrative structures, procedures, policies, and conduct. To achieve this, there is a need for reorganization of government administration. This requires fewer levels of management, greater autonomy of offices and divisions, performance incentives, goal-oriented staff, introduction of budgets based on double-entry bookkeeping; awareness of costs, the use of outside contractors for peripheral work, and greater cooperation with the private sector.

The Desired Outcomes

The outcomes of a restructured system should be a more economical, efficient, and effective government. This would include customer-oriented behavior, economical completion of work, sound decision making, more flexible behavior, more mobility among personnel, and greater employee job satisfaction.

Although all levels of government—federal, state, and local—need reform, the prospects for reform vary according to the level of government. It is difficult to reform the federal and state ministries because of their political environment. For example, specialized departments inside ministries cannot be controlled with managerial methods very easily.

Reform at the municipal level is somewhat easier and more necessary—local authorities must be reformed extensively. Included in reform efforts should be internal services such as personnel departments, accounting and auditing departments, as well as auxiliary services such as printing. Specialist departments including social welfare, urban planning, and civil engineering should also be reformed. This brings us to the question: How can government agencies be restructured?

TEN POINTS IN A REFORM PROGRAM

Downsize Administration

Over the past decades, local and state governments, as well as private firms, followed the basic premise that "bigger is better." It was believed that government functions could be more effectively managed simply by means of large agencies having many employees. The result was an extensive bureaucracy with a large administrative structure, protracted decision making, and sluggish action.

In response to the failure of bureaucratic structures, businesses have begun to embrace the principle that "small is beautiful." An example is a small holding company, umbrella organization, or board of directors that oversees clearly structured and flexible profit centers. The advantages of decentralized management such as this include division of labor between strategic planning and operational tasks, greater independence and personal responsibility, increased employee motivation, and improved coordination of tasks through an improved information system.

When applied to government institutions, the result is lean government, resulting in fewer hierarchies with fewer divisions and departments. The reduction of government begins with the transfer of nongovernmental tasks to subordinate administrations or outsourcing them to publicly owned enterprises. This would focus government ministries again on fundamental political affairs, law making, decrees, and edicts as well as supervisory matters.

Reduce the Management Burden

Executives in government agencies are often overloaded. This creates a bottleneck in the political and administrative process. The obligation of managing "everything" results in information overflow and makes it difficult for executives to focus on strategic goals. Leadership requires setting fundamental goals, developing strategies, and making and implementing decisions.

However, the actual implementation of decisions lies less in the top administrative levels than in the middle and lower ones. Administrative functions currently performed at the ministerial level should be transferred to subordinate agencies. These agencies should be self-reliant and responsible for carrying out their tasks.

A consequence of reallocation of work, such as described previously, is that the political responsibility of the minister for decisions in a decentralized system can only extend to what actually lies in his area of influence. This includes the political and legal objectives of the ministry, the selection of agency heads, and the organization of the agency.

Removing upper management from operation tasks means freeing ministries of them. This should lead to a situation in which the managers within the respective agencies further delegate the operational tasks to their employees.

Make Offices Autonomous

Greater independence for individual public administrative authorities such as provincial offices and local agencies means governmental management without a centralized bureaucracy and increased latitude in decision making. Discretionary decision making should exist to the extent that even "make or buy" decisions can be made at the lowest level. In this same spirit, less urgent political and legal objectives should be assigned to third parties—for example, independent professionals, specialists, and small businesses. The tasks of planning, specification, allocation, and supervision, however, still remain the responsibility of the state or local administrations. It follows that administrative personnel deal less with the actual performance of tasks and more with their supervision.

Independent work means increased personal responsibility. This requires a compensation system that encourages managers to accept responsibility and also does not permit poor performance to escape negative consequences. As part of the accountability system, top management positions with extensive independence and responsibility should be filled for limited terms.

Provide Achievement Incentives

Civil service legislation is not on the agenda of most local governments. Nevertheless, possibilities present themselves for promoting personnel efficiency and initiative.

Delegating jobs to employees within an independent and autonomous system of work permits latitude in structuring incentives. To implement this, the style of leadership between supervisors and employees must change. Decentralized, job-specific management should replace leadership by centralized directives as much as possible.

Additional achievement incentives that should be instituted are career incentives, continuing education for junior staff, creating a sense of group affiliation, employee suggestion programs, performance bonuses, and vertical and regional job mobility to reduce dependence on local job opportunities. Another possibility is a profit-sharing system to improve the motivation of both supervisors and employees.

Merge Responsibility for Performance and Resources

The traditional separation of specialized and general functions is incompatible with modern management methods and contributes to the fact that services are not viewed as a whole. Specialization by creating support services or central departments does indeed have the undeniable advantage of work division, provides substantial benefits, and ensures a unified administration; but dependency, redundancy, domineering conduct, and rivalry also result. To counter this, specialized processes must instead proceed with a view toward personnel, organizational, and financial resources; responsibility for the means used and the results achieved must be combined. In other words, processes must be integrated as a whole in the organization.

To make this system work, managers with strong economic or managerial backgrounds must participate more in decision making, especially on the executive level. Authority for making decisions in the areas of personnel management, organization, finance, information systems, auditing, and accounting should be transferred to these people.

A result of tying performance and resource responsibility is that central departments or support services are limited because their functions are integrated into the functional divisions. Where such support services still need to exist as separate departments, they should be structured as profit centers, each with an independently managed budget.

Staffing Guidelines

From the point of view of leaner management, three levels of organization are appropriate: (1) leadership, (2) divisions, and (3) departments.

In the ministries the top management consists of the Minister and the Director General; in the subordinate authorities, the agency head, who is either the President or Director, and his deputy. In the larger public agencies, the leadership also has a staff, which usually includes advisors in personnel, media, internal services, and financial control. In addition to providing support, the staff helps with the coordination of the divisions.

The divisions should be presided over by a division head supported by a deputy division head. Each division head has a staff of advisors, including a controller or attorney, who devote time to personnel, organizational, financial, legal, and informational issues.

Reducing the number of departments and restructuring into fewer, larger ones within a division should make it possible to combine work. This process would be made easier by a simplification of regulations, which should be particularly useful for the middle and lower-level managers.

The larger departments could become teams whose advantages lie in unifying employees into larger work areas. This would strengthen interdisciplinary work, provide more possibilities for job substitution, create easier dispatching within work units, and permit the creation of project groups. The overall result should be more flexibility.

Introduce Budgets and Double-Entry Bookkeeping

Traditional budgeting that has a fiscal orientation does not adequately reflect productivity. Questions regarding the merit of internal production versus outside purchases; the choice of buying, renting or leasing of buildings or vehicles; the valuation of assets; the expense of making, installing and carrying out laws; optimal agency size; and other general economic considerations remain unanswered or require separate calculations. The most serious problem is that politicians and agency personnel are not aware of the cost implications of administrative actions.

The divisions perform public tasks. As such, they require their own budgets, which they can administer themselves, even though their budgets are integrated into the budgets of the local or state government.

Following international developments in budgeting and accounting, budgets should make use of double-entry bookkeeping. The divisions receive current budgets, including planned expenditures for personnel, materials, interest, depreciation, and allocations, as well as anticipated proceeds from taxes, assets, and payments. The investment budgets indicate planned expenditures for investments, inventories, reserves, equities, amortizations, and appropriations to funds and budget revenue arising from assets, reserves, loans, and planned credit intake.

At the end of the year in both budgets, the actual expenditures are compared with what was initially planned. Asset accounting will report on the assets (administrative and financial resources) and the liabilities (equity and debt capital) as of December 31 of each year. To make flexible management possible, budgets should contain comprehensive appropriations and reasonable collateral information.

Develop a Performance Base on Costs and Performance

The public authorities are considered by law to be part of the executive component of government. This should be maintained. From the perspective of business administration, they form a service organization because they provide diverse services such as counseling centers, state universities, teaching and research institutions, and public schools, among others.

To accomplish these services the organizations that deliver them develop ways of acquiring resources along with the services they provide. These administrative tasks must be compared with their costs. In other words, costs must be clearly separated from budget expenditures and must also include items such as depreciation, equity capital, and reserves for future pensions. This would permit cost comparisons between comparable agencies over various periods of time. In establishing the cost of administration, the institutional efficiency of administrative action can be determined.

Allocate Assignments Externally

Division of work promotes synergistic effects. The performance of related tasks within one institution leads to the positive effects of economies of scope and scale and, under certain circumstances, improvement in performance and cost reduction. Public administrators should investigate which tasks in which areas and with which characteristics can be diversified at what cost. This examination would have to occur in three steps.

First, administrators should determine indispensable work—for example, municipal administration. Then, they should identify peripheral tasks such as conducting investigations and gathering statistics, and connected tasks such as building cleaning and printing. Second, administrators should identify those responsible for the work, its implementation, and financing. Third, they should generate alternatives available by contracting of peripheral and related tasks to other public agencies, to public enterprises, to mixed-economy enterprises (for example, public traffic organizations, banking, public housing), or to private third parties. This transfer to the private sector does not represent a privatization of public tasks if the public administration bears ultimate responsibility for public work.

Cooperate with the Private Sector

Even the central tasks of the public administration should be evaluated to determine whether they can be planned, implemented, or financed together with the private sector. Public-private partnerships can be fulfilled on a contract basis or by a mixed-economy enterprise.

There are a variety of models that can be used for contracted cooperation between the public and private parties. These include the operation model in which the public work sponsor remains the direct owner of the facilities, the management of project model, strategic alliances, the leasing model, and tenancy or concession models. In this and the mixed-economy enterprise, where government collaborates with the private sector, an important requirement is that a balance exist between the public duty and welfare and the profit orientation of the private partner.

PROBLEMS IN REALIZING THE REFORMS

Bureaucratic Culture

It is difficult to implement the reform proposals presented here. Governments have a bureaucratic culture, and they resist change. Indeed, it takes a long time for new ideas to be accepted, let alone acted on. There are several reasons for this.

First, there is a strong set of constraints provided by law, including budgetary legislation, employment legislation, and laws regarding the organization of public administration. To change the management of the various levels of government means changes in the laws that govern them. Second, there are strong political groups and organizations that want their goals realized. Reform, then, is a political process. Third, many workers in public administration are highly specialized and do not have extensive knowledge of business administration principles. For most of them, "saving money" means reducing services but not working more economically, efficiently, or effectively.

Plans Instead of Real Actions

Almost all cities in Germany want to reform their administrations, but there is not a homogeneous procedure for doing so. Most of them choose one specific area of their administration and organize a pilot program to gain experience and understand which management style will be most acceptable to the local government. The pilot programs are currently being implemented in some places, but at the federal and state levels, there is discussion of reform but no meaningful implementation.

Fundamental Changes

To realize the reforms and to find a new management style for the public sector requires change in governmental structures, procedures, and behavior. In the future employees will have to look to economic success, think in terms of cost and performance indicators, make decisions and bear the responsibility for them, and work efficiently to be competitive. Heads of departments will have to believe in staff members, and motivated employees will have to cooperate with department heads and colleagues in order to have a fruitful and productive workplace. Finally, it is necessary that special training courses and advanced training programs support the reform effort.

Making Differences Matter: A New Paradigm for Managing Diversity

David A. Thomas
Robin J. Ely

Why should companies concern themselves with diversity? Until recently, many managers answered this question with the assertion that discrimination is wrong, both legally and morally. But today managers are voicing a second notion as well. A more diverse workforce, they say, will increase organizational effectiveness. It will lift morale, bring greater access to new segments of the marketplace, and enhance productivity. In short, they claim, diversity will be good for business.

　　Yet if this is true—and we believe it is—where are the positive impacts of diversity? Numerous and varied initiatives to increase diversity in corporate America have been under way for more than two decades. Rarely, however, have those efforts spurred leaps in organizational effectiveness. Instead, many attempts to increase diversity in the workplace have backfired, sometimes even heightening tensions among employees and hindering a company's performance.

This article offers an explanation for why diversity efforts are not fulfilling their promise, and presents a new paradigm for understanding—and leveraging—diversity. It is our belief that there is a distinct way to unleash the powerful benefits of a diverse workforce. Although these benefits include increased profitability, they go beyond financial measures to encompass learning, creativity, flexibility, organizational and individual growth, and the ability of a company to adjust rapidly and successfully to market changes. The desired transformation, however, requires a fundamental change in the attitudes and behaviors of an organization's leadership. And that will come only when senior managers abandon an underlying and flawed assumption about diversity and replace it with a broader understanding.

Most people assume that workplace diversity is about increasing racial, national, gender, or class representation—in other words, recruiting and retaining more people from traditionally underrepresented "identity groups." Taking this commonly held assumption as a starting point, we set out six years ago to investigate its link to organizational effectiveness. We soon found that thinking of diversity simply in terms of identity-group representation inhibited effectiveness.

Organizations usually take one of two paths in managing diversity. In the name of equality and fairness, they encourage (and expect) women and people of color to blend in. Or they set them apart in jobs that relate specifically to their backgrounds, assigning them, for example, to areas that require them to interface with clients or customers of the same identity group. African American M.B.A.'s often find themselves marketing products to inner-city communities; Hispanics frequently market to Hispanics or work for Latin American subsidiaries. In those kinds of cases, companies are operating on the assumption that the main virtue identity groups have to offer is a knowledge of their own people. This assumption is limited—and limiting—and detrimental to diversity efforts.

What we suggest here is that diversity goes beyond increasing the number of different identity group affiliations on the payroll to recognizing that such an effort is merely the first step in managing a diverse workforce for the organization's utmost benefit. Diversity should be understood as *the varied perspectives and approaches to work* that members of different identity groups bring.

Women, Hispanics, Asian Americans, African Americans, Native Americans—these groups and others outside the mainstream of corporate America don't bring with them just their "insider information." They bring different, important, and competitively relevant knowledge and perspectives about how to actually *do work*—how to design processes, reach goals, frame tasks, create effective teams, communicate ideas, and lead. When allowed to, members of these groups can help companies grow and improve by challenging basic assumptions about an organization's functions, strategies, operations, practices, and procedures. And in doing so, they are able to bring more of their whole selves to the workplace and identify more fully with the work they do, setting in motion a virtuous circle. Certainly, individuals can be expected to contribute to a company their firsthand familiarity with niche markets. But only when companies start thinking about diversity more holistically—as providing fresh and meaningful approaches to work—and stop assuming that diversity relates simply to how a person looks or where he or she comes from, will they be able to reap its full rewards.

Two perspectives have guided most diversity initiatives to date: the *discrimination-and-fairness paradigm* and the *access-and-legitimacy paradigm*. But we have identified a new, emerging approach to this complex management issue. This approach, which we call the *learning-and-effectiveness paradigm*, incorporates aspects of the first two paradigms but goes beyond them by concretely connecting diversity to approaches to work. Our goal is to help business leaders see what their own approach to diversity currently is and how it may already have influenced their companies' diversity efforts. Managers can learn to assess whether they need to change their diversity initiatives and, if so, how to accomplish that change.

The following discussion will also cite several examples of how connecting the new definition of diversity to the actual *doing* of work has led some organizations to markedly better performance. The organizations differ in many ways—none are in the same industry, for instance—but they are united by one similarity: Their leaders realize that increasing demographic variation does not in itself increase organizational effectiveness. They realize that it is *how* a company defines diversity— and *what it does* with the experiences of being a diverse organization—that delivers on the promise.

THE DISCRIMINATION-AND-FAIRNESS PARADIGM

Using the discrimination-and-fairness paradigm is perhaps thus far the dominant way of understanding diversity. Leaders who look at diversity through this lens usually focus on equal opportunity, fair treatment, recruitment, and compliance with federal Equal Employment Opportunity requirements. The paradigm's underlying logic can be expressed as follows:

> Prejudice has kept members of certain demographic groups out of organizations such as ours. As a matter of fairness and to comply with federal mandates, we need to work toward restructuring the makeup of our organization to let it more closely reflect that of society. We need managerial processes that ensure that all our employees are treated equally and with respect and that some are not given unfair advantage over others.

Although it resembles the thinking behind traditional affirmative-action efforts, the discrimination-and-fairness paradigm does go beyond a simple concern with numbers. Companies that operate with this philosophical orientation often institute mentoring and career-development programs specifically for the women and people of color in their ranks and train other employees to respect cultural differences. Under this paradigm, nevertheless, progress in diversity is measured by how well the company achieves its recruitment and retention goals rather than by the degree to which conditions in the company allow employees to draw on their personal assets and perspectives to do their work more effectively. The staff, one might say, gets diversified, but the work does not.

What are some of the common characteristics of companies that have used the discrimination-and-fairness paradigm successfully to increase their demographic diversity? Our research indicates that they are usually run by leaders who value due process and equal treatment of all employees and who have the authority to use top-down directives to enforce initiatives based on those attitudes. Such companies are often bureaucratic in structure, with control processes in place for monitoring, measuring, and rewarding individual performance. And finally, they are often organizations with entrenched, easily observable cultures, in which values like fairness are widespread and deeply inculcated and codes of conduct are clear and unambiguous. (Perhaps the most extreme example of an organization in which all these factors are at work is the United States Army.)

Without doubt, there are benefits to this paradigm: it does tend to increase demographic diversity in an organization, and it often succeeds in promoting fair treatment. But it also has significant limitations. The first of these is that its color-blind, gender-blind ideal is to some degree built on the implicit assumption that "we are all the same" or "we aspire to being all the same." Under this paradigm, it is not desirable for diversification of the workforce to influence the organization's work or culture. The company should operate as if every person were of the same race, gender, and nationality. It is unlikely that leaders who manage diversity under this paradigm will explore how people's differences generate a potential diversity of effective ways of working, leading, viewing the market, managing people, and learning.

Not only does the discrimination-and-fairness paradigm insist that everyone is the same, but, with its emphasis on equal treatment, it puts pressure on employees to make sure that important differences among them do not count. Genuine disagreements about work definition, therefore, are sometimes wrongly interpreted through this paradigm's fairness-unfairness lens—especially when honest disagreements are accompanied by tense debate. A female employee who insists, for example, that a company's advertising strategy is not appropriate for all ethnic segments in the marketplace might feel she is violating the code of assimilation upon which the paradigm is built. Moreover, if she were then to defend her opinion by citing, let us say, her personal knowledge of the ethnic group the company wanted to reach, she might risk being perceived as importing inappropriate attitudes into an organization that prides itself on being blind to cultural differences.

Workplace paradigms channel organizational thinking in powerful ways. By limiting the ability of employees to acknowledge openly their work-related but culturally based differences, the paradigm actually undermines the organization's capacity to learn about and improve its own strategies, processes, and practices. And it also keeps people from identifying strongly and personally with their work—a critical source of motivation and self-regulation in any business environment.

As an illustration of the paradigm's weaknesses, consider the case of Iversen Dunham, an international consulting firm that focuses on foreign and domestic economic-development policy. (Like all the examples in this article, the company is real, but its name is disguised.) Not long ago, the firm's managers asked us to help them understand why race relations had become a divisive issue precisely at a time when Iversen was receiving accolades for its diversity efforts. Indeed, other organizations had even begun to use the firm to benchmark their own diversity programs.

Iversen's diversity efforts had begun in the early 1970s, when senior managers decided to pursue greater racial and gender diversity in the firm's higher ranks. (The firm's leaders were strongly committed to the cause of social justice.) Women and people of color were hired and charted on career paths toward becoming project leaders. High performers among those who had left the firm were persuaded to return in senior roles. By 1989, about 50% of Iversen's project leaders and professionals were women, and 30% were people of color. The 13-member management committee, once exclusively white and male, included five women and four people of color. Additionally, Iversen had developed a strong contingent of foreign nationals.

It was at about this time, however, that tensions began to surface. Senior managers found it hard to believe that, after all the effort to create a fair and mutually respectful work community, some staff members could still be claiming that Iversen had racial discrimination problems. The management invited us to study the firm and deliver an outsider's assessment of its problem.

We had been inside the firm for only a short time when it became clear that Iversen's leaders viewed the dynamics of diversity through the lens of the discrimination-and-fairness paradigm. But where they saw racial discord, we discerned clashing approaches to the actual work of consulting. Why? Our research showed that tensions were strongest among midlevel project leaders. Surveys and interviews indicated that white project leaders welcomed demographic diversity as a general sign of progress but that they also thought the new employees were somehow changing the company, pulling it away from its original culture and its mission. Common criticisms were that African American and Hispanic staff made problems too complex by linking issues the organization had traditionally regarded as unrelated and that they brought on projects that seemed to require greater cultural sensitivity. White male project leaders also complained that their peers who were women and people of color were undermining one of Iversen's traditional strengths: its hard-core quantitative orientation. For instance, minority project leaders had suggested that Iversen consultants collect information and seek input from others in the client company besides senior managers—that is, from the rank and file and from middle managers. Some had urged Iversen to expand its consulting approach to include the gathering and analysis of qualitative data through interviewing and observation. Indeed, these project leaders had even challenged one of Iversen's long-standing, core assumptions: that the firm's reports were objective. They urged Iversen Dunham to recognize and address the subjective aspect of its analyses; the firm could, for example, include in its reports to clients dissenting Iversen views, if any existed.

For their part, project leaders who were women and people of color felt that they were not accorded the same level of authority to carry out that work as their white male peers. Moreover, they sensed that those peers were skeptical of their opinions, and they resented that doubts were not voiced openly.

Meanwhile, there also was some concern expressed about tension between white managers and nonwhite subordinates, who claimed they were being treated unfairly. But our analysis suggested that the manager-subordinate conflicts were not numerous enough to warrant the attention they were drawing from top management. We believed it was significant that senior managers found it easier to focus on this second type of conflict than on midlevel conflicts about project choice and project definition. Indeed, Iversen Dunham's focus seemed to be a result of the firm's reliance on its particular diversity paradigm and the emphasis on fairness and equality. It was relatively easy to diagnose problems in light of those concepts and to devise a solution: just get managers to treat their subordinates more fairly.

In contrast, it was difficult to diagnose peer-to-peer tensions in the framework of this model. Such conflicts were about the very nature of Iversen's work, not simply unfair treatment. Yes, they were related to identity-group affiliations, but they were not symptomatic of classic racism. It was Iversen's paradigm that led managers to interpret them as such. Remember, we were asked to assess what was supposed to be a racial discrimination problem. Iversen's discrimination-and-fairness paradigm had created a kind of cognitive blind spot; and, as a result, the company's leadership could not frame the problem accurately or solve it effectively. Instead, the company needed a cultural shift—it needed to grasp what to do with its diversity once it had achieved the numbers. If all Iversen Dunham employees were to contribute to the fullest extent, the company would need a paradigm that would encourage open and explicit discussion of what identity-group differences really mean and how they can be used as sources of individual and organizational effectiveness.

Today, mainly because of senior managers' resistance to such a cultural transformation, Iversen continues to struggle with the tensions arising from the diversity of its workforce.

THE ACCESS-AND-LEGITIMACY PARADIGM

In the competitive climate of the 1980s and 1990s, a new rhetoric and rationale for managing diversity emerged. If the discrimination-and-fairness paradigm can be said to have idealized assimilation and color- and gender-blind conformism, the access-and-legitimacy paradigm was predicated on the acceptance and celebration of differences. The underlying motivation of the access-and-legitimacy paradigm can be expressed this way:

> We are living in an increasingly multicultural country, and new ethnic groups are quickly gaining consumer power. Our company needs a demographically more diverse workforce to help us gain access to these differentiated segments. We need employees with multilingual skills in order to understand and serve our customers better and to gain legitimacy with them. Diversity isn't just fair; it makes business sense.

Where this paradigm has taken hold, organizations have pushed for access to—and legitimacy with—a more diverse clientele by matching the demographics of the organization to those of critical consumer or constituent groups. In some cases, the effort has led to substantial increases in organizational diversity. In investment banks, for example, municipal finance departments have long led corporate finance departments in pursuing demographic diversity because of the typical makeup of the administration of city halls and county boards. Many consumer-products companies that have used market segmentation based on gender, racial, and other demographic differences have also frequently created dedicated marketing positions for each segment. The paradigm has therefore led to new professional and managerial opportunities for women and people of color.

What are the common characteristics of organizations that have successfully used the access-and-legitimacy paradigm to increase their demographic diversity? There is but one: such companies almost always operate in a business environment in which there is increased diversity among customers, clients, or the labor pool—and therefore a clear opportunity or an imminent threat to the company.

Again, the paradigm has its strengths. Its market-based motivation and the potential for competitive advantage that it suggests are often qualities an entire company can understand and therefore support. But the paradigm is perhaps more notable for its limitations. In their pursuit of niche markets, access-and-legitimacy organizations tend to emphasize the role of cultural differences in a company without really analyzing those differences to see how they actually affect the work that is done. Whereas discrimination-and-fairness leaders are too quick to subvert differences in the interest of preserving harmony, access-and-legitimacy leaders are too quick to push staff with niche capabilities into differentiated pigeonholes without trying to understand what those capabilities really are and how they could be integrated into the company's mainstream work. To illustrate our point, we present the case of Access Capital.

Access Capital International is a U.S. investment bank that in the early 1980s launched an aggressive plan to expand into Europe. Initially, however, Access encountered serious problems opening offices in international markets; the people from the United States who were installed abroad lacked credibility, were ignorant of local cultural norms and market conditions, and simply couldn't seem to connect with native clients. Access responded by hiring Europeans who had attended North American business schools and by assigning them in teams to the foreign offices. This strategy was a marked success. Before long, the leaders of Access could take enormous pride in the fact that their European operations were highly profitable and staffed by a truly international corps of professionals. They took to calling the company "the best investment bank in the world."

Several years passed. Access's foreign offices continued to thrive, but some leaders were beginning to sense that the company was not fully benefiting from its diversity efforts. Indeed, some even suspected that the bank had made itself vulnerable because of how it had chosen to manage diversity. A senior executive from the United States explains:

> If the French team all resigned tomorrow, what would we do? I'm not sure what we *could* do! We've never attempted to learn what these differences and cultural competencies really are, how they change the process of doing business. What is the German country team actually doing? We don't know. We know they're good, but we don't know the subtleties of how they do what they do. We assumed—and I think correctly—that culture makes a difference, but that's about as far as we went. We hired Europeans with American M.B.A.'s because we didn't know why we couldn't do business in Europe—we just assumed there was something cultural about why we couldn't connect. And ten years later, we still don't know what it is. If we knew, then perhaps we could take it and teach it. Which part of the investment banking process is universal and which part of it draws upon particular cultural competencies? What are the commonalities and differences? I may not be German, but maybe I could do better at understanding what it means to be an American doing business in Germany. Our company's biggest failing is that the department heads in London and the directors of the various country teams have never talked about these cultural identity issues openly. We know enough to *use* people's cultural strengths, as it were, but we never seemed to learn from them.

Access's story makes an important point about the main limitation of the access-and-legitimacy paradigm: under its influence, the motivation for diversity usually emerges from very immediate and often crisis-oriented needs for access and legitimacy—in this case, the need to broker deals in European markets. However, once the organization appears to be achieving its goal, the leaders seldom go on to identify and analyze the culturally based skills, beliefs, and practices that worked so well. Nor do they consider how the organization can incorporate and learn from those skills, beliefs, or practices in order to capitalize on diversity in the long run.

Under the access-and-legitimacy paradigm, it was as if the bank's country teams had become little spin-off companies in their own right, doing their own exotic, slightly mysterious cultural-diversity thing in a niche market of their own, using competencies that for some reason could not become more fully integrated into the larger organization's understanding of itself. Difference was valued within Access Capital—hence the development of country teams in the first place—but not valued enough that the organization would try to integrate it into the very core of its culture and into its business practices.

Finally, the access-and-legitimacy paradigm can leave some employees feeling exploited. Many organizations using this paradigm have diversified only in those areas in which they interact with particular niche-market segments. In time, many individuals recruited for this function have come to feel devalued and used as they begin to sense that opportunities in other parts of the organization are closed to them. Often the larger organization regards the experience of these employees as more limited or specialized, even though many of them in fact started their careers in the mainstream market before moving to special markets where their cultural backgrounds were a recognized asset. Also, many of these people say that when companies have needed to downsize or narrow their marketing focus, it is the special departments that are often the first to go. That situation creates tenuous and ultimately untenable career paths for employees in the special departments.

THE EMERGING PARADIGM: CONNECTING DIVERSITY TO WORK PERSPECTIVES

Recently, in the course of our research, we have encountered a small number of organizations that, having relied initially on one of the above paradigms to guide their diversity efforts, have come to believe that they are not making the most of their own pluralism. These organizations, like Access Capital, recognize that employees frequently make decisions and choices at work that draw upon their cultural background—choices made because of their identity-group affiliations. The companies have also developed an outlook on diversity that enables them to *incorporate* employees' perspectives into the main work of the organization and to enhance work by rethinking primary tasks and redefining markets, products, strategies, missions, business practices, and even cultures. Such companies are using the learning-and-effectiveness paradigm for managing diversity and, by doing so, are tapping diversity's true benefits.

The Research

This article is based on a three-part research effort that began in 1990. Our subject was diversity; but, more specifically, we sought to understand three management challenges under that heading. First, how do organizations successfully achieve and sustain racial and gender diversity in their executive and middle-management ranks? Second, what is the impact of diversity on an organization's practices, processes, and performance? And, finally, how do leaders influence whether diversity becomes an enhancing or detracting element in the organization?

Over the following six years, we worked particularly closely with three organizations that had attained a high degree of demographic diversity: a small urban law firm, a community bank, and a 200-person consulting firm. In addition, we studied nine other companies in varying stages of diversifying their workforces. The group included two financial-services firms, three *Fortune* 500 manufacturing companies, two midsize high-technology companies, a private foundation, and a university medical center. In each case, we based our analysis on interviews, surveys, archival data, and observation. It is from this work that the third paradigm for managing diversity emerged and with it our belief that old and limiting assumptions about the meaning of diversity must be abandoned before its true potential can be realized as a powerful way to increase organizational effectiveness.

A case in point is Dewey & Levin, a small public-interest law firm located in a northeastern U.S. city. Although Dewey & Levin had long been a profitable practice, by the mid-1980s its all-white legal staff had become concerned that the women they represented in employment-related disputes were exclusively white. The firm's attorneys viewed that fact as a deficiency in light of their mandate to advocate on behalf of all women. Using the thinking behind the access-and-legitimacy paradigm, they also saw it as bad for business.

Shortly thereafter, the firm hired a Hispanic female attorney. The partners' hope, simply put, was that she would bring in clients from her own community and also demonstrate the firm's commitment to representing all women. But something even bigger than that happened. The new attorney introduced ideas to Dewey & Levin about what kinds of cases it should take on. Senior managers were open to those ideas and pursued them with great success. More women of color were hired, and they, too, brought fresh perspectives. The firm now pursues cases that its previously all-white legal staff would not have thought relevant or appropriate because the link between the firm's mission and the employment issues involved in the cases would not have been obvious to them. For example, the firm has pursued precedent-setting litigation that challenges English-only policies—an area that it once would have ignored because such policies did not fall under the purview of traditional affirmative-action work. Yet it now sees a link between English-only policies and employment issues for a large group of women—primarily recent immigrants— whom it had previously failed to serve adequately. As one of the white principals explains, the demographic composition of Dewey & Levin "has affected the work in terms of expanding notions of what are [relevant] issues and taking on issues and framing them in creative ways that would have never been done [with an all-white staff]. It's really changed the substance—and in that sense enhanced the quality—of our work."

Dewey & Levin's increased business success has reinforced its commitment to diversity. In addition, people of color at the firm uniformly report feeling respected, not simply "brought along as window dressing." Many of the new attorneys say their perspectives are heard with a kind of openness and interest they have never experienced before in a work setting. Not surprisingly, the firm has had little difficulty attracting and retaining a competent and diverse professional staff.

If the discrimination-and-fairness paradigm is organized around the theme of assimilation—in which the aim is to achieve a demographically representative workforce whose members treat one another exactly the same—then the access-and-legitimacy paradigm can be regarded as coalescing around an almost opposite concept: differentiation, in which the objective is to place different people where their demographic characteristics match those of important constituents and markets.

The emerging paradigm, in contrast to both, organizes itself around the overarching theme of integration. Assimilation goes too far in pursuing sameness. Differentiation, as we have shown, overshoots in the other direction. The new model for managing diversity transcends both. Like the fairness paradigm, it promotes equal opportunity for all individuals. And like the access paradigm, it acknowledges cultural differences among people and recognizes the value in those differences. Yet this new model for managing diversity lets the organization internalize differences among employees so that it learns and grows because of them. Indeed, with the model fully in place, members of the organization can say, We are all on the same team, *with* our differences—not *despite* them.

EIGHT PRECONDITIONS FOR MAKING THE PARADIGM SHIFT

Dewey & Levin may be atypical in its eagerness to open itself up to change and engage in a long-term transformation process. We remain convinced, however, that unless organizations that are currently in the grip of the other two paradigms can revise their view of diversity so as to avoid cognitive blind spots, opportunities will be missed, tensions will most likely be misdiagnosed, and companies will continue to find the potential benefits of diversity elusive.

Hence the question arises: What is it about the law firm of Dewey & Levin and other emerging third-paradigm companies that enables them to make the most of their diversity? Our research suggests that there are eight preconditions that help to position organizations to use identity-group differences in the service of organizational learning, growth, and renewal.

1. *The leadership must understand that a diverse workforce will embody different perspectives and approaches to work, and must truly value variety of opinion and insight.* We know of a financial services company that once assumed that the only successful sales model was one that utilized aggressive, rapid-fire cold calls. (Indeed, its incentive system rewarded salespeople in large part for the number of calls made.) An internal review of the company's diversity initiatives, however, showed that the company's first- and third-most-profitable employees were women who were most likely to use a sales technique based on the slow but sure building of relationships. The company's top management has now made the link between different identity groups and different approaches to how work gets done and has come to see that there is more than one right way to get positive results.

2. *The leadership must recognize both the learning opportunities and the challenges that the expression of different perspectives presents for an organization.* In other words, the second precondition is a leadership that is committed to persevering during the long process of learning and relearning that the new paradigm requires.

3. *The organizational culture must create an expectation of high standards of performance from everyone.* Such a culture isn't one that expects less from some employees than from others. Some organizations expect women and people of color to underperform—a negative assumption that too often becomes a self-fulfilling prophecy. To move to the third paradigm, a company must believe that all its members can and should contribute fully.

4. *The organizational culture must stimulate personal development.* Such a culture brings out people's full range of useful knowledge and skills—usually through the careful design of jobs that allow people to grow and develop but also through training and education programs.

5. *The organizational culture must encourage openness.* Such a culture instills a high tolerance for debate and supports constructive conflict on work-related matters.

6. *The culture must make workers feel valued.* If this precondition is met, workers feel committed to—and empowered within—the organization

and therefore feel comfortable taking the initiative to apply their skills and experiences in new ways to enhance their job performance.

7. *The organization must have a well-articulated and widely understood mission.* Such a mission enables people to be clear about what the company is trying to accomplish. It grounds and guides discussions about work-related changes that staff members might suggest. Being clear about the company's mission helps keep discussions about work differences from degenerating into debates about the validity of people's perspectives. A clear mission provides a focal point that keeps the discussion centered on accomplishment of goals.

8. *The organization must have a relatively egalitarian, nonbureaucratic structure.* It's important to have a structure that promotes the exchange of ideas and welcomes constructive challenges to the usual way of doing things—from any employee with valuable experience. Forward-thinking leaders in bureaucratic organizations must retain the organization's efficiency-promoting control systems and chains of command while finding ways to reshape the change-resisting mind-set of the classic bureaucratic model. They need to separate the enabling elements of bureaucracy (the ability to get things done) from disabling elements of bureaucracy (those that create resistance to experimentation).

FIRST INTERSTATE BANK: A PARADIGM SHIFT IN PROGRESS

All eight preconditions do not have to be in place in order to begin a shift from the first or second diversity orientations toward the learning-and-effectiveness paradigm. But most should be. First Interstate Bank, a midsize bank operating in a midwestern city, illustrates this point.

First Interstate, admittedly, is not a typical bank. It's client base is a minority community, and its mission is expressly to serve that base through "the development of a highly talented workforce." The bank is unique in other ways: its leadership welcomes constructive criticism; its structure is relatively egalitarian and non-bureaucratic; and its culture is open-minded. Nevertheless, First Interstate had long enforced a policy that loan officers had to hold college degrees. Those without were hired only for support-staff jobs and were never promoted beyond or outside support functions.

Two years ago, however, the support staff began to challenge the policy. Many of them had been with First Interstate for many years and, with the company's active support, had improved their skills through training. Others had expanded their skills on the job, again with the bank's encouragement, learning to run credit checks, prepare presentations for clients, and even calculate the algorithms necessary for many loan decisions. As a result, some people on the support staff were doing many of the same tasks as loan officers. Why, then, they wondered, couldn't they receive commensurate rewards in title and compensation?

This questioning led to a series of contentious meetings between the support staff and the bank's senior managers. It soon became clear that the problem called for managing diversity—diversity based not on race or gender but on class. The support personnel were uniformly from lower socio-economic communities than were the college-educated loan officers. Regardless, the principle was the same as for race- or gender-based diversity problems. The support staff had different ideas about how the work of the bank should be done. They argued that those among them with the requisite skills should be allowed to rise through the ranks to professional positions, and they believed their ideas were not being heard or accepted.

Their beliefs challenged assumptions that the company's leadership had long held about which employees should have the authority to deal with customers and about how much responsibility administrative employees should ultimately receive. In order to take up this challenge, the bank would have to be open to exploring the requirements that a new perspective would impose on it. It would need to consider the possibility of mapping out an educational and career path for people without degrees—a path that could put such workers on the road to becoming loan officers. In other words, the leadership would have to transform itself willingly and embrace fluidity in policies that in times past had been clearly stated and unquestioningly held.

Today the bank's leadership is undergoing just such a transformation. The going, however, is far from easy. The bank's senior managers now must look beyond the tensions and acrimony sparked by the debate over differing work perspectives and consider the bank's new direction an important learning and growth opportunity.

SHIFT COMPLETE: THIRD-PARADIGM COMPANIES IN ACTION

First Interstate is a shift in progress; but, in addition to Dewey & Levin, there are several organizations we know of for which the shift is complete. In these cases, company leaders have played a critical role as facilitators and tone setters. We have observed in particular that in organizations that have adopted the new perspective, leaders and managers—and, following in their tracks, employees in general—are taking four kinds of action.

They Are Making the Mental Connection

First, in organizations that have adopted the new perspective, the leaders are actively seeking opportunities to explore how identity-group differences affect relationships among workers and affect the way work gets done. They are investing considerable time and energy in understanding how identity-group memberships take on social meanings in the organization and how those meanings manifest themselves in the way work is defined, assigned, and accomplished. When there is no proactive search to understand, then learning from diversity, if it happens at all, can occur only reactively—that is, in response to diversity-related crises.

The situation at Iversen Dunham illustrates the missed opportunities resulting from that scenario. Rather than seeing differences in the way project leaders defined and approached their work as an opportunity to gain new insights and develop new approaches to achieving its mission, the firm remained entrenched in its traditional ways, able to arbitrate such differences only by thinking about what was fair and what was racist. With this quite limited view of the role race can play in an organization, discussions about the topic become fraught with fear and defensiveness, and everyone misses out on insights about how race might influence work in positive ways.

A second case, however, illustrates how some leaders using the new paradigm have been able to envision—and make—the connection between cultural diversity and the company's work. A vice president of Mastiff, a large national insurance company, received a complaint from one of the managers in her unit, an African American man. The manager wanted to demote an African American woman he had hired for a leadership position from another Mastiff division just three months before. He told the vice president he was profoundly disappointed with the performance of his new hire.

"I hired her because I was pretty certain she had tremendous leadership skill," he said. "I knew she had a management style that was very open and empowering. I was also sure she'd have a great impact on the rest of the management team. But she hasn't done any of that."

Surprised, the vice president tried to find out from him what he thought the problem was, but she was not getting any answers that she felt really defined or illuminated the root of the problem. Privately, it puzzled her that someone would decide to demote a 15-year veteran of the company—and a minority woman at that—so soon after bringing her to his unit.

The vice president probed further. In the course of the conversation, the manager happened to mention that he knew the new employee from church and was familiar with the way she handled leadership there and in other community settings. In those less formal situations, he had seen her perform as an extremely effective, sensitive, and influential leader.

That is when the vice president made an interpretive leap. "If that's what you know about her," the vice president said to the manager, "then the question for us is, why can't she bring those skills to work here?" The vice president decided to arrange a meeting with all three present to ask this very question directly. In the meeting, the African American woman explained, "I didn't think I would last long if I acted that way here. My personal style of leadership—that particular style—works well if you have the permission to do it fully; then you can just do it and not have to look over your shoulder."

Pointing to the manager who had planned to fire her, she added, "He's right. The style of leadership I use outside this company can definitely be effective. But I've been at Mastiff for 15 years. I know this organization, and I know if I brought that piece of myself—if I became that authentic—I just wouldn't survive here."

What this example illustrates is that the vice president's learning-and-effectiveness paradigm led her to explore and then make the link between cultural diversity and work style. What was occurring, she realized, was a mismatch between the cultural background of the recently promoted woman and the cultural environment of her work setting. It had little to do with private attitudes or feelings, or gender issues, or some inherent lack of leadership ability. The source of the underperformance was that the newly promoted woman had a certain style and the organization's culture did not support her in expressing it comfortably. The vice president's paradigm led her to ask new questions and to seek out new information, but, more important, it also led her to interpret existing information differently.

The two senior managers began to realize that part of the African American woman's inability to see herself as a leader at work was that she had for so long been undervalued in the organization. And, in a sense, she had become used to splitting herself off from who she was in her own community. In the 15 years she had been at Mastiff, she had done her job well as an individual contributor, but she had never received any signals that her bosses wanted her to draw on her cultural competencies in order to lead effectively.

They Are Legitimating Open Discussion

Leaders and managers who have adopted the new paradigm are taking the initiative to "green light" open discussion about how identity-group memberships inform and influence an employee's experience and the organization's behavior. They are encouraging people to make *explicit* use of background cultural experience and the pools of knowledge gained outside the organization to inform and enhance their work. Individuals often do use their cultural competencies at work, but in a closeted, almost embarrassed, way. The unfortunate result is that the opportunity for collective and organizational learning and improvement is lost.

The case of a Chinese woman who worked as a chemist at Torinno Food Company illustrates this point. Linda was part of a product development group at Torinno when a problem arose with the flavoring of a new soup. After the group had made a number of scientific attempts to correct the problem, Linda came up with the solution by "setting aside my chemistry and drawing on my understanding of Chinese cooking." She did not, however, share with her colleagues—all of them white males—the real source of her inspiration for the solution for fear that it would set her apart or that they might consider her unprofessional. Overlaid on the cultural issue, of course, was a gender issue (women cooking) as well as a work-family issue (women doing *home* cooking in a chemistry lab). All of these themes had erected unspoken boundaries that Linda knew could be career-damaging for her to cross. After solving the problem, she simply went back to the so-called scientific way of doing things.

Senior managers at Torinno Foods in fact had made a substantial commitment to diversifying the workforce through a program designed to teach employees to value the contributions of all its members. Yet Linda's perceptions indicate that, in the actual day-to-day context of work, the program had failed—and in precisely one of those areas where it would have been important for it to have worked. It had failed to affirm someone's identity-group experiences as a legitimate source of insight into her work. It is likely that this organization will miss future opportunities to take full advantage of the talent of employees such as Linda. When people believe that they must suggest and apply their ideas covertly, the organization also misses opportunities to discuss, debate, refine, and build on those ideas fully. In addition, because individuals like Linda will continue to think that they must hide parts of themselves in order to fit in, they will find it difficult to engage fully not only in their work but also in their workplace relationships. That kind of situation can breed resentment and misunderstanding, fueling tensions that can further obstruct productive work relationships.

They Actively Work Against Forms of Dominance and Subordination That Inhibit Full Contribution

Companies in which the third paradigm is emerging have leaders and managers who take responsibility for removing the barriers that block employees from using the full range of their competencies, cultural or otherwise. Racism, homophobia, sexism, and sexual harassment are the most obvious forms of dominance that decrease individual and organizational effectiveness—and third-paradigm leaders have zero tolerance for them. In addition, the leaders are aware that organizations can create their own unique patterns of dominance and subordination based on the presumed superiority and entitlement of some groups over others. It is not uncommon, for instance, to find organizations in which one functional area considers itself better than another. Members of the presumed inferior group frequently describe the organization in the very terms used by those who experience identity group discrimination. Regardless of the source of the oppression, the result is diminished performance and commitment from employees.

What can leaders do to prevent those kinds of behaviors beyond explicitly forbidding any forms of dominance? They can and should test their own assumptions about the competencies of all members of the workforce because negative assumptions are often unconsciously communicated in powerful—albeit nonverbal—ways. For example, senior managers at Delta Manufacturing had for years allowed productivity and quality at their inner city plants to lag well behind the levels of other plants. When the company's chief executive officer began to question why the problem was never addressed, he came to realize that, in his heart, he had believed that inner-city workers, most of whom were African American or Hispanic, were not capable of doing better than subpar. In the end, the CEO and his senior management team were able to reverse their reasoning and take responsibility for improving the situation. The result was a sharp increase in the performance of the inner-city plants and a message to the entire organization about the capabilities of its entire workforce.

At Mastiff, the insurance company discussed earlier, the vice president and her manager decided to work with the recently promoted African American woman rather than demote her. They realized that their unit was really a pocket inside the larger organization: they did not have to wait for the rest of the organization to make a paradigm shift in order for their particular unit to change. So they met again to think about how to create conditions within their unit that would move the woman toward seeing her leadership position as encompassing all her skills. They assured her that her authentic style of leadership was precisely what they wanted her to bring to the job. They wanted her to be able to use whatever aspects of herself she thought would make her more effective in her work because the whole purpose was to do the job effectively, not to fit some preset traditional formula of how to behave. They let her know that, as a management team, they would try to adjust and change and support her. And they would deal with whatever consequences resulted from her exercising her decision rights in new ways.

Another example of this line of action—working against forms of dominance and subordination to enable full contribution—is the way the CEO of a major chemical company modified the attendance rules for his company's annual strategy conference. In the past, the conference had been attended only by senior executives, a relatively homogeneous group of white men. The company had been working hard on increasing the representation of women and people of color in its ranks, and the CEO could have left it at that. But he reckoned that, unless steps were taken, it would be ten years before the conferences tapped into the insights and perspectives of his newly diverse workforce. So he took the bold step of opening the conference to people from across all levels of the hierarchy, bringing together a diagonal slice of the organization. He also asked the conference organizers to come up with specific interventions, such as small group meetings before the larger session, to ensure that the new attendees would be comfortable enough to enter discussions. The result was that strategy-conference participants heard a much broader, richer, and livelier discussion about future scenarios for the company.

They Are Making Sure That Organizational Trust Stays Intact

Few things are faster at killing a shift to a new way of thinking about diversity than feelings of broken trust. Therefore, managers of organizations that are successfully shifting to the learning-and-effectiveness paradigm take one more step: they make sure their organizations remain "safe" places for employees to be themselves. These managers recognize that tensions naturally arise as an organization begins to make room for diversity, starts to experiment with process and product ideas, and learns to reappraise its mission in light of suggestions from newly empowered constituents in the company. But as people put more of themselves out and open up about new feelings and ideas, the dynamics of the learning-and-effectiveness paradigm can produce temporary vulnerabilities. Managers who have helped their organizations make the change successfully have consistently demonstrated their commitment to the process and to all employees by setting a tone of honest discourse, by acknowledging tensions, and by resolving them sensitively and swiftly.

Our research over the past six years indicates that one cardinal limitation is at the root of companies' inability to attain the expected performance benefits of higher levels of diversity: the leadership's vision of the purpose of a diversified workforce. We have described the two most dominant orientations toward diversity and some of their consequences and limitations, together with a new framework for understanding and managing diversity. The learning-and-effectiveness paradigm we have outlined here is, undoubtedly, still in an emergent phase in those few organizations that embody it. We expect that as more organizations take on the challenge of truly engaging their diversity, new and unforeseen dilemmas will arise. Thus, perhaps more than anything else, a shift toward this paradigm requires a high-level commitment to learning more about the environment, structure, and tasks of one's organization, and giving improvement-generating change greater priority than the security of what is familiar. This is not an easy challenge, but we remain convinced that unless organizations take this step, any diversity initiative will fall short of fulfilling its rich promise.

Women Managers
in a Global Economy

Nancy J. Adler

"The best reason for believing that more women will be in charge before long is that in a ferociously competitive global economy, no company can afford to waste valuable brainpower simply because it's wearing a skirt." So wrote Anne B. Fisher in the September 21, 1992, issue of *Fortune* magazine. But a four-part study of women international managers suggests that her belief is not borne out by companies' behavior in the global marketplace.

The first part of the study tallied the number of women that North American firms assign to expatriate management positions. The study polled 686 major Canadian and U.S. firms that had at least one major operation located outside of North America.

Altogether, these firms reported that women filled 402 of 13,348 international management positions, or about 3 percent. Put another way, these firms sent 32 male managers abroad for every woman manager. In comparison, women hold 37 percent of domestic U.S. management positions, 12 times as many as they hold abroad.

Three percent of expatriate management positions is not as poor a showing as one might think. Ninety percent of the women international managers identified in the survey were the first women their companies had ever sent abroad; many had assumed their posts within the previous five years. In this light, 3 percent might be viewed as the start of a trend.

More recent research suggests that the percentage of women executives serving abroad has doubled since the study concluded in 1987. Still, the absolute number of women international managers remains small. Given the global competitive pressures business face, why don't companies assign more women internationally?

They don't because managers and executives base decisions about assigning women overseas on myth instead of fact, as the rest of the study showed. Interviews with human resource vice-presidents and managers from many large North American companies revealed that firms resist assigning women overseas because they assume certain things about female managers' characteristics and about the competitive conditions that women managers face when they go abroad. More than half of the companies cited such beliefs as the reasons they hesitate to send women abroad, although many of the firms are quick to promote women into domestic management positions.

"Women Managers in a Global Economy" by Nancy J. Adler from *Training and Development* (April 1994): 31–36. Reprinted by permission of Blackwell Publishers.

Here are the most common beliefs held by companies about women in international management:

- Women do not want to be international managers.
- Women in dual-career marriages are poor candidates for overseas assignments.
- Foreigners' unwillingness to accept women as managers dooms women international managers to failure.

Research has revealed these assumptions to be false, yet executives continue to base decisions on them that are neither effective nor equitable.

MYTH 1: WOMEN'S RELUCTANCE

This myth seems to have evolved, at least in part, from companies' experiences with male expatriates. A large body of research has shown that when men are assigned overseas and are accompanied by their nonworking spouses, wives' inability to adjust is the single biggest reason that assignments fail. Responses from human resource executives indicate that companies have confused a role (unemployed spouse) with a gender (female) and concluded that women do not adjust well to life abroad, and so would prefer to avoid international assignments.

This myth that women do not want to serve abroad was tested by surveying more than a thousand graduating MBAs. The results revealed no significant difference between female and male MBAs' interest in pursuing international careers. More than four out of five MBAs—both women and men—want an international assignment at some time during their career. Women and men are equally interested in international management, including expatriate assignments.

A later phase of the study showed that women both prepare and position themselves for international assignments. A survey of 100 women international managers from major North American firms showed that, as a group, they are very well-educated—almost all held graduate degrees. Most had extensive international interests and experiences before assuming their expatriate posts; many spoke two or three languages.

Many of these women said they explored the possibility of an international assignment during their original job interview and eliminated companies that would not consider sending them. Others said they tried to be in the right place at the right time. For example, one woman who predicted that Hong Kong would be her firm's next major business center arranged to assume responsibility for the Hong Kong desk in New York, leaving the rest of Asia to a male colleague. The strategy paid off: Within a year, the company elevated its Hong Kong operations to a regional center and sent her to Asia as the firm's first woman international manager.

Rather than resisting international assignments most women expatriates reported that they had to overcome corporate resistance before being sent abroad. Most women said it had never occurred to their companies' managers to consider women for overseas posts. Four out of five women reported that they initially suggested the idea of an international assignment to the company. Some said they kept mentioning the idea to their bosses until they won international positions. Others said their companies offered them international positions as a last resort, after all male candidates turned the assignments down.

Here are some typical comments from female international managers about how they obtained their first overseas assignments.

- "Management assumed that women didn't have the physical stamina to survive in the tropics. They claimed I couldn't hack it in Malaysia."

- "My company didn't want to send a woman to that 'horrible part of the world.' They think Bangkok is an excellent place to send single men, but not a woman."

- "Every advance in responsibility is because the Americans had no choice. I've never been chosen over someone else."

- "They never would have considered me. But then the financial manager in Tokyo had a heart attack, and they had to send someone. So they sent me, on a month's notice, as a temporary until they could find a man to fill the permanent position. It worked out, and I stayed."

MYTH 2: THE "PROBLEM" OF DUAL-CAREER MARRIAGES

More than three-quarters of the human resource executives interviewed cited dual-career marriages as a reason that companies avoid sending women executives abroad. Many suggested that the problems posed by assigning overseas a married woman with an employed husband "can't be solved." (Left unsaid was the fact that many companies frequently assign men with working wives to international posts.)

But responses of women international managers interviewed indicate that couples' career problems can indeed be ironed out. About half the women expats were married; they and their spouses had reconciled career conflicts in different ways. Some opted for commuter marriages, at least for a while. Some spouses had "portable" careers that enabled them to work anywhere; others found positions overseas.

As a sidenote, the few women expatriates who had children reaped an unexpected benefit from their overseas posts: household help. Traditionally, companies supply their expatriate managers with housekeeping services, live-in child-care givers and, often, drivers. According to international manager/moms, this windfall gave them more time to attend to business than they had back home.

MYTH 3: WOMEN MANAGERS AND FOREIGN PREJUDICE

Is historic discrimination against local women a valid basis for predicting expatriate women's success or failure as international managers? Many firms believe so. Almost three-quarters of human resource managers interviewed said that foreigners are so prejudiced against women that women managers would not succeed if they were sent.

To investigate this myth, we surveyed more than 100 women managers from major North American firms who were on international assignments in countries around the world.

Almost all the women managers (97 percent) reported that their international assignments were successful. This success rate is considerably higher than that of North American male expatriates.

Their companies' actions corroborate that assessment. Most companies promoted the women on the basis of their performance abroad. Many companies offered them other international assignments after the first one. And most of the firms, after experimenting with their first female international manager, decided to send other women abroad.

Women and Transnational Corporations

The extent to which firms fill international positions with female executive talent depends to some degree on a firm's status as a global enterprise.

Firms evolve through stages of internationalization. The first step (after the domestic phase) is the international phase, in which companies export products and services abroad but retain highly centralized structures. At the next phase, the multinational phase, firms organize around global lines of business, but largely keep their management hierarchies in place.

Firms at these two phases of internationalization are much less likely to assign female managers internationally than are firms that have evolved to the final, transnational phase.

Truly transnational firms—which are characterized by highly integrated, worldwide operations and are staffed by highly diverse workforces—have the strongest record for deploying female managers around the globe. A firm's transnational character allows it organizational freedoms and imposes competitive demands not present in domestic, international, or multinational environments.

The extremely competitive global business environment forces transnational firms to select the very best people available regardless of gender; transnationals cannot afford to overlook any source of management talent. So transnational firms are more likely to send women on overseas assignments than are firms at other stages of internationalization.

The outstanding success of female international managers in all areas—Africa, the Americas, Asia, Europe, and the Middle East—is encouraging firms both to continue sending women abroad and to begin promoting more local women into management.

Domestic firms have to stick closely to local norms on hiring—or not hiring—women managers. Transnationals are not limited by these norms; their transnational natures allow them organizational flexibility that is not present in firms that are in earlier stages of internationalization. In addition to having women as expatriate managers, transnationals can and do hire local women as managers—even in countries in which the local companies rarely do so. By hiring women, transnationals can act as role models for local firms in countries that have not seriously considered promoting women into managerial positions.

Most local firms have traditionally been structured as hierarchies, but transnationals are increasingly organized into networks of equals. Recent research suggests that women work particularly well in such networks. Not surprisingly, transnational firms benefit from the increasingly important collaborative and participative skills women tend to bring to the workplace.

Innovation is a key factor in global competitiveness. And a key source of innovation is well-managed diversity, including gender diversity. Women bring diversity to transnational corporations that have been primarily male.

Transnational corporations thus include more women than their predecessors and benefit from women's professional contributions in new ways. They can benefit from women's increased representation at all levels of the organization as well as from women's unique ways of contributing to the organization, which complement those of men.

If the third myth were true, we would expect the women international managers interviewed to report difficulties abroad related to their gender. This is not the case. Almost half of the international women managers (42 percent) describe their gender as an advantage; 16 percent find both advantages and disadvantages to being female; 22 percent see it as irrelevant. Only 20 percent describe their gender as a disadvantage.

One pattern became clear: Male or female, foreigners are seen as foreigners. A woman who is a foreigner (a *gaijin*, as the Japanese say) is not expected to act like a local woman. The cultural norms that limit local women's access to managerial positions do not apply to foreign women. The comments of women international managers bear this out:

- "They can tell that I am not Japanese, and they do not expect me to act as a Japanese woman. They will allow and condone behavior in foreign women that would be absolutely unacceptable in their own women."
- "Will I have problems? No! There is a double standard between expats and local women. The Pakistanis test you, but you enter as a respected person."
- "Hong Kong is very cosmopolitan. I'm seen as an expat, not as an Asian, even though I am an Asian American."

These findings indicate that clients' acceptance of women expatriate managers hinges much more on nationality than it does on gender. Local managers see female expatriates as foreigners who happen to be women, not as women who happen to be foreigners.

Some women find that being female has no effect at all on their professional life, especially in Asia:

- "There are many expat and foreign women in top positions here in Hong Kong. If you are good at what you do, they accept you. One Chinese woman told me, Americans are always watching you. One mistake and you are done. Chinese take a while to accept you and then stop testing you."
- "There's no difference. They respect professionalism . . . including in Japan. There is no problem in Asia."

"If anything, women expats are likely to find a warmer welcome in many nations because they are a novelty. Among the advantages, women international managers said that because of their gender they are more visible, are accorded higher social status, and benefit from a "halo effect"—host-nation clients know that women expats are rare, so they assume the women are outstanding. Local managers assume that women expatriates would not have been sent unless they are "the best."

As one women international manager assigned to Indonesia noted, "It's easier being a woman here than in any place in the world, including New York City . . . I

Advice for Aspiring Expats

Women who aspire to international assignments should keep the following recommendations in mind:

- Be persistent. Educate your company about the possibilities of sending women abroad. Root out unfounded assumptions that might influence decisions about overseas assignments. Point out reasons why the firm must grant women the same status and support it gives to male employees.

- Be excellent. Sending women abroad is perceived as risky, so no woman will be selected unless she is seen as technically and professionally excellent. Beyond becoming well qualified, it helps to arrange to be in the right place at the right time.

- Address private-life issues directly. Contact other international women for help. Single expatriates must devise strategies for dealing with potential loneliness. Married managers and their working spouses must discuss the implications for both careers—preferably before the possibility of an international assignment becomes a reality.

never get the comments I got in New York, like 'What is a nice woman like you doing in this job?' "

The more different the expats are from their overseas clients, the more of an advantage they seem to gain. For example, Caucasian women (the vast majority of the sample) serving in Japan reported a greater advantage than counterparts serving in the United Kingdom.

Do the same advantages hold true for North American women of non-Caucasian backgrounds? The sample included too few minority women to draw conclusions, but the few black women expats interviewed did well in their overseas assignments.

Expat women all around the globe report that foreign clients are curious about them, want to meet them, and tend to remember them.

- "It's the visibility as an expat, and even more as a woman. I stick in their minds. I know I've gotten more business than my two male colleagues . . . [My Japanese clients] are extra interested in me."

- "Being a woman is never a detriment. [In Thailand] they remembered me better—fantastic for a marketing position. It's better working with Asians than with the Dutch, British, or Americans."

- "In India and Pakistan, being a woman helps in marketing and client contact. I got in to see customers because they had never seen a female banker before . . . Having a female banker adds value [for] the client."

- "It's an advantage that attracts attention. Japanese are interested in meeting a *gaijin*, a foreign woman. Women attract more clients. On calls to clients, they elevate me, give me more rank. If anything, the problem for men and women, is youth, not gender."

"Women expats also report that strong interpersonal and social skills give them an advantage. Many said that local male clients talk more easily with them about a wider range of topics than they do with their male North American counterparts. Several women expatriates discussed this aspect of their interactions with host-country business associates:

- "Women are better at putting people at ease . . . The traditional woman's role . . . inspires confidence and trust, less suspicion, not threatening."
- "I often take advantage of being a woman. I'm more supportive than my male colleagues . . . [My Indonesian clients] relax and talk more. And 50 percent of my effectiveness is based on volunteered information."
- "Women are better at treating men sensitively, and they just like you. One of my Korean clients told me, 'I really enjoyed . . . working with you.' "

Women often receive special treatment not given to their male counterparts. According to a female international manager in Hong Kong, "Single female expats travel easier and are treated better. Never hassled. No safety issues. Local offices take better care of you. They meet you, take you through customs . . . It's the combination of treating you like a lady and a professional."

HOME-COMPANY HURDLES

Unfortunately, North American companies often perpetuate policies and practices that rip the halo off the heads of their women expats rather than enable them to build on the advantages they bring to their overseas posts.

Because many foreign managers lack experience with women international managers, host-country managers may assume that newly arrived female expats are not managers. If male colleagues from the home company make clear the role and responsibilities of the women manager, smooth working relationships are quickly established. If male colleagues fail to clarify the status of the female expat, the challenge to her credibility, authority, and responsibility becomes chronic and undermines her effectiveness. Several women whose companies failed to clarify their roles discussed the problem:

- "I speak Chinese, which is a plus. But they'd talk to the men, not to me. They'd assume that I, as a woman, had no authority. The Chinese want to deal with . . . top-level people, and there is always a man at a higher level.
- "It took extra time to establish credibility with the Japanese and Chinese. One Japanese manager said to me, 'When I first met you, I thought you would not be any good because you were a woman.' "

Companies hobble their female expats in other ways. To assuage their nervousness about sending women abroad, some companies limit the length of a woman's assignment to six months or a year, rather than offering her the more standard two to three years.

Temporary status comes across to foreign colleagues and clients as a lack of confidence and commitment, and foreigners fail to take the woman manager seriously. That sets the woman manager up for failure.

- "It is very important to clients that I am permanent. It increases trust, and that's critical."

- "After offering me the job, they hesitated: 'Could a woman work with the Chinese?' So my job [in Hong Kong] was defined as temporary, a one-year position to train a Chinese man to replace me. I succeeded and became permanent."

A similar problem occurs when a home company limits a woman's professional opportunities and job scope after she is abroad. For example, some companies, out of supposed concern for the woman's safety, bar her from traveling to remote, rural, or underdeveloped areas, which limits the scope of her responsibility. More than half of women international managers report difficulties in persuading their home companies to give them the same latitude accorded their male counterparts. Some of their comments:

- "My problem is overwhelmingly with Americans. They identify it as a male market . . . geisha girls. . . ."
- "The Americans wouldn't let me on the drilling rigs, because they said there were no accommodations for a woman. Everyone blames it on something else. They gave me different work. They had me on the sidelines, not planning and communicating with drilling people. It's the expat Americans, not the Thais, who'll go to someone else before they come to me."

A few companies limit women to working only internally with company employees, rather than externally with clients. These companies assume that their own employees are somehow less prejudiced than are outsiders. In reality, women often find the opposite to be true.

"It was somewhat difficult internally," said a woman expat in Hong Kong. "They feel threatened, hesitant to do what I say, resentful. They assume I don't have the credibility a man would have. Perhaps it's harder internally than externally, because client relationships are one-on-one, and internally it's more of a group. Or perhaps it's harder because they have to live with it longer internally. Or perhaps it's because they fear that I'm setting a precedent, or because they fear criticism from their peers."

In sum, biased working conditions perpetuated by home companies posed far more problems for female expats than presumed "foreign prejudice" against women.

RECOMMENDATIONS

With all these data as a backdrop, companies need to rethink the ways they make decisions about assigning women managers internationally. Here are some points for company decision-makers to keep in mind.

- Consider women for international assignments as often as men. Do not assume that women managers will not want to go abroad; ask them. Women are as interested as men are in foreign assignments.
- Abandon all assumptions about foreign acceptance of women managers. Do not assume that foreigners will treat women expats the same way they treat local women.
- Do not confuse the role of a spouse with that of a manager. Although the single most common reason for male expatriates' failure and early return from international assignments is wives' dissatisfaction, this does not mean that women cannot cope in a foreign environment. The ambiguous role of expatriate spouse is difficult to play, regardless of gender.

- Offer flexible benefits packages. Most expatriate benefits packages were designed to meet the needs of a family with an employed husband, a non-employed wife, and children. Companies should modify their benefits packages to meet the needs of managers who are single (female or male) or in dual-career marriages.

- Create and support innovative company policies. Such modifications might include increased lead time in announcing assignments, executive-search services for the partner in dual-career couples, and allowances for "staying connected"—including telephone and airfare expenses—for couples who choose some form of commuting.

- Give women international managers every opportunity to succeed. Accord them full status and arm them with appropriate titles to signal the company's commitment to them. Don't tie their hands with temporary or experimental assignments. Train male colleagues to underscore female managers' roles to foreign clients and colleagues.

ARCHAIC "LUXURY"

Global competition is, and will continue to be, intense in the 1990s. Companies cannot afford to pass over qualified people just because their gender does not fit the traditional managerial profile. Successful companies will select both women and men to manage their cross-border operations.

The option of limiting international management to one gender has become an archaic luxury that no company can afford. The only remaining question is how quickly and effectively companies will increase the number and use of women in their worldwide managerial workforces.

Balancing the Work/Home Interface: A European Perspective

Reading 14

ORGANIZATIONS AND FAMILIES IN TRANSITION

Suzan Lewis
Cary L. Cooper

Families and employing organizations throughout the industrialized world are changing fundamentally and rapidly, both in terms of structure and in terms of expectations. However, work and family policies and practices within organizations and wider societies, and the values and assumptions which underpin them, are

"Balancing the Work/Home Interface: A European Perspective" by Suzan Lewis and Cary L. Cooper from *Human Resource Management Review*, Vol. 5, No. 4, 1995, pp. 289–305. Reprinted by permission of Cary L. Cooper.

changing more slowly (Kanter 1989). The failure to reflect and build upon rapid social change poses threats to occupational health and has far reaching implications for human resources management (Cooper and Lewis 1994).

Within organizations, globalization, the drive for more productivity and quality, downsizing and the need for a flexible workforce which can respond rapidly to new technologies and changing markets create new challenges. The nature of work is shifting towards more accountability, responsibility, and autonomy at the working level. These shifts demand more commitment from employees in terms of intrinsic motivation and the ability to be self motivating and self managing. To meet the needs for a committed, innovative and unstressed workforce, it is essential to empower workers to lead balanced lives by responding to contemporary family and social trends.

The once traditional family pattern of breadwinner father, homemaker mother, and children is now a minority form in much of the industrialized world (Lewis et al. 1992). In the UK, for example, 60 per cent of couples with children have both parents in employment, compared with 43% in 1973 (GHS 1994). Forty two per cent of lone mothers are also in employment, often full time (Bartholomew, Hibbert, and Sidaway 1992). A growing number of working women and men of all ages also have caring responsibilities for elderly or disabled relatives (Brannen et al. 1994; Neal et al. 1993). With the increasing numbers of dual earner and single parent families, high rates of divorce, medical advances and the growing elderly population, most adult family members combine employment with family caring at some stage in their life cycle (Lewis and Cooper 1987).

Both women's and men's family roles are changing dramatically, although the trends are more marked in women, with men continuing to endorse more traditional views than women on gender roles and particularly domestic work (Newell 1993). Although still more attached to family than men, women are increasingly valuing career and paid work over absorption in family (Wilkinson 1994). However, this has not led to a whole hearted acceptance of the traditional male work ethic, with its emphasis on total dedication of time to the workplace. Indeed, there is evidence that more men, as well as women are valuing shorter working hours and would trade income for shorter hours to spend time with family and achieve a more balanced life (Schor 1991). One suggestion is that this may be a reaction to the excessive competitiveness of the 1980s (Bruce and Reed 1994).

The shift towards the greater valuing of both work and family involvement for men and women has numerous potential advantages. A balanced life can provide multiple sources of satisfaction (Baruch and Barnett 1983; Noor 1994), contribute towards quality of life and well being of men and women, and of those for whom they care (Neal, Chapman, Ingersoll-Dayton, and Amlen 1993; Wagner and Neal 1994) and enable people to make an optimum contribution at work (Ganster and Schaubroeck 1991). Currently, however, combining of family and employment roles often creates stress, overload, and conflict (Lewis and Cooper 1987, 1988a, 1988b; Neal et al. 1993). A number of factors relating to the way work and family are socially and historically constructed, and to current organizational and social contexts, contribute to the appraisal of work and family demands as sources of stress. These include:

- Assumptions about the dichotomy of work and family and the prevailing male model of work which assumes that ideal employees work full time and continuously, implying that they have the back up of a full time help mate to take care of family work (Pleck 1977; Cook 1992; Bruce and Reed 1994).

- The greater valuing of public than private roles in many societies. For example, family roles, especially for men, are expected to be of secondary importance to economic roles (Bailyn 1992).

- Job insecurity which creates reluctance on the part of employees to ask for family needs to be taken into consideration.

- Tensions between new and old models of work, and between long and short term attitudes towards flexibility in the workplace. Many organizations are interpreting the need for flexibility in terms of an expendable workforce. This creates unpredictable work schedules, stress, and financial insecurity for families, and may therefore have negative consequences for employees and organizations in the longer term. Furthermore, temporary workers may not develop the commitment and ability to work in a co-ordinated way with team members, which may be crucial to organizational survival in the future (Bridges 1994).

- Cuts in public expenditure and the emphasis on 'care in the community', which relies on the informal care given by family members, particularly women. This is increasingly problematic as more women are employed and are thus not available to play the role of community carer (Finch and Mason 1993).

RECONCILING WORK AND FAMILY: A EUROPEAN PERSPECTIVE

The European Union (EU), an international body with considerable potential for initiating cross national and political action (Moss forthcoming) has a long standing concern with what it terms the *reconciliation* between paid work and family life (European Commission 1993, 1994). This arises from the EU goal of gender equality in the labor force, expressed in Article 119 of the Treaty of Rome, although economic goals (e.g., the optimum use of social resources) and quality of life goals (benefits to individual workers and their families) are also articulated (Moss forthcoming). Moss notes that the term reconciliation has been criticized as implying the need to restore a harmonious relationship between work and family which once existed and is now lost, but argues that the European Commission (the administrative arm of the Union) is quite clear that the term does not imply restoration, but rather, an attempt to harmonize different activities and interests so they can be conducted with minimum stress and disadvantage. This implies the need to seek accommodation between the needs and interests of employers, employees, families, and others. In the pursuit of reconciliation the EU has sought to influence social policy in member states (see Moss forthcoming, for an overview of EU activities in this area) particularly on matters such as parental leave, childcare and working time, but also to encourage changes in the environment, structure and organization of work to make it more responsive to the needs of children (currently its main focus in relation to families) (European Commission 1994). The promoting of increased participation of men in family care is also on the EU agenda as a prerequisite for wider change towards equal opportunities (European Commission 1995). The EU has identified social partners who share responsibility for reconciliation of work and family life, including national and local governments, management and labor, and individuals. Although no guidance is provided on the respective responsibilities of each partner, it is apparent that in this framework workplace change is regarded as one strand within a collaborative process of achieving reconciliation.

The response of EU member states to the goal of reconciliation have not been unanimous. The UK government in particular has stood against many of the recommended reforms because of assumed costs to industry, refusing, for example, to implement statutory parental leave. Nevertheless, European law has exerted some influence on UK social policy. For example, maternity leave entitlements have been extended to cover all women, as the result of an EU directive, and a recent House of Lords decision that it is unlawful to require a 16 hour working week for employees to qualify for unfair dismissal or redundancy pay after 2 years employment, was based on European law, and has the potential to improve conditions for those who work part time to fit in their family work (J. Lewis forthcoming). Other EU member states recognise a public responsibility for family care, as evidenced by public provision of childcare and statutory rights to parental leaves. These rights are often supplemented by collective agreements, and some employers build on these by developing a range of "family friendly" practices such as flexible forms of work, additional leaves and assistance with family care (Hogg and Harker 1992).

The European perspective stresses partnerships, but the importance of workplace change within this framework cannot be overstated. For example, in Sweden, (a recent member of the EU), where parental leave rights have long been available, the take up by men remains substantially lower than that for women (Haas and Hwang 1995). Haas and Hwang (1995) argue that this is because workplaces remain deeply gendered in their expectations of appropriate behavior. Initiatives to change organizational policies and practices, and the assumptions which underpin them thus remain crucial in Europe as elsewhere.

In the US, as in the UK, families and children are considered to be a private concern. Bailyn (1992) argues that in the US any government help is seen as a sign of personal failure or stigma. This is less so in the UK, where, for example, government help with family health care is taken for granted. In the US the focus has been on the role of employers in providing work family policies, and as employers rather than government also provide health care benefits this has come to be regarded as part of the corporate welfare system (Gonyea and Googins forthcoming). Nevertheless, advocates of work family policies are increasingly debating the role of government and other bodies in addressing these issues, rather than regarding it solely as a business issue (Lambert 1993) and the Family and Medical Leave Act represents a step in the direction of government involvement. The main drive in the US, and to a large extent, the UK, however, has been towards persuading employers to implement policies and practices to enable people to balance work and personal lives, and hence the business case for change has been developed and applied to a greater extent than social arguments.

Clearly different approaches to work and family issues are likely to continue, both within Europe and between Europe and elsewhere, and to a certain extent these remain appropriate given different historical, social and political contexts. Nevertheless, we operate in a global economy and interchanges of ideas and perspectives will be fruitful. We would argue, moreover, that the different perspectives are not necessarily very different in their implications. As discussed above, workplace culture change remains an important goal within the European partnership approach, while the limits to corporate responsibility for family well being is increasingly being debated in the US despite the tradition of corporate welfare systems. We recognize that a business case for organizational change to support work and family is essential, but propose that a broadening of the business argument to include wider social partners is necessary to take account of recent changes in families and organizations. A broader approach would take account of the needs of all stakeholders. We define stakeholders here as all those with an interest in organizations, including, for example, employer, employees, unions, family members, customers or clients, suppliers, investors and others (RSA 1994). This approach has the potential to incorporate the spirit of the different perspectives on work and family by broadening debates on social partnerships as well as highlighting the need for fundamental organizational culture change. It is based on a systems model which conceptualizes work organizations and families as interrelated sub systems which also are influenced by wider social contexts.

THE COSTS OF NOT ATTENDING TO WORK/FAMILY ISSUES

One reason for emphasizing a broad partnership approach is that work and family issues have potential costs for individual, organizations, families, and communities. Multiple roles in work and family in non responsive employing organizations, can create conflict and stress leading to poor mental and physical health, job and life dissatisfaction, family conflicts and breakup (Lewis and Cooper 1987, 1988a, 1988b; Neal et al. 1993; Googins and Bowden 1987; Bacharach, Bamberger, and Conley 1991; Frone, Russell, and Cooper 1992). Individuals pay a price in terms of stress related illnesses and reduced quality of life (Lewis and Cooper 1988a; 1988b; Jones and Fletcher 1993; Wagner and Neal 1994). Organizations which do not respond to work family needs also bear the costs in terms of absenteeism (Goff, Mount, and Jamison 1992), "presenteeism" or lack of psychological availability at work (Cooper and Williams 1994; Hall and Parker 1993), accidents and loss of productivity (Ganster and Schaubroeck 1991), high turnover (Grover and Crooker 1995), and wasted human potential (Wagner and Neal 1994). For example, in 1993 alone the average cost of absence from work in the UK was £513 for each employee; a total of 11 billion pounds for the UK economy as a whole (CBI 1994). In addition, the Confederation of British Industry report states that mental illness/stress among non manual staff, and poor motivation among manual workers are strong causes of absence. It is not known exactly what proportion of sickness absence and other costs can be attributed directly or indirectly to work family stress. Nevertheless, where cost benefit analyses of responses to work and family issues have been carried out they generally demonstrate that the benefits to organization outweigh the costs (e.g., Hillage and Simkin 1992). However, the range of outcomes measured in such analyses tend to be narrow, largely because of the difficulty in measuring concepts such as productivity (Googins and Gonyea 1992), although absenteeism and turnover can be more easily assessed. It is therefore unlikely that the full costs to employers of ignoring the work and family interface has been calculated (Holterman 1995). Furthermore researchers need to consider ways of operationalizing and quantifying broader costs, including wider social influences which impact on organizations, such as family breakdown and other stressors which can spill over to affect people at work (Barnett 1994). Holterman (1995) argues that a full cost benefit analysis of family friendly policies would take account of benefits and costs for employers, employees, families, and the whole economy, but notes that no research has yet been this ambitious.

Lack of balance in peoples' lives also affects families. Family members need support for care of children and others; time and energy at the end of the day to interact with family; and for a secure income for family support (Holt and Thaulow forthcoming). Long hours of work can increase conflict from work to family and negatively affect life satisfaction (Judge, Boudreau, and Bretz 1994). Stress experienced by employees in the workplace can also spill over to affect their family members (Jones and Fletcher 1993; Cartwright and Cooper 1994). In two parent families where both parents have highly demanding jobs, and single parent families working in organizations which are not responsive to their family priorities, parents may have too little time to spend with children. There is growing evidence that work family conflict affects parents' mood and parent child interaction, which in turn affects children's behavior (Barling 1986, 1994; MacEwen and Barling 1991). Families may also suffer when jobs are insecure or unpredictable. Children's distress may be reflected in ill health, poor performance at school or anti-social behavior, and we do not know the costs of these to society. Problems at home and family stress inevitably feeds back into the experience of work, generating greater need for support (Greenhaus and Parasuraman 1994). We need to know more about the impacts of new ways of working on families. As Giele (1995) points out, the well being of future generations is not a trivial concern, but equally important to the future of nations as continued economic viability or national defense.

Finally, there are important implications of work and family stress for the wider society. Stress related illnesses can be costly for society in terms of health service costs. Unless people are empowered to contribute to work and family, there will also be a severe crisis in caring. The elderly and vulnerable, as well as children, may be damaged unless employees are enabled to work in ways which do not preclude time for family, and are supported by an infrastructure of quality child and other care (Finch and Mason 1993; Lazsco and Noden 1992). Employment experiences can affect the quality of care provided. Although some studies have found that employed and non employed caregivers provide similar levels of care (e.g., Body and Schoonover 1986), researchers may not see those employed family members whose jobs prevent them from taking on the role of carer. Longitudinal research (Dwyer, Henretta, Coward, and Barton 1992) indicates that employment can reduce the likelihood that adult children will begin to provide assistance to elderly parents. Research needs to consider these issues, and also the extent to which current models of work and the time demands of combining work and family preclude time for involvement in community activities, which could lead to the collapse of community support systems. The costs to organizations of these wider impacts of work and family are more difficult to measure than some immediate business concerns, but their significance cannot be overlooked.

LIMITATIONS OF FAMILY-FRIENDLY POLICIES AND PRACTICES

To what extent are workplace developments taking account of current trends and promoting the reconciliation of work and family? A growing number of organizations are responding to work/family issues, with policies including childcare or eldercare assistance, and a range of "non standard" or flexible forms of work. These policies have been shown to be effective in meeting some employee needs (Thomas and Ganster 1995; Shinn et al. 1989) and to be of benefit to organizations in terms of reduced absenteeism, enhanced recruitment and retention, and organizational attachment (Goff et al. 1992; Truman 1986; Bretz and Judge 1994; Grover and Crooker 1995). There are, however, several limitations to the family-friendly provisions currently available, which reduce their potential wider impact. These include:

- *Limited access.* These initiatives have mostly been introduced into larger organizations. As such, the majority of employees, especially those with the greatest needs, may be unaffected by these developments (Brannen et al. 1994; Lambert 1993; Seyler, Monroe, and Garand 1995).

- *Most initiatives are targeted at women and particularly mothers of young children* (Brannen et al. 1994; Seyler et al. 1995; Bruce and Reed 1994). This overlooks the diversity in family needs, consequently, policies tend to enable women to continue in employment while also carrying out their traditional caring roles. The take-up of benefits by men is low, not least because many workplace cultures, and particularly line managers still implicitly, if not explicitly, define 'the family' as a concern of women workers (Haas and Hwang 1995).

- *Family friendly initiatives do not challenge traditional organizational values.* They tend to be regarded as benefits for marginalized workers rather than being integrated into mainstream thinking. The ideal of "standard" full time, inflexible work (Bruce and Reed 1994; Raabe forthcoming), the notion that time in the workplace symbolizes commitment (Hewitt 1993; Lewis and Taylor forthcoming; Bailyn 1993), and the prevailing model of hierarchical and unbroken careers, all remain largely untouched.

- *Formal work family policies do not necessarily alter informal practices.* Informal practice appears to be heavily influenced by the gender composition of the workforce and can be a powerful factor for, or barrier to, flexibility (Holt & Thaulow forthcoming).

- *Organizations alone cannot support the social change needed for the reconciliation of work and family.* Social as well as organizational policy needs to reflect changing realities. In countries which accept the dual earner family as the norm social policy is directed as safeguarding the quality of childcare and ensuring that parents have time for family care (Madsen 1994; Tauberman 1994). However, family policy in the UK and US tends to be based on the assumption that male breadwinner families remain the norm (Pascal 1986; Giele 1995), with a subsequent lack of support for work and family. Employers may take steps to assist their own employees, but cannot provide overall entitlements or an infrastructure of quality care for all dependents.

BEYOND "FAMILY FRIENDLY" TOWARDS RECONCILIATION

It is increasingly being argued that for wider change to occur to meet the needs of today's workforce and contemporary organizations, there is a need to move away from a benefits approach of "family friendly" policies towards systemic change within organizations (Bailyn 1993; Hall and Parker 1993; Gonyea and Googins forthcoming). This is articulated as a need for synergy between the needs of various groups (Bailyn 1993) or mutual flexibility in work (Gonyea and Googins forthcoming; Hall and Parker 1993). Flexibility here is defined with regard to the needs of all stakeholders rather than just from the perspective of employers' short term needs. This approach recognises the diverse needs and identities of workers, including their family roles, involves an emphasis on the rights and responsibilities of both employers and employees, moves away from beliefs that there is one best way in accomplishing business goals, and seeks ways of meeting goals in ways which will meet the needs of businesses and workers. This approach implicitly recognizes that many long standing assumptions about work and family are social and historical constructs, open to renegotiation and reconstruction to meet current needs. We argue that this process of deconstruction is necessary for the reconciliation of work and family, but that it should take place within a partnership framework.

AN AGENDA FOR CHANGE

There now needs to be a forum for discussion where all stakeholders can develop a shared vision of the sort of organizations, families and society we wish to develop and support. The need is particularly great now, not least because of the effects that the pace of economic changes is having on the way companies manage their human resources. They offer scope to become more people friendly, or more alienating.

The necessary changes will involve a number of steps:

- *The integration of work family issues into core thinking and strategic planning in organizations.* Organizations need to be proactive. They need to anticipate the changing needs of the workforce in strategic planning (Cooper and Lewis 1994; Bailyn 1993; Gonyea and Googins forthcoming). This will entail at the very least a recognition that the ways in which organizations have operated in the past are not necessarily appropriate to today's workplace.

- *Organizations will need to question traditional ways of working to reflect the contemporary, diverse, workforce.* It is not necessarily the most rational decision outcomes which are acted upon in organizations, but often the decision outcome favored by the most powerful individual or groups of individuals (Pettigrew 1973). Often these are men with non-career wives or women without family commitments. For example, in a recent study of over 1300 US male executives over 50% of those who were married had non working wives. Although these men reported some interference of work with family, they reported little interference from family to work (Judge et al. 1994). It is unlikely that this group will have an understanding of the work family issues confronting more typical members of the workforce, nor will they be able to share the cognitive appraisal of standard ways of working as stressful. More diversity in decision making may help to focus organizations on issues relating to the achievement of balance in people's lives.

- *A rethinking of notions of time.* The assignment of value to *time* is a process of social construction, involving an interplay between situational and structural factors which vary across time and place. Currently, men's time is valued more than women's time, and time in the market place more than time with family. These values reflect cultural ideologies, values and beliefs (Schor 1991; Hewitt 1993). They influence the sexual division of labor, and the assumed rights of employers to demand excess time which would otherwise be given to family, community, or leisure activities. A critical evaluation of the ways in which values are assigned to time will be a necessary precursor to changes to benefit all stakeholders. Within the workplace the definition of time as symbolic of productivity, commitment and value, marginalizes those who work shorter or more flexible hours and obscures the fact that long hours at the workplace reflect inefficiency (Lewis and Taylor forthcoming). Different ways of thinking about time in the workplace might include a focus on quality of outcome rather than quantity of time spent on activities.

- *Developing flexibility and autonomy.* It is only in the context of new ways of thinking about *time* that genuine flexibility can be achieved and atypical workers can be valued as highly as those working in traditional ways. To achieve this, there needs to be openness about the expectations of particular jobs and the demands they make on incumbents' personal lives as a means of clarifying boundaries (Bailyn 1993) and a non zero sum model of commitment which acknowledges that people can be highly committed to both work and family and make valuable contributions to both (Thoits 1987; Gilbert 1985; Quick et al. 1990).

- *Redefining careers.* A separation of career stage from age and a valuing of a wider range of career patterns is needed. Organizations need people who can do different types of work at different times and be flexible in a way which is not encouraged by the traditional career ladder. If careers, as well as time and commitment, can be redefined, this will have important effects. For example, a temporary lower time investment at work to enable individuals to meet family needs, would reduce only the tasks which people are allocated at a particular stage and not undermine what they can achieve in the future. This will be easier to achieve in flatter, less hierarchical organizations (Bailyn 1993).

- *New approaches to management.* Bruce and Reed (1994) argue that traditional management theory and subsequent supervisor behavior presume a work family split and assumes that a concern for family will interfere with organizational needs. They argue that traditionally supervisors have tended to think in terms of forcing workers to prioritise career or family rather than considering ways of helping them to integrate and manage both. Managing a flexible workforce requires trust, involves support rather than control, and collaboration rather than confrontation, in finding mutually acceptable ways of achieving goals. Supervisors must still expect workers to meet standards of performance and achieve strategic goals. However, this need not involve a prescription of the best way of achieving these goals which denies autonomy to manage work and family demands (Bailyn 1993).

- *Reconstructing notions of equality.* It is important to clarify the forms of equality we wish to pursue. Definitions of equal opportunities in terms of treating people the same has led to policies to enable women to act like men in the workplace, rather than a questioning of the appropriateness of current forms of work for today's men as well as women, parents as well as others. There is now a growing awareness of the need to manage diversity and that this involves not treating people the same, but recognizing differences and seeking equity and fairness to harness the potential of all the workforce (Parker and Hall 1993; Herriott and Pemberton 1995). Collaboration and mutual problem solving may be necessary for a mutual appreciation of what individual employees need to enable them to make an optimum contribution in the workplace. This will include a questioning of the prevalent assumption that family is the legitimate concern of women, not men, which overlooks evidence that, for example, lack of flexibility at work is a significant source of stress for fathers of young children as well as mothers (Lewis and Cooper 1987). The assumption that family is not the concern of men both reinforces and is reinforced by the continuing inequality in the sexual division of domestic labor (Newell 1993), which in turn is reinforced by gendered expectations in the workplace, so family roles will also have to be considered in wider debates. At wider community level, a consideration of equity would also take account of the growing gap between those in and out of work. The long hours of work expected in many organizations, especially at higher levels, together with the poor conditions attached to part time work and rising unemployment, create a situation in which some people are working too many hours and unable to make time for family, while others have too little work and offer little security for families.

- *Deconstructing success.* Success is another dynamic and changing concept and it is useful to reflect on its meaning in the context of current changes and tensions. As Handy (1994) points out, successes such as the invention of the motor car or of new manufacturing technology were made without thought to the long terms consequences of pollution or a redundant workforce. It is important to consider the possible long term impact of the ways in which we currently define success. The emphasis tends to be on profits and responsibilities to shareholders which are assumed to be independent of other needs. In the UK an increasing regard to corporate social responsibility, with organizations considering the impact of their operations on a wider range of stakeholders was identified as an emerging issue in a national survey of management training and development needs (Institute of Management 1994), and a report on ways of achieving sustainable business growth in the face of substantial global competition argues that tomorrow's company will adopt an inclusive approach to the definition of success (RSA 1994), considering all stakeholder (RSA 1994).

- *Public policy support and partnership with industry.* Public policy makers also need to recognize the changes in family structures and to adapt to meet the needs of these families. Change is particularly necessary in those societies in which public policy continues to assume the breadwinner family as the norm.

An infrastructure of quality childcare, eldercare and other care is a basic need of all working families. Government has an important role to play here, in partnership with local government and employers if appropriate, to ensure that local needs are met. Social policy makers also need to consider the value of statutory entitlement to appropriate paid leaves for family care. Lack of provision for family leaves is based on the assumption that one family member (usually a women) is either not employed or that their income in not necessary for family upkeep. Holterman (1995) analyses the costs of providing leaves and points out that there are benefits as well as costs to these provisions, for employers and for the economy as a whole. Apart from the more obvious advantages of potential for greater gender equity, reduced stress and absenteeism, there is some evidence that parental leave encourages androgynous behavior (Hwang and Haas 1995) and androgyny, manifested in co-operative collegiate management styles is increasingly recognised as a characteristic of good managers (Institute of Management 1994).

Public policy makers can also play an important role in the reconciliation process by ensuring equal employment protection for those who work what are currently constructed as atypical hours to enable them to achieve a balance between work and family (J. Lewis forthcoming). This would discourage organizations from regarding part of the workforce as peripheral and expendable but may be opposed on the grounds of limiting competitiveness. However the law already defines what are legitimate forms of competitiveness. For example, competitiveness on the grounds of child labor is not acceptable in the Western world, and certain levels of health and safety are also prescribed. Lewis (forthcoming) argues that if we accept the principle of equality of opportunities it should also be acceptable to define the boundaries of competitiveness, with regard to the type of society we wish to live in. He argues that the law can have a role in providing equality of opportunities by promoting diverse opportunities conducive to the reconciliation of work and family. In the UK for example, discrimination law has been used to challenge individual employers' decisions not to offer certain forms of flexible work. Nevertheless, if business perceives such intervention as unwelcome and constraining there will be a reluctance to change. This underlines the importance of making the broader business case as clearly as possible. Ideally the establishment of a range of options for meeting the interrelated needs of business, employees and families will be reached by collaboration and problem solving by all social partners.

IMPLICATIONS FOR RESEARCH

There is a burgeoning research literature on work and family issues, but in times of rapid social change it cannot be assumed that findings are of more than transitory significance. In particular, it is important to chart the impact of new ways of working, including the casualization of the labor market, as well as initiatives designed to help workers balance work and family obligations, on individuals, organizations, families, and communities. Most research on the impact of work and family policies has focused on the organizational perspective (Raabe 1990; Lambert 1993). An expansion of research orientations is now needed to examine the perspectives of multiple stakeholders and the interrelationships between the experiences of each group.

It is important to identify and investigate assumptions which underpin different ways of working (Raabe forthcoming). For example, the perpetuation of traditional ways of working are often based on an assumption that they are related to profit, and that investors are interested only in profits and not the means by which they are achieved. The 'ethical investment' movement and growing concerns about issues such as the environment imply that this may not be wholly true. Research is needed to explore investors' attitudes to organizational policies which are detrimental to family life. Such research may also help to raise consciousness about these issues.

The importance of clarifying definitions for research is also apparent. Organizations, family and family friendly policies are all illusive terms in the current context, while concepts of success, time and equality are all shifting. An objective of gender equality or challenging broader social inequalities is currently not explicit in family friendly rationales. It is important to clarify the outcomes desired from the reorganization of work and the criteria of success before evaluation can take place.

Evidence of cost effectiveness for employers is still needed, although it has been noted that employers often implement other policies with a good rationale but scant evidence (Lambert 1993). A major challenge for research is to design measures of cost effectiveness, which go beyond the measurement of the more easily quantifiable business outcomes to include costs and benefits of broader social outcomes.

Work and family researchers must also attend to social policy issues. Cross national comparisons monitoring different impacts of social policies on child-care, family leaves, the rights of atypical workers and other policies in interaction with workplace practice, will help to inform national debates. Research on social movements and influencing processes may also be applied to work family issues. There may be a role here for action research, with the objective of hastening the policy changes needed to support workers, families, organizations and communities.

Shifts in family and organizational structures and values are giving rise to tensions which are likely to be important drivers of change towards the 21st century. They present challenges and opportunities to human resource management and the reorganization of work, in ways which have the potential to benefit all stakeholders whether in a European or a US context.

References

BACHARACH, S.B., BAMBERGER, P. and CONLEY, S. (1991), "Work Home Conflict Among Nurses and Engineers: Mediating the Impact of Job Stress on Burnout and Satisfaction at Work," *Journal of Organizational Behaviour* 12: 39–53.

BAILYN, L. (1992), "Issues of Work and Family in Different National Contexts: How the United States, Britain, and Sweden Respond," *Human Resource Management* 31, 201–8.

——— (1993), *Breaking the Mold. Women, Men, and Time in the New Corporate World*. New York: Free Press.

BARLING, J. (1986), "Fathers' Work Experiences, the Father Child Relationship and Children's Behaviour," *Journal of Occupational Behaviour* 7, 1–8.

——— (1994), "Work and Family: In Search of More Effective Workplace Interventions," in Cooper, C.L., and Rousseau, D.M. eds., *Trends in Organizational Behavior* (Vol. 1). Chichester: John Wiley & Sons.

BARNETT, R. (1994), "Home to Work Spillover Revisited," *Journal of Marriage and the Family* 56, 647–56.

BARTHOLOMEW, R., HIBBERT, A. and SIDAWAY, J. (1992), "Lone Parents and the Labour Market: Evidence from the Labour Force Survey," *Employment Gazette* 100, 559–78.

BARUCH, G. and BARNETT, R. (1983), *Lifeprints: New Patterns of Love and Work for Today's Women*. New York: McGraw Hill.

BRANNEN, J., MESZAROS, P., MOSS, H. and POLAND, G. (1994), *Employment and Family Life: A Review of Research in the UK (1980–1994)*. London: Department of Employment.

BRETZ, R.D. and JUDGE, T.A. (1994), "The Role of Human Resource Systems in Job Applicant Decision Processes," *Journal of Management* 20, 531–51.

BRODY, E.M. and SCHOONOVER, C.B. (1986), "Patterns of Parent Care When Adult Daughters Work and When They Do Not," *The Gerontologist*.

BRUCE, W. and REED, C. (1994), "Preparing Supervisors for the Future Workforce: The Dual Income Couple and the Work Family Dichotomy," *Public Administration Review* 54, 36–43.

CARTWRIGHT, S. and COOPER, C.L. (1994), *No Hassle: Taking the Stress Out of Work*. London: Century Books.

CBI. (1994), *Sickness Absence in Industry*. London: CBI/PERCOM.

COOK, A. (1992), "Can Work Requirements Change to Accommodate the Needs of Dual-Earner Families?" in Lewis, S., Izraeli, D., and Hootsmans, H. eds., *Dual-Earner Families: International Perspectives*. London: Sage Publications.

COOPER, C.L. and LEWIS, S. (1994), *Managing the New Work Force*. San Diego: Pfeiffer & Co.

——— and WILLIAMS, S. (1994), *Creating Healthy Work Organizations*. Chichester: John Wiley & Sons.

DWYER, J.W., HENRETTA, J.C., COWARD, R.T. and BARTON, A.J. (1992), "Changes in the Helping Behaviors of Adult Children as Caregivers," *Research on Aging* 14, 351–75.

European Commission. (1993), *European Social Policy: Options of the Future*. Luxembourg: Office for Official Publications of the European Communities.

——— (1994), *European Social Policy: A Way Forward for the Union*. Luxembourg: Office for Official Publications of the European Communities.

——— (1995), *Men as Carers: Towards a Culture of Responsibility, Sharing and Reciprocity between Women and Men in the Care and Upbringing of Children*. Brussels: European Commission Equal Opportunities Unit.

FINCH, J. and MASON, J. (1993), *Negotiating Family Responsibilities*. London: Routledge.

FRONE, M.R., RUSSELL, M. and COOPER, M.L. (1992), "Antecedents and Outcomes of Work Family Conflict: Testing a Model of Work Family Interface," *Journal of Applied Psychology* 77, 65–78.

GANSTER, D.C. and SCHAUBROECK, J. (1991), "Work Stress and Employee Health," *Journal of Management,* 17, 235–71.

GHS. (1994), *General Household Survey.* London: HMSO.

GIELE, J. (1995), "Women's Changing Lives and the Emergence of Family Policy." in Gordon, T. and Kauppinen-Toropainen, K. eds., *Unresolved Dilemmas: Women, Work and the Family in the United States, Europe and the Former Soviet Union.* Aldershot: Avebury.

GILBERT, L. (1985), *Men in Dual Career Families.* Hillsdale, NJ: Lawrence Erlbaum.

GOFF, S.J., MOUNT, M.K. and JAMISON, R.L. (1992), "Employer Supported Childcare, Work/Family Conflict and Absenteeism: A Field Study. *Personnel Psychology* 43, 793–809.

GONYEA, J. and GOOGINS, B. (1992), "Linking the Worlds of Work and Family: Beyond the Productivity Trap," *Human Resource Management* 31, 209–26.

——— (forthcoming), "The Restructuring of Work and Family in the United States: A New Challenge for American Corporations." in Lewis, S. and Lewis, J. eds., *Rethinking Employment: The Work Family Challenge.* London: Sage.

GOOGINS, B. and BURDEN, D. (1987), "Vulnerability of Working Parents: Balancing Work and Home Roles." *Social Work* 32, 295–300.

GREENHAUS, J. and BEUTELL, N. (1985), "Sources of Conflict between Work and Family Roles," *Academy of Management Review* 10, 76–88.

GREENHAUS, G. and PARASURAMAN, S. (1994), "Work Family Conflict, Social Support and Well Being." in Davidson, M. and Burke, R. eds., *Women in Management: Issues in Research.* London: Paul Chapman Publishing.

GROVER, S.L. and CROOKER, K.J. (1995), "Who Appreciates Family Responsive Human Resource Policies: The Impact of Family Friendly Policies on the Organizational Attachment of Parents and Non Parents," *Personnel Psychology* 48, 271–88.

HAAS, L. and HWANG, P. (1995), "Company Culture and Men's Usage of Family Leaves in Sweden," *Family Relations* 44, 28–36.

HALL, D.T. (1990), "Promoting Work Family Balance," *Organizational Dynamics* 18, 5–18.

——— and PARKER, V.A. (1993), "The Role of Workplace Flexibility in Managing Diversity," *Organizational Dynamics* 21, 5–18.

HANDY, C. (1994), *The Empty Raincoat.* London: Hutchinsons.

HERRIOT, P. and PEMBERTON, C. (1995), *Competitive Advantage through Diversity.* London: Sage.

HEWITT, P. (1993), *About Time: The Revolution in Work and Family Life.* London: Rivers Oram Press.

HILLAGE, J. and SIMKIN, C. (1992), *Family Friendly Working: New Hope or Old Hype,* IMS Report 224. Brighton: Institute of Manpower Studies.

HOGG, C. and HARKER, L. (1992), *The Family Friendly Employer: Examples from Europe.* London: The Daycare Trust.

HOLT, H. and THAULOW, T. (forthcoming), "Formal and Informal Flexibility in the Workplace." in Lewis, S. and Lewis, J. eds., *Rethinking Employment: The Work Family Challenge.* London: Sage Publications.

HOLTERMAN, S. (1995), "The Costs and Benefits to British Employers of Measures to Promote Equality of Opportunity," *Gender, Work, and Organization* 2, 102–112.

Institute of Management. (1994), *Management to the Millennium: The Cannon and Taylor Working Party Reports.* Corby: Institute of Management.

JONES, F. and FLETCHER, B. (1993), "An Empirical Study of Occupational Stress in Working Couples," *Human Relations* 46, 881–903.

JUDGE, T.A., BOUDREAU, J.W. and BRETZ, R.D. (1994), "Job and Life Attitudes of Male Executives," *Journal of Applied Psychology* 79, 767–82.

KANTER, R.M. (1989), *When Giants Learn to Dance. Mastering the Challenge of Strategy, Management and Careers in the 1990s.* New York: Routledge.

LAMBERT, S. (1993), "Workplace Policies as Social Policy," *Social Services Review* 12, 237–60.

LAZSCO, F. and NODEN, S. (1992), "Elder Care and the Labor Market." in Lazsco, F. and Victor, C. eds., *Social Policy and Elderly People.* Aldershot: Avebury.

LEWIS, J. (forthcoming), "Work Family Reconciliation and the Law: Intrusion or Empowerment?" Lewis, S. and Lewis, J. eds., *Rethinking Employment: The Work Family Challenge.* London: Sage Publications.

LEWIS, S. and COOPER, C.L. (1987), "Stress in Two Earner Couples and Stage in the Life Cycle," *Journal of Occupational Psychology* 60, 289–303.

———— (1988a), "The Transition to Parenthood in Two Earner Couples," *Psychological Medicine* 18, 477–86.

———— (1988b), "Stress in Dual Earner Families," in Gutek, B.A., Stromberg, A.H., and Larwood L. eds., *Women and Work: An Annual Review* (Vol. 3). Beverly Hills: Sage Publications.

LEWIS, S., IZREALI, D. and HOOTSMANS, H. (1992), *Dual-Earner Families. International Perspectives*. London: Sage.

LEWIS, S. and TAYLOR, K. (forthcoming), "Evaluating the Impact of Family Friendly Employment Policies: A Case Study." in Lewis, S. and Lewis, J. eds., *The Work Family Challenge: Rethinking Employment*. London: Sage Publications.

MADSEN, A.L. (1994), "Danish Policies With Respect to Children and Families With Children," in Arves-Pares, B. ed. *Building Family Welfare*. Stockholm: The Network of Nordic Focal Points of the International Year of the Family.

McEWEN, K. and BARLING, J. (1991), "Effects of Maternal Employment Experiences on Children's Behavior Mood, Cognitive Difficulties, and Parenting Behavior," *Journal of Marriage and the Family* 53, 635–44.

MOSS, P. (forthcoming), "Reconciling Employment and Family Responsibilities: A European Perspective," in Lewis, S. and Lewis, J. *Rethinking Employment: The Work Family Challenge*. London: Sage Publications.

NEAL, M., CHAPMAN, N., INGERSOLL-DAYTON, B. and AMLEN, A. (1993), *Balancing Work and Caregiving for Children, Adults, and Elders*. London: Sage Publications.

NEWELL, S. (1993), "The Superwoman Syndrome: Gender Differences in Attitudes towards Equal Opportunities at Work and towards Domestic Responsibilities at Home," *Work, Employment and Society* 7, 275–89.

NOOR, N.M. (1994), "Children and Well Being: A Comparison of Employed and Non Employed Women," *Work and Stress* 8, 36–46.

PASCALL, G. (1986), *Social Policy: A Feminist Analysis*. London: Tavistock.

PETTIGREW, A. (1993), *The Politics of Organizational Decision Making*. London: Tavistock.

PLECK, J. (1977), "The Work Family Role System," *Social Problems* 24, 417–27.

QUICK, J., NELSON, D. and QUICK, J.D. (1990), *Stress and Challenge at the Top: The Paradox of the Healthy Executive*. Chichester: Wiley.

RAABE, P. (1990), "The Organisational Effects of Workplace Family Policies: Past Weaknesses and Recent Progress towards Research," *Journal of Social Issues* 11, 477–91.

———— (forthcoming), "Constructing Pluralistic Work and Career Arrangements That are Family and Work Friendly," in Lewis, S. and Lewis, J. eds., *Rethinking Employment: The Work Family Challenge*. London: Sage Publications.

RSA. (1994), *Tomorrow's Company: The Case for an Inclusive Approach*, Royal Society of Arts Report. London: Royal Society of Arts.

SCHOR, J. (1991), *The Overworked American*. New York: Basic Books.

SEYLER, D.L., MONROE, P.A. and GARAND, J.C. (1995), "Balancing Work and Family: The Role of Employer Supported Childcare Benefits," *Journal of Family Issues* 16, 170–93.

SHINN, M., WONG, N.W., SIMKO, P.A. and ORTIZ-TORRES, B. (1989), "Promoting the Well Being of Working Parents: Coping, Social Support and Flexible Job Schedules," *American Journal of Community Psychology* 17, 31–55.

TAUBERMAN, A.C. (1994), "Swedish Family Policy: Main Steps and Present Conditions," in Arves-Pares, B. ed., *Building Family Welfare*. Stockholm: The Network of Nordic Focal Points of the International Year of the Family.

THOITS, P.A. (1987), "Multiple Identities and Psychological Well Being: A Reformulation and Test of the Social Isolation Hypothesis," *American Sociological Review* 48, 174–87.

THOMAS, L.T. and GANSTER, D.C. (1995), "Impact of Family Supportive Work Variables on Work Family Conflict and Strain: A Control Perspective," *Journal of Applied Psychology* 80, 6–15.

TRUMAN, C. (1986), *Overcoming the Career Break: A Positive Approach*. Sheffield: Training Services Agency.

WAGNER, D.L. and NEAL, M.B. (1994), "Caregiving and Work: Consequences, Correlates and Workplace Responses," *Educational Gerontology* 20, 645–63.

WILKINSON, H. (1994), *No Turning Back: Generations and the Genderquake*. London: Demos.

Part V

CASES IN INTERNATIONAL ORGANIZATIONAL BEHAVIOR

A Cultural Clash in the Entertainment Industry

Anne Marie Francesco
Barry Allen Gold

CULTURE AND IDEOLOGY

"We're going to ruin your culture just like we ruined our own!" Jay Leno's humorous promotion for his Tonight Show on the European NBA Super Channel sounded like a threat to French Minister of Culture Jacques Toubon. In Toubon's opinion, the United States entertainment industry wants to dominate the world by any means. Toubon's opinion is shared by many of the French. For instance, French film producer Marin Karmitz, whose credits include the critically acclaimed *Blue*, sees a battle developing. According to Karmitz,

> Of course the U.S. movie industry is a big business, but behind the industrial aspect, there is also an ideological one. Sound and pictures have always been used for propaganda, and the real battle at the moment is over who is going to be allowed to control the world's images, and so sell a certain lifestyle, a certain culture, certain products and certain ideas. With the globalization of satellite and cable systems, that is what is at stake (Stevenson 1994).

The view from the Continent is that Hollywood is the enemy—trying to standardize world entertainment tastes and bring levels down to the lowest common denominator. As writer/philosopher Regis Debray sees it, "The American empire will pass, like the others. Let's at least make sure it does not leave irreparable damage to our creative abilities behind it" (Cohen 1994). Daniel Toscan du Plantier, president of Unifrance, the French government–funded marketing and publicity association, sees the distinction between the French and Americans differently. He sees the United States as a market that reasons in terms of profit, compared with France, where the people are often driven by intangible values. The result is French films that explore emotion, ideas, passion, and existential dilemmas compared with an American cinema that is obsessed with sex, violence, and fast action.

From the American viewpoint, Jack Valenti, president of the Motion Picture Association of America (MPAA) accused the European Union of "flagrant protectionism." American movie makers viewed the French attitude as "little more than a

---

Source: Anne Marie Francesco and Barry Allen Gold. The situations depicted in this case are intended to stimulate classroom discussion rather than suggest administrative solutions to the issues raised.

mask for inept film making—weak scripts, slow narrative, sloppy characterization and an overarching dullness that can be stupefying" (Cohen 1994). The pragmatic American approach, despite producing some "art films" or serious movies such as *Schindler's List*, is to view movies and other entertainment as commodities. The objective is to create a product, market and distribute it, and make as much money as possible.

If the approaches to movie making are so different, why are the French worried about the American influence on their cinema? Shouldn't the French movie-goers prefer their own movies rather than the "crass" American products?

> Providing a graphic illustration of what troubled the French during the GATT talks, France's greatest living film actor makes a fool of himself on water skis in 'My Father, the Hero.' In this latest example of that all-American art form known as 'le re-make,' Gerard Depardieu also wears loud shirts, cavorts on a Jet Ski, lets American teen-agers get the better of him and imitates Maurice Chevalier singing 'Thank Heaven for Little Girls.' Many words could describe what he does here, but 'hero' is not one of them (Maslin 1994).

Despite the cultural differences, some American artists are well received in France. In addition to the acting of Jerry Lewis, films directed by Woody Allen and Robert Altman are popular. An interesting example is the American novelist Paul Auster. Auster's symbol-laden novels sell about 20,000 copies a year in the United States and are purchased mainly by intellectuals. In France his novels sell 50,000 copies annually, and he is recognized on the street as a celebrity. It can be argued, however, that these artists are a small minority and have achieved acclaim in France because they capture European sensibilities in their work.

CULTURE AND POLITICS

In France culture is also often very closely linked to politics. A recent example was the appointment of a music director for the Paris National Opera. With great expectations, Argentine-born Daniel Barenboim was appointed music director under a conservative government. He was summarily dismissed before the debut of the new opera house when the socialists returned to power in 1988. His successor, South Korean–born Myung-Whun Chung met a similar fate. He was dismissed in August 1994 after the conservatives won parliamentary elections.

However, in an interview unrelated to these events, Cultural Minister Toubon emphasized that "the foreigner does not understand that the cultural politics of the left and the right are the same in France. Here culture transcends political differences. It is a part of the national consensus" (Suleiman 1993).

In the United States appointments to similar posts are usually unaffected by national politics; the board of a cultural institution appoints artistic directors according to aesthetic preferences, not the ideology of a national political party.

GENERAL AGREEMENT ON TARIFFS AND TRADE

The views that met head on in the 1993 General Agreement on Tariffs and Trade (GATT) talks were based on extreme interpretations of each country's culture and strategy. As a result, after seven years of negotiations, the GATT agreement was almost derailed.

France spearheaded the group of European countries that fought to have audiovisual products excluded from the GATT as part of a "cultural exception." American President Bill Clinton insisted that audiovisual services must be included in the agreement and that there be no "unacceptable restrictions" on these products.

At the time, the French government was spending $350 million to subsidize the French film industry, the largest in Europe. The United States objected to the subsidies as well as French taxes and quotas on American-made movies, television programs, and music recordings, which were used to support the French film industry. In practical terms, the American movie product that the French patron paid to see was taxed, with the benefit going to the French movie makers.

In the final days of the negotiation, chief U.S. trade negotiator Mickey Kantor feared that the entire agreement would be lost if the United States did not drop the demand for a completely open European market. Consequently, when the agreement was signed by 117 countries in December 1993, films and television were entirely excluded. The French won out in their desire to protect their industry and to preserve what they viewed as their cultural identity.

ECONOMIC REALITIES

How will this exclusion of television and film from the GATT impact the American entertainment industry? American movie makers now have a huge percentage of the Western European market (more than 80%) and more than half of the French market (57%). France is the third largest foreign market for American movies after Japan and Germany. The U.S. movie industry makes more than half of its money from distributing films outside the United States, and this percentage has been increasing yearly.

In contrast, foreign language films in the United States capture less than 2% of box office receipts, with the French getting about half of that. In dollar terms, in 1992, the value of audiovisual exports to Europe was US$3.66 billion compared with European exports to the United States valued at US$288 million.

In 1993, of the 100 most-attended films worldwide, 88 were American, with the highest ranking non-American entry, the French *Les Visiteurs*, only at number 27.

A UNI-CULTURE?

The cultural relationships between the two countries have become more complex recently. For instance, Disney has formed a unit to dub, market, and distribute French films in the United States. In part this is an attempt to lessen tensions with the French and reduce their opposition to Disney releases. Another aspect of this decision is that Disney, a partner in the EuroDisney theme park, which many Europeans criticize, needs to improve its image in France.

Many Hollywood studios have remade French films such as *Three Men and a Baby* and *The Vanishing* that have either never been released in the United States or that have very limited distribution. The studios believe that American actors—and the absence of dubbing—are more attractive to U.S. audiences. At the same time, however, Hollywood is casting more foreign actors in made-for-America movies. At work here is a business philosophy that argues, "Why cast an American actor when Gerard Depardieu can make them laugh in at least two languages?" (Natale 1994)

Just as foreign actors are becoming more sought after for American films, the European filmmakers are no longer filming solely in their native lands. For example, one of Frenchman Betrand Tavernier's recent films was bilingual (English and French), starring Dirk Bogarde. Polish filmmaker Krszystof Kieslowski made two recent films in France, and Italian Bernardo Bertolucci and German Win Wenders have made films on many different continents.

At one point in time, there was a clear distinction: Films from Europe were "art," whereas those from Hollywood were merely entertainment. More recently this distinction is not so clear. With American remakes of European films and a strong Hollywood influence on directors such as Jean-Jacques Beineix (*Diva*) and Luc Besson (*Nikita*), the two approaches appear to be moving toward a common direction.

And as for Jack Valenti, who was so opposed to the cultural exception in the GATT talks, his advice to the French is, "Invade the American market!" (Woodrow and Valenti 1994)

References

ANDREWS, N. (1993), "Identity Crisis in the Euro-movies—Nigel Andrews Explains Why it is Becoming More and More Difficult to Tell European and Hollywood Films Apart," *Financial Times*, (December 18).

BEGLEY, A. (1992), "Case of the Brooklyn Symbolist", *The New York Times Magazine*, (August 30).

"Clinton Rejects French Bid for GATT Concession," (1993), *The Reuter European Community Report*, (October 15).

COHEN, R. (1994), "Aux Armes! France Rallies to Battle Sly and T. Rex," *The New York Times*, (Arts and Leisure Section), (January 2).

FRODON, J-M. (1993), "World Commercial Negotiations and Their Repercussions in France" *(Les Negociations sur le Commerce Mondial et Leurs Repercussions en France)*, *Le Monde*, (December 10).

HOFSTEDE, G. (1980), *Culture's Consequences: International Differences in World Related Values*. Beverly Hills, CA: Sage.

KAPLAN, D. (1993), "How GATT Wrote an Unhappy Ending for Hollywood," *The Gazette* (Montreal), (December 17).

KING, T. (1994), "Disney's Miramax to Form Unit to Dub, Market, Distribute French Films in U.S.," *The Wall Street Journal*, (October 10).

MASLIN, J. (1994), "Depardieu's Bahamian Vacation," *The New York Times*, (February 4).

NATALE, R. (1994), "Hollywood Dit Willkommen, Bienvenido," *The New York Times*, (Arts and Leisure Section), (February 20).

STEVENSON, R. (1994), "Lights! Camera! Europe!" *The New York Times*, (Business Section), (February 6).

SULEIMAN, E. (1993), "GATT Debate: Why America has so Little Interest in France," *(Debats GATT: Pourqoi la France Interesse si peu l'Amerique)*, *Le Monde*, (December 8).

THOMAS, A. (1993), "The Audiovisual Negotiations Seen by the French Negotiator: First, An Internal Fight for Europe," *(Les Negociations sur l'Audiovisuel Vues par le Neogociateur Francais: D'Abord une Bataille Interne a l'Europe)*, *Agence France Presse*, (December 19).

WOODROW, A. and VALENTI, J. (1994), "An Interview with the Patron of American Studios Jack Valenti: 'Competition promotes quality,'" *(Un Entretien avec le Patron des Studios Americains Jack Valenti: "La concurrence stimule la Qualite")*, *Le Monde*, (February 15).

YOUNG, J. (1994), "The Best French Films You'll Never See," *The New York Times*, (Arts and Leisure Section), (October 30).

Conscience or the Competitive Edge? (A)

Kate Button
Christopher K. Bart

The plane touched down at Bombay airport on time. Olivia Jones made her way through the usual immigration bureaucracy without incident and was finally ushered into a waiting limousine, complete with uniformed chauffeur and soft black leather seats. Her already considerable excitement at being in India for the first time was mounting. As she cruised the dark city streets, she asked her chauffeur why so few cars had their headlights on at night. The driver responded that most drivers believed that headlights use too much petrol! Finally, she arrived at her hotel, a black marble monolith, grandiose and decadent in its splendour, towering above the bay.

The goal of her four-day trip was to sample and select swatches of woven cotton from the mills in and around Bombay, to be used in the following season's youthwear collection of shirts, trousers, and underwear. She was thus treated with the utmost deference by her hosts, who were invariably Indian factory owners, or British agents for Indian mills. For three days she was ferried from one air-conditioned office to another, sipping iced tea or chilled lemonade, poring over leatherbound swatch catalogs, which featured every type of stripe and design possible. On the fourth day, Jones made a request that she knew would cause some anxiety in the camp. "I want to see a factory," she declared.

After much consultation and several attempts at dissuasion, she was once again ushered into a limousine and driven through a part of the city she had not previously seen. Gradually, the hotel and the western shops dissolved into the background and Jones entered downtown Bombay. All around was a sprawling shantytown, constructed from sheets of corrugated iron and panels of cardboard boxes. Dust flew in spirals everywhere among the dirt roads and open drains. The car crawled along the unsealed roads behind carts hauled by man and beast alike, laden to overflowing with straw or city refuse—the treasure of the ghetto. More than once the limousine had to halt and wait while a lumbering white bull crossed the road.

Finally, in the very heart of the ghetto, the car came to a stop. "Are you sure you want to do this?" asked her host. Determined not to be faint-hearted, Jones got out of the car.

White-skinned, blue-eyed, and blond, clad in a city suit and stiletto-heeled shoes, and carrying a briefcase, Jones was indeed conspicuous. It was hardly surprising that the inhabitants of the area found her an interesting and amusing subject, as she teetered along the dusty street and stepped gingerly over the open sewers.

Her host led her down an alley, between the shacks and open doors and inky black interiors. Some shelters, Jones was told, were restaurants, where at lunchtime people would gather on the rush mat floors and eat rice together. In the doorway of one shack there was a table which served as a counter, laden with ancient cans of baked beans, sardines, and rusted tins of a fluorescent green substance that might have been peas. The eyes of the young man behind the counter were smiling and proud as he beckoned her forward to view his wares.

As Jones turned another corner, she saw an old man in the middle of the street, clad in a waist cloth, sitting in a large tin bucket. He had a tin can in his hand with which he poured water from the bucket over his head and shoulders. Beside him two little girls played in brilliant white nylon dresses, bedecked with ribbons and lace. They posed for her with smiling faces, delighted at having their photograph taken in their best frocks. The men and women moved around her with great dignity and grace, Jones thought.

Finally, her host led her up a precarious wooden ladder to a floor above the street. At the top Jones was warned not to stand straight as the ceiling was just 5 feet high. There, in a room not 20 feet by 40 feet, twenty men were sitting at treadle sewing machines, bent over yards of white cloth. Between them on the floor were rush mats, some occupied by sleeping workers awaiting their next shift. Jones learned that these men were on a 24-hour rotation, 12 hours on and 12 hours off, every day for 6 months of the year. For the remaining 6 months they returned to their families in the countryside to work the land, planting and building with the money they had earned in the city. The shirts they were working on were for an order she had placed 4 weeks earlier in London, an order of which she had been particularly proud because of the low price she had succeeded in negotiating. Jones reflected that this sight was the most humbling experience of her life. When she questioned her host about these conditions, she was told that they were typical for her industry—and for most of the third world, as well.

Eventually, she left the heat, dust, and din of the little shirt factory and returned to the protected, air-conditioned world of the limousine.

"What I've experienced today and the role I've played in creating that living hell will stay with me forever," she thought. Later in the day, she asked herself whether what she had seen was an inevitable consequence of pricing policies that enabled the British customer to purchase shirts at £12.99 instead of £13.99 and at the same time allowed the company to make its mandatory 56% profit margin? Were her negotiating skills—the result of many years of training—an indirect cause of the terrible conditions she had seen?

When Jones returned to the U.K., she considered her position and the options open to her as a buyer for a large, publicly traded, retail chain operating in a highly competitive environment. Her dilemma was twofold: Can an ambitious employee afford to exercise a social conscience in his or her career? And can career-minded individuals truly make a difference without jeopardizing their future?

Conscience or the Competitive Edge? (B)

Olivia Jones described her subsequent decision as follows:

"The alternatives for me were perfectly clear, if somewhat unrealistic: I could stipulate a standard of working conditions to be enforced at any factory employed, and offer to pay an inflated price for merchandise in an effort to fund the necessary improvements. This would mean having to increase the margins in other sections of the range and explaining to my controller exactly why prices had risen.

"There was, of course, no guarantee that the extra cash would make its way safely into the hands of the worker or improve his working conditions. Even exercising my greatest faith in human nature, I could see the wealthy factory owner getting increasingly fatter and some other keen and able buyer being promoted into my highly coveted position!

"I could refuse to buy from India. This would mean I would have to find alternative sources at equally low prices to justify my action. There was always Macau, where I knew conditions were worse if anything, or Hong Kong, where conditions were certainly better, from what I had seen, but prices were much higher. I had to ask myself if I would truly be improving the plight of the workers by denying them the enormous orders that I usually put through their factories. Or would I simply be salving my own conscience by righteously congratulating myself at not dealing in slave labour? Doubtless my production schedule would be snapped up eagerly by the next buyer who was hungry for cheap labour and fast turnaround.

"I could consider speaking to the powers that be and ask their advice. After all, the group was proud of its philanthropic reputation and had promoted its charity work and sponsorship of various causes, including Wimbledon Football Club and Miss World. This in mind, I approached my line manager, who laughed at my idealistic naivety and made it quite clear that I should hold my tongue if I knew what was good for me.

"It seemed I had but two choices. Either I quit the company and look for an employer which would be more responsible in its attitude towards sourcing merchandise, or I could continue to buy as before, but aware of the consequences and exercising a conscience wherever possible. I won't bother to list my excuses for opting for the latter choice.

"I believe that there is no solution, no generalization which can be used as a precedent in this type of scenario. I don't know to this day what action I could have taken to improve the lives of those individuals whom I felt I had compromised.

"Every day, in various work situations, employees, and specifically managers, come up against questions of conscience versus the status quo. It may be that you are encouraged to show prejudice against an individual or group of employees due to their race, colour or clique; maybe your boss asked you to lie to camouflage an embarrassing error and insinuate that the fault lies with someone else; maybe your employer's policy requires you to screw a client or a supplier to close a deal and maintain the bottom line.

"Each case is different and demands its own evaluation. Each man and woman must draw their own set of rules and regulations to suit their own situation and conscience.

"It takes brave individuals to jeopardize their careers for a cause but it is thanks to those who do take a stand that great feats of humanitarian work are successfully undertaken and completed. We should all evaluate the choices that are open to us and be true to ourselves. Let your conscience be your guide within the realms of reality.

"The most important lesson that I learned from the episode was that, above all, you have to learn to live with the choices that you make."

Case 3

James Brunner

Buckeye Glass Company in China

In November 1988, Buckeye Glass sent a highly skilled team to Qinhuangdao, People's Republic of China, to negotiate a joint venture for the manufacture of glassware. The team consisted of John Brickley, Vice President of Marketing; Bob Caines, Production Manager; and Steve Miller, Chief Engineer. Brickley had carefully selected an interpreter, Ling Sida, who knew Mandarin Chinese, the dialect spoken in Northern China, as he was concerned that a language barrier might arise.

COMPANY BACKGROUND

Buckeye Glass headquartered in Columbus, Ohio, produced glassware, including wide and narrow mouth containers, and glass prescription ware. It had more than 25,000 customers worldwide in diverse industries such as food processing, liquor, beer, wine, cosmetics, soft drinks, and proprietary and prescription drugs. Its 10 month worldwide sales in 1988 were $3.0 billion, and it had plants in Europe, Asia, and North and South America, employing 44,000 people. Its earnings had been flat for the past 5 years and management was exploring new avenues for growth of sales and earnings. The plant being considered for construction in China would produce all types of glassware under the name of Buckeye, its brand name worldwide. It is known as a high-quality producer and a leader in its field.

Year	Sales (billion)	Profits (million)
1988*	$3.0	$120
1987	$3.4	$138
1986	$3.0	$140
1985	$3.0	$136
1984	$2.8	$135

*10 months

QINHUANGDAO

Qinhuangdao is a Chinese international port city in Northern China. Located on the Bohai Sea, it is only 277 kilometers (166 miles) southeast of Beijing and serves as the gateway to the capital as it has a large, modern harbor, which is ice and salt free. The weather is milder than inland, and its beaches at Beidaihe attract thousands annually, including leading government officials from Beijing.

By 1988 Qinhuangdao had developed into an important economic center and was the glass capital of the People's Republic of China. It is one of 14 coastal cities opened to the outside world in 1984 and has a new economic and technical development site which had attracted foreign investors from the United States, Australia, and several other countries. This site had a 12,000-unit Swedish program controlled telephone system. One of the companies located there manufactured silicon solar batteries, and another, special tubing for refrigerators and buses. There were 25 glass factories in the area producing laminated glass, thermal glass, medical glassware, fiberglass, and heat-absorbing glass. These companies engage in lateral economic cooperation and pool both technologies and skilled personnel, thereby enhancing the quality and efficiency of production. The area is rich in quartz, a major ingredient in the manufacturing of glass.

TRIP TO QINHUANGDAO

The Buckeye Glass team had flown for 26 hours and stayed overnight in Beijing at the Great Wall Hotel. The next morning they traveled by train for six hours to Qinhuangdao. Enroute they discussed their plans and were anxious to meet the Chinese and begin negotiating as soon as possible.

When they arrived there, they were greeted warmly by their Chinese hosts and escorted to the Jinshan Hotel, expressly reserved for foreigners. They found to their surprise that their accommodations were comparable to those of first-class hotels in the United States. The rooms were complete with comfortable beds, baths, televisions, and telephones. Wake-up service and a dining room were available for meals, which were served in both Chinese and Western styles.

Pleased by their surroundings and encouraged by the congeniality of their hosts at dinner that night they retired; confident that the meeting scheduled for the next day would establish a beneficial working relationship with the Chinese. At 10 P.M. strains of Brahm's lullaby flowed from the intercom system, and the negotiators slept peacefully after their arduous journey as they began to adjust to their jet lag.

The Chinese arrived promptly at 9 A.M. The Chinese delegation was led by Tien Chao, the Deputy Director of the Foreign Affairs Office. Through his interpreter, he introduced the others in his party. Pi Zhao, Director of the Xia Xian Glass Factory, the leading glass manufacturer in China, and Mah Ai-qi, his personal secretary and interpreter. Tien Chao was tall, thin, erect, and very dignified in bearing. After formal introductions and an exchange of pleasantries, the group left for a tour of Xia Xian Glass Factory's manufacturing facilities.

Arriving at the factory, the group was greeted by Poh Jiwei, the Managing Director, who escorted them on a tour of the facilities. The Americans were surprised by what awaited them. The floor of the factory was dirty, and there was a large number of glass container crates located haphazardly on the floor. Groups of employees were loitering, playing cards, conversing, and laughing, while others were engaged in various work activities. Surprised at the minimal level of activity in the plant, Caines asked through their interpreter, Ling Sida, "Why aren't all these people working or are some of them on break?"

Poh Jiwei smiled and replied proudly, "Our plant has met its production quota for the year; but these men report in each day to be with their friends and do whatever work is planned for that day. You know, in China we provide jobs for all our people and unemployment is nonexistent. When we receive our new quota from the government, production will begin again at a higher level."

Caines, still perplexed, replied, "Wouldn't it be more profitable to close down some of the production facilities and lay off at least some of the workers until the new quotas are announced and thereby increase the profits of the company?"

Poh Jiwei replied politely as he smiled, "In China, we do what is best for the workers in order to give them steady incomes. Our concern is more about the workers, than the income of the factory."

Caines, noting that some workers were arriving late, asked, "I've known that Chinese factories practice this *iron rice bowl* concept whereby all workers are assured they will have jobs. But some of them are late in arriving for work. Aren't they expected to be on time?" Poh Jiwei smiled and replied, "Well, in the past we have not enforced your Western-style work ethic of being punctual, but we are beginning to change. But please understand that the middle-aged and elderly workers are hard to change and they resist this new approach. The younger workers, however, agree that punctuality should lead to increased productivity, and are willing to accept these changes. In fact we now give bonuses to those who exceed their quotas and stay on their jobs until closing time. You may be interested to know that our workers retire when they reach the age of 55, and we have only a few older workers in the factory."

As the tour progressed, Caines continued to be amazed by the antiquated machinery in operation, but was startled when they came to an installation which had the latest container glass manufacturing technology. When he openly praised the equipment, Poh Jiwei smiled broadly and replied humbly to the surprise of the Americans, "Oh, our factory is very ill-equipped, with few modern machines unlike those you have in your country." Brickley, confused by Poh Jiwei's statement since they had just viewed a great deal of modern machinery, quickly assured Poh that the plant was indeed impressive and very well equipped.

After the tour of the plant, the Buckeye executives were escorted to a conference room which was plainly decorated, had 24 chairs arranged around the walls of the room, and a conference table with 10 chairs. They were invited to be seated at the table, and were served tea by their hosts. Pi Zhao thanked the Buckeye team for visiting the plant and commented for five minutes upon their proposed relationship with Buckeye Glass. He elaborated upon the economic development plans of the People's Republic of China and noted that even though the government had not given top priority to glass container production, it looked favorably upon the possibility of building a plant in Qinhuangdao for that purpose. He stressed the need for the development of a long-term relationship and hoped those present could become "old friends." After elaborating further for 20 minutes, he sat down.

John Brickley immediately stood up and responded by expressing his sincere appreciation for the plant tour, and also his hope that a close relationship could be developed with the Chinese in this endeavor. He stressed how a glass manufacturing plant would be beneficial to the economic progress of the country as well as the living standards of the Chinese. He profusely thanked Poh Jiwei for the tour of the factory and continued to elaborate for about 10 minutes on this relationship and its mutual benefits.

After he finished, Tien Chao proposed that after lunch they should tour Qinhuangdao and visit the eastern section of the Great Wall of China. He proudly stated that the sea end of the wall was in Qinhuangdao and at one time had been more than 23,000 meters long, but that only 2300 meters of it still existed. He stated it had been originally constructed by Emperor Qin Shi Huang of the Qin dynasty, commencing in 221 B.C. He also announced, "We should visit other features of interest, such as the 'Old Dragon's Head' at the sea end of the wall, the park and, of course, the beach in Beidaihe."

The rest of the afternoon was, therefore, spent touring the area. A photographer went with the party to photograph the Americans at the various points of interest, which were proudly described in detail by Tien Chao through an interpreter. (Appendix 1 provides a brief review of Chinese culture and negotiating styles.) Brickley was frustrated as he wanted to discuss the proposed joint venture. He attempted not to show his impatience, and expressed interest in the special features of the region. At 6 P.M. they returned to the hotel. The Chinese joined them for dinner and left promptly at 8 P.M.

Initial Meeting

The next morning, the Chinese delegation arrived promptly and escorted the Buckeye team to the hotel's meeting room. The Chinese delegation now consisted of 12 members, including Pi Zhao, the Director of Xin Xian Glass Factory, its plant manager, two assistant plant managers, several engineers, and the interpreter. The Chinese arranged themselves on one side of the table and the Buckeye Glass team was seated opposite them. After they were served tea, Brickley rose, thanked the Chinese for inviting them, and described the services of his company.

Brickley then introduced Caines who elaborated for approximately 20 minutes upon the history of Buckeye Glass, its premier position in the worldwide market in the production of containers for a wide range of industries such as food, soft drinks, beer, cosmetics, and pharmaceuticals, and how profitable they had been internationally. He then turned to Steve Miller who introduced the engineers. As a team, they presented a slide presentation of the company's production and sales facilities, and a statistical review of sales and profits for the previous decade. They continued by elaborating on the technological capabilities of Buckeye Glass. Brickley then rose and commented at length about the strong managerial team which the company had. He elaborated upon the integration of the marketing, finance, and production activities at Buckeye Glass, which he explained had been highly effective in thrusting the company into a leading position in the international glass container industry.

He commented briefly upon his opinions concerning observations made the previous day in the factory, and noted that his company could assist the Chinese by introducing its production workers and managers to Western concepts of production and marketing. He emphasized the need for management to introduce Western management know-how and methods in the Xia Xian Glass Factory in order that it could effectively serve the needs of the Chinese people.

During his presentation, the Chinese seemed somewhat passive, but occasionally asked questions and probed for information. Brickley and the other members of the Buckeye Glass team carefully and patiently answered the questions raised. They also endeavored to sense the priorities of the Chinese concerning the various types of problems that they had and what they wanted the American team to do. In their discussions, it became evident that breakage was a major problem as the Chinese workers were not well trained in the use of the equipment. Further, they learned that Xia Xian's customers wanted different types of glass containers than were being produced in this plant, but the company was still manufacturing ware no longer in heavy demand. They had a sizable overaged inventory of these outmoded containers.

Further, the Chinese noted that their products were not meeting the quality specifications demanded by foreign buyers. Thus, it was evident that a quality control training program was essential. Poh Jiwei observed further that the corregated shipping containers for the glass products were inferior and oftentimes broke in shipment, which then led to damaged merchandise.

While Brickley was aware of these problems, he had no idea of the order in which the Chinese would prioritize them, and specifically, which of Buckeye's services were considered to be the most important to the Chinese.

After the discussion had continued for three hours, Pi Zhao suggested that they break for lunch; and that after lunch they should go on a sightseeing tour of Yanshan University, a new educational institution founded in the 1980s to train engineering and technical students in the latest scientific developments and technology. Pi Zhao assured the Buckeye team that he would like to meet the next day to discuss the possibility of signing a letter of intent. The meeting then adjourned.

The next morning promptly at 9 A.M. Tien Chao, Pi Zhao, and Poh Jiwei arrived with their interpreter and three engineers. They escorted the Buckeye Glass executives to the conference room and they arranged themselves on one side of the table while the Americans occupied the other. Through his interpreter, Tien Chao expressed his appreciation to the Americans for their informative presentation and announced that they were interested in signing a letter of intent. Tien Chao observed that the Xia Xian Glass Factory had inadequate equipment and elaborated on a low level of skill possessed by the production workers as well as the managers. Brickley silently concurred with Tien Chao's observations concerning the workers, but he was surprised to hear this comment concerning the managers as some of them were present at the meeting. Further, Tien Chao expressed his admiration of the Buckeye Glass executives, acknowledging that the company was one of the leading glass manufacturers in the world, and that his company was humbly appreciative of the opportunity to join them in a joint venture. Brickley was amazed at this sense of humbleness by the Chinese as he didn't feel that they were as inferior as Tien Chao was suggesting.

Tien continued. "We feel that the time has arrived for us to sign a letter of intent and to express the general principles under which our venture will operate. Our objective is the modernization of the Xia Xian plant in Qinhuangdao and propose that it be located in the new economic and technical development zone. Further,

Buckeye Glass will provide for managerial training of the Chinese managers and also for the factory workers and service staff of the joint venture." He paused and then announced, "Further, Buckeye Glass will provide for the transfer of technology to improve the product's quality and performance, reduce production costs, and conserve energy and materials. This technology should also enable the company to expand the exportation of glass containers and thereby increase the foreign exchange revenues of the Xia Xian Glass Factory. Finally Buckeye will be the marketing agent for the joint venture, not only in China but on a worldwide basis."

Brickley was silently pleased. On second thought, he was somewhat perplexed as the objectives proposed were very broad and outlined the general principles of the accord without spelling out the specific details. Nevertheless, he thanked Tien Chao and added, "I think it's important that we also include the specific details of our mutual obligations in order to avoid any misunderstandings in the future."

Tien Chao smiled and replied, "We appreciate your concern, but it is not necessary to specify the particulars of the joint venture at this point. But we need to reach a general agreement on the principles in your letter of interest."

As the executives of Buckeye Glass were surprised at the Chinese proposed letter of intent, they began to fire questions concerning the specific details. Tien Chao again smiled and asserted, "The details can be worked out later but first we must come to an agreement on general principles. We propose that we break for a period of time in order that you may have an opportunity to review our broad objectives, I propose that we meet again after lunch."

The meeting adjourned and the two groups went to separate meeting rooms. The Buckeye team met in Brickley's room and after pouring each a cup of tea, Brickley, exasperated, stated, "Well this certainly isn't what I expected. I thought we could reach some general agreement on the specific details. Evidently the Chinese are only interested in general principles. Frankly, I'm concerned they didn't specify the time period for the joint venture and the financial details. How much each of us is going to have to put up front is also up in the air. What products are to be produced? This is certainly different than any joint venture I've ever written in the United States. I propose that we come up with recommendations so that we can get this show on the road." Brickley noted further, "After listening to their monologue, I'm sure glad that I took notes, but I'm not certain what their priorities are. There is a lot we can bring to the table, but it would be helpful if we knew their priorities. I will press that issue after lunch."

At noon, Tien Chao and his team met Brickley and his associates, and they went to the dining room. While the Chinese remained reserved and occasionally talked among themselves, the atmosphere was still friendly. After lunch they adjourned again to the conference room and Brickley stated their concern about the missing details and made some specific suggestions. Tien Chao commented, "I know we are old friends, but you are insisting upon being very specific about the details and are not willing to agree only on the general principles. We regret this and don't understand why." Brickley's interpreter told him the Chinese felt he was behaving dishonorably and acted as though he did not trust the Chinese. Brickley feeling intimidated quickly responded, "I'm disappointed we can't agree. However, if it is not customary in China to be specific in a letter of agreement but only to reach agreement only on the general principles, we will go along to demonstrate our sincerity. After we have signed it, I would like to give it to the press in order that my company may publicize it in the United States as it will be good publicity and will demonstrate Buckeye's interest in economic development in the People's Republic of China."

Tien Chao agreed, but asked that no dates be stated concerning when it was to commence and that no mention be made of the investment that would be involved, nor the city in China in which it was to be located.

Brickley knew that the Chinese had mixed feelings about publicity and preferred to maintain secrecy in the negotiating process as they had a mistrust of publicity and perceived it as a form of pressure. Moreover, he sensed that they were concerned that their superiors might feel they were endeavoring to promote themselves. On the other hand, he thought that if he didn't publicize the agreement, the Chinese might be offended. He was aware that they might sense a violation of confidentiality if he revealed too much. It was a minor dilemma for him. Brickley paused, and then agreed to all of these stipulations with the exception that the city should be specified as it was known in the United States that his company had representatives in Qinhuangdao. Tien Chao agreed reluctantly.

The next day they met again and signed a joint agreement, which Brickley recognized was not binding on either parties, but at least served as a basis for commencing the substantive negotiations. He personally felt quite gratified with the progress made, as the Chinese indicated that they were now willing to work out the specific details.

Formal Banquet

That evening the Chinese team escorted the Buckeye Glass representatives to a Chinese banquet to celebrate the signing of the letter of intent. Brickley was surprised to observe that place cards had been arranged on the tables in order to facilitate the seating arrangements. He was seated next to Tien Chao's left and the Chinese were interspersed among the Americans around two tables. When the first course consisting of braised prawns were served, the Chinese to the right of a Buckeye executive served him a portion of the prawns. While they were awaiting the second course, Tien Chao gave a speech lauding Sino-American relations and the signing completed that afternoon. As he closed he offered a toast of Mao Tai wine to the Buckeye Glass team. Brickley, aware of the effect of Mao Tai, which has a 40% alcoholic content, toasted cautiously.

Following this, in sequence, scallops fried in tomato sauce, sautéed conch, fillet of fish stir-fried, pork steak fried, crabmeat stir-fried, heart of rape with mushroom, and sea slugs were served. During each of these seven courses, the Chinese served the Americans saying, "Quing, Quing" ("please, please").

During the course of the two-hour banquet, innumberable toasts were made by the Chinese and the Buckeye team reciprocated, oftentimes going from table to table to present toasts. Both teams used the white wine on the table for their toasts on these occasions, rather than the Mao Tai. However, when Tien Chao offered his toasts, Brickley followed protocol, and drank the complete glass of wine, on the urging by Tien Chao, who proposed. *"Ganbei"* ("bottoms up").

During the dinner, the conversation naturally turned to the different cuisines of the various regions of the People's Republic of China. Miller asked facetiously if it was true that the Chinese in Southern China ate dog, snake, and monkey brains. Tien Chao smiled broadly and replied affirmatively. Encouraged by Tien Chao's smile. Miller began joking about some of the other delicacies that appeared on the menu; such as heart of rape on mushrooms and the sea slugs. The Chinese apparently enjoyed this humorous approach as they were grinning and nodding their heads in response. Encouraged, the Americans began to tell Western jokes. Apparently, the atmosphere was friendly and relaxed.

Brickley, encouraged by this feeling of cordiality, sensed that the time was appropriate to again address the subject of the joint venture. Turning to Tien Chao, he said, "With our technology and investment, Buckeye Glass can pull China from its backwardness and make it a world power." Tien Chao replied. "Yes, yes. Buckeye Glass is a world leader, and a very powerful company from the United States. Xia Xian certainly must make use of a liaison with it."

Encouraged by Tien Chao's reply, Brickley continued, expounding upon the mutual benefit that this joint venture would provide both parties. He observed that Buckeye Glass could train the management of Xia Xian in modern managerial techniques and assist them in training their workers to use Western technology. He noted further that their close contacts would enable Buckeye to establish a foothold in the Chinese market and become a major power in the glass industry in the Pacific Basin countries.

While the guests were eating the stir-fried crabmeat course, Tien Chao rose and commented on the close ties being established with Buckeye Glass. He then presented Brickley a gift of two Chinese exercise balls, which he stated had been in use in China since the fourteenth century and were used to stimulate important acupressure points below the wrist. He then demonstrated that they emitted soft chiming sounds in two different pitches to calm the nerves and soothe the soul. Tien Chao then gave Brickley a 4 × 6 foot tapestry of the Great Wall. Brickley thanked him profusely, but was embarrassed as he had no gifts to reciprocate this show of friendship and cordial relations.

After the pastry had been served, the next course consisted of soup, rice and fruit. The Americans found the soup to be delicious and each took two servings of the rice as they especially enjoyed it. Tien Chao listened politely as Brickley sipped his tea. After a third cup, Tien Chao rose and thanked the Buckeye executives for attending the dinner. The hosts escorted them back to their room and quickly departed.

POLITICAL AND ECONOMIC ENVIRONMENT

That night, Brickley reflected on the economic and political environment of the PRC in order to gain a broader perspective. He was aware that the PRC had a population of more than a billion and that its economic system was being developed aggressively by the government. He noted that labor was inexpensive and quite abundant without any problem of labor strikes. Further, he was aware that although raw materials and other supplies were less costly than in some countries, there were some difficulties in their procurement. He had heard that in the PRC the availability of materials and supplies was oftentimes dependent upon connections which one had with others. These relationships in China were referred to as *guanxi*, and Brickley was aware that if one formed such ties, they signified close bonding. This permitted either party to call upon the other for any favors if they were within the power of a *guanxi* member to grant, and he would be obligated to do so. Further, he knew that *guanxi* ties were also important for getting things done when working with the governmental bureaucracy, as the PRC does not have an institutionalized legal system. Therefore, getting favorable interpretations by bureaucrats was dependent largely upon whom one knew and who had *guanxi* with whom.

Moreover, he noted that the PRC had a culture which traditionally shunned legal considerations and stressed rather the ethical and moral principles of everyday living; and that formal agreements were based more upon moral obligations than the law. He also recognized that although the PRC was a socialist country, it suffered from political instability, and the recent open door policy was primarily the endeavor of their senior leader Deng Xiaoping. Brickley knew that in November, 1983, Deng had launched a movement to put his mark on China's new emerging economic development. He had devised a five-year plan to purge the Communist party's 40 million members of 1 million leftists, most of whom were ill educated. This had been accomplished through a reedification program of self criticism and prescribed study. Deng endeavored to clear the way for his protégés to rise to positions of power in order to ensure continuation of his economic, political and open-door policies.

In October 1987, Zhao Ziyang became the party general's secretary succeeding Deng and a sixth five-year plan was announced. Deng, however, remained a paramount figure in the decision-making process and was encouraging some capitalistic practices to be adopted in China, such as using quotas and holding managers accountable for the profitability of their factories.

In general, China's semiclosed economy was modified to an open economy with international exchanges encouraged. In moving toward a market mechanism for setting prices, however, inflation surged in 1988 to an unofficial but acknowledged annual rate of nearly 50% in cities. There was evidence that government officials were capitalizing on entrepreneurism by accepting bribes and engaging in other unsavory activities. The economy was clearly overheated, industrial output had risen 7% in the first half, and investment in capital construction had increased 14%. China's inefficient factories were unable to keep up with the demand for goods and thereby added to the inflationary pressures. Demand for consumer goods was far outstripping supply, and black market activities were thriving with inflationary price rises as a consequence.

The government attempted to slow the economy by controlling the money supply, but this had proven to be ineffective as the money supply rose 30% in the first five months of 1988. Finally, in order to get better control on the economy and slow down the inflationary pressures, in October 1988, the state council announced that as of December 1, it would reduce investment in a variety of nonessential industries, ranging from textile processing to consumer electronics and plastics. However, this would not apply to projects involving foreigners or those in priority areas such as energy and transportation. It was anticipated that the roll back would be huge and that Beijing would cut back capital investment in 1989 by 50 billion Chinese yuan (13.5 billion dollars). Fortunately for Buckeye Glass, this would not pertain to glass containers but rather involved such products as cotton textiles, rubber goods, tractors, television sets, and those which consumed too much energy such as irons, vacuum cleaners, and rice cookers. The crux of the problem was that the Chinese enterprises were state owned and the managers were not inclined to think in terms of economic efficiency.

Substantive Negotiations

Negotiations commenced promptly the next day and continued for two days. Both teams had copies of the Law of the PRC on Joint Ventures. (See Exhibit C3-1.) On occasion, the Chinese would engage in detailed questioning about topics which apparently were not too significant. Brickley sensed that this stalling tactic was used to gain time to enable the Chinese to elicit the comments of their superiors concerning various parts of the contract. He observed that when points requiring clarification arose, the Chinese during informal breaks would gather around the Buckeye Glass interpreter in order to attempt to persuade her to get concessions for the Chinese or to clarify Buckeye's proposals. Further, when the Americans expressed their

Exhibit C3-1

The Law of the People's Republic of China on Joint Ventures Using Chinese and Foreign Investment (adopted in 1979 at the second session of the Fifth National People's Congress)

1. Foreign companies and individuals within the territory of the People's Republic of China may incorporate themselves into joint ventures with Chinese companies or other Chinese entities with the objective of expanding international economic co-operation and technological exchange.

2. The Foreign Investment Commission must authorize joint ventures, and if approved, ventures are required to register with the General Administration for Industry and Commerce of the PRC, which will then issue a license within 3 months.

3. Joint ventures shall have limited liability and the foreign parties will contribute not less than 25% of the registered capital.

4. The participants will share profits, risks, and losses of the joint venture in proportion to their capital contributions.

5. The equity of each party may be capital goods, industrial property rights, cash, etc., in the ventures.

6. The contributors of technology or equipment contributed run the risk of forfeiture or damages if the technology or equipment contributed is not truly advanced and appropriate for Chinese needs. If losses are caused by deception through the intentional provision of outdated equipment or technology, compensation must be paid for the losses.

7. Investments by the Chinese participants may include the right of use of a site but it shall not constitute a part of the investment as the joint venture shall pay the Chinese government for its use.

8. A joint venture will have a Board of Directors and the Chairman of the board is to be appointed by the Chinese participants. The foreign parties may appoint 2 Vice-Presidents. These do not necessarily have to be Chinese but must be approved by the partners to the joint venture.

9. A joint venture agreement must stipulate procedures for the employment and discharge of the workers and staff members and comply with Chinese laws.

10. The net profit of a joint venture shall be distributed in proportion to the parties' respective investment shares after deductions for reserve funds. Bonuses and welfare funds for the workers and the expansion funds of the venture and the profit or losses shall be in accordance with the capital investment of the parties involved and be subject to the tax laws of the People's Republic of China and expatriation.

11. Joint ventures must maintain open accounts in a bank approved by the Bank of China.

12. All foreign exchange transactions shall be in accordance with the foreign exchange regulations of the People's Republic of China.

13. Joint ventures may borrow funds directly from foreign banks. Appropriate insurance will be provided by Chinese insurance companies. A joint venture equipped with up-to-date technology by world standards may apply for a reduction of or an exemption from income tax for the first 2 or 3 profit-making years.

14. A joint venture is encouraged to market its products outside China through direct channels, its associated agencies, or Chinese foreign trade establishments. Its products may also be distributed on the Chinese market.

15. The contract period of a joint venture must be agreed upon by both parties and may be extended subject to authorization by the Foreign Investment Commission.

16. Disputes which cannot be settled through consultation may be settled through consultation or arbitration by an arbitral body of Chinese or arbitral body agreed upon by the parties.

views on a point under negotiation, Tien Chao would say, "We'll take note of your position," but then go on to the next issue under discussion. Brickley sensed that this indicated that the Chinese did not agree, but wished to avoid confrontations.

He also noted that the Chinese were extremely sensitive when pricing was being discussed and were apparently concerned that they might be given unfavorable treatment or were being cheated. From his interpreter, Brickley learned that this was true and that the Chinese were apprehensive that their superior would deal with them harshly if favorable terms were not obtained. Brickley also noted that in order to gain concessions from the Chinese, it was necessary to give one in return, thereby engaging in a face-saving action.

American Hosted Dinner

That evening, the Buckeye Glass executive hosted a dinner for the Chinese. The menu was simpler than the Chinese banquet as the Buckeye executives felt that the Chinese meal was too exotic for their tastes and digestion. Speeches were again given by Tien Chao and Brickley and frequent toasts were offered. Miller again told some Western jokes accompanied by friendly backslapping. The Buckeye executives attempted to lighten the ongoing formal conversation by steering it to familiar topics, such as the families of the Chinese, personal tastes and ideas, and sexual patterns in China. The Chinese responded with much smiling and laughter even though their replies to the questioning were vague.

Proposed Joint Venture Contract

After a long weekend, during which the Americans and Chinese separately developed proposals for the joint venture, the Buckeye team were the first to present their terms for negotiations. Brickley submitted the financial requirements as he and his team perceived them (see Table C3-1) and their terms for the joint venture (see Exhibit C3-2).

T a b l e C 3 - 1   Proposed Joint Venture, Dragon Glass Company: Financial Requirements (U.S. $000)

First year capital		Loan from Bank of China	$ 200
Working capital	$898	Long-term debt	400
Installations and equipment	790	Total liabilities	600
New $450			
Old 40			
Factory	800	Net worth	
Land		First 2 year loss	200
Technology	550	Initial capital	2338
Total	$2738	Total	$3038
Partners' Investments			
Xia Xian Glass Company	55%	Buckeye Glass	25%
Factory	$ 400	Factory	$ 400
Installations and equipment	490	Technology	550
New $750		Cash/equivalent	102
Old 40			
Cash/equivalent	396		
Total	$1286	Total	$1052

Exhibit C3-2   Proposed Joint Venture

Name: Dragon Glass Company.

Capital Contributions: 55% of the capital for the venture should be provided by the Xia Xian Glass Factory and 25% by the Buckeye Glass Company. In meeting this requirement, the Chinese were to obtain the right to use a site in the Qinhuangdao Economic Development Zone. It was agreed that the joint venture should rent the property from the Chinese government. Buckeye Glass was to invest $400,000 in the building and installations.

Training: Buckeye Glass was also to provide for training of the joint venture's managers and engineers in the United States for a period of 3 months.

Marketing: Buckeye Glass shall be the sole sales agent in the world market and provide for the maximum market penetration by its products internally in China and in the Pacific Basin countries, with the objective of 40% being sold domestically and the remaining 60% in the export market.

Pricing: The prices established in the world market would provide a 20% after tax return on the total investment of each party to the contract.

Technology: Technology provided by Buckeye Glass shall comply with the technology transfer regulations of the People's Republic of China and provide for the improvement of product quality and performance, reduce production costs, and increase foreign revenues. The value of the technology in the first year shall be $550,000.

Imported Materials: All silica and related production materials imported will not be subject to the standard 12% import duty if used for exported products, but a duty will be applied to those used for glassware produced for domestic sales. An 18% tax of value-added nature on domestic sales shall be levied. Sales in the world market shall provide a 20% after-tax return on the total investment of each party to the contract.

Work Force: The work force shall consist of the normal staff of production workers and include staff employees including engineers, office workers and managers. The joint venture shall not hire additional workers for the factory or office workers without the approval of the Board of Directors.

The initial work force for the plant shall be limited to 200 factory workers and 50 service employees in the offices, including the managers.

Wage Compensation: The direct salary and benefits for the workers shall be determined by the Chinese government. The range for factory workers in the first year will be for 1200 Yuan and in the second year 1800 Yuan and will be for 2000 hours annually.

The annual wage rate for the production workers will include direct and fringe benefits. The wage rate will be modified after the first year in conformity with those paid in other Chinese corporations for production workers by the Board of Directors.

Technology Confidentiality: The joint venture partners will be obliged to maintain confidentiality of the technology and shall be required during the life of the joint venture and beyond. Damages for the breach of contract will be pursuant to the Foreign Economic Contract Law and recoverable against a contract transferee who discloses the confidential information.

Expansion: The joint venture should secure from the Chinese government an additional 10 acres for expansion of this manufacturing facility.

Board of Directors: The management of the joint venture shall consist of 7 members on a Board of Directors, 4 of whom will be appointed by the Chinese and 3 by the Buckeye Glass Company. The board will follow modern management principles and establish a 5 year marketing and production plan. A planning budget shall be developed for the same period of time. It will be the responsibility of the joint venture board to specify the types and numbers of workers and managers for the venture.

Taxation: With approval of the tax authorities, the joint venture may be exempt from taxation for the first 2 profit-making years and granted a 50% tax reduction for the

Exhibit C3-2   Proposed Joint Venture (cont)

following 5 years. A profit-making year shall be defined as the year in which a joint venture realizes profits after the accumulated operating losses from prior years have been deducted. Further, as this joint venture is in a Special Investment Zone, the tax rate applicable to the enterprise shall be 15%, and no withholding tax on repatriated profits shall be levied.

Currency: This joint venture will use Renminbi (RMB) to calculate its income and tax liabilities. It may maintain its accounting records and books in dollars.

Negotiations Concluded

As Brickley was willing to negotiate and make concessions, he was puzzled that the Chinese did not present their terms. He commented on the key issues of the joint venture agreement and the Chinese listened intently. As they were passive and remained silent, Brickley couldn't tell whether they agreed or not with his proposal, and the team was perplexed about how to cope with these periods of silence. Tien Chao thanked him and proposed they continue their discussions at 2 P.M. that afternoon. He was most concerned about the confidentiality of the transfer of technology in China as he knew there were no comprehensive commercial laws to protect his company, and China did not have trade secret laws. He had been told that the Chinese, on occasion, take technology and copy it. Moreover, he was aware margins initially would be nonexistent for goods sold on the world markets, and the joint venture would undoubtedly incur losses until the company could become more efficient.

In the afternoon session, the Chinese were cordial but remained passive. Tien Chao observed, "We have reviewed your proposal and can agree on most of its provisions. However, the value placed on the technology is far greater than we believe can be justified. As you have already paid for its development, we insist that in the spirit of friendship, a much lower figure be used. Further, we believe that Buckeye Glass should contribute all of the money for the investment in installations and equipment as we are providing labor at a considerably lower level than can be obtained elsewhere. We will cover the cost of the factory in our investment. We believe that 80% of the goods should be sold in the export market. Before proceeding, we wish to resolve these issues."

Brickley then endeavored to explain that although his company had already invested in the glass technology, that on world markets it would be valued at this level. Further, he was quite puzzled by the large percentage of output which was to be destined for the export market as he had assumed the Chinese were interested in raising the standards of living of the people in the PRC. Obviously the need for foreign hard currency was more paramount. Discussion continued for another hour, at which time Tien Chao then proposed they adjourn and meet the next morning. At the meeting Tien Chao presented Xia Xian's proposal. Buckeye Glass was to invest 35% of the capital in the form of cash, installations, and technology. He specified that the technology must be advanced, lead to improved product quality and performance, and contribute to export expansion.

Brickley thereupon assured him that the technology proposed would do all these things, but insisted that the most advanced technology would not be appropriate at this time in China. He agreed that the value of the property in the buildings should be fixed by the People's government of Qinhuangdao according to a relative industry index. When Brickley inquired concerning the availability of silica and other raw materials for this project the Chinese were evasive, but assured him their "connections" would be able to find the necessary materials at reasonable prices.

To relieve some of the tension, Mr. Brickley and his team avoided the topics about which the two groups were in most disagreement; and again emphasized the great mutual benefits which would result from this venture. The afternoon meeting ended well. There were still some disagreements remaining; however, much ground had been covered. The remaining differences were considered by the Buckeye Glass negotiators to be minor, and they agreed to go back over them for the discussion on the next day, but Brickley was becoming impatient, as he thought about the considerable investment his company had made in order to conduct these negotiations in Qinhuangdao. Buckeye had already committed more than $25,000 for lodging, food, transportation and other expenses, and at least another million could be required for the equity capital.

The next morning the negotiators met again and to Brickley's dismay, the Chinese were adamant and refused to modify their terms. However, Tien Chao proposed that production be expanded to include containers for the wine and soft drink industries rather than only for food. This astounded Brickley, as these industries were expanding rapidly and naturally he wanted to be involved in the early phase of development of these markets. He knew that the Chinese had strong loyalty to their initial suppliers and it was essential to establish these relationships before other foreign competitors entered the Chinese market. "What do we do now to break this impasse?" he agonized to his team. "What concessions can we make to enable the Chinese to save face and alter this position?"

Brickley was aware that any joint agreement proposal would be subject to review by not only the Chinese government but also his legal department. At least another year would be required to formalize the agreement. His team had been in China for two weeks and the potential for profit in the long run was in the millions after the shakedown period in the first two years. He perceived several options at this point. They could drop the idea and move on to more promising ventures in the short run, make some concessions, and bring in an agent who resided on a permanent basis in Beijing who had strong Chinese ties, as he was a successful Chinese negotiator; they could offer to invite the Chinese to come to America as Buckeye's guests in order to visit the corporate plant and observe the technology and training facilities, or they could set a date for departure with the objective of forcing the Chinese to move off dead center and reach an agreement on the terms. He murmured to himself, "Patience, John, getting a joint venture signed in the PRC is like building Rome—it takes longer than a day! Freight trains move faster than negotiations in the PRC!"

APPENDIX 1: CHINESE CULTURE AND NEGOTIATING STYLES

Face

Paramount to an understanding of Chinese behavior in relationships is an understanding of face behavior. In China, face has two forms: *lien* and *mien-tzu*. *Lien* refers to one's moral character and is a person's most precious possession. Without it, one cannot function in society. It is earned by fulfilling one's duties and other obligations. *Mien-tzu* refers to a person's reputation or prestige and is based on personal accomplishments, political status, or bureaucratic power. It also refers to one's ability to deal smoothly with people face-to-face. Face enhancement can be attained by acts of generosity in terms of time, gifts, or praise of others.

Face is the cooperative manner in which people behave toward one another in order to avoid loss of self-respect or prestige by either party. While the concept of face is often a fiction in practice, it retains its importance in actual dealings. For example, given a situation in which two people are bargaining with each other, one must win and the other must lose. Each side expects that the other will consider face in the transaction. In reality, both sides know at the end who has won and who has lost, but the winner makes token concessions to save the loser's face. This is important in that it allows the loser to win in that he or she has been respected by the other, the winning party. Without the saving of face, the loser will be justly offended and avoid dealing with the winner in the future. This avoidance reaction carries with it obvious consequences and hinders any potential ongoing business relationship.

Another aspect of face is similar to the Western concept of being a good sport, or being a good winner. Modesty over one's own achievement and appreciation of the loser's skill and effort are central to saving face.

Face most often requires little effort but merely an attention to courtesy in relationships with others, yet will have a great positive effect upon the recipient. If lost, face will have a negative effect: which, if shown by the loser, results in still further loss of face. With the exception of a show of controlled anger by a person in authority, such as by a policeman, loss of self control, sulking, and displays of anger or frustration create further loss of face rather than drawing respect or conciliation.

When face has been lost, the loser will prefer to avoid the winner and ignore the face-losing incident as though it never occurred. In circumstances in which the two parties must continue a relationship, the loser will return to formal and polite etiquette, pretending that the incident had not occurred. The other party should accommodate the loser's preference and not refer again to the incident. Face involves a high degree of self-control, social consciousness, and concern for others.

Smiling and Laughter

Laughter and smiling in Chinese culture represent the universal reaction to pleasure and humor. In addition, they are also a common response to negative occurrences, such as death and other misfortunes. When embarrassed or in the wrong, the Chinese frequently respond with laughter or smiling which will persist if another person continues to speak of an embarrassing topic or does not ignore the wrong. Westerners are often confused and shocked by this behavior, which is alien to them. It is important to remember that smiling and laughter in these situations are not exhibitions of glee but are rather a part of the concept of face when used in response to a negative or unpleasant situation.

Guanxi (The Value of an Ongoing Relationship)

Guanxi is the word that describes the intricate, pervasive network of personal relations which every Chinese cultivates with energy, subtlety, and imagination. *Guanxi* is the currency of getting things done and getting ahead in Chinese society. *Guanxi* is a relationship between two people containing implicit mutual obligation, assurances, and intimacy and is the perceived value of an ongoing relationship and its future possibilities that typically govern Chinese attitudes toward long-term business. If a relationship of trust and mutual benefit is developed, an excellent foundation will be built to future business with the Chinese. *Guanxi* ties are also helpful in dealing with the Chinese bureaucracy as personal interpretations are used in lieu of legal interpretations.

Due to cultural differences and language barriers, the visitors to China are not in a position to cultivate *guanxi* with the depth possible between two Chinese. Regardless, *guanxi* is an important aspect of interrelations in China and deserves attention so that good friendly relations may be developed. These connections are essential to get things accomplished.

Formal and Informal Relations

At present it is likely that the majority of social contacts foreigners have with the Chinese are on a more formal than informal level. Informality in China relates not to social pretension or artifice, but to the concept of face. Great attention is paid to observance of formal or social behavior and corresponding norms. The social level is the level of form and proper etiquette where face is far more important than fact. It is considered both gauche and rude to allow one's personal feelings and opinions to surface here to the detriment of the social ambience. It is much more important to compliment a person or to avoid an embarrassing or sensitive subject than it is to express an honest opinion if honesty is at the expense of another's feelings. Directness, honesty, and individualism that run counter to social conventions and basic considerations of politeness have no place on the social level; emotions and private relationships tend to be kept private in Chinese society.

Chinese Etiquette for Social Functions

Ceremonies and rules of ceremony have traditionally held a place of great importance in Chinese culture. Confucianism perpetuated and strengthened these traditions by providing the public with an identity, mask, or persona with which a person is best equipped to deal with the world with a minimum of friction. Confucianism consists of broad rules of conduct evolved to aid and guide interpersonal relations. Confucius assembled all the details of etiquette practiced at the courts of the feudal lords during the period c. 551–479 B.C. These rules of etiquette are called the *li* and have long since become a complete way of life for the Chinese.

The *li* may appear overly formalistic to Westerners at first glance. Upon closer inspection it is apparent that the rules of etiquette play a very important role in regulating interpersonal relations. Some basic rules of behavior are as follows:

- A host should always escort a guest out to his car or other mode of transportation and watch until the guest is out of sight.
- Physical expression is minimal by Western standards. A handshake is polite, but backslapping and other enthusiastic grasping is a source of embarrassment.
- At cultural functions and other performances, audience approval of performers is often subdued by American standards. Although the accepted manner of expressing approval varies between functions and age groups, applause is often polite, rather than roaring and bravo-like cheers.
- A person should keep control over his or her temper at all times.
- One should avoid blunt, direct, or abrupt discussion, particularly when the subject is awkward; delicate hints are often used to broach such a topic.
- It is a sign of respect to allow another to take the seat of honor (left of host), or to be asked to proceed through a door first.
- The serving of tea often signals the end of an interview or meeting. However, it is also served during extended meetings to quench the thirst of the negotiators.

Case 4

Rus Wane Equipment: Joint Venture in Russia (A)

Stanislav Shekshnia
Sheila M. Puffer

"John, yesterday Lev presented me with a candidate for the human resource manager's position. Tomorrow he is going to ask the board to appoint Sasha Neresyan. What do you think?" Ronald Chapman, Wane Machines, Inc.'s country manager for Russia, was querying John Swift, deputy general manager of Rus Wane Equipment, as they discussed Wane's Russian joint venture on the eve of its third anniversary in November 1993.

The question came as quite a surprise to John, who had virtually given up hope that the human resource manager position would be filled and who would never have considered 30-year-old Sasha as a candidate for the job. Not that Sasha lacked desirable qualities as an employee. He had joined Rus Wane in June 1992 as a customs clearance officer and had subsequently earned a very good reputation in the company by skillfully negotiating with bureaucratic and often corrupt Russian government officials who could turn importing of crucial goods and components into a nightmare for the joint venture. Before joining Rus Wane, Sasha had retired from the Army with the rank of captain, having worked in the Middle East using his background as a military translator. His excellent communications skills and fluency in English had helped him build good relations with many local and all expatriate Rus Wane employees.

But being a good customs clearance officer, John thought, hardly makes one a qualified human resource professional. As Ron paused, John wondered aloud: "Will Sasha be respected by senior Rus Wane managers, even though he is at least 20 years younger than they are? And what does he know about HR practices?" John did not have the answers to these questions, but he knew that Sasha was a smart and hard-working young man. What really bothered John was the fact that Sasha

"Rus Wane Equipment: Joint Venture in Russia" by Stanislav Shekshnia and Sheila Puffer from *The Case Research Journal*, 1995. Reprinted by permission of the North American Case Research Association. The authors gratefully acknowledge the valuable suggestions of editor John Seeger, three anonymous reviewers, and Northeastern colleague Daniel J. McCarthy. This case was written solely for the purpose of stimulating student discussion. All events and individuals are real, but names and industry have been disguised.

had been brought to Rus Wane by the general manager, Lev Novikov, who had been a long-time patient and friend of Dr. Neresyan, Sasha's father. This hiring proposal was the latest episode contributing to the strained relations between the Russian general manager of the joint venture and his American deputy general manager.

THE U.S. PARTNER, WANE MACHINES, INC.

During its 150 years of operation, Wane Machines, Inc. had grown from a one-person, one-invention workshop in New York City into a multibillion-dollar multinational corporation with manufacturing, sales, and service operations in dozens of countries. Wane had always remained in one industry, engaging in the manufacture, installation, and maintenance of large-scale heating and cooling equipment for office and apartment buildings. In the late 1890s, Wane began its international expansion by setting up operations in Europe. From the outset, its strategy had been to be recognized as a local company in every market it entered and to establish long-term relationships with customers by providing a complete package of services, including product maintenance, repair, and upgrading. Following this strategy consistently for nearly a hundred years, Wane Machines became a global market leader with a network of more than 50 companies operating in 160 countries.

Wane Machines had four regional divisions: domestic (the United States and Canada), Europe, Latin America, and Asia. In the 1980s domestic operations lost its sales leadership to the European division, as the market for new construction in the United States dropped precipitously during the severe economic recession. After a decade of spectacular growth, the European market also declined sharply in the early 1990s as the United Kingdom, and later France and Germany, entered an economic recession. To attempt future growth, Wane management began to explore the markets that had begun to open in Eastern Europe and the Soviet Union. In 1989 Ronald Chapman was appointed Wane's country manager for the Soviet Union. Ron, who had a Harvard MBA and 20 years' experience with Wane, was charged with studying the Soviet market and setting up Wane's operations in Moscow and St. Petersburg. Before this assignment, he had managed Wane's joint venture in Taiwan after working in Japan and Hong Kong for 10 years. In his new function, Chapman reported to the area vice president for Central and Eastern Europe, who was located in Wane's European division in Brussels.

ENTERING THE USSR MARKET

The Soviet market was not total terra incognita for Wane, as the company had been exporting its products to the USSR through its Austrian company since the early 1970s. During that period Wane sold its high-quality heating and cooling equipment for installation in several Soviet government buildings as well as an American-built hotel. However, it could not penetrate the huge domestic market for several reasons. The ruble could not be converted to hard currency to pay for imported goods, few Soviet enterprises had access to hard currency, and until 1988 all purchases of imports were controlled by government foreign trade organizations with whom enterprises were required to negotiate for imported equipment and other supplies.

By the late 1980s the market potential in the USSR for Wane's products was the largest in the world, as 85% of the country's 290 million people lived in apartment complexes, most of which required upgrading of their large-scale heating and cooling systems. In addition, more housing was planned under President Gorbachev's "Housing 2000" program, announced in 1986 with the goal of providing every Soviet family with a separate apartment by the year 2000. This would be a massive undertaking, as some 25% of families lived in communal apartments in which they shared kitchen and bathroom facilities with other families. Because of these conditions, demand for large-scale heating and cooling systems was expected to double through the remainder of the century.

According to the Ministry of Building Equipment Manufacturing, in the late 1980s annual demand for large heating and cooling equipment was approximately 100,000 units, while Soviet enterprises manufactured a total of 60,000 units. Production planning, resource allocation, and customer selection were all controlled centrally by government bodies such as Gosplan, the state planning ministry, and Gossnab, the government supply organization. The domestic heating and cooling industry was fragmented: Manufacturing plants were under the Ministry of Building Equipment Manufacturing, installation units were attached to the State Construction Committee, and maintenance services were operated by local civic authorities. The major cities of Moscow, St. Petersburg, and Kiev had their own manufacturing facilities and installation units.

For more than 20 years, Soviet factories had been manufacturing the same, unimproved heating and cooling products for the domestic market, having little incentive or ability to upgrade them under the system of central planning. Artificially low prices were established by state authorities with little regard to actual costs or customer demand. For their part, customers, who were construction ministries and building management organizations attached to local governments, paid for goods not with their own money, but with funds allocated by the government. They were usually glad to receive the scarce equipment, even though it was of poor quality and low reliability.

FORMATION OF THE JOINT VENTURE

In 1989 the Soviet Ministry of Foreign Trade put Wane in touch with NLZ, a medium-sized factory located just outside Moscow that manufactured heating and cooling equipment similar to Wane's, but of lower quality. In February 1990, after what appeared to Wane's management as lengthy and sometimes frustrating negotiations, a joint venture called Rus Wane Equipment was formed, with the primary purpose of establishing a new plant to manufacture products virtually identical to Wane's European models. Registered as a Soviet–Belgian joint venture, the new company had initial capital funds of US$11.5 million. Wane contributed $8 million in hard currency and equipment for the new factory to be built with the Soviet partner. The latter contributed use of the facilities in the existing plant to manufacture components, as well as the site for the new factory. Whether NLZ or the government owned the land was unclear, however, because of ambiguous legislation on property. Wane Machines had a 57% share of the joint venture, and NLZ, 43%. At about the same time, Wane signed a second joint venture with a St. Petersburg partner to install and service Rus Wane's products in western Russia.

Wane's strategy for Russia consisted of three major elements. First, they did not expect to make money for the first three years. Second, they planned to develop export potential for Eastern Europe. Third, Wane hoped that the Russian ruble would become a convertible currency in the near future.

The highest governing body of the Rus Wane joint venture was the board of directors. The chairman of the board was Wane Europe's area vice president for Central and Eastern Europe. The other board members were the legal counsel of Wane Europe; Wane's country manager for the Soviet Union, Ron Chapman; Rus Wane Equipment's general manager, Lev Novikov; and an official from the Soviet ministry of building equipment manufacturing. The board of directors met quarterly to review developments since the last quarter's meeting, to review business plans and the progress made toward achieving them, to approve capital expenditures, and to appoint direct reports. Organization charts depicting the Rus Wane Equipment joint venture and its relationship with Wane Machines are provided in Figures C4-1 and C4-2.

At the time of Wane's initial negotiations, joint ventures were the primary form of market entry into the Soviet Union. The Joint Venture Law of 1987 had opened the door for foreign investment in the USSR and accorded preferential taxation status and other privileges to foreign joint ventures. Initially, Soviet law restricted foreign ownership of joint ventures to a maximum of 49%, and the head of the operation was required to be a Soviet citizen. In 1988, these provisos were withdrawn by the Russian government, permitting greater foreign ownership and control.

Although Soviet law no longer required a Soviet citizen to hold the most senior position, Wane's policy throughout the world was to put local managers in charge, because they were believed to be the most knowledgeable and capable individuals to run local operations. Therefore, Lev Novikov, a 58-year-old mechanical engineer by training, was appointed general manager of Rus Wane Equipment. He also remained general manager of the Soviet partner, NLZ, a position he had held for 15 of

Figure C4-1 Rus Wane Equipment's Organization Chart

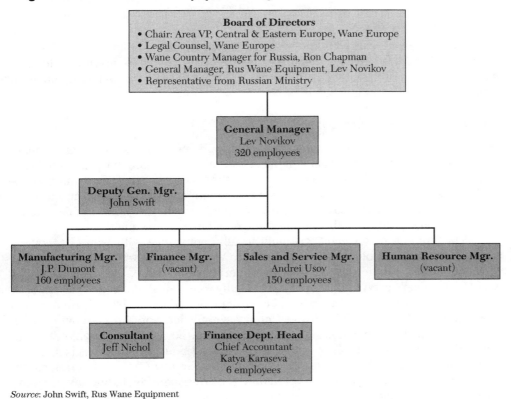

Source: John Swift, Rus Wane Equipment

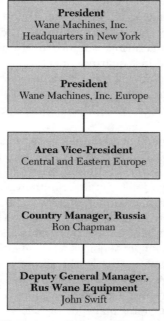

Figure C4-2 Wane
Machines, Inc.'s Organization
Chart (Abridged)

Source: John Swift, Rus Wane Equipment

the 25 years he had worked in the industry. His experience, enthusiasm, and strong leadership led Wane's management to view him as the driving force who could manage construction of the new manufacturing facility and see it through to completion under very difficult circumstances.

CONSTRUCTION OF THE PLANT

In October 1990, shortly after the joint venture agreement was signed, Wane's management took the bold step of beginning construction of a plant in the Moscow area to produce heating and cooling equipment for the Russian market. The multimillion-dollar investment was one of the first major commitments by a Western firm to manufacture products in Russia, since most companies were unwilling to take such a risk in Russia's highly unstable political and economic environment.

The state-of-the-art plant was built in full compliance with Wane's specifications, making it technologically comparable to Wane's European facilities. The plant was completed in June 1992, an extremely short period of time, especially in the Soviet Union, where such building projects usually took years, and sometimes as long as a decade. Furthermore, the external environment at the time of construction was marked by the breakup of the Soviet Union; severely deteriorating economic conditions in Russia, including monthly inflation exceeding 20%; disintegration of the centralized resource allocation system; and confusing and vacillating legislation on corporate taxation, business development, and the status of foreign operations. Inconsistent government policy on foreign direct investment, including taxation and ownership rights, along with erratic domestic policy concerning government subsidies, business law, and ownership of property, contributed to the external problems confronting international firms in Russia.

Rus Wane Equipment's plant was designed to manufacture Wane's European models of heating and cooling equipment, with minor modifications for the Russian market. Product characteristics, such as length of service and number of callbacks per unit, showed that the quality of Wane's products was more than four times that of Russian competitors', requiring half the energy to operate. Wane maintained a pricing policy not to exceed twice the price of the grossly inferior Russian models. The first product was scheduled to be shipped from the new factory in June 1993, and full capacity of 5,000 units annually was projected for 1995.

In August 1993, only six weeks behind schedule, Rus Wane Equipment celebrated its first shipment with toasts of Moet champagne and Stolichnaya vodka. By September the factory was fully operational, with an available production capacity of 85 units per month. Most of the joint venture's office employees and factory workers came from NLZ, the Russian partner. A select group, they were full of enthusiasm for working on the joint venture and looked forward to excellent working conditions in the new plant as well as democratic and participative Western management methods.

SALES AND SERVICE OPERATIONS

While the plant was under construction, Rus Wane also set up an organization to sell, install, and maintain Wane's imported and locally produced equipment. Field personnel, who numbered 150, were recruited from various Moscow installation and service agencies. This part of the business was quite successful, offering Western-style maintenance service to numerous foreign organizations and some Russian companies that could afford it.

EARLY OBSTACLES

Construction of a state-of-the-art manufacturing facility and establishment of a sales and service network were achievements that few joint ventures had accomplished in Russia up to that time. However, reaching these goals by no means guaranteed Rus Wane's success. Among the obstacles confronting the firm once it became operational were an unexpected downturn in demand, difficulty in securing reliable suppliers, and an unpredictable legal and economic environment.

Despite the Soviet Union's vast market potential, much of Rus Wane's production capacity sat idle in the initial months because of weak customer demand. As a result, only 17 units were manufactured in September, 12 were completed in October, and 15 were planned for November. As Russia and the other countries of the former Soviet Union entered a severe economic crisis, new construction declined dramatically and demand for heating and cooling systems plummeted. No one had exact data, but Rus Wane's management estimated annual domestic sales in Russia to be 6,000 units, while the total combined capacity of domestic manufacturers was 30,000 to 40,000 units.

Under this tremendous supply pressure, aggravated by the extremely difficult financial position of most of their customers, price became a major factor in the purchase decision. Rus Wane's product, sold even at zero profit margin, was still nearly twice as expensive as domestic equipment because of small production runs and costs associated with the sophisticated design. Prospective Russian customers, primarily state or municipally owned construction and engineering enterprises, were caught in a squeeze. They suffered a cash shortage resulting from sharply reduced government subsidies of their operations, and hyperinflation had eroded their purchasing power. A limited number of price-tolerant and quality-sensitive customers, such as commercial banks, foreign hotels, and joint ventures, appreciated the quality of Rus Wane's products. Even those, however, often preferred to buy competitors' systems manufactured in Western Europe, considering the foreign origin to be more prestigious. High inflation of the ruble, along with its devaluation against foreign currencies, eliminated virtually all cost advantages of manufacturing in Russia and did not allow Rus Wane to sell profitably to customers outside the country as it had planned.

Developing relationships with reliable domestic suppliers was an objective that proved challenging to implement. The company carefully sought out enterprises that had produced for the military sector because they had been held to higher quality standards and stricter delivery schedules than other enterprises under the former central planning system. Such enterprises also often had idle capacity and faced layoffs resulting from drastic cuts in government orders, and hence were eager to find customers. However, even these suppliers were not easily able to meet Rus Wane's standards, and they required a considerable amount of Rus Wane's time and energy for training and monitoring.

Like other companies operating in the Russian market, Rus Wane had to struggle with a constantly changing legal framework and unpredictable government policy. For example, in 1992 the Russian government froze the company's bank account for six months. The State bank had run out of cash and arbitrarily withheld payments owed to Russian and foreign enterprises. In another unfortunate financial incident, Rus Wane was forced to pay $1.5 million in taxes on their new factory building when the Russian government introduced a value-added tax, even though the building had been completed well before the introduction of the tax.

In spite of such problems, the company was growing and its management systems were being developed. With significant cash flows from its sales and service field operations compensating for the losses in manufacturing, Rus Wane was a profitable organization overall, with 320 employees and monthly revenues of $600,000.

STAFFING KEY MANAGERIAL POSITIONS

According to the joint venture agreement, Wane Machines was responsible for sending three experienced executives to serve as Rus Wane's deputy general manager, manufacturing manager, and financial manager for the first two to three years. Russian nationals would take over the positions at the end of this initial period. The major objectives of this policy were to provide "assistance in technology and management skills transfer, management systems and processes development, and local personnel coaching." Two other senior management positions, sales and service manager and human resources manager, were to be filled by local nationals from the beginning because they involved regular contact with Russian customers or workers at various levels, thus requiring a thorough knowledge of local culture and employment practices.

An experienced local manager had been found to fill the sales and service manager's position, but the remaining key managerial positions had been harder to fill. Wane fell behind schedule in sending its expatriates to Russia, and Lev Novikov, the general manager, delayed hiring a local for the human resources position, preferring to administer that function himself.

John Swift, a 35-year-old American, was appointed as Rus Wane's deputy general manager in late 1991. For nearly 10 months, while seeking suitable accommodations for his family, he commuted frequently from European headquarters in Brussels; he finally settled in Moscow in September 1992. John had joined Wane in 1989 after graduating from business school. He then completed the corporate management development program and worked for two years in Western Europe as a field operations manager. Before 1991 John had never been to Russia nor, he said, had he ever had any intention of going there. He was, however, ambitious, and readily accepted the job offer, seeing it as a valuable career move. As deputy general manager, he reported to Lev Novikov, the joint venture's general manager, and was responsible for supervising technology transfer, sales, pricing, and personnel. He also served as the liaison between the joint venture and Wane's European headquarters, and reported to Ron Chapman, Wane's country manager for Russia.

Jean-Pierre Dumont, Rus Wane's manufacturing manager, had 15 years of engineering experience with Wane Machines in his native France, but the Russian appointment was his first management position. Like John Swift he had little prior knowledge of Russia, yet he was equally eager to take the job. He explained: "It's very rare these days that an engineer gets a chance to work in a factory created from scratch. I am lucky to get this chance and I'm not going to miss it."

Convincing an experienced financial manager to relocate to Russia was not an easy task. After an intensive and lengthy search, Jeff Nichol, a 27-year-old Englishman who had been working at Wane for two years as a corporate auditor, was selected in October 1991. Because of Jeff's limited experience, Ron Chapman sent him for training in Brussels for six months before going to Russia. In the meantime, Lev appointed Katya Karaseva, NLZ's chief accountant, to head Rus Wane's finance department. Katya had worked in the industry for 24 years, 17 of them with Lev.

Wane's Russia country manager, Ron Chapman, worked out of Wane's European headquarters in Brussels but flew to Russia at least once a month to visit Wane's St. Petersburg joint venture as well as Rus Wane Equipment in Moscow, where he would review the joint venture's situation with the general manager, Lev Novikov, and his deputy, John Swift.

TENSIONS IN THE FINANCE DEPARTMENT

When Jeff Nichol arrived at Rus Wane in the spring of 1992, Lev suggested that he be a consultant for a while rather than immediately assuming the duties of financial manager, citing his young age, his need to adjust to the local culture, and his lack of Russian language abilities. Ron accepted the arrangement because he wanted Jeff to spend some of his time at the St. Petersburg joint venture. For a while, Jeff traveled between Moscow and St. Petersburg, spending most of his time learning the Russian language, becoming acquainted with Russian accounting systems, and developing financial procedures for both joint ventures.

Early in 1993, when a financial manager had been recruited for the St. Petersburg operation, Jeff decided it was the right time for him to become financial manager at Rus Wane. John Swift fully supported him. By that time Rus Wane had eight employees in the finance department: Jeff, Katya, and six accountants, most of whom came from NLZ. Unfortunately, this small group was unable to work smoothly together. As John explained to Ron: "We've got total confusion in the finance department: people don't know who's the boss, Katya does what she wants, and Jeff is running out of patience. His contract expires in March and I don't think he's looking forward to staying any longer. Ron, we can't allow this situation to continue—the company needs a financial manager."

To compound the problem, the accountants expressed their disappointment to John that Western management practices that they had hoped would give them greater participation in decision making had not been implemented. They also complained about not being rewarded on merit, and the fact that the Westerners, whom they considered to be doing comparable work, were receiving substantially higher compensation.

From the beginning, communication between Jeff and Katya had not been easy. The language barrier—he did not speak Russian and she did not speak English—was not the only problem. Several times Jeff had organized training sessions for Rus Wane's finance personnel, yet each time Katya had found excuses not to participate. When, after a year at the joint venture, Jeff had become conversational in Russian, communication between him and Katya failed to improve in any meaningful way. Even though they worked virtually side by side, with Katya in a private office and Jeff in an adjacent common area, they communicated only through interoffice mail.

Jeff made a number of appeals to Lev to try to get his point across. He wrote several memos, with copies to the vice president of finance for Wane Europe, in which he described Katya's mistakes, but the general manager never replied and continued to show his full support for Katya. In addition, the finance staff had been expanding, yet Jeff had never been involved in the selection process. When he raised the issue with Lev, the latter responded that hiring was his problem, not Jeff's.

DISCORD OVER THE GENERAL MANAGER

In February 1993, John Swift sent a memo to Lev suggesting that he propose Jeff's appointment as acting financial manager to Rus Wane's board of directors for approval, as required by company policy. Lev did not respond. A month later John raised the issue again and received the categorical reply: "He cannot be a financial manager." Without challenging that conclusion, John forwarded his suggestion to Ron Chapman who had shown full understanding of John's viewpoint. The subject of the financial manager's appointment was put on the agenda for the next board meeting. However, the day before the meeting, the item was withdrawn from the agenda. Ron later explained to John that Lev had convinced him not to be in a hurry to appoint Jeff to the position.

Meanwhile, tensions in the finance department continued to escalate. The joint venture experienced some delays in consolidating its first business plan, as well as difficulties in cash management and inventory control. On several occasions Jeff openly expressed his low opinion of his Russian colleagues' professional qualifications. These problems deeply concerned the deputy general manager, but the country manager did not take the matter seriously. Nor did Ron seem to be concerned about other signs of poor morale. For example, the first Russian hired as a salesperson, who had been trained in the United States and Western Europe and was highly respected in the company, left to work for a Russian trading venture. In addition, turnover in the factory was 5% a month.

In a discussion the two had about the finance department, Ron assessed the situation quite differently from John: "I think you're dramatizing the situation, John. Rus Wane has an excellent cost accounting system, our corporate financial software has been successfully introduced, and the skills of the finance people have improved tremendously."

"Yes, but Jeff has done it all himself," John replied.

"That's because he doesn't know how to delegate. He needs to work at improving his management style. I am beginning to understand why Lev can't see him as a financial manager. Jeff doesn't know how to manage people and he is becoming paranoid about Katya. I'm afraid that if on Saturday night his girlfriend doesn't show up for a date, he'll find a way to blame it on Katya. By the way, John, Lev is looking for a financial manager from the outside. It could be a good solution."

John was unpleasantly surprised to hear about the proposal. Lev had mentioned nothing about it to him. "You know, Ron, it's always very difficult to communicate with Lev. First, he doesn't like to share any information with me and he prefers to make all the decisions himself. And second, he is simply never here. The last time I saw him was ten days ago."

Although Lev had officially become a full-time employee of Rus Wane Equipment in January 1993, he had never resigned from his position as general manager of NLZ, which was still manufacturing its old product next door to the joint venture's new plant. Some people at Rus Wane were concerned about the situation; their perception was that their general manager was also their competitor's general manager. There had been rumors about the old plant being in a difficult financial situation, but no one had reliable information. Yet it was well known that NLZ had been going through the process of privatization, as mandated by the government, and Lev had been leading it. A major task would be to determine what percentage of shares would be owned by various managers and other employees.

John thought that there was a clear conflict of interest between Lev's role at the old factory and his position in the joint venture. He tried to raise the issue with Ron during one of his monthly visits: "Lev is preoccupied with his own interests, not Rus Wane's. When you are not here, he spends all his time at the old factory trying to turn it into his private property."

Ron angrily interrupted: "Let's drop the subject. This is not your responsibility, John."

HIRING A HUMAN RESOURCE MANAGER

John suppressed his instinctive response, feeling his anger growing. On several previous occasions he had tried to raise the subject of Lev Novikov's management style with Ron, but the latter never wanted to discuss it. Now, totally frustrated with personnel management issues at the joint venture, John shifted to another sore point: "As you know, Ron, we still don't have a human resource manager here at Rus Wane. I believe Lev hasn't filled the position on purpose. He wants to continue to do things the old Soviet way—to run the company like a tsar."

Ron looked up sharply: "That's a pretty strong statement, John. You've got to have facts to prove it."

John was sure he had the facts. A human resource manager was supposed to have been hired three years ago—just as soon as the joint venture was official—in order to organize the selection process for other positions. However, Lev had decided to manage this function himself. As a result, all of the joint venture's senior managers other than the expatriates, and most of the lower-level managers, had come from NLZ. John considered this move a dangerous mistake. What was worse, he believed, was that quite a few senior managers' relatives had also been hired. The most notable, Lev's son, had already built an astonishing career within 12 months, starting as an assistant, becoming purchasing manager, and then going to Western Europe for 18 months' practical training. John had strongly opposed the decision to send Novikov junior abroad, arguing that there had been better candidates and that Rus Wane's reputation among its employees for fairness and democracy would suffer. Ron had ignored these concerns, and, just as he had anticipated, John began to detect silent but strong disapproval and disappointment from employees.

Unhappy with Lev's hiring practices, John championed the introduction of selection and hiring procedures that had been developed for Russian operations by Wane's European headquarters (Exhibit C4-1). The procedures for implementing Wane's standard corporate practices—preparing job requisitions, advertising vacant positions, evaluating candidates' résumés, and having human resource and line managers conduct interviews—had been approved by Ron Chapman and were supposed to be mandatory at Rus Wane. However, the Russian managers ignored the procedures. For instance, a week before John's meeting with Ron, an angry Jean-Pierre Dumont told John that a new machine operator had been hired for the factory without his knowledge. It took John some time to find out that the 18-year-old new employee was the son of a local customs officer who often cleared shipments for Rus Wane. The young man had no manufacturing skills and was eligible for the army draft the following spring.

When John described the incident to Ron, he got a rather philosophical reply: "Well, you've got to remember the specifics of the country you are operating in. Russia has an Asian culture and European faces should not mislead you. American standards do not always work here. If hiring people you have known for a long time, and therefore trust, is a local custom, you can't change it overnight. And you probably don't need to change it."

John didn't challenge his boss, but he saw no reason to change his mind about hiring practices. He strongly believed that hiring friends and relatives was equally bad whether one was in the United States, China, or Russia. Now Ron was telling him that Lev was going to appoint his doctor's son as human resource manager. John had always regarded a human resource manager as one of the primary business officers responsible for enforcing high ethical standards in the company. Would Sasha be able to fulfill such an important responsibility? How much credibility would he have? And how independent would he be from his boss and likely mentor? These were some of the questions for which John did not have a ready answer.

PROSPECTS FOR THE FUTURE

This latest hiring decision only added to John Swift's growing frustration over the management of the joint venture. He had been appointed to provide expertise in Western management systems and to coach local personnel. Yet his attempts had been foiled at virtually every turn. He didn't know who was more to blame—Lev, for sticking to his former Soviet practices, or Ron, for letting Lev get away with such seemingly counterproductive behavior.

All of these issues contributed to John's worries about the future of Rus Wane Equipment. With the prospect of privatization turning NLZ into more of a competitor than a partner, and the advantages of joint ventures declining as a result of changing government legislation, John wondered whether Rus Wane had the right organizational structure and management systems in place to be a viable player in Russia's rapidly changing business environment. And not the least of his worries was whether there would be a place for him at Rus Wane that would allow him to be taken seriously.

Exhibit C4-1

Wane Machines, Inc.'s Human Resources Policies for Rus Wane Equipment

Recruitment and Selection Process

The following recruitment and selection principles have been established in order to assist company management in hiring the best qualified employees. It is the responsibility of the Human Resources Department to manage and facilitate recruitment and selection in collaboration with line management, with the final decision on selecting and hiring candidates made by line management. It is also the responsibility of company management to ensure that these principles are followed and to maintain their effectiveness.

1. *Identification of job openings.* The number of positions to be staffed in the company is primarily determined by the workforce forecast established every year as part of the business plan. Input is then provided by line management throughout the year with necessary adjustments to the plan made in order for the HR Department to take action in recruitment and selection. Any vacancy or opening due to resignation, termination or other reasons will be filled according to line management's request. A final list of job openings is then established and updated as necessary. A job requisition form must be signed by line management and the General Manager before every recruiting action.

2. *Determination of job requirements.* In close collaboration with line management, each position to be staffed is documented as follows:

   - A list of professional and technical requirements as well as a list of personal traits required to do the job (strengths, personality, background experience, etc.).

   - A written job description outlining the basic responsibilities of the position, and the main tasks to fulfill position responsibilities and deliver the expected results.

   These two documents will be established jointly with the HR Department and approved by line management.

3. *Attracting applicants.* A list of possible human resources outsourcing options is presented below. One or several sources listed may be used with consideration given to availability, costs, and likelihood of success.

   - Spontaneous, unsolicited candidacies are examined and acknowledged. A curriculum vitae and letter of intention are necessary documentation.

   - Advertisements for jobs may be inserted in local or national newspapers: they advertise not only the content of the job through a short description, but also the required profile of the candidate. A description of the company is also recommended.

   - State employment agencies: Contracts to conduct employee searches can be used with recognized agencies. Company needs are specified in a job requirements position description.

   - Educational institutions: The company should develop and maintain regular and frequent contacts with local or national technical and nontechnical institutions considered as potential sources of job candidates. Background on the company should be presented to students. Job postings may be sent to these schools.

   - Private employee search firms: Restricted to managerial positions, private employee search firms may be used for candidate searches and screening interviews. The search must be cost effective, with conditions of the services rendered clearly stated in a contract.

   The use of one of these options should result in a list of candidates for consideration, as well as detailed information about the candidates recorded on forms.

4. *Prescreening.* The Human Resources Manager establishes a final list of candidates by eliminating applicants whose profile does not meet requirements. At this stage, the Human Resources Department informs candidates who are not selected for interviews that they are no longer under consideration.

5. *Screening interviews.* The Human Resources Manager contacts the eligible candidates for interviews to assess:

   ■ Their knowledge of the company (product, service and culture, as appropriate). Additional information may be given to answer candidates' questions.

   ■ Their background (education and experience) to determine whether it is consistent with their application. This step helps answer the question, "Can the individual perform the job?"

   ■ The motivation of the applicant to perform the job in the company and to develop within the company's culture. This step helps answer the question, "Will he/she do the job?"

6. *Level of approval for recruitment for senior positions.* The General Manager will be involved in any recruitment for a position reporting directly to him/her, and will make the final decision. The General Manager will also interview candidates for positions reporting to his/her direct reports. Approval by the General Manager will be necessary before filling such positions.

7. *Preselection.* The interviews will be reported in a written evaluation of the candidate by the HR manager using the appropriate forms. These forms are reviewed with the line manager involved in the recruitment process, and a list of candidates to be interviewed is then established jointly.

8. *Interview with line Management.* The preselected candidates are called for interviews with the line manager. The purpose of the interview is to determine again whether professional aptitude based on experience and skills (technical and nontechnical) will enable the applicant to perform the work. Also, the interviewer assesses the candidate's motivation to work for the company and to meet the company's overall requirements (personal fit with the culture, etc.). At the end of these interviews, evaluation forms are filled out by the interviewer.

9. *Evaluation of candidates and hiring decision.* A joint evaluation of the candidates by the line manager and the human resources manager is conducted using evaluation forms, and a ranking of the candidates is completed.

10. *Hiring decision.* The line manager makes the final decision to hire one of the candidates interviewed based on an assessment of their capabilities and potential for development in the company. At the stage, the HR manager informs the unsuccessful candidates by letter of the company's decision. The selected candidate is also informed by the HR manager.

11. *Offer to the candidate.* A formal offer is prepared by the HR manager in cooperation with the line manager. The offer (including the contract and conditions of employment, etc.) is extended to the selected candidate. At the same time, administrative documents are given to the future employee to begin the employment registration process.

12. *Integration in the company.* The human resources manager assists the line manager in facilitating the newcomer's integration into the company.

    A welcome guide is given to the new employee upon his/her arrival in addition to all necessary documents, identification badges, punch cards, safety brochures, internal regulations, etc. Mandatory company training (e.g., safety) and any special training are coordinated by the HR manager in the new employee's first few days.

13. *New-employee feedback meeting.* Six weeks after the starting date of employment, the human resources manager invites the new employee for a feedback meeting to determine how well he/she is adapting to the work place. Any obstacles are addressed in accordance with company policies.

The HR manager provides feedback to the new employee's supervisor and follows up on any decisions made to ease the newcomer's integration into the company.

Rus Wane Equipment: Joint Venture in Russia (B)

EPILOGUE

John resisted Sasha's appointment as human resources manager, but to no avail. Sasha turned out to be very enthusiastic about his job, and was willing to learn and introduce new things. To John's surprise, Sasha was very independent in his actions and did not seem to be afraid to challenge Lev Novikov. He made sure that everyone in the company followed the hiring procedure developed by Wane, and worked quite well with John.

John was subsequently transferred to the United States, and was not replaced. Jeff Nichol was appointed by the board of directors as Rus Wane's financial manager. However, his relations with Lev and Katya did not improve, and he asked for a transfer four months after assuming the position. Wane Machines sent a new financial manager, a 59-year-old Indian national whom Lev Novikov had interviewed and approved of.

Rus Wane Equipment continued to struggle with low demand and poor collections, but no major top management changes were made. Ron Chapman remained country manager for Russia. The company converted from joint venture status to a joint stock company in 1994, since joint ventures no longer enjoyed special tax or other benefits from the Russian government. A joint stock company was similar to a conventional Western limited liability company.

NLZ was privatized into an employee-owned company, with the state owning no shares. Some employees later sold their stock to Lev for cash. How much stock Lev personally owned was unknown, but he was rumored to have more than 50% ownership of NLZ.

In early 1995, Lev left Rus Wane Equipment and returned to work exclusively for NLZ. No Rus Wane employees followed him. Ron Chapman moved to Moscow and became acting general manager of Rus Wane, while retaining his job as country manager for Russia. Wane Machines planned to merge Rus Wane Equipment with Wane's newly created service enterprise in Moscow.

Case 5

The Careless Collaborators

Sara L. Keck
Anne Marie Francesco

As my flight from Milan to Chicago took off, I sat wondering whether I was really as insensitive to the cultural differences of colleagues as I felt. Despite the best of plans and intentions to accommodate, facilitate, and negotiate, the week's meeting in Milan had been another disaster in terms of reestablishing rapport with other team members and accomplishing productive joint research. Doubting the value of my continued membership in the group both to myself and to the team, once again I had to decide whether continued work on the international research project was worth the resources dedicated to it. The long flight home in the business class seats might be a physically comfortable one, but one likely to be fraught with meditation over the right thing to do for the team and for myself. What should I do now? Drop out of the project or continue on? If I continued, I had to find a way to address my problems in the group.

Susan's Background

Susan was a professor of management at a large state university with a growing international reputation when the invitation was first extended to join a relatively small but prestigious research group. She had received her doctorate from Columbia University after spending several years as a management consultant.

Susan's background was very broad in international experience, teaching, and research. She had been married to an Iranian for many years, had lived with her husband's family in Iran, and had taught English as a second language in Iran. After completing her doctorate, she had visited universities and/or guest-lectured in several countries, including Germany, Great Britain, the Czech Republic, Italy, France, and Belgium.

Most recently, her university had chosen her to teach in a faculty development program at the University of Indonesia because the directors of the program recognized her expertise and experience abroad.

Thoughts About Business and Academia

Work on the academic project was not that different from work on business teams. Susan had extensive experience in working on teams as a consultant. She had been both a team member and leader for several projects during her time as a management consultant. Her familiarity with teams in both business and academia led her to draw multiple parallels between such teams. First, teams are often drawn from offices across geographic areas such as the project she worked on in Boise, Idaho. The members on that project came from Denver, San Francisco, Los Angeles, and Dallas. Coordination efforts were extremely important and difficult on that project, as well. Firms also form teams across national boundaries. Susan remembered a software development project on which she had worked as a consultant to design and program a system that served the needs of a multinational corporation with multiple national accounting systems.

Second, the interaction with the academic team could facilitate or damage team performance just as it could for business teams. Smoothly operating teams of any kind can lead to superior performance. Unaddressed conflicts, unclear or unacceptable roles, unbalanced power relationships, or weak members can become problems on any type of team. There was one unfortunate team problem when Susan worked on a client project: An unaddressed conflict between two team leaders who had opposing views about how best to solve a design problem led to endless bickering and a near failure to complete the project on time.

Third, both academic and business teams have a mission to accomplish and performance requirements against which to benchmark. Susan remembered well all the performance requirements from the consulting teams. On the whole, the research team's mission and execution did not seem that different from those of business teams'.

The Team's Background

The group, International Strategy Research Group (ISRG), had formed itself with the purpose of conducting scholarly research over national boundaries with members from multiple nations. The first project had been directed toward the managerial effects of the 1992 European Integration. Although the second project never quite got off the ground, the third project, the current one, was to be a very important one because it was funded by the European Union (EU) and because it addressed some controversial theoretical issues: the stability of transnational strategies in certain industries of importance to EU countries, for example.

The book from the first project had been well received by both scholars and managers throughout continental Europe and the United Kingdom. Despite variation in English language skills on the team (the book was written in English) and fighting among some members, the first book was of high quality and was completed on time. This first project included a group of eight professors from France, Germany, Italy, Britain, and Sweden. This original group considered themselves to be a very closely knit cohort of researchers who had personal as well as professional ties.

The second project was just getting started when Susan met Professor Kent Peters at an international conference on managing the global economy. Kent had spearheaded the final writing and completion of the first book on European Integration. Kent and Susan met at several subsequent conferences. During a trip to Britain in January 1992, they met again, and in the course of conversation, Susan mentioned that she would be traveling to the Czech Republic (then Czechoslovakia). Kent considered this a golden opportunity for the ISRG group to have interviews conducted for the second project on organizational change in Eastern and Central Europe.

Susan's Experience

I was absolutely delighted to have been asked to join the prestigious group with a controversial research agenda, and I considered the invitation evidence of the recognition of my scholarly research as well as my ability to interact well across cultures. I made preparations and conducted the Czech interviews. Unfortunately, that project never got off the ground because the European members were unable to obtain funding.

The ISRG group seemed to be signaling their continued respect for my work by asking me to join the third project, which did receive generous funding from the European Commission. While the grant would not cover expenses incurred outside the EU by Americans and funding would have to obtained elsewhere, I was still enthusiastic about participation because the study was interesting, and it was an opportunity to work in a very unusual multinational group of diverse scholars from multiple perspectives, including comparative management, strategy, and organizational behavior.

Indeed, it was a group that was diverse on multiple dimensions. There was, of course, diversity of national backgrounds. But beyond this was diversity of type of institution, individual age and academic experience, and academic discipline. I had noticed that there were only three other women in the group of 15 people, and none of these women, including myself, were of senior academic rank.

THE FIRST MEETING: LYON, FRANCE

The first meeting for the third project took place in June 1993 in Lyon, France. Because the French team had obtained the EU funding, the French members hosted the first meeting and set the team in motion. The third project was to be conducted by representatives of Sweden, France, Germany, Italy, Portugal, Spain, Britain, Belgium, and the United States. Canada was to be included if someone could be recruited to carry out the work. This broad representation of countries and universities was new for the team. This is the first time the ISRG group had been so large and unwieldy, but the project was broad in intention within the EU grant. The monetary value of the EU grant was very high, and consequently, the size of the group was justified both from the work load and from the approval of the EU.

Each member was sent a preliminary copy of the questionnaire and asked by the project coordinator to conduct at least one pilot interview in her or his respective country. Not everyone was as fast out of the blocks as Kent and Susan. Kent, representing the British team, and Susan, being the only American member, had conducted interviews in Britain and the United States before this meeting. No one else conducted any pilot interviews.

Susan's Experience in Lyon

I planned for this first meeting in Lyon with the level of enthusiasm normally reserved for sabbatical leaves. I took a course in French, conducted pilot interviews, and rearranged my other summer obligations to avoid conflict with other responsibilities. I even convinced a friend to take my dog for the summer so that I could combine the travel to the Lyon meeting with my travel to Indonesia to minimize costs my own university would have to pay.

I began to wonder whether I was communicating well with my colleagues from the very first day in Lyon. The meetings were to begin on Monday. Despite arriving in Lyon on Saturday so that I could completely adjust to the time change, I did not see a single one of my colleagues until late on Monday afternoon. Had I misunderstood? Well, perhaps. The Monday start date meant that each would travel to Lyon on that day. The meetings would actually begin on Tuesday morning. Monday evening was spent in groups of colleagues who went out to dinner in casual restaurants in the historic part of Lyon. On the whole, the first day was unproductive but jolly good fun!

I had a strong theoretical as well as statistical training in my doctoral program at Columbia University, so each step of the research process was of interest to me as well as something to which

I could contribute. Though I was disappointed that I was not part of the original theory building and felt a little like a "free loader," I was not overly concerned because I knew I could contribute to the empirical steps of the project. In addition, the team had expressed an interest in publishing the results in American journals, something of which the other members had done very little. I felt I could carry my weight as a team member by also contributing what I knew about the publication values and process of American journals.

But, I was to be surprised once again that week. Had I misunderstood once again? Had I been insensitive? Had I communicated inadequately? The team seemed not to accept descriptions of the review process, forecasts of needs for positioning of articles to maximize likelihood of publication, and so on. My suggestions about statistical rigor, methods for sample selection, and choice of sample size were all rejected as irrelevant or even wrong.

The week ended in disappointment. I had not carried my weight in the prestigious group and apparently had not used my academic knowledge and personal style to be accepted into the group. If the work was to be aimed at American publications but without American conventions, how successful would this project be? Kent assured me that the project would still be very valuable with or without statistical rigor and urged me to stay on the team despite the initial disappointment.

The evening activities in Lyon continued to be friendly, but the meetings during the day were a bit strained. The groups tended to break into national groupings. The Swedish dined together, the French went to their homes each evening, and the British and I formed a clique. The Italians and Germans preferred to go their own way.

I left Lyon, headed to Indonesia, with a sense of dread. If I could not adapt to my colleagues who shared a common historical and cultural background, how could I possibly survive a summer in Jakarta? The cross-cultural techniques I had learned did not seem to be helping, and the little French I knew helped only with taxi drivers and waiters.

Susan's New Position

In the months that followed, Susan moved to a new position at another university that equally valued international research and the development of its international reputation. Because the research and contacts seemed to be valued at the university, she decided to forge on with less than perfect enthusiasm.

Perhaps it was just as well that the project was not the first priority for her. The French team had continued on without her, failing to mail out important updates in the questionnaire, notification that industries had been chosen, and an announcement that interviews were to proceed in the first industry. When Susan learned from Kent that the other project members were receiving instructions, she became very uncomfortable with her role on the team. The planning had proceeded without her, although she had performed the detailed analyses assigned for each member at the end of the Lyon meeting and had sent the results to the French coordinator. Susan decided to call Kent in Great Britain to seek his opinion and advice. Susan was convinced that she had done something wrong. Kent's response was that everything was fine and that Susan should prepare for their next meeting.

THE SECOND MEETING: ESTORIL, PORTUGAL

Plans were in place to attend the July 1994 meeting in Estoril, outside Lisbon, Portugal. Again, no one appeared until late afternoon on Monday. Professor Pierre Simone, the senior professor of the French contingency, adjourned Monday's meeting. He preferred to have a swim. "Tomorrow, then, at 8:30 A.M." were his dismissive words. A night of revery was to begin the proceedings once again.

This rough beginning was fortuitous of events to come. A whole series of unfortunate interactions occurred as the week progressed.

Susan's Experience

At least at this meeting, if the meetings were dismal, there would be the beach!

Tuesday morning, I left the meeting for a few minutes and returned to witness a pubic dressing down of a senior German professor by the junior French professor who was the project administrator. "Are you not capable of completing your interviews? Do you need help? We need for you to get moving," Antoine said to Professor Ditmar Schwartz as I entered the room. Academic rank notwithstanding, the senior German professor had been publicly reprimanded.

The second incident also occurred on Tuesday, when Kent asked who would be responsible for editing the book. "The book is to be written in English, so it makes sense that a native speaker of English should edit it. We have some very capable scholars in our group, but their written English skills vary widely. The editor cannot be just anyone," Kent emphasized. "What are you suggesting, Kent?" Pierre Simone countered. "Are you suggesting that we cannot speak English well? Why do you always think the English speakers are the best in the group? Look around this group and you will see that is not the case!"

"Pierre, you misunderstand my intention," Kent responded defensively. "I am merely suggesting that we avoid the disaster we faced last time when the Italians' chapter had to be rewritten at the last minute because the English was incomprehensible!"

"No, Kent, you intend to take all the royalties for yourself again as you did last time for doing nothing but merely editing the book. No, you will not selfishly take all profits this time!"

In uncharacteristic directness, Kent threatened, "Then you go ahead and try to sell this book, something you will be unsuccessful in. But, do not come to me at the last minute for help for you surely will not get it from me."

Stunned, the room sat silently. When I finally got my breath back, I mumbled under my breath, "I thought only Americans argued in this way publicly."

Tuesday evening was spent, as usual, in small groups looking for the quintessential memorable meal and entertainment. This time though, palpable resentment hung in the air, at least between the French and the British/American group. The French were not asked to join us nor did they extend an invitation. The new Spanish members went out with the French. The German professor had his meal in the hotel, claiming he wanted to watch the football match on television.

Shockingly, Wednesday turned out to be worse than Tuesday. I unwittingly became the lightening rod by suggesting the team make plans for presentations of the theoretical ideas and preliminary results. I already knew where Pierre stood on the issue because I had corresponded with him via fax regarding a deadline the previous March for a very prestigious conference. In a salty response which began with "Mrs. Hepburn, I will decide where and when this material will be presented, not you," Pierre made his position perfectly clear. I thought it rather insulting that Pierre had not used my professional title of "professor" or "doctor" in the correspondence and wondered whether it reflected a gender bias toward me as a woman. At a minimum, it seemed a friendly first name might have been appropriate.

Despite Pierre's response, it seemed that the decision should not be a unilateral one but a joint, team-level one. So, I thought it was appropriate to bring it up again before the whole group. Kent actually brought it up, and the French members were immediately against it. The Swedish, British, and Italian members favored it. The Spanish and Portuguese were rather silent on the matter. The conversation around this topic was as unpleasant as the previous day's. Personal insults were hurled.

Pierre suggested in sum that the only people who were in a hurry were the young, inexperienced members who could not be trusted to conduct an acceptable presentation. So, he proposed a compromise under the following restrictions: Nontenured professors could present as long as (1) they restricted their contents to industry facts and (2) they were accompanied by a senior professor from the group. Needless to say, feathers were ruffled on all sides. Having presented multiple times at the most visible of national meetings in the field, I did not feel I needed to be chaperoned by senior faculty. The other nontenured professors shared my feelings of indignity.

"I was not treated like this when I was a student," I fumed indignantly to Kent. "I certainly do not have to stand for this now. This project is not worth this insult! Let them get someone else to do the American interviews, if they can. I challenge them to find a qualified faculty member in the

United States who will put up with this nonsense. Am I this incompetent? Perhaps this is pure male chauvinism. No matter what the reason, I will not be back for another ISRG meeting," I vowed as we assessed our positions in the group. Apparently, I had spoken for the entire group of nontenured faculty on the project. Interestingly, this nontenured group was composed of all women.

Feelings of failure again dominated my thoughts as I packed to head for home. "This is a waste of scarce research time and money," I thought as I assessed the lack of achievements during the week. "I have several other projects I neglected in favor of ISRG. I will just get back to those. I will call Kent on Monday and tell him that I am withdrawing from the team."

Upon hearing of my decision, Kent immediately apologized on behalf of the whole team and urged continued participation in the project. "This will be very good for your career when it is complete," he said. "Please reconsider and don't make any decisions to leave the team without consulting me. I don't understand what is going on in the minds of the French. We need you on the team for the North American comparison."

Kent's words appealed to my analytical as well as emotional side. I knew it was good for me to remain on the team but doubted the cost, and I shared this with Kent. "If it will help, I can do two things for you," Kent volunteered. "First, I will send you all the material I receive from the French so that you need not rely upon them. Second, I will pay for your expenses from my budget so that you will not have to cover your expenses which are higher than most of ours anyway." This conversation helped address several concerns. After thinking about Kent's generous offer, I decided to renew my interest in the project but to work on it only after completing several others that had high potential for early completion. The enthusiasm was not to return, however.

THE THIRD MEETING: MILAN, ITALY

In December 1994, Susan received funding from her university and had time to conduct some of the interviews. Apparently Susan was not the only team member who lacked total commitment. Each team was to have completed 30 interviews by the third meeting, which took place in January 1995 in Milan. Only the British and German teams accomplished the task as set out in Estoril. The other teams, including the French team, seemed to have completed only about half of the intended interviews. The Milan meeting promised to be another difficult one.

The French were on time this meeting, but several other teams were missing on Monday afternoon. Despite the 3:00 P.M. scheduled start time, only the British and French had arrived at the hotel. Susan had brought a laptop and some papers to review so that she would have something to do while waiting at the hotel for the rest of the members.

After a very brief meeting lasting only minutes, the assembled group was dismissed and asked to meet promptly at 8:30 A.M. on Tuesday morning. The meeting was adjourned to the hotel lobby for casual conversation until dinner time. Predictions of doom issued from Susan and each of the British members.

Susan's Experience

Then, Tuesday morning offered another surprise from the French for me. A professor from a Canadian university, Frederick Wise, had arrived at the meeting. Not introduced nor explained, I wondered what was up. Anthony, the French professor responsible for acquiring the EU grant, addressed requests for interviews with specific American firms to Frederick who was smoothly noncommittal. "I will look into it," he responded often.

That evening at the hotel bar over Spumante, I was decidedly American in my directness toward Frederick. "So, Frederick, have you been asked to do the American interviews?"

"Well, that is what I wanted to talk to you about, Susan. How would you feel about my doing some interviews in the United States?"

This lack of finesse and diplomacy on the part of the French was revealing. "I have no problem with your doing any of them, Frederick. I would prefer that you not do any interviews in firms I have already contacted and planned on. But, the more disturbing issue is that the French have left this to you and me to work out. Why have they done this?"

Frederick responded, "Of course, I would not want to interfere in any way with your role. Perhaps, I could do interviews in Canada just across the border. I have made no commitment. We will see how the week progresses."

"How could I have come so far from my original role in this group? Is it something I have done? Is it because I am a woman? Is it because I was introduced by Kent?" I wondered after Frederick had gone. So much for the honor of participating in such a prestigious group.

Susan's Decision

In the year I had been in the group, I had the opportunity to have my professional pride wounded. But, just as seriously, I wondered whether the situation had arisen from a lack of cultural sensitivity and understanding. I also wondered whether I was qualified to teach others about cross-cultural issues, much less participate in a sophisticated multinational research project.

But, how should I decide whether to continue with the group? Certainly I had to consider whether the project could actually be executed given the requirements of the team leaders and the effort needed to complete the project. And, if I spent the time needed on this project, how would it affect my other work? I really needed to weigh the potential benefits of continuing versus the costs of quitting. How would my professional reputation be affected if I left the group? What impact would it have on my career? Would I be disappointed with myself for quitting or would it be a relief?

I resolved to speak with other colleagues about this when I arrived home. In the meantime, I reclined my spacious seat to enjoy the trip home.

APPENDIX

Researchers of culture have provided different frameworks for viewing average behavior or values of different cultures. Although these frameworks do not describe every individual within a particular culture, they do provide an indication of what an average person might be like. They can be used as a good starting point for understanding what to expect from someone from a particular culture. We give a summary of how three cultural researchers categorize people from the United States, France, and England here. To gain a greater understanding of these theories, it is recommended that the reader refer to the works cited in this discussion.

Gannon's Metaphors

Martin Gannon from the United States used a metaphor to describe each of 17 cultures. In his book (Gannon 1994), he describes in detail how the metaphor can be used to explain and understand the behavior of each culture. The following summary provides the metaphor and a brief description of the culture as explained by Gannon.

The United States The metaphor for the United States is American football. Within the game we see some of the major cultural characteristics of Americans: movement, speed, aggressiveness, and competitive specialization. Although Americans are highly individualistic, the "huddling" behavior of football can be used as a metaphor to show how they function within groups. The huddling or group behavior is a societal mechanism for coordinating activities; thus Americans can be intensely committed to a group for a short time in order to accomplish certain goals. They then move on.

Americans are also very numbers oriented and use standardized rankings for judging performance. Some other cultural characteristics that are manifest in the football metaphor include time-obsessed, monochronic, nationalistic, ethnocentric, and religious. People from the United States generally value profits, fame, glory, equal opportunity, independence, individual initiative, and self-reliance.

France   The metaphor used to describe the French is French wine. The process of wine making is a complex one, a blending of science and art that has evolved over the centuries. Gannon uses this process of wine making to explain the complex, sometimes seemingly contradictory, French people. The French believe in their own cultural superiority and in their very pure and proud country. Just as there is a hierarchy of wines, so too is there a hierarchy of society, a centralized social structure. The person at the top of the hierarchy is the most important and has the power to make most, if not all, decisions.

The French have a need to control and refine life. This is manifest in bureaucratic institutions where risk taking is not encouraged. French people are hard working, argumentative, individualistic, and honorable. They enjoy life and nurture relationships but are wary of outsiders.

England   The traditional British house is the metaphor Gannon selects for the British. Both the house and the people are raised in the one "right way": to be properly British. The house is built as the people behave—in a traditional manner. There is a firmness and a respect and strong desire for privacy. We would also expect a certain orderliness. Some of the other British characteristics include resourcefulness, diplomacy, leadership, good graces, unexcitability, reserve, and patience.

Hofstede's Dimensions of Cultural Values

Dutch researcher Geert Hofstede (1980) undertook to compare work-related values of employees of IBM in more than 40 countries. Using his studies, he constructed four dimensions of cultural values that could be used to describe the preferences of people in the various cultures he studied. The first of these dimensions was power distance (PD), the degree to which people accept inequalities in power distribution. A high score indicates that people accept the fact that power is not equal among individuals. The second dimension, uncertainty avoidance (UA), is the degree to which people in a society are accepting of ambiguity and risk taking behavior. A country with a high UA score has people who seek security and try to avoid risky situations. The third dimension is individualism/collectivism (I/C). In an individualistic society each person is expected to be self-reliant and does things on his or her own; a collective society is group oriented. People do things as expected by the society or by the clan. The fourth dimension, masculinity/femininity (M/F), describes what things people value. A masculine society has "tough" values, money, status, and things. A feminine society has "tender" values, quality of life and the nature of relationships.

The following chart indicates where the United States, France, and England scored on Hofstede's four dimensions:

	PD	*UA*	*I/C*	*M/F*
United States	Low	Low	I	M
France	High	High	I	F
England	Low	Low	I	M

Trompenaars' Dimensions

Fons Trompenaars (1993), also from the Netherlands, developed a set of dimensions to describe cultural values. His studies were based on surveys of thousands of managers in 28 countries over a 10-year period. The dimensions that he developed were based on the work of American anthropologists Kluckhohn and Strodtbeck (1961). Five of his dimensions are particularly relevant to business situations (Hoecklin 1995).

The first dimension, universalism versus particularism (U/P), indicates how a society applies rules of morals and ethics. In a universal society, rules and contracts are developed that can apply in any situation. A particularist culture, in contrast, looks at relationships and circumstances in a particular case to decide what is right. The second dimension, individualism versus collectivism (I/C), is similar to Hofstede's. The third dimension is neutral versus affective relationships (N/A). In neutral cultures, expression of emotion is more restrained, certain emotions are considered to be improper to exhibit in certain situations. In an affective culture, emotions are expressed more naturally.

Trompenaars' fourth dimension is specific versus diffuse relationships (S/D). In a specific society, people generally have larger public spaces (or lives), and the access to these is very open. Their private spaces are smaller and more difficult to access. In a diffuse culture, public spaces are relatively smaller, whereas private spaces are relatively larger. It is more difficult to access the public space but once one does, access to the private space often comes along with it.

The fifth dimension is achievement versus ascription (Ac/As). In an achievement culture, status and power are derived from what an individual has done. In an ascription society, the emphasis is on who the person is.

The following chart gives the relative scores of the United States, France, and England on Trompenaars' dimensions.

	U/P	*I/C*	*N/A*	*S/D*	*Ac/As*
United States	U	I	N/A	S	Ac
France	U/P	C	N/A	S	Ac/As
England	U	I	N	S	Ac

Note: When both ends of the dimension have been given, it indicates a score that is approximately in the middle.
Source: Based on dimensional scoring given in Hoecklin, L. (1995), *Managing Cultural Differences: Strategies for Competitive Advantage*. Reading, MA: Addison-Wesley.

References

GANNON, M. J. (1994), *Understanding Global Cultures*. Thousand Oaks, CA: Sage Publications.
HOECKLIN, L. (1995), *Managing Cultural Differences: Strategies for Competitive Advantage*. Reading, MA: Addison-Wesley.
HOFSTEDE, G. (1980), *Culture's Consequences: International Differences in Work-Related Values*. Newbury Park, CA: Sage Publications.
KLUCKHOHN, S. H. and STRODTBECK, F. L. (1961), *Variations in Value Orientation*. Evanston, IL: Row, Peterson.
TROMPENAARS, F. (1993), *Riding the Waves of Culture: Understanding Diversity in Global Business*. London: The Economist Books.

Case

Portrait of a Young Russian Capitalist

"I want to make profit, not a salary"—Max Levin

IN THE BEGINNING

Beginning with the collapse of communism in 1988 and accelerating with the breakup of the Soviet Union in 1992, Russia has experienced dramatic changes. In May 1988, as part of *Perestroika*, Mikhail Gorbachev passed the Law of Cooperation. For the first time since the 1917 Revolution—excluding 1922 to 1929—this law permitted Soviet citizens to form private partnerships. In 1992, with the breakup of the USSR, Russia's parliament, under the guidance of President Boris Yeltsin, passed the State Privatization Program, which was intended to increase privatization and assist the transition to a market economy.

But, the road to capitalism has been rocky. The October 11, 1994 *New York Times* began a front page article:

> The ruble is crashing amid mounting fears of renewed inflation, and the fledgling stock market is still smarting from its first big downturn. Bankers and entrepreneurs are being gunned down in the streets. There is little financial regulation and considerable fraud.

> But for American and other foreign investors, those unpleasant realities are becoming far less important than their growing sense that Russia presents a business opportunity so big that they can no longer afford to hold back.

A CAPITALIST'S BACKGROUND

Family

Maxim "Max" Levin is a 25-year-old Moscovite. His family is Jewish. Under communism they never experienced overt discrimination; religion was simply not discussed. In postcommunist Russia, Max claims, "I can be proud to be a Jew," but

---

Copyright © 1997 Barry Allen Gold. Presented at the 1996 annual meeting of the North American Case Research Association.

considers himself assimilated into Russian society and does not practice any religion.

Max describes his family's economic status under the communist regime and in 1994 as upper-middle class; for many years they have had a high, steady, secure income. Before *Perestroika*, Max's father was an upper-level manager at a state-owned petroleum refinery and then became a high-ranking government official at the Ministry of Petroleum Refining. In 1989, he became a manager at a Soviet–German joint venture refinery in Moscow. As a result of these positions, he developed many personal connections with government officials and private businesspeople. Yet, even with the liberalized political climate, he remained very concerned with which individuals and groups possessed power and control in government and industry.

Max's mother is a physician. Under communism, she earned a high salary compared with other occupations and worked in a state hospital. Soviet physicians—who never had the high status and generous salaries of medical doctors in the United States—still earn comparatively modest salaries under privatization. Beginning in 1991 Dr. Levin worked in a public clinic in Moscow.

Education

In September 1987, after secondary school, Max enrolled in the Moscow Finance Institute—renamed the State Finance Academy in 1992—to study for a degree in finance. In June 1988 he entered the Soviet Army for two years as then required by Soviet law for all 18-year-old men. His army duty was reduced to 14 months when the law was changed. Max views himself as fortunate: Because of the change he avoided duty in the USSR's war with Afghanistan. Overall, his assessment of his military experience is positive; he learned discipline and matured rapidly.

Work

When he returned to school after the military in September 1989, business opportunities were beginning to open as a result of economic policies designed to create private enterprise and markets. In October 1989, with the aid of his father's business connections, Max took a part-time job in Moscow at Neftechimbank.

When Max joined Neftechimbank in 1989, it was small and mainly provided services to state-owned industries. However, as a result of privatization and the resultant growth of the petroleum industry—the bank's major client and shareholder—within a few months the bank experienced rapid growth. A year later, it was one of the largest banks in Russia. Because of the remarkable growth, work at the bank offered many opportunities and valuable experiences. For instance, as part of his training, Max was rotated among the various divisions and got an overview of banking. In addition, substantial customer growth provided Max with many personal connections with people starting businesses.

While working part-time at Neftechimbank, Max attended classes full-time in finance, accounting, and auditing. As in Russian society generally, change was occurring quickly at the Academy. For example, Price Waterhouse, one of the "Big Six" world accounting firms, presented seminars on Western accounting practices to the Academy's students. This immersion into capitalist techniques was unthinkable a year earlier.

COMPANY FOUNDING—1991

Capitalism was spreading. In 1991 Max left the bank. He and Sergey Kamaroff, a fellow student, formed a partnership with Vladimir Smirov, a friend and student at the Moscow State Technical Institute, with the intention of starting a business.

They had no particular business in mind and no capital (there were no requirements for shareholders' capital at the time). According to Max, "In 1991 everyone tried to do *something* in business. They wanted to take advantage of opportunities." For many people a major enticement was greed: *the opportunity to get rich quick.* Max and his partners knew people who, by setting up trading companies, became millionaires in a short time. This was comparatively easy to do in 1991, at the beginning of privatization, because there were few government regulations concerning private businesses. However, there was considerable risk: State control over the economy was still strong, and many of the new entrepreneurs violated the state monopoly on foreign trade with the prospect and, in some cases, the actuality of arrest.

Six months passed and the new corporation was inactive. The partners, who were among the first Academy students to form a corporation, still had no specific business in mind and almost no models to emulate. It slowly became clear to them that they wanted to blend "theory and practice"—to use what they were learning in school as a basis of their business.

The partners decided to translate into Russian a 50-page pamphlet written in English on how to read American corporate financial statements. They sold the translation to a small publishing company and now had some capital. Considering the success of the pamphlet, their training, and banking experience, they decided to open an accounting firm. They envisioned a growing market as companies formed, the government required more standardized financial reporting, and American and European companies began to do business in Russia, because Russian and Western accounting principles were not the same.

In March 1992 the company leased a small office in an unfashionable part of Moscow. They selected the name Marillion Accounting Firm after the novelist Tolkien to symbolize "truth." At this time they had one computer and two small business clients.

COMPANY GROWTH—1992

In May 1992 Max's father suggested that they contact a Soviet–Italian joint venture company—the general manager was his college classmate. This was their first major client. The task was to set up an accounting system for the company that had been operating for two years. Because it was a sizable job, they hired two fellow students to work for them. (One of the new employees, Ilya Popov, became a partner a short time later.) All of them worked at the joint venture company for a month; it was difficult to straighten out the books which had been neglected for the past two years. The fees they earned went to pay salaries and rent.

In December 1992, because of a growing staff, they required more space and relocated to a hotel in Moscow. Also, more elaborate, presentable offices were needed to meet with current and potential clients. At this time, they had six employees and six clients, and every quarter showed modest revenue growth.

A few weeks after moving into the hotel, members of the Russian Mafia "visited" them. Although they made threats, the firm's small size and limited operations were of no interest to the Mafia. They never returned.

Another significant early client was a watch manufacturing firm. Ilya had good relationships with the manager of the company, which was a state enterprise. After several months of negotiations Marillion won the account. Ilya, a talented accountant, personally managed the watch company account. Eventually, Ilya and several new accountants relocated to the watch firm's offices, while Max and Vladimir worked on other accounts and sought new business.

The Insurance Industry

At this time, the three principals reorganized the company into a limited partnership with no outside shareholders. Shortly after, in summer 1992, the firm's emphasis shifted from general accounting to auditing joint ventures and limited partnerships. Also at this time, there was a change in the structure of the Russian insurance industry. Like every other industry, insurance in the Soviet Union was a state monopoly. In 1992 it was privatized, and no regulations governing insurance or standard accounting practices for insurers existed. The State Insurance Supervisory Service was formed at this time to regulate the insurance industry. The three partners viewed this as a strategic niche and decided to make insurance auditing a specialty because of their background and the emerging opportunities. It was particularly attractive because there were few competitors.

They met with several executives of the State Insurance Company, Rosgosstrackh. The discussion focused on the services they had developed and anticipated changes in government oversight of insurance companies. Marillion signed an agreement with Rosgosstrackh and got an approval from the State Insurance Supervisory Service for developing a Chart of Accounts. This was a formal mandate to set up accounting systems for insurance companies.

At this time, in addition to changes in the insurance industry, there were also changes in the Russian accounting system intended to make it more like Western accounting. Few accountants in Russia knew much about the new procedures. This enhanced the opportunity for Max and his partners. In August 1992 they began work on the Chart, which would incorporate Western accounting principles.

By December 1992 the system Marillion developed was approved and implemented. It was the first accounting system of its type in Russia and became a model for other insurance firms. Max and his partners published a pamphlet describing how to set up an accounting system for the insurance industry. They sold the book to a private publisher before the government officially printed it. This publication made the company well known and generated new business. Eventually, these guidelines were adopted by the State Insurance Supervisory Service and were codified in an official policy manual.

By December 1992, revenues were sufficient for the business to pay salaries to the principals and retain modest earnings.

In January 1993, under a new set of government regulations, every insurance company was required to adopt the new accounting practices. Marillion acquired more insurance companies as clients; Max and Sergey were now responsible for the insurance business. Ilya continued to supervise the work with the watch company, the joint ventures, and several small accounts. By April 1993 they had 10 insurance companies and 20 firms in other industries as clients.

In May 1993 Marillion moved to a larger office in a more desirable location. At this time they attracted another large client: a holding company that managed trading companies, a bank, and an insurance company.

THE COMPANY—1994

By 1994 the firm had a staff of 20 with 40 clients and was continuing to grow. Revenue was at a record high. In addition to drawing salaries, the partners split a substantial profit. In July 1994, they moved to a larger office opposite the Kremlin. This office was closer to the holding company that was their largest client. However, despite rapid growth, they were still a small company compared with the Big Six auditing firms that opened in Russia in 1992. Nevertheless, they had certain competitive advantages. In one case, Marillion was in competition with KPMG and won the account because they knew more about Russian companies. In addition, KPMG charged very high fees by Russian standards. Also, Marillion had developed a good reputation.

In September 1993, after graduating from the Moscow State Finance Academy, Max decided that it would be an advantage to know more about American business practices, particularly accounting and finance. He enrolled in an MBA program in the United States. After beginning graduate studies Max returned to Moscow to manage the company actively during the summer but otherwise limited his involvement to an investor.

In February 1994 Max incorporated a branch office of Marillion in New York City. By February 1995 the branch had one client to which it consulted regarding investments in Russian businesses.

THE FUTURE

The partners developed short- and long-range plans to develop the business. For the short term, Marillion hired a computer programmer to develop software for insurance companies. They also started to consult with foreign companies in Russia. Long-term plans included involvement in the Russian stock market as consultants for companies that wanted to obtain a listing or invest in the stock market. Finally, they planned to merge Marillion with other small companies to become more competitive with the Big Six.

Taxes

In 1994 the Russian tax rate, which is progressive, was 60% on personal income and 35% for corporate revenue. There was a 23% VAT (value-added tax) and many other taxes on specific goods and services. These high rates were part of a program to stem hyper-inflation. But high taxes have adverse effects on entrepreneurial activity. As a result, rather than not enter business or pay the tax, Russian businesspeople looked for ways to avoid taxes. For example, many entrepreneurs were paid in U.S. dollars "off-the-books" to avoid taxes and reduce the effects of hyper-inflation. In 1995, the Russian government began to close tax law loopholes.

The Mafia

In the mid-1990s the Mafia was a real problem for Russian businesses. As noted previously, when Marillion moved to its second location in a hotel in Moscow, the Mafia visited Max and his partners. Though nothing happened, the Mafia was a genuine concern. Mafia killings of businesspeople were frequent. Despite the fact that they were well publicized, they increased and the government did little to prevent Mafia activities. Citizens, Max among them, viewed the government as colluding with the Mafia and benefiting from their activities. Ironically, Max viewed the Mafia as contributing to the maintenance of order in Russian society, which became fragmented and lawless after the collapse of Communism.

For a Russian businessperson, as a practical matter to prevent drawing attention, it was not wise to purchase a Mercedes or otherwise display wealth. The Mafia was attracted to success, which increased the likelihood that a business would be infiltrated. According to Max, if you were successful and advertised it, "before too long you would be the employee and the Mafia would be your boss." Or worse. In early October 1994 an executive of the insurance company that gave Max's firm one of their first major insurance accounts was shot dead by the Mafia on a Moscow street.

Reflection and Action

In February 1995 Max's optimism of five years earlier was tinged with the realization that conducting business in the new Russian economy was not as easy as it had first appeared. In addition to the Mafia, domestic political and economic instability created uncertainty.

Russian culture also posed threats to the development of a new economic order. On April 11, 1995, the *New York Times* printed an article with the headline, "Latest Films for $2: Video Piracy Booms in Russia." The story recounted how Russian merchants sold counterfit copies of Academy Award–winning films such as *Pulp Fiction* and *Forrest Gump.* Svetlana Abromovna, a senior researcher at the Institute of Civil Law in Moscow, who has studied intellectual property rights for 30 years said:

> 'There is a law against this kind of theft. But there are many laws in Russia that nobody takes seriously. There are no penalties.' Ms. Abromovna continued, 'Private property—whether it is land, a car or somebody else's idea—is still the hardest thing for Russians today to understand. In principle everyone is for it. But in fact, nothing is harder than convincing a Russian to leave other people's property alone.'

Max, who maintained frequent contact with his partners in Russia, now also had a view of events in Russia from abroad. This complicated his decision making. He would receive his MBA from an American university in May 1995. He wondered: "Should I stay in the United States and be a consultant with American firms interested in doing business in Russia, or should I return to Russia and rejoin my partners to develop Marillion?"

Case

J. Stewart Black

Yutaka Nakamura: A Foreigner in His Native Land

As he neared the top of the stairs that would lead him to the subway train and his hour and a half commute to his office, Yutaka Nakamura hesitated and then quickly moved aside to allow the mass of morning commuters to push their way down to the most punctual and safe mass transit system in the world. As he stood there at the top of the stairs watching the mass of humanity before him, he reflected on the past six months since he and his family had returned to Japan from their

"Yutaka Nakamura: A Foreigner in His Native Land" by J. Stewart Black from *International Management: Text and Cases* 3rd. ed. Paul Beamish, Allen Morrison, Phillip Rosenweig (eds.), Illinois: Irwin. Copyright © 1997 by J. Stewart Black. Reprinted by permission of the author.

overseas assignment in the United States. Once again, this morning his wife had cried and asked him to request another transfer overseas. After listening to his wife, Yutaka pushed back the carefully prepared breakfast his wife had made. Like most mornings lately, he left for work without eating much and with a throbbing headache left over from the previous night's drinking and socializing. As he stood there knowing that he needed to hurry down the stairs in order to catch the train that would put him into Tokyo and at his office precisely ten minutes before nine o'clock, Yutaka wondered what direction his life should take.

BACKGROUND

Yutaka, 44, prior to being sent to a key subsidiary in California four years ago, was in the sales department in a large electronics firm. He was hired directly after graduating from Tokyo University, the most prestigious university in all of Japan. His wife Chizuru, 40, was a graduate of Sofia University and the daughter of a former parliament member of Japan's Lower House. Yutaka and Chizuru met when they were both employees in the same department of the electronics firm. After they were married, they waited a few years to have their first child, Kenichi, now 14 and a very bright and outgoing teenager. Three years after Kenichi was born, they had their daughter, Yukimi. Yutaka felt he had a fairly typical middle-class Japanese life. Given that he worked in one of the largest electronics firms in the world, with operations in over 100 different countries, it was not surprising that Yutaka was asked to fill an overseas position in the marketing and sales department in southern California. He was given the position of co-vice president of marketing. Although it took some effort, Yutaka adjusted to living and working in southern California with its much more leisurely paced life and work style compared to Tokyo.

At first Chizuru had trouble adjusting to living in the United States. It took her several months before her English was sufficiently proficient for her to go grocery shopping, driving, and otherwise to take care of various family needs. Chizuru's English was much more labored than that of the other family members, but she eventually reached the point where she felt comfortable talking with the various neighbors who lived around them.

The children, on the other hand, quickly adjusted to the California lifestyle. In particular, Kenichi enjoyed whatever time he could at the beach, where he learned how to surf. Both children did extremely well in school and after their first year were completely age-proficient in English. The children attended normal American schools during the weekday, but on weekends spent one and a half days in a special Japanese school. Chizuru also had correspondence work sent from Japan and spent weekends helping the children with math, science, and Japanese reading and writing.

In general, the Nakamuras enjoyed their new lifestyle, the three-bedroom, 2,600 sq. ft. house, the two cars, the weekends of picnics, museums, and camping, the evenings spent together barbecuing in the backyard, and the yearly holiday back to Japan.

In spite of the fact they enjoyed their life in America, when it came time to return to Japan, all of the family members were excited to return. Other than checking on schools back in Tokyo, little thought was given to preparing for the re-entry and readjustment back to Japan. After all, they were going home.

PROBLEMS SINCE RETURN

Unfortunately, things had not gone as smoothly as they had anticipated since their return to Japan. The kids, Chizuru, and Yutaka had their own particular problems in adjusting to life back in Japan.

The Children

Although Kenichi and Yukimi had spent weekends in a special Japanese school while they were overseas, when they returned, it became very clear they were somewhat behind in several key areas. In particular, they were behind in math, science, and written Japanese. As a consequence, Chizuru hired a special private tutor to help the children with these subjects. She was most concerned that Kenichi was not adequately prepared for the upcoming high school exam. She hoped he would be able to enter an "escalator" high school (i.e., those particularly well-known for facilitating their graduates in entering a prestigious Japanese university). However, soon after their return, Chizuru began to get phone calls from the children's teachers and school administrators. In particular, Kenichi's teacher commented that he asked too many questions during class, and that his memorization skills seemed to be quite poor. Kenichi also seemed unwilling to accept facts as stated by the teacher, and constantly wanted to know the logic behind various statements.

Yukimi adjusted somewhat more easily than Kenichi to school. However, not long after they returned to Japan, she complained that her classmates were calling her *Gaijin*, which translated means foreigner.

Both children commented that their peers ridiculed some of their clothes, which they had purchased while they were in California. Some of their teachers commented that both Yukimi and Kenichi were not as proficient as they should be in the variations of their speech needed when speaking to individuals of differing status. Kenichi also complained several times that he didn't get jokes told at school because he did not understand the particular slang expression that was being used. Chizuru was disappointed to find that the children's English ability actually worked against them in their English classes. In particular, Kenichi had difficulty because he felt his English teacher had terrible pronunciation. A couple of times Kenichi offered a correct pronunciation, only to be ridiculed by his teacher and his classmates. Eventually, Kenichi had to consciously try to forget correct English pronunciation, and pronounce English words with a strong Japanese accent.

One Sunday morning, before going off to a special weekend class at a nearby *Juku*, or cram school, Kenichi asked his mother if his father would play catch with him with the half hour he had before he needed to go. Chizuru replied that his father was asleep and tired from the long hours of work. At this Kenichi exploded and burst out that his father was never around. They used to go to museums and the park and camping when they lived in the United States, now it was clear his father loved his job more than he loved his children. In tears, Kenichi ran out of the house and off to his cram session.

Above all these developments, one of the most disturbing had only recently emerged. Chizuru knew that both of the children had enjoyed much of their experience in the United States; however, lately she found them criticizing California and the United States to their friends. In fact, one day she overheard Yukimi telling a classmate that she hated America; she hated Americans; and she hated her parents for making her live in that foreign country. This 180-degree turn in attitude seriously troubled Chizuru, but she didn't know what to do about it or what it meant.

Chizuru Nakamura

Chizuru had her own difficulties adjusting to Japan. It had taken her about a year to begin to feel comfortable in the United States, but she now missed many things about their life in California. One of the most interesting aspects of life in the United States was the parties she and Yutaka attended and hosted together. When they hosted parties at their California home, her role was quite different than back in Japan. In the United States when they hosted a party, both she and Yutaka would plan the event and then greet the guests at the door. Throughout the night guests would comment to Chizuru how lovely her home was, how wonderful the dinner was, and how beautiful she looked. These compliments were, at first, somewhat strange to her, but over time became a very important source of pride and satisfaction. In addition, during dinners, as was customary, Chizuru rarely sat by her husband. Instead she was often placed next to other spouses as well as other executives and clients with whom her husband associated. Many of these guests commented directly and indirectly about Chizuru's intelligent insights concerning international affairs. After some time, Chizuru found that she quite enjoyed both attending and hosting these social interactions. Instead of simply being relegated to the kitchen and bringing in various dishes for the guests only to quickly disappear again as was the custom in Japan, Chizuru found she played an important role in the social standing of her husband, and that she had an importance in her own right.

When she returned to Japan, of course, these social interactions were completely out of the question. Yutaka rarely brought friends home, and when he did, he brought them without their wives. Her role was not that of hostess as much as it was that of waitress. Chizuru longed for her life back in the U.S. On top of losing her broader role in life, Chizuru felt she lost her husband upon returning to Japan. During their time in the United States, Chizuru had felt that she had rediscovered the man she had fallen in love with and married over 17 years ago. Many times they would talk together at night or take walks in their quiet suburban neighborhood. Especially during the last two years of their overseas assignment, Chizuru and Yutaka would often go out for dinner, see a show, or attend a cultural event. Unfortunately, those times were long gone now.

When Chizuru had first returned to Japan, she tried to re-establish relationships with some of her friends. However, whenever she tried to tell them of her experiences in the U.S., they quickly seemed disinterested and on some occasions actually accused her of showing off. This hurt Chizuru deeply. In her heart, she was simply trying to share something that was very important to her with her friends in order to reconnect with them after the long absence.

In addition to these social difficulties, Chizuru often found herself depressed because of the difficulties the children were having at school. Chizuru had prided herself on the fact that she had kept the children involved in Japanese curriculum during their stay in the United States through correspondence work and the weekend Japanese classes. She was very disappointed and frustrated to find that once they had returned, the children were still somewhat behind in critical areas. Also, despite her best efforts, the children had not yet adjusted well to the new schools, and it was becoming increasingly doubtful that Kenichi would be able to pass the test and enter one of the more prestigious high schools. She was convinced that women in her neighborhood were talking about what a poor mother she was, and the disservice she had brought upon her children by not keeping them up-to-date in their schoolwork while overseas.

Chizuru had also found many other points of frustration during the six months since they had returned to Japan. Although she was unaware of it at first, many of the Western clothes she had purchased while in California had brighter colors than those in Japan. It had first occurred to her that her style of dress had changed when she had visited the market the first week after their return. As she was in the market buying fruits and vegetables for dinner that evening, she overheard one of her neighbors whisper to another that she must think herself better than the Japanese. After all, she was not wearing a traditional apron that all the women in that neighborhood wore when visiting the market.

The daily visits to the market were by themselves another irritant to Chizuru. In America, she had been able to shop once a week, or once every two weeks, because the refrigerator she had was large enough to store plenty of food. Going to the grocery store only once every week or two reduced the time she spent shopping and gave her more time to enjoy various activities. Now she had to spend two hours every day grocery shopping and had to spend nearly twice as much money on food because of its high cost in Japan. The high cost caused her to change the family's diet. For example, Yutaka, as well as the children, had come to like steak and other meats, but they were so expensive in Japan that Chizuru had to cut back dramatically on their purchase.

Another frustration concerned Chizuru's English language ability. In an effort to keep her language ability that she had worked so hard to achieve from declining, Chizuru joined an English class a month or so after returning to Japan. She very much enjoyed the classes until one day her sister-in-law commented that it was perhaps her attending English classes that was contributing to her children's difficulty in school. The fact that her sister-in-law would think such a thing made Chizuru wonder if she really was at the heart of her children's difficulties at school.

Her sister-in-law was not the only one with whom Chizuru had had difficulties since her return. Recently Chizuru's mother-in-law had asked her to come over. Although the request had seemed rather innocent at the time and her mother-in-law wanted nothing more than to chat, Chizuru discovered that it was a test of her loyalty. Her delay in going to visit her mother-in-law caused serious problems for a period of about two weeks. Yutaka had strongly criticized her for being so self-centered and not visiting his mother until the day after she called.

The cumulative effect of all these incidents was almost more than Chizuru could bear. One night after her husband arrived home at about 11:30 p.m., Chizuru in tears complained that she felt like Cinderella in reverse. All the wonderful things that she had come to enjoy were suddenly taken away from her, including her Prince Charming. When Yutaka replied that there was nothing that could be done, she begged him to seek another international assignment.

Yutaka Nakamura

Incidents big and small had taken their toll on Yutaka since his return to Japan. Often he had difficulty sleeping, and most mornings he headed to work with a throbbing headache. His wife was also worried because of his poor appetite. Yet, by many standards these were the typical ailments of a Japanese salaryman. Still, Chizuru encouraged Yutaka to take better care of himself. Yutaka was a little resentful of her concern and complaints. It seemed to him that on Sundays, his only free day at home, when he wanted to sleep, all he received was complaints from the family about his unwillingness to spend time with them. No matter what he did, someone was complaining.

Complaints also showed up rather frequently at work. For example, not long after he had returned home to Japan, he was reading a *Newsweek* on the train into work, just as he had often done before his assignment to America. However, once he got in his office, several of his peers chided him for showing off his language skills and reading an English news magazine instead of reading one of the more traditional Japanese news magazines. Surprised and hurt by this, Yutaka decided that from then on, even though he would continue to read *Newsweek* in order to pass the time on the train, he would hide it before entering the office so as not to offend his peers.

He was also frustrated about the slow decision-making process in Japan. In the United States it had been uncomfortable at first to make important decisions on his own, but he soon grew to enjoy the autonomy and responsibility. Back in Japan, even simple decisions, such as approving a minor promotion budget, required him to talk to dozens of people. In fact, the more people he talked to, the more people that were suggested for him to talk to. Often the people who were suggested seemed totally unrelated to the issue on which Yutaka was working. However, he was reminded that in Japan relationships are what makes businesses function. As a consequence, even though someone's opinion may not always directly bear on a particular project, it was important to stay connected with that person and for that person to feel that their opinion would be considered.

This emphasis on relationships also required after-hours socializing at least three nights a week until approximately 11:30 or 12 midnight. This socializing was particularly difficult for Yutaka to readjust to. The frequency was nothing short of exhausting. Twice he had fallen asleep on the train and had to stay in a hotel at the end of the line until he could take an early train home the next morning.

The commute in Japan was a far cry from his 20-minute commute in his comfortable car in California. Although he resented the complaints of his family about the time he spent at work, Yutaka was also frustrated with the long hours he spent away from his family. In fact, some days it felt as though he were wasting his entire life traveling on cram-packed, noisy trains.

Some days the train was so crowded that Yutaka could doze off without any worry of falling over. Some days after the long commute to or from work, life back in California seemed like a fading dream. Memories of going to museums, going to the beach, camping, and barbecues on the back patio were harder to recall. Now, it seemed to him that he was stuck in "no man's land." He no longer had the love and companionship of his family, and he also didn't feel completely accepted by his Japanese coworkers. It seemed to him that whatever direction he turned, any effort to try to please one group would alienate and displease another group. It was like being caught in an ever-tightening vice and there was no way out.

He felt frustrated almost on a daily basis at work because the marketing and negotiation skills that he had worked so hard to develop in the United States were going virtually unutilized back in Japan. Yutaka had gained great knowledge and insights into methods of integrating promotion print media and electronic media into unified marketing strategies. Unfortunately, in the general affairs department, these skills were not needed. Yutaka had also gained a great knowledge of how to negotiate effectively with Americans. He had mentioned his insights in this area several times to various people throughout the organization, but the only time he was allowed to utilize these skills was simply as a translator in a high-level meeting between a potential American supplier and the purchasing department. Yutaka had thought to himself that he had not worked so hard at understanding Americans' negotiation tactics and thinking only to simply translate words, rather than to formulate negotiation strategy.

Yutaka was rudely awakened from these reflections as someone crashed into him in their hurry down the steps to the subway. Unavoidably, Yutaka found himself running down the steps in order not to lose his balance. As he paid for his ticket and headed through the turnstile toward the tracks, he couldn't help but feel isolated and alone, despite being surrounded by 120 million Japanese.

Suddenly over the loudspeaker came the announcement that the train was arriving. As Yutaka looked down the track he saw the solitary beam of the approaching train. He wondered to himself how he should resolve these feelings he felt inside.

Should he ask for a transfer to another overseas assignment? If he did, he might become a permanent international assignee, rotating from one international assignment to another. This would virtually lock him out of any major advancement. Also, if he ever chose to return to Japan, it would probably be much more difficult the next time. Each time away would likely contribute to a deeper chasm between him and his home country and coworkers. Also, if the children went away again, this time it would be impossible for them to pass the entrance exams and get into a prestigious Japanese university. This would virtually guarantee that they would have to enter a foreign university. However, even if they went to a prestigious foreign university, such as Oxford, Harvard, or one of the grand ecoles in France, Yutaka doubted that they would ever be able to work for a large Japanese corporation. If they were given such a job, he doubted if they would ever be able to reach a position of any significance.

Yutaka worried that another overseas assignment would take his children away from both sets of grandparents. He had already heard enough from his mother about the pain she had suffered while the children were away. On the other hand, an international transfer could bring back the lifestyle and time together he and his wife and children had once enjoyed.

Part of him wanted to request a transfer, but another part of him deep inside recalled various stories he heard as a youth in Japan—a story of a 40-year-old son who dressed in a diaper and crawled across the floor so his parents would not feel old, a story of a son who laid naked beside his parents so that the mosquitoes would only attack him. These and other stories of self-sacrifice—for many the essence of the Japanese spirit—caused him to think about the responsibility he had to simply *gammon* or "hang in there."

As the train grew near, its flickering light sparked another alternative that would free him from disappointing someone no matter what choice he made. Yutaka flirted with this image longer than he had ever done before.

Case

Giordano Holdings Ltd.

Richard C. Wei

Four kinds of values we indoctrinate into people through preaching,
through role modeling, through communications, through just interact-
ing. You do not need systems. If whatever [we] do, [we] think whether
it's good for "value for the customer" or whether it's good for service, for
simplicity, for speed—if whatever we do are improvements of this—we
do not need systems! We channel everybody to this same direction. Sys-
tems become onerous. . . . If whatever you do, you improve upon those
four values, then you do not need any more systems. That is the whole
value of Giordano.

Jimmy Lai
Chairman and Founder, Giordano Holdings Ltd.[1]

Giordano is a retailer of men's casual apparel in East and Southeast Asia. It operates retail outlets in China, Hong Kong, Malaysia, New Zealand, the Philippines,
Singapore, South Korea, and Taiwan and has two distributors in Japan. Its sales
grew at an annual rate of 35% from HK$712 million (US$92.4 million) in 1989 to
HK$2,334 million (US$303.1 million) in 1993. (See Table C8-1.) In a recent survey of
Hong Kong businesses, Giordano was voted the most innovative in responding to
customer needs and the company that others most try to emulate.[2]

COMPANY BACKGROUND[3]

Giordano Limited was incorporated in 1980.[4] In 1981, it began to sell, in Hong Kong,
certain types of casual apparel manufactured predominantly for the U.S. market by
the Comitex Group, a Kong-based garment manufacturer. Initially, Giordano Limited concentrated on the wholesale trade of high margin products under the Gior-

"Giordano Holdings Ltd." by Richard C. Wei. Copyright © 1994 by the President and Fellows of Harvard College. Harvard Business School Case 9-495-002. This case was prepared by Richard C. Wei under the supervision of Professor D. Quinn Mills as the basis for class disscusion rather than to illustrate either effective or ineffective handling of
an administrative situation. Reprinted by permission of Harvard Business School.

Table C8-1 Financial Highlights (Amounts expressed in HK$ thousands)

	1993	1992	1991	1990	1989
Turnover	2,334,135	1,661,364	1,169,622	892,337	711,564
Turnover increase (%)	40.5	42.0	31.1	25.4	42.8
Profit after tax	137,632	115,091	85,130	45,501	28,734
Profit after tax increase (%)	19.6	35.2	87.1	58.4	35.8
Shareholders' funds	454,697	361,677	283,239	58,630	34,861
Working capital	297,379	238,905	219,262	9,467	(23,638)
Total debt to equity ratio	0.8	1.1	0.6	4.6	7.3
Bank borrowings to equity ratio	0.1	0.0	0.0	0.0	0.0
Inventory turnover (days)	5.9	86	76	71	73
Return on total assets (%)	16.7	15.4	18.3	13.8	10.0
Return on average equity (%)	33.7	35.7	49.8	97.3	142.1
Return on sales (%)	5.9	6.9	7.3	5.1	4.0
Earnings per share (cents)	22.0	19.0	15.8	10.1	6.4
Cash dividend per share (cents)	9.0	7.5	5.0		0.0

dano brand in Hong Kong but in 1983, it scaled back its wholesale operation and began to set up its own retail shops in Hong Kong. It also began to distribute, through a joint venture, Giordano products in Taiwan. In 1985, it opened its first retail outlet in Singapore.

Despite these efforts, sales remained low and the business was unprofitable. In 1986, the company decided to reposition Giordano Limited under a new management team. It also adopted a goal of maximizing unit sales instead of maximizing price margin through a "value for money" policy and an increased commitment to customer service. As a result, sales increased substantially.

In 1988, the company established East Jean to take over the business of the joint venture in Taiwan and to undertake the exclusive distribution, through the company's retail outlets, of Giordano products. In 1989, it set up a small franchise in the Philippines. In 1990, the company entered into a distribution agreement for the sale of its products through Giordano counters at Aoyama stores throughout Japan.

Table C8-2 Operations Highlights

	1993	1992	1991	1990	1989
No. of retail outlets directly managed by the group	257	191	160	143	116
Total no. of retail outlets	738	614	236	148	118
Retail floor area directly managed by the group (sq. ft.)	209,500	139,500	99,800	90,400	68,900
Sales per sq. ft.(HK$)	12,600	12,200	10,900	10,000	8,800
No. of employees	2,330	2,104	1,477	1,437	1,298
Comparable store sales increase (%)	15	25	25	22	17
No. of sales associates	1,502	1,207	794	700	619

Table C8-3   Regional Highlights

	Hong Kong		Singapore		Taiwan	
	1993	**1992**	**1993**	**1992**	**1993**	**1992**
Net sales (HK$m)	777.7	652.8	277.5	168.9	1,003.3	615.1
Sales per sq. ft. (HK$)	21,200	21,100	15,100	13,200	9,900	8,800
Comparable store sales increase (%)	6	16	11	27	28	37
Retail floor area (sq. ft.)	41,900	33,100	23,600	16,900	134,900	81,800
No. of sales associates	479	497	206	186	780	484
No. of outlets (shops & counters)	46	37	29	16	174	129

Aoyama, a chain store operator specializing in menswear, has an extensive retail network of stores in Japan.

From the beginning, Giordano Holdings Limited and its subsidiaries were part of the Comitex Group. By the beginning of 1990, Giordano's retailing business had reached a sufficient size (see Tables C8-1 and C8-2) such that the directors of Comitex considered it appropriate to separate it from those operations of the Comitex Group, engaged primarily in manufacturing sweaters for the U.S. market. On May 6, 1991, Giordano Holdings Limited ceased to be a subsidiary of the Comitex Group. As part of the separation, two manufacturing companies were acquired from Comitex. (See Figure C8-1) At the end of May 1991, Giordano was taken public.

MANAGEMENT VALUES

Trial and Error

Company founder Jimmy Lai is a fervent believer in management by trial and error:

> We make no assumptions about business; we don't go into business thinking that we know something better than other people; we try to make people believe that we can only learn through trial and error because the market is changing too fast these days . . . Information, technology, and innovation . . . stimulate the consumer much more than ever before . . .

Table C8-4   Consolidated Profit and Loss Account

	1993	*1992*
Turnover	2,334,135	1,661,364
Operating profit	180,481	155,969
Share of loss of an associated company	(13,815)	(10,400)
Profit before taxation	166,666	145,569
Taxation	(29,034)	(30,478)
Profit attributable to the members	137,632	115,091
Appropriation:		
Dividends	(57,098)	(46,545)
Retained profit for the year	80,534	68,546
Earnings per share (cents)	22	19

T a b l e   C 8 - 5   Manufacturing Divisions

	Knitwear Division			Woven Division		
	1993	**1992**	**1991**	**1993**	**1992**	**1991**
Sales (HK$m)	349.3	347.5	325.6	144.4	101.9	48.8
Workers	2,591	2,696	2,342	758	692	198
Monthly capacity at year end						
(thousand dozens)	68	62	51			
(thousand pieces)				200	130	47
Percentage of sales to:						
Giordano	57	64	66	77	56	82
Japan	19	14	19	8	11	4
China	15	12	—	12	24	—
USA	—	1	5	—	—	1
Korea	—	1	2	—	1	3
Taiwan	1	3	6	—	3	—
Others	8	5	2	3	5	10

If we adopt the past successful way of doing business, we will only be keeping ourselves in the dark; we have to search in the dark, not stay there . . . Tomorrow's market is different. We are in business to solve problems. When the markets change, even the same problem will have different human connections, market positions, all that is related to other things in the market, so the solution has to be different. . . . We have to fix the market position, like . . . demographics, geography, price range, what kind of customer, but that does not mean we know what to do. . . .

The only thing to do is through trial and error, which has made the way we conduct business very flexible. We make a lot of mistakes, but mistakes are very important for us because they are an indicator of what is not possible at the moment and leave us the possibility of trying what is right. That is the basic philosophy that we have introduced into the management.

It does not matter that we are brought up with the idea that we should not make mistakes and with the idea that we should know what we are doing; we are in a world of not knowing, in a world of continually trying to stumble into something which becomes a solution to the problem. That's what I try to get a lot of people to [understand]. A lot of people have hang-ups, especially the MBAs. They come to work for me and point out that according to this or that equation, . . . That's all rubbish. The market does not have an equation. The solution of yesterday does not apply even to the same problem of today just because the relationship of the problem has changed.

With trial and error inevitably come mistakes and failures. On how Giordano deals with employees making mistakes, Lai said,

A lot of people go into business thinking we are in pursuit of perfection. No. We are in an imperfect world. We only have the choice between the more perfect or less perfect, the more imperfect or the less imperfect. We have people who work for us for a couple of months and leave. They become depressed when they make mistakes. They take mistakes as a burden, not as enlightenment. It's very difficult to tell people that if you make mistakes on the right side, the possibility is on the left. That's why the mistake is so important. . . .

I always have to make people comfortable about making mistakes by role-modeling it. Like in a meeting, I say, "Look, I have made this mistake. I'm sorry for that. I hope everybody learns from this." If I can make mistakes, who the hell do you think you are that you can't make mistakes? The more I make myself equal and common to them, the more comfortable they would do what I encourage them to do.

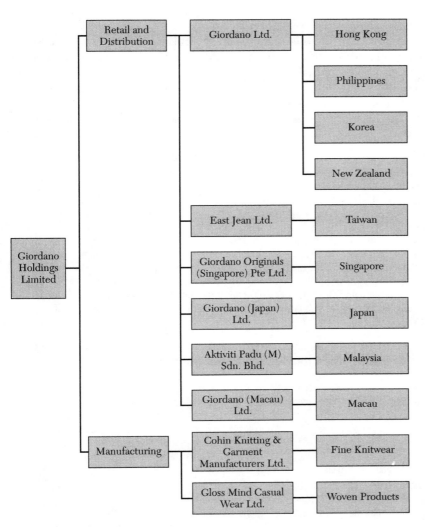

Figure C8-1 Corporate Structure

Empowerment

Lai strongly believed that it is important to empower people, to allow employees to make mistakes, for if everyone contributes and participates, any mistakes will be minimized. And people can make mistakes only when they have decision-making ability. He used a "tasteful" analogy:

> In Giordano, we have maybe 1,000 people in Hong Kong. I tell those guys that if I'm the one who gets the recipe to bake a cake and if I put salt instead of sugar, the whole cake will be spoiled. It's not edible. If I am the only one who can make decisions and you guys are going to carry out my decisions, no matter what obstacles or barriers that you have you won't dare to tell me. You will only do what I told you. After eight months, the cake is baked. It's disastrous. It could be a fatal mistake. . . . For instance, if 10% of the people make mistakes and put salt instead of sugar, the cake is still edible. . . . If we delegate the decision-making to everyone, the consequences of a mistake will be so small and so frequent, it is harmless. It's like the cake with 10% salt and 90% sugar. It might even taste better!

Simplicity

Simplicity as a value at Giordano is reflected in several ways. Corporate headquarters are located in a nondescript commercial building in Kowloon. Employees work in cubicles separated by waist-high or shoulder-high partition panels; managers and executives, including CEO Peter Lau, have slightly larger cubicles. The accouterments of power that define an executive's position are very much pared down.

Simplicity, in fact, is key to the company's basic culture, as Jimmy Lai describes:

> We [must] be simple enough so we can react to the market's change fast enough. If our organization and the things we do are so complicated, it would take a long time and a long process for whatever decisions we have to make and whatever things we have to make. Even if we make a perfect solution [but it is] too late, what good is it? Even if we have a perfect, complicated company . . . what good is it? We have to sacrifice thinking that we can do a lot of things but focus on a very few things and make it as simple as possible. How can we make a three-layer process into one layer? How can we make two departments into one? The more simplified is the structure, the more flexible it is, the more reactive it is to market changes. And that is very important, because the market changes a lot these days. Simplicity is reflected in the way we work, in the way we merchandise our goods. You'll see no more than 100 items in a Giordano store. Our core items are 17; you go to any retailer: they have 200–300 items. It takes them more time to react. So simplicity in the way we manage, in the way we communicate, in the way we process things [is what we strive for].

Furthermore, simplicity in Lai's view also applies to communication between managers and employees. The more straightforward it is, the less effort is spent deciphering the message.

> The most important simplicity is in communications among people, among staff, and among associates. The simplest communication is the most trusting communication that we do not have to second guess. If you say something and I have to second guess it for half a day and it costs $3,000 for an executive a day, that's $1,500. Who is going to pay for it? . . . People tend to be, if not cynical, skeptical. It is the human side of it that I always preach. I always try to role-model it. I really try to "de-hang-up-tize" it.
>
> Management is communications; management is the network of communications. Yet in this network, we have this trust there. It is like a computer network which has bugs; you have to debug it. Distrust is bugs in the network of communications. Management is communications, no more than that. Internal communications interact with external communications; that is management.

Service

When Giordano first began to focus on providing good customer service, it was not easy. Lai recalled,

> In 1987, service in Hong Kong was terrible. Absolutely pathetic. . . . The problem with service is that people do not stay with you; they can so easily find jobs because the pay is so low. So I decided to double the salary [to] make sure those guys won't be able to leave! Overnight, we raised the salaries 40%, we doubled the incentive/commission so those guys almost had an 80% increase overnight. So we attracted the best people in the service industry in our company. [According to Terry Ng, the director of business development, the turnover rate of Giordano's sales force is about 50%, much lower than the industry average of 75%.]
>
> Having the heart and the will to [provide good] service does not mean that [they] know how; we got to give those guys tools also. "Serving people is a low job, a mean job"—we got to make sure that kind of hang-up is not there. We build centers for training. We've invested a lot of money in training to make sure we turn the peddlers into professionals. We are not just serving our customers, we are managing our customers' needs. If we think we are serving our customers, we are like servants. In Chinese terms, that is very mean. But if we think that we are managers, managing the needs of customers, that is something else. The incentives come first, the psycho-

logical training come second. Make people feel proud of their job so that they are happy about it. If they do not have pride, they cannot reflect it to the customer.

"Why do we have to invest so much in service? But maybe service is not what people want." That is the question asked by people surrounding me. I tell those guys if today we stop buying any shirts, does anybody worry about not having any shirt to wear? No. We do not buy things because we need them; we have a lot of shirts in the wardrobe. But those are not exciting anymore. We buy things because we want a good feeling. . . . We are in an affluent society. Is a good feeling from service different from a good feeling from a product? [It's the] same! We are not just selling a product; service is part of our product. Good service gives people a good feeling. That kind of thing people slowly, slowly accept. We are not just a shirt retailer, we are not just an apparel retailer. We are also a service retailer because we sell feeling. Let's make the guy feel good coming in here! Let's make the guy feel good leaving our shop! We were the first to change from plastic bags to paper bags, which cost three times as much. This was not because of any environmental orientation that we had! Because people are so environment conscious that if we give them a plastic bag, they do not like it.

People

One reason Giordano has done well in a fast changing market is because it has won the hearts and dedication of its employees. Lai explained how:

We are very sure that our greatest asset is our people. We always tell them that if they leave tonight and don't come back tomorrow, the $4 billion that this company is worth is zero. Our responsibility is to make sure that [they] will come back in the morning. For this we have to delineate an external customer and an internal customer.

The external customers of course are the people who come to the shop to buy. The internal customers are the guys who are next in line. . . . To every head of a department, their staff are their customers; their problem is my problem. I have to make sure those guys are happy working there. I have to make sure those guys have a better deal than anywhere. A committed person is 10 times better than someone who is not committed. How do we make someone committed? To make sure that the guy has a better deal than anywhere. He is a customer, too. He comes to find employment; he comes to make a deal with me. So if I make the best deal for him, he will forget the rest and be totally devoted. So it is very important for us as managers that the people who work for us are our customers and for those who work in the company to think that the guy who is next in line—his problem you have to solve before you pass on work to him. By doing this, we cut a lot of bullshit, we cut a lot of meetings. . . .

That is why we are very focused on the people who work for us. They are our customers. I'm never a boss; I am just somebody who makes sure that the people who work there have the best environment, the best pay, the best opportunities, and they are happy. Because people do not get paid through money; they get paid from the happiness of the working environment, from the encouragement, from the winning. To do this is very easy to say but very difficult to do, because everybody has an ego, especially [managers]. I tell those managers, "If you are always right, they [i.e., subordinates] are always wrong, you always win, they always lose—how much do you have to pay someone to be a loser everyday?" You have to make the guy a winner; the guy might even work for nothing! It is an intangible payment, not the pecuniary payment which we have to create in addition to the pecuniary payment. Only when they get the best deal do we get the best people! The smarter the people, the more they think for themselves, the more they want a better deal. I believe that having the best people I will have the best company, regardless what I do. You cannot make anything out of dummies. Someone who does not know what is good for him can't be good for you. . . .

Finding the right people is very important. I have been running it for over four years. I only go there maybe once every two months for senior staff seminars because I am not a very good manager myself. I do not have the patience to manage; I am just entrepreneurial. I start off new businesses. . . .

As an entrepreneur, I have to make sure I do not have an ego; I have to recognize that other people are better managers than I am. I do not draw a salary at Giordano but the CEO makes over $5 million, so I make sure that people don't think I have privileges. I do not want people to think I am smarter, I am better. No, I have shortcomings, but my shortcomings are what you guys are coming in to compensate for.

After I finish a company, I lose the motivation to go to work. I have to make sure I do not let my ego in my way, because if I use my ego, I will impose my ego on other people and make other people losers. The only way I can motivate other people is to use other people's egos, not my own. If I have to use other people's ego, I have to hide my own or get rid of it. The only way you can motivate other people is to use other people's ego. Because motivation is what management is.

We release [those not performing well] right away if they do not fit. Once we accept somebody, we try to work very hard before we release them. We make sure that the people surrounding him know how much effort is being put into him; when we dismiss him, it is in tacit agreement with the people who work around him. Not for his good but for the people staying there. Whatever we do to the person who is leaving reflects the people who work there. If we treat them ill, [those staying] know that we will not treat them better. . . . They know enough chances and opportunities are being given to this person to change. So [they] feel undisturbed and that it was just. . . . A very small percentage [leaves voluntarily or involuntarily]. We can improve on this. If we put more effort, we might have less people leaving. Maybe a turnover of a few percent per year, or maybe more. But the percentage is deceiving because we release people at the early stage . . . actually those very new.

Speed

Lai also values speed:

Can we make things more speedy? Let's not count months, let's not count weeks, let's count days and hours. If we save one day out of a hundred-day selling season, we have one more percent of selling time. Simplicity and speed are actually the same thing; the more simplified, the more speedy it becomes.

COMPETITIVE STRENGTHS

By the end of 1993 Giordano has become one of the largest retailers in the region. Management attributed the company's success to its focus on the following areas:

Value for Money

Lai explained the rationale for Giordano's "Value for Money" policy this way:

Consumers are buying a lot more than they ever did. Through the purchases they have made, they have learned a lot better about what value is. Out of ignorance, people chose the label. But the label does not matter, so the business has become value driven, because when people recognize value, that is the only game in town. So for us, we always ask ourselves, "Can we make it better today than yesterday? Can we sell it cheaper today than yesterday? Can we deliver it faster than yesterday? Can we make it more convenient for the customer to buy today than yesterday?" That is all value, because convenience is value for the customer, time is value for the customer, . . . value for money is very important for us today with the transparency of information.

Customer Service

The company places great emphasis on customer service. All sales personnel, including those working in franchise outlets, receive extensive training. In most outlets, sales associates can make simple alterations, such as hemming, on the spot. Furthermore, goods purchased in Hong Kong may be exchanged or returned for full refund, in contrast to the typical policy of no exchanges and refunds practiced by most retailers in this region. [Also see previous discussion on service.]

Stock Replenishment

In a market such as Hong Kong where rent is expensive, idle space is a luxury very few retailers can afford. "We make sure the places for which we are paying a lot of money are sitting with goods that walk," noted Lai. "There is no back stock room in a Giordano store; every square foot is dedicated to providing sales opportunity. The back stock room at Giordano is replaced by a central Distribution Center."[5]

To make this scheme work requires skillful application of information technology. All merchandise is bar-coded. When a customer purchases an item in a Giordano outlet, the bar code information, identifying size, color, style, and price, is recorded by the store's P.O.S. cash register and transmitted to the company's main computer. The information is then sent to the sales department and the Distribution Center where, at the end of the day, sales information is compiled store by store. This sales information then becomes the store's orders for the following day. Orders are filled during late night hours and by early morning the Giordano trucks begin delivery. Before stores reopen, new inventory is already on the shelves. Lai compared Giordano's feat in this regard to competitors and elaborated on the use of information:

> We are the only one, I think, who can replenish goods within two weeks instead of three or four months. [It allows us to] do a lot of testing on our goods, and whatever sells in the shop not only the salespeople, not only headquarters staff, not only the manufacturing people but everyone involved shares the same information. So psychologically, everyone is prepared for what is going to happen. If yellow T-shirts are selling well, the factories may get the yellow dye ready in case orders for more yellow T-shirts come in.

> Things are being done simultaneously instead of serially, and that is what we call nonlinear way of sharing information. That is actually the core reason of our success. By being able to replenish goods in such a short time, we can eliminate a lot of mistakes. [There are] retailers who are still using the projections of the last experience for the next season. Nobody is a prophet, especially when the market changes so fast. We change from a projective business into a reactive business by having more statistics, by having more people. We kind of have a "mug shot": We have the goods ready preseason. We have all the salespeople come in to buy the goods [we are planning to sell] for the next season at half price. We get feedback from at least 1,000. We go to Taiwan, and that's another 1,000. We go to China, another 300. When we get all the figures in, we are quite sure what sells and what does not sell.

> We do not have to guess whatever that sells; the first day we know what sells and right away place the order. We don't place orders just because information comes in. We call up the sales associates and ask them, "Why are we selling so many? How do you feel?" Hard facts are not enough; information includes feelings. We [humans] do not make decisions out of dispassionate rationale; we make decisions out of passionate rationale, a feeling of heart and mind; got to get the feeling. Combine the hard facts and figures and the feelings, then place the orders. We are still refining.

> Why is it so important to have the ability to react to information? If we make 300 dozen tape-recorders, put them in the shops, sell them in one day and cannot replenish, [what good is having the information]? We know we can sell something but we do not know how [many] we can sell. The potential of the information remains a mystery to us because we can't utilize it.

Further flexibility is achieved by producing garments in raw form and having only some of the garments dyed or printed for sale in the stores. The remaining inventory is finished later pending sales performance by color.

Product Focus

In successful businesses, management is always tempted to expand into more products and services to meet customers' every need, but Giordano has remained focused on one specific area. Lai explained:

We never allow our expansion to expand beyond the intensity of the management. We have to keep our intensity at the highest because competition is very intense. We have to manage our business more intensely in order to compete. The narrower the focus, the higher the intensity. There is always a devil to tempt us to do more than what we can manage, but once we do that, we retreat, retrench, we align ourselves. After I left [management], they tried to expand into kids' clothing, then retrenched. After one or two years, they tried woman's apparel and retrenched again. I let them try and as long as we learn from our mistakes, that's fine.

VENTURE IN CHINA

Giordano has a 20% ownership interest in Tiger Enterprises Limited, a joint venture set up for the purpose of marketing Giordano products in China. In 1993, Tiger Enterprises suffered a loss of HK$68.9 million (US$8.9 million); Giordano's share of the loss was HK$13.8 million (US$1.8 million). Commenting on the loss, Lai said,

We proliferated too much; we lost focus. We were the first ones there. We thought we would take the opportunity to expand. It wasn't something we believe in but we did it anyway. We are retrenching. We would like to contain ourselves in Canton and have a focus in Canton and give franchise licenses in other areas. We have to prepare. . . . Make sure that the shops we want are being run intensely, professionally, so we can stand up to any competition. So we stick to being a regional retailer.

It is not just the business infrastructure [that is problematic in China], not just the physical infrastructure, but the moral fabric of the marketplace that is something that will take a long time to build.

Endnotes

1. Jimmy Lai, interviewed in May 1994 for this case, is no longer involved with the day-to-day operations of the company; he is running a new publication called *Next Magazine*. He remains, however, the company's largest shareholder, owning almost 37% of the shares outstanding.

2. "Money in the Bank," *Far Eastern Economic Review*, December 30, 1993 and January 6, 1994.

3. Prospectus, Giordano Holdings Limited, May 28, 1991.

4. When asked how he had chosen the name Giordano, Jimmy Lai explained, "I was still quite an unsophisticated businessman at that time. I thought if I used an Italian name, people would think it was an Italian product. The name was from a pizza place in New York. I was thinking about a name; there was the name on a napkin. I put it in my pocket and gave it to the [marketing] director . . . If I were to do it again, I would not use Giordano. I would use a name simpler to pronounce and easier to remember. To be honest, I would use 'O.K.'!"

5. Company literature.

Case

Francisco de Narváez at Tía

Stacy Palestrant

Late one blustery evening in April 1992, 38-year-old Francisco de Narváez (hereafter referred to as "Narváez") paced in front of the Tía store on the Avenida Santa Fe in Buenos Aires. Tía, which employed 3,900 people and was the only national retail chain in Argentina, offered its customers an assortment of food and general merchandise in its 45 stores. (See Figure C9-1 for 1992 Tía locations and Figure C9-2 for selected Tía financial information and past store growth.) The store Narváez faced was boarded shut; it would re-open in two months to become the prototype for other Tía units in Argentina's five largest cities—making Narváez's vision a reality. As the grandson of one of the two Tía founders, he knew all too well the cost of the transformation he had spearheaded. Three years earlier, when he became general manager of the chain, he initiated a change process that had exacted a heavy toll.

TIA'S HISTORY

In 1933, Narváez's maternal grandfather, Carlos Steuer, founded Te-Ta, in Prague, Czechoslovakia. "Te-Ta" meant "aunt" in Czech, and the stores were fashioned after the successful Woolworth's five-and-dime concept.[1] They were filled with, among other things, little treats for children: trinkets, dolls, colored pencils, and candies— what a "favorite aunt" might buy for her nieces and nephews. This mix of quality merchandise at good value proved highly successful, and Steuer with his friend, Federico Deutsch, soon opened branches in Yugoslavia and Romania. Shortly thereafter, however, the war engulfing Europe caused the families to flee to Argentina, where they and six other Czech friends, who had worked at Te-Ta, hoped to settle and replicate their success. By 1947, this dream was realized: They had opened five stores offering the same kinds of goods provided in Czechoslovakia. This merchandise was unique for Argentines—never before had they been able to find so many inexpensive, "essential" items under one roof. All of the merchandise was displayed in thematic islands, each with its own cashier. However, "Te-Ta" means "breast" in Spanish, so the company name was changed to Tía, the Spanish word for aunt.

Figure C9-1 Location of Tía Stores, 1992

Even though the founders did not speak much Spanish, they spent a great deal of time visiting the stores, talking to customers and observing how the merchandise did. Informal business discussions occurred daily when the families dined, went to the movies, or vacationed together. In its early years, Tía was run by a committee of six. Responsibility for business matters was shared by all, although they knew the final decisions were made by either Steuer or Deutsch. Children helped too, and were relied upon particularly as translators from Czech into Spanish. Indeed, Steuer's daughter, Doris, remembered that "My Daddy says . . ." was the preamble to many of her conversations with Tía suppliers. "It was very exciting when we opened our first store in Buenos Aires," she remembered. "All of us would chip in and help. Even though we weren't all family, we had such a communal atmosphere that we felt like family!"

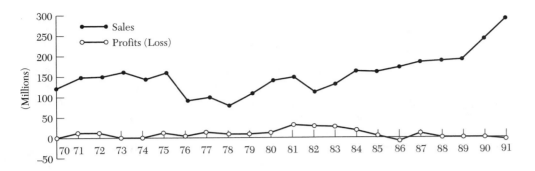

Year	# of Stores	Year	# of Stores	Year	# of Stores	Year	# of Stores	Year	# of Stores
1947	1	1956	7	1965	14	1974	21	1983	26
1948	2	1957	8	1966	14	1975	21	1984	30
1949	3	1958	8	1967	15	1976	21	1985	31
1950	3	1959	10	1968	15	1977	21	1986	32
1951	4	1960	10	1969	16	1978	23	1987	35
1952	5	1961	11	1970	17	1979	23	1988	38
1953	6	1962	11	1971	18	1980	23	1989	44
1954	7	1963	12	1972	20	1981	23	1990	45
1955	7	1964	13	1973	22	1982	24	1991	45

Figure C9-2 Tía's Selected Financial Information in Millions of Dollars, 1970–1991 and Number of Stores 1947–1991

The business flourished, particularly in an economic environment characterized by customer demand vastly exceeding supplier capability and the absence of aggressive competition. By 1966, Tía had opened 14 stores, and its annual profits were US$2.1 million. For customers, shopping "Casa Tía,"[2] had become a tradition.

Francisco de Narváez Begins at Tía

In 1970, at the age of 17, Narváez, Doris Steuer's son, began working at Tía, in the administration and finance departments. Narváez commented, "Working at Tía seemed the obvious thing to do. I had grown up hearing about it and my older brother, Carlos, was already working there. Plus, I greatly respected my grandfather and was eager for the opportunity to work in his company." Soon after Narváez started at Tía, however, Deutsch died and in 1972, Steuer passed away. "The sense of loss was immense," Doris Steuer said. "We missed their charismatic leadership and wisdom. Tía was not the same without them."

Doris Steuer and Gustavo Andres ("Andy"), Deutsch's[3] son, became the majority shareholders (owners) and decided that a committee of four men, who had been with Tía since its founding, would run Tía. Although Deutsch, who had become president, was responsible for making final decisions, he left the day-to-day business to the committee. One long-time Tía employee described the committee:

We called them 'the Czechs' since they had all come from Prague. They would have closed door meetings for several hours and then emerge to proclaim a decision. Hardly ever would they explain to us how the decision was made. Their decision-making process was very secretive and seemed even more so since it was all in Czech. Ironically they soon lost control of the stores because they rarely left the head office.

Meanwhile, Narváez was working in the warehouse installing a computerized inventory control system. He then moved into the operations department (i.e. store management and logistics) as an assistant manager in three different Tía stores, including a new Tía hypermarket in which food, a relatively new product line to Tía, came to account for 50% of the sales. In 1976, he returned to the head office to manage Tía's first team of auditors hired to evaluate operations. While there, he became increasingly critical of Tía's leadership. He said, "Since I was always complaining, the committee considered me a troublemaker. I routinely had a different opinion on everything from merchandise to the taste of the office coffee. Looking back, I was used by my peers to create conflict and deliver messages. To be sure, I had no solutions—I was part of the whole mess."

Eventually exasperated, Narváez left Tía in 1977 (his brother Carlos de Narváez remained and joined the committee in 1980). He went to work with an old high school friend's cattle brokerage business in which he acquired 25% equity. There Narváez felt that he was finally given the opportunity to "get things done properly."

In 1981, when a committee member became ill, Deutsch and Steuer asked Narváez to return to Tía. At this point Tía had 23 stores and its annual profits were $28 million. Narváez accepted their request, on the conditon that he would be allowed to work his way up from the bottom. Thus Narváez became an assistant in the commercial (i.e. purchasing and merchandising) department. Narváez remarked:

> The head office was split by a corridor with commercial on one side and operations on the other. The commercial department was the seat of power. Nothing happened without their permission. For the first eight months they only let me do accounting paperwork. I didn't have an opportunity to buy a product or fix a price.

When the ill committee member died, Steuer and Deutsch urged Narváez to join the committee. By this time, Deutsch was devoting much of his attention to the management of his passion, a charter airline he had founded in 1976, Lineas Aereas Privadas Argentinas (LAPA). After some prodding, Narváez agreed to join, and decided to focus on information systems, accounting, and to a lesser extent, the purchasing process.

While each committee member had individual pet projects, the division of labor was unclear, which worried Narváez. As he expressed to his brother: "I'm getting frustrated by the lack of defined sectors and how everybody is involved in everything. Nobody has responsibility for anything." Although Carlos de Narváez agreed that much needed to be changed, others observed that he was simply more "diplomatic" than Narváez. Besides, Carlos de Narváez was working in real estate, leasing and new site construction, areas in which he did not get much interference. When the committee decided not to invest in new sites, Carlos de Narváez received financing from his grandmother to build two new stores. And, Narváez had to admit with chagrin, somehow Tía was "successful and making money without any big problems."

THE AWAKENING

Success was not to last. In early 1986, Tía experienced its first ever monthly loss. Initially many contended that the loss could be attributed to either accounting or inventory "errors." No sooner had they made these assertions then they had to admit that the "numbers were true." The committee held a meeting that, for the first time, brought store managers and buyers together. All sorts of ideas were proposed, from an aggressive advertising campaign to firing low-level employees. As Narváez listened, he noticed that everyone seemed to think that Tía had an internal operational problem. Narváez lamented, "No one questioned Tía's position in the market. It seemed as if we had lost sight of our identity. *I* wasn't sure what our identity was at that point."

In the ensuing months, Deutsch and Narváez began to speculate that Tía was experiencing the effect of Argentina's newly democratic government's *Plan Austral*, a fiscal "austerity" program launched to tame the country's wild inflation. By mid-1986, the plan had failed and hyperinflation returned—along with profits for Tía. This episode led Narváez to believe that Tía didn't know how to make money in a stable economy. As he explained to Deutsch:

> I am convinced that with democracy in place, the government will eventually implement a stable economy. Then the customers who select a government will select where they are going to shop—I am sure they are not going to pick us. The only reason we are making money is because inflation makes our inventories "worth" more and more, and our cash flow is valued at increasingly higher rates. We are not earning money as *retailers*; we are just traders [of our working capital] in the financial market.

Beginning to Think Strategically

Concerned that Tía needed more in-depth understanding of its customers, Narváez hired Monica Kleiman, a leading marketing research consultant in Argentina. Starting in January 1987, she began systematic interviews of Tía customers in Buenos Aires.

Narváez arranged for Kleiman to present her results to a meeting of 30 employees from the operations and commercial departments. She told them that in the last decade, Tía had developed a reputation for lack of service, quality, and value. Kleiman noted that many Tía customers felt that its only positive attribute was its low-priced products. She relayed what one customer had told her; "When I come out of a Tía store, I hide my Tía shopping bag because I don't want any of my friends to see it." Tía was still popular for special event occasions such as back-to-school and Christmas. Kleiman asked for questions at the end of her presentation and was confronted with silence. After she left the room, debate erupted. "Where did she do the interviews?" one store manager demanded. "She might know about the retail industry," shouted another, "but she doesn't know about Tía, and we're different." Narváez ended the meeting with a question: "Will Tía survive to the year 2000 if we continue to do business as we are doing it now?" Later that evening Narváez said to Deutsch:

> If I were to do the presentation again, I would have found out the results beforehand and prepared questions to help facilitate a discussion. Even I found it hard to believe that the customers were saying such bad things about us. I think everyone was frustrated because Monica [Kleiman] did not offer us solutions to the problems she presented.

Narváez realized that he needed to know more about the concepts that Kleiman had introduced to him, such as market, positioning, and image. The two agreed to meet weekly for several months, and Narváez began to understand Tía's market and competition. He decided to commission Kleiman to research Tía's reputation outside of Buenos Aires, in what Argentines called "the interior."

During one of their sessions Kleiman asked about Tía's organizational chart. Narváez looked at her blankly. After Kleiman explained what she meant by an organizational chart, Narváez attempted to draw one. As Kleiman recounted:

> He needed to tape together several pieces of paper so he could draw a complex chart. There were lines crossing in all different directions. According to the chart, everyone had more than one boss and none of the positions had a clear definition of their responsibilities. There was some kind of circular thing going on.

After his attempt to draw an organizational chart, Narváez requested an "internal assessment" of Tía.

The Interior and Internal Culture Studies

When Kleiman was ready to report her results in March 1988, Narváez decided that Kleiman should first present only to Deutsch, Steuer, and Carlos de Narváez and himself. Regarding Tía's reputation in the interior, Kleiman had good news to report: customers were incredibly loyal to Tía and depended on the stores for the majority of their goods. Many customers in a small town in northern Argentina had testified that during the worse days of hyperinflation, only Tía had continued to sell milk and flour. But in the four largest cities (besides Buenos Aires), Cordoba, Rosario, Mar del Plata and Mendoza, customer attitudes mirrored those of their counterparts in Buenos Aires.

Kleiman concluded by holding up a chart (see Figure C9-3), noting:

> Market diagnosis shows that where the markets are more competitive and the customers are more sophisticated, Tía sells less and doesn't make a profit. On the other hand, 62% of your profit comes from the interior of the country. The projection of this chart into the future indicates that, by the end of the century, Tía will be pushed into small towns in the remote areas of the country. The store will do well there, but only until the competition arrives, and then it will be out.

Then Kleiman turned to the internal assessment:

> Tía's internal culture sustains much tension and quarrels due to the confrontation between the departments. Departments have no clear assignment of responsibilities and positions. As a result people are continually fighting for power. The managing committee does not help the situation. They are accused of making high-handed and anarchic decisions. Mid-level employees are extremely frustrated since they feel their proposals are not heard. They feel their personal development is limited because top positions are occupied for life. In Tía's job hierarchy, the lower the level, the higher the tension and frustration. This situation is a time bomb.

Figure C9-3   Revenue and Profit Distribution by Region, 1988

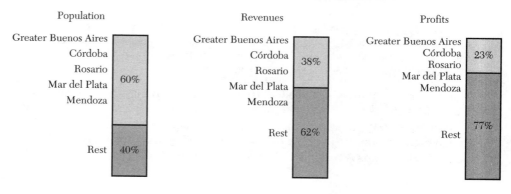

"What can be done?" exclaimed Steuer. Kleiman suggested implementing a formal organizational structure with distinct departments, positions, and responsibilities. She also advised that a strategic commercial planning group and a human resource department be established immediately. At the end of the emotionally draining meeting, Narváez proposed that only the results of the interior study be presented to the rest of the top management team, since the internal culture findings were much too sensitive.

Internal Tensions

Over the next weeks, Deutsch, Steuer, Carlos de Narváez, and Narváez held long discussions about Kleiman's recommendations. Steuer and Deutsch, who travelled extensively in Europe and the United States, were aware that Tía was "out of fashion." Carlos de Narváez was sympathetic to much of what Kleiman presented because of his involvement with new site construction. He had come to believe that the Tía stores should reflect a more contemporary image.

At one meeting Steuer said, "We'll agree to a business strategy change but we don't want any management changes." And, Deutsch informed Narváez, "We trust you and Carlos with these changes. We hope both of you can improve Tía's image and performance." Deutsch and Steuer thought that the brothers might make the perfect team: Carlos de Narváez was the "creative" one, while Narváez was the "fixer." Yet, Narváez began to feel that he and Carlos de Narváez did not share the same management style or philosophy—that the two were sending mixed messages to the staff. Whenever Narváez would make a policy decision, other managers would approach his brother saying, "What is he doing? He's crazy. He's going to change things for the worse."

As the divide between the brothers widened, Narváez finally confronted Deutsch and Steuer in September, 1988:

> There needs to be one person willing to take responsibility for all of the decisions—both the right ones and the wrong ones. Maybe we should hire someone from the outside to run the company. Tía needs to change and if it doesn't change then I don't want to be part of it.

Neither Deutsch nor Steuer would hear of an outsider running Tía, although Deutsch was willing to designate Narváez as Tía's primary manager. Steuer, however, felt uncomfortable choosing between her two sons. With a pained expression, she remembered her untenable position:

> I really felt that I had to make a difference between my sentiment and my head. There are two 'families' that come up in my life all the time, the business and the family. After all I must choose the company, because if anything is wrong with the company it will be critical for my family.

Steuer proposed a compromise: Carlos de Narváez could be in charge of opening new Tía stores plus assume responsibility for constructing and managing Paseo Alcorta, a 100,000 square meter luxury mall in Buenos Aires, in which the family had a majority of the control. Meanwhile Narváez would manage more of the details concerning Tía.

Accepting this compromise and knowing his mother was "trying to be good to both of us and to satisfy each of us," Narváez changed the organization chart. Carlos de Narváez's new role was to "help implement Francisco's decisions." In a matter of months, this arrangement failed, and Narváez asked his brother to leave Tía. He refused. Narváez then "picked up the telephone and called a truck company. Half an hour later, Carlos' desk was carried onto the truck and I let him go. Period."

FRANCISCO DE NARVÁEZ'S
FIRST YEAR AS GENERAL MANAGER

Upon becoming Tía's general manager in 1989, Narváez set out to achieve two key objectives: make Tía market driven and professionally managed. The idea of being market driven was appealing. Steuer commented:

> We had to prepare ourselves for world class competition. I think I frustrated them [Tía management] sometimes because I had been sending articles about Wal-Mart and giving them samples of products we could import. They would tell me that I was trying to introduce products Argentina wasn't ready for yet. But the founders had wanted a company with the spirit of growth. Just like his grandfather. Narváez had a vision of the future that included growth and globalization; he loves greatness.

"When Francisco became general manager I wanted Tía to become one of the leaders in retailing not simply in Argentina, but also in Latin America," Deutsch elaborated. "We were already located in Uruguay and Ecuador and have always had our sights on Brazil."

Having Tía be professionally managed was more controversial. "Professional management implied a terrible break from the family tradition," Steuer said. "What will our grandchildren do if they can't work at Tía?" Narváez responded: "Whoever is capable of working at Tía will have the same chances as anyone else from the outside." He himself had resigned his hereditary rights as a minority shareholder (owner) of the company. Moreover, he began calling his mother and Deutsch "the shareholders" in professional settings.

The Perils of Change

Problems persisted despite the supportive tone of the discussions between the "general manager" and "shareholders." Narváez summed up his first year:

> I had 22 people reporting to me and was spending 16-18 hours in the office trying to talk to everyone and get decisions made. Hyperinflation was making the economy crazy—it was sometimes 200%. We would make a major decision in the morning and then have to reconsider in the afternoon. The economic situation made it impossible for me to think about our long-term objectives. I was consumed with our day-to-day activities. I was lonely, often deeply confused and depressed.

To help him deal with the overload of information and decisions that needed to be made, he formed the ComiTía (a pun on the word *comite*, the name for the head committee of Argentine political parties), which was comprised of the directors of all the departments—including two members of the former Tía executive committee—and Narváez. The ComiTía was to meet weekly and each director was to provide a report on the progress of his department. Narváez said he hoped the team "would understand the whole business and take responsibility for sharing the opportunities and risks of running Tía."

Narváez asked people in the head office to undertake numerous studies, from why checkout lines were so long to how employees were evaluated and promoted. One employee recalled, Narváez "gave us permission to ask questions, but no answers were provided." Narváez hit a wall of resistance: "I would make suggestions about how to improve Tía and watch them write my ideas down, but it never amounted to anything."

Narváez tried to introduce the practice of sharing store level profit and loss statements with employees, only to discover that the relevant financials were imprecise. He instituted an assessment process to evaluate the commercial department's buying decisions because, "It was ridiculous. We had managers in the north complaining about getting swim suits, and it never drops below 60-70° up there. We had managers in the south complaining about getting swim suits, and it never goes above 0° down there." They spent hours debating the merits of whether to buy more sewing kits than pencils for the stores.

Meanwhile, Narváez had thought carefully about Kleiman's recommendations to create commercial planning and human resources departments, and ultimately decided to hire new people to establish them. To some potential new recruits, Tía was an undesirable place to work. Narváez realized, "I could only offer them a promise of the future, a fantasy of how I wanted to change things. I would say, 'Join us and you might come out with something.'" Many turned him down.

The New Hires

One person enticed by Narváez's dream was 28-year-old Marcelo López, hired to start the commercial planning department. López had previously been a product manager at Molinos, the largest food company in Argentina. He spent much of his time in the fall of 1989 reading and analyzing Kleiman's reports to understand Tía's competitive position and alternatives in the market.

The newly created human resource department's director was another new hire who "spoke about managing by objectives" Narváez recalled. "I had never heard that phrase." Based on the new director's suggestion, Sandra Barragat was hired as his assistant. She was responsible for developing an aggressive schedule of training programs for all employees.

For the operations department, Narváez hired a senior manager from Unilever. He was unofficially put in charge of the department. The previous head retained his title but lost his authority. Assisting the man from Unilever, as an "advisor," was 34-year-old Guillermo Bustos, whom Narváez had hired away from Carrefour, a French hypermarket chain that had been in Argentina since 1980. Bustos, who had worked for Carrefour for five years and had become one of the first Argentines named a manager, brought with him a thorough understanding of retail strategies, competitive issues and product assortment. Bustos was particularly knowledgeable about engendering cooperation between operations and commercial departments—one of Carrefour's strengths. Bustos explained that at Carrefour he was responsible for the textile department as a "business unit," which meant managing human resources, buying, and setting the margins. During his interview with Narváez, Bustos mentioned that he had begun his career working in *his* father's business. Narváez also hired 27-year-old Alejandro Ocampo from Carrefour. His task was to work with a consultant from Arthur Andersen and create a basic management information system from which store level profit and loss statements could be generated.

Narváez was pleased with the performance of his new hires. "He had given us permission to commit transgressions against the culture if necessary," remarked Barragat, "and we did." Bustos, for example, had initiated a study of the relationship between one Tía store and its supply warehouse, and based on this analysis Narváez revamped Tía's operations department to improve logistics and encourage more initiative at the store level. At the same time, Narváez observed that, while his other new hires interacted extensively with the Tía staff, López, the commercial planning director, remained a mystery. As one staffer noted, "He is a strange animal. All he does is sit in an office and read notes. He only meets with the top guys of the company, and he is not responsible for anything."

Losing Tía's Core

Narváez noticed a festering tension between the long-standing Tía employees and the new hires. This divide was particularly noticeable during his newly established weekly meetings for top management, designed to encourage discussion about what "change" meant for Tía. As Narváez commented, the "old timers seemed to feel that the status quo was good enough, especially since Tía was doing remarkably well due to the 200% inflation and interest costs running between 40-60% a day."

One manager described the "subtle boycotting" that began to occur. "The older employees' grapevine passed around rumors that the new hires were crazy. People were shocked with what they were doing and they were critical of the salaries they were being paid." Around this time, López mentioned to Narváez that there was grumbling in the top ranks about "vision" and "strategy." "The old guard think they know enough. They say, 'We are the champions, Tía is the best.' They think Kleiman's assessment is a lie," López said. And that, López claimed, made it very hard to work at Tía—yet very interesting. He concluded, "They seem to be slowing down the process of change."

Narváez understood López' sentiments. After a year of watching the friction mount between the "old" and the "new" guard, Narváez became exasperated:

> Tía would never get anywhere with these people. Sometimes I thought they were just playing with me, since I was so much younger. They had been my teachers and mentors. They knew so much about the business, and I think they looked at me and thought, 'We'll let him go and try it his way, but he'll return to our method soon.' I suddenly realized that my combination of old and new people was never going to work. I was just losing time. So one day in mid November [1990], I fired 29 [of the 30] people who had key positions in the company. Many were from the operations department.

Narváez's action was shocking. As Barragat explained:

> The original Czech people were the untouchables. Who would dare touch them if they were hired by the founders of the company? There is a cruel irony in the way life turns out. Many of the people fired had taught Francisco about the company from the time he was young. And it was Francisco who asked them to leave.

On the Monday after the firing, Narváez met Steuer and Deutsch, whom he had not spoken to since the firings but who had received many irate phone calls in the meantime. When they asked Narváez about the situation, he stated, "There is no way around it. We were going to die trying to change the thing—to make it happen if they remained." Since Deutsch and Steuer subscribed to a philosophy of change and progress, they were understanding of Narváez's actions. As Steuer noted, "I'm very much avant-garde about this—I don't try to keep back or cry, I always want to go on." Deutsch assured Narváez of their support and explained that he saw himself as "serving in an advisory role."

Christmas 1990

With a virtually nonexistent top staff and the Christmas season nearing, Narváez was forced to focus on the short term. He began by making the director of the operations department the director of the commercial department. Then he restructured the operations department: five regions were created to replace what previously had been 11 regions, each with four stores (see Figures C9-4 and C9-5 for organizational charts). Bustos became the regional manager for Buenos Aires with its 13 stores; Narváez with Ocampo as assistant temporarily became the manager for the north and south regions with eight stores each. Two regional managers were yet to

Figure C9-4 Organizational Chart of the Senior Management Team, 1990

Figure C9-5 Organizational Chart of the Commercial and Operations Department, 1990

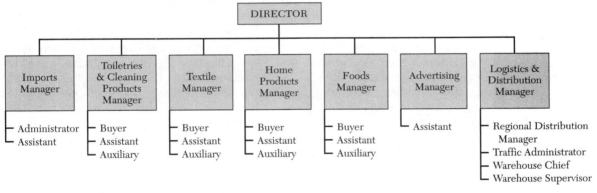

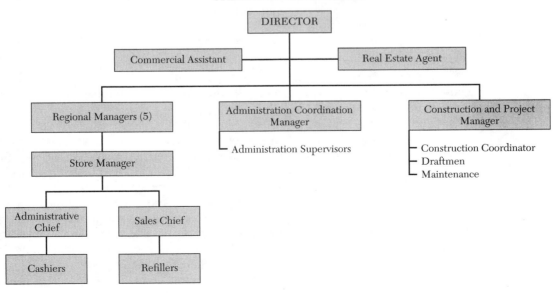

be assigned. "It was an incredible challenge!" commented Bustos. "All of us came from different places, and we brought with us the work style of our previous employers. It was difficult having one cohesive working group, but somehow we managed during the Christmas season." Indeed, Narváez could hardly believe the results—Tía had actually succeeded and it made a profit:

> For the first time, I really got the feeling that I could challenge people—in areas where they did not have the slightest experience. But if they used common sense, they could make it happen. I also came to believe in the virtues of hands-on learning! Basically I had to provide my employees with a clear goal and political support along with the authority, resources, and responsibilities. And then I had to tell them *go*.

As a close friend of Narváez observed, "He empowers people, but he is a ruthless evaluator at the same time."

The Second Round of Firing

Coming down from the Christmas high, Narváez still felt that his drive for change was being slowed; and thus, he began to examine the role of employees lower in the organization. Bustos and his colleagues had been running an experiment in a store in the northern town of Resistencia for six months. According to Bustos, their objective was to create a customer-focused company by changing the "mentality of the store managers to think like business owners." They had found 114 different job titles in a store that had only 120 employees. As one manager lamented; "There were 20 different ways to do the same things. Our efforts to restructure the store and create a prototype for change were thwarted at every turn. Even with all the authority, they [the store management] couldn't seem to make things happen." One of the regional managers was not surprised by their failure: "The store manager's job had become a cardboard job. Their responsibility was to keep the stores stocked, and that was about it. All the other decisions were made centrally." Narváez was determined, but resistance to change still thrived—and so over the course of the next few months he fired an additional 200 people, recalling:

> Many people I fired had 25 years of experience. Collectively it was 5000 years of Tía experience that I got rid of. In a certain moment, the company lost its culture. Everything. The good and the bad. I fired everyone from cashiers to assistant store managers—people who had in the past effectively run the company. And now if they did not agree with a certain decision, they would not do it. It was a hard decision to make, and I still live with it every day. It's nonsense to think about it in a just way. There's no justice.

Narváez personally informed the majority of people that they were fired, because he found many of the managers were "unwilling or incapable of handling what some referred to as these 'killing' sessions."

When Narváez met again with the shareholders, Deutsch said, "If you say that certain people have to leave, then I agree with you. Whatever is good for the company is good for me. I'm not all that sentimental." Steuer, though supportive, spoke more personally about the effect of the firings: "I did not like walking down the corridors of Tía headquarters seeing so many unfamiliar faces. I felt strange walking through the offices. I think it is very important to know the Tía people. I care for them. It took me a while to get used to it." Reflecting on this period, Narváez was moved by the shareholders' support: "I wanted to keep their [the shareholders'] confidence and the power they had let me have. I tried to protect them. I made decisions that went over my authority, but they asked no questions."

After collective soul-searching and discussion, some of the new hires also left the company. Narváez said, "They were the kind of people who have to go by the book. If the book is not written, then they tread water." Narváez decided to promote Barragat to the position of director of human resources, and he himself temporarily assumed the position of commercial director. On the recommendation of Bustos, Narváez hired Marcelo Nalda, also from Carrefour, in February. Nalda was hired to become the manager of the Buenos Aires region with its 13 stores. Ocampo was promoted to regional manager of the northeast region, with its 13 stores.

The Dinosaurs

In February 1991, Narváez met with Barragat to discuss a project he had been contemplating. He wanted to "send a message" to the Tía staff: "The staff should know that we are inviting everyone to participate in the changing of Tía. This is not an exclusive club." Barragat agreed with Narváez's initiative. She was encountering difficulty getting even the "Chicago boys"[4] to embrace the new initiatives for more investment and training in their people.

Barragat pondered whether she should "divide Francisco's message of change into smaller increments or to give it to the staff all at once." After consulting with her colleagues, she chose the latter and decided that a film would be the best medium. Three weeks later, everyone working in the head office gathered at a nearby movie theater. Barragat had also distributed copies of the film to Tía store managers throughout the country to view with their employees. The mood was festive as the film began. Most of the employees assumed they were about to preview Tía's new TV campaign, about which there was much anticipation.

The film began with dinosaurs roaming the screen as the narrator described their colossal size and how they existed so long without enemies, then intoned: "The world's condition changed and the dinosaurs died. Their end was swift and painful." Images of modern technology now flashed and the narrator continued: "If we don't open the window and look out at our customers, Tía will have the same fate." Then the film showed Narváez, sitting at his office desk, who stated, "Everyone should move onward and forward. Challenge one another with your ideas to make Tía a better place." The movie ended with clips from Tía's TV campaign, with its uplifting music and images. As people left the theater, Barragat and some assistants passed out "Tía is a part of me" buttons, the slogan of their new campaign.

While Barragat distributed the buttons, she heard snatches of conversation. One person said, "I feel like my job is in jeopardy. If this company is going to change so much, will I still be with it?" Other conversations focused on "how Tía could change itself." Still other people seemed resistant: "Wasn't that just a bit too dramatic? I don't think Tía is in such bad shape."

THE REPOSITIONING COMMENCES

Shortly thereafter, Narváez met with López, Bustos, Ocampo and Nalda who had been meeting regularly to hammer out a change strategy. Although thoroughly familiar with Kleiman's studies and projections, they were having difficulty developing plans to address Tía's shortcomings. They seemed trapped by the format of Tía's current stores. As one manager put it, "We were stuck in the middle of nowhere." Recalled López, "We seemed to be changing the location of cashiers, furniture and the colors. We always returned to the same basic layout, the same merchandise. We were going round and round." The solution, the group decided, was "outside help, a consultant, someone who could offer us perspective," as Bustos put it. This seemed particularly critical since Wal-Mart and Toys R Us were rumored to be considering a move to Argentina.

Outside Help

In March 1991, Narváez and López flew to New York to meet with William Sands, president of Factors, a retail strategy consulting firm based in Columbus, Ohio. The Tía team outlined their situation to Sands. By June, Sands had visited Buenos Aires several times. Working with a translator, he became well versed in the Kleiman material and learned about Tía's most important competitors (two Argentine supermarket chains that offered general merchandise, albeit in limited assortment). Sands concluded Tía had a business problem, not a layout problem. Convinced, Narváez proclaimed that "Tía was dead" and Sands was given a mandate to develop a plan to address Kleiman's findings—what came to be called "the repositioning."

Narváez knew that he had to assign an internal point person for coordinating the repositioning project, and the most probable candidate was López. Narváez hesitated: "While Marcelo [López] understands conceptually what we are trying to do, he has never operated a store. On the other hand, I can choose someone who knows a lot about running stores and infuse him with the concept." In response, Bustos noted that they could not afford to lose the concept itself and that López could do a quick study of operations. Thus, Narváez selected López, telling him, "You've created the plans on paper. It is time to build this vision in real terms. You will report directly to me."

Reactions of the Operations and Commercial Departments

Sands and López proposed a two-pronged strategy. One would be the "demand strategy" for the interior; the other would be the "convenience strategy" for the five primary urban centers (see Table C9-1 for Tía's strategy and Table C9-2 for profile

Table C9-1   Tía Strategy

	Convenience Strategy	*Demand Strategy*
LOCATION	Neighborhood commercial area Transfer center Pedestrian area—no transport Area of influence: 3 to 5 blocks	Only commercial center Pedestrian area Area of influence: whole town or city
ASSORTMENT	Reliable supplier, but not integral Target: the family Limited assortment Development of top brands	Reliable and integral supplier Target: the family Large and spacious
PRICE	Optimum relationship cost– benefit = value	The best price (area of influence)
ENVIRONMENT AND DISPLAY	The product/merchandise define and direct the concept and have priority over elements used for the display. Introduction rigorously follows the consumers' sequence of selection	
SERVICE	High standard of service (speed)	Adequate level of service
COMMUNICATION	According to defined positioning: Tía resolves all daily needs with quality, at the most convenient price and with an efficient level of service	

Table C9-2   Profile of Typical Tía Customers

Convenience Strategy: Customer Profile	Demand Strategy: Customer Profile
Rosie	**Rosita**
25/40 years old	25/50 years old
Married with children	Married with children
Completed high school	Maybe finished high school
Works outside her home	More time available
Little time available	Slower pace of life, but better quality
Limited income	Limited income
Interested in brands	Social life (neighbors)
Expectations of a better living standard	Does not accumulate things
Poor image of Tia	Has less available/has less to choose from Appreciates the value Tia offers and is comfortable with it

of typical customers.) In July, the two met with Narváez, proposing they hold a meeting with the commercial department to obtain data on its buying policy. López added that operations people should be invited since the work of the two departments was so intertwined. Narváez consented to the meeting although he would be out of town. Upon his return he received a description of the meeting from Sands:

> The meeting was a disaster. We went in hoping to hear what the buyers thought about their products, how competitive they were and what their new ideas were. The commercial side maintained there was no problem with their buying program. They said everything was "perfect." It's clear that over the years they have developed strong relationships with their suppliers and are comfortable maintaining the status quo.
>
> When the operations people heard this, they became enraged and accused the buyers of being oblivious to the customers' needs. The operations guys have always known that there are big problems with products, assortment and replenishment since they are in the stores. They pointed out that of course the commercial side does not have any problems with the merchandise since they aren't in the stores.

After hearing this, Narváez remained silent for a few minutes and then told López and Sands, "We're taking it down too low. These people can't fly with our vision. They are not the players—they are the troops. They do what they are told." Reflecting on the experience, Sands offered another reason why the commercial department was resistant: "They seemed to think that Marcelo [López] and I had flown in from somewhere, that we had put together a strategy and we would bang it around for a little while before we disappeared."

Defining New Objectives

In October, 1991, López and Sands made a presentation to the ComiTía. They began by reviewing some of the principles that Kleiman and Narváez had already proposed:

- Tía's market should be segmented into: the developing market, the interior, and the developed market, urban centers.

- The operations department must become the heart of the company. The role of the head office should become servicing and facilitating store management. A thorough review of all organizational structures, processes, and policies should be made to ensure that store managers focus first and foremost on target customers.

- All employees should be trained to be team and customer service oriented. Store personnel's merchandising and inventory management skills should be upgraded.

Then they began to elaborate on and provide more details about implementation:

- Tía should become the reliable supplier of daily use personal and household goods of good quality, affordable price and with an efficient level of service.

- Stores in Argentina's interior should be transformed into hyperstores, whereas those in the cities should become convenience stores.

- The assortment of merchandise in both markets should have to be widened and deepened and cover four main categories or "worlds": Body, Home, Spirit, and Food (see Figure C9-6).

Figure C9-6 Sand's Proposed Product Categories

The Four Worlds

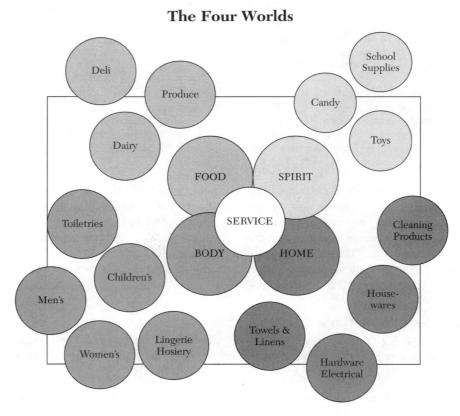

Then, Sands and López presented drawings depicting the proposed layouts of the stores. The traditional island format would be changed to aisles organized around each of the four "worlds," and the cashiers would move to the front of the stores. As the presentation came to an end, everyone except Narváez broke into debate. "Willy [Bustos] and some of the operations guys got it like that," one participant at the meeting observed, snapping his fingers. "Willy, who is usually more reserved and thoughtful, was electric, far ahead of the pack in the vision." López was nervous about the discussion: "I had warned Bill [Sands] not to talk about details. Everybody was so involved in the details. For example, they argued about how big the shopping carts should be. They talked about colors and textures for the interior of the store. It was chaos."

Suddenly, Narváez pushed his chair back from the table and left the room without a word; the others fell silent. "Didn't he approve of the presentation?" Sands asked. López responded, "I don't know, but if he isn't able to see these concepts then there is no way it will work. You have to talk about dreams with Francisco. He needs to fly." Thirty minutes later, Narváez returned, sat down, and looked at the strained faces around the table. When asked where he had gone, Narváez smiled wryly and told them that he had slipped into the store below the headquarters and had paced back and forth between the islands, observing the random merchandise and long lines of people. "As I walked around," he recalled, "I tried to implement Bill [Sand]'s suggestions in my imagination. It was the first time I saw the animal. My first reaction was negative—it wasn't exactly what I thought it would look like. Then I imagined the specifics of the new merchandise and layout. We're going to do this!" As one manager recalled, that was the turning point. "When Francisco is in a meeting, it is his meeting and no one else's, even though he tries to share the power and evoke contributions. When he speaks, he must be right."

They decided that the prototype of the convenience style Tía store would open June 29th, 1992 in an existing store on Avenida Santa Fe. The date was chosen because it is customary for Argentine employers to distribute bonuses of up to one month's pay on June 30th. Narváez decided to close the store while the renovations were in progress. "There is symbolic value to closing this store," he told those around the table. "It is the store beneath the headquarters and now it will shut down as we begin to transform Tía's image." The last item of business was to decide when to start transforming the stores of the interior, which would have a different format. They agreed to wait six months before beginning that project. The pressure was on. Despite the continued hyperinflation and its particular benefits to the company, Tía was in fact losing money due to the $10 million it was paying in severance to those who had been fired.

Too Much Change?

The repositioning team of Sands and López, which now regularly reported to the ComiTía, expanded to include Bustos and an architect responsible for design and construction. When the two groups met together, Narváez encouraged debate: "He likes to play ping pong with ideas," noted Bustos; "If a shoot-out begins, I'll play the sheriff," López recalled Narváez saying. One of their toughest decisions concerned who to designate as manager of the new repositioned store. Narváez was adamant that they hire someone from the outside: "Everybody questioned my decision to hire a manager from Carrefour. I did not think we could risk transferring anything from the old culture of Tía—even the good." Narváez's opinion prevailed, although many did not agree. They argued that it was wrong to send a signal that "everybody had to be new." Despite the repositioning team's differences, everyone seemed to get along, even though, Bustos jokingly grimaced, "We were eating breakfast, lunch, and dinner together." The managers began to gain a new respect for Narváez. "When I joined the company, I didn't really think much of Narváez. He was just the son of one of the owners. But then I started to realize how knowledgeable he is. He is daring and capable of making dramatic decisions. And he is capable of recognizing his mistakes."

Yet by January 1992, it became apparent to López, Bustos, and Barragat that Narváez was slowing down the change process, and they confronted him. Bustos reminded Narváez of the recent time when López proposed eliminating some traditional Tía merchandise: "You went crazy when he suggested dropping the little sewing kits!" Long ago, "Rosie," the prototypical metropolitan customer, had sworn off such items. While everyone laughed, the point had been made: Narváez was still drawn to the "old" Tía assortment—and construction, layout, and decoration. Narváez himself had begun to sense that the ComiTía and repositioning team did not like to make decisions without him. When he got involved, however, it would take weeks to decide the smallest issues. López informed him:

> You say you need another week, but then *everyone* needs another week; but if you decide in a day, then *everyone* decides in a day. I feel like I'm part of a family, not a business. You're the father, and whenever you speak, we all shut up, pay attention: we say, together, 'OK, Daddy.'

At the same time, Narváez needed to address another grave concern. The combined investments of the Steuer and Deutsch families were in financial jeopardy. Feeling as if there was no alternative, in March, 1992, Narváez set up a separate office in the Tía headquarters to concentrate his efforts on making sense of the families' portfolio of diverse companies, some of which were grossly underperforming. During the previous two decades, the two families had embarked on a diversification spree and had acquired companies that ran the gambit from a radio station to textile mills. The diversity of their acquisitions was due to Argentina's closed economy, which had made the prospects for developing new retail formats limited.

"He was dealing with Tía 20% of the time and 80% of his time was devoted to the other situation," commented Bustos. Not having Narváez present to make important decisions was making the ComiTía and the repositioning team nervous. Bustos and López decided that due to the situation, it would be beneficial if López reported to Bustos rather than Narváez. Most agreed with Narváez's decision. As one of his peers described, "Willy [Bustos] is very pragmatic. He always takes a straightforward position. He sets fair but demanding standards, and he takes care of people. He works to get the consensus of the other players on important issues."

WHAT'S IN A NAME?

One of the issues to be decided as a part of the repositioning campaign was the name of the new store. The matter was still being discussed just two months before the store opening. The repositioning team considered three options: keeping the name Tía, adding a "descriptor" to Tía, or determining a brand-new name. To explore the possibility of adding a descriptor, they hired a market research firm to create some new names and test them for customer response. "We are looking for a name that conveys the things we are adding to Tía: efficiency, good quality, low-priced items, cleanliness and order," López told the market researchers. The results showed that "Express" was the most popular new name, conveying service and reliability. "Francisco's going to suffer between making an emotional decision and a rational decision," Barragat predicted. López advocated lobbying Narváez with the new name proposal: "We have to be extremist and push a new name, because in the end he will compromise and decide to add a descriptor."

When they spoke to Narváez about it, his visceral reaction was, "It will be called Tía. We can't lose our heritage. As Kleiman found, the name Tía is like Coca-Cola in Argentina." The team encouraged him to think about it. Curious to hear what the other Tía employees had to say about the name change, Narváez walked down the hallways polling everyone he saw. "Though he seemed open-minded in style, I didn't think he was really," declared one manager in the operations department. Adriana Ferro, the manager of publicity, shared her opinion, and pointed out, "The customers need to perceive the change." Someone else suggested: "To give a name to something is to have access to a different concept, and this new Tía is clearly a new concept."

Narváez sought refuge and inspiration in the unopened store that rainy night in April. He knew that the issue of what to name the chain was volatile. Tía was almost the "family" name. As he turned from the darkened windows of the "old/new store," he wondered if this was a decision he could, or should, make. "These days when I attend ComiTía meetings, I can't figure out when to get involved. I feel like I'm losing power, but then I see the value-added everyone in the room brings to the problem. I did not anticipate that change would be so painful. But, I don't know of anything that I could have done differently."

Endnotes

1. According to Jorge Forteza, a consultant with Booz-Allen Argentina, the Tía stores were "nicer than a Woolworth's. They were closer in format to two French chains, Prisunic and Monoprix, shops targeted to the real middle class."

2. Literally translated "Casa Tía" means House of Tía. The Argentines had bestowed this name on the chain of stores connoting their sense that Tía was an institution for which they held affection.

3. Henceforth reference to "Steuer" implies Doris Steuer and "Deutsch" implies Gustavo Deutsch.

4. Many at Tía had begun to refer to the new hires as the "Chicago boys." The term is a reference to the Latin American finance ministers who had trained under Milton Friedman, a free-market economist at the University of Chicago.

Case 10

From Saatchi & Saatchi PLC to Cordiant PLC: Rapid Change at a Global Advertising Agency

Barry Allen Gold

The headline of *Barron's* (August 8, 1994) read:

Getting It Together
After briefly reigning as the world's largest ad agency, Saatchi & Saatchi flamed out. Now it's winning big accounts again—and making profits.

THE FOUNDING OF SAATCHI AND SAATCHI

Saatchi & Saatchi PLC was founded in 1970 by Maurice and Charles Saatchi.[1] The brothers were in their mid-twenties; Maurice had recently earned a degree in sociology from the London School of Economics, and Charles had been a copywriter in a small advertising agency. In the beginning, Maurice was the administrator and Charles handled the creative side of the business.

From the start, the Saatchis planned to create a large advertising agency. With revenues still meager, they acquired small firms in the early 1970s in France, Holland, and Belgium. Although these acquisitions were not successful, the Saatchis continued to approach other agencies with buyout offers. They also aggressively tried to entice rival agencies' large accounts. This was against the practice of mainstream London firms; but the Saatchis did not join the professional advertising society that enforced this rule.

1975 was an important year for the fledgling agency: Saatchi & Saatchi came to public attention with two advertisement campaigns. The first was a "pregnant man" advertisement for the British Health Education council. The second was a campaign for the Conservative Party that featured the slogan "Labour Is Not Working," which is credited with helping Margaret Thatcher become prime minister.

Copyright © Barry Allen Gold, presented at the Annual Meeting of the North American Case Research Association in Colorado Springs, Colorado, November 1996.

RAPID GROWTH

Also in 1975, in a reverse takeover of Compton Advertising, an American agency, the Saatchis became officers of the fourth ranked ad agency in the United Kingdom. Compton had prestigious international clients like Procter & Gamble and United Biscuits. From this base, the Saatchis continued to absorb British agencies until the end of the decade.

In 1982 Saatchi & Saatchi was the largest advertising agency in Britain. Although it had many multinational accounts, Saatchi had to have European and American agencies assume the responsibilities for those accounts outside the United Kingdom. In the advertising industry, splitting accounts often resulted in the larger firm taking over the entire account.

In an effort to prevent losing multinational accounts, in 1982 Saatchi acquired Compton Advertising. This made it the 13th largest agency in the United States; additional acquisitions followed in Europe and the United States. Before long, Saatchi was recognized as the foremost proponent of global advertising and had won awards for its global advertisements for British Airways. Global advertisements use the same visual and audio material throughout the world; the underlying assumption is that certain products—blue jeans, beer, air travel—are used in the same way in all countries and cultures. As a result, one advertisement fits the globe; customization to local values and preferences is not necessary. Among the benefits of the global approach are cost reductions by producing one commercial instead of many, and the creation of a single, potentially universal theme for the advertiser.

THE GLOBAL AGENCY

In May 1986, Saatchi & Saatchi acquired Ted Bates, the third largest agency in the United States. With billings of almost $7 billion, this made it the largest advertising agency in the world. However, it also created conflict of interest issues: Within its various companies Saatchi now provided services for corporations with competitive products. For example, with the acquisition of Ted Bates they added Colgate-Palmolive and Quaker Oats while in existing units they had Procter & Gamble and General Mills. To avoid conflict of interest, more than $400 million in billings departed; but, within a short time, the group had added more than $450 million in billings. Another problem with the acquisition was that the extremely high price that Saatchi paid for Bates created a negative financial market reaction.

During this time, Saatchi & Saatchi diversified its services by acquiring Hay Consultants for more than $100 million. This altered its business mix to 70% advertising and 30% consulting.

In 1986 Saatchi & Saatchi employed more than 13,000 people worldwide in 150 offices in 57 countries. Advertising billings were about $7 billion, with 65% of revenue coming from the United States, 26% from the United Kingdom, 9% from Europe, and 3% from the rest of the world.

THE COSTS OF RAPID GROWTH

By June 1988 the prospects for Saatchi & Saatchi had changed dramatically.[2] Initiated by an attempt to raise capital that many analysts thought would dilute future earnings, the London financial community raised fundamental questions about Saatchi's business strategy. First, it was claimed that the globalization strategy—to have one advertisement throughout an increasingly homogeneous global marketplace—was simplistic and self-serving. The feasibility of global advertising was questioned by those who thought the Saatchis underemphasized the importance of national differences and viewed local campaigns as more effective. In addition, one analyst pointed out that only 20% of Saatchi's business was global. Second, the diversification plan was attacked on the basis that most major clients, especially multinational corporations, saw little advantage in purchasing multiple services from one vendor because there were limited savings and a possible sacrifice of quality. Finally, the management style of decentralization—every unit operated autonomously with local management responsible for profit and growth—was viewed by some analysts as preventing Saatchi from using the synergy among the units to leverage its position in the industry.

These critical observations accurately identified weaknesses in Saatchi & Saatchi. In addition, costs grew faster than revenues in the advertising division, thus reducing margins. Similarly, the price earnings ratio of the consulting division had fallen significantly and was below its rivals. Finally, in their attempt to respond to their critics, the Saatchis began to examine whether the agencies' structure was appropriate for its strategy.

In addition to these issues being raised by outsiders, in 1988 two key employees left the firm to pursue their own business interests. Investors viewed these departures with alarm because these executives worked well with the Saatchi brothers and contributed to their success.

To improve the situation at Bates, Charles and Maurice merged it with Backer and Spielvogel. The intention was to develop a new strategic direction and inject new creative talent. The results were mixed. The agency won new accounts but never regained the confidence of the financial markets.

A second acquisition created more serious problems. In 1988 Charles and Maurice tried to bid for the Midland Bank, the third largest bank in England. This would have been the largest acquisition for Saatchi & Saatchi: Midland had a market capitalization of $2 billion, whereas Saatchi & Saatchi was capitalized at $1 billion. The rationale for entering the banking industry was that, like advertising, banking was highly fragmented. Deregulation would permit the Saatchis to use technology to globalize it much as they had the advertising business. However, the financial community viewed the difficulties of Midland Bank differently than Charles and Maurice did. Most investors thought the bank's problem was too much Latin American debt, which would not be solved by creating a global bank. The result was that Saatchi & Saatchi's stock dropped sharply and the acquisition did not occur.

After this and another failed acquisition attempt, the strategy shifted to become the leading management services company in the world, evenly divided between consulting and advertising.

SAATCHI & SAATCHI—1988 TO 1994

In 1987 Saatchi & Saatchi's American depository receipts (the equivalent of three shares on the London market) were $343.[3] By August 1994 they had dropped 98% to 7 1/8, the result of giving out shares to debtholders, a 1 to 10 reverse split, a rights offering, and the evaluation of Saatchi's prospects by financial analysts.

The steep drop in stock price was indicative of the management problems at the agency. For example, in addition to excessive debt, Charles and Maurice drew large salaries, and the concept of decentralized management devolved into fiefdoms that contradicted the idea of a global agency. In effect, instead of working together, the various agencies that had been acquired were competitors, resulting in low productivity and high salary costs. The various agencies also lost large accounts such as Jeep and Helene Curtis. In addition, at this time, Charles began withdrawing from the company to devote himself to amassing a world-class art collection.

In 1989 Saatchi hired Robert Louis-Dreyfus, a member of one of France's wealthiest families and a business turnaround specialist, as chief executive officer. Louis-Dreyfus brought along Charles Scott as his right-hand man and financial director. Underperforming or miscellaneous businesses were sold, the agencies were reorganized into networks, and excess staff was fired. During this time, Maurice, who as the chairman was still very active in the business, began what became a bitter feud with Charles Scott.

Although there were some highly successful advertisements during this period, such as the champagne glasses on the Lexus automobile, the creative energies of the agency appeared to be near exhaustion. *Barron's* reported that in March 1994,

> Bill Muirhead parachuted into the New York office of advertising giant Saatchi & Saatchi. His assignment: to help turn the slumbering operation around. "It all seemed so terribly quiet, dull and sleepy," he recalls, speaking in the broad tones of his native Australia. "People were just sitting around in their offices with the doors closed, not talking to each other, not doing anything terribly creative." So Muirhead decided to deliver a Down Under wake-up call. One afternoon that first week, he and a colleague went out into the central atrium of Saatchi's elegant office building on Hudson Street and really "let rip," screaming themselves hoarse for a couple of minutes.
>
> But it didn't work. "No one paid any attention," quips Muirhead. "No one even bothered to come and see what was happening."

Louis-Dreyfus left in early 1993 and was replaced by Charles Scott. The Saatchis thought of both Dreyfus and Scott derisively as "bean counters" who, nevertheless, helped straighten out the business. But this attitude intensified the dispute between Maurice and Scott, which centered on the effect of cost cutting on the profitability of the company. Reflecting his disdain for Scott's management style, Maurice told a reporter from the *London Sunday Times*, "We lost market share, we lost good people and we spent £37 million on severance for nothing."

But, in addition to cutting staff, Scott had also removed Charles and Maurice from their extremely expensive offices to more cost-effective quarters, saving $1.8 million. This and other acts exacerbated the situation; the conflict was between creativity and cost control. Maurice gained allies in the agency world, and Scott was supported by institutional investors. Martin Sorrell, who had been Saatchi's chief financial officer, said "Maurice thought he could do Charlie's job, and Charlie thought he could do Maurice's."

The battle between Maurice Saatchi and Charles Scott continued until institutional stockholders and the board intervened. They pointed out that large accounts were becoming worried by the conflict and that, in general, Saatchi & Saatchi's image was becoming more tarnished. But the board concluded that the departure of either man would harm the company by driving away clients, bankers, and institutional investors.

Eventually, through a series of structural and incentive adjustments (e.g., Maurice's compensation was renegotiated to make it tied to the firm's performance), the conflict was resolved—at least publicly. Also at this time, aggressive shifts in personnel were made to the U.S. market—where Saatchi had been lagging—as well as other restructurings to improve costs and relations with clients.

A feature article about Saatchi & Saatchi in *Barron's* (August 8, 1994), concluded:

At the Saatchi annual meeting in June, Maurice acknowledged that stockholders "must sometimes feel a little like the characters in Beckett's *Waiting for Godot*, who wait for a change in their fortunes. And wait. And wait." Unlike the predicament faced by those characters, however, fortunes at Saatchi are at last changing, and it won't take long for that to be fully apparent, by the ad community and investors as well. This time next year, Muirhead should have plenty to holler about, and perhaps some of his colleagues will be hollering with him.

Profits for the first six months of 1994 showed a marked improvement and investors had renewed interest in the stock. In addition to changing management, Saatchi became more creative and won large accounts, such as the European ads for Compaq computers, Warner-Lambert, Philip Morris's Miller beer, Cunard, Qantas, and the British Lottery.

DECEMBER 1994

The headline of *The New York Times* (December 17, 1994) read:

Chairman Is Deposed At Saatchi
Co-Founder's Fall Ends Years of Rifts: Saatchi's Chairman Is Forced Out by Large Shareholders

Despite improved financial performance, large institutional investors remained uncomfortable Waiting For Godot. In early December 1994 shareholders proposed that Maurice's compensation package should be reviewed and perhaps he should be removed as chairman.

Publicly, there was ambivalence concerning Maurice's role. On one hand, investors—including Harris Associates of Chicago, the State of Wisconsin Investment Board, and large British investors—agreed with the *Barron's* assessment that Saatchi & Saatchi was on the road to recovery. One knowledgeable person claimed that the major shareholders' view was, "We feel the company is so attractive. We would rather try to impact significant changes at the holding company than throw away long-term gains." Shareholders thought that the 5% to 6% operating margins could rapidly improve to 9% to 10%. Some credited Maurice with considerable strengths: He was creative and had political and business connections that were invaluable. On the other hand, his compensation package was exorbitant and unrelated to his performance. To make matters worse, at about this time, Maurice's lavish lifestyle was described in detail in a magazine article. Among other major expenses, he flooded 13 acres of his property to make a lake with three islands.

On December 16, 1994, the board deposed Maurice as chairman of Saatchi & Saatchi. In a display of ambivalence, the board offered him the opportunity to stay as president of the company, a largely honorary position, and as chairman of the Saatchi & Saatchi advertising subsidiary. Some analysts speculated that this was an attempt to placate major clients such as Mars, British Airways, and the Mirror Group Newspapers, who warned in letters to the board that they would consider leaving the agency if Maurice was ousted. For example, John and Forrest Mars, the billionaire brothers who own the Mars company, wrote:

We insist that our advertising agencies have their top people involved in the business. We are pleased that you [Maurice] have been able to do this and if you were not fulfilling that role our business would suffer significantly. We might, and probably would have to transfer our business to your competitors.

Despite this type of close relationship between Maurice and major clients, David Herro of Harris Associates said, "The last impediment to rebuilding this company is gone. This is what needed to happen for the company to enter the next phase in its rebuilding. The company is now in a great position to go forward. Mr. Saatchi's resignation will ensure this company can return to the top of the class."

The removal of Maurice as chairman created speculation that he and Charles might leave the company and form a new agency. Indeed, early in 1995 Charles rejected the offer to stay in a largely honorary role and left the company. Of course, this intensified concern that major Saatchi & Saatchi clients might follow the Saatchis to a new agency.

In early January 1995 three senior Saatchi & Saatchi executives left the agency, claiming that it was no longer run by ad people but by financial types. They also resigned as a protest against the ouster of Maurice. It was also reported that Charles Saatchi, who was a consultant to Saatchi & Saatchi, was about to leave and join his brother in forming a new agency.

On January 11, 1995, Maurice announced that he was forming a new agency—The New Saatchi Agency—with the three other top Saatchi executives who left earlier in the month. This again intensified rumors that major clients were soon to leave Saatchi & Saatchi and that Maurice would actively court them and do everything possible to damage Saatchi & Saatchi.

Investment manager David Herro's reaction to these developments was, "The board made the right decision, Mr. Saatchi violated his fiduciary responsibility. The only thing that shareholders did was voice an opinion."

On January 15, 1995, Charles approached individuals close to the Saatchi & Saatchi board with an unexpected proposition: Maurice would consider returning to run Saatchi & Saatchi Advertising Worldwide. Part of this plan was that in two years Maurice would break Saatchi & Saatchi away and run it as an independent company. Maurice said, "I was approached by one of the largest clients of Saatchi & Saatchi PLC, a client with whom I have had a long, personal relationship. They were profoundly disturbed by recent events. They wanted their team back on their business." The offer of Maurice's return was considered and dismissed after a three-hour unscheduled board meeting.

In an attempt to prevent the Saatchis from starting a new agency, Saatchi & Saatchi sued the brothers, claiming, among other things, that if they took Saatchi & Saatchi clients they would violate the terms of their employment contract. After a few months of preliminary hearings, the lawsuit was dropped because Saatchi & Saatchi determined that it would be expensive and disruptive to their business.

Another effect of the turmoil was that Saatchi & Saatchi's stock price tumbled. Before Charles was ousted, the American depository receipts sold on the New York Stock Exchange for $7.25. On January 10, 1995, they were selling for $5.375.

MARS FLIES SOUTH WITH BRITISH AIRWAYS

In mid-January 1995 Charles Saatchi invited 40 Saatchi & Saatchi employees to his London home and asked them to consider joining his new firm, which would begin operations in May 1995. Many of these employees worked on the British Airways account, which had been placed in review. But Charles Scott was able to convince them to stay at Saatchi & Saatchi, pointing out that there was no guarantee that the New Saatchi agency would win the account. He also guaranteed the employees their salary for at least one year to ensure their remaining with the agency.

On February 20, 1995, Saatchi & Saatchi announced that its holding company would be called Cordiant. The Saatchi & Saatchi name, which had served as the name for both the holding company and the agency, would only be retained for the agency.

After putting its account under review, Mars dismissed Saatchi & Saatchi. The headline in The Wall Street Journal (February 22, 1995) read:

**Mars Deals Saatchi a Mighty Blow
By Pulling $400 Million Account**

Mars was one of the founding clients at Ted Bates Worldwide, and the relationship between Mars and Bates spanned almost 40 years. Bates developed such memorable ads for Mars as the M&M slogan "The milk chocolate melts in your mouth, not in your hand."

Wendy Smyth, the acting chief operating officer of Saatchi & Saatchi in London said, "We didn't actually believe they would've taken all the business away. So be it. We have to get on with life." A few weeks later, British Airways, Mirror Newspaper Group, and other large clients had either left or were putting their accounts in review.

NEW CHALLENGES

In the view of some analysts, the real impact of departures such as Mars and British Airways would be on the ability of the various Cordiant agencies to win new business. Another issue facing Cordiant was the restructuring of its agencies as a result of the departure of major accounts. For instance, some Bates offices had only Mars as a client; these offices had to be either disbanded or assigned new accounts. Yet another issue confronting the company was leadership: Who could reinvigorate the creative side of the firm and regain the confidence of investors?

Charles Scott, Cordiant's CEO and Saatchi's acting chairman, had a lot to do in the coming months.

Endnotes

1. This section draws extensively on Collis, D. (1987), *Saatchi & Saatchi Company PLC*. Cambridge, MA: Harvard University.

2. This section draws extensively on Avis, A. and Ghoshal, S. (1989), *Saatchi and Saatchi Plc*. Fontainebleau, France: INSEAD.

3. Information from this point on is from articles in *Barron's*, *The New York Times*, and *The Wall Street Journal* from 1988 to 1996.

Ellen Moore (A):
Living and Working in Bahrain

Gail Ellement
Martha Maznevski

The General Manager had offered me a choice of two positions in the Operations area. I had considered the matter carefully, and was about to meet with him to tell him I would accept the Accounts Control position. The job was much more challenging than the Customer Services post, but I knew I could learn the systems and procedures quickly and I would have a great opportunity to contribute to the success of the Operations area.

It was November 1989, and Ellen Moore was just completing her second year as an expatriate manager at the offices of a large American financial institution in Manama, Bahrain. After graduating with an MBA from a leading business school, Ellen had joined her husband, who was working as an expatriate manager at an offshore bank in Bahrain. Being highly qualified and capable, she had easily found a demanding position and had worked on increasingly complex projects since she had begun at the company. She was looking forward to the challenges of the Accounts Control position.

ELLEN MOORE

Ellen graduated as the top female from her high school when she was 16, and immediately began working full time for the main branch of one of the largest banks in the country. By the end of four years, she had become a corporate accounts officer and managed over twenty large accounts.

I remember I was always making everything into a game, a challenge. One of my first jobs was filing checks. I started having a competition with the woman at the adjacent desk who had been filing for years, except she didn't know I was competing with her. When she realized it, we both started competing in earnest. Before long, people used to come over just to watch us fly through these stacks of checks. When I moved to the next job, I used to see how fast I could add up columns of numbers while handling phone conversations. I always had to do something to keep myself challenged.

While working full time at the bank, Ellen achieved a Fellowship in the Institute of Bankers after completing demanding courses and exams. She went on to work in banking and insurance with one of her former corporate clients from the bank. When she was subsequently promoted to manage their financial reporting department, she was both the first female and the youngest person the company had ever had in that position.

Since she had begun working full time, Ellen had been taking courses towards a bachelor's degree at night in one of the city's universities. In 1983 she decided to stop working for two years to complete her Bachelor's Degree. After she graduated with a major in accounting and minors in marketing and management, she entered the MBA program.

I decided to go straight into the MBA program for several reasons. First, I wanted to update myself. I had taken my undergraduate courses over ten years and wanted to obtain knowledge on contemporary views. Second, I wanted to tie some pieces together—my night school degree left my ideas somewhat fragmented. Third, I wasn't impressed with the interviews I had after I finished the Bachelor's degree, and fourth I was out of work anyway. Finally, my father had already told everyone that I had my MBA, and I decided I really couldn't disappoint him.

Just after Ellen had begun the two year MBA program, her husband was offered a position with an affiliate of his bank, posted in Bahrain beginning the next spring. They sat down and examined potential opportunities that would be available for Ellen once she completed her MBA. They discovered that women could work and assume positions of responsibility in Bahrain, and decided they could both benefit from the move. Her husband moved to Bahrain in March, while Ellen remained to complete her masters. Ellen followed, with MBA in hand, 18 months later.

BAHRAIN

Bahrain is an archipelago of 33 islands located in the Persian Gulf (see Figure C11-1). The main island, Bahrain, comprises 85% of the almost 700 square kilometers of the country, and is the location of the capital city, Manama. Several of the islands are joined by causeways, and in 1987 the 25 kilometer King Fahad Causeway linked the principal island to the mainland of Saudi Arabia, marking the end of island isolation for the country. In 1971, Bahrain gained full independence from Britain, ending a relationship that had lasted for almost a century. Of the population of over 400,000 people, about one third were foreigners.

Bahrain has had a prosperous history. Historically, it has been sought after by many countries for its lush vegetation, fresh water, and pearls. Many traditional crafts and industries were still practiced, including pottery, basket-making, fabric-weaving, pearl-diving, dhow (fishing boat) building, and fishing. Bahrain was the pearl capital of the world for many centuries. Fortunately, just as the pearl industry collapsed with the advent of cultured pearls from Japan, Bahrain struck its first oil.

Since the 1930's, the oil industry had been the largest contributor to Bahrain's Gross National Product. The country was the first in the Persian Gulf to have an oil industry, established with a discovery in 1932. Production at that time was 9600 barrels a day. Eventually, crude output had reached over 40,000 barrels a day. Bahrain's oil products included crude oil, natural gas, methanol and ammonia, and refined products like gasoline, jet fuels, kerosene, and asphalts.

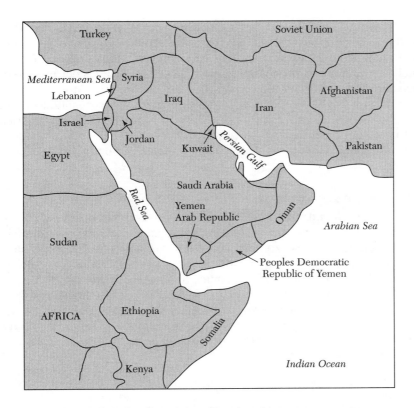

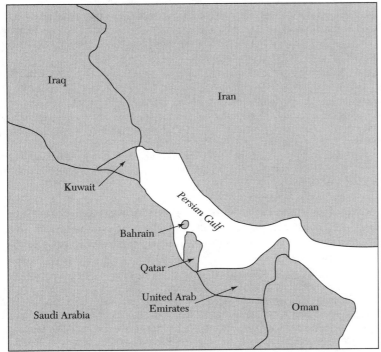

Figure C11-1 Maps of the Middle East

The Bahraini government had been aware for several years that the oil reserves were being seriously depleted. It was determined to diversify the country's economy away from a dependence on one resource. Industries established since 1971 included aluminum processing, shipbuilding, iron and steel processing, and furniture and door manufacturing. Offshore banking began in 1975. Since Bahraini nationals did not have the expertise to develop these industries alone, expatriates from around the world, particularly from Western Europe and North America, were invited to conduct business in Bahrain. By the late 1980s, the country was a major business and financial center, housing many Middle East branch offices of international firms.

Expatriates in Bahrain

Since Bahrain was an attractive base from which to conduct business, it was a temporary home to many expatriates. Housing compounds, schools, services, shopping and leisure activities all catered to many international cultures. Expatriates lived under residence permits, gained only on the basis of recruitment for a specialist position which could not be filled by a qualified and available Bahraini citizen.

To Ellen, one of the most interesting roles of expatriate managers was that of teacher. The Arab nations had been industrialized for little more than two decades, and had suddenly found themselves needing to compete in a global market. Ellen believed that one of her main reasons for working in Bahrain was to train its nationals eventually to take over her job.

> Usually the teaching part was very interesting. When I first arrived in the office, I was amazed to see many staff members with micro computers on their desks, yet they did not know the first thing about operating the equipment. When I inquired about the availability of computer courses, I was informed by a British expatriate manager that 'as these were personal computers, any person should be able to use them, and as such, courses aren't necessary.' It was clear to me that courses were very necessary when the computer knowledge of most employees consisted of little more than knowing where the on/off switch was located on a microcomputer.
>
> Although it was outside of office policy, I held "Ellen's Introduction to Computers" after office hours, just to get people comfortable with the machines and to teach them a few basics.
>
> Sometimes the amount of energy you had to put into the teaching was frustrating in that results were not immediately evident. I often worked jointly with one of the Bahraini managers who really didn't know how to develop projects and prepare reports. Although I wasn't responsible for him, I spent a great deal of time with him, helping him improve his work. Initially there was resistance on his part, because he was not prepared to subordinate himself to an expatriate, let alone a woman. But eventually he came around and we achieved some great results working together.

The range of cultures represented in Bahrain was vast. Expatriate managers interacted not only with Arabic nationals, but also with managers from other parts of the world, and with workers from developing countries who provided a large part of the unskilled labor force.

> The inequality among nationalities was one issue I found very difficult to deal with during my stay in Bahrain. The third world immigrants were considered to be the lowest level possible in the pecking order, just slightly lower than nationals from countries outside the Gulf. Gulf Arabs, being of Bedouin origin, maintained a suspicious attitude towards "citified" Arabs. Europeans and North Americans were regarded much more highly. These inequalities had a major impact on daily life, including the availability of jobs and what relations would develop or not develop between supervisors and subordinates. Although I was well acquainted with the racial problems in North America, I haven't seen anything compared to the situation in Bahrain. It wasn't unusual

for someone to be exploited and discarded, as any expendable and easily replaceable resource would be, because of their nationality.

Although many expatriates and their families spent their time in Bahrain immersed in their own cultural compounds, social groups, and activities, Ellen believed that her interaction with the various cultures was one of the most valuable elements of her international experience.

MANAGING IN BAHRAIN

Several aspects of the Middle Eastern culture had tremendous impact on the way business was managed, even in Western firms located in Bahrain. It seemed to Ellen, for example, that "truth" to a Bahraini employee was subject to an Arab interpretation, which was formed over hundreds of years of cultural evolution. What Western managers considered to be "proof" of an argument or "factual" evidence could be flatly denied by a Bahraini: if something was not believed it did not exist. As well, it seemed that the concept of "time" differed between Middle Eastern and Western cultures. Schedules and deadlines, while sacred to Western managers, commanded little respect from Bahraini employees. The two areas that had the most impact on Ellen's managing in a company in Bahrain were the Islamic religion and the traditional attitude towards women.

Islam

Most Bahrainis are practicing Muslims. According to the Muslim faith, the universe was created by Allah who prescribed a code of life called Islam and the Qur'an is the literal, unchanged World of Allah preserved exactly as transcribed by Muhammad. Muhammad's own acts as a prophet form the basis for Islamic law, and are second in authority only to the Qur'an. The five Pillars of Islam are belief, prayer, fasting, almsgiving and pilgrimage. Muslims pray five times a day. During Ramadan, the ninth month of the Islamic calendar, Muslims must fast from food, drink, smoking and sexual activity from dawn until dusk, in order to master the urges which sustain and procreate life. All Muslims are obliged to give a certain proportion of their wealth in alms for charitable purposes; the Qur'an stresses that the poor have a just claim on the wealth of the prosperous. Finally, if possible, all Muslims should make a pilgrimage to Mecca during their lives, in a spirit of total sacrifice of personal comforts, acquisition of wealth, and other matters of worldly significance.

> Certainly the Muslim religion had a tremendous impact on my daily working life. The first time I walked into the women's washroom at work I noticed a tap about three inches off the floor over a drain. I found this rather puzzling; I wondered if it was for the cleaning crew. When a woman came in, I asked her about the tap, and she explained that before going to the prayer room, everyone had to wash all uncovered parts of their bodies. The tap was for washing their feet and legs.
>
> One time I was looking for one of my employees, Mohammed, who had a report due to me that afternoon. I searched for him at his desk and other likely spots throughout the office, but to no avail, he just wasn't around. I had had difficulties with Mohammed's work before, when he would submit documents long after deadlines, and I was certain he was attempting to slack off once again. I bumped into one of Mohammed's friends, and asked if he knew Mohammed's whereabouts. When he informed me that Mohammed was in the prayer room, I wasn't sure how to respond. I didn't know if this prayer room activity was very personal and if I could ask questions, such as the length of time one generally spends in prayer. But I needed to know how long Mo-

hammed would be away from his desk. Throwing caution to the wind, I asked the employee how long Mohammed was likely to be in prayers and he told me it usually takes about ten minutes. It wasn't that I felt I didn't have the right to know where my employee was or how long he would be away, I just wasn't certain my authority as a manager allowed me the right to ask questions about such a personal activity as praying.

During Ramadan, the hours of business are shortened by law. It is absolutely illegal for any Muslim to work past two o'clock in the afternoon, unless special permits are obtained from the Ministry of Labor. Unfortunately, business coming in to an American firm does not stop at two, and a majority of the non-Muslim workers are required to take up the slack.

Unlike religion in Western civilization, Islam permeates every function of human endeavour. There does not exist a separation of church, state, and judiciary. Indeed, in purist circles, the question does not arise. The hybrid systems existing in certain Arab countries are considered aberrations created by Western colonial influences. Accordingly, to function successfully, the expatriate must understand and learn to accept a very different structuring of a society.

Women in Bahrain

Bahrain tended to be more progressive than many Middle Eastern countries in its attitude towards women. Although traditions were strong, Bahraini women had some freedom. For example, all women could work outside the home, although the hours they could work were restricted both by convention and by the labor laws. They could only work if their husbands, fathers, or brothers permitted them, and could not take potential employment away from men. Work outside the home was to be conducted in addition to, not instead of, duties performed inside the home, such as child-rearing and cooking. Most women who worked held secretarial or clerical positions; very few worked in management.

Bahraini women were permitted to wear a variety of outfits, from the conservative full length black robe with head scarf which covers the head and hair, to below-the-knee skirts and dresses without head covering.

Arabic women who sincerely want change and more decision-making power over their own lives face an almost impossible task, as the male influence is perpetuated not only by men, but also by women who are afraid to alter views they understand and with which they have been brought up all their lives. I once asked a female co-worker the reason why one of the women in the office, who had previously been "uncovered", was now sporting a scarf over her head. The response was that this woman had just been married, and although her husband did not request that she become "covered", she personally did not feel as though she was a married woman without the head scarf. So she simply asked her husband to demand that she wear a scarf on her head. It was a really interesting situation: some of the more liberal Bahraini women were very upset that she had asked her husband to make this demand. They saw it as negating many of the progressive steps the women's movement had made in recent years.

Although Bahrainis had been exposed to Western cultures for the two decades of industrial expansion, they were still uncomfortable with Western notions of gender equality and less traditional roles for women.

One day a taxi driver leaned back against his seat and, while keeping one eye on the road ahead, turned to ask me, "How many sons do you have?" I replied that I didn't have any children. His heartfelt response of "I'm so sorry" and the way he shook his head in sympathy were something my North American upbringing didn't prepare me for. My taxi driver's response typifies the attitude projected towards women, whether they are expatriates from Europe or North America, or are Bahrainis. Women are meant to have children, preferably sons. Although Bahrain is progressive in many ways, attitudes on the role of women in society run long and deep, and it is quite unlikely these sentiments will alter in the near, or even distant, future.

Another time I was greeted with gales of laughter when I revealed to the women in the office that my husband performed most of the culinary chores in our household. They assumed I was telling a joke, and when I insisted that he really did most of the cooking, they sat in silent disbelief. Finally, one woman spoke up and informed the group that she didn't think her husband even knew where the kitchen was in their house, let alone would ever be caught touching a cooking utensil. The group nodded in agreement. Although these women have successful business careers—as clerks, but in the workforce nonetheless—they believe women should perform all household tasks without the assistance of their husbands. The discovery that this belief holds true in Bahrain is not remarkable as I know many North American and European businesswomen who believe the same to be true. What is pertinent is these women allow themselves to be completely dominated by the men in their lives.

The one concept I faced daily but never accepted was that my husband was regarded as the sole decision maker in our household. He and I view our marriage as a partnership in which we participate equally in all decisions. But when the maintenance manager for our housing compound came by, repairs were completed efficiently only if I preceded my request with "my husband wants the following to be completed." It's a phrase I hated to use as it went against every rational thought I possess, but I frequently had to resort to it.

These attitudes also affected how Ellen was treated as a manager by Bahraini managers:

One manager, I'll call him Fahad, believed that women were only capable of fulfilling secretarial and coffee serving functions. One day I was sitting at my desk, concentrating on some documents. I didn't notice Fahad having a discussion with another male manager nearby. When I looked up from my papers, Fahad noticed me and immediately began talking in French to the other manager. Although my French was a bit rusty, my comprehension was still quite serviceable. I waited for a few moments and then broke into their discussion in French. Fahad was completely dismayed. Over the next few years, Fahad and I worked together on several projects. At first, he was pompous and wouldn't listen to anything I presented. It was a difficult situation, but I was determined to remain above his negative comments. I ignored his obvious prejudice towards me, remained outwardly calm when he disregarded my ideas, and proceeded to prove myself with my work. It took a lot of effort and patience but, in time, Fahad and I not only worked out our differences, but worked as a successful team on a number of major projects. Although this situation had a happy ending, I really would have preferred to have directed all that energy and effort towards more productive issues.

Bahraini nationals were not the only ones who perpetuated the traditional roles of women in society. Many of the expatriates, particularly those from Commonwealth countries, tended to view their roles as "the colonial charged with the responsibility to look after the developing country." This was reflected in an official publication for new expatriates that stated: "Wives of overseas employees are normally sponsored by their husbands' employers, and their Residence Permits are processed at the same time. . . ." However, wives were not permitted to work unless they could obtain a work permit for themselves.

The first question I was often asked at business receptions was "What company is your husband with?" When I replied that I worked as well, I received the glazed over look as they assumed I occupied myself with coffee mornings, beach, tennis and other leisure activities as did the majority of expatriate wives.

Social gatherings were always risky. At typical business and social receptions the men served themselves first, after which the women selected their food. Then women and men positioned themselves on opposite sides of the room. The women discussed "feminine" topics, such as babies and recipes, while the men discussed the fall (or rise) of the dollar and the big deal of the day. At one Bahraini business gathering, I hesitated in choosing sides: should I conform and remain with the women? But most of these women did not work outside their homes, and, consequently, they spoke and understood very little English. I joined the men. Contrary to what I expected, I was given a gracious welcome.

However, on another occasion I was bored with the female conversation, so I ventured over to the forbidden male side to join a group of bankers discussing correspondent banking courses. When I entered the discussion, a British bank general manager turned his nose up at me. He motioned towards the other side of the room, and told me I should join the women. He implied that their discussion was obviously over my head. I quickly informed him that although I personally had found the banking courses difficult to complete while holding a full time banking position, I not only managed to complete the program and obtain my Fellowship, but at the time was the youngest employee of my bank ever to be awarded the diploma. The man did a quick turnabout, was thoroughly embarrassed, and apologized profusely. Although it was nice to turn the tables on the man, I was more than a little frustrated with the feeling that I almost had to wear my resume on my sleeve to get any form of respect from the men, whether European, North American, or Arab.

A small percentage of Bahraini women had completed university degrees in North America and Europe. While residing in these Western cultures, they were permitted to function as did their Western counterparts. For example, they could visit or phone friends when they wished without first obtaining permission. After completing their education, many of these women were qualified for management positions; however, upon returning to Bahrain they were required to resume their traditional female roles.

The notion of pink MBA diplomas for women and blue for men is very real. Although any MBA graduate in North America, male or female, is generally considered to have attained a certain level of business sense, I had to constantly "prove" myself to some individuals who appeared to believe that women attended a special segregated section of the university with appropriately tailored courses.

Ellen discovered that, despite being a woman, she was accepted by Bahrainis as a manager as a result of her Western nationality, her education, and her management position in the company.

Many of my male Arabic peers accepted me as they would any expatriate manager. For example, when a male employee returned from a holiday, he would typically visit each department, calling upon the other male employees with a greeting and a handshake. Although he might greet a female co-worker, he would never shake her hand. However, because of my management position in the company and my status as a Western expatriate, male staff members gave me the same enthusiastic greeting and handshake normally reserved for their male counterparts.

Ellen also found herself facilitating Bahraini women's positions in the workplace.

As I was the only female in a senior management position in our office, I was often asked by the female employees to speak to their male superiors about problems and issues they experienced in their departments. I also had to provide a role model for the women because there were no female Bahraini managers. Some of them came to me not just to discuss career issues but to discuss life issues. There was just no one else in a similar position for them to talk to. On the other hand, male managers would ask me to discuss sensitive issues, such as hygiene, with their female staff members.

The government of Bahrain introduced legislation that restricted the amount of overtime hours women could work. Although the move was being praised by the (female) Director of Social Development as recognition of the contribution women were making to Bahraini industry, Ellen saw it as further discriminatory treatment restricting the choices of women in Bahrain. Her published letter to the editor of the *Gulf Daily News* read:

. . .How the discriminatory treatment of women in this regulation can be seen as recognition of the immense contribution women make to the Bahrain workforce is beyond comprehension. Discrimination of any portion of the population in the labor legislation does not recognize anything but the obvious prejudice. If the working women in Bahrain want to receive acknowledgement of their indispensable impact on the Bahrain economy, it should be through an increase in the number of management positions available to qualified women, not through regulations limiting the hours they work. All this regulation means is that women are still regarded as second class citizens who need the strong arm tactics of the government to help them settle disputes over working hours. Government officials could really show appreciation to the working women in Bahrain by making sure that companies hire and promote based on skill rather than gender. But there is little likelihood of that occurring.

The letter was signed with a pseudonym, but the day it was published one of Ellen's female employees showed her the letter and claimed "if I didn't know better, Ellen, I'd think you wrote this letter."

CAREER DECISIONS

When Ellen first arrived in Bahrain, she had great expectations that she would work somewhere where she could make a difference. She received several offers for positions and turned down, among others, a university and a high profile brokerage house. She decided to take a position as a Special Projects Coordinator at a large American financial institution.

> In fact, the records will show I was actually hired as a "Financial Analyst", but this title was given solely because at that time, the government had decided that expatriate women shouldn't be allowed to take potential positions away from Bahrain nationals. The expertise required as a Financial Analyst enabled the company to obtain a work permit for me as I had the required experience and academic credentials, although I performed few duties as an analyst.

In her special projects role, Ellen learned a great deal about international finance. She conducted efficiency studies on various operating departments. She used her systems expertise to investigate and improve the company's micro computer usage, and developed a payroll program which was subsequently integrated into the company's international systems. She was a member of the Strategic Review Committee, and produced a report outlining the long term goals for the Middle East market, which she then presented to the Senior Vice President of Europe, Middle East, and Africa.

After one year, Ellen was rewarded for her achievements by a promotion to Manager of Business Planning and Development, a position which reported directly to the Vice President and General Manager. She designed the role herself, and was able to be creative and quite influential in the company. During her year in this role, she was involved in a diverse range of activities. She managed the Quality Assurance department, coordinated a product launch, developed and managed a senior management information system, was an active participant in all senior management meetings, and launched an employee newsletter.

At the end of her second year in Bahrain, Ellen was informed that two positions in Operations would soon be available, and the General Manager, a European expatriate, asked if she would be interested in joining the area. She had previously only worked in staff positions, and quickly decided to accept the challenge and learning experience of a line post. Both positions were in senior management, and both had responsibility for approximately thirty employees.

The first position was for Manager of Accounts Control, which covered the Credit, Collection and Authorization departments. The manager's role was to ensure that appropriate information was used to authorize spending by clients, to compile results of client payment, and to inform management of non-payment issues. The manager also supervised in-house staff and representatives in other Gulf countries for the collection of withheld payments.

The second post was Manager of Customer Services, New Accounts, and Establishment Services. The manager's role was to ensure that new clients were worthy and that international quality standards were met in all Customer Service activity. The manager also worked with two other departments: with Marketing to ensure that budgets were met, and with Sales to manage relationships with the many affiliate outlets of the service.

After speaking with the two current managers and considering the options carefully, Ellen decided that she would prefer working in the Accounts Control area. The job was more oriented to financial information, the manager had more influence on operations at the company, and she would have the opportunity to travel to other countries to supervise staff. Although she was not familiar with the systems and procedures, she knew she could learn them quickly. Ellen went into her meeting with the General Manager excited about the new challenges.

Ellen Meets with the General Manager

Ellen told the General Manager she had decided to take the Accounts Control position, and outlined her reasons. Then she waited for his affirmation and for the details of when she would begin.

"I'm afraid I've reconsidered the offer," the General Manager announced. "Although I know you would probably do a terrific job in the Accounts Control position, I can't offer it to you. It involves periodic travel into Saudi Arabia, and women are not allowed to travel there alone." He went on to tell Ellen how she would be subject to discriminatory practices, would not be able to gain the respect of the company's Saudi Arabian clients, and would experience difficulty travelling there.

Ellen was astonished. She quickly pointed out to him that many businesswomen were representatives of American firms in Saudi Arabia. She described one woman she knew of who was the sole representative of a large American bank in the Eastern Province of Saudi Arabia who frequently travelled there alone. She explained that other women's experiences in Saudi Arabia showed professional men there treated professional women as neither male nor female, but as businesspeople. Besides, she continued, there were no other candidates in the company for either position. She reminded the General Manager of the pride the company took in its quality standards and how senior management salaries were in part determined by assuring quality in their departments. Although the company was an equal opportunity employer in its home country, the United States, she believed the spirit of the policy should extend to all international offices.

The General Manager informed her that his decision reflected his desire to address the interests of both herself and the company. He was worried, he said, that Ellen would have trouble obtaining entry visas to allow her to conduct business in Saudi Arabia, and that the customers would not accept her. Also, if there were ever any hostile outbreaks, he believed she would be in danger, and he could not have lived with that possibility.

Ellen stated that as a woman, she believed she was at lower risk of danger than her Western male counterparts since in the event of hostility, the Saudi Arabians would most likely secure her safety. There was much greater probability that a male representative of the firm would be held as a hostage.

The General Manager was adamant. Regardless of her wishes, the company needed Ellen in the Customer Service position. New Accounts had only recently been added to the department, and the bottom line responsibility was thus doubled from what it had been in the past. The General Manager said he wanted someone he could trust and depend upon to handle the pressure of New Accounts, which had a high international profile.

Ellen was offered the Customer Service position, then dismissed from the meeting. In frustration, she began to consider her options.

Take the Customer Services Position   The General Manager obviously expected her to take the position. It would mean increased responsibility and challenge. Except for a position in high school where she managed a force of sixty student police, Ellen had not yet supervised more than four employees at any time in her professional career. On the other hand, it went against her values to accept the post since it had been offered as a result of gender roles when all consideration should have been placed on competence. She knew she had the abilities and qualifications for the position. She viewed the entire situation as yet another example of how the business community in Bahrain had difficulty accepting and acknowledging the contributions of women to international management, and didn't want to abandon her values by accepting the position.

Fight Back   There were two approaches which would permit Ellen to take the matter further. She could go to the General Manager's superior, the Senior Vice President of Europe, Middle East, and Africa. She had had several dealings with him, and had once presented a report to him with which he was very impressed. But she wasn't sure she could count on his sympathy regarding her travelling to Saudi Arabia as his knowledge of the region was limited, and he generally relied on local management's decisions on such issues. She could consider filing a grievance against the company. There were provisions in Bahraini Labor Law that would have permitted this option in her case. However, she understood that the Labor Tribunals, unlike those held in Western countries, did not try cases based on precedents or rules of evidence. In other words, the judge would apply a hodgepodge of his own subjective criteria to reach a decision.

Stay in the Business Planning and Development Job   Although the General Manager had not mentioned it as an option, Ellen could request that she remain in her current position. It would mean not giving in to the General Manager's prejudices. Since she had been considering the two Operations positions, though, she had been looking forward to moving on to something new.

Leave the Company   Ellen knew she was qualified for many positions in the financial center of Bahrain and could likely obtain work with another company. She was not sure, though, whether leaving her present company under these circumstances would jeopardize her chances of finding work elsewhere. Furthermore, to obtain a post at a new company would require a letter of permission from her current employer, who, as her sponsor in Bahrain, had to sanction her move to a new employer who would become her new sponsor. She was not sure that she would be able to make those arrangements considering the situation.

> I always tell my employees "If you wake up one morning and discover you don't like your job, come to see me immediately. If the problem is with the tasks of the job, I'll see if I can modify your tasks. If the problem is with the department or you want a change, I'll assist you in getting another position in the company. If the problem is with the company, then I'll help you write your resume." I have stated this credo to all my employees in every post I've held. Generally, they

don't believe that their manager would actually assist with resume writing, but when the opportunity arises, and it has, and I do come through as promised, the impact on the remaining employees is priceless. Employees will provide much more effort towards a cause that is supported by someone looking out for their personal welfare.

Ellen's superior did not have the same attitude towards his employees. As she considered her options, Ellen realized that no move could be made without a compromise either in her career or her values. Which choice was she most willing to make?

Ellen Moore (B)

What decision did you make and why?

I accepted the Customer Services position because I was looking for a win-win situation. The Customer Services post was, despite everything, a promotion. Fighting back was not really an option. I would never have received the Accounts Control position, no matter how hard I fought. There was no doubt of this at all. The General Manager had already made up his mind. Any effort I might have made to fight for the Accounts Control post would have compromised my effectiveness in the company, as I would be perceived as someone unwilling to accept senior management decisions.

I could have left the company, but that action would have placed me in a difficult situation, as my husband still had one year remaining on his contract and I wanted to continue working in Bahrain. I could have looked for a post with another company in Bahrain, but the economic situation had changed, and a number of companies were closing, so there was a limited number of available jobs.

When I was making the decision regarding the position I would prefer, the discussion involved three people: the General Manager, the Director of Operations, and me. No one else was aware of this discussion. If the issue had been in the public forum, and if everyone knew I had unsuccessfully requested the Accounts Control position, I would have been perceived to have lost face. It would have been difficult, if not impossible, to work there afterwards and to maintain the level of respect I had in the company. If everyone had known about the situation, I probably would have had to fight the General Manager's decision. One reason which allowed me to work so effectively was that people had a high degree of respect for me. They felt that I had approval, tremendous approval, from senior management. If they saw that I wanted this particular position and that senior management disagreed, for whatever reason, they would assume that senior management no longer held me in the same regard.

I actually did receive a portion of the Accounts Control area because one segment, New Accounts, had been moved from Accounts Control to the area which was under my responsibility. Management had been reviewing the move during this decision process. I also received a high degree of international exposure from my Customer Service post. My reports and documents, and the statistics from my group, went to all international centers, so it was a high profile post. Interestingly, the majority of my clients were from Saudi Arabia, and I dealt with them personally when they occasionally visited our center, and when they called by phone. I didn't experience any problems when I personally handled their accounts. In fact, as I was the Senior Manager, these clients actually were pleased when I would take the time to deal with them directly. They understood that they were receiving professional attention.

I left the job and the company after three months in the Customer Service post. I was working seven days a week, seventeen hours a day when I woke up one morning and realized that I didn't want to go to work. I recognized the signal I had always asked my employees to be aware of. I tried to salvage the situation. I phoned the Senior Vice President in Europe to see if there might be an available post in the United Kingdom. I knew him because I had made a successful presentation to him. He was keen, very enthusiastic. He found a post in London which was exactly what I was looking for at the time, but the company couldn't get the required work permit. He was very embarrassed. By this time, the people in the Bahrain unit found out I was looking and I could no longer remain with the company. I did some private consulting for about six months, assisting a company to obtain research on the Bahrain market, as well as designing the office layout and systems.

How did you decide which job to take?
I really did not have a choice. I had to accept the Customer Service post or leave the company. I could not stay where I was, as this option had not been offered. Basically, I sat down and thought about what was important to me. I said okay, it is a line position, and I want a line position; tick one in the "pro" column. Is there an appropriate number of staff reporting to me? Tick another in the "pro" column, and so on. I didn't actually make a list, but I reviewed the pro's and con's of accepting the Customer Service post, and made what I felt was a slight compromise to my values at the time. That was how I came to accept the decision.

Did you compromise your values?
I don't really think so, because I was looking for a senior management position, and this post provided that opportunity. There were times, however, when I would sit back and think, perhaps I did compromise. But, it's all relative. If that situation had occurred in North America, then, yes, it would definitely be a compromise. But given that same situation and in Bahrain, I don't believe I compromised my values. I was just incredibly fortunate to get the positions I did receive.

I have been asked if I have any regrets regarding my move to Bahrain or with my decision to take the Customer Service post. In both cases, I believe the experiences have been generally positive influences on my career. I am not looking for easy ways out or quick jumps up the corporate ladder. I expect to work hard and hope that my efforts will be recognized. When situations arise where I must compromise slightly, I evaluate my decision carefully, and once satisfied that I am not compromising more than is appropriate, I accept the situation and move on from there.

What was your experience when you returned to North America?
My husband remained in Bahrain when I returned to North America to look for a new post, rent a house, and get us settled. We were moving to Toronto, a city where I had not lived before. Everyone seemed so cold and unfriendly. I really was not prepared for this atmosphere, and it took a while for me to get used to it. And although I am a Canadian, when I returned I didn't really feel the same attachment towards Canada. I felt more like a citizen of the world. That is how both my husband and I feel right now. We're not really attached to Bahrain, although our hearts are still

there with our friends. Our hearts are also here in Canada with our parents, families and friends, but we don't feel the same nationalistic ties that we felt before.

Also, someone recently commented to me about how much easier it would be to be accepted in a similar professional role in North America. My response was "Don't be so sure. Think again!" I've been a guinea pig in most places where I have worked. I'm the youngest to do, or the first to be, or the only female ever. I'm always breaking new ground, and it's very, very difficult. In fact, I believe I was accepted more readily as a professional in Bahrain by the Arab men because I had education and experience, and I was in a senior position. Here, having an MBA isn't necessarily a ticket towards acceptance. Also, I am now working in the railroad industry and in Information Systems, both fields typically dominated by men. I have had to prove myself here once again.

How do women get international experience?

In my opinion, there are two ways that you can get a position in international business. The first is that you can enter a country on a visitor's visa, which is usually valid for several weeks for most countries. During your stay, you should go to recruitment agencies and companies. This method allows you to see what the country is like in terms of both lifestyle and working environment. You may find out that, although the country appears to be exactly what you want and looks great in a movie, it may not meet your expectations. The other route is to seek work in your own country from a company which has a large international operation. Over time, you may obtain a post within its international system. This option is much more difficult these days, particularly as firms tighten their expenses, and, therefore, limit the number of available international posts.

Do you think that if you had worked for this company in the United States, it would have transferred you to Bahrain?

Probably not. We had a small percentage of people who were placed on international assignment. The company doesn't normally hire through its international posting system for the level of position at which I was hired. It is very expensive to transfer employees internationally, they generally attempt to hire locally. I was, therefore, a local hire for that company.

What tips would you have for women about being effective in management positions?

I believe that it is very important not to become complacent once you attain the next level on the way up the ladder. Never assume that you will be automatically given the respect normally accorded to your position. For example, when I am introduced to someone in business as "Here is Ellen," I immediately stick my hand out and say, "Hello my name is Ellen Moore, I'm the Manager of X Group for Company Y". If I am introduced as "here's Ellen" by one of my employees, I'll add "and X (the staff member) is a member of my team working on your project." You have to eliminate any ambiguity in such situations.

I strongly believe that women can obtain recognition for their efforts by understanding that they are employees first, and women second. While I was in Bahrain, I was generally regarded by Arab males as a professional, not as a female. I work very hard to ensure that I am professional at all times. I believe that treating people, at any level, from any background, with respect will usually create a positive atmosphere.

Although I am normally very professional, I will play the stereotypical feminine role when required. If I must state to the housing compound manager that "my husband would like this repair", I'll do that. I am very pragmatic, and recognize that sometimes I must resort to play-acting to get something accomplished, without being totally ridiculous about it. However, I'm not about to "sell my soul to the devil".

Do you have any ideas about how men can help women in international business? Or have you worked with any men who have been particularly helpful?

Yes, but I think it's not just in international business, I think it's anywhere. Men often talk about the mentors they have had in their careers who have assisted them in their progress up the ladder. Women very rarely have that source of assistance. There are few women in senior positions at this time; therefore, there are few role models. In my current position, I am often regarded as a role model by female employees at lower levels. I am very cognizant of this fact and strive to maintain a positive image. For example, although I may be frustrated by some aspects of my work, I will portray a positive outlook to my employees. I believe that employees can become disconcerted by negative views expressed by management. That is not to say that I hide reality, but there's a difference between communicating a realistic and pessimistic view. I take my responsibility as a role model very seriously.

It is very difficult for most men in senior positions to become a mentor for a woman. Constant justifications of the relationship are necessary because many people perceive it as being something entirely different. As a result, the majority of men don't enter into these situations. But, while I was in Bahrain, a director of another area reporting to the General Manager often discussed business tactics with me. He and I talked about our views on management styles, as well as the future direction of the company. He was there for me when I needed assistance, and when I wanted to bounce an idea off someone. I think that a coach is what most women don't have, a person with whom they can discuss their ideas, someone who has been there before and who is willing to share his knowledge and expertise.

What is your feeling about imposing your value system or your beliefs regarding women's roles in a culture like that in Bahrain? For example, why did you write the letter to the editor of the local newspaper?

I wrote that letter because I felt very strongly about the interpretation made by the Director of Social Development. She believed that the inclusion of women in this labour legislation indicated that their contributions to the workforce were being recognized. I didn't write the letter in an effort to influence anyone's views regarding the legislation itself; that would have been a completely unrealistic purpose. I wrote the letter in order to provide an alternative viewpoint. I had often seen in Bahrain that individuals would accept the views of others without thoroughly understanding or examining all the issues, and I wanted to do my part to prevent that from occurring with this situation.

I am generally a very enthusiastic person, and people tend to follow my lead. I have to be very careful with that side of myself. I would like to believe that I have made some positive changes within my small group of colleagues. But one has to recognize that, at the same time, there is a limited amount of change possible, particularly changes for Bahraini women.

As a North American woman I was generally accorded a high degree of professional respect by Arab males in Bahrain. I have been asked if I believe the same respect would be shown to women with an Arab background who were born in North America. My response is that I don't believe they would be treated equally. Their Arab background would be considered primarily, and as Arab women, their role in society would be set forth by long standing traditional values. There are numerous changes I would like to see for Arab women, but I am realistic at the same time.

As well, individuals from Western countries often incorrectly perceive that a country such as Bahrain is similar to any Western country because of the presence of office buildings and Western firms. They don't understand that as a guest in someone's country, you must respect the cultural values of the host country. I recently read of a North American woman working in Bahrain who said that, although she knew the custom was to wear more conservative clothing, she insisted on wearing shorts in public and didn't care that people stared at her. One Bahraini women confided in me that when a woman wears such clothing in public, it is the same as if she were walking up to all the people she meets and slapping them across the face. I wonder if that woman would feel as comfortable wearing her shorts if she took the time to understand the impact of her attire on the people she met on the street. This blatant disrespect for cultural values, while indicating a lack of acceptance for local customs, also demonstrates why many individuals from the West fail to succeed in foreign countries.

You said you were generally respected as a professional by the Arab men. Yet we hear of situations where, for example, a female bank manager working in North America is not invited by Arab male clients to attend a meeting. What are your views on this issue?

Although there could be other factors involved here, my understanding of this type of situation is that the Arab clients are not concerned with the fact that she is a woman. Instead, they most likely believe that her position in the bank is a low level post with limited decision making power. In Bahrain, for example, the leaders of the country are fairly accessible to the people. Given that one can meet with the leader of a country, within a business environment one should be permitted to meet with the president of a given firm. In business I have found most Arab men would like to ensure that they are accorded respect by North American firms, which generally means they wish to meet with senior management who have the authority to make decisions. Individuals from Western countries may interpret these requests incorrectly.

You said that there were no Americans in this American company, you were the token North American?

Yes. Well, I'm Canadian. Most of the executives were European or from other countries in the Middle East, a situation which is not unusual for large multinational firms. The remaining staff were locally hired in Bahrain.

How about your personal relationship?

When we first met over fifteen years ago, my husband and I decided that our relationship was a partnership, and as partners that we would make decisions jointly. And, we recognized early on that we would both have very demanding careers. We sat down and tried to determine, believe it or not it actually took months to accomplish this, what criteria we would use to choose a city, if that situation occurred during our careers. How would we decide if we were offered posts in different cities?

We first thought we should base our decision on salary, with the highest paying job determining the city. But we quickly eliminated that factor as a determinant as I might have a job that pays more today, but if the post is a dead end with no promise of a future, it isn't worth a high investment. We finally decided the position which offered the most long term growth opportunity would be our primary decision criterion. And, that is how we have handled these situations. We actually sit down and say: Well, this is what I've been presented with by this recruitment agency or by this company, and your job is currently at this level. We evaluate the pro's and con's of each posting, and the long term benefits. As well, another key determinant is that good posts would have to be available for both my husband and me in whatever city we select. We seem to go through this decision process fairly often. In fact, we're going through it again. My husband just left for England to be Vice President for an American bank. He is going on a short term contract, but we will be evaluating our alternatives shortly when we have more information on the scope of his post.

My husband and I have a partnership in which each of us respects and assists the other person at all times. For example, he does all the cleaning, dusting, washing the dishes, buying the groceries and the cooking. At one point, a few years ago, I was cooking our dinners about three or four times a week, but I recently haven't had the time as my job has become much more demanding. We know that sometimes my job is more demanding, and sometimes his job requires more of his time. And we share the work in the house based on demands made on our time by our current work situation. We joke about who is the better cook; for example, there are some recipes which I usually prepared and he had his specialty dishes. It happened a few times that he prepared one of my dishes and would say "I think I make it better than you", and I would say, "Really? I guess that one should be your dish from now on." So, little by little I started giving him a few more recipes, but he loves it. He is not cooking our dinners and hating it, he really likes contributing to our relationship in this way.

I think that both people in a relationship have to be flexible, and be willing to make compromises. They have to recognize the needs of each other and understand that these needs will change as time goes on. We often go out for dinner, just so we have special time together, to talk about everything, with no interruptions or television to take us away from each other. We don't fight like most couples I know. We talk about issues, and generally attempt to make decisions based on the "us" rather than the "you" or "I". For example, this Christmas I would like to go to a beach for a holiday. I have not had a holiday for so long, and just need a holiday where I can completely relax. He, on the other hand, would like me to go to London to be with him. We have decided to compromise. I am going to London, and will relax and do nothing much while he is at work during the days. Then, we are planning to take a beach holiday sometime in February or March.

We have also made a conscious decision not to have children. I guess I have had a lot of time to think about this decision. I remember when I was in elementary school some of my friends had mothers who worked, and these friends would come home from school and no one would be there. I would come home, and my mother was there to hear about my day at school, and her presence was very special. This comparison was always at the back of my mind.

On the other hand, I recognized that in order to be truly successful at anything, you have to devote a fair amount of time to that effort. For example, someone training to be the best at a certain sport will have to give up something else, like being a great pianist. Both goals would require more time than is ever available. Alternatively, someone could choose to be adequate at the sport and to have average skills playing the piano, and that would be perfectly alright as long as the person recognized, and accepted, the fact that he or she would not be the best at either the sport or the piano. I view having children in a similar fashion. Although I agree that you can have children and also work, you have to recognize that you simply can't be the best at both. For example, an out-of-town business trip may come up on the day that the child has a school recital. Time is required to be the best at anything, and, I determined I couldn't be the best in work and the best with children. Together, my husband and I decided to choose each other and our career accomplishments.

However, you could decide to compromise, to go half way for both career and children. You could say I don't necessarily want to be the best in my career, half way is fine. But then you still have to say it's half way for the children as well. So you have to realize that you certainly can't be the best at both, but you could choose to have both. If you choose to accept that you won't be the best at both that's fine. I personally don't know how anyone who is raising children could consciously choose this route.

Case

John E. Walsh, Jr.

Managing a Diverse Work Force in Indonesia

INDONESIAN ENTERPRISES

Paul Korsvald, the general manager of a large Norwegian paper company's subsidiary, Indonesian Enterprises, had several decisions to make before the day was over. His first decision was whether to build a small mosque next to his corrugated carton plant near Jakarta, Java. Among the Indonesian Enterprise workers, 34 were Chinese and were primarily Confucians and Buddists, 4 were Javanese Christians, and 2 of Indian extraction were Hindus. The other 352 plant workers and supervisors and the 48 office managers, and workers under him said they were Muslims (see Appendix). Many, however, were not strict followers. They practiced an Islam that had been blended with Hindu, Buddhist, and other beliefs. Jim Sterba (*The Wall Street Journal*, September 29, 1987) observes:

> Islam is different in the world's largest Moslem nation, Indonesia. It has a sense of humor. It doesn't seem so stern and insistent. It is more tolerant than Islam elsewhere.

This toleration was attributed by scholars to Indonesia's vast diverse land and population. The country, comprising 13,677 islands of which 6,000 are populated and covering 3,200 miles, has a population of more than 180 million people of 366 different ethnic groups. Although 250 different languages are spoken, Bhasa Indonesia is the official language taught in the schools. Half of the population was Javanese and two thirds of all Indonesians lived in Java, which constituted 7% of the land mass.

Friday is the holiest day of the week for Muslims, and the company was required by custom to permit workers, especially the men, to attend noon prayers and collective recitals of the Koran. Although government offices closed at 11:00 A.M. on Fridays, Indonesian Enterprises' policy was to close the plant and offices from 11:30 A.M. until 2:30 A.M. only. Paul Korsvald observed that typically fewer than 20 Muslim factory and office workers returned to work on Friday. Many excuses were given by the others such as it was impossible to catch a bus or services were longer than expected.

Actually, after services was a time for workers to visit with friends to gossip and learn what had taken place during the week. It was also a time to bargain, barter, and buy a variety of goods and food sold near the mosque.

What bothered Paul Korsvald most was the loss in production output and paying people for not working. The average monthly salary for factory workers was approximately US$100; for office workers, it was US$150 for a six-day work week. The day began at 7:00 A.M. and ended at 3:30 P.M. including an hour-and-a-half for lunch.

How could he meet the religious needs of the Muslims and non-Muslims without losing production output and keeping costs down? To build a mosque would cost about US$30,000. Four thousand dollars of this would be spent to purchase and transport sacred stones from Mecca. If Korsvald decided to buy the mosque, he would then have to obtain the services of the local hadji (one who had made the pilgrimage to Mecca) for US$15 to bless the ground before construction began. In addition, he would be required to purchase a goat for sacrifice for about US$20. The goat's head would be buried near the mosque; the remainder given to the workers for a feast. He would also have to provide onions and green peppers to be placed on a stick to keep the rains away on the opening day of the mosque.

If he decided not to build the mosque, Paul Korsvald could also continue the current practice or he could rent seven buses for three hours, at a cost of US$50 per bus. While the buses would probably arrive on time to take the employees to the mosque, Korsvald was unsure if employees would return to the factory on the buses.

THE POSSIBLE PURCHASE OF CALL OR PRAYER CALL CLOCKS

Korsvald was faced with another dilemma as well: whether to buy from Maruem Murakemi and Company, Ltd. either ten semi-automatic prayer call clocks or fully automatic prayer call clocks, or some combination of the two. Good Muslims are required to pray five times a day, first in the morning when they arise, before lunch, mid-afternoon, after sunset and before retiring. This schedule did not have to be followed to the letter, for according to the Koran, "When ye journey about the earth, it is no crime to you that you come short in prayer if you fear that those that disbelieve will set upon you." Typically, employees would pray whenever they had spare time. However, by not praying at the prescribed times, some of the reward was lost. According to Muslim tradition, every corner of Allah's universe was equally pure, so the employees would spread their prayer rugs wherever they were when they decided to pray. Standing erect with their hands on either side of their face and their thumbs touching the lobes of their ears, they would begin, "God is most great." Still standing, they would continue with the opening Ayat (passage from the holy Koran):

Praise belongs to God, Lord of the Worlds,
The Compassionate, the Merciful.
King of the day of Judgment.

Tis thee we worship and thee we ask for help.
Guide us in the straight path.
The path of those whom thou hast favored.
Not the path of those who incur thine anger
Nor of those who go astray.

Unfortunately for Paul Korsvald, the prayers continued from noon to afternoon, because each Muslim employee would wait until he or she had spare time. If Paul Korsvald bought the semi-automatic clocks for US$30 and the fully automatic for US$35 and placed them in prominent locations throughout the plant and office, the clocks could be synchronized to proclaim an Azan (prayer call) ten minutes before noon and at 2:40 in the afternoon.

Another option existed. He could eliminate the lunch hour, the practice of the Dutch-owned companies, and end the working day at 2:00 P.M. Rather than buy the clocks, he would make it known through supervisors that plant operations would cease ten minutes before noon for prayers.

THE NEED TO INCREASE
PRODUCTIVITY DURING RAMADAN

A third decision confronting Korsvald dealt with solving the problem of low productivity of employees during Ramadan, the holy month of fasting and the ninth month in the Arabian calendar. In this month, Muhammed, according to Muslim tradition, received the holy Koran from God as guidance for his people and made his hyiria from Mecca to Medina. From dawn to dusk, during this period Muslims abstain from food and drink. Among those automatically exempted were the sick, the very old, very young, pregnant and nursing women, soldiers in war, and persons on long trips. Although no one in Indonesia is legally compelled to fast, many Muslim employees did.

When Ramadan fell during the hottest season, fasting took its toll. Employees, observing tradition, were noticeably nervous, excitable, and prone to flare-ups of temper. Korsvald estimated that productivity in the plant and office declined 20–30%. Korsvald had identified three options to address this issue and suspected there were others. First, he could start the plant at 3:30 in the afternoon and end at midnight. Second, he could close the plant for two weeks and require employees to take their vacations during this time. Third, he could require only those Muslim employees who were fasting to take vacations.

SELECTING THE MANAGER
OF THE ACCOUNTING DEPARTMENT

A fourth decision had nothing to do with religion. He had to decide whether Mr. Abukar, a native Javan, or Mr. James Lee, an Indonesian of Chinese nationality, should be appointed to the position of manager of the accounting department. In Norway, promotion decisions were primarily based upon employee's prior work performance. However, discussions with other Western general managers operating in Java and researchers from *Business International* revealed a consensus that decisions on promotions in Indonesia placed more importance on ethnic background, personalities, and individual circumstances. Thus, managers in Indonesia had to consider whether a prospective manager was Javanese, an outer islander, Chinese, or Indian. Although Indonesia's motto is "Unity in Diversity," it made a difference for instance if a prospective manager was Javanese, Sumatran, or Moluccan.

The Javanese are considered an agrarian-based conservative people proud of their traditions and strong family ties. They value harmony and sensitivity to others, characteristics that historians attribute to feudal influences. Additionally, they are reluctant to convey information that could displease business associations or cause conflicts.

The outer Islanders, the Bataks of Sumatra and the Moluccans, are more prone to say what they think. The Dutch set up large tobacco, rubber, and palm oil estates in Northern Sumatra, so modern agricultural developments were concentrated there. Because these products were produced primarily for export in contrast to rice production in Java, which is consumed locally, natives possessed greater experience in international trade. The straightforwardness of the outer islanders complemented the style of Western managers, resulting in a disproportionate number of outer islanders holding key positions in foreign companies in Java.

While the Chinese accounted for less than 2% of the population, they played a key role in business and owned, according to reliable sources, more than 50% of the nation's private capital. Despite high levels of education and administrative experience, they were excluded from the bureaucracy and the military, which was dominated by the Javanese.

The official ideology of the Indonesian government was Pancasila, which consisted of five principles affirming belief in one God, humanitarianism, national unity, democracy, and social justice. A balance between national unity and social justice proved difficult. Any foreign company having too many Chinese executives would be vulnerable to resentment from indigenous Indonesians (pribumi) workers, and the Indonesian government might intervene and press for social justice. While Indians were also vulnerable to resentment they were too small a group to constitute a threat.

Paul Korsvald had many issues to consider. James Lee was older, and age was important to Indonesians. He was unquestionably the best qualified of the two, technically and in managerial experience. He had more years of work experience with the company. Lee, fearing a backlash from the pribumi staff, might fail to give them firm orders to take disciplinary actions when needed.

On the other hand, Mr. Abukar was reasonably competent technically, pleasant to all employees and well-liked by the Indonesian accounting staff. He came from a respectable family, with several relatives working as lower level executives in the government. Further, the promotion would help him financially, because he had a large family to support. In the past, he had been extremely loyal to the company. He had been reluctant, however, to assume authority, make decisions, and work overtime. Due to a dearth of pribumi managers, it would not be difficult for Mr. Abukar to find another job at a higher salary.

Korsvald could seek a consensus (mufakat) of his key executives through tedious consultation (muskawarah). Whatever choice this consensus brought about, he risked shaming the candidate (malu) in front of others if he did not handle the promotion well. Under no circumstances did he want to create malu.

THE NEED TO FORMULATE POLICIES

His last decision was how to formulate a policy covering responsibilities of his employees to achieve results, to reduce kickbacks, and to determine under what circumstances loans would be made to employees.

The frequent cases of stomach ulcers and heart attacks among European and American managers in Indonesia, he thought, resulted from their failure to counteract djamkeret ("dj" pronounced like "j") or rubber time. He observed that Indonesians could not be rushed and would leave an employer who tried to make them move faster or work harder. When asked, "When will the job be finished," adherents to djamkeret would simply reply, "sometime during the next few days." Modern plants with international commitments could not operate this way. So, he needed a policy that could dampen the excuses of djamkeret.

European companies operating in Asia have been offering bribes and kickbacks since the 1600s when the British East India Company won duty-free treatment for its exports by giving Mongol rulers expensive gifts including rare paintings and carvings. Korsvald, however, had difficulty adjusting to the succession of kickbacks and payoffs necessary to conduct business in Indonesia. On one occasion, his sales manager had to send twelve bottles of scotch for a party given by a purchasing agent of a large corporate customer. On another, he had to give US$10,000 to the large corporate customer's local director. In the latter case, he was surprised to receive a silver tray as a gift from the local director. Last year on Christmas morning, he awoke to find a Christmas tree brightly lit and heavy with gleaming ornaments. On it was a card from another company's director to whom he had been forced to make kickbacks for years. "Muslim economics require that the wealth of her people be widely shared," he mused, "it insists that acquisitions and competitiveness be balanced by fair play and compassion."

In addition to kickbacks to customers, many foreign businessmen in Indonesia felt it was necessary to place someone in power in the Indonesian government associated with their company. It was rumored the family of the president of Indonesia owned shares in 15 companies including a hotel, a flour mill, and two cement factories. The president's brother strongly denied any favoritism and added that several charitable foundations were set up with business earnings.

Trading on influence was not considered corrupt unless it involved excesses. To maintain a low profile, distant relatives of top military and government officials were placed as heads or directors of companies rather than members of their immediate families.

Korsvald observed that the Chinese were adaptable. If they had to give gifts to generals or make deposits to an official's Singapore bank account and become friends for life, they did so. According to Barry Newman in *The Wall Street Journal*, April 14, 1978):

> The strategy of gift giving has been perfected by Cukongs of Indonesia, about 30 moneyed Chinese who have made fortunes for themselves and, as it happens, for the country's ruling elite. "We don't worry," says a manager in one of their many companies. "We have information first hand. We know what's going on." Occasionally, when there is money to be made, a Cukong will take a fellow Chinese for a ride on his coattails.

Korsvald wondered if kickbacks and payoffs to high officials known as the "untouchables" should be continued by his company. Frequently, he had trouble determining whether middlemen who received bribes from the company to give to his ranking officials still had influence. He was never sure how much to pay or if he was paying the right person. His experience in Indonesia convinced him that establishing good personal relations and trust did not always entail a payoff.

Lower-level civil servants continually practiced the ancient Indonesian form of social commerce called the "sticky handshake." Traditionally, funds acquired through extortion were called "smooth money," "lubricating money" or "rule 2000" (it will cost you 2,000 rupiahs). More recently, they have been labeled "illegal levies" and were required for everything from processing a passport to exporting corrugated boxes. It would be almost impossible to stop "illegal levies," because low-level civil servants needed them to live. Nevertheless, the National Command for the Restoration of Security and Order, a government body, was, at present, trying to ban illegal levies. The response was a combination of outrage and jealousy from civil servants who believed that the higher-ups were taking more and not spreading it around. Although Indonesian Enterprises' workers were better paid than civil servants, they, too, sought ways to increase their incomes. Any items the company had in stock that could be sold easily, like glue and starch, had to be closely monitored and physically secured, or they would be stolen.

Korsvald knew compassion was necessary and could produce practical results each morning. He provided free bottles of "vitasoy," soy bean milk processed in Indonesia by the Hong Kong Soy Bean Products Company of Hong Kong, to mitigate the effects on his employees of malnutrition and tuberculosis, both common ailments in Indonesia. The result was an increase in worker productivity.

Sometimes, though, his compassion created problems. He gave 25 corrugated boxes to one employee who said he wanted the boxes for moving to a new home. Later, he discovered that the boxes were sold to a woman going to Pakistan. When Korsvald confronted the employee, the employee became nervous and started to cry. "My wife was sick and I needed the money," the employee sobbed, "I'm not a criminal." Korsvald knew it would be difficult to fire the employee because of strict Indonesian labor laws, so he returned the money to the woman and treated the payment as an advance loan to the employee. Later, the employee sent flowers to Korsvald.

He wondered about what other policies he should prepare for purchasing and advancing loans. Should his purchasing agent be responsible for all purchases up to a certain amount, say $300 in Indonesian rupiahs? Should the purchasing agent be able to further delegate authority to other departments? Should he let a policy on advance loans be made by the comptroller? Weren't there inherent dangers?

In one Western company in Jakarta, when loan policies were delegated to a pribumi comptroller, salary advances had more than quadrupled. The chief executive called in the comptroller to find out if the report was in error. It was not.

The comptroller said that, rather than follow the policy blindly, cases were judged individually. The company's new chief engineer needed a large sum of money to pay three years' rent advance for the house he had just leased and such advances were normal in Jakarta. A one-year advance in pay was made to an older employee who was making his pilgrimage to Mecca (Haj), which every devout Muslim was required to do at least once in his or her life. While the comptroller gave explanations for each advance in salary, the chief executive noticed a loan of four months' salary to a recently hired factory worker. When the comptroller was questioned about this advance he said, "The man is my brother-in-law, and my wife would be embarrassed if I didn't grant him this favor."

Korsvald wanted policies that would prevent such a problem from occurring in Indonesian Enterprises.

APPENDIX: ISLAM AND THE KORAN

The word *Islam* literally means submission to the will of anybody, but in a religious sense it is properly defined as acceptance of what has been ordered or commanded by God via a man named Muhammed. The principles that regulate the life of Muslims in their relationship with God are called the Five Pillars of Islam. The first pillar is Islam's creed, "There is no God but Allah and Muhammed is his prophet." The second pillar is prayer and Muslims are required to be constant in prayer which under normal conditions means praying five times a day. The third pillar of Islam is charity. Those with money should help those who are less fortunate. The fourth pillar is the observance of Ramadan the ninth month of the Arabian Calendar. Ramadan commemorates God's making Muhammed a prophet and ten years later Muhammed's Hijiah flight from Mecca to Medina. The fifth pillar of Islam is pilgrimage. Once during a lifetime a Muslim is expected to visit Mecca.

The word *Koran* literally means "that which is read," but to Muslims it is the sacred book that contains the word of God as revealed to Muhammed. The book consists of 114 chapters, 6,000 verses, and over 80,000 words. There is no specific order except the shorter chapters are at the beginning. It contains information pertaining to prophets and the people to whom they were sent. It also contains laws, dogmas, and ethical ideas. In addition, it is considered by Muslims as a first-rate piece of literature. Many Muslim writers copy its style which they consider a miracle of eloquence. In many parts it is rhymed and unlike ordinary prose, it is chanted rather than read. During daily prayers Muslims usually recite the opening chapter of the Koran and any other part they like.

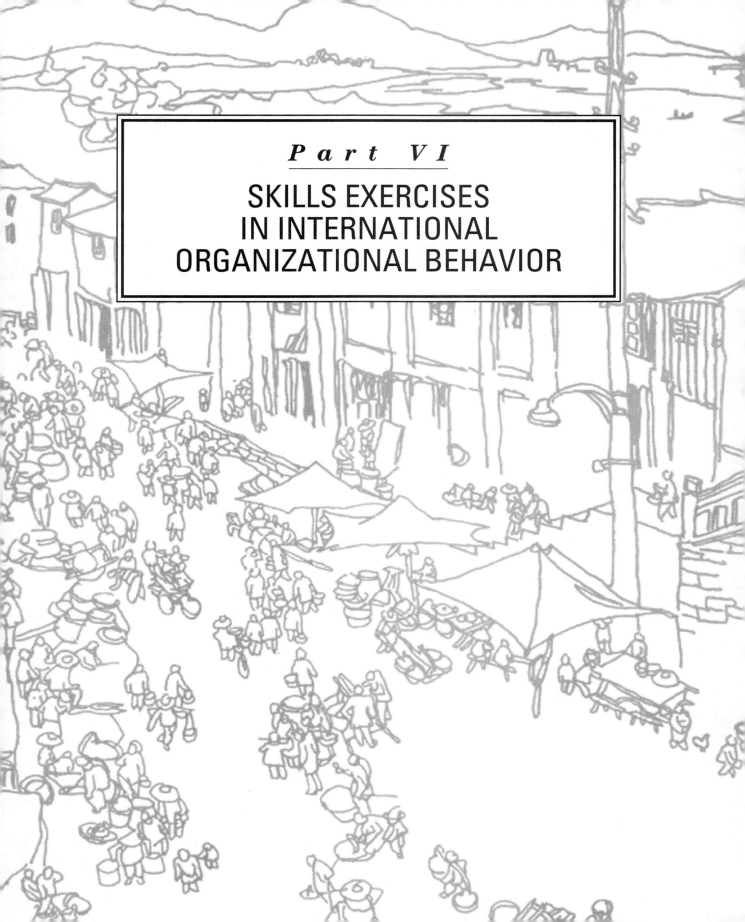

Part VI

SKILLS EXERCISES IN INTERNATIONAL ORGANIZATIONAL BEHAVIOR

International Awareness Survey

Uzoamaka P. Anakwe
Anne Marie Francesco

The environment in which organizations operate in different countries varies. This survey is designed as a learning tool to gauge your knowledge of some environmental and cultural factors that could influence successful overseas operations. The survey is organized into four sections: culture, education, government, and economy.

DIRECTIONS

Following is a list of statements describing various aspects of a country's culture. Circle TRUE if the statement is generally accurate and FALSE if the statement is generally not accurate. If the question asks for specific information, fill it in. Your instructor will tell you which countries are to be included in the survey. Be sure to answer all the questions in the survey as accurately as you can on the basis of your current knowledge.

CULTURE

1. People believe that hard work leads to high achievement.

Country 1	TRUE	FALSE
Country 2	TRUE	FALSE
Country 3	TRUE	FALSE

2. Children are taught to conform and be "team players."

Country 1	TRUE	FALSE
Country 2	TRUE	FALSE
Country 3	TRUE	FALSE

3. Women are expected to be subservient to men.

Country 1	TRUE	FALSE
Country 2	TRUE	FALSE
Country 3	TRUE	FALSE

4. People are comfortable taking orders from those with higher positions.

Country 1	TRUE	FALSE
Country 2	TRUE	FALSE
Country 3	TRUE	FALSE

5. Men and women are given equal employment opportunities.

Country 1	TRUE	FALSE
Country 2	TRUE	FALSE
Country 3	TRUE	FALSE

6. People in the society are comfortable taking risks.

Country 1	TRUE	FALSE
Country 2	TRUE	FALSE
Country 3	TRUE	FALSE

7. The society values working together as a group.

Country 1	TRUE	FALSE
Country 2	TRUE	FALSE
Country 3	TRUE	FALSE

8. Work is considered an important part of people's lives.

Country 1	TRUE	FALSE
Country 2	TRUE	FALSE
Country 3	TRUE	FALSE

9. Being independent is valued.

Country 1	TRUE	FALSE
Country 2	TRUE	FALSE
Country 3	TRUE	FALSE

10. In this society, there are clear rules as to how one should behave.

Country 1	TRUE	FALSE
Country 2	TRUE	FALSE
Country 3	TRUE	FALSE

11. People sit or stand close to one another in carrying out their daily activities.

Country 1	TRUE	FALSE
Country 2	TRUE	FALSE
Country 3	TRUE	FALSE

12. People like to socialize and get to know each other before doing business.

Country 1	TRUE	FALSE
Country 2	TRUE	FALSE
Country 3	TRUE	FALSE

13. Not being on time for meetings or for conducting daily business activities is acceptable.

Country 1	TRUE	FALSE
Country 2	TRUE	FALSE
Country 3	TRUE	FALSE

14. People do not schedule more than one activity at a time.

Country 1	TRUE	FALSE
Country 2	TRUE	FALSE
Country 3	TRUE	FALSE

15. People feel comfortable questioning their supervisor's decisions.

Country 1	TRUE	FALSE
Country 2	TRUE	FALSE
Country 3	TRUE	FALSE

16. People value being direct and speaking their mind freely.

Country 1	TRUE	FALSE
Country 2	TRUE	FALSE
Country 3	TRUE	FALSE

17. Personal characteristics such as age, gender, and family background
    determine who will get ahead.
    Country 1   TRUE   FALSE
    Country 2   TRUE   FALSE
    Country 3   TRUE   FALSE

18. People welcome specific directives from someone with higher authority
    in carrying out their work.
    Country 1   TRUE   FALSE
    Country 2   TRUE   FALSE
    Country 3   TRUE   FALSE

19. People rely mainly on the use of words to convey meaning.
    Country 1   TRUE   FALSE
    Country 2   TRUE   FALSE
    Country 3   TRUE   FALSE

20. The official language is_____
    Country 1   Specify_____
    Country 2   Specify_____
    Country 3   Specify_____

21. Business is conducted in the following languages:
    Country 1   Specify_____
    Country 2   Specify_____
    Country 3   Specify_____

EDUCATION

1. The literacy level is more than 80%.
   Country 1   TRUE   FALSE
   Country 2   TRUE   FALSE
   Country 3   TRUE   FALSE

2. The percentage of population with high school education is more
   than 80%.
   Country 1   TRUE   FALSE
   Country 2   TRUE   FALSE
   Country 3   TRUE   FALSE

GOVERNMENT

1. Citizens know when the country will have new leadership.
   Country 1   TRUE   FALSE
   Country 2   TRUE   FALSE
   Country 3   TRUE   FALSE

2. There is a stable government.
   Country 1   TRUE   FALSE
   Country 2   TRUE   FALSE
   Country 3   TRUE   FALSE

3. The government encourages investment from other countries.
   Country 1   TRUE   FALSE
   Country 2   TRUE   FALSE
   Country 3   TRUE   FALSE

4. The government provides incentives for foreign companies to invest in this country.

Country 1	TRUE	FALSE
Country 2	TRUE	FALSE
Country 3	TRUE	FALSE

ECONOMY

1. The percentage of the population below the poverty level is greater than 30%.

Country 1	TRUE	FALSE
Country 2	TRUE	FALSE
Country 3	TRUE	FALSE

2. The infrastructure is well developed.

Country 1	TRUE	FALSE
Country 2	TRUE	FALSE
Country 3	TRUE	FALSE

3. People are ready to work for low wages.

Country 1	TRUE	FALSE
Country 2	TRUE	FALSE
Country 3	TRUE	FALSE

4. The country has the following natural resources (list three for each country)

Country 1	Specify_____
Country 2	Specify_____
Country 3	Specify_____

5. The average per capita annual income is (expressed in dollars)

Country 1	Specify_____
Country 2	Specify_____
Country 3	Specify_____

6. The country's national currency is

Country 1	Specify_____
Country 2	Specify_____
Country 3	Specify_____

The Owl: Cross-Cultural Sensitivity

Theodore Gochenour

Purpose

To experience and understand how cultural values influence behavior and relationships.

Group Size

Any number of groups of five to seven members.

Time Required

50 minutes or more.

Preparation Required

In a previous class session, roles need to be assigned: three X-ians and two Americans/Westerners per group. Larger classes may have one or two observers per group. X-ians must meet for about an hour prior to class to prepare for the role-playing. Americans/Westerners meet for no more than 15 minutes before the role-play begins.

Room Arrangement Requirements

Circles of five chairs set up in various places around the room.

EXERCISE SCHEDULE

1. **Preparation (pre-class)**
   X-ians, Americans/Westerners, and observers roles are assigned. Each group reads only its role sheet. Observers read both role sheets.

	Unit Time	Total Time
2. **Role-play, Part 1**	**15 min**	**15 min**

   X-ians take their places in groups of chairs and wait for the American/Western couple to arrive. Then the conversation begins.

	Unit Time	*Total Time*

3. **Time out**   5 min   20 min

The instructor signals time up and the American/Western couple leaves the room while X-ians remain.

4. **Role-play, Part 2**   25 min   25 min

The Americans/Westerners return and make their request. X-ians give a "yes" or "no" reply.

5. **Class discussion**   25+ min   50 min

The instructor will lead a discussion on the exercise covering the following areas:

   a.   Which groups got a "yes"? Which ones got a "no"?
   b.   What were the reasons for the "success" or "failure"?
   c.   What did the Americans/Westerners understand about Culture X?
   d.   How does this exercise relate to stereotyping?

ROLE FOR "THE OWL"

Briefing 1: To be read ONLY by the Americans/Westerners

You are two Americans/Westerners, male and female, both of you well-known journalists.

Both of you have master's degrees in journalism from recognized schools, and have spent several years in international travel and reporting on political, cultural, and artistic subjects in a number of countries.

Never at a loss to detect a possible "story," you are pleased to encounter three people in a restaurant in Athens whom you have met once before briefly. You do not remember their names, but do remember that they are from Country X, a rather exotic and unusual place not often visited by foreigners. Country X is one of those places in the world about which there are more legends than facts. It is known, however, to be a society with highly developed arts, literature, and gardens (which are apparently some kind of art form), with an atmosphere of being inaccessible and not too interested in getting into the world tourism business. One of the intriguing things about which speculation sometimes appears in the Sunday Supplements is the X-ian Queen's Garden Festival, which takes place apparently once a year, and which no one has ever visited or photographed. To do so, especially to be the first, would be a true journalistic "coup."

In this exercise, you will approach the X-ians at their restaurant table and ask to join them. Talk with them for about 15 minutes. Then, find a pretext and leave the table for two or three minutes and decide together what would be the best way to approach your real subject: Can you get permission to observe the next Queen's Garden Festival and do a story with pictures?

Try not to let your conversation run on too long. After you return from your two or three minutes of conferring, make your request to the X-ians. You will get a "yes" or "no" answer. At that point, the exercise is over, and you then excuse yourselves again and leave.

ROLE FOR "THE OWL"

Briefing 2: To be read ONLY by X-ians

You are a member of Country X, an ancient land of high culture which has, in the course of the centuries, tended to develop along somewhat isolationist lines. X-ians have a deep and complete acceptance of a way of life that no outside influence has altered in any appreciable way for many years due to the sense of perfection and harmony of life that each X-ian derives from her/his culture.

In Country X, women are the natural leaders, administrators, heads of households, principal artistic creators, owners of wealth through whom inheritance functions, and rulers of the state. Men rarely work outside the home—where they keep house, cook, mind children, etc.—and then only in menial positions where heavy labor is required. Among X-ian women, education is important, with a high percentage going on to the university level. Among men, there is little interest and no encouragement to go beyond basic literacy. In all respects, women know themselves to be superior to men, and are acknowledged to be superior by the men, both in individual attitudes and as expressed institutionally. There is a well-known expression, for example, which goes, "Don't send a man on a woman's errand."

Knowing much of the outside world—and rendered somewhat uncomfortable by what they know of male-female relationships in many other countries—X-ians have tended to withdraw into themselves. In Country X, marriage is between two women, forming what is known as the Bond. The two women (the Bond) then may wish to receive jointly a man into their household, for purposes of creating children, for tending the home, etc. Two women in the Bond are equal in all respects, jointly agree in all decisions, and mutually have responsibility for a man, should he be affiliated with them. Relating to a Bond, a man is legally regarded as an entity, having protection from the Bond. The man is considered "cherished" by the Bond. The women are "married"; his relationship is to the Bond, whereby he is "cherished." A state of being "cherished" is considered very desirable among men.

The artistic powers of X-ian women are famous, particularly in having developed the design and care of gardens into a unique art form. In Country X, the Queen's Garden is open once a year on her birthday to the women of the country (no men allowed) in celebration of the natural processes of growth and rebirth. No foreigners have been able, so far, to observe this Queen's Garden Festival, though there is no law to the contrary that would prevent it from happening.

X-ians share with some cultures of the world a marked discomfort with prolonged eye contact. They, of course, look at another person with brief, polite glances when they are in conversation, but do not hold another person's eyes with their own. In Country X, one is very careful not to "stare," since it is very impolite, and considered to be the worst kind of aggressiveness.

You are an X-ian Bond, Ms. Alef and Ms. Beh, with your Cherished Man Peh. Ms. Alef holds an important position in the Ministry of Foreign Affairs as Directress of Cultural Affairs. Ms. Beh holds a position, also in the Ministry of Foreign Affairs, as Special Assistant to the Minister. Both women are distantly related to the Queen. Cherished Man Peh has been taken along by the two women of the Bond on one of their official trips outside Country X. The three of you are now in a restaurant in Athens, and have been spotted by an American/Western couple whom you have met once before but do not know very well.

When speaking with the Americans/Westerners, you must limit your vocabulary to words of only one or two syllables. The purposes for this are: (1) your native language is that of Country X, and thus it is quite natural for you to be limited in your command of English, and (2) by making you conscious of your language, it is an easy way to prevent a use of vocabulary and concepts that people rarely use except as sociologists and anthropologists.

This American/Western couple will attempt to gain your help in getting permission to observe the next Queen's Garden Festival. They will talk with you for about fifteen minutes. At that time, on some pretext, the American/Western couple will excuse themselves for a few minutes, then return to the three of you. At that time they will ask you for your help.

You must decide whether to say "yes" or "no." Basically, you should decide "yes" if, in your judgment, the Americans/Westerners have shown cultural sensitivity to what X-ians like. This means looking for and considering three main things:

1. The American/Western woman must be the one asking for permission, and she must ask the X-ian Bond (not Peh). The men in the role play (both the American/Western man and Peh) must not be involved in the request.

2. You must decide how thoughtful the Americans/Westerners have been about your limitations in use of English. They should not just rattle on when it is obvious by your speech that you may not understand them very well. If they show sensitivity in this, it will be one factor toward saying "yes."

3. The Americans/Westerners must also show sensitivity to your customs in eye contact. If they continue to "stare" at you during the conversation (and the request), then your answer would be "no."

Skill Exercise 3

The East-West Game (Emperor's Pot)

Donald Batchelder

Purpose

To explore dynamics of cross-cultural interactions when one group wants something from the other.

Group Size

An even number of groups with 10 to 19 people in each group.

Time Required

One class period of 90 minutes, or two class periods of 50 minutes each.

EXERCISE SCHEDULE

		Unit Time	Total Time
1.	**Groups form**	**5 min**	**5 min**

1. **Groups form** — Students are assigned a group, either "West" or "East." If the class is large enough to have more than one East/West group, each East group is paired with a West group. Within each group, role assignments are made. Participants within each group decide who will play which role.

2. **Groups prepare** **30+ min** **35 min** — Groups discuss what their culture and behaviors will be like and they practice various interactions. This part may be done the class before, or assigned as a group project for outside class.

3. **Role play** **20 min** **55 min** — A delegation from the East visits the West group, while simultaneously a delegation from the West visits the East group.

4. **Debrief** **20+ min** **75 min** — Instructor leads a discussion on what occurred. What was it like to play a part in your culture? How different was it from your own culture? How well did the West group do in asking the favor of the East group? Were members sensitive to cultural differences? How can cultural insensitivity get in the way of business negotiations?

EAST GROUP

Instructions: Situational note: The West will be sending delegates to your culture to find a way to persuade you to relinquish the national treasure. You will observe their style and make notes on your assumptions, based on the way they behave and talk in your culture during the Phase II negotiations. At the same time (Phase II), a delegation of your people will visit the West (to their embassy, let's assume), where their officials will try to persuade some of your people on their home ground.

Only To Be Read By the East Group

Your group represents an ancient Eastern culture. You are poor but proud.

A highly treasured artifact is in your possession. It dates back to A.D. 400. It is a national treasure, in fact THE national treasure. Culturally, you cannot give it up under any circumstances. The other side (West) wants it. Their delegation is under strong pressure from the West to return with the artifact. (You may wish to identify one key behavior that, if demonstrated by the West, will win the treasure.)

However, it is in the nature of your culture to be very agreeable, to be very polite, to try always to answer affirmatively, whether you mean it or not. You never come out directly with a flat negative in the negotiations. You never tell their delegates that they will never get the artifact. You dissemble if necessary; you seem to agree and go along, because culturally you never wish to offend.

Culturally, it is important for you to avoid strong, direct eye contact with the delegates or visitors from the West. You look them in the eye, but never a fixed, hard, direct look of any duration.

Typically, even your negotiating team (your delegates to the West) will practice the ancient art of dealing through a third party. Example: One of you has the role of Chief Spokesman (a senior scholar and official), who may act as one of your delegates to the West, or may negotiate at home with the delegates from the West. And while he will do some of the talking in either situation, he will defer often to one of the other members of your group, allowing that other person to carry on some, if not most, of the conversation with the other side. The West will not understand what dynamic is operating here, but that is its problem.

Your list of cultural values follows. A staff person in your room will help with questions during the Phase I planned period. During that time, you will sort out your various roles, decide who and how many should go to the West, and who should remain in the East to negotiate with the West delegates. You should decide on your approach in Phase II.

Roles:

Chief Spokesman

Minister of Education and Culture

Security Officer

Political Officer

Protocol Officer

Information Officer

Recorder: to list all the assumptions and values of other side

Astrologer/timekeeper: to keep each phase exactly on schedule

GOD (Group Organizational Director):

the overall organizer of East

Most Honored Grandmother

Spokesman #2 (most honored)

Advisers: all others

East Cultural Traits (These are the items governing your behavior)

WE Performance is conditioned by role in society, as opposed to individualism.

OVERLAPPING EGO Expectations/morality of community more important than those of the individual. Individual always in social role. Cannot do anything to conflict with group.

FORM Outward form is of major importance. Manners extremely important. Must participate in activities considered important by group, even if one disagrees.

PASSIVISM Confucian idea of endurance is prevalent. Acceptance of fate, life, etc.

PRAGMATISM Confucian or community morality is applied to social issues and problems.

PROGRESS Change is both negative and positive. Technical change is necessary; social change is bad.

NATURE Nature is considered beautiful/good. Conformity to rule of nature considered good.

EFFICIENCY Considered less important than higher values such as form, face, conformity to custom.

TIME Not precisely measured, except in business/science. Time not a primary consideration. The present, not the future, is given utmost consideration.

HISTORY History is seen as a cyclical phenomenon rather than a linear progression.

HUMILITY Humility is related to social status. One never takes advantage of one's rank. One must always defer to another of higher social rank, must always try to appear humble. Persons of higher rank must even make attempts to defer to and honor special inferiors.

DISCIPLINE Pre-school: much freedom, little discipline. School age: discipline begins at home and from teachers in school. Considered a function of the school system at this age rather than a function of the parents. Adulthood: many responsibilities to family and community. Old age: great freedom, shown much respect, considered to have great wisdom.

MOBILITY Important because of duties to family and community.

WORK A means to an end rather than an end in itself. Has no value in itself.

MONEY Saving for the sake of saving is seldom considered a virtue. Some attitudes toward money involve concepts of "face"—i.e., spending an entire year's income for elaborate ceremonies, wedding, etc., to increase or maintain family prestige. Price is regarded as an index of quality.

AGE Great reverence for age, which means wisdom, authority, great perspective on life. Age brings certain privileges (a girl is not a woman until married and a mother). One always uses honorific terms when addressing an elder.

EDUCATION A discipline and a reflection on family prestige. Means of raising whole family's status. Confucian idea of education to create the true gentleman.

AUTHORITY Confucian values stress the cautions. Obedience to authority. Individual rights bear little consideration. Vertically organized hierarchy regarded as most orderly and harmonious.

MORAL SUPERIORITY A moral smugness stemming from a conviction that East's people are a special people with a set of values and conditions that have made them unique.

WEST GROUP

Instructions: Situational note: When told, you will send your delegation to the East. While they are negotiating, this team will also be recording observations about the ways in which the Easterners operate and making assumptions about them. At the same time, a delegation from the East will come to the West. During the visit you will try to persuade their delegates about the merits of your case for the artifact and to simultaneously find out from them what the price might be, etc.

Only To Be Read By West Group

Your group represents an authentic Western culture. You are rich and powerful.

A highly treasured artifact is in the possession of the East. It is a most valuable part of their ancient cultural heritage, and although they are a poor country, they will be reluctant to give it up. You have been assigned the task, however, by your national museum, with strong urging from the government itself, to obtain this national treasure for your country's own collection. Money is no problem.

Thus your task is to assemble a delegation and send it to the East. You decide who goes, how many, what approach they should use . . . as long as the approach appears to you to be compatible with the cultural values listed on the next page. In plainest terms, your group has been sent to the East to bring back the artifact at whatever cost, although you cannot come right out and say this during negotiations with the East. They are known as shrewd traders, even though they are relatively poor, but you have been instructed to operate on the supposition that "every man has his price."

Culturally, it is important for you and your negotiators to figure out which approaches are acceptable on the other side, in order to smooth out the path to your objective of gaining the artifact. At the same time, you should try to stay within the value system defined for you in the next pages.

Typically, you tend to be success-oriented, hard-working and efficient; you plan ahead and try to use time productively.

Your list of cultural values follows. There will be a staff person in your room to help with questions during the Phase I planning period. During that time, you will sort out, consult the value list, decide who and how many should go to the East to negotiate, and who and how many should remain in the West to negotiate with their delegation.

Roles:

Curator of National Museum (expert on Oriental Art)

Diplomatic Officer

Public Relations person

CIA agent posing as an Area Studies specialist

Journalist

Chief of your task group (forceful administrator)

Recorder: to list all assumptions, values, etc., of other side

Timekeeper: to keep each phase of exercise exactly on schedule

GOD (Group Organizational Director): organizer of the West

Advisers: all others

West Cultural Traits (These are the items governing your role behavior)

"I" Ego-centrism

INDIVIDUALISM Self-reliance. Initiative expected from each. Status achieved by own efforts. Economic, social, political equal opportunity regarded as right of individual. Achievement is good and requires competitiveness. Competition expected.

SOCIAL CONFORMITY Outward conformity to opinions of others and to dress has certain value in society.

ACTIVISM Being active, especially in face of uncertainty, is a virtue. Achievement and goal-oriented activities are strongly stressed.

PRAGMATISM Practical ingenuity applied to social as well as materialistic problems.

PROGRESS Change in itself is good. Improvement, especially personal, is a duty. Man is supposed to work in order to control nature.

EFFICIENCY Applies not only to machines but to social organizations and personalities.

TIME Precisely measured and must be used productively and efficiently.

HISTORY Seen as a linear progression.

AGGRESSIVENESS Ambition, competition, self-assertiveness to achieve success are emphasized. High status, once attained, does not confer right to treat lower class as "inferior." Personal excelling is good, but empty boasts and boasting about success are bad.

DISCIPLINE Pre-school: discipline from parents. School age: increased freedom and responsibility. Adulthood: time of greatest freedom. Old age: considered less productive, less active, an epoch of incapability, less freedom.

MOBILITY Great physical and social mobility seen as good.

WORK Valued as an end in itself. Personal effort and energy output are good. Laziness is bad.

MONEY An economic tool, plus a yardstick for social status, influence and power satisfaction.

YOUTH Highly valued. Old people wish they were young again. Elders feel outmoded by rapid change.

EDUCATION Means to an end. Reflections on family prestige. Means to attain skill, money, status.

AUTHORITY Rules/law generally obeyed, but don't like to be ordered to obey. Authorities must not infringe upon individual rights. Mild suspicion of authority.

MORAL SUPERIORITY A moral smugness stemming from convictions that West's people are a special people with a set of values and conditions that have made them unique.

Skill Exercise 4

Race From Outer Space: An Awareness Activity

Dorothy Goler Cash

Goals

I. To compare qualities and skills needed to lead a single racial group and those needed to lead a mixed racial group.

II. To increase awareness of social values and how these may differ among people and groups.

Group Size

Twelve to fifteen members (preferably both male and female).

Time Required

One and one-half to two hours.

Materials

    I.   Newsprint and felt-tipped markers for each group and for the facilitator.

   II.   Masking tape for each group.

Physical Setting

A room large enough for three small groups to meet privately, with a place to hang newsprint.

PROCESS

    I.   The facilitator divides the participants into three groups of four to five members each (extra members become observers):

       1. People from Alpha

       2. People from Beta

       3. People from Gamma.

       The facilitator gives three sheets of newsprint, markers, and tape to each group.

   II.   The facilitator explains that each group is a race of creatures from one of three planets. On each planet all creatures are alike—they look alike, their religion and social class are alike; the only difference is that some are male and some are female. Each group will have fifteen minutes to develop a profile of its race on newsprint by responding to the following items (the facilitator posts the guidelines and reads them aloud):

      1.   Describe your physical appearance.

      2.   Briefly describe your religion or spiritual/moral beliefs.

      3.   Describe the physical environment in which you live.

      4.   Describe the socio-economic structure of your society.

      5.   What is expected of females in your society?

      6.   What is expected of males in your society?

  III.   At the end of fifteen minutes, each group is directed to choose one of its race to present a profile report to the other groups. (Three minutes per group.)

  IV.   Following the three groups' reports, the facilitator initiates a discussion of similarities and differences among the three races. (Ten minutes.)

   V.   Next, each race is given ten minutes to list the five most important personal qualities and the five most important skills needed to become a leader of that race. These characteristics are listed on newsprint by each group.

  VI.   The races compare their lists, and characteristics are tallied. For example:

Qualities	A	B	G	Skills	A	B	G
1. Strong	X			1. Communicates	X	X	
2. Brave	X		X	2. Listens			X
3. (etc.)				3. (etc.)			
4.				4.			
5.				5.			

VII. The facilitator explains that a war of the planets will destroy Alpha, Beta, and Gamma and that the races must take their possessions and leave to pioneer a new planet that is uninhabited, on which they can all live together. He redivides the participants into three groups with approximately equal numbers of people from Alpha, Beta, and Gamma in each group. They are given ten minutes to get acquainted and reiterate their similarities and differences.

VIII. The group must then decide which qualities and skills on the tally sheets they must have available in order to lead this racially mixed group. (One-half hour.)

IX. Each group reports on its discussion, then the facilitator leads a general discussion of leadership demands in the new situation and how these might differ from the previous situation. (Twenty minutes.)

VARIATIONS

I. Two or three characteristics (step II) can be provided for each group by the facilitator.

II. The male–female aspect can be eliminated to establish the races as unisex.

III. Each group can select a group leader who best represents the posted qualities and skills, after step VIII.

IV. Additional questions concerning education, politics, families, etc., can be added to the profile.

Skill Exercise 5

How Many Things Do You Like To Do At Once? An Introduction To Monochronic and Polychronic Time

Allen C. Bluedorn
Carol Felker Kaufman
Paul M. Lane

Right now you are reading this article in one of two fundamentally different ways. You may be reading and deliberately doing nothing else, or you may be reading and watching television or eating or conducting a conversation or perhaps doing all of

"How many things do you like to do at once? An introduction to monochronoic and polychronic time" by Allen C. Bluedorn, Carol Felker Kaufman, and Paul M. Lane from *Academy of Management Executive*, 1992, Vol. 6, No. 4. Reprinted by permission of Academy of Management.

these while you read. The former approach, focusing entirely on one task, is the *monochronic* approach to life: do one thing at a time. The latter approaches, simultaneously being actively involved in two or more activities, are termed *polychronic* approaches. And as is implied by the word "approaches," there are degrees of polychronicity, ranging from people who tend to be very monochronic to those who are extremely polychronic.[1]

A question that often arises about the idea of polychronicity concerns the meaning of "simultaneously" and "at once." For example, is working on three different projects during a one-hour period an example of polychronic or monochronic behavior? Are they actually carried out at the same time, or are the parts of one activity interspersed or "dovetailed" with the others? Actually, both patterns are considered to be polychronic time use.

If three projects are dealt with completely and in sequence—A is begun and completed before B is started, B is begun and started before C, and C is begun and completed before any other project is started—the behavior is clearly monochronic, extremely monochronic. However, if the following intermittent pattern occurs—resume A from a previous time, stop A and begin B, stop B and return to A, stop A and begin C, stop C and return to B, etc., always making progress on each task, albeit slowly—a much more polychronic behavior pattern is being followed. Even more polychronic would be someone who is writing a letter, talking on the phone, eating an apple, and listening to the *War of 1812 Overture* simultaneously.

In addition to the directly observable patterning of your activities, your subjective reactions to events are also indicators of polychronicity. Compare, for example, two managers who are both planning to write a report in the morning. Both begin writing, and after thirty minutes, both managers receive a phone call. Manager A regards the phone call as an interruption and attempts to reschedule the call for a time later in the day. Manager B answers the phone, has a complete conversation with the caller, and returns to work on the report after the call. Manager A is relatively monochronic because unplanned, unscheduled events are considered interruptions that should be minimized and not allowed to interfere with scheduled activities. Manager B is relatively polychronic because the unscheduled event was handled as a normal part of life, of equal or greater importance than planned activities (i.e., writing the report).

Thus, we need not consider the concept of "simultaneous," of "at the same time" as an absolute. Were we to do so, we would not be able to speak of degrees of polychronicity and would be forced to classify people as being either polychronic or monochronic. Instead, we can identify time use behavior more accurately along the monochronic/polychronic continuum presented in Figure S5-1.

Individuals vary in their orientation along this continuum as do organizations and entire cultures. You will soon be able to identify your own orientation along this continuum as well as recognize how monochronic or polychronic the cultures of your employing organization and department are.[2]

Many of these fundamental variations are so subtle that they often go unrecognized because they exist beneath the level of conscious awareness. Differences in patterns related to time horizon, pace, and punctuality can be found as well as tendencies to use time monochronically or polychronically. However, individuals are sometimes unaware of the particular aspects of their "time personalities," although they can readily report actual time use preferences and behaviors. Furthermore, polychronicity is important, not only because it is a fundamental distinction in and of itself, but because pioneering research indicates that it is related to many of our other important behaviors and attitudes.

Figure S5-1   **Monochronic/Polychronic Time Use Continuum**

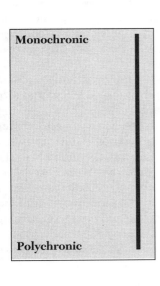

One activity is engaged in during a given time period.

Some activities may be performed simultaneously or intermittently, while other activities are performed one at a time. Individuals may vary along a continuum in the amount of their time spent in either polychronic or monchronic time use.

Two or more activities are engaged in simultaneously or intermittently during a given time period.

Anthropologist Edward Hall has observed that differences in space utilization and the priorities given to human relationships over task accomplishment vary with monochronic and polychronic cultural orientations.[3] His observations indicate that people with a monochronic orientation are task-oriented, emphasize promptness and a concern for others' privacy, stick to their plans, seldom borrow or lend private property, and are accustomed to short-term relationships with other people. Conversely, people with a polychronic orientation tend to change plans, borrow and lend things frequently, emphasize relationships rather than tasks and privacy, and build long-term relationships with family members, friends, and business partners. Because of these relationships and polychronicity's stature as a core defining characteristic of temporal attitudes and behaviors, an understanding of monochronic and polychronic orientations is vital to understanding our own behaviors, the ability to manage in the international arena, and the ability to manage in an increasingly culturally diverse workplace.

HOW POLYCHRONIC ARE YOU?

Researchers Carol Kaufman, Paul Lane, and Jay Lindquist conducted an extensive survey of polychronic time use in which they examined individuals' tendencies to use time either polychronically or monochronically. They developed a scale, the Polychronic Attitude Index (PAI), which attempted to capture the respondent's general attitude toward performing more than one activity at a time.[4] Respondents were also requested to report the likelihood of their participation in some specific types of activity combinations. As anticipated, several activity combinations were found to be significantly correlated with the PAI. Thus, one's score on the PAI provides a preliminary indication of whether an individual has the potential and desire to combine activities in the same block of time. In contrast, prior research on polychronicity has been primarily qualitative and observational.

Kaufman, Lane, and Lindquist's work produced the four-item scale presented in Figure S5-2. We suggest that you complete the four-item scale right now and then score yourself. By completing this scale you will gain a better understanding of the monochronic/polychronic continuum and learn about an element of your own personality most people do not know about themselves.

Kaufman, et al.'s survey was completed by 310 employed adults in southern New Jersey. Their sample is fairly representative of the general U.S. population and provides the only existing baseline against which your response may be compared. The mean score in their sample was 3.128, which you can use as a point of comparison for your own score. Kaufman, et al. found that polychronic time use was negatively correlated with role overload (the more polychronic the individual, the less role overload the individual tended to experience), and positively correlated with education (the higher the education level, the more polychronic the respondent tended to be), working more than 40 hours per week (the more polychronic tended to work more than 40 hours per week), and social group and club membership (the more polychronic were more likely to belong to social groups and clubs). Polychronic time use was not, however, correlated with gender (contrary to Hall's suggestion), age, income, or marital status.

HOW POLYCHRONIC ARE YOUR DEPARTMENT AND ORGANIZATION?

After Kaufman, et al. had completed the first phases of their work, Bluedorn built upon it to develop a five-item scale for measuring the monochronic/polychronic continuum as a component of organizational culture.[5] Unlike Kaufman, et al.'s original scale, his scale asks respondents to report on the general time use orientations they perceive in their departments and organizations rather than about their own individual orientations. This scale, tested in a sample of 205 employees drawn from a medium-size bank in Missouri, is presented in Figure S5-3. We suggest that you complete the scale in Figure S5-3 for both your department and your entire organization at this time. Then follow the instructions to score your department and organization.

The results in Figure S5-3 reveal your perceptions of your department's and organization's location on the monochronic/polychronic continuum (they will not necessarily be at the same place on the continuum). To determine the "real" locations of your department and organization on the continuum, a survey drawn from a large sample of your department and organization would be necessary. However, your perception by itself is still useful because you can now use it to compare to your own orientation, as measured by the scale in Figure S5-2, your perceptions of your department and organization in Figure S5-3. We suggest that you now plot your results from Figure S5-2 and Figure S5-3 on the scales in Figure S5-4, which will allow you to compare your personal time use orientation with that which you perceive in your department and organization.[6]

The more polychronic the department, the more externally focused it tended to be. The more polychronic departments also tended to have longer time horizons. These results, which should be considered preliminary findings, may indicate that more polychronic individuals would also have better matches with departments that have longer time horizons and more of an external orientation.

Please consider how you feel about the following statements. Circle your choice on the scale provided: strongly agree, agree, neutral, disagree, or strongly disagree.

I do not like to juggle several activities at the same time.	Strongly Disagree 5 pts	Disagree 4 pts	Neutral 3 pts	Agree 2 pts	Strongly Agree 1 pt
People should not try to do many things at once.	Strongly Disagree 5 pts	Disagree 4 pts	Neutral 3 pts	Agree 2 pts	Strongly Agree 1 pt
When I sit down at my desk, I work on one project at a time.	Strongly Disagree 5 pts	Disagree 4 pts	Neutral 3 pts	Agree 2 pts	Strongly Agree 1 pt
I am comfortable doing several things at the same time.	Strongly Disagree 1 pt	Disagree 2 pts	Neutral 3 pts	Agree 4 pts	Strongly Agree 5 pts

Add up your points, and divide the total by 4. Then plot your score on the scale below.

1.0	1.5	2.0	2.5	3.0	3.5	4.0	4.5	5.0
Monochronic								Polychronic

The lower the score (below 3.0) the more monochronic your organization or department; and the higher the score, (above 3.0) the more polychronic.

Figure S5-2 Polychronic Attitude Index

MANAGERIAL IMPLICATIONS

Although the monochronic-polychronic distinction creates as many potential implications for behavior and action as there are people, three behavioral domains are particularly prominent: individual time management, supervision/coordination, and cultural diversity.

Individual Time Management

Much of traditional prescriptive time management emphasizes a monochronic orientation. To wit: In an orderly fashion carefully plan your day by organizing a schedule based on your priorities with a specific allotment of time allocated for each activity. Kaufman, et al. have suggested that more polychronically oriented consumers may be more successfully marketed to by learning which types of activities they would like to have combined with others. For example, many people may like to drive and conduct business at the same time (cars and cellular phones) or watch the news and a ball game at the same time (picture-in-picture televisions). Their idea of identifying

Please use the following scale to indicate the extent to which you agree or disagree that each statement is true about 1) your organization and 2) your department.

		Strongly Disagree	Somewhat Disagree	Slightly Disagree	Neutral	Slightly Agree	Somewhat Agree	Strongly Agree
We like to juggle several activities at the same time.	Organization	1 pt	2 pts	3 pts	4 pts	5 pts	6 pts	7 pts
	Department	1 pt	2 pts	3 pts	4 pts	5 pts	6 pts	7 pts
We would rather complete an entire project everyday than complete parts of several projects.	Organization	7 pts	6 pts	5 pts	4 pts	3 pts	2 pts	1 pt
	Department	7 pts	6 pts	5 pts	4 pts	3 pts	2 pts	1 pt
We believe people should try to do many things at once.	Organization	1 pt	2 pts	3 pts	4 pts	5 pts	6 pts	7 pts
	Department	1 pt	2 pts	3 pts	4 pts	5 pts	6 pts	7 pts
When we work by ourselves, we usually work on one project at a time.	Organization	7 pts	6 pts	5 pts	4 pts	3 pts	2 pts	1 pt
	Department	7 pts	6 pts	5 pts	4 pts	3 pts	2 pts	1 pt
We prefer to do one thing at a time.	Organization	7 pts	6 pts	5 pts	4 pts	3 pts	2 pts	1 pt
	Department	7 pts	6 pts	5 pts	4 pts	3 pts	2 pts	1 pt

Add up your points, for our organization, and your department. Divide each total by 5. Then plot both scores on the scale below.

```
1.0   1.5   2.0   2.5   3.0   3.5   4.0   4.5   5.0   5.5   6.0   6.5   7.0
Monochronic                                                   Polychronic
```

The lower the score (below 4.0) the more monochronic your organization or department; and the higher the score, (above 4.0) the more polychronic.

Figure S5-3 **Monochronic/Polychronic Orientation Scale**

activities whose combination is attractive to customers can readily be extended to the personal time management enterprise through a series of questions.

- Which activities require your undivided attention?
- Which activities do you prefer to do in combination with other tasks?
- Which activities do you prefer to have grouped together?
- Which activities would you prefer not to be grouped together?

Candid answers to these questions and their corollaries can lead to a more sophisticated approach to time management by moving beyond the general use of priorities to establish schedules. Using this approach in addition to priorities estab-

To compare your individual Monochronic/Polychronic orientation with your department and organization, copy your scores from the three scales onto this chart.

Individual

1.0	1.5	2.0	2.5	3.0	3.5	4.0	4.5	5.0

Monochronic   Polychronic

Department

1.0	1.5	2.0	2.5	3.0	3.5	4.0	4.5	5.0	5.5	6.0	6.5	7.0

Monochronic   Polychronic

Organization

1.0	1.5	2.0	2.5	3.0	3.5	4.0	4.5	5.0	5.5	6.0	6.5	7.0

Monochronic   Polychronic

To interpret the scores, rather than using exact numerical values, use general comparisons such as "middle of the scale" or "clearly above" or "clearly below" the midpoint.

Figure S5-4 Orientation Comparison

The closer your individual preference score is to that of your organization or department, the closer your "fit" or "match" in terms of the monochronic/polychronic orientation, but the closeness of the match may indicate more than just a fit or misfit with the monochronic/polychronic continuum alone. Bluedorn's bank study revealed some very large correlations between a department's polychronicity and the extent to which it emphasizes an external focus (on customers, suppliers, changing technologies, etc.) rather than an internal focus (interpersonal relations and development, rules, procedures, etc.).

lishes multiple criteria for deciding what things you plan to do when. By identifying which types of things seem to go together and which do not, a self-managed process of job enrichment can accompany the more traditional time management task.

Your own orientation—relatively monochronic or relatively polychronic—will naturally make some of the preceding questions and issues easier to deal with than others, and it will also lead you to different ways to deal with them.[7]

If you are relatively polychronic, you may find it more difficult giving an activity your undivided attention than will your monochronic counterpart. Conversely, if you are relatively monochronic, you may have more difficulty than your polychronic colleague grouping certain tasks together to be performed during the same time period; and the more diverse the activities, the more difficulty you are likely to have grouping them together.

Earlier in this article we discussed behaviors associated with monochronic and polychronic orientations, one of which was the individual's degree of flexibility in regard to plans and schedules. The time management fundamental of the daily To-Do list that identifies your activities and assigns priorities to them is a plan and a schedule. Given the association of polychronic orientations with greater flexibility toward plans and schedules, polychronic individuals may be more flexible in their approach to the To-Do list.

First, they are likely to be less precise in scheduling completion times for tasks, if they even use them at all. Second, they should be more likely to modify the items on their lists (add, postpone, delete) as well as alter item priorities as the day proceeds; but this flexibility is neither a universal advantage nor a disadvantage. Flexibility in one situation may lead to the exploitation of an unanticipated opportunity, but in other situations it may lead to unproductive dithering. Third, the practice of using priorities to say no to lower priority requests, especially when the requested activities involve interaction with other people, should be more difficult for more polychronic people too.

Supervision and Coordination

Regardless of whether you are a first-line supervisor managing a single work group or a CEO managing multiple divisions or departments, the polychronicity issues described for individual time management have direct analogues at these higher levels. Which tasks and assignments do your people seem to be able to handle simultaneously (e.g., selling computers and teaching customers how to use them), and which do they have trouble handling if assigned together (e.g., selling computers and repairing them)? Which tasks do they like to handle simultaneously and which ones are better if given one at a time (e.g., taking inventory)? And which tasks might the organization be able to *learn* to handle simultaneously (e.g., designing new computers and repairing current models), giving it competitive advantages in any environment where time-based competition exists?

All of these issues imply the universal management activity of *delegation*, an act that can be influenced by your own monochronic/polychronic orientation as well as that of your subordinate.

Or consider the very monochronic boss. He is so insistent on a tightly planned schedule—everything has its time and only one thing at a time is scheduled—that he delegates almost everything to ensure his ability to be working on only one task at a time. The resulting avalanche of delegated tasks may overwhelm the constantly inundated subordinate, especially if the subordinate has a relatively monochronic orientation too. The subordinate in this case will gain very little in terms of skill en-

> Although similarity between delegator's and subordinate's degree of polychronicity would seem to be the obvious route to harmony and successful delegation outcomes, the issue may be more complex than it appears at first glance. For example, an extremely polychronic boss may so enjoy the stimulation of multiple activities carried out simultaneously or in a short period that she fails to delegate enough tasks to subordinates. Not only would polychronic subordinates be potentially experiencing a too-monochronic environment for their own work satisfaction, but they would not be developing skills in a variety of activities, which is a major benefit and purpose of delegation.

hancement from the delegated tasks and will probably feel continuously overwhelmed and miserable.

Overall, you need to recognize your own orientation and that of your subordinate because you must take *both* into account to successfully delegate over the long term. If you and your subordinates differ in orientation, do not consider such differences impediments. Such differences may actually be complementary and provide opportunities to improve the results of delegation in your department.

Cultural Diversity

" ... when people or groups with different [temporal] perspectives interact, conflicts often arise. Misunderstandings occur when intention and action are judged, by different participants, on different temporal scales. Values are attached to these scales. *The differences in temporal perspective often go unrecognized by the participants.* [Emphasis added] But the differing temporal scales have values associated with them nonetheless, and the temporally divergent actions lead to value inferences by the participants about each other."[8] Thus has James Jones succinctly described the *raison d'etre* for understanding temporal concepts such as monochronic/polychronic orientation when working with culturally diverse groups. To illustrate the problems that may occur if you do not understand these temporal differences, put yourself into the following situation.

You are a sales representative for a U.S-based company that is attempting to expand into overseas markets. As part of the expansion effort, you are travelling around the world to call on several potential customers. Your itinerary includes appointments in New York, Paris, Berlin, Tunis, and Seoul. You want to make a good impression on your firm's prospective clients in each location, but you are far from an expert on France and Germany, let alone Tunisia and South Korea. Thus, you are quite anxious about how people in these different cultures will react to your behavior, and you are equally concerned about your own abilities to attribute the correct meanings to the treatment you will receive from the French, Germans, Tunisians, and Koreans.

That there will be language differences is obvious, but you were recently briefed that some of the greatest non-language difficulties in cross-cultural interactions are those arising from differences in beliefs, values, and behaviors concerning time. For example, what does it mean when a French manager keeps you waiting for thirty minutes after your scheduled appointment time? Does it mean the same thing that it means when an American or a Korean manager keeps you waiting? Similarly, should you end your appointment at the scheduled time if you have not covered everything you want to discuss, or should you attempt to continue your meeting even if you would be going beyond your scheduled time allotment? And should you try to keep going in Tunis, but not in Berlin?

Although you may not know the exact answers to the questions raised in the scenario, you have a competitive advantage over anyone who does not even know that there are questions, that there may be a difference in these matters between cultures, and that these differences are often crucial differences.

It is hackneyed now to expound on the increasingly diverse nature of the American workforce, let alone the greater diversity of the global economy. But if, as analysts such as Hall and Jones assert, the temporal components of culture are the most fundamental, recognizing and understanding those components, and hence the differences among cultures concerning them, becomes essential for productive cross-cultural management and interaction.

For example, when a relatively monochronic North American interacts with a more polychronic Latin American, misinterpretations and misattributions of behavior, if not friction and conflict, are likely to occur unless some attention has been paid to identifying and learning such differences in temporal behavior and norms. The situation may be even more complex in interactions with the Japanese who tend to be monochronic in their use of technology and in dealing with non-Japanese, but who are very polychronic in respect to most other matters. Similarly, misunderstandings may occur among major subcultures within the United States.[9] And monochronic/polychronic time use, however important, is but one of many ways cultures may differ temporally. If people coming from different cultures and traditions understand these differences, or even that there may be differences, conflicts related to polychronicity and other temporal differences can be managed more effectively.

CONCLUSION

The more polychronically oriented among you have not only finished this article, but have also finished lunch or are about to change the subject of your conversation; the more monochronically oriented are about to begin lunch or will now make that phone call. Either way, you have learned about one of the subtler yet more profound ways individuals can differ from one another.

As we have seen, an understanding of the monochronic/polychronic continuum can lead to better self-management as well as better management of our organizations and our relationships with people from different cultures and traditions. Given the increasingly international nature of business and management, the strategic competitive advantages will be held by the individuals, companies, and nations who learn how to successfully manage cultural diversity. And temporal differences such as monochronic/polychronic orientations are among the most basic cultural differences to manage.

Endnotes

[1]Edward T. Hall developed the concepts of monochronic and polychronic time and presented them most extensively in his book, *The Dance of Life: The Other Dimension of Time*, which was published in 1983 by Anchor Press. Additional material is provided in *Understanding Cultural Differences* by Edward T. Hall and Mildred Reed Hall, published in 1990 by Intercultural Press.

[2]Some time writers (not all) such as James W. Gentry, Gary Ko, and Jeffrey J. Stoltman in "Measures of Personal Time Orientation," in Jean-Charles Chebat and Van Venkatesan (eds), *Time and Consumer Behavior*, (Val Motin, Quebec, Canada: Universite du Quebec a Montreal, 1990) reserve the use of the word "orientation" to refer to an individual's relative emphasis on the past, present, or future. Throughout this article we have used "orientation" in its more traditional, more generic sense of establishing a location or position with respect to some phenomenon.

[3]See Hall and Hall, Endnote 1.

[4]Kaufman, Lane, and Lindquist's research is reported in their article, "Exploring More Than 24 Hours a Day: A Preliminary Investigation of Polychronic Time Use," *Journal of Consumer Research*, 18, 1991, 392–401. The scale presented in Exhibit 2 produced an alpha reliability coefficient of 0.67 in their study.

[5]Allen Bluedorn's study is reported in the working paper, "Time and the Competing Values Model of Culture: Adding the Fourth Dimension," which is available from him at the University of Missouri-Columbia. The scale in Exhibit 3 produced an alpha reliability coefficient of 0.74 in the bank sample, and he is currently involved in research on a large insurance company to see if his results will replicate.

[6]Carol Kaufman, Paul Lane, and Jay Lindquist provide a much more extensive discussion of matching individual and organizational time styles and orientations in their article, "Time Congruity in the Organization: A Proposed/Quality of Life Framework," which is forthcoming in *The Journal of Business and Psychology*.

[7]We would like to thank the following individuals who suggested some of the implications of MP orientation for individual time management: Kevin Adam, Barbara Braungardt, Greg Boivin, Steven Briggs, James Dawes, Matthew Harper, Mary Hass, Mike Ondracek, and Julie Witte.

[8]The quotation is from page 27 of James M. Jones' article, "Cultural Differences in Temporal Perspectives," in J.E. McGrath (ed), *The Social Psychology of Time*, (Newbury Park, CA: Sage Publications, 1988).

[9]The relative orientations of North and Latin Americans are taken from Hall, *The Dance of Life*. The description of the Japanese is from Edward T. Hall and Mildred Reed Hall, *Hidden Differences: Doing Business With the Japanese*, which was published in 1987 by Anchor Press/Doubleday.

Double-Loop Thinking:
Seeing Two Perspectives

Anne B. Pedersen

OBJECTIVE

To analyze a cross-cultural encounter from at least two perspectives, that is, from the viewpoints *of both* those involved.

Participants

1–30.

Materials

Handouts, paper and pencil/flip chart or chalkboard.

Setting

No special requirements.

Time

50–70 minutes.

RATIONALE

The incident provided below describes a cross-cultural encounter between two students, one the participant identifies with and the second, "the other."

The situation is examined first from "your" perspective and then from the perspective of "the other," with a distinction being made between the facts of the encounter and the inferences about it made by each. What you learn during this exercise is a way to see the incident, your role in it, and the values governing your behavior more accurately from the perspective of the other person.

PROCEDURE

There are at least three ways to administer it:

1. Provide both the Incident and Analysis Handouts to participants, let them work on the exercise alone, and then share and discuss their reactions in small groups and/or as a whole group.

2. Ask participants to read only the Incident Handout. Then lead a discussion (based on the Analysis Handout) in which, with the help of a flip chart or chalkboard, you analyze the incident with them in the framework of double-loop thinking as discussed in the exercise.

3. Do the same as in #2, but provide the participants with the Analysis Handout to aid them in following the discussion.

INCIDENT HANDOUT

To begin, it is important to describe a conflict situation as completely as possible. Ilse has volunteered her problem.

You, Ilse, of German descent, and Leilani, from Hawaii, are first-year students at Chandler Engineering College. Both of you had requested single rooms in the college dormitory. However, because of unavailability, you were assigned as roommates.

From the start, the relationship seemed less than amicable. You created rules to divide ownership of the living space into equal parts. Your share was orderly and tidy. Leilani, on the other hand, stapled and taped colorful posters helter-skelter on the plaster wall, played rock music Polynesian style, and chatted with her island friends sprawled three or four deep on her bed, which normally could not be seen anyway due to clothes, clutter, and debris.

One morning after you left for class, Leilani remembered an important essay was due. She needed a dictionary for the task and took one from your shelf, without permission. As the day was warm, she gathered up her materials and left the dorm to write in the sun on the lawn. Joined by friends on the blanket, the dictionary was soon lost among the pile of multiple texts.

You returned shortly thereafter to find the wide empty space on the bookshelf. During the blowup that followed, Leilani responded:

I needed the dictionary just then. Books are to be used, not just looked at. Do you expect them to be ornaments? You are stingy, mean, obsessed; you value control over everything. Well, you won't control me. Someday, you'll find friends are more important than books.

You, Ilse, replied:

The dictionary is mine. I spend my money on books not junk music, like you, and I take care of them. If you had a dictionary, you wouldn't know where it was. You are totally irresponsible. In your crowd, everyone just helps themselves. No respect for other people. And you abuse my books too. All you value is friendships. Well, you don't have mine. Good fences make good friendships.

ANALYSIS HANDOUT

A. This handout constitutes a guide to the application of double-loop thinking to the Ilse/Leilani incident. In analyzing the incident we ask you to take the role of Ilse.

B. *Objective Behaviors.* Note which statements in the incident are statements of fact, i.e., which refer to observable behavior. Make a list of specific behaviors for both yourself (Ilse) and Leilani. This list may look like the following:

Specific Behaviors

Ilse (yourself)	Leilani
1. requested a single room	1. requested a single room
2. created rules	2. stapled and taped wall posters to plaster
3. careful with possessions	3. played rock music Polynesian style
4. left for class	4. cluttered up her bed
5. returned to find her dictionary missing	5. took Ilse's dictionary and left dorm

C. *Inferences*. It is also important to note which statements are inferences, i.e., judgments made or conclusions drawn based on what happened. These commonly involved such things as expectations, values, and/or attributions of causality between events. Make a list of inferences found in your problem description. The list might look like the following (you can add others if you wish):

Inferences

Leilani infers that Ilse (yourself)	Ilse infers that Leilani
1. is stingy, mean, and obsessed with rules	1. is irresponsible and careless of possessions
2. expects books to be ornaments	2. is disrespectful of others
3. overvalues control	3. abuses Ilse's books
4. undervalues friendship	4. overvalues friendships

D. *Your Personal Perspective of Yourself*. An analysis of the encounter within a consistent framework will make your task easier. Below is a simple matrix to help you order your information.

My Personal Perspective of

Behavior	Expectation	Value
Myself		
Leilani		

To complete this matrix you need an accurate assessment of your own values and expectations as they influenced your behavior in the interaction. (This personal perspective of your behavior may look like the following.)

My Personal Perspective of Myself

Behavior	Expectation	Value
creates rules, careful with books	to know where my books are	orderliness and responsibility

E. *Your Personal Perspective of the Other (Leilani).* Following the procedure outlined in D, above, begin an inventory of the values and expectations that may support the behavior of the other person. Your initial list of inference phrases will prove helpful in generating alternative interpretations. Choose the most likely one. The resulting sequence is *your personal perspective of Leilani's behavior*. This is a process of inference. Your conclusion may be confirmed or refuted through further communication and/or repeated observation. It might look like the following:

My Personal Perspective of Leilani

Behavior	Expectation	Value
takes my dictionary without asking	will abuse the property of others	orderliness and responsibility

F. *Your Personal Perspective of Someone You Know from a Different Culture.* At some point in the not-too-distant past, you will likely have interacted with a person who behaved differently from yourself in a cross-cultural encounter. Exercise your analytical skill by graphing the interaction from *your* perspective on the model below.

My Personal Perspective of

Behavior	Expectation	Value
Myself		
Different other		

G. *"Double-Loop" Thinking.* A more advanced stage in describing a cross-cultural event involves what is known as double-loop thinking, that is, knowing and understanding what the other person thinks of your behavior, expectations, and values. In simpler terms, it is called *taking the perspective of the other*. It is a relatively complex and difficult skill to master, involving patience, considerateness, time, and a certain tolerance for ambiguity.

Taking the perspective of another builds upon the assessment of the situation from your perspective. In other words, it is a further step away from perceiving the reality of the situation solely *as you see it*.

Staying with the same example of differing treatment of personal property, taking the perspective of another may be graphed in the following way:

Taking the Perspective of Another (Leilani)

Behavior	Expectation	Value
creates rules careful with books	to hoard information and property	control, possessions more important than people

This analysis necessarily involves a conjecture based on inference. As in making analyses from your personal perspective, this hypothesis must be checked (preferably with the other) to be confirmed or discarded. Making successive approximations closer and closer to what is accurate is the central ingredient of effective perspective taking.

H. *Practicing Double-Loop Thinking*. Here are a number of ways.

1. Continue to experiment with (and graph) taking Leilani's perspective, using the other inferences listed above, e.g., about friendship. Develop more inferences.

2. Assume Leilani's role and take (and graph) her perspective on Ilse.

3. Use the incident that you chose to describe in item F above relative to your personal perspective on a different other. Generate a number of alternative interpretations that the other person could plausibly draw about you. Choose the most likely and graph.

Taking the Persepective of a Different Other

Behavior	Expectation	Value
The other's perspective of me		

In short, an accurate description of a cross-cultural encounter involves identification of your own perspective and, further, taking the perspective of the other.

In summary, the steps to follow are:

1. Describe the situation.
2. Objectively list the behaviors of both participants (don't use adjectives).
3. List statements of inference.
4. Relate the behaviors to the underlying expectations and values from your perspective. (Use the suggested matrix.)
5. Attempt to understand the other's thinking about *your* behavior, expectations, and values, i.e., take another's perspective. (Use the suggested matrix.)
6. Expand "taking the other's perspective" to an encounter you have had with someone from a different culture. Confirm or reject your understanding through further communication and/or repeated observation.
7. Learn double-loop thinking.
8. Practice double-loop thinking.

I. *The final step*, of course, is to (a) assess the accuracy of your perspective on the other's perception of you and (b) explore ways in which you can modify your behavior to stimulate in the other an even more accurate (and more positive as well) perception.

Make a list and discuss with others who are doing this exercise effective ways to pursue these goals. Note: One of the simplest is to take the step suggested in item G above: check and/or confirm directly your perspective with the different other.

"Facts" or "Feel"?

Indrei Ratiu

OBJECTIVE

To understand that some people—and some cultures—require a great deal more information than others to make a decision. That is, some people and cultures are "low-context" while others are "high-context."

Participants

Any number of adults

Materials

Pencils. Three handouts.

Time

1–2 hours, depending on group size.

PROCEDURES

1. Pass out Handout 1. Ask readers to note the main characteristics of high-context and low-context cultures.

2. Invite participants to list on the chalkboard (or flip chart) the main characteristics of high- and low-context cultures. After this is done, pass out Handout 2: Analytical vs. Intuitive Thinking, which is a summary of these two approaches or "ways of reading the map." Then synthesize the two lists.

3. Read through the list of situations identified in Handout 3: Daily Tasks, and quickly check each one "Low" or "High" according to whether you personally feel you would respond intuitively (high-context) or analytically (low-context) to that situation.

4. Now go back over the list of situations, and for each one invite both high- and low-context participants to tell what they might do in each situation.

" 'Facts' or 'Feel'?" by Indrei Ratiu from *Experiential Activities for Intercultural Learning*, pp. 57–63. Vol. 1, ed. by H. Seelye. Reprinted by permission of Intercultural Press, Inc., Yarmouth, ME.

This activity was inspired by Edward T. Hall's *Beyond Culture*. New York: Doubleday/Anchor, 1977.

HANDOUT 1: HIGH- AND LOW-CONTEXT CULTURES

Let us use a "map" metaphor for a moment. Imagine that a certain traveler constantly refers to the map as a means of orientation while another traveler prefers to keep the map in his or her head only as a general idea rather than a detailed record of every feature in the terrain. Of this second traveler, we say that he or she prefers to work intuitively, using hunch or feel and relying on sense of direction.

This second traveler makes the first traveler feel uneasy. "How does this intuitive person know he or she is on the right track?" the first traveler will ask. The first traveler needs specific evidence or indicators, needs to check with the map to get clear directions. To him or her, the intuitive person seems to work almost by magic, and that feels risky.

We call this first traveler analytical, using facts and figures and relying on spoken language and past experience (the map is, after all, a distillation of other people's experience) in order to move about.

The contrast illustrated here is fundamental in some human psychological paradigms. It is the contrast between the thinking and feeling dimensions of Carl Jung's psychological types. It is the contrast between the modes of operation of the "adult" and "little professor" ego states in transactional analysis. It is the contrast between the left and the right hemispheres of the human brain as identified by R. Ornstein and others.

The different modes of thinking exhibited by the two travelers is prevalent among human cultures, and this can be seen in their use of language. Anthropologist Edward T. Hall calls this contrast in the cultural sphere that between low-context (LC) and high-context (HC) cultures.

In *Beyond Culture*, Hall (1977) describes the contrast as follows:

> A high-context (HC) communication or message is one in which most of the information is either in the physical context or internalized in the person, while very little is in the coded, explicit, transmitted part of the message. A low-context (LC) communication is just the opposite: i.e., the mass of information is vested in the explicit code. Twins who have grown up together can and do communicate more economically (HC) than two lawyers in a courtroom during a trial (LC), a mathematician programming a computer, two politicians drafting legislation, two administrators writing a regulation, or a child trying to explain to his mother why he got into a fight.
>
> Although no culture exists exclusively at one end of the scale, some are high while others are low. American culture, while not at the bottom, is towards the lower end of the scale. We [Americans] are still considerably above the German-Swiss, the Germans, and the Scandinavians in the amount of contexting needed in everyday life. While complex, multi-institutional cultures (those that are technologically advanced) might be thought of as inevitably LC, this is not always true. China, the possessor of a great and complex culture, is on the high-context end of the scale (91).

A high-context communicator is thus sensitive to situational or contextual data, what we would describe as information that is implicit in the situation, and requires relatively little content or explicit information in order to understand what is going on.

A low-context communicator is highly sensitive to standardized data from which he or she can generalize and requires a large amount of content, or explicit information, in order to understand what is going on.

The intuitive, "feely" traveler who keeps the map in his or her head is high-context, while the analytical, "factual" one who has it constantly in hand is low-context.

The activity which follows makes the assumption that our psychological type is partly innate and partly learned: each of us engages in both intuitive and analytical processes many times each day, but for reasons that are partly cultural (i.e., learned), partly innate, and partly situational, we tend to have preferences for one approach rather than another.

HANDOUT 2: ANALYTICAL VS. INTUITIVE THINKING

Analytical

- Relies on prior knowledge and experience
- Deductive (or inductive)
- Mind is in control
- Collects data in light of prior knowledge and experience
- Appropriate where circumstances are predictable and familiar
- Planning/theory-oriented
- Explicit (i.e., verbal)
- Rational
- Content-oriented (low-context)
- Linear
- Concerned with patterns of events
- Sensitive to causality (i.e., events related to each other over time)

Intuitive

- Relies on immediate sense data of the moment
- Intuitive
- Mind is not in control
- Regards data collecting as an objective in itself
- Appropriate where circumstances are upredictable and unfamiliar
- Action/event-oriented
- Implicit (i.e., nonverbal)
- Nonrational
- Context-oriented (high-context)
- Holistic (big picture)
- Concerned with "shape" of events
- Sensitive to synchronicity (i.e., events occurring together)

HANDOUT 3: DAILY TASKS

a. Getting yourself from an office to another location in town
b. Finding out who is married to whom at a party
c. Determining the mood of a meeting
d. Finding out where to catch the bus and when
e. Identifying people's professions
f. Deciding when it is time to leave a dinner party
g. Deciding how many people are in favor of a resolution
h. Deciding on the right moment to ask for a raise in salary
i. Picking winning numbers in a lottery

j. Identifying a market need for a product

k. Identifying people's state of health

l. Deciding how much time is needed in getting to the airport

m. Knowing what your partner is thinking at a given moment

n. Preparing the annual budget

o. Finding out train times at the station

Skill Exercise 8

Bribery in International Business

Dorothy Marcic

Purpose

To discuss issues related to ethical behavior in international business dealings.

Group Size

Any number of groups of 4–6 members.

Time Required

One class period.

Preparation Required

Students read mini-cases and decide what action should be taken in each one.

CASES

1. You are driving to a nearby country from your job as a manager of a foreign subsidiary. In your car are a number of rather expensive gifts for family and friends in the country you are visiting. When you cross the border, the customs official tells you the duty will be equivalent to $200. Then he smiles, how-

ever, hands back your passport and quietly suggests you put a smaller sum, say $20, in the passport and hand it back to him.

What do you do?

2. You have been hired as an independent consultant on a United States development grant. Part of your job involves working with the Ministry of Health in a developing country. Your assignment is to help standardize some procedures to test for various diseases in the population. After two weeks on the job, a higher-level manager complains to you that money donated by the World Health Organization to the ministry for purchasing vaccines has actually been used to buy expensive computers for top-ranking officials.

What do you do?

3. You have been trying for several months to privatize what was formerly a state-owned business. The company has been doing well and will likely do better in private hands. Unfortunately, the paperwork is slow and it may take many more months to finish. An official who can help suggests that if you pay expenses for him and his family to visit the parent company in the United States (plus a two-week vacation at Disney World and in New York City), the paperwork can be completed within one week.

What do you do?

4. One of your top managers in a Middle Eastern country has been kidnapped by a terrorist group that has demanded a ransom of $2 million, plus food assistance for refugees in a specified camp. If the ransom is not paid, they threaten to kill him.

What do you do?

5. On a business trip to a developing country, you see a nice leather briefcase (which you badly need) for a reasonable price in the local currency (the equivalent of $200 on the standard exchange rate). In this country, however, it is difficult for the locals to get U.S. dollars or other hard currency. The shop clerk offers you the briefcase for $100 if you pay in U.S. dollars.

What do you do?

6. You are the manager of a foreign subsidiary and have brought your car with you from the U.S. Because it is a foreign-purchased car, you must go through a complicated web of lines and bureaucracy (and you yourself must do it—no one can do it for you), which takes anywhere from 20 to 40 hours during business hours. One official tells you, however, that he can "help" if you "loan" him $100 and buy him some good U.S. bourbon.

What do you do?

7. Your company has been trying to get foreign contracts in this developing country for several months. Yesterday, the brother-in-law of the Finance Minister offered to work as a consultant to help you secure contracts. He charges one and one-half times more than anyone else in a similar situation.

What do you do?

8. You have been working as the director of the foreign subsidiary for several months. This week, you learned several valued employees have part-time businesses that they run while on the job. One of them exchanges foreign currency for employees and visitors. Another rents a few cars to visitors. And so on. You are told this has been acceptable behavior for years.

    What do you do?

9. As manager of a foreign subsidiary, you recently discovered your chief of operations has authorized a very convoluted accounting system, most likely to hide many costs that go to his pocket. Right now, you have no real proof, but rumors are circulating to that effect as well. This chief, however, has close ties to officials in the government who can make or break your company in this country.

    What do you do?

10. You have been hired to do some management training in a developing country. The costs of the program are almost entirely covered by a U.S. government agency. The people responsible for setting up one of the programs in a large company tell you they want the program to be held in a resort hotel (which is not much more expensive than any other) in a beautiful part of the country. Further, because they are so busy with all the changes in their country, they cannot come to a five-day program, which is what has been funded. Could you please make it a little longer each day and shorten it to three days? You would get paid the same.

    What do you do?

11. You have been hired by an investment firm funded by U.S. dollars. Your job is to fund companies in several former communist countries. If you do not meet your quota for each of three months, you will lose your job, or at least have your salary severely cut back. One of the countries is still run by communists, though they have changed the name of their political party. They want you to fund three companies that would still be tightly controlled by the state. You know they would hire their relatives to run those companies. Yet, if you don't fund them, no other opportunities will exist for you in this country.

    What do you do?

12. Your new job is to secure contracts with foreign governments in several developing countries. One of your colleagues takes you aside one day to give you "tips" on how to make sure you get the contracts you are after. He tells you what each nationality likes to hear, to soothe their egos or other psychological needs. For example, people in one country like to be told they will have a better image with the U.S. government if they contract with your company (of course, this is not true). If you tell them these things, he says, they will most definitely give you the contracts. If not, someone in another company will tell them similar things and they will get the contracts.

    What do you do?

13. You have been asked to be on the board of directors of a large telecommunications company about to be privatized. The two main organizers of the project, former government officials, have asked that their names not be used until after all the governmental approval is set, as they are concerned with being accused of using undue influence in other privatization projects.

What do you do?

14. You are the manager of a foreign company in a country where bribery is common. You have been told an important shipment has arrived but it will take up to six months to clear the paperwork. However, you were informed casually that a "tip" of $200 would cut the time to three days.

What do you do?

Skill Exercise 9

Babel: Interpersonal Communication

Phillip M. Ericson

Goals

    I. To examine language barriers, which contribute to breakdowns in communication.

    II. To demonstrate the anxieties and frustrations that may be felt when communicating under difficult circumstances.

    VIII. To illustrate the impact of nonverbal communication when verbal communication is ineffective and/or restricted.

Group Size

An unlimited number of equal-sized groups of four, six, or eight members each.

Time Required

Approximately two hours.

"Babel: Interpersonal Communication" by Philip M. Ericson from *A Handbook of Structured Experiences for Human Relations Training*, Vol. V. pp. 16–17. Copyright © 1975 by Pfeiffer, an imprint of Jossey-Bass Inc., Publishers.

Physical Setting

A room large enough for the groups to meet comfortably.

Materials

    I. A pencil and paper for each participant.

    II. A blindfold for each group member.

PROCESS

    I. The facilitator divides the large group into subgroups.

    II. When the groups have assembled, the facilitator announces that each group is to create a language of its own. This language must be significantly different from English and must include the following:

        1. a greeting

        2. description of some object, person, or event

        3. an evaluative statement about an object or a person

        4. a farewell.

Group members must be able to "speak" their group's language at the end of this step. (Forty-five minutes.)

    III. Within each language group, members number themselves sequentially, i.e., 1,2,3,4, etc. The facilitator announces the location of a new group to be composed of all participants numbered 1. He likewise forms new groups of participants numbered 2,3,4, and so on.

    IV. The facilitator directs members to pair off in the new groups. Each member must teach his new language to his partner without using English or any other recognized language. (Twenty minutes).

    V. The facilitator distributes a blindfold to each group. A blindfolded volunteer from each group teaches his language to the group. A second volunteer repeats this task. (Twenty minutes.)

    VI. The facilitator distributes blindfolds to all remaining participants. Participants are told to stand in their second groups, and all chairs are moved aside. Participants blindfold themselves and are instructed to find their original groups without the use of any conventional language or people's names.

    VII. When the original groups have been re-formed, the facilitator instructs them to discuss the activity and to answer the following questions:

        1. What did this experience illustrate about communication?

        2. How did you feel during the experience?

        3. What did you learn about yourself from it?

    VIII. The facilitator leads a general discussion on the problems faced by people who do not understand a language and on the difficulties that blind people may have in communicating.

VARIATIONS

    I. The requirements for the new vocabulary can be changed to make the task more difficult or less difficult.

    II. All participants can be blindfolded for step V.

    III. Real language can be used. The phrases can be preset.

Ugli Orange Case

Robert J. House

Purpose:
To practice negotiation skills in a conflict situation.

Group Size:
Any number of groups with three members.

Time Required:
40 minutes.

Related Topics:
Interpersonal Communication

EXERCISE SCHEDULE

	Unit Time	Total Time
1. **Groups form**	5 min	5 min

Form groups of three members. One person will be Dr. Roland, one will be Dr. Jones, and the third will be an observer.

2. **Read roles**	5 min	10 min

Roland and Jones read only their own roles, while the observer reads both.

3. **Role-play**	10 min	20 min

Instructor announces: "I am Mr./Ms. Cardoza, the owner of the remaining Ugli oranges. My fruit-export firm is based in South America. My country does not have diplomatic relations with your country, although we do have strong trade relations."

Groups spend about 10 minutes meeting with the other firm's representative and decide on a course of action. Be prepared to answer the following questions:

	Unit Time	*Total Time*

1. What do you plan to do?
2. If you want to buy the oranges, what price will you offer?
3. To whom and how will the oranges be delivered?

4. **Observers report**   **10+ min**   **30 min**
   Observers report the solutions reached. Groups describe decision-making process used.

5. **Class discussion**   **10 min**   **40 min**
   The instructor will lead a discussion on the exercise, addressing the following questions:
   a. Which groups had the most trust? How did that influence behavior?
   b. Which groups shared more information? Why?
   c. How are trust and disclosure important in negotiations?

ROLE OF "DR. ROLAND"

You are Dr. P. W. Roland. You work as a research biologist for a pharmaceutical firm. The firm is under contract with the government to do research on methods to combat enemy uses of biological warfare.

Recently several World War II experimental nerve gas bombs were moved from the United States to a small island just off the U.S. coast in the Pacific. In the process of transporting them, two of the bombs developed a leak. The leak is presently controlled by government scientists, who believe that the gas will permeate the bomb chambers within two weeks. They know of no method of preventing the gas from getting into the atmosphere and spreading to other islands, and very likely to the West Coast as well. If this occurs, it is likely that several thousand people will incur serious brain damage or die.

You've developed a synthetic vapor that will neutralize the nerve gas if it is injected into the bomb chamber before the gas leaks out. The vapor is made with a chemical taken from the rind of the Ugli orange, a very rare fruit. Unfortunately, only 4,000 of these oranges were produced this season.

You've been informed on good evidence that a Mr./Ms. R. H. Cardoza, a fruit exporter in South America, is in possession of 3,000 Ugli oranges. The chemicals from the rinds of all 3,000 oranges would be sufficient to neutralize the gas if the serum is developed and injected efficiently. You have been informed that the rinds of these oranges are in good condition.

You have also been informed that Dr. J. W. Jones is also urgently seeking purchase of Ugli oranges, and s/he is aware of Cardoza's possession of the 3,000 available. Dr. Jones works for a firm with which your firm is highly competitive. There is a great deal of industrial espionage in the pharmaceutical industry. Over the years, your firm and Dr. Jones' have sued each other for violations of industrial espionage laws and infringement of patent rights several times. Litigation on two suits is still in process.

The federal government has asked your firm for assistance. You've been authorized by your firm to approach Cardoza to purchase the 3,000 Ugli oranges. You have been told s/he will sell them to the highest bidder. Your firm has authorized you to bid as high as $250,000 to obtain the rinds of the oranges.

Before approaching Cardoza, you have decided to talk to Dr. Jones to influence him/her not to prevent you from purchasing the oranges.

ROLE OF "DR. JONES"

You are Dr. J. W. Jones, a biological research scientist employed by a pharmaceutical firm. You have recently developed a synthetic chemical useful for curing and preventing Rudosen. Rudosen is a disease contracted by pregnant women. If not caught in the first four weeks of pregnancy, the disease causes serious brain, eye, and ear damage to the unborn child. Recently there has been an outbreak of Rudosen in your state, and several thousand women have contracted the disease. You have found, with volunteer patients, that your recently developed synthetic serum cures Rudosen in its early stages. Unfortunately, the serum is made from the juice of the Ugli orange, which is a very rare fruit. Only a small quantity (approximately 4,000) of these oranges were produced last season. No additional Ugli oranges will be available until next season, which will be too late to cure the present Rudosen victims.

You've demonstrated that your synthetic serum is in no way harmful to pregnant women. Consequently, there are no side effects. The Food and Drug Administration has approved production and distribution of the serum as a cure for Rudosen. Unfortunately, the present outbreak was unexpected, and your firm had not planned on having the compound serum available for six months. Your firm holds the patent on the synthetic serum, and it is expected to be a highly profitable product when it is generally available to the public.

You have recently been informed on good evidence that Mr./Ms. R. H. Cardoza, a South American fruit exporter, is in possession of 3,000 Ugli oranges in good condition. If you could obtain the juice of all 3,000, you would be able to both cure present victims and provide sufficient inoculation for the remaining pregnant women in the state. No other state currently has a Rudosen threat.

You have recently been informed that Dr. P. W. Roland is also urgently seeking Ugli oranges and is also aware of Cardoza's possession of the 3,000 available. Dr. Roland is employed by a competing pharmaceutical firm. S/he has been working on biological warfare research for the past several years. There is a great deal of industrial espionage in the pharmaceutical industry. Over the past several years, Dr. Roland's firm and yours have sued each other for infringement of patent rights and espionage law violations several times.

You've been authorized by your firm to approach Cardoza to purchase the 3,000 Ugli oranges. You have been told s/he will sell them to the highest bidder. Your firm has authorized you to bid as high as $250,000 to obtain the juice of the 3,000 available oranges.

Work Values Exercise

Carol Wolf

OBJECTIVES

- To get people to think and talk about their own values and life histories as they relate to work, including the cultural patterns embodied therein.
- To explore the ways in which the group or organization reflects or stimulates conflict with the values of individual members of subgroups.
- To engage in values clarification (individual and group).

Setting

Sufficient space for large- and small-group discussions.

Participants

Individual, small groups (3–5), or large group.

Time

1 hour.

Materials

Flip chart, markers. Participants need pen and paper. Handouts 1 and 2.

RATIONALE

Diverse groups of people often have very different ideas about the meaning and purpose of work. Some of these differences are culturally based, others may stem from different life experiences. Quite often, these differences are unspoken, or even outside of awareness—yet they are often the root of assumptions, judgments, and conflicts in the workplace. Understanding personal and organizational value systems is a critical component in the development of diversity awareness and the bringing about of organizational change. Highlighting core organizational values, or uncovering what may be unspoken or hidden values, can help groups and individuals to bet-

"Work Values Exercise" by Carol Wolf from *Experiential Activities for Intercultural Learning.* Reprinted by permission of Intercultural Press, Inc., Yarmouth, ME.

ter understand what enables (or disables) teamwork and effective organizational alignment. The "Work Values Exercise" helps participants take the first steps in building a foundation based on the valuing of diverse perspectives and skills. (Note: The group must be at a point in their development where open dialogue about differences is acceptable.)

PROCEDURE

1. Have participants break into small groups (3–4 members each). Ask them to respond to and discuss their answers to each of the questions listed in Handout 1. (Approximately 20 minutes. Facilitator should make sure they don't get stuck on the first subject.) In the meantime, put the definition of "value" on a flip chart and post the list of work values.

2. Distribute Handout 2. Based on their previous discussions, ask participants to pick their three most important values from Handout 2 and, continuing in their groups, do all or some of the following:
   a. Talk about the values they chose, why they picked them, and what they mean for them.
   b. Discuss how they believe their values differ from the values of their group (organization) as a whole.
   c. Talk about what needs to change in order for them to feel more comfortable with/committed to the group.

OUTCOMES

Information gleaned from this exercise can be used as lead-in to a variety of areas, including improving reward and motivation policies, evaluating employee performance, improving team building, diagnosing work conflicts, or clarifying group identity.

HANDOUT 1

Questions

1. When was the first time in your life that you worked? Describe what you did. How did you know it was work?
2. What was positive about this experience? What was negative?
3. What did you learn from this and subsequent experiences about yourself and work? (For example, why you work, what you need in order to work well.)
4. What messages or lessons did you get from your family about work? Who taught you? How?

Examples

"I learned that I can't stand tedious jobs" (work value: variety).

"I learned that the people I work with are important" (work value: relationships).

HANDOUT 2

Definition of "Value"

A principle or quality intrinsically valuable or desirable (Webster's Ninth New Collegiate Dictionary).

Work Values

Respect
Communication
Clear purpose
Relationships—working with others
Individual achievement
Challenging work
Contribution to goals/sense of accomplishment
Recognition
Rewards
Security
Chance to develop/improve
Efficiency
Good pay/benefits
Variety of work
Control over work
Environment/surroundings
Others:

Japanese Decision-Making Exercise (Ringi/Nemawashi)

William Van Buskirk

Goals

1. To give students the opportunity to work through a meaningful task in the manner of Japanese consensual decision making.
2. To compare their own experiences of group decision making with the Japanese approach.

Preparation (optional)

Background reading: chapter 3 of *The False Promise of the Japanese Miracle*, by P. Sethi, N. Namiki and C. Swanson.

EXERCISE SCHEDULE

	Unit Time	Total Time
1. **Introduction**	5 min	5 min

Instructor explains the processes of Ringi and Nemawashi and sets up the structure of the exercise. Group composition includes group leaders (Kacho) and student manager (Bucho).

2. **Primary groups meet**	20 min	25 min

Groups of four of six members design a final exam format that is likely to be a valuable learning tool and basis of evaluation.

3. **Secondary groups meet**	20 min	45 min

New groups of four to six members continue with assignment as above, using what was discussed in primary groups as a basis. These are called secondary groups (Kacho). After this session, groups can meet in whatever way they want. The professor will give guidance during one or two open-ended class sessions. Outside class meetings occur at the instigation of the group leaders and the student manager.

	Unit Time	Total Time

4. **Whole class decides**   **30 min (new class)**

   Generation of a Ringi document specifying the content of the exam. Document must be signed by all students in the class. Instructor discusses what problems, if any, this document might cause with university administration.

5. **Evaluation**   **15 min**   **45 min**

   Evaluation of the exercise. How much did it resemble the descriptions of Ringi and Nemawashi found in the literature? What difficulties did we encounter? Were those difficulties likely to be present in the Japanese context? If so, how would they likely be managed? This evaluation may be done in the context of class discussions and as part of the final exam.

Skill Exercise 13

Onion, Iceberg, Endive, or?: Mapping Organizational Culture

Barry Allen Gold

Purpose

To understand how external and internal influences contribute to an organization's culture and ways to change organizational culture.

Group Size and Structure

Any number. Form groups of five for creation of an organizational culture map. Each group selects a member who reports the results of the discussion to the class.

Time Required

90 minutes. The first hour is for developing a culture map. The remaining time is for discussing each group's map. If necessary, the times can be cut in half.

Materials

Chalkboard or newsprint for presenting images of culture and the culture map.

IMAGES OF ORGANIZATIONAL CULTURE

Organizational culture can be thought of as a concrete image. For example, the idea of culture—national and organizational—as represented by an onion or iceberg—suggests that many layers of culture are below the surface of organizational behavior.

Another approach is to view culture as a metaphor. For example, a metaphor for American culture is football, because of the blend of group and individual performance found throughout American life. A metaphor for Japanese culture is a garden, which captures the careful mixture of ingredients that maintains a group oriented culture.

Organizational culture is composed of elements of many external cultures, including national, regional, and local. These cultures reflect religious values, ethnic group values, and social class preferences, which are important elements of culture.

A university reflects these and other cultural sources in its architecture, geographic location, language, curriculum, customs, ceremonies, rituals, and vision of its students' futures.

For example, in the United States there is a wide range of organizational cultures in higher education. Some schools are known for their nationally ranked athletic teams, whereas others earn their reputations exclusively as a result of academic excellence. Underlying many universities and colleges are religious values either because they were influential in its founding or are still important to the institution. These differences can affect the core values and behavior of students, faculty and administrators.

Finally, within universities there are subcultures. Subcultures often form around academic majors such as music, premedicine, accounting, and theater. Subcultures have their own images and metaphors.

GROUP ACTIVITY

Step 1

Each group of five should develop an image or metaphor for the culture of the university. The following questions are guidelines for each level of culture.

Manifestations: Observable Elements

- What are the distinguishing artifacts of the students?
- What artifacts represent the culture of the faculty?
- What artifacts are present in the university?

Expressed Values: Explanations of the Manifest Elements

- What is the mission of the university?
- What are the goals of the university?
- If the university has a motto, what is it and what does it mean?

Basic Assumptions: Foundations of Culture

- What are the underlying value assumptions of the university?
- Are there different assumptions for different subcultures within the university?
- Are some assumptions so deep that they are not apparent to most members of the university?

MAPPING ORGANIZATIONAL CULTURE

Step 2

Using the data generated from the group discussion, each group should create a visual representation of the culture of the university that displays the following:

- the influence of external cultures,
- central components of the internal culture and subcultures,
- areas in which the internal and external cultures achieve a consensus on the goals of the university, and
- areas in which the various cultures are in either disagreement or conflict.

Step 3

Indicate on the map elements of the culture that are manifestations, expressed values, and basic assumptions.

CHANGING THE CULTURE

Step 4

Based on the preceding information, the groups should answer the following:

- How has the culture of the university changed over the past several years?
- Is the culture of the university changing now?
- What influenced the amount and type of change?
- How does the culture change, or lack of it, affect the future of the university?

MAPPING CULTURE CHANGE

Step 5

Using the culture map, the group should consider ways that the culture can be changed by discussing the following:

- How can artifacts of culture be changed?
- How can expressed values be changed?
- How can basic assumptions be changed?
- How can the influence of the various external and internal cultural influences be changed?
- What image or metaphor would represent a significant change of the culture?
- What management skills are necessary to implement the suggested changes?

CLASS DISCUSSION

Step 6

Each group's reporter presents the image or metaphor of culture developed and major themes from the small group discussion to the entire class. A facilitator, either the instructor or a student, moderates the presentation of each group's product and records the major points on a chalkboard or flipchart.

Step 7

The entire class then considers the following questions:

- What aspects of the culture explain either the similarities or differences in the group's cultural images?
- How has the culture of the school affected the small group discussion and the overall conduct of the exercise?
- How does the organizational culture affect daily life for the average student in the university?

Step 8

The facilitator concludes the exercise—with assistance from the class—by combining elements of each group's presentation and the class discussion into a model of the university's culture.

Skill Exercise 14

Dimensions of National Culture and Effective Leadership Patterns: Hofstede Revisited

Peter Dorfman

Purpose

To measure value systems.

Group Size

Any number.

Time Required

20 minutes.

EXERCISE SCHEDULE

	Unit Time	*Total Time*
1. **Preparation** Complete inventory.		
2. **Class discussion** Instructor leads a discussion on Hofstede's value system.	20+ min	20+ min

In the questionnaire below, please indicate the extent to which you agree or disagree with each statement. For example, if you strongly agree with a particular statement, circle the 5 next to the statement.

1 = strongly disagree

2 = disagree

3 = neither agree nor disagree

4 = agree

5 = strongly agree

Questionnaire	strongly disagree				strongly agree
1. It is important to have job instructions spelled out in detail so that employees always know what they are expected to do.	1	2	3	4	5
2. Managers expect employees to closely follow instructions and procedures.	1	2	3	4	5
3. Rules and regulations are important because they inform employees what the organization expects of them.	1	2	3	4	5
4. Standard operating procedures are helpful to employees on the job.	1	2	3	4	5
5. Instructions for operations are important for employees on the job.	1	2	3	4	5
6. Group welfare is more important than individual rewards.	1	2	3	4	5
7. Group success is more important than individual success.	1	2	3	4	5
8. Being accepted by the members of your work group is very important.	1	2	3	4	5
9. Employees should pursue their own goals only after considering the welfare of the group.	1	2	3	4	5
10. Managers should encourage group loyalty even if individual goals suffer.	1	2	3	4	5
11. Individuals may be expected to give up their goals in order to benefit group success.	1	2	3	4	5
12. Managers should make most decisions without consulting subordinates.	1	2	3	4	5
13. Managers should frequently use authority and power when dealing with subordinates.	1	2	3	4	5
14. Managers should seldom ask for the opinions of employees.	1	2	3	4	5
15 Managers should avoid off-the-job social contacts with employees.	1	2	3	4	5
16. Employees should not disagree with management decisions.	1	2	3	4	5
17. Managers should not delegate important tasks to employees.	1	2	3	4	5

Questionnaire	strongly disagree				strongly agree
18. Managers should help employees with their family problems.	1	2	3	4	5
19. Managers should see to it that employees are adequately clothed and fed.	1	2	3	4	5
20. A manager should help employees solve their personal problems.	1	2	3	4	5
21. Management should see that all employees receive health care.	1	2	3	4	5
22. Management should see that children of employees have an adequate education.	1	2	3	4	5
23. Management should provide legal assistance for employees who get into trouble with the law.	1	2	3	4	5
24. Managers should take care of their employees as they would their children.	1	2	3	4	5
25. Meetings are usually run more effectively when they are chaired by a man.	1	2	3	4	5
26. It is more important for men to have a professional career than it is for women to have a professional career.	1	2	3	4	5
27. Men usually solve problems with logical analysis; women usually solve problems with intuition.	1	2	3	4	5
28. Solving organizational problems usually requires an active, forcible approach, which is typical of men.	1	2	3	4	5
29. It is preferable to have a man, rather than a woman, in a high-level position.	1	2	3	4	5

BACKGROUND WORK VALUES

Geert Hofstede examined international differences in work-related values and came up with the four dimensions: power distance, uncertainty avoidance, individualism and masculinity. Below are brief definitions of each of the four dimensions.

POWER DISTANCE (PD) measures human inequality in organizations, looking at the boss's decision-making style, employees' fear of disagreeing with the superior, and how subordinates prefer a boss to make decisions. Power distance assesses the interpersonal power or influence between lower- and higher-ranking employees, as perceived by the less powerful one. Essentially, it looks at how less powerful people validate the power structure. Cultures with a low score tend to respect individuals, strive for equality and value happiness. Those with a high score look to servitude and tact of lesser individuals, while allowing great privileges to those with influence. Other characteristics of low-scored cultures are that managers tend to consult subordinates when making decisions, perceived work ethic is stronger, close supervision is evaluated negatively by subordinates, and employees are cooperative. High scorers are less likely to have managers consult subordinates, and employees are reluctant to trust each other.

UNCERTAINTY AVOIDANCE (UA) explains each society's Search for Truth and the anxiety people feel in a situation with conflicting values or unstructured outcomes. Cultures with high uncertainty avoidance try to minimize the anxiety with a thorough set of strict laws and behavior norms. To ease the discomfort on the philosophical level, there is a belief in One Truth, the One Way. Low uncertainty avoidance cultures tend to have fewer rules and more acceptance of diversity of thought and behavior. Organizations, too, try to avoid uncertainty by creating rules, rituals and technology that give the illusion of predictability. Even group decision-making, however, is a means for avoiding risk because no one is held accountable. Countries that have low UA tend to have less emotional resistance to change, a stronger achievement motivation, a preference for managerial careers over specialist fields, and hope for success. On the other hand, countries with high UA tend to have more emotional resistance to change, weaker achievement motivation, a preference for specialist careers over managerial, and a fear of failure.

INDIVIDUALISM (I) looks at the degree to which people are part of groups or on their own. In collective societies, everyone is born into a strong clan of uncles, aunts and cousins (even third and fourth) who are part of one unit. Each person contributes to the group and at some time receives care from the group. Loyalties are to the group above everything else. In more individualistic societies, people are more or less on their own and are expected to take care of themselves and their immediate family. In collective countries (with a low I score), there is often an emotional dependence on the company, managers aspire to conformity and orderliness, group decisions are considered better than individual ones, and managers value security in their work. In societies with a high I score, though, there is more emotional independence from the company; managers aspire to leadership and variety; managers seek input from others, but individual decisions are still seen as better; and managers value autonomy in their work.

MASCULINITY (M) versus its opposite, femininity, examines how roles are distributed between the sexes. The predominant pattern of socialization worldwide is for men to be more assertive and women to be more nurturing. In countries with high M scores, the successful manager is seen as more male—aggressive, competitive, just and tough—and not as feminine—soft, yielding, intuitive and emotional (as the stereotypes define it). In countries with high M scores, earnings, recognition and advancement are important to employees, work is more central to people's lives, achievement is defined in terms of wealth and professional success, people prefer

Table S14-1 Cultural Dimension Scores for Ten Countries

	PD	ID	MA	UA	LT
USA	40L	91H	62H	46L	29L
Germany	35L	67H	66H	65M	31M
Japan	54M	46M	95H	92H	80H
France	68H	71H	43M	86H	30*L
Netherlands	38L	80H	14L	53M	44M
Hong Kong	68H	25L	57H	29L	96H
Indonesia	78H	14L	46M	48L	25*L
West Africa	77H	20L	46M	54M	16L
Russia	95**H	50**M	40*L	90**H	10**L
China	80**H	20**L	50**M	60**M	118H

PD=Power Distance; ID=Individualism; MA=Masculinity; UA=Uncertainty Avoidance;
LT=Long-Term Orientation H=top third, M=medium third, L=bottom third (among 53 countries and regions for the first four dimensions; among 23 countries for the fifth)

*Excerpted from Geert Hofstede (1993), *Academy of Management Executive*, 7(1), 81–94. Used with permission.

**estimated

more salary rather than fewer working hours, "Theory X" gets some acceptance, and there is higher job stress. In societies with low M scores, on the other hand, cooperation and security are valued by employees, work is less central to people's lives, achievement is defined in terms of human interactions, people prefer fewer working hours rather than more salary, "Theory X" is less accepted, and there is lower job stress.

Management in the Year 2200

Hiroaki Izumi

Purpose
To explore issues in management in other cultures.

Group Size
Any number of groups of four to six people.

Time Required
50 minutes.

EXERCISE SCHEDULE

1. **Pre-class**
   Read background and answer questions.

	Unit Time	Total Time
2. **Group discussions**	20 min	20 min

   Groups of four to six answer questions.

| 3. **Class discussion** | 30 min | 50 min |

   Groups report results and instructor leads discussion on issues of "cross-cultural" management.

"Management in the year 2200" by Hiroaki Izumi. Reprinted by permission of City University of Hong Kong.

Background

The year is 2200 A.D. During the past two centuries, Earth has achieved interstellar travel at faster-than-light warp speed. Because of overcrowding and depletion of resources on Earth during the second half of the 22nd century, we began to colonize other planets in other star systems. People were sent out to assist in civilizing uninhabited planets and to extract their resources for shipping back to the industries in our home solar system. About 100 years ago, a major political upheaval on Earth put most of the colonies out of touch with us for about 75 years. They no longer were able to ship resources to Earth so they began interstellar commerce amongst themselves. They continued to extract resources but they also began some limited industrialization themselves. The level of development on these colonies could be compared to that of LDCs on Earth during the 20th century, but at a much higher level of technological sophistication.

Recently, about the year 2175, when contact was re-established with the Earth colonies, interstellar trade with them was also re-established. Earth is trying to regain the lost commercial trade that existed prior to the political problems and loss of contact. But the situation has changed. The colonies no longer act as colonies, but more like nations on their own. They have tariff barriers, their own commercial laws and codes based on the old common law ideas, political parties and full governments, their own corporations and business infrastructures, their own educational systems, and their own market structures. In fact, during almost one generation of separation from Earth, each of the colonies began to develop their own human subcultures based on the conditions that existed on their planet.

One planet that recently regained contact with Earth is in the Orion constellation of stars. It is the only colony in that area, so the colony is known as the Orion colony and the people on the planet as Orions.

The Orion colony is rather strange by Earth standards. The planet is relatively new in geological terms and still has Ice Age conditions. The climate is very harsh due to the cold weather. It is, however, rich in certain rare elements trapped in pockets in the ice. Before losing contact with Earth, the Orions traded in the rare elements that they extracted from the ice by mechanical means. The equipment is highly sophisticated and fully automated. Unfortunately, even automated equipment must be maintained and serviced. Furthermore, the ice must be prospected using labor-intensive methods in which individuals must go out on the ice and run specialized sensing equipment, which has a very limited life-span.

> **Earth, surprisingly, has not changed much in how we do business, our diversity of political parties and ideologies, our lifestyles, our mores and norms, and our knowledge of how to deal with strange cultures. We still tend to be slightly xenophobic, too concerned with making money, living for the short term with emphasis on quick return on investments (though there is some improvement in favoring long-term investments among some groups), and we haven't improved our production and marketing skills much. We've only improved our production methodologies.**

Because of the cold weather and great physical endurance needed for prospecting and servicing and maintaining the equipment, most of the field workers are women who are much better suited to the work. Women's better physical heat retention, smaller size, greater manual dexterity, and greater muscle endurance provide them with physiological advantages that cannot be matched by men. Having recognized these qualities early on, Orion women were better technically educated than Orion men. Because of their technical expertise and educational advantages, they also quickly took over control of much of the organizational management positions, with women generally being the top executives. The men were relegated to lower-level positions in the large mining organizations, the small-business market system, lower level education system, clerical work, or house-husbands. In fact, one could say that the traditional Earth-type sex relationships were reversed on the Orion colony.

This has led to some interesting conditions concerning the Orion culture. First, a strong feminist culture exists. Women like to be seen as individualistic, independent, and stoic, but at the same time very feminine in appearance. The frontier mentality of individualism and independence runs strong in both the female and the male population. Small nuclear families that often stay together for many years are the norm.

The language is the same as the Interlingua used on Earth, so they have no real communication problem. People from Earth do find the common usage of the language a little strange. Instead of the subject-verb-object sentence structure used on Earth, Orions tend to leave out the subject and start sentences with verbs. A linguist from Earth might consider this a sign of a high level of action orientation in the society. Orions say it is because they generally know who they are talking to during a conversation.

Everyone is literate and highly educated through the education system based on lesson transmission to children at home. Children receive their lessons on the three-dimensional holographic, interactive television network, which is the same system used for entertainment in the home and communication with those outside. Because education is free and widely available, it could be depreciated. But survival on the ice, work, and independence depends on good education, so it is appreciated and even valued. With its wide availability, everyone has achieved a high level of education for a colony in the boondocks.

> The Orions spend much of their free time trying to achieve higher self-actualization through greater education. You might even say they have a thirst for exploration of new territories, new ideas, new levels of understanding, and their own minds.

They live in underground family dwellings that are connected to others by 3-D holographic video-telephone, computerized delivery systems connected to all major stores and services, and computerized pneumatic shuttle service-like individualized train compartments. Dwellings are grouped in sets of three called a module. These sets of three dwellings are, in turn, connected to a more widely spaced grouping of three other family modules. These sets of three modules are called blocks. Nine blocks make up a district. Some districts are made up on strictly commercial units, also structured in the modular system of modules-blocks-districts. An indeterminate number of districts make up one Orion city. Everything in these cities is underground, but the high-technology infrastructure allows for rapid communication, transport, and intra-city commerce. Unfortunately, this superb infrastructure tends to break down in inter-city commerce. While communication over the ice is no problem most of the time, transportation across it is often interrupted by icestorms, shifting ice and icequakes, electromagnetic storms, and static-electricity storms.

> The nuclear families of a dwelling module is the core of the culture, and each modular group of families tries to be as self-sufficient as possible because they could easily be cut off from the rest of the district or city by a major disaster. The people in each module are so close that they often share child-care duties, work duties, religions, and sometimes even spouses.

In terms of the old Hofstede culture analysis, the module dwellers would be described as moderate in Individualism, low in Power Distance, low in Uncertainty Avoidance, and high in Femininity. This means that they have slight collectivist tendencies based on the modular dwelling system. The low Power Distance characteristic arises from the individualistic and equalizing tendencies of the frontier culture; out on the ice, your status doesn't matter. They have to have low Uncertainty Avoidance. It's a risky life in the colonies, especially on the Orion ice. High Uncertainty Avoidance people wouldn't last. The high Femininity level results from the frontier mentality also. Because they have to always look out for each other when people are working on the ice, they tend to be greatly concerned for others and their own quality of life. They also emphasize relationships over acquisition of money and material goods because they have most of what they need. They also have learned that being too assertive on the ice can be fatal.

As for other value dimensions, they believe in harmony with nature (especially the ice), have a "present" Time Orientation (They really don't have much of a past and they don't know what is going to happen in the future), and a "doing" Activity Orientation (They like to work and accomplish things). Living on the ice with a high Femininity Behavior Orientation, they have come to believe that people are generally good. They have a slight Group Orientation in their belief concerning people's relationship with others due to their modular dwelling system. The modular dwelling system has also contributed to their "mixed" Conception of Space. In one module, there is really little private space. But with those outside, they tend to stress privacy.

> The tendency for family modules to be somewhat private towards other modules or strangers allows them to hold many different philosophical beliefs without conflict between philosophies.

Their religions are generally eclectic and very individualized. There is no real common system of religions. The only consistent religious factor is that families in one module tend to hold similar religious or philosophical beliefs. In general, people from one module will not ask people from another module about their private lives, but will accept people on face value. A cultural norm, though, is that if you are visiting another module where the values differ from your own, you will accept the values, beliefs, and behaviors of that module as your own as long as you are a guest in that module. Thus the beliefs and values of the people must allow for adaptability and tolerance. You cannot visit another module and push your values and behaviors on them, nor can you use them yourself. Such behavior would constitute a gross violation of social norms. You would no longer be welcome in that module.

The demographics of Orion colony show that the mean age of the people is about 50 Earth years and they have a life span of about 150. So the population pattern tends to be tulip shaped. They normally don't start families until at least 40 Earth years. Starting families is not a problem because the sexes are almost evenly balanced. The tulip-shaped demographics and equal number of sexes resulted from the Orions' belief in birth control to regulate population and sex of children.

The government of Orion colony is based on a modular structure of city-states. Each Orion city-state has its own separate form of democratic government, but they all send representatives to a planetary council in the largest city of Intbus.

Within each city-state, the exact form of government can vary, but they are generally democratic structures based on representation by districts. Districts usually have no need for government, per se, but they usually do have ad hoc working committees to get things done on a group basis. These ad hoc committees spring up and then disband on a need basis. The lack of a strong governmental tendency at the district level can be attributed to the Orions' general dislike of extensive government interference. Modules like to be left alone, as do districts. If anything needs to be done on a group basis, the people would rather solve the problem on an ad hoc consensus and involvement basis. So committees for special projects are always springing up and then disappearing. They can work in an ad hoc manner because of the highly accommodative nature, low Power Distance, high Femininity Behavior Orientation, present Time Orientation, slight Group Orientation, and "doing" Activity Orientation of the Orions.

Their business systems also tend to be highly modular. Even the large firms are based on a modular structure, with each module handling a function, production, or geographic area.

These business modules are highly flexible in that a single functional module from the support core could be transplanted into another business organization without much trouble. Production modules, which constitute the technical core of industrial organizations, could be easily assigned to produce different products if they were provided with the correct equipment. Geographic business modules of the marketing function could easily be reassigned responsibility for a different geographic region without too much trouble. Thus Orion business organizations are highly flexible and loosely connected.

Each major business organization is made up of a central core module that coordinates the work of all other modules; functional, production, and geographic modules; and sourcing modules. Within these modules, the workers generally work in teams with very little hierarchy. The modules can be said to have lean, flat structures with little bureaucracy. Usually everyone is on the same level and the leadership works in a facilitative rather than directive manner.

The functional modules are normally production, marketing, finance, and accounting. The only type of function that they really lack is the Research and Development (R&D) function. Businesses in the Orion colony do not conduct R&D because they have not yet produced significant technological research expertise. The sourcing modules are closely interlinked modules that supply resources and materials to the technical core of the main organization. Each of these sourcing modules are smaller organizations in their own right. They are linked with the major business organization through a commonality in organizational missions, philosophies, goals, and objectives. These smaller sourcing modules are, however, expendable to the major business organization. If they are no longer needed because the major business organization has changed its business or its organizational mission, the services of the sourcing modules may be sold to another major business or they may be left on their own.

Production systems in businesses tend to be highly modular. The production equipment is fashioned to take advantage of the flexible manufacturing systems technology. One piece of equipment can often be used for manufacturing several different items. All of this equipment is fully automated. The work of production team members is to service, maintain, control, and modify the equipment to obtain the best performance from the equipment.

The Orion economy is dominated by the major conglomerate businesses that extract rare elements. Using mining as their cash cow, these businesses have diversified into industrial goods production, consumer goods production, and services. Surrounding these major conglomerates are many medium-sized sourcing modules. Servicing these sourcing modules are small-sized independent firms. Other specialized services and goods are provided by other small independent firms. For consumer retailing, boutiques or small shops are the norm. The only exception is food, which is centrally produced and distributed directly to homes. Most of these businesses can be considered relatively young, except for the major conglomerates, which got their start when the planet was colonized.

People shop when they have to. Foodstuffs are delivered to their homes, so weekly grocery shopping is unnecessary. Clothing and other household goods are bought at the small boutiques in the shopping districts. Purchases are made on an electronic credit transfer system through the central city computer. Purchases are usually made by males, who often stay home and raise children. Open hours of the stores differ by district, and at least one shopping district is open at any time of the day since being underground means there is no night or day.

Industrial goods are purchased by firms directly from other firms using the electronic credit transfer system of the central city computer. Supply contracts are usually not used. Deals are often consummated by a simple shake of hands. These agreements are generally renegotiated every six Earth months. Distribution of industrial goods occurs through a separate underground transportation network than is used by commuters or retail goods. The transportation system is fully automated, very efficient, and reliable.

Research of the Orion colony has shown that they have a desire to trade with Earth for new Earth clothing fashions, educational material, fresh Earth foods brought to Orion in stasis chambers that keep them fresh forever, the latest industrial equipment, the latest consumer technology, and the latest transportation technology.

Shipping bulk goods to Orion colony takes two Earth months, but small packages and people can get there in two Earth weeks. Communication with Earth is even quicker. Electronic messages sent by subspace radio can reach Earth in two days. This does not indicate, though, a lag in communication—it is not instantaneous.

QUESTION

You are a middle-level manager in a large conglomerate based on Earth. You have been given responsibility for the exploitation of an ex-colony in the Orion star cluster. The top management directive to your department is to develop a strategy for the commercial exploitation of the Orion colony. They want you to tell them how to go about benefitting from Earth's recent contact with this planet; how should they invest their time and money? What kinds of problems are they likely to face in dealing with these people? And what can you do to overcome these problems? Remember, you'll have to come up with some hypotheses concerning how Orions do business. You'll have to make some intelligent and supportable guesses at how they structure and carry out various business functions.

GLOSSARY

achievement society A society that emphasizes attainment of position and influence. Competence determines who occupies a particular position. People in more powerful positions hold them because of their skills, knowledge, and talents.

activity orientation The categorization of a culture according to whether it is a doing, being, or containing/controlling culture.

affective culture A culture that believes expressing emotions is natural and appropriate. Not to express emotions may be considered dishonest.

affective-intuitive conflict style A style for handling conflict that is more common in high-context cultures. This approach uses circumlocution or flowery speech to make an emotional appeal, and ambiguity and understatement to diffuse conflict.

affective communication style The verbal communication style in which the speaker is process oriented and receiver focused.

affirmative action An attempt to make up for past systematic discrimination against women and minorities through a quota employment system.

agreement In the negotiation process, the parties come to a mutually acceptable solution.

ambivalent leadership A leadership style that a culture with contradictory norms and values produces. Alternating between opposite values

and behaviors is not the product of inadequate understanding of human nature, but rather consists of difficulty acting in a consistent, coherent way in response to the diverse, sometimes conflicting, values of a complex, heterogeneous, society.

artifacts The most visible and observable elements of organizational culture; the concrete aspects of an organization that symbolizes its culture. These include material aspects of the organization such as its architecture, physical layout, and decoration. A second type of artifact is slogans, organizational stories, myths, corporate heroes, rites, rituals, and ceremonies.

ascriptive culture A culture that believes people are born into influence. Those in power naturally have the right to be there because of their personal characteristics.

axiomatic-deductive conflict style A style of handling conflict that reasons from the general to the specific, going from basic ideas to their implications.

barriers to change Those factors that prevent an organization from appropriately modifying to new conditions. Rigidity that can stifle and eventually kill an organization.

basic assumptions The foundations of a culture: shared ideas and beliefs about the world and society as a whole that guide people's thoughts and actions.

basic human nature Analysis of a culture based on the assessment of

that culture's belief in people as good, evil, or neutral/mixed.

basic underlying assumptions Unconscious beliefs and values that structure feelings, perceptions, thoughts, and actions that members of a culture view as the only correct understanding of life.

being culture A culture that emphasizes enjoying life and working for the moment; people work to live rather than live to work.

bicultural group A group in which two or more members from each of two distinct cultures come together.

boundaryless organization Breaks the traditional demarcations of authority, political, communication, and task specialization found in bureaucracies and other organizational structures. Features of a boundaryless organization include a widespread use of project teams, interfunctional teams, networks, and similar structural mechanisms, thus reducing boundaries that typically separate organizational functions and hierarchical levels.

brownouts Expatriates who finish their assignments but do so ineffectively.

bureaucracy In this type of organization, each position has fixed official duties. Conduct is governed by impersonal rules and regulations. Effort is coordinated through a hierarchy of levels of authority. Order and reliability are maintained through written communication and files. Employment is a full-time occupation for members

621

of the organization. Appointment to office is made by superiors. Promotion is based upon merit.

centralization When decisions are made by a few people—usually those at the top—an organization is centralized.

Chinese family business A family business structure, usually one of two types. The first type is small businesses that include only family members. The second type is controlled by family members but also employs nonfamily members and operates as a clan or extended family, which permits it to grow considerably larger than businesses that restrict themselves to family members.

chromatics Communication through colors.

chronemics The use of time in a culture. Two dominant patterns are characteristic: monochronic time schedule and polychronic time schedule.

code of ethics Although these are not laws, they codify behavior that is unacceptable under certain conditions. Organizations expect their members to adhere to them or suffer penalties.

codetermination Worker representatives hold decision-making roles on corporate boards. Popular in Germany, it has permitted German industry to adjust effectively and peacefully to economic change.

collectivist society A society that values the overall good of the group. The expectation is that people subordinate their individual interests and needs for the benefit of the group. Because being part of the group is so important, it is very clear how people in the group should behave.

communication The process of transmitting thoughts or ideas from one person to another. Central to groups because it is the major mechanism for achieving their goals. Culture affects communication in

groups by shaping roles and statuses and the interactions among them.

comparative method A technique for the systematic study of behavior in multiple cultures whose aim is to reduce reliance on a single set of values.

compensation and benefits Develops and administers the salary system and other forms of remuneration such as vacation and sick pay, health insurance, and pension funds.

complexity The extent to which an organization has subparts. Three important components of complexity are horizontal differentiation, vertical or hierarchical differentiation, and spatial dispersion.

compromise In negotiations, the requirement that all parties give up something in order to reach a decision.

conceptual approach to ethics Focuses on the meaning of key ideas in ethics such as obligation, justice, virtue, and responsibility. The emphasis is to refine definitions of important ethical concepts through philosophical analysis.

Confucian work dynamism Organizations that have concern with the future. They consider how their current actions could influence future generations, for example, value is placed on thrift and persistence.

containing/controlling culture A culture that emphasizes rationality and logic. People restrain their desires to try to achieve a mind/body balance.

content theories Motivation theories that focus on the "what," identifying factors that cause people to put effort into work.

context Hall developed the concept of context to explain differences in communication styles among cultures. He defined context as the information that surrounds an event, and is therefore inextricably bound

up with the meaning of that event. Cultures can be categorized on a scale from high- to low-context.

contextual style A verbal communication style that focuses on the "role" of the speaker, and meanings are expressed for the purpose of emphasizing certain role relationships.

contingency theories The view that there are multiple causes of behavior.

conversational overlaps This occurs when more than one person speaks at the same time.

core group Consists of several employees from different cultural backgrounds who meet regularly. The group members discuss their attitudes, feelings, and beliefs about cultural differences and how they influence work behavior.

corporate social responsibility theory This theory holds that the obligation of business is to maximize profits for the company's stakeholders, such as suppliers, customers, employees, stockholders, and the local community.

cross-cultural communication Occurs when people from more than one culture communicate with each other. Noise develops due to differences in language, values, and attitudes, among other factors.

cross-cultural negotiations Occurs when members of different cultures negotiate with each other.

cross-cultural training (CCT) Prepares an expatriate to live and work in a different culture because coping with a new environment can be much more challenging than dealing with a new job. An organization can choose an appropriate CCT method using three situational factors of the expatriate's assignment: culture novelty, degree of interaction with host country nationals, and job novelty.

cultural ethical relativism   The doctrine that what is right or wrong, good or bad, depends on one's culture. If the values of a society support certain acts as ethical and morally correct, then they are acceptable behavior for that society.

cultural determinism   The position that all behavior is the product of culture. Ignores economic, political, technological, and biological factors as plausible explanations.

culture   The way of life of a group of people.

culture-free approach   It states that because of technology, policies, rules, organizational structure, and other variables that contribute to efficiency and effectiveness, the role of national culture in shaping organizational behavior, and therefore the need to understand it, is irrelevant for management.

culture shock   An adverse or confused reaction to behavior in other cultures, challenges understandings between ourselves and others. What is "normal" behavior becomes problematic.

decode   In the communication process, the receiver interprets the meaning of the symbols used by the sender to understand or comprehend the meaning of the message.

descriptive approach to ethics   The study of ethics using the methods and theories of social science. Researchers study the ethics of a particular society or corporation and explain their effect on behavior without making judgments regarding their correctness.

descriptive organization theories   An attempt to portray organizations realistically.

determinist organization theories   Through logical argument, inductive and deductive theories, and empirical research, management scholars and sociologists have argued that one variable explains more of the structural aspects of organizations than others.

dialectical theory   An approach to understanding development and change in organizations. The balance of power between opposing entities determines stability or change. If the struggles and accommodations continually taking place between these parties are maintaining the balance of power, stability reigns. If one side gains enough power to tip the scales and engage the status quo, change occurs.

diffuse culture   In this type of culture, the public space is relatively smaller and more carefully guarded than the private space.

direct communication style   The speaker tries to convey true feelings through the choice of words.

distributive justice   The issue of how rewards can be distributed in a fair manner: (1) An outcome to input ratio should be relatively equal for every employee; (2) an equality norm in which each employee receives the same outcomes regardless of inputs; and (3) a need norm suggests each employee be given outcomes according to his or her need.

diversity   A range of differences, including gender, race, ethnicity, and age—characteristics that might be apparent from looking at someone. It also includes differences that are not visible, such as education, professional background, functional area of expertise, sexual preference, and religion. All of these differences are important because they affect how individuals behave within an organization.

doing culture   A culture in which the emphasis is on action, achievement, and working.

dysfunction   A negative outcome of an organization.

efficiency perspective   The key concept is corporate social responsibility—argues that the obligation of business is to maximize profits for shareholders.

Eiffel Tower culture   A classic bureaucratic structure that emphasizes a division of labor and coordination through a hierarchy of authority, and relies on planning to accomplish its goals.

elaborate communication style   In communication, the quantity of talk is relatively high, description includes great detail, and there is often repetition. The use of metaphors, similes, and proverbs is frequent, many adjectives modify the same noun, and verbal elaboration and exaggeration are typical.

encode   In the communication process, a message is expressed in an understandable format for the receiver.

entitlement norm   The rights of individuals in society to seek out, obtain, and maintain gainful employment. Every individual has the right to work and be an active participant in his or her employment.

equal employment opportunity   Prohibition of discrimination on the basis of such variables as race, gender, ethnicity, religion, color, age, disability, pregnancy, national origin, and citizenship status.

Equity Theory   The basic premise of this theory is that people try to balance their inputs and outcomes in relation to others.

espoused values   The public values and principles that the organization's leaders announce it intends to achieve. They include mission statements, goals, and ideals.

ethical universalism   Maintains that there are universal and objective ethical rules located deep within a culture that also apply across societies.

ethics   Moral standards, not governed by law, that focus on the human consequences of actions. Ethics often require behavior that meets higher standards than that established by law, including selfless behavior rather than calculated action intended to produce a tangible benefit.

ethnocentrism The belief that the group to which one belongs is the primary group, and all other groups are rated according to how they compare to the primary group.

evolutionary theory Borrows key ideas from biological evolutionary theory and views change as a continuous cycle of variation, selection, and retention. The creation of new forms of organizations emerge by blind or random change. The evolutionary selection of organizations occurs through the competition for scarce resources, and external forces select entities that best fit the resource base of an environmental niche.

exacting communication style A communication style in which the emphasis is on precision and using the right amount of words to convey the desired meaning.

expatriates Employees who work outside their home countries.

expatriate failures Those who do not remain abroad for the duration of their assignment.

Expectancy Theory A theory of motivation that rests on important assumptions about people's behavior. (1) Behavior is a result of personal and environmental factors. (2) People's decisions about whether to belong to an organization and how much effort to put into performing influence their behavior in organizations. (3) Because of different needs, people seek different rewards from the organization. (4) People decide how to behave on the basis of beliefs about what leads to the most desirable outcomes.

experience In organizations, it is a factor that can cause barriers to arise due to differences in life events between two individuals. When two people are from different cultures, it is likely that their life experiences have varied in many ways. Lacking a common body of experience is likely to make communication more difficult.

expressed values level Represents how people in the culture explain the manifest level of their culture.

expressive-oriented In high-context cultures, people do not separate person from issue in conflicts.

external-oriented society The society tries to harmonize with the environment and have more focus on the "other."

external sources of change Events in the environment that are usually beyond the organization's control. They can affect the organization immediately, influence other elements in its environment that then affect it, or make their impact in the future.

face Usually identified as exclusively part of Asian culture, it is found in many cultures. Face is an ethical concept that is part of the general culture and internalized rather than an institutionalized code of ethics. Saving one's face and that of other group members is of central importance in highly integrated and authoritarian cultures. A behavior that protects harmony, tolerance, and solidarity.

facial gazing Looking at the counterpart's face. Eye contact is one of the most intense forms of facial gazing.

factual-inductive conflict style A style used to handle conflict that focuses on relevant facts and moves toward a conclusion using an inductive approach.

family organizational culture An organization that emphasizes personal, face-to-face relationships. It is hierarchical with an authority structure based on power differentials commonly experienced between parents and children.

feedback In the communication process, the reversal of the initial sender/receiver roles to let the sender know if his message was received and understood.

feminine culture A culture that places importance on "tender" values such as personal relationships, care for others, the quality of life, and service. Gender roles are less distinct and often equal.

Five-Stage Group Development Model Theory of group development that views groups as experiencing five distinct phases: (1) Forming, (2) Storming, (3) Norming, (4) Performing, (5) Adjourning.

followers Group members who do not have leadership roles.

formal group This type of group reflects the idea that pooling resources for decision making is superior to individual effort. In most instances management appoints a leader, membership is mandatory, and rules govern behavior.

formalization The extent that rules, policies, and procedures govern organization members' behavior. The more extensive the documentation of appropriate behavior, the more formalized the organization.

future-oriented society A society that emphasizes the long term. Uses the past and present to gain future advantage.

geographical location A situational factor for negotiators in deciding where to hold a negotiation.

global company A centralized company that follows a strategy built on global-scale cost advantage.

globalization The transcendence of previous geographic, economic, political, and cultural boundaries towards a new world order. Increasing awareness of activities in other parts of the world.

goal setting theory A theory of motivation that involves the effect that goal setting has on performance. Based on the idea that people are motivated by intentions to work toward a goal.

group A number of people who are in contact with one another and who are aware of some significant commonality.

group culture The basis can be membership in a formal or informal group, an occupation, union membership, ethnic or religious background, or membership in a department that provides common experiences. The groups maintain themselves just as subcultures do through shared symbols, ceremonies, rituals, and values, which become a means for establishing a group's identity that differentiates itself from other groups.

group decisions Groups pool the skills, talents, and experiences of many people instead of relying on one decision maker. Group decision making, the active participation of many people, increases the likelihood of decision implementation.

group-oriented society A society in which a positive relationship to the collective is important.

group structure The patterns of interaction among members. Elements that compose structures are rules, norms, roles, and statuses. These concepts are useful for understanding groups in all cultures.

groupthink A group decision-making process that occurs when members of a highly cohesive group are unable to evaluate each other's inputs critically.

guest workers In Germany, after World War II when there was a shortage of men, industry recruited workers from abroad with the intention that these workers would eventually go back to their homeland. The foreign worker population increased dramatically since that time.

guided missile culture An egalitarian culture that is impersonal and task oriented. This culture is egalitarian because it employs experts in technical fields. Experts work on projects together rather than take directives from superiors. Technical expertise reduces emotional elements in the culture, producing a bureaucratic culture based on knowledge rather than position or on emotional ties.

habit Regular, stable patterns of events over time that are taken for granted and become mindless actions. All organizations engage in habitual behaviors.

haptics Communication through the use of bodily contact.

harmony A factor when analyzing cultures and their relation to nature. A culture that is in harmony with nature attempts to orient behavior to coexist with nature.

hierarchical society A society that values group relationships, but emphasizes the relative rankings of groups within an organization or society as a whole, making them more class conscious than group societies.

Herzberg's Motivation-Hygiene Theory Developed in the 1950s and 1960s and built on Maslow's theory, the premise of Herzberg's theory is that satisfaction and dissatisfaction are two dimensions rather than opposite ends of a single dimension.

heterarchy A form of multinational organization that utilizes aspects of markets and hierarchies.

heterogeneity Diversity in the workforce.

high-contact culture High-contact cultures usually are in warmer climates, have a greater interpersonal orientation, and are seen as interpersonally "warm."

high-context (HC) communication One type of communication in which most of the information is either in the physical context or internalized in the person, while very little is in the coded, explicit, transmitted part of the message.

home culture consensus Values widely shared by the home culture and therefore are maintained in an ethical decision.

homogeneous Cultures and groups that contain members who have the same backgrounds and generally understand events and the world in general more similarly than other types.

horizontal differentiation The way that tasks performed by the organization are divided.

hygiene factors Also called extrinsic or context factors, are factors outside the job itself that influence the worker.

immediate environment Forces in an organization with which it is continually in contact and that can create pressures for change. Some examples of these forces are domestic competition, population trends, social trends, governmental actions.

incubator culture It attempts to minimize organizational structure and culture and develops with this mind-set: "If organizations are to be tolerated at all, they should be there to serve as incubators for self-expression and self-fulfillment." Minimal organizational structure facilitates a culture that is egalitarian, personal, and highly creative. In most cases, incubator cultures are in knowledge and science industries.

indirect communication style The speaker selects words to hide his real feelings.

individual change When the behavior of a person is different as a result of new information, training, experience, or rearrangement of an organization's structure.

individual ethical relativism   The view that there is no absolute principle of right and wrong, good or bad, in any social situation. The individuals in a particular situation determine what is right and wrong. In its extreme form, ethics are a personal judgment independent of societal norms and values.

individualistic society   The people in this type of society relate to each other through personal characteristics and achievements. People have concern for themselves and their families, rather than others. The individual is important, and each person's rights are valued. The society structures laws and rules to preserve the rights of the individual and to allow individual development and achievement.

informal groups   Evolve naturally in organizations, often without the awareness of management. People who work together in a functional area, across specializations, or as a result of frequent contact can form relationships based on similar experiences, common interests, and friendship. Informal groups vary in their contribution to an organization's goals.

information exchange   The stage in the negotiation process when each party states an initial position, usually in a presentation, followed by questions, answers, and discussion.

initial offer   In negotiation, the beginning statement of intent made by each party, is influenced by culture.

inputs   In Equity Theory, these are what someone brings to a situation. An employee's inputs include education, previous work experience, personality, and personal characteristics.

institutional theory   A theory that views the primary source of change as external and beyond the control of management.

instrumental orientation   The orientation of people in low-context cultures who view conflict in the world in analytic, linear logic terms, and separate issues from people.

instrumental style   The verbal communication style in which the sender uses goal-oriented, sender-focused language.

integrative solution   The outcome of a win-win agreement; all parties achieve their objectives.

internal change factors   An organization's technical production system, political processes, and culture. At times these factors exert strong and direct pressures for change. At other times, when the organization is in equilibrium, internal factors maintain organizational stability but retain the potential for creating change.

internal organizational culture   Artifacts, values, and basic assumptions that create meaning for organizational insiders and present it to those outside the organization.

internal-oriented culture   A culture that believes nature is controllable. The individual or his group is in control of a situation.

international contingency model of leadership   The reasoning supporting the model, which provides general guidelines for international managers, not a scientific theory, is that different leadership styles fit various national cultures.

international firm   A firm that develops products and innovations in their domestic market and then transports them to foreign affiliates.

international human resource management (IHRM)   Includes three major areas: (1) The management of human resources in global corporations; (2) the management of expatriate employees; (3) the comparison of human resource management (HRM)

practices in a variety of different countries. Includes recruiting and selecting employees, providing orientation and training, evaluating performance, administering a compensation system, and handling other aspects of labor relations.

international organizational behavior   The study of behavior in organizations around the world.

interpretive scheme   A way to make sense of the arrangements of positions and activities in an organization. It acts as a perceptual filter, embodied in stories and myths, that creates meaning out of routine, frequently experienced events, as well as unique situations.

intimate zone   A distance of less than 18 inches (46 cm) that is used by very close friends.

intracultural negotiation   Members of one culture negotiate with each other.

job enrichment   Application of Herzberg's Motivation-Hygiene Theory, to motivate workers, a job must include many motivation factors.

kinesic behavior   Communication through body movements, including facial expression, gestures, and posture.

labor relations   Identifies and defines the roles of management and workers in the workplace.

laws   Imposing mandatory compliance accompanied by formal punitive sanctions.

leadership   Leadership is a management style that focuses on creativity, vision, and long-term organizational development, rather than routine operations.

Learned Needs Theory   McClelland proposed that three major needs influence people's behavior. These needs are not instinctive desires, but learned. The learned needs, which help explain individual differences in motivation, are need for achievement, need for power, and need for affiliation.

life-cycle theory   A development theory that borrows concepts from fields as diverse as biology, child development, and moral development. The central view of life-cycle theory is that the developing organization has within it an underlying form, logic, program, or code that regulates change and moves the group from a given point of departure toward an end that is prefigured in the present state.

long-term oriented   Societies that have concern with the future. Values are thrift and persistence.

lose-lose solution   In negotiation, all parties must give up something. A compromise is a lose-lose solution.

low-contact cultures   People in these cultures prefer to stand farther apart and touch infrequently. These cultures are often in cooler climate zones, and people there are task oriented and interpersonally "cool."

low-context (LC) communication Communication in which the mass of the information is vested in the explicit, coded, transmitted part of the message rather than in the physical context.

macro-level change typology   A theory that provides a larger framework for understanding the processes of organizational change. These theories identify processes that create change independent of national culture and, to some extent, managerial action.

managing diversity training program   The major focus of this training is raising levels of awareness and sensitivity to diversity issues. The time required for the program varies from a few hours to a few days.

manifest culture   Easily observable elements of a culture,

such as behaviors, language, music, food, and technology.

maquiladoras   International manufacturing and processing facilities in Mexico.

masculine society   The "tough" values such as success, money, assertiveness, and competition are dominant in such societies, and there are often significant differences between men's and women's roles.

Maslow's Hierarchy of Needs   A theory of general motivation developed by Maslow that theorized an individual would try to satisfy one category of needs at a time and that the hierarchical order of needs is the same for everyone.

mastery culture   A culture that attempts to change aspects of the environment through technology when necessary or desirable.

matrix organization   A type of organic structure. Instead of a bureaucratic authority structure with employees accountable to one supervisor, an employee reports to more than one supervisor.

mechanistic organization   A centralized organization that is highly formalized and specialized with a micro division of labor.

micro division of tasks   A type of job specialization by breaking jobs into their smallest components that individuals can perform well with low levels of education and training.

mixed orientation   A society with a tendency to believe people are basically good, however, in some situations they do behave in an evil manner.

mixed society   In space orientation, this society's views on space fall somewhere between public and private societies, with a combination of public and private spaces.

monochronic time schedule (M-time)   A culture where things are

done in a linear fashion one activity at a time. Time schedules are important, and an appointment is treated seriously. Time is seen as something that can be controlled or wasted by people.

monolithic organization   An organization that is predominately homogeneous. People who are different from the majority often work only in a limited number of positions or departments. Because people with different backgrounds do not hold positions throughout the organization, to survive minority group members usually follow the organizational norms set by the majority. Intergroup conflict is relatively low because the organization is so homogeneous; however, discrimination and prejudice are common.

motivation   The amount of effort that an individual puts into doing something.

motivation factors   Also called intrinsic or content factors, these are aspects of the job itself, including achievement, recognition, interesting work, responsibility, advancement, and growth. The presence or absence of these factors influences the satisfaction and motivation of workers.

multicultural groups   Groups that contain members of three or more ethnic backgrounds.

multicultural teams   Groups that contain workers from different cultural groups who learn how to maximize their effectiveness by taking full advantage of their differences.

multinational firm   A firm whose focus is on a strategy that is primarily country oriented and locally responsive. Their structures are decentralized.

multiple structures   Complex structures that contain both bureaucratic administration and more organic structures. In addition to requiring more coordination, these types of organizations often experience conflict as a result of the coexistence of different structures.

negotiation   The process of bargaining between two or more parties to reach a solution that is mutually acceptable.

neutral culture   People in this type of culture try to control emotion so as not to interfere with judgment. Expressing emotion at a culturally inappropriate time may be considered irrational.

neutral orientation   A cautious approach toward people in general in order to protect yourself, because although the belief is that people are mostly good, they can act in evil ways.

noise   Factors responsible for distortion and interruption that enter the communication process.

nonrational elements of culture   A theory about how much leaders can manage organizational culture holds that these nonrational elements are behaviors not grounded in empirical data or distorted to serve a particular group's interests. These include destructive or negative emotions, erroneous beliefs, and idiosyncratic interpretations of the organization's past, present, and future. Leaders are unable to control these aspects of organizational culture.

nonverbal communication   The part of the message other than the words, such as facial expressions, gestures, and tone of voice. Nonverbal meanings in different cultures vary tremendously.

nonverbal tactics   Negotiating behaviors other than the words used, for example, tone of voice, facial expressions, gestures, and body position.

normative approach to ethics   This approach constructs arguments

in defense of basic moral positions and prescribing correct ethical behavior. These arguments may rely on social science studies and conceptual clarification, but they focus primarily on the rationale for a particular position, often on the basis of logic as much as empirical evidence.

normative organizational theories   These theories attempt to formulate the way organizations ought to function.

norms   Guides of behavior and beliefs that are informal, usually unstated, and taken for granted by group members. Groups generate their own norms rather than have norms forced upon them.

obligation norm   A belief that holds all individuals in society have a duty with respect to working. This norm includes the notion that everyone has a duty to contribute to society by working, a duty to save for their own future, and the duty to value one's work, whatever its nature.

oculesics   Communication through eye contact and gaze.

open systems   Organizations interact with their environment rather than exist independently of surrounding influences. Organizations continuously require inputs from the environment in the form of raw materials, human resources, finance, and ideas. After the inputs are transformed through a variety of processes, an organization returns output to the environment in the form of products, services, and knowledge.

organic structure   Decentralized organizations that have low formalization and specialization based on depth of knowledge. Flexible and change oriented, creativity is fostered. Knowledge and ability determine participation in decision making and problem solving rather than position titles. Decision making is decentralized, and there is

an attempt to involve lower-level participants in decision making whenever possible. Communication channels operate vertically and horizontally.

organization development (OD)   The application of social science research and theories to create more "rational" organizations. OD involves attempting to improve organizational efficiency and effectiveness, create organizational "health," and build capacity to change continuously.

organization structure change   The deliberate rearrangement of the positions, departments, or other major units of an organization.

organizational behavior modification   The application of Reinforcement Theory to motivate workers in organizations. A four step process: (1) Ensure workers know the behaviors they are expected to carry out as part of the job; (2) train observers and have them record the workers' correct and incorrect behaviors; (3) reinforce workers who practice correct behaviors and provide corrective feedback; (4) evaluate the effects of the program on behavior.

organizational change   The reconfiguration of the components of an organization to increase efficiency and effectiveness. Change can occur at the level of the individual, group, or organizational structure.

organizational culture   The basic assumptions of an organization as it learns to cope with problems of external adaptation and internal integration. These assumptions work well enough to be considered valid and, therefore, to be taught to new members as the correct way to perceive, think, and feel in relation to those problems. To the members of the organization, it is the "natural" way of understanding the business world and taking action.

organizational structure   The arrangement of positions in an organization. Positions, or roles, are intentionally structured to accomplish the goals of the organization. The basic components of structure are complexity, centralization, and formalization.

outcomes   In Equity Theory, what one takes from a situation—for example, pay, benefits, working conditions, coworker relationships, and training opportunities.

particularist society   A society that is more contingency oriented, believing circumstances and relationships are more important in deciding what is right or good.

past-oriented culture   A culture that emphasizes tradition and uses time-honored approaches. Tradition and history are important.

path-goal model of leadership
This model attempts to explain how the behavior of a leader influences the satisfaction and performance of subordinates dependent on aspects of a situation. The task of leadership is to strengthen subordinates' perception of the ties among effort, performance, and desired outcomes. To do this a leader should adapt her style to various situations. The four leadership behaviors follow: (1) directive leadership, (2) supportive leadership, (3) participative leadership, and (4) achievement-oriented leadership.

perception   An individual's personal view of the world. Whether it is correct or not, it is a person's definition of reality.

performance evaluation   The systematic appraisal of employees' performance within the organization. Its purposes are to provide information for organizational decisions such as promotions and salary increases and to give feedback to employees to help them develop and improve.

personal communication style   A verbal communication style that focuses on the speaker.

personal zone   The distance from 18 inches to about 4 feet (46 cm to 1.22 m), used for close working situations or to give instructions.

persuasion   In the negotiation process, the parties try to convince their counterparts to accept their proposals. This might involve the parties consciously trying to work toward a mutually acceptable solution or one party using persuasive arguments to influence the other.

plural organization   A type of organization that includes a wider variety of people, and management makes a greater effort to include people who differ from the majority.

polychronic time schedule (P-time)   People tend to do several things at the same time. In a P-time culture, schedules are subordinate to personal relationships.

population ecology   A theory that views the primary source of change as external and beyond the control of management. For example, similar to natural selection in biology, population ecology views the environment as selecting those types of organizational forms that survive. Organizations do not adapt; instead, certain types fail and are replaced with different types.

power distance   The extent to which less powerful members of organizations accept that power is unequally distributed. It ranges from small to large. Suggests that national cultures low on power distance— those most likely to question the leader's actions—would be the least supportive followers, whereas cultures high on power distance would be the most supportive of a group leader's efforts.

practical approach to conflict   A variant of the normative perspective, involves developing a set of normative guidelines for resolving conflicts of interest to improve societal well-being.

preparation stage   Negotiators plan how to approach the actual negotiation and try to learn as much as possible about their negotiating partner. This stage typically takes place at the home office before the face-to-face meeting. The negotiators must understand their own positions and anticipate the positions of the other party through considering each party's objectives, needs, and interests.

present-oriented culture   A culture that focuses on the short-term—what is going on now, including activities and relationships.

primary socialization   The specific culture that one learns while growing up. A complex, nonexplicit, prolonged process of learning appropriate age, gender, ethnic, and social class behavior from families, friends, schools, religious institutions, and media.

private society   In this type of society, it is important for each person to have his or her own space.

process motivation theories
These theories focus on the "how," the steps an individual takes in putting forth effort.

proxemics   The use of space, either personal or office, to communicate.

public society   In this type of society, space belongs to all.

public zone   Distances over 12 feet (over 3.66 m), used infrequently for formal occasions such as for a speech.

punctuated equilibrium model   A theory of group development. The first meeting is important for the group because it sets the climate for the group and establishes its leadership. This is followed by a period of equilibrium, which is routine group functioning that changes abruptly at the midpoint of the group's allotted time. This equilibrium is disrupted by recognition that the task must be completed and creates a revolutionary change in the group's arrangements. The new arrangements shift to a task orientation that results in project completion.

receiver The person who is the recipient of the sender's message in the communication process.

recruitment The process through which an organization takes in new members. Involves attracting a pool of qualified applicants for the positions available.

Reinforcement or Learning Theory The premise of this theory is that the environment determines people's behavior. As people grow from children into adults, what they learn is a result of the outcomes of their behavior. If individuals receive a reward for what they do, it is likely they will repeat it.

relation to nature Kluckhohn and Strodtbeck's concept to analyze a culture as to how it relates to nature either through subjugation to it, harmony with it, or mastery of it.

relationship-building stage The negotiating parties begin their discussion, typically at one of their offices or at a mutually acceptable neutral location. The objective is for the parties to get to know one another.

resource limitations Societies and organizations within them have varying levels of scarce resources— human, financial, intellectual.

reverse culture shock The disorientation experienced by a returning expatriate.

ringisei A Japanese term that means participation in group decision making.

role conflict Within an organization, group members often occupy multiple roles with different statuses. When the demands of the various roles are incompatible, role conflict occurs.

roles Sets of norms that define what behavior is appropriate for and expected of various positions within a group.

room arrangements A situational factor for negotiations that includes the physical setup of the place for the negotiations.

rules Guidelines for expected behavior that the organization imposes on group members and can formally sanction for disobedience.

secondary socialization Occurs after primary socialization and usually equips people with the knowledge, skills, and behavior to achieve adult roles successfully, particularly occupational roles.

selection Process through which an organization takes in new members. Requires choosing from the recruitment pool the candidate whose qualifications most closely match the job requirements.

selection of negotiators Involves choosing the number of people and exactly who will represent a team. The number chosen often reflects the organization's national culture.

sender The person who initiates the communication process.

sequential culture Cultures in which people do one thing at a time, make appointments and arrive on time, and generally stick to schedules.

short-term oriented A society's values are toward the immediate past and present. There is respect for tradition and fulfilling social obligations, but the here and now is most important.

silence In negotiating, a period of nonresponsiveness, used to reflect on what has been said, what should be said, or if a problem arises. The Japanese consider this a normal part of conversation.

simple organizational structure There is little need for elaborate

coordination because the organization is not complex; top management supervises through direct supervision. There is also centralization in top management with employees exerting little independent decision making or influence. The organization's goals are those of its top manager, who is frequently also its owner.

social control mechanism Through culture—particularly a strong, effective culture—the organization defines the reality that organization members experience. It socializes new members into a particular way of doing things and periodically resocializes its long-term members. For example, organizational rites and ceremonies reward and reinforce desired behavior as well as demonstrate and legitimate the organizational power structure.

social power Authority or the ability to have others follow directives without question.

social zone A distance of 4 to 12 feet (1.22 to 3.66 m), used in most American business situations.

socio-emotional leader Also known as the relationship or maintenance leader, focuses on the emotional and social aspects of a group. They encourage and praise others, resolve conflicts, and engage in behavior that facilitates the group's work. This leader role focuses on constructing and maintaining group cohesion.

space orientation A method of looking at differences in culture by indicating how people relate to the ownership of space, either public, private or mixed.

spatial dispersion A variable of organizational structure that is a component of complexity. The activities of an organization can be in one place or in different locations on either the basis of power centers, that is, hierarchy or specialization.

specific culture   People in this type of culture usually have large public spaces and relatively smaller private spaces. There is a separation between the public and private spaces, and the private space tends to remain more private, with access to it limited.

status   The rank of the role in the hierarchy of the group.

stereotyping   A shortcut to "understanding" someone by categorizing her as a member of a particular group, and then assigning her the characteristics of that group. Stereotyped characteristics may be based on data learned from other sources.

subculture   A separate set of cultural norms that set a group apart from the larger group. Contributing to subculture formation are age, gender, race, ethnic background, religion, and national culture. Subcultures contain their own rituals and ceremonies that have distinct meaning for their members and create ingroup identification.

succinct communication style   A communication style in which people are comfortable with a relatively low quantity of talk. Understatements, pauses, and silence convey meaning.

symbolic meaning system Selective interpretations of societal and organizational traditions, customs, rituals, and artifacts that contribute to organizational culture. The leader interprets and shapes the larger culture to the needs of the organization. Its products are particular ways of doing things in organizations in different cultures and a distinctive organizational identity.

subjugation orientation   A society's tendency for people to do several activities simultaneously, the time for appointments is approximate, and interpersonal relationships are more important than schedules.

task leader   Also called the initiating leader, focuses the group on

goal achievement. Task leaders clarify the goals, present information, ask other members for information, and evaluate the group's progress toward making a decision. The task leader's efforts aim toward specific outcomes.

team   A type of group that uses self-management techniques to achieve goals to which its members express high commitment. Teams have more cohesiveness and responsibility and use member talents more effectively than do other groups.

teleological organizational theory This theory relies on the philosophical doctrine that a purpose or goal is the final cause for guiding the movement of an organization. Emphasis is on goal achievement, and it underlies much managerial and organizational behavior theory.

time limits   The real or presumed deadlines under which negotiating parties operate. The expected time for a negotiation varies with culture.

time orientation   A society's focus on the past, present, or future.

token group   A group that consists of members with the same background with the exception of one member who is different in some significant way. The token member probably interprets things differently from the other group members.

tradition   A preference for acting based on custom and precedent. The most compelling reason for adherence to tradition is that the practices it prescribes have worked sufficiently well to warrant continuing them.

training and development Planned individual learning, organization development, and career development. It is a recognized professional field known as human resource development.

transformational leadership   A more commonly found type of leadership than charisma, especially

in contemporary business organizations in which a leader acts as a teacher, role model, and inspirational figure to create conditions under which subordinates enthusiastically contribute to the organization. It also includes a focus on the nonroutine aspects of an organization, including establishing a vision for the organization's future, making decisions with long-term consequences, creating an organizational culture, and initiating and managing change.

transmit   In the communication process, the message is sent via a medium such as voice, fax, memo, or e-mail.

transnational firm   A firm that avoids dichotomous structures such as product based or geography based, centralized or decentralized, independent or dependent. It attempts to achieve solutions tailored to specific situations, and differentiated structures replace systemwide structures. This type of firm creates high levels of interdependence among countries and cultures.

Two-Factor Theory   The premise for Herzberg's Motivation-Hygiene Theory that satisfaction and dissatisfaction are two dimensions rather than opposite ends of a single dimension.

uncertainty avoidance   A measure that indicates a culture's preferred amount of structure, ranging from strong to weak. Strong uncertainty avoidance cultures prefer more structure, resulting in explicit rules of behavior, either written or unwritten. Weak uncertainty avoidance cultures favor unstructured situations. The culture is more flexible and easy-going.

universal culture   In this type of culture, people believe the definition of goodness or truth applies to every situation. Judgments are made without regard to circumstance.

urgency   A factor that determines which course of action will be used to resolve ethical conflicts. The more urgent the need for resolution, the more likely actions such as avoidance, forcing, or accommodation will be chosen because infiltration, education, negotiation, and collaboration take extended time.

value judgments   Culturally biased assessments of behavior.

values orientations   Indicators of how different societies cope with various issues or problems.

variations   In the Kluckhohn and Strodtbeck framework, a culture favors one or more of the approaches associated with a particular values orientation.

verbal negotiation tactics Spoken negotiating behaviors such as initial offer made, promises, threats, and recommendations.

vertical differentiation   The number of levels in an organization. A measure of this is the number of levels between the highest and lowest position in an organization. The assumption is that the higher the level, the greater the authority of the position.

win-lose solution   In negotiation, one party receives all it wants by forcing or demanding the other to concede defeat.

win-win solution   In negotiation, all parties are able to achieve their objectives.

INDEX

633